This volume is a welcome new edition of a highly successful and well-acclaimed text, written by authors who combine a strong academic pedigree with practical application. As such, it represents one of the best foundation texts for students of small business and entrepreneurship and an excellent building block for subsequent specialised study. At the same time, its clarity of organisation and uncluttered style makes it accessible to all.

David Smallbone, *Professor of Small Business and Entrepreneurship and Associate Director of the Small Business Research Centre at Kingston University, UK*

This book is fresh and innovative and is true to the real sense of the entrepreneurial spirit in that it encourages thinking out of the box. The authors have managed to combine substance, depth and creativity.

Spinder Dhaliwal, *author of* Making a Fortune – Learning from the Asian Phenomenon; *Lecturer in Entrepreneurship, School of Management, University of Surrey, UK*

This text provides a valuable combination of theoretical and practical perspectives in this essential area of business studies. It goes beyond the usual 'how to start a new business' approach to address the wider economic and policy implications. The authors consolidate many of the key debates in enterprise studies (e.g. are entrepreneurs made or born?) and provide a wealth and variety of bite-sized case studies and examples drawn from SMEs and larger organisations. The text will be useful to students, academics and policy makers as well as business leaders. This new edition incorporates fresh and useful sections on the stages of business formation without sacrificing its overall theoretical rigour.

Peter Vlachos, *Senior Lecturer, Business School, University of Greenwich, UK*

This is a very comprehensive and practical book giving us real and deep insight into entrepreneurship and small business. The new edition of *Understanding Enterprise, Entrepreneurship and Small Business* enriches the field, putting more attention on competitive entrepreneurs and social entrepreneurship.

Professor Kiril Todorov, *Chairman, Bulgarian Association for Management Development and Entrepreneurship (BAMDE); Professor of Entrepreneurship, Faculty of Business, University of National and World Economy, Sofia, Bulgaria*

Understanding Enterprise provides a very comprehensive overview of the landscape of small business, enterprise and entrepreneurship, dealing with issues of definition, relationships, features and contributions to personal, social and economic development ... The authors have done an excellent job of integrating and linking the existing knowledge base about small business, enterprise and entrepreneurship, outlining the different typologies of enterprise and small business, presenting the internal and external factors and influences which give rise to their emergence and development within society (both at the individual and firm level) and providing key insights to policymakers and other professionals working to support the 'enterprise phenomenon'.

Lois Stevenson, *Visiting Research Fellow, International Development Research Centre, Middle East Regional Office, Cairo, Egypt*

This is a very comprehensive book, embracing the essence of enterprise and entrepreneurship. It is a must for everyone who is interested in the fascinating world of entrepreneurship and small business.

Rob van der Horst, *Past President, International Council for Small Business (ICSB)*

Understanding Enterprise

Entrepreneurship and Small Business

Third Edition

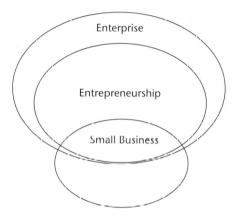

Simon Bridge, Ken O'Neill & Frank Martin

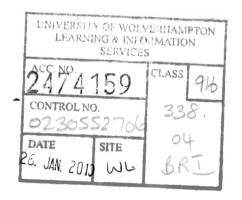
palgrave
macmillan

First edition 1998
Second edition 2003
Third edition 2009

First published 1998 by
PALGRAVE MACMILLAN

Palgrave Macmillan in the UK is an imprint of Macmillian Publishers Limited, registered in England, company number 785998, of Houndmills, Basingstoke, Hampshire RG21 6XS.

Palgrave Macmillan in the US is a division of St Martin's Press LLC, 175 Fifth Avenue, New York, NY 10010.

Palgrave Macmillan is the global academic imprint of the above companies and has companies and representatives throughout the world.

Palgrave® and Macmillan® are registered trademarks in the United States, the United Kingdom, Europe and other countries.

ISBN-13: 978-0-230-55270-8
ISBN-10: 0-230-55270-6

This book is printed on paper suitable for recycling and made from fully managed and sustained forest sources. Logging, pulping and manufacturing processes are expected to conform to the environmental regulations of the country of origin.

A catalogue record for this book is available from the British Library.

A catalog record for this book is available from the Library of Congress.

10   9   8   7   6   5   4   3   2
18   17   16   15   14   13   12   11   10   09

Printed and bound in China

Contents

Figures, tables, illustrations and cases

Figures

Tables

Illustrations

Cases

Preface

This is a book about enterprise and entrepreneurship and their relationship to small business. Throughout history many people have been enterprising and small businesses have been with us for many years. Recently however they have been seen as particularly economically beneficial. The world has been changing, and the role of the individual has become increasingly more important, with individual entrepreneurship becoming ever more necessary for economic success. This process has been referred to as the development of an enterprise culture and its benefits have been widely sought. Enterprise and its associated concepts of entrepreneurship and small business have therefore all been widely promoted and their development supported.

In many countries in the closing decades of the last century a new industry developed. It was the industry of enterprise promotion and support. It was developed by government departments, by local economic and enterprise agencies, by community initiatives, by private organisations and by academic institutions. This process is also being repeated in other countries, such as those of Central and Eastern Europe, with less well-developed market economies and where enterprise development is seen as a key route to economic growth.

For those working in this field, especially when they are new to it, there can be considerable confusion about what is involved. The language used is not clearly defined and many key words, with the word 'enterprise' itself being a prime example, have more than one meaning and are used differently by different people or in different contexts. The new industry has developed theories, policies and practices of its own, often without a clear objective or strategy. This may be typical of an emerging field but for those unfamiliar with it, and even for many who have some familiarity, it is hard to grasp what is being done and why. Nevertheless the industry will continue to grow and employment in it is already substantial, so that those working in it or close to it need to try to make sense of it.

Until relatively recently comprehensive overviews of the subject have not been available. A lot of research has been done, but it has of necessity been rather specialised, often not very widely published and usually of a piecemeal nature. The books and pamphlets, guides and courses that were available on the subject of enterprise and small business often focused mainly on how to start a business: a relevant subject for those who are thinking of doing just that, but not so useful for those seeking a wider insight into enterprise and its associated concepts in order better to understand, promote or support it. This book therefore attempts to address their needs.

Who should read this book

This book is targeted at students of enterprise at universities, business schools and other further and higher education establishments; at researchers and teaching staff; at policy makers and staff of business support organisations; and at the informed public. It aims to provide a foundation text for the study of enterprise and entrepreneurship and a perspective on broader aspects of enterprise. It seeks to be helpful both to those who might, at some stage, want to start a business and to those who might want to work with, but not in, such businesses. It has been written in the UK but much of its content should be relevant in all countries where people, for whatever reason, wish to know more about enterprise and its context. It seeks to present them with a sound introduction to the key concepts and issues as a grounding for understanding and work in this area, and as a starting point for further explorations of more specialised elements.

Aspects of the book have been specifically written for students who need a broad introduction to the whole field of enterprise, such as those doing an entrepreneurship option on a Bachelors or Masters course. It provides students and lecturers with cases and questions, summaries and suggestions for further reading. The three parts of the book, covering different aspects of the subject, may have different relevance to different students. Those wanting an introduction to the subject should read Part I; those wanting also to know about entrepreneurship and small businesses should use Part II; and those wanting also to know about the promotion of, and support for, enterprise should study Part III.

The structure of the book

A word about the structure of the book might also be helpful. We have tried, in all the main chapters, to start by summarising the contents and the key concepts covered in the chapter together with, for those who are using the book for study, a list of the key learning objectives of the chapter. Where, in addition to text, the chapter contains relevant material in table or figure form this is described as such and separately numbered. Three other types of information are, however, also used. Additional illustrative material which is thought to be relevant as an accompaniment to the text, but not an integral part of it, has been placed in a box and numbered as an illustration. Where this additional material is in the form of an example of something described in the text which can be used as a case for subsequent questions to test or reinforce understanding, this has also been boxed but separately labelled as a case study. The third type of material is stand-alone quotations which we have also used to add examples or emphasis. We hope that in this way we have provided relevant illustrations and examples in a way which gives the reader some choice and variety instead of just more unadorned text.

We have not started, however, with any definitions. Despite a desire on the part of some readers to start with an explanation of the terminology, in this field we are dealing with words which can and do have more than one meaning or use. Because we are looking at enterprise as it is, rather than as we might wish it to be, we should not try to impose our own interpretation or our own vocabulary on it. Therefore in Chapter 2 we explore how the words 'enterprise', and associated concepts such as 'entrepreneurship', are used by different people and what they appear to mean in different contexts. Chapter 6 offers some of the more commonly found definitions of a small business.

Changes in the second and third editions

This is the third edition of our book, written some ten years after the first edition and five years after the second. In these periods there have been new developments in enterprise thinking which we have on each occasion endeavoured to include. In the second edition we tried to recognise the continuing increase in attention being given to entrepreneurship and the focus now being directed by some people onto the entrepreneur instead of the business. We also recognised the distinction now being drawn between entrepreneurship strategies, with their focus on more business starts, and small business strategies with their focus on maintaining and growing the existing business stock. We also included a summary of the findings of the Global Entrepreneurship Monitor (GEM), which has recently been researching differences in the levels of entrepreneurship amongst countries and their implications.

For the third edition, in addition to updating some of the earlier material, we have recognised the increasing focus being given to entrepreneurship as well as to small businesses. This appears to be not only because greater recognition is being given to the importance of the entrepreneur, but also because of a tendency to use the word 'entrepreneurship' not just to refer to the process of business start-up, but in a wider sense almost synonymously with 'enterprise'. Thus there seems to be a greater emphasis on entrepreneurship in government policy statements and in naming initiatives, but this sometimes seems to reflect an evolution of language, rather than a change of emphasis. We have also in the third edition given more attention to social enterprise and social entrepreneurship (in Chapter 5) and we have restructured Part II to give a clearer coverage of the distinctive features of small businesses in Chapter 6 and of the various stages of the entrepreneurial process of business formation and development in Chapters 7 and 8.

We have also made some changes to our broad conclusions, in particular about the effectiveness of many interventions designed to promote enterprise. Earlier we had noted comments that, 'despite an increase in academic knowledge, or even perhaps because of it, there has also been a growth in ignorance about entrepreneurship and small and medium enterprises.'[1] We had concluded that, while there appeared to be no strong body of evidence to say that intervention worked, there was also no clear evidence that it didn't. Now, however, we feel that the balance of the evidence is that much intervention has not worked and has not had any significant effect on its overall targets such as levels of entrepreneurship or of business performance.

Thank you

One other significant change from the second to the third edition is that Stan Cromie has now retired and wants to follow other pursuits. We are very grateful for all the work he put into the first two editions and for letting us take forward that work into the third. Simon and Ken are also grateful to Frank Martin for agreeing to take his place.

In our work of writing, and re-writing, this book we have been conscious of many people who have helped and encouraged us. We owe them considerable thanks. We would like especially to highlight the patience and support shown by our wives, and to some extent our work colleagues, who have had to put up with our application to this instead of to other tasks, and who have tolerated the many phone calls and interruptions which do not seem to reduce for later editions. We are very grateful to all of them.

Simon Bridge
Ken O'Neill
Frank Martin
Belfast and Stirling

Reference

1. A. A. Gibb, 'SME Policy, Academic Research and the Growth of Ignorance, Mythical Concepts, Myths, Assumptions, Rituals and Confusions' *International Small Business Journal*, 18(3) (April–June 2000), p. 31.

Acknowledgements

The authors and publisher gratefully acknowledge the following for permission to reproduce copyright material in the third edition of this book.

Chapter 1. UK unemployment (millions), CSO/ONS; composition of the European business stock 1998, from the Sixth Report of the European Observatory for SMEs, with permission of the Office for Official Publications of the European Communities; Self-employed and employers in the UK, from the UK Labour Force Surveys, with the permission of the Controller of HMSO; reasons for the re-emergence of small-scale enterprise, based on D. J. Storey, *Understanding the Small Business Sector* (London: Routledge, 1994), p.35; an excerpt from business articles in the *Observer*, from J. Walters 'Turbulence Ahead for City's Airline' and S. Caulkin, 'Dismembering the Body Corporate', both *Observer*, 15 September, 1996; an excerpt from T. Peters, 'Travel the Independent Road' © *Independent on Sunday*, 2 January 1994; A view of Birch, from 'Twenty Years of Job Creation Research: What Have We Learned?' *40th ICSB World Conference, 1995*, by B. A. Kirchoff.

Chapter 2. J. B. Cunningham and J. Lischeron, 'Defining Entrepreneurship', *Journal of Small Business Management* (January 1991), p.47; influences on the development of entrepreneurial ideas and ambitions at different stages of life, A. A. Gibb, 'Enterprise Culture: Its Meaning and Implications for Education and Training', *Journal of European Industrial Training* (1987), p.13; the components of enterprise culture from Gibb (1987), *ibid.*, p.14; the focus of learning from Gibb (1987) *ibid.*, p.17; entrepreneurial v. corporatist management – some contrasts, from Gibb (1987) *ibid.*, pp.21–2; pathfinder initiatives 2, from *Building a Stronger Economy – The Pathfinder Process* (Belfast: Department of Economic Development, 1987, now Department of Enterprise, Trade and Investment 2008).

Chapter 3. Three types of small business owner, from R. W. Hornaday, 'Dropping the E-Words from Small Business Research', *Journal of Small Business Management,* vol. 28 (1990), pp.22–33; talent, temperament and technique, from W. K. Bolton and J. L. Thompson, *Entrepreneurs: Talent, Temperament and Technique* (Oxford: Butterworth Heinemann, 2000), p.30; promotional material used by the Department of Trade and Industry; what makes an entrepreneur, from 'Risky Business' in *Holland Herald,* the inflight magazine of KLM, with permission from Malcolm Brown and Ken Wilkie; framework for identifying enterprise competency, from S. Caird, 'Problems with the Identification of Enterprise Competencies', *Management Education and Development,* vol. 13 (1992), p.16, © Sage Publications; intentions model of entrepreneurial potential, from N. F. Krueger, *Prescriptions for Opportunity: Communities Can Create Potential* *for Entrepreneurs* (Washington, DC: Small Business Foundation of America, Working Paper 93–03, 1995); Ethnic sponsorship as a Sustainable Competitive Advantage (SCA), from P. B. Greene, 'The Resource Based Approach to Ethnic Business Sponsorship: A Consideration of Ismaili-Pakistani Immigrants', *Journal of Small Business Management,* vol. 35 (1997), p.66, published by Blackwell Publishing.

Chapter 4. Suggested influences on the level of enterprise in people and their businesses, from H. Pompe, M. Bruyn and J. Keok, 'Entrepreneurs in Small Business and International Comparative Perspective', *The 13th International Small Business Congress, London, 1986;* an Eclectic Theory of Entrepreneurship: Policies, Institutions and Culture, by D. Audretsch, R. Thurik, I. Verheul and S. Wennekers (eds) published in *Entrepreneurship; Determinants and Policy in a European–US Comparison (*Dordrecht, the Netherlands and Norwell, MA, USA: Kluwer Academic Publishers, 2000) p.19; key features associated with entrepreneurship initiation, from A. Morrison 'Initiating Entrepreneurship', in S. Carter and D. Evans (eds) *Enterprise and Small Business: Principles, Practice and Policy* (London: Financial Times/Prentice Hall, 2000), p.106, Pearson Education Limited; key differences between collectivist and individualist societies, from G. Hofstede, *Cultures and Organisations* (London: HarperCollins Publishers, 1994), pp.67 and 73; demand side determinants of entrepreneurship, from D. Audretsch, R. Thurik, I. Verheul and S. Wennekers (eds) published in *Entrepreneurship; Determinants and Policy in a European–US Comparison (*Dordrecht, the Netherlands and Norwell, MA, USA: Kluwer Academic Publishers, 2000), p.23; participation by men and women in the UK labour market, with permission from the Office for National Statistics, Government Statistical Service (GSS); early stage entrepreneurial activity (TEA) for 42 nations by income/regional groups, N. Bosma, K. Jones, E. Autio and J. Levie, from the *Global Entrepreneurship Monitor 2007 Executive Report 2007*, p.15; early stage entrepreneurial activity rates and per capita GDP, N. Bosma, K. Jones, E. Autio and J. Levie, from the *Global Entrepreneurship Monitor2007 Executive Report 2007*, p.12; GEM conceptual model, from A. L. Zacharakis, W. D. Bygrave and D. A. Shepherd in *Global Entrepreneurship Monitor, National Entrepreneurship Assessment;* United States of America, 2000 Executive Report (Kansas City, MO: Kauffman Centre for Entrepreneurial Leadership, 2000), p.5 (by permission from the Kauffman Centre).

Chapter 5. Autonomous and community entrepreneurs, adapted from B. Johannisson and A. Nilsson, 'Community Entrepreneurs: Networking for Local Development', *Entrepreneurship and Regional Development,* vol. 1, no. 1 (1989), p.5, with permission from Taylor & Francis.

Chapter 6. A statistical profile of business enterprises in the UK, BERR Enterprise Directorate Analytical Unit by permission of the Office of Public Sector Information (OPSI), 2008; three dimensions of habitual entrepreneurs, from P. Rosa, 'Entrepreneurial Process of Business Cluster Formation and Growth by Habitual Entrepreneurs', *Entrepreneurship: Theory and Practice,* vol. 22 (1998), pp.48–51, Baylor University, by permission from Blackwell Publishing; different criteria by which family businesses have been defined, based on, R. K. Z. Heck and E. Scannell-Trent 'The Prevalence of Family Businesses – From a Household Sample', *Family Business Review*, 1999, 12, pp.210–11, Blackwell Publishing; advantages and disadvantages of family controlled enterprises, from M. F. R. Kets de Vries, 'The Dynamics of Family Controlled Firms: The Good News and the Bad

News', *Organisational Dynamics*, 1993, 21, p.69 with permission from Elsevier Business and Management; transactions between family and business, from K. Stafford et al, 'A Research Model of Sustainable Family Business', *Family Business Review,* vol. 12 (1999), p.204, reprinted with permission from The Family Firm Institute, Inc., all rights reserved.

Chapter 7. The five stages of business growth, from N. C. Churchill and V. L. Lewis, 'Growing Concerns: The Five Stages of Small Firm Growth', *Harvard Business Review,* May–June (1983), pp.31, 32, 34 and 40; growth process as reflected in possible growth paths, from E. Garnsey, 'A New Theory of the Growth of the Firm', *41st World Conference of ICSB, Stockholm*, June 1996, p.4; the Greiner growth model, from L. E. Greiner, 'Evolution and Revolution as Organisations Grow', *Harvard Business Review*, July–August 1972, quoted in P. Burns, *Entrepreneurship and Small Business* (Basingstoke: Palgrave, 2007), p.240; influences on the entrepreneurial decision, from A. C. Cooper, 'Technical Entrepreneurship; What Do We Know?', *R & D Management,* vol. 3 (1973), pp.59–64; new technology adoption rate, in B. Bygrave, 'Building an Entrepreneurial Economy; Lessons from the United States', *Wall Street Journal*, June 1997, quoted in *Business Strategy Review* 1998; vol. 9, no. 2, p.11; business opportunities in technology, in *Mobile Data Association Newsletter*, January, 2007; entrepreneurial success, from R. Peterson and R. Rondstadt, 'A Silent Strength: Entrepreneurial Know Who', *The 16th ESBS, efmd IMD Report* (86/4), p.11; the self-employment spectrum, from R. Lessem, 'Getting Into Self-Employment', *Management Education and Development*, spring (1984), p.31, © Sage Publications; the four dimensions of management development, from R. E. Boyatzis, *The Competent Manager: A Model for Effective Performance* (New York: Wiley, 1982); an analysis of a start-up business, from M. Scott and R. Bruce, 'Five Stages of Growth in Small Business', *Long Range Planning,* vol. 20 (1987), p.48, © 1987 Elsevier Science Ltd; debt structure by country, from P. Burns and O. Whitehouse, *Financing Enterprise in Europe 2* (Milton Keynes: 3i Enterprise Centre); the layers of the small business support network, from A. A. Gibb, 'Towards the Building of Entrepreneurial Models of Support for Small Business', paper presented at the *National Small Firms Policy and Research Conference* (Cambridge, 1988); small business problems, from 'Problems Facing Small Firms', *Nat West/Small Business Research Trust Quarterly Survey of Small Business in Britain,* vol. 17 (2001), p.20, reproduced with permission from the Small Business Research Trust; the ingredients of failure, from P. Burns, *Entrepreneurship and Small Business* (London: Palgrave Macmillan 2002), p.271, reproduced with permission of Palgrave Macmillan.

Chapter 8. Managing factors and stages, from N. C. Churchill, 'The Six Key Phases of Company Growth', in 'Mastering Enterprise', © *Financial Times,* 20 February 1997, p.3; breakout by ethnic entrepreneurs, from M. Ram, 'Ethnic Minority Enterprise: An Overview and Research Agenda', *Journal of Entrepreneurial Behaviour and Research,* 1997, 3, pp.145–56; management weaknesses as a constraint on growth: internal barriers to growth (percentage of respondents citing factor as important), from Binder Hamlyn and the London Business School, 'The Quest for Growth', reprinted from *Managing to Grow* (London: CBI, 1995), p.11; constraints for small business growth, from ESRC Centre for Business Research, *The State of the British Enterprise* (Cambridge: Cambridge Small Business Research Centre, 1992); constraints on small business growth, from A. Cosh and A. Hughes (eds), *Enterprising Britain: Growth, Innovation and Public Policy in the Small* *and Medium Sized Enterprise Sector 1994–1997* (Cambridge: Small Business Research Centre, University of Cambridge, 1992); business survival rates: percentage of enterprises surviving after one, two, and five years, by country, reproduced from the *Third Annual Report of the European Observatory for SMEs* (Zoetermeer, The Netherlands: EIM Small Business Research and Consultancy, 1995), p.87.

Chapter 9. 'Who is the entrepreneur?', adapted with permission from *Intrapreneuring* (New York: Harper & Row, 1985), pp.54–6, by Gifford Pinchot III; new products at 3M, from R. Mitchell, 'Masters of Innovation: How 3M Keeps Its New Products Coming', *Business Week*, 1989; 10 April: pp.58–63; slightly modified version of T. Heller, 'Loosely Coupled Systems for Corporate Entrepreneurship', *Entrepreneurship: Theory and Practice*, vol. 24 (1999), pp.25–31, Baylor University, publisher of *Entrepreneurship Theory and Practice*, reproduced by permission of Blackwell Publishing; the old and new paradigm at Baxi, based on J. Balogun and V. Hope-Hailey, *Exploring Strategic Change,* copyright © Prentice-Hall 1999, reprinted by permission of Pearson Education Limited; a motivational framework, based on T. Peters and R. H. Waterman, *In Search of Excellence* (London: Harper & Row, 1982); manager mindset and behaviour for innovation, from © The ForeSight Group Diagram, S. Hamngatan 37, 41106 Göteborg, Sweden.

Chapter 10. Objectives of small firm policy, from D. J. Storey, *Understanding the Small Business Sector* (London: Routledge/Cengage, 1994), p.260; a view of market imperfections, their causes and actions taken, developed from D. Keeble and S. Walker, 'New Firms, Small Firms and Dead Firms: Spatial Patterns and Determinants in the United Kingdom', *Regional Studies,* vol. 28 (1994), pp.411–27 and P. Westhead and A. Moyes, 'Reflections on Thatcher's Britain: Evidence from New Production Firm Registrations 1980–88', *Entrepreneurship and Regional Development,* vol. 4 (1992), pp.21–36; Policy Rationale 1: an OECD View, extracts from a personal communication from members of an OECD Working Party on SMEs called with recognition to the Organisation for Economic Cooperation and Development, Paris (OECD/DSTI/IND, 2000); Policy Rationale 2, an OECD View, the role of SMEs: findings and issues, *ibid*; small business growth stunted by reluctance to seek advice, from Business Link Press Release, 8 October 2001, with permission from Business Link; Variations in business start-up rates across the UK, from www.hm-treasury.gov.uk/press/2000, with permission from the Controller of HMSO; the rationale for an industrial policy, from an address by Mary Harney, Tanaiste and Minister for Enterprise to Dail Eireann on 18 June 1998, reproduced with the permission of the Department of Enterprise and Employment, Dublin.

Chapter 11. Does location matter for innovation? a comparison of high tech firms in Israel and Ireland, with permission from the Northern Ireland Economic Research Centre, Belfast, 2001; the start-up failure myth, from A. A. Gibb, 'SME Policy, Academic Research and the Growth of Ignorance: Mythical Concepts, Myths, Assumptions, Rituals and Confusions', *The International Small Business Journal*, vol. 18 (2000), pp.22–3, and A. A. Gibb, 'SME Policy, Mythical Concepts, Myths, Assumptions, Rituals and Confusions', 21st ISBA National Small Firms Conference, Durham, 1998, p.12.

Chapter 12. The small business service's performance framework, House of Commons, Committee of Public Accounts, *Supporting Small Business,* reproduced by permission under Parliamentary licence; linking entrepreneurship and economic growth from A. Lundstrom and L. Stephenson, *Entrepreneurship Policy in the Future*, Vol. 1 of the Entrepreneurship for the Future series (Stockholm: Swedish Foundation for Small Business Research, 2001); the UK Small Business Service, based on 'Finance for Small Firms: An Eighth Report' (London: Bank of England, 2001), pp.21–2; UK government SME policies, adapted from D. Storey, *Understanding the Small Firms Sector* (London: Routledge, 1994), p.269; policy fields and instruments, adapted from K. de Lind Van Wijngaarden and R. Van der Horst, 'A Comparison of SME Policy in the EU Member States', *Business Growth and Profitability*, 1996, vol. 2, no. 1, p.40; 'The Dirty Dozen' from 'Help for Small Firms to Beat Bureaucrats' by Claire Oldfield, *The Sunday Times* © Times Newspapers Limited, 14 November 1999; public sector initiatives for high-tech businesses, The Cruickshank Review, The Social Investment Task Force and government initiatives for deprived areas, all from 'Finance for Small Firms: An Eighth Report' (London: Bank of England, 2001), with kind permission of the Bank of England; a letter from David Irwin, the Chief Executive to the Institute of Business Advisers and others on 9 May 2001, with the kind permission of the Business Link.

Chapter 13. The difference between evaluation and appraisal, from 'Appraisal and Evaluation in Central Government: The Green Book' (London: The Stationery Office, 1997), pp.96–7, with permission from the Controller of HMSO; two types of evaluation from J. Curran, 'What is Small Business Policy in the UK for? Evaluating and Assessing Small Business Policies', *International Small Business Journal,* 2000, vol. 18, no.3, pp.38–9; a coherent framework, from House of Commons Committee of Public Accounts, 'Supporting Small Business', 11th Report of Session 2006–7, HC 262, 6 February 2007, p.3, by permission under Parliamentary licence; why workers in smaller businesses are less likely to receive training, from S. Fraser, D. Storey, J. Frankish and R. Roberts, 'The Relationship Between Training and Small Business Training: An Analysis of the Barclays Bank Small Firms Training Loans Scheme', Paper presented at the 23rd ISBA National Small Firms Policy and Research Conference, Aberdeen, 2000, pp.1–2; measuring performance, from A. Lundstrom and L. Stevenson, *Entrepreneurship Policy in the Future* (Stockholm: Swedish Foundation for Small Business Research, 2001), pp.144–6, with permission from the Swedish Foundation for Small Business Research.

Introduction

This book seeks to introduce the concepts of enterprise, entrepreneurship and small business and their interrelationships. It is not intended to be a comprehensive theoretical study, but instead tries to provide a practical guide to these subjects for those working in this field, be they students, promotion and support agency staff, civil servants, advisers, counsellors, trainers or academics. It aims to provide a guide to the key facts, ideas, concepts, theories and thinking about enterprise and entrepreneurship, to look at their relationship to small businesses, and to consider the methods that are used to promote them.

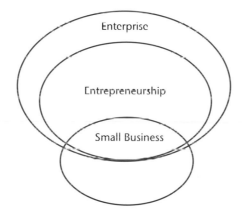

The word 'enterprise' is much used in a variety of contexts and with a wide range of meanings. Within this range there are narrow meanings of the word specifically related to business, and there are wider meanings indicating a way of behaving that can apply in a variety of contexts, including business. The narrower meanings are closely linked to business entrepreneurship, and in turn the concepts of enterprise and entrepreneurship embrace much that would be considered to be expressions of small business activity. Indeed, the words enterprise, entrepreneurship and small business often appear to be used interchangeably; but it is also argued that there are many small businesses that do not demonstrate much enterprise.

The variety of uses made of the words 'enterprise' and entrepreneurship and the variety of contexts in which they are applied are indicative of the appeal of the concepts and their various applications. Evidently, one of the main reasons for this appeal is jobs. Small businesses are frequently net creators of jobs, more so than big businesses. Those, therefore, who wish to encourage and promote more jobs are interested in small businesses and often in what can be done to develop more of them. It is this process of business formation and development that is often referred to as entrepreneurship, which therefore forms, for many people, an important sub-set of enterprise.

The book consists of three parts. Part I starts with a largely historical examination of why the concepts of enterprise and entrepreneurship have been presented by many people as things that are desirable and worth pursuing in practice. It then explores the variety of ways in which the words are used and the spectrum of meanings they can have. In particular it refers to the narrow and broad definitions, which see enterprise respectively as being just business entrepreneurialism or as the qualities which enable people to be creative and adaptable in the face of economic and social change. It presents a number of theories about enterprising behaviour in individuals, looking at the external environment in which individuals and groups operate and at the influences that cultural, economic and political conditions can have on enterprise. The link between entrepreneurship and economic success is also explored.

Part II focuses on the narrow but important view of enterprise as small businesses and their formation and development. This is often the reason why people are interested in enterprise. There are many varieties of small business, which differ from each other as much as they differ from larger businesses. Small businesses should not be viewed, however, as smaller versions of large businesses. They have many distinctive features, and those who wish to understand and influence the development of small businesses need to be aware of these distinctions. As businesses are formed and developed they face different issues, first in the stages of their formation and start–up and then in their subsequent development through survival and growth and/or decline and termination. Mature businesses can also benefit from corporate entrepreneurship, or 'intrapreneurship', which is the application of enterprise inside larger businesses.

If enterprise, entrepreneurship and small business are beneficial then there will be a wish that there should be more of them. In Part III the issues of reasons and ways to promote enterprise are explored. A distinction is made between the concepts of entrepreneurship policy and small business policy, where the former can be said to focus mainly on business formation and the latter on business development. Small businesses are important for a variety of reasons including their contributions to economic diversity, social stability and support for other businesses.

Attention has been focused on small businesses in particular because of the indicated links between them and job creation. Governments, especially in times of high unemployment, want more jobs and are prepared therefore to intervene to secure the development of more enterprise.

Part III starts by considering the reasons for intervention and the benefits sought from it. It then considers a number of theories and assumptions about the nature of the enterprise process in order to see how intervention might work and what interventions might be successful. The possible areas for intervention and the forms it might take are examined; this is followed by a look at the issues of evaluating interventions and the results indicated by some of the relevant research.

An important theme highlighted in the book is the need to look at enterprise and small business formation and development from the perspective of the individual entrepreneur who is the agent of change, instead of using only the business as the main focus of attention. The final chapter in the book therefore attempts to take a wider view of what has been presented on enterprise and its relevance to the economic future of individuals.

The concept of enterprise

Part I of this book looks at concepts of enterprise and entrepreneurship, and the small businesses with which they are often associated, and considers why they have been and are the focus of considerable attention, what they are interpreted to mean, and what appear to be the main influences on them.

Chapter 1 starts with a largely historical examination of why enterprise and entrepreneurship have been presented by many as desirable and worth pursuing and why, therefore, they are the subject of considerable interest in government, academic and business circles.

Chapter 2 explores the concepts of enterprise and entrepreneurship and the variety of ways in which the words are used, and looks at the spectrum of meanings they can have. In particular it refers to two definitions: a 'narrow' definition, in which enterprise means the same as business entrepreneurship and is specifically concerned with the start-up and development of business; and a 'broad' definition, which considers enterprise, and sometimes entrepreneurship, as the behaviour resulting from the exercise of a set of attributes that can be demonstrated in a variety of different contexts.

Chapters 3 and 4 look at the factors which have been thought to influence enterprise and entrepreneurship. There are many factors which can be categorised in a number of ways but here, in order to provide some structure for presenting them, the factors are broadly categorised as internal or external to the individual. Chapter 3 considers the internal factors and looks at a number of theories about enterprising behaviour and what it is in individuals that influences them to engage in enterprising acts. Chapter 4 considers the environment external to individuals and groups, and at the influences that economic, cultural and political conditions can have on their behaviour individually and collectively.

In practice, as the boundaries distinguishing internal and external influences are not absolute, there are areas of overlap. Those theories which include aspects of both sets of influences are also reviewed in Chapter 4, thus developing some of the separate ideas presented earlier.

A number of important aspects and perceptions of enterprise do not however fit into the categories of internal and external. They are therefore presented separately in Chapter 5 which looks at some of these perceptions, at some enterprise connotations, at the possible disadvantages of enterprise and at possible aspects of its future development. It also considers that aspect of enterprise which is often called social enterprise.

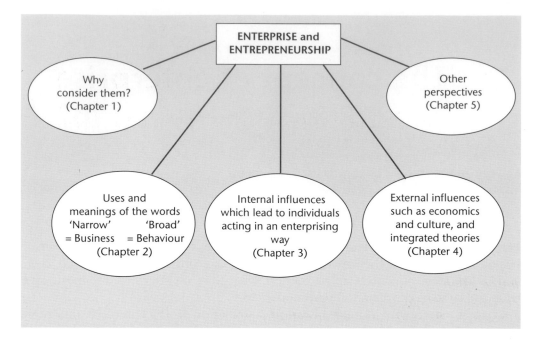

CHAPTER 1
Why talk about enterprise and entrepreneurship?

Contents

KEY CONCEPTS

This chapter covers:

- The expectation people have of employment and the desire by governments to maintain full employment.
- The trends in work, in employment and in self-employment, and the ending of an expectation of a job for life.
- Birch's finding in the United States that small businesses created the majority of net new jobs.
- The extent to which small businesses predominate in the world's economies.
- The attractiveness of 'enterprise' as a source of employment and other economic benefits.
- The increasing use also of the term 'entrepreneurship' in this context.

LEARNING OBJECTIVES

By the end of this chapter the reader should:

- Understand why the current interest in enterprise and entrepreneurship has arisen and why they have become a focus of government policy.
- Appreciate the economic significance of the small businesses sector.
- Be aware of the trends in the structure of employment.

Introduction

Chapter 1 introduces the subjects of enterprise and entrepreneurship by considering why they have become popular. It explores how and when the concept of enterprise gained its present desirability, when this also came to be described as entrepreneurship, and why together they have become the subject of considerable interest in government, academic and business circles. This largely historical explanation provides a background for the subsequent chapters which consider what enterprise and entrepreneurship are and what factors are thought to influence them.

The passion for enterprise

> The implementation of this strategy will lead to what the President [of the European Commission] referred to as 'Enterprise Europe'.
>
> Commission Working Paper SEC(2000)771, Brussels, 2000.
>
> The central economic policy issue will be widening and deepening the enterprise culture.
>
> Gordon Brown, UK Chancellor of the Exchequer, 2001.
>
> Working together we can do more to enhance Britain's great entrepreneurial culture – ensuring that there is no no-go area for enterprise in any part of Britain.
>
> Gordon Brown, as Chancellor of the Exchequer, launching 'Enterprising Britain' in 2004.

There are a number of generally recognised human rights but the one that probably commands the greatest recognition, if not the greatest observance, is the right to freedom. But can a government ensure freedom for its subjects? Good laws, it has been said, can promote freedom, whereas bad laws can restrict it. Despite its recognition as a right, laws cannot therefore, of themselves, ensure freedom; they can only help to set the conditions in which it can exist.

Another human benefit sometimes recognised as a right is an education. Education, however, differs from freedom in that, whether it is seen as a right or not, a government can take steps to provide at least a basic education for its citizens. An education, it is generally recognised, is within a government's gift.

But can the same be said of work, and is the right to work the same as the right to a job? That 'everyone has the right to work' is enshrined in the Universal Declaration of Human Rights signed by the members of the United Nations. The desirability of full employment as a political objective is often debated, however, not so much because people do not want full employment, but because questions are raised about the practicality of achieving it and the implications it might have. Is employment like health or education, where a government can provide a basic level of service or provision for everyone? Or is it more like freedom, in respect of which a government's powers are

---

ILLUSTRATION 1.1
The right to a job

The other day one of the authors was having a Saturday morning coffee in his favourite café. He happened to know the two people at the adjacent table. He had said hello to them when they came in before resuming his attempts to solve the crossword in the daily paper. Suddenly something one of them said impinged on his consciousness. 'Everyone', she said, 'has the right to a job.' What are the implications of that, he wondered; how can such a right be ensured and how does it fit into an enterprise culture?

---

more negative than positive: where it has the power to deny freedom but cannot itself directly provide freedom for everyone? Can a government provide a basic job for everyone who wants one? Governments do directly create some jobs but, at least in Western societies, they are not the main sources of direct employment and they cannot themselves create enough jobs for everyone who might want one.

It is businesses that create most jobs. Governments can encourage businesses to create jobs, they can try to provide a supportive environment for the creation of jobs and they can legislate for people to have an equal opportunity to get the jobs that do exist, but that is not the same as offering the right to a job. That would mean that everyone who wanted a job could have one, but how can a government maintain that when it can't actually create enough jobs itself? If a government cannot create enough jobs then is it practical to talk about the 'right to a job'?

For many people a key feature of the communist-inspired systems of government was that they guaranteed a job for everyone. Actually, it would seem that was not really the case; it might be more accurate to say that they provided everyone with an employment contract and a wage, whether or not they really had a full job to do at their official place of employment. But to achieve even that required centrally controlled economies, which are now largely deemed to have failed. A job for everyone who wants one nevertheless remains a very desirable aspiration.

Earlier in the last century, after the upheavals of the Industrial Revolution and the First World War, there did seem to be some prospect that a job for everyone might become the norm. Then, in the Western world at least, there were the traumas of the 1930s. Following the Wall Street crash in 1929 it appeared that there were indeed fundamental problems with the structure of capitalist economies in maintaining full, or nearly full, employment. However, by the end of that decade major job creation initiatives had produced significant reductions in unemployment and John Maynard Keynes had in theory suggested how unemployment might continue to be controlled. In addition, by 1940, there was again a war which increased the demand for armaments and other requirements for the military struggle and brought an end to the remaining unemployment.

After that war economic prospects seemed to be much better. Keynesian economic theory seemed to be working, the experiences in the 1930s of practical employment creation seemed still to be valid, and in Britain unemployment seemed to be relatively steady at about a quarter of a million. This was a manageable figure, which offered support to the view that full employment was realistically achievable. Alarm bells did not ring loudly when by the end of the 1960s this figure had doubled to about half a million. Although history is lived forwards it is viewed backwards, and it is only in retrospect therefore that it would now seem that this was a turning point. Half a million now looks like a relatively small figure and it was during the 1970s, when the figure grew to one and a half million, and the 1980s, when it rose again, to 3 million, that notions about the practicality of achieving sustained full employment were finally shattered (Figure 1.1).

What was going on? One person who has studied this matter is Charles Handy. He saw that what was happening in the 1970s and 1980s was a fundamental restructuring of work. For millennia of human history the major source of jobs was agriculture. Then, with increases in industrial production and agricultural efficiency, work for many became based in industry through the process which came to be known as the Industrial Revolution. Was that revolution itself, however, now being superseded?

In his introduction to *The Future of Work*, Handy points out that it was during the 1970s that visible changes began to appear in what had until then been the normal working life.[1] Large organisations began to decline and concepts such as redundancy and long-term unemployment became more familiar. Britain, along with other countries such as the United States and France, was no longer primarily an industrial nation. Since the early 1970s the aggregate profits from the service sector had exceeded those from manufacturing. Internationally it was the same. Similar changes had taken place throughout the industrialised world. The problem for many, however, was not the change to new jobs but that the generation of these new jobs did not seem to be keeping pace with the reduction in the old ones.

In this situation there was a natural tendency to look back to the 1930s when job creation measures had worked and to try to repeat that prescription. A number of solutions were proposed. Expanding the business sector was one solution considered,

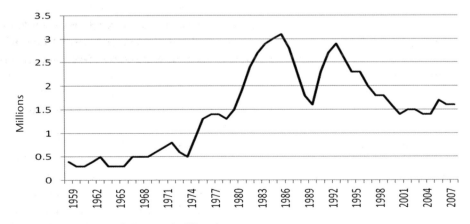

Figure 1.1 UK unemployment (millions)

Source: CSO/ONS, Labour Market Statistics.

although to an extent business output was already expanding, but through increases in productivity not in jobs. Some businesses were simultaneously increasing output and shedding jobs – a phenomenon referred to as 'jobless growth'. Other suggestions included expanding government employment to take up the slack in jobs – a Keynesian type of solution that suggested increased government spending on infrastructure, health and education. That looked problematic, however, because of the numbers who would have to be employed, the cost and the potential impact on inflation. Governments struggled to find something that might work and certainly still hoped that business would make a major contribution, but they were not looking at small businesses. These had been seen as a 'vanishing breed' and any efforts to preserve them 'had more to do with democratic and political values than with economic efficiency'.[2]

Discovering the importance of small businesses

It was in this situation in 1979 that David Birch published the results of his research into employment in the United States. He concluded that small firms, defined as those with 100 employees or fewer, had in the early 1970s created over 80 per cent of net new jobs. Net new jobs is the difference between the total of new jobs created and the total of jobs lost during the same period, and is sometimes used as a reasonable indicator of economic growth. The implication was that, in the United States, it was small firms which were responsible for much of the economic growth and were the prime source of employment creation. Many people discounted Birch's work when it was first published, as his conclusion was contrary to the perceived wisdom of the time. Nevertheless, the issue was important enough to stimulate others to try to replicate his work. (See Case 1.1 for a more detailed view on Birch and Chapter 7 for further reference to the validity of Birch's findings.)

While the statistical debate still continues, it can be seen that it was the work of Birch, followed by that of others, that challenged the previously held common belief that economic benefits such as jobs and growth came always from big business, and that small business was almost incidental to this. This work led to a recognition that the bulk of the new jobs being created to maintain or increase employment levels was actually coming from small businesses. While it is not all small businesses which create additional jobs and it is the case that many small businesses are in the service sector, where work is generally more labour intensive than in the manufacturing sector, that does not detract from the perceived value of the small business sector as an important source of employment. It has also been shown that small businesses can provide other economic benefits, such as a relatively greater rate of innovation.[3]

This process did not only apply in America. In Europe (the then 15 countries of the EU plus Iceland, Liechtenstein, Norway and Switzerland) for instance, by 1998 the number of enterprises in the non-primary private sector reached almost 20 million, of which 99.8 per cent were SMEs (small and medium-sized enterprises – for definition see Chapter 6).[4] In 2006 in the then 27 countries of the EU, nearly 90 per cent of businesses were micro-businesses and SMEs accounted for over 60 per cent of employment. Table 1.1 shows these figures in more detail.

Therefore those looking for an expansion of business employment, or even for

Table 1.1 Composition of the European (EU27) and UK business stock in 2006

Business size: (number of employees)		Micro (>10)	Small (10-49)	Medium (50-249)	Large (250+)
EU	by number of enterprises:	87.3%	10.8%	1.6%	0.3%
	by employment:	30.6%	18.6%	14.2%	36.6%
UK	by number of enterprises:	95.3%	3.9%	0.6%	0.2%
	by employment:	25.5%	12.0%	10.2%	52.4%

Source: UK figures from a press release of the Department of Business, Enterprise and Regulatory Reform, 22 August 2007. EU figures based on a sample survey for the 2007 report of the Observatory of European SMEs,http://ec.europa.eu/enterprise/enterprise_policy/analysis/observatory_en.htm (accessed 16 January 2008). Reproduced with the permission of the office for official publications of the European Communities.

the maintenance of existing employment levels, looked increasingly to small businesses to do this. Small businesses became a focus of interest and policy-makers wanted to know more about them. They were seen as a fundamental component of any effort to increase employment. There was a desire to promote more of them and consequently to understand and promote the concept of 'enterprise' that was thought to underlie them. Enterprise was becoming a vogue word, and the number of businesses and the extent of self-employment were increasing, as shown for the UK in Table 1.2 (although part of the increase may have been due to factors such as the tax changes in the 1980s which led to many contract workers being re-classed as self-employed).

Essentially what Birch had done was to challenge a particular assumption that the future was a continuation of the past and had shown it to be wrong. He looked at what was already happening and demonstrated that it was not what many experts had assumed. Others have also highlighted aspects of the present and used them to suggest that there are changes that many have not perceived. At the same time as Birch was publishing his work, Alvin Toffler was writing *The Third Wave* in which he described large-scale industrial mass production as 'second wave' industry and forecast that both the office and the factory would be revolutionised over the future decades in a way that would affect the structure of industry, the size of work units and even the location of work.[5] In effect, Toffler analysed reasons for the change

Table 1.2 Self-employed and employers in the UK

Year	Total (million)
1951	1.65
1961	1.72
1971	1.79
1981	2.06
1991	3.30
2001	3.15

Source: UK Labour Force Survey. Reproduced with the permission of the Controller of HMSO.

Table 1.3 Reasons for the re-emergence of small-scale enterprise

Supply	Demand
Technological changes	Structural changes
• New products	• Demand for service
• New industries	• Demand for variety
Fragmentation/cost advantage	Uncertainty of demand
• Subcontracting	• Individual customer requirements
Labour force/unemployment	Macro economic conditions
• Redundancy	• Unemployment
• Education	
Government	Economic developments
• Privatisation	• Services
• Deregulation	• Just-in-time
• Tax benefit	• Niches

Source: based on D. J. Storey, *Understanding the Small Business Sector* (London: Routledge, 1994) p. 35.

that gave rise to the developments Birch had recorded. Table 1.3 also indicates some of the reasons for the re-emergence of the small business.

The recent recognition given to small businesses might initially have been largely for the employment they create but other economic benefits of small businesses have also been recognised:

- *Individual outlet.* The small firm provides a productive outlet for the energies of those enterprising people who set great store by economic independence. Many of them are antipathetic or not suited to employment in a large organisation, but have much to contribute to the vitality of the economy. In industries where the optimum size of the production unit or the sales outlet is small, the most efficient form of organisation is often a small firm. For this reason many important trades and industries consist mainly of small businesses.

- *Specialist supplier.* Many small firms act as specialist suppliers to large companies of parts, sub-assemblies or components, produced at lower cost than the large companies could achieve. Small firms add greatly to the variety of products and services offered to the consumer because they can flourish in a limited or specialised market which it would not be worthwhile or economic for a large firm to enter.

- *Competition.* In an economy in which even larger, multi-product firms are emerging, small firms provide competition, both actual and potential, and provide some check on monopoly profits and on the inefficiency which monopoly breeds. In this way they contribute to the efficient working of the economic system as a whole.

- *Consumer choice.* The small business sector, in generating competition, also widens choice for consumers. This is particularly true when considering products or services tailored to the desires of individuals or small groups of consumers, since larger firms tend to look for opportunity for large-scale production and ignore specialist niches.

- *Seedbed for new industries.* The small firm sector is the traditional breeding ground for new industries – that is for innovation writ large. Small firms provide the means of entry into business for new entrepreneurial talent and the seedbed from which new large companies will grow to challenge and stimulate the established leaders of industry.

- *Source of innovation.* The view that large firms dominate in the process of innovation has been, until recently, the prevalent one. Over the last 25 years, however, various empirical studies have revealed that 'small firms can keep up with large firms in the field of innovation', albeit to varying extents in different sectors.[6] Rothwell deduces that 'the relative importance of firms of different sizes to innovation in a particular industry is likely to depend on the age of that industry.'[7] While there is no overall consensus on the circumstances of when small firms demonstrate superiority or otherwise, it seems incontrovertible that small firms, in spite of relatively low expenditure on research and development by the sector as a whole, are an important source of innovation in products, techniques and services.

- *Source of stability.* The sector is also perceived as contributing to economic and social stability, not only through its employment-creating capacity, but also by offering a means of social and community cohesion. Indeed in the United States, when the Small Business Administration was being created over 50 years ago, the sector was described as vital 'to the security of the nation'.

Employment trends

Charles Handy also talked about the 'shamrock organisation'.[8] It had been the assumption, he suggested, that an organisation should do as much as possible in-house with its own permanent workforce. Indeed, vertical and horizontal integration was seen as the norm for business development. However organisations in future would most likely have three distinct categories of people working for them, like the three leaves of a shamrock. The first category was the professional core, the second was the contractual fringe and the third was the, mostly part-time, flexible labour force. The result, he suggested, was that in the UK already by the end of the 1980s about a third of the paid workforce were part-timers or self-employed, and this could rise to 50 per cent by the end of the century. Subsequent experience has confirmed this trend. The proportion of part-time workers in organisations and self-employed workers contracted to them has increased, with consequent changes in employee loyalty and in expectations about length of service.

A generation ago Handy said we used to work for 47 hours a week, for 47 weeks a year and for 47 years, or about 100,000 hours in a lifetime.[9] Now he suggested this may be down to 50,000 hours for someone just starting work. This may be 37 x 37 x 37, or it could still be 47 hours a week for 47 weeks a year but only for 25 years in an intense professional job, or possibly 22 hours a week for 47 weeks a year for 50 years of part-time work extending well into one's sixties as it is a continuing part, but not the whole, of life.

The 50,000-hour job was just one of the unanticipated outcomes of the shamrock organisation although, with more people living into their eighties and nineties,

---

ILLUSTRATION 1.2
Contracting out in the 1990s

'Contract out everything except your soul!', exhorted management expert Tom Peters.

The airline is going to examine every part of its operation and decide which services it can buy more cheaply elsewhere. ... Over the past four years ... it has contracted out its security arrangements, heavy engineering and much of its catering. It has recruited small external 'franchise' airlines to fly several routes on its behalf. ... 'There is no part of the operation that we are not going to look at', said one source.

Rolls-Royce last year signed a deal with EDS to provide all its IT needs for 10 years.

J P Morgan is paying a consortium of suppliers $7bn over seven years.

Source: Excerpts from business articles in the *Observer* © on one Sunday in 1996.[10].

---

the pensions 'time bomb' has meant that many people cannot now afford early retirement and need to find further employment after their first careers. It was nevertheless clear that the employee society had changed fundamentally and would not readily change back. Half as many people in the core of the business, paid twice as much and producing three times as much, may make economic sense for a business, but what did it mean for the assumption of permanent jobs for life? Other attitudes to employment will be needed. Those not in the core will not have a permanent job but will have portfolio careers moving from job to job or from contract to contract. They will have to find such work, to contract to do it, and to manage its delivery. Such a situation will require behaviour that has been described as enterprising.

Tom Peters also looked at trends in business organisation. He foresaw the time when the organisation as we know it would not exist. Instead there would be smaller, flat and flexible network organisations. To get beyond your own brain-dead management, he said you must subcontract everything. The future, he went on to suggest, even for larger organisations, is to deconstruct the organisation and to organise work by small teams. Otherwise the responsiveness needed for true competitiveness would be impossible to achieve.

Changes in the organisation of many businesses are already clear. The hands-on management style, flexible structures and consequent fast response times of small firms can be very beneficial in the rapidly changing modern world, and bigger businesses have sought to benefit from them. In effect they have been diminishing the disadvantages of bigness by contracting out many production and service functions. As Mintzberg notes:

This is what NASA did in the 1960s, when its attention was focused on the Apollo project, whose singular goal was to put an American on the moon before 1970. NASA conducted much of its own development work but contracted production out to independent manufacturing firms.[11]

It is also possible to contract in. Self-employed people can take on specific responsibilities 'within' large businesses, working in effect for a price not for a wage. This form of organisation is not new. Clawson shows that it was an important aspect of industrial organisation in textiles, transport and iron and steel in the transition from craft organisations to the fully fledged factory in eighteenth-century Britain.[12]

There is another discernible trend among large organisations: the creation of federal structures. As large organisations divest themselves of their divisions in pursuit of the benefits of smallness, the task of managing all divisions from the centre – and a much reduced centre, at that – becomes increasingly problematic. An example of this can be seen in *chaebols* (conglomerate businesses) such as Hyundai and Daewoo in Korea, which have had to divest and restructure as the competitiveness and viability of their parts became confused. The solution can be to create a federation, or network, of connected units in which the core organisation acts on behalf of its constituent parts. This only works when the centre:

> genuinely is at the middle of things and is not a polite word for the top ... the centre must cling to its key functions of new people and new money, but its decisions have to be made in consultation with, and on behalf of, the chiefs of the parts.[13]

While such arrangements do provide large organisations with greater flexibility, they have potential drawbacks. They can mean a lessening of commitment on both sides, with employees and subcontractors having to look out themselves for the best deals and for new opportunities. A lessening of paternalism may be accompanied by a lessening of employee loyalty. It can be increasingly a case of everyone for himself or herself.

This trend has been assisted more recently by the application of information and communication technology (ICT) to provide the Internet and facilitate the emergence of significant numbers of knowledge-based and Internet businesses. They, and sometimes other new technology-based businesses, have been referred to as the 'new economy' and they are typically small businesses that each concentrate on an aspect of the overall process and communicate electronically, and often deliver their product or service the same way. This is very different from the 'old economy' of traditional businesses such as chemicals and heavy engineering, where the technology requires the majority of the process workers to be physically present on the same site. However, it could be said that the new economy has precedents such as the clock industry in the nineteenth century when, instead of big manufacturers building complete clocks there were, in places such as Clerkenwell in the east of London, assemblers of clocks who bought the necessary components from an array of local small manufacturers who each specialised in the supply of one sort of component.

These developments have major implications for individuals. If a job for life is no longer either the norm or a realistic aspiration, if even securing a succession of different jobs may not always be easy, if businesses will contract out work rather than employing people to do it, and if those who do have jobs will be working in smaller, more independent business teams or individually, then people themselves will have to be more proactive in arranging and managing their own economic activity. If there will no longer always be an employer to find work, to arrange materials and facilities and to pay wages, then people will have to do it themselves. There will be an increase in the number of people, either from want or necessity, who will be thinking and acting to establish their own smaller work units. That process has also been called 'enterprise', and the changes outlined above have stimulated a desire for more of it and an exploration of what it involved.

> People do realise that job security is gone, but many don't realise what it has been replaced by. The driving force of a career must come from the individual, not the organisation.
>
> Professor Homa Babrami.[14]

As well as individuals perceiving the advantage of being able to fend more for themselves, there has also been an interest in reversing the apparent tendency of many people to look to government, or at least to someone else, for the provision of whatever seems to be missing in society. Some saw this change as the essence of what in the UK was called Thatcherism and, in the United States, Reaganism, but, whatever its label, there has been, in many developed countries, a reduction in the perception of government as the universal provider. There have as a result been corresponding moves to make individuals more aware of their own ability to do things, to accept responsibility and to foster more communal and social development. This has been called an 'enterprise culture', and associated with it are views that there are general economic and social benefits to be gained from having a more enterprising culture, society, family or person. 'Enterprise' has in consequence been on many agendas.

Evolving theory

In parallel with these changes in economies, there were also changes in economic thinking. It used to be assumed that the key factors in production were land, labour and capital, and that economies of scale would mean that large businesses would always be more competitive than small ones. In the middle of the twentieth century, if governments had a concern for small businesses, it was to preserve some of them from large company and large union monopolies, often for largely social reasons. Small businesses were not then thought to be special in economic terms. For instance a book first published in the 1950s called *Business Enterprise* acknowledges that some businesses are small, but it only considers them as a category when looking at the merits and disadvantages of large organisations.[15] Even in its 1967 edition it does not consider that small businesses merited a section or even a chapter of their own.

As technological change speeded up, and as innovation seemed to gain in importance, knowledge began to be seen as a necessary component in the economic equation. But even when knowledge was recognised as a key factor in wealth creation alongside land, labour and capital, theory still seemed to favour larger businesses which were supposed to have advantages in affording the R&D expenditure on which innovation was thought to depend. However when reality showed that, despite the theory, large businesses were not all-powerful and that innovation was often found in clusters of small businesses, the prevailing economic theories began to be reassessed. The places where knowledge was being generated were often not where it was being exploited. Universities, research institutes and large firms were generating the knowledge but it was being exploited by entrepreneurs in, for example, spin-outs which bred more spin-outs. As it became apparent that knowledge was often being exploited better through smaller firms than in larger ones, the importance of the individual entrepreneur, and of entrepreneurial capital, also gained recognition.

Entrepreneurship was seen as the otherwise missing ingredient and as the fifth key economic factor: the factor which commercialised knowledge spill-over and spin-outs, which saw and pursued opportunities, and which built knowledge economies.

The role of entrepreneurship and small business has evolved considerably since the Second World War. What was once considered to be a perhaps necessary drain on western economies has become a central strategic instrument for competitiveness in global markets. Just as it has been important to understand how to manage entrepreneurial firms, it has now become at least as important to understand how to achieve an entrepreneurial society. While this emphasis on small entrepreneurial firms as engines of dynamic efficiency may seem startling after decades of looking at the corporate giants as engines of growth and development, it may not be so new. Before the country was even half a century old, Alexis de Tocqueville, in 1835, reported, 'What astonishes me in the United States is not so much the marvellous grandeur of some undertakings as the innumerable multitude of small ones.'

Acs and Audretsch[16]

Thus not only did the practical observations of Birch and others highlight the importance of small businesses in job creation, but research began to recognise the importance of entrepreneurship as the key link between knowledge and its commercial exploitation, a link upon which economic growth and wealth creation depend. Attention therefore began to be focused on entrepreneurship as well as on small businesses.

The changes in theory and perception mentioned above were not apparent initially, they were not instantaneous, and they did not proceed smoothly. Nevertheless they were, and are still, being felt, and the responses that were perceived as necessary to accommodate them were described as 'enterprise'. Whether it was a move at government level to promote more small business, or an individual entrepreneurial response to changed employment-market conditions, or something in between, the word 'enterprise' came to be attached to it. 'Enterprise' became seen as an important part of the way forward to a stronger economy, to a less dependent society and to a more prosperous future. Then, at the end of the twentieth century, the term entrepreneurship began to widen its meaning and to be used also in this context. For instance in the UK the Labour government which came to power in 1997 often referred to its entrepreneurship agenda. This indicated that the meaning of entrepreneurship was broadening, as it apparently became fashionable to use it sometimes as a synonym for enterprise. This change in terminology did not appear however to indicate any change in policy objectives, which still variously covered encouraging new starts and supporting existing businesses.

Conclusions

For all these reasons 'enterprise', or 'entrepreneurship' in some interpretations, became the thing to explore, to understand and to promote. This resulted in a growth of research about 'enterprise' topics, a proliferation of courses or programmes with 'enterprise' in their title, and an increased readiness to apply the label 'enterprise' to anything remotely connected to small business or to the attitudes or behaviour perceived to be associated with it. It began to be seen almost as some sort of universal cure-all for economic ills.

What enterprise, or sometimes entrepreneurship, consisted of was not always clear, however. For some the terms would appear to have meant simply small business and the activity of starting and running a small business. For others enterprise, and increasingly also entrepreneurship, related to a set of personal qualities that made their holders more ready than others to seek their own solutions to economic or other problems. In this wider sense, an enterprising, or entrepreneurial, person was one who saw opportunities not problems, who looked to the future and not to the past, who was more creative than analytical and who was more active than passive. There was, however, a spectrum of ways in which the words were used, rather than one narrow definition.

To address only one definition of enterprise or of entrepreneurship would not be relevant to other uses of the words. The first part of this book therefore addresses the question 'What is enterprise?' by looking at the range of contexts in which the words have been used and the spectrum of different meanings that these usages imply. It explores some of the components associated with these concepts and examines the ideas associated with enterprise and entrepreneurship from a number of different perspectives. It concludes by considering the implication of some current and potential future developments in society on our need for enterprise or for aspects of it.

Those wishing to study enterprise or entrepreneurship are often interested in one or other of two key aspects. As noted, the words are often used to refer to small business or to the process of their formation, and for many policy makers this aspect would appear to be of prime importance. In Part II of this book, therefore, small business is explored from the point of view not of the small business practitioner or the person thinking of starting a business, which is the approach taken by many writers on the subject, but from the point of view of someone who might desire to encourage more such businesses and might question what constitutes a small business and what particular insights are helpful in understanding small businesses. The issues of small business growth and other associated concepts such as innovation are also linked in to this.

The second aspect, covered in Part III, is the issue of how to promote the growth of enterprise and entrepreneurship, and within that the growth of small businesses in general and in particular. The possible reasons for such external interventions are considered, together with some of the more common or useful theories and assumptions about intervention in enterprise or small business development. Specific intervention categories and methods are then explored, together with some indication of their apparent results. Evaluating the effectiveness of such measures is crucial to determining the efficiency and effectiveness of intervention, and so this part concludes by considering the possibilities, limitations and pitfalls of measuring and evaluating results.

THE KEY POINTS OF CHAPTER 1

- The last 30 years have been a time when a number of parallel developments have become clear.

- Following the relatively successful attempts in countries such as the UK to address unemployment in the 1930s, and the apparent ease of maintaining virtually full employment after the Second World War, a belief had arisen that permanent full employment was possible and that it was the duty of the government to maintain that position.

- However in the 1970s and 1980s unemployment, in particular in the UK, rose considerably, without apparently being susceptible to government attempts to reverse it. Actually employment was not falling, but the number looking for employment was rising.

- Another development was that industry, the traditional main source of employment, was itself changing. It was actually increasing its output, but through increased productivity, not through increased numbers of employees. Expanding output no longer automatically increased employment.

- Birch, however, showed that, at least in the United States, the bigger businesses were actually losing jobs, and that the source of the increased number of jobs needed to maintain employment levels was small businesses. Governments therefore wanted to promote more small business development, in order to maintain economies and to promote more employment.

- Other commentators showed that the structure of employment itself was changing. The mass, long-term employment resulting from the Industrial Revolution was being replaced by a much more flexible employment structure.

- The development of information and communication technology, combined with the increased need for inputs of knowledge rather than physical effort, have facilitated the interactive supply of input from remote locations. This has enabled small suppliers in the 'new economy' to operate remotely from their customers instead having to be co-located on or close to the same production site.

- The implication of this was that business would be increasingly likely to be offering to people not jobs, but tasks to undertake. People therefore would need skills and aptitudes for utilising opportunities to be paid a fee for an amount of work done, instead of finding jobs in which they would then be paid for an amount of time spent. They would have to be more flexible themselves, and more prepared and able to find their own sources of such work. In other words, they would have to be more enterprising.

- In addition to the benefits to individuals of being more enterprising, there are also perceived benefits to society of a more enterprising culture in general that would result in less dependence on government to address all society's ills.

- At the end of the twentieth century the term entrepreneurship also was increasingly being used in this context.

CASE 1.1

A view of Birch

Since David Birch first published his research on job creation by size of firm in 1979, a great deal of public attention has focused upon small firms' role in economic growth. His original research provided a measure of job creation in the US from 1969 to 1976 and concluded that small firms created the majority of net new jobs. Subsequently, the US Small Business Administration has built a similar database and has produced job creation statistics from 1976 to 1990. Thus, a continuous series of job creation statistics exists for 20 years.

Other researchers have used different data sources and methods to examine job creation categorised by size of firm. Some have emulated Birch's research data and methodology and have come to the same conclusions as he. Still others have found new data sources that purport to be better than his. Some of these sources show similar results. More recently, others have criticised Birch's sources and methodologies suggesting that both are incorrect.

Neo-classical economics' theoretical constructs

Birch's *The Job Generation Process*[17] created quite a stir among economists when it reported that most net new jobs were created by small firms not large corporations. This finding was contrary to all previous economic analyses in the US. Few economists understood Birch's work because he used a new data source, Dun & Bradstreet data files, instead of US Department of Labour or Bureau of the Census data. Furthermore, he analysed the employment history of millions of firms individually rather than using the classified data on which mainstream economists relied.

But no one criticised Birch for violation of theoretical constructs, for there is no economic theory about firm size and job creation activity and little mainstream economic theory that addresses firm size at all. Neo-classical economic theory, the foundation of mainstream economic theory in the US, does not incorporate any constructs about small firms except one. That one is an assumption rooted in the ideas of Adam Smith[18] and well known as the theory of 'economies of scale'. Economies of scale simply states that as production volume increases, the cost per unit of output declines. Thus, the larger production organisation will have the lower cost of production. Although it is empirically logical, and can be supported by engineering calculations, the theory is troubled by non-linearity in its structure and has been a consistent source of discord in the ranks of macro and micro economists. Nevertheless, it is a theory, and it is violated by Birch's findings since it is illogical that an economy will have most of its new jobs created by small firms when large firms have lower costs of production. In a competitive market, small firms with higher costs will have lower profits and therefore are unlikely (or unable) to expand their operations.

There is a second economic theory construct, Gibrat's law,[19] that seems to be violated by Birch's findings. Gibrat's law states that all firms grow at the same rate regardless of their size. If this is true, large firms' job creation must necessarily be greater than small firms' because large firms have a larger employment base at the start of any time period.

Interestingly, neither of these theoretical bases was used to object to Birch's research. It is not clear even today, 15 years later (at the time Kirchhoff was writing), why theoretical critiques have not emerged. It can only be assumed that the absence of debate indicates that Birch's research has been ignored because his results were of minor importance in the minds of most mainstream economists. This is because firm size is of no importance in the neo-classical theory model. Firm size is determined by the operation of markets. Smaller size firms have higher costs of production because of economies of scale and must struggle to survive in a market dominated by large firms. Firm size is not a cause of anything in the neo-classical model. Firm size is considered to be a dependent variable and is simply not a variable of any significance.

Thus, there is an absence of neo-classical theoretical constructs to provide a domain for examining job creation research. In fact, many mainstream economists do not understand why the topic is even being discussed. This has led to misunderstanding and conflict among proponents and opponents of the small firm job creation hypothesis. The motives of both sides seem clear. Small business believers have gained much public attention and some policy initiatives to assist their cause. The large business believers have watched their influence wane within society and have become the brunt of much criticism during the recent years of 'down-sizing.' In the US and Canada, a wave of social antagonism is sweeping over large corporations while small business owners have become heroes of job creation. In response, recent job creation research has emerged challenging the appropriateness of all previous research in an effort to regain the long held view that large firms create the majority of new jobs.

Emergence of dynamic methodologies

Most researchers have been trained in the classical scientific method that states a hypothesis must be proposed prior to empirical testing. One reason the classical scientific thinkers have for their view is that theory provides a domain within which empirical methods are designed and applied. Without theory to guide empirical methods, methods become arbitrary. Those who merely 'massage data' to extract meaning are scorned as second rate researchers by the classical thinkers.

On the other hand, it is argued by some that empirical research results lead theory development. In this manner, the job creation empirical research of the last 20 years has clearly challenged mainstream economic theory but no new theory has emerged. Still, this research is full of differing data sources, research methodologies and procedures. Not surprisingly, it is empirical research without theoretical foundations and as dictated by classical thought, it is full of conflict without resolution since there is no agreement on what is being tested and why. In other words, the absence of theory leads to confusion in job creation research.

For this reason, determining what we have learned from job creation research requires a theoretical foundation. Adoption of a theoretical domain will provide a basis for evaluating the arguments that are being advanced today. The theoretical domain proposed is Schumpeter's theory of economic development modified into a typology called 'dynamic capitalism.'

Creative destruction

Schumpeter[20] argues that the main mechanism of economic development in a capitalist economy is creative destruction. Creative destruction occurs when an entrepreneur forms a new firm that uses an innovation(s) to enter an existing market dominated by a few large suppliers. The innovative new firm will grow through the dual processes of (1) increasing overall demand for the products (services) offered in the market and (2) taking market share from the existing suppliers. Thus, while the new firm expands overall economic activity, it also redistributes wealth by destroying market structure and shifting market shares from existing large firms to itself. This creation of new wealth combined with destruction of market structures is called 'creative destruction'.

Schumpeter's theory is quite different from the neo-classical model with its equilibrium market structures. In fact the two theories defy comparison. The neo-classical model is built on a static concept – market equilibrium. Creative destruction is built upon dynamics, deliberate entrepreneurship efforts to change market structures. However, dynamics are difficult to model in mathematics and therefore cannot be developed into predictive models useful for policy-making. Since prediction is an attractive component of economic theory, Schumpeter has traditionally been largely ignored in the US and Canada (see also Chapter 2).

Source: From the start of *Twenty Years Of Job Creation Research: What Have We Learned* by B. A. Kirchhoff, from the 40th International Council for Small Business World Conference, Sydney, 1995.

Points raised

This piece by Bruce Kirchhoff provides some background to Birch's work and high-lights how both his methods and findings differed from those of the more traditional economists. It indicates the potential of dynamic theory, such as that advanced by Schumpeter, to explain the strength of small businesses, in contrast to the static neo-classical model which does not.

QUESTIONS, ESSAY AND DISCUSSION TOPICS

- Why is enterprise now a popular subject for study?
- What are the benefits of enterprise?
- Can governments deliver full employment and, if not, what can they do?
- Explain the reason for the rapid growth in the number of SMEs in the latter part of the twentieth century.
- Provide examples of large firms downsizing and small firm growth in your local area.
- According to economic theory (see Case 1.1), larger firms should have better economies of scale than smaller ones yet, according to Birch, smaller firms create more jobs than larger ones. Do you think that this is correct and, if so, why?

Suggestions for further reading and information

R. Gavron, M. Cowling, G. Holtham and A. Westall, *The Entrepreneurial Society* (London: Institute for Public Policy Research, 1998).
C. Handy, *The Future of Work* (Oxford: Basil Blackwell, 1984).
C. Handy, *The Age of Unreason* (London: Arrow, 1990).
A. Toffler, *The Third Wave* (London: William Collins, 1980).
J. A. Schumpeter, *The Theory of Economic Development* (Cambridge, Mass.: Harvard University Press, 1934) and *Capitalism, Socialism and Democracy* (London: Allen and Unwin, 5th edition, 1976).
Z. J. Acs and D. B. Audretsch, *The Emergence of the Entrepreneurial Society* (Stockholm: Swedish Foundation for Small Business Research, Presentation for the acceptance of the 2001 International Award for Entrepreneurship and Small Business Research, April 2001).
http://www.smallbusinessportal.co.uk – The Small Business Research Portal 'has been designed to provide links to Internet sites that will be helpful to fellow small business researchers, policy-makers and support agencies'.

References

1. C. Handy, *The Future of Work* (Oxford: Basil Blackwell, 1984) p. ix.
2. I. Verheul, S. Wennekers, D. Audretsch and R. Thurik, *Research Report – An Eclectic Theory of*

Entrepreneurship: Policies, Institutions and Culture (Zoetermeer Holland: EIM/Small Business Research and Consultancy, 1999), p. 8.

3. For instance see in Z. J. Acs and D. B. Audretsch, *Innovation and Small Firms* (Cambridge, Mass.: MIT Press, 1990).

4. Sixth Report of the European Observatory for SMEs (Luxembourg, 2001).

5. A. Toffler, *The Third Wave* (London: William Collins, 1980).

6. See D. Deekins and M. Friel, *Entrepreneurship and Small Firms* (London: McGraw-Hill, 2006), p. 121.

7. Ibid.

8. C. Handy, *The Age of Unreason* (London: Arrow, 1990).

9. C. Handy, *The Age of Unreason*, pp. 34–5.

10. From J. Walters, 'Turbulence Ahead for City's Airline' and S. Caulkin, 'Dismembering the Body Corporate' (both in *Observer* ©, 15 September 1996).

11. H. Mintzberg, *The Structuring of Organisations* (Englewood Cliffs, New Jersey: Prentice-Hall, 1979), p. 131.

12. D. Clawson, *Bureaucracy and the Labour Process: The Transformation of US Industry, 1860–1920* (New York: Monthly Review Press, 1980).

13. C. Handy, *The Age of Unreason*, p. 98.

14. Quoted in T. Peters, 'Travel the Independent Road' (*Independent on Sunday*, 2 January 1994).

15. R. S. Edwards and H. Townsend, *Business Enterprise: Its Growth and Organisation* (London: Macmillan, 1958).

16. Z. J. Acs and D. B. Audretsch, *The Emergence of the Entrepreneurial Society* (Stockholm: Swedish Foundation for Small Business Research, Presentation for the acceptance of the 2001 International Award for Entrepreneurship and Small Business Research, April 2001), pp. 26–7.

17. D. Birch, *The Job Generation Process* (Cambridge, MA: MIT Programme on Neighborhood and Regional Change, 1979).

18. A. Smith, *An Inquiry into the Nature and Causes of the Wealth of Nations* (New York: Modern Library, 1937) (first published in 1776).

19. R. Gibrat, *Les Inégalités Economiques* (Paris: Editions Sirey, 1931).

20. J. A. Schumpeter, *The Theory of Economic Development* (Cambridge, MA: Harvard University Press, 1951) (first published in 1934); *Capitalism, Socialism and Democracy*, fifth edition (London: Allen and Unwin, 1976).

CHAPTER 2

Enterprise and entrepreneurship: what do they mean?

Contents

KEY CONCEPTS

This chapter covers:

- The spectrum of meanings of the words 'enterprise' and 'entrepreneurship' which, judging from the contexts in which they are used, range from the narrow to the very broad.

- The 'narrow' meanings refer specifically to business and in this context can refer to starting a business, being in business or growing and developing a business, and the word enterprise can even refer to a business itself.

- The 'broad' meanings refer to attitudes and skills which, when possessed by individuals, lead them to exhibit innovative behaviour, including business entrepreneurialism.

> - How these attributes and skills often differ from many of those fostered by traditional education or by larger corporate businesses.
>
> ## LEARNING OBJECTIVES
>
> By the end of this chapter the reader should:
>
> - Be aware of how the words enterprise and entrepreneurship are often used and the range of meanings they can have.
> - Understand the distinctions between the 'narrow' and 'broad' ranges of meaning.
> - Understand the differences between enterprise or entrepreneurial attitudes and skills and those fostered by traditional education or by larger corporate businesses.

Introduction

> Enterprise – Undertaking, esp. bold or difficult one; readiness to engage in such undertakings; enterprising, showing courage or imaginativeness.
>
> Entrepreneur – Person in effective control of commercial undertaking; one who undertakes an enterprise, with chance of profit or loss.
>
> *The Oxford Handy Dictionary*

As Chapter 1 indicated, by the end of the twentieth century enterprise and entrepreneurship had become attractive concepts for many people. They were being promoted, not least by governments, because it was thought that they were necessary for economic growth and future employment opportunities. Enterprise and/or entrepreneurship have been popular labels for a variety of initiatives but, in this varied exchange, the terms have been used in different ways and they have not had commonly accepted precise definitions. This chapter therefore considers the meanings that have apparently been given to these words and explores the sometimes different things they have come to mean.

Like many fashionable labels, these words appear sometimes to have been applied more for the cachet they bring with them than for the appropriateness of their application. Dictionary definitions of are some help, but language evolves and the meaning of words can change as their usage develops. This book is concerned *inter alia* with understanding what people actually mean when they use these words and their implications, rather than with trying to isolate an abstract concept of 'enterprise' or 'entrepreneurship' and to impose single uniform meanings for them. In this chapter, therefore, some of the key usages are considered and the meaning, or meanings of their authors extracted or deduced.

Examples of 'enterprise' usage

ILLUSTRATION 2.1
Enterprise

The British sense of enterprise

BERR: The Department of Business, Enterprise and Regulatory Reform

The Enterprise Initiative for Industry

Scottish Enterprise

The Enterprise Investment Scheme

Enterprise Ireland

Enterprise Directorate-General

Local Enterprise Agencies

Enterprise in Higher Education

Science Enterprise Challenge

Young Enterprise

and even

The Starship *Enterprise*

International economic agenda

The word enterprise appears in many international contexts, but mainly in the context of economics and business. Smaller businesses are referred to almost universally as small and medium-sized enterprises, usually abbreviated to SMEs. Many bodies with an economic remit have an enterprise policy which is often focused on the needs of business. The EU and the OECD are examples of this.

The European Union

'In his communication to the European Council at Lisbon, the President of the Commission called for the European Union, building on the stability that had been achieved and taking advantage of the favourable economic outlook, to take action to ensure stable economic growth, full employment and social cohesion. The communication pointed to the important role which has to be played by enterprise policy in fulfilling this ambition and in ensuring that Enterprise Europe meets the challenge of the knowledge economy.'[1]

'The European Union's commitment to help create a climate in which enterprise, industry and innovation can thrive is officially stated in EC Article 157' (in Title XVI of the EC Treaty). 'EU enterprise policy today is tailored to the needs of the entire business community and its environment. Its history has been shaped by work in three key policy areas: small and medium-sized enterprises (SMEs), innovation and competitiveness, including single market opportunities and benefits.'[2]

OECD (Organisation for Economic Co-operation and Development)

'The OECD brings together the governments of countries committed to democracy and the market economy from around the world'. It has a membership of 30 countries and its departments include the Directorate for Financial and Enterprise Affairs and the Centre for Entrepreneurship, SMEs and Local Development. The prime objective of the Directorate for Financial and Enterprise Affairs is 'to identify policies and best practices designed to keep markets open, competitive and sustainable', while the Centre for Entrepreneurship, SMEs and Local Development 'aims at disseminating best practice on the design, implementation, evaluation and promotion of entrepreneurship and SME policies and local development initiatives'.[3]

UK government initiatives

Lord Young, when he was the UK Secretary of State for Employment, said that: 'We must have an enterprise culture, not a dependency culture.' When he was asked what he meant by enterprise he described it as: 'Get up and go – not sitting back and accepting it. Think positive and things can happen; if you are passive and think negative then nothing happens. It's a mental attitude.'[4]

In 2002 the Chancellor of the Exchequer, the Secretary of State for Education and Skills and the Secretary of State for Trade and Industry jointly commissioned Howard Davies to produce his review of *Enterprise and the Economy in Education* in which he said:

> It is also likely that young people in education now will face greater economic uncertainty and more frequent change in their future working lives than did their predecessors. Against that background, all young people will need more enterprising skills and attitudes, not just to set up businesses (or enter self-employment), but also to build their own careers and to stay employable. In addition enterprise may be seen as a set of skills, attributes and capabilities which can help weaken the link between economic uncertainty and social exclusion.[5]

In 2007 the Shadow Chancellor George Osborne commissioned a report on the decline of Britain's small business sector under the Labour government. According to the authors of the report its main objective was 'to develop a set of policy guidelines that would improve the culture of enterprise in the UK and thus contribute towards making Britain the enterprise capital of the world'.[6]

In the UK the former Department of Trade and Industry (DTI) is now the Department of Business, Enterprise and Regulatory Reform (BERR). In 1988 the DTI launched its Enterprise Initiative, which brought together many of the schemes of support provided by the DTI for industry and commerce. At its launch the DTI considered whether its plans were 'an industrial policy', but concluded that:

the phrase itself is unfortunate, because it appears to concentrate on industry rather than consider all the factors which affect the ability of industry and commerce to create wealth; it also carries the flavour of the DTI taking responsibility for the fortunes of individual industries and companies. It will be obvious that neither is consistent with the philosophy of this paper. ... But the government has a coherent set of policies towards industry and commerce. That set of policies is better described as an enterprise strategy than an industrial policy.[7]

The DTI described its objectives as follows:

The needs and demands of society can only be met by increasing prosperity. The prime objective of the Department is to assist this process throughout the economy and then to champion all the people who make it happen, rather than just individual sectors, industries or companies. ... We seek to:
- produce a more competitive market by encouraging competition and tackling restrictive practices, cartels and monopolies;
- secure a more efficient market by improving the provision of information to business about new methods and opportunities;
- create a larger market by privatisation and deregulation;
- increase confidence in the working of markets by achieving a fair level of protection for the individual consumer and investor.

We will encourage the transfer of technologies and co-operative research, the spread of management education and the growth of links between schools and the world of work. Our objective will be to produce a climate which promotes enterprise and prosperity.[8]

In the 1988 White Paper describing the role of DTI, encouraging enterprise was described as 'one of the major economic goals of the Government'. 'Enterprise', the DTI said:

is fundamental to a dynamic and growing economy. Lack of enterprise played a major part in the relative decline of the British economy; its return has played a major role in the recent economic revival. The key to continued economic success lies in the further encouragement of the enterprise of our people. ... The change of approach is reflected throughout DTI's activities. DTI will be the Department for Enterprise.[9]

These examples are all taken from UK government initiatives and publications. The major thrust of government industrial policy in the UK under the Conservatives in the 1980s and 1990s was the creation of a climate that stimulated enterprise and thereby sought to increase prosperity. In this context, as the above examples show either explicitly or by implication, the concept of enterprise was concerned with business, with the creation of new businesses or with the development of existing ones. In 1997 the Labour government took over. One if its priorities was to create an environment conducive to stimulating entrepreneurship, and since its arrival it has taken steps to attempt to tackle barriers to enterprise and entrepreneurship by addressing economic, political, legal and cultural issues in order to boost rates of entrepreneurial activity.[10] These initiatives have been in support of the overall aim of economic improvement which was expected to come from business development which, in turn, was to come from more enterprise and entrepreneurship.

Regional and local enterprise organisations

The Local Enterprise Companies (LECs) in Scotland, and the former Training and Enterprise Councils (TECs) in England and Wales, were formed as the result of central government initiative. However there are many examples of enterprise organisations formed as a result of regional and local initiatives.

Scottish Enterprise is Scotland's main economic development agency, funded by the Scottish government. It is the successor to the Scottish Development Agency and its mission is 'to help the people and businesses of Scotland succeed'. In doing so, it aims 'to build a world-class economy'.[11]

Enterprising Nottinghamshire is an initiative designed to promote an awareness and understanding of the creative potential of people. Its aim was 'to develop and encourage an enterprising culture in Nottinghamshire', and a presentation on its achievements indicated that: 'an Enterprising Person was someone who displays initiative, makes decisions, manages resources, shows drive and determination, influences others and monitors progress.'[12]

Then there are local enterprise agencies, many of which have been around for some time. Their formation was due not primarily to a central government policy, but to a series of local initiatives. Their aims are therefore relatively diverse. One example is the London Enterprise Agency (LEntA), which:

exists to enable a group of the UK's leading companies to work together to tackle some of the economic and employment issues facing inner-London. ... The LEntA member companies aim to foster job and wealth creation, and to improve the economic prospects of the least advantaged among inner-London's residents.[13]

CASE 2.1
The Scottish Institute for Enterprise

The Scottish Institute for Enterprise (SIE) was established with support from the Science Enterprise Challenge. Its mission is 'to stimulate, educate, facilitate and create enterprising individuals with the skills to contribute to a Smart Successful Scotland'. It works with all 19 higher education institutions in Scotland and provides 'a free service for all of Scotland's students to encourage enterprising spirit and skills, and help start-up companies become the businesses of tomorrow'. It aims 'to inspire students and spark their curiosity with a number of events and activities throughout the year'. Its three major events are its Business Plan Competition, Social Enterprise Conference and International Student Enterprise Summit. Its activities range from developing an awareness and involvement with social enterprise to considering gender issues in the student–business workplace.

For a student with a business idea who needs support, SIE is readily available with four regional business advisers. They act as mentors and provide professional advice and excellent networks, and do all in their ability to help the business get on its feet. SIE also hosts a range of master classes for expert advice on a range of topics. In partnership with Scottish Enterprise it can also fund the filing of intellectual property for students and graduates.

> Most importantly, we want to emphasise to every student in Scotland that no matter what their degree, interests or current involvement with business, they can discover a world of potential and make enterprise an active part in their life.

Source: taken from the SIE web site: www.sie.ac.uk (accessed 17 January 2008).

Local Enterprise Agencies vary greatly in size and in the range of services offered. But they all have one thing in common, one core activity: counselling of clients looking for advice in starting up or expanding small businesses.

Source: Business in the Community booklet.[14]

Enterprise Northern Ireland is the organisation formed to represent the network of local enterprise agencies (LEAs) in Northern Ireland. Those agencies are 'independent locally-based not for profit companies which have been established, often in partnership with local councils, to support local business and enterprise development. By working together through Enterprise Northern Ireland, LEAs can offer a service of consistent standard across Northern Ireland.'[15]

Higher Education

rise in Higher Education (EHE) initiative was introduced by the Secretary
oyment in December 1987. According to the Training Agency:

> aim of EHE is to assist institutions of higher education develop enter-
> ing graduates in partnership with employers. There are as many definitions
> of 'enterprise' as there are people defining the word! However, there is a great
> deal of common ground, and most people would agree that the enterprising
> person is resourceful, adaptable, creative, innovative and dynamic. He or she
> may also be entrepreneurial. However, the qualities of enterprise are as useful in
> the employee as the employer, and equally important in the public, private and
> voluntary sectors. ... The broad aims of the initiative are that:
>
> - Every person seeking a higher education qualification should be able to
>   develop competencies and aptitudes relevant to enterprise.
> - These competencies and aptitudes should be acquired at least through project
>   based work, designed to be undertaken in a real economic setting, which
>   should be jointly assessed by employers and the student's higher education
>   institution.[16]

The aim of the Enterprise in Higher Education programme in one university was
described as:

> to provide the opportunity for all full-time undergraduate students to acquire
> enterprise competencies, without compromising academic and intellectual stan-
> dards. Students will be afforded the chance to develop both personal skills, such
> as leadership, creativity, problem analysis and solving, self awareness and flexi-
> bility; and interpersonal skills such as team building, negotiation and
> persuasion, conflict resolution and all forms of communication including IT.

This was also expanded as:

> giving all full-time undergraduate students the opportunity to develop their enter-
> prise competencies as an integral part of their academic programme. The university
> has chosen to adopt a broad definition of enterprise, based on personal transferable
> skills. These include:
>
> - Communication skills: written reports, oral presentations, media awareness
> - Group-work skills: leadership, teamwork, group dynamics
> - Personal skills: self-awareness and self-appraisal
> - Organisational skills: time-management, task management, objective setting
> - Interpersonal skills: listening, negotiation and persuasion, mutual confidence
>   and respect
> - Problem-solving: problem analysis, creative thinking and decision making
> - Social and community awareness: sensitivity to others, moral and ethical
>   bases of decision making
> - Resource management skills: economic awareness, costing and budgeting.'[17]

After the Enterprise in Higher Education initiative, another attempt made by the UK government was the Science Enterprise Challenge. Its aim was 'to establish a network of centres in the UK universities, specialising in the teaching and practice of commercialisation and entrepreneurialism in the field of science and technology'.[18] In the first round of funding, 12 science enterprise centres were established in UK universities and the initiative, under its new name of Enterprise Educators UK, by 2008 supported almost 80 institutions 'to develop their practice, network with peers, and collaborate in enterprise and entrepreneurship teaching and research across all curriculum areas'.[19] (See Case 2.1.)

Young Enterprise

Young Enterprise has its origins in the Junior Achievement organisation in the United States. In the UK it is a national educational charity, founded in 1963, with the mission of providing young people from 5 to 25 with an exciting, imaginative and practical business experience, enabling them to develop their personal and interpersonal skills, knowledge and understanding of business objectives and the wealth creation process. It does this by, *inter alia*, giving young people the chance to learn from setting up and running their own companies during one academic year. By 2008 almost 500,000 students from schools and colleges were participating each year in the UK, supported by businesses and volunteers. The benefits the charity delivers to its participating 'achievers' include improving their business knowledge, influencing their career and study preferences, improving their attitudes and skills such as the ability to work in a team and self-confidence, and supporting qualifications in business core skills.

Young Enterprise therefore sees 'enterprise' primarily in the context of business, but within that context it is concerned with the acquisition of attitudes and skills that involve discovery, confidence and achievement, as well as the specific business skills of marketing, finance, communication and organisation.

Other examples

An enterprise culture is one in which every individual understands that the world does not owe him or her a living, and so we act together accordingly, all working for the success of UK plc. The gross national product is earned by companies. Successful companies which regularly make profits and grow are the flagships of the enterprise culture. Directors who lead those successful companies are heroes of the enterprise culture. Any of our products or services which lead the world are the pride of the enterprise culture.

In an enterprise culture we expect that some of the wealth will be used for public goods and services, but we believe that wealth-creation comes first.

Peter Morgan[20]

How is the 'enterprise culture' to be regarded? Just like some handy little slogan? A simple shorthand way for describing developing small business activity? Some

visdom about such? Small businesses' new guiding spirit? Or just some
'd party political trademark? Maybe the latest populist catchphrase? A
sed euphemism which glosses over something else?

John Ritchie[21]

Une can be enterprising both by making a million before one's fortieth birthday
and by shepherding passengers out of a burning aeroplane.[22]

Enterprise is having ideas and imagination and using them.[23]

The mission of the Starship *Enterprise* is 'to boldly go where no man has gone
before'.

These examples of the word 'enterprise' demonstrate that the word has, in normal
usage, a wide variety of meanings. In some cases its meaning is limited to the business context, but in others, for instance when applied to the *Starship Enterprise*, it
is an attitude to life, an attitude of exploring, of developing, of leading and of
taking initiatives, which, while it may help in the business context, has much
wider relevance.

Examples of 'entrepreneurship' usage

The word entrepreneurship has been used to refer mainly to the process of starting or
running a business. This usage is, for instance, referred to in the GEM definition of
entrepreneurship (see Chapter 4) which is 'any attempt to create a new business enterprise or to expand an existing business by an individual, a team of individuals or an
established business'.[24] It is also the basis of Shane's approach: 'Entrepreneurship is an
activity that involves the discovery, evaluation, and exploitation of opportunities to
introduce new goods and services, ways of organising, markets, processes, and raw
materials through organising efforts that previously had not existed.'[25] Now however
it is often being used with a somewhat wider meaning.

Entrepreneurship education

The concept of entrepreneurship has been moving away from one which is just
concerned with the act of new venture creation or growth, and this can be seen, for
instance, in the context of entrepreneurship education, which has become very
popular. A definition of entrepreneurship used in Harvard is: 'Entrepreneurship is the
pursuit of opportunity beyond the resources you currently control'[26] and recently, in
Northern Ireland, the government's Entrepreneurship and Education Action Plan
offered a definition of entrepreneurship as 'the ability of an individual, possessing a
range of essential skills and attributes, to make a unique, innovative and creative

contribution in the world of work, whether in employment or self-employment'.[27] This approach is also used by Allan Gibb who has said that:

> Entrepreneurship relates to ways in which people, in all kinds of organisations behave in order to cope with and take advantage of uncertainty and complexity and how in turn this becomes embodied in: ways of doing things; ways of seeing things; ways of feeling things; ways of communicating things; and ways of learning things.[28]

These two, somewhat different, approaches to the meaning of entrepreneurship were picked up by the EU Working Group which looked at entrepreneurship education in preparation for the Lisbon Strategy. The Group's definition of 'education and training for entrepreneurship' therefore included two components:

- 'A broader concept of education for entrepreneurial attributes and skills, which involves developing certain personal qualities and is not directly focused on the creation of new businesses, and
- A more specific concept of training in how to create a business.'[29]

And also in the context of education, a paper on evaluating entrepreneurship education did not distinguish between the words 'enterprise' and 'entrepreneurship' but often used them jointly and treated them more or less as one concept. It did suggest that there are three different roles which might be assigned to enterprise and/or entrepreneurship education programmes depending on whether the aim was:

- To learn to understand entrepreneurship (What do entrepreneurs do? What is entrepreneurship? Why are entrepreneurs needed?), or
- To learn to become entrepreneurial (I need to take responsibility for my learning, career and life. How to do it?), or
- To learn to become an entrepreneur (Can I become an entrepreneur? How to become an entrepreneur? Managing the business).[30]

In recognition of the extent of entrepreneurship in the UK the National Council for Graduate Entrepreneurship (NCGE) was formed in 2004 'with the aim of raising the profile of entrepreneurship and the option of starting your own business as a career choice amongst students and graduates'. 'The Council is not only focused on graduates starting businesses, but on understanding, developing and promoting a culture of entrepreneurship within Higher Education through research, education and facilitation' and it 'aims to become the national focal point for graduate entrepreneurship'.[31]

'Entrepreneurship is 'I've earned it', not 'I deserve it'.
David Hall, in an Institute of Business Advisers
breakfast presentation, Belfast 2003

The field of entrepreneurship is 'an intellectual onion. You peel it back layer by layer and when you get to the centre, there is nothing there, but you are crying'.
A senior faculty member at Harvard Business School in 1983[32]

Social entrepreneurship

Another application of the word entrepreneurship which has become noticeable recently has been in the term 'social entrepreneurship'. Increasingly the social economy, and the wider third sector of which it is a part, are being recognised as a significant and beneficial part of an economy. The difference between it and the private sector is that private sector businesses are formed primarily to make money for their founders and/or owners whereas third sector organisations, while they have to generate financial income to pay for their costs, are formed primarily to achieve other purposes, which are often social in nature. Nevertheless the process of starting or growing third sector organisations still requires entrepreneurship and those who do it are therefore referred to as social entrepreneurs. Like private sector entrepreneurs, they are being enterprising in the achievement of personal objectives, and if they differ, it is only in the extent to which their objectives are focused on personal enrichment. (See also Social Enterprise and the Social Economy in Chapter 5.)

Narrow and broad meanings of enterprise and entrepreneurship

> Endeavour to be firm (10 letters)
>
> (Crossword clue)[33]

In many of the examples examined above the implication is that 'enterprise' is seen, at least primarily, as connected with the promotion of business generally, or of small business and/or business starts in particular. Some of the examples however suggest that, on occasion, it can have a wider meaning. Writing on 'enterprise culture' the author of an OECD monograph indicated that

> there are, in effect, two definitions of, or approaches to, the word 'enterprise' and the practice of it. One, which can be termed a 'narrow' one, regards enterprise as business entrepreneurialism, and sees its promotion and development within education and training systems as an issue of curriculum development which enables young people to learn, usually on an experiential basis, about business start-up and management. The second approach, which can be termed the 'broad' one, regards enterprise as a group of qualities and competencies that enable individuals, organisations, communities, societies and cultures to be flexible, creative, and adaptable in the face of, and as contributors to, rapid social and economic change.[34]

In answer to the question 'What do we mean by enterprise?', another commentator replied:

> Two schools of theory and practice are evident, each based on different although not contradictory answers to the question. They can be called the

'economy school' and the 'education school'. The 'economy school' says that enterprise is what entrepreneurs do and entrepreneurs create business and jobs and wealth and those things all contribute to, indeed they comprise, the economy. ... The 'education school' says that enterprise has a broader meaning and application than that. ... It says that many types of initiative which need to be taken, many types of responsibility which need to be discharged and many types of problems which need to be resolved require the individual to act in an 'enterprising' manner. Thus this school sees business-type entrepreneurialism as just one context in which people act in 'enterprising' ways. It says that enterprise involves using the imagination, being creative, taking responsibilities, organising, identifying ideas, making decisions, dealing with others in a wide range of contexts. It says that as society becomes more complex and as it changes towards greater complexity, people need to be more and more enterprising. At the heart of this approach is, therefore, personal development and, in particular, the development of self-confidence.[35]

Now entrepreneurship, like enterprise, also seems to have a range of meanings. Whereas it was once used primarily to refer to the process of business formation or growth, in a way similar to the narrow meaning of enterprise, it clearly now can have a wider application which is similar to the broader meaning of enterprise.

The narrower view of enterprise and entrepreneurship: business creation and development

> The carrying out of new combinations (of means of production) we call 'enterprise'; and the individuals whose function it is to carry them out we call 'entrepreneurs'.
>
> Joseph Schumpeter[36]

The 'narrow' or 'economy' school view is the one behind many of the examples quoted in the introduction to this chapter. In that context it is not possible to explore enterprise without also examining 'entrepreneurialism' and 'entrepreneurship', because frequently the words are used interchangeably, and have a common root.

There have been, of course, examples of entrepreneurs and entrepreneurial behaviour from very early times. As Bolton and Thompson point out, one type of entrepreneur who has appeared consistently throughout history has been the merchant entrepreneur, some of whom made the Great Silk Road into the market-driven highway it became.[37] They did not describe themselves as entrepreneurs though, and nor did they appear to have had a concept of entrepreneurship.

The evolution of that concept can be traced back to an Irish economist living in France called Richard Cantillon, who introduced the word into economic literature in his 'Essai sur la nature de commerce en général', said to have been written in 1734 but not published until 1755, 21 years after his death. The word is derived from the French *entreprendre* meaning 'to take between' and entrepreneur referred originally to a 'go-between' or broker. Cantillon's implicit concept of the entrepreneur is a broad one, but it is based on the entrepreneur as a person with the foresight and confidence to operate in conditions when costs may be known but rewards are uncertain.

Jean-Baptiste Say (1767–1832), the first professor of economics in Europe, produced a narrower definition of the entrepreneur that involved the combination and co-ordination of the factors of production to accommodate the unexpected and overcome problems. It was however earlier, in 1776, that the capitalist concept had been first described as a relatively complete theory by Adam Smith in his book *The Wealth of Nations*.[38] This work was the foundation of the classical capitalist economic theory, and it identified the capitalist as the owner or manager who, from basic resources of land, labour and capital, constructed successful industrial enterprises. By the middle of the next century the word 'entrepreneur' was being used to indicate the owner-manager of an industrial enterprise.

By the start of the twentieth century a further refinement in theory of the capitalist economy had been developed by the neo-classical school, in particular by Leon Walras and Alfred Marshall. Its key component is that of market equilibrium, when supply equals demand in a perfectly competitive market. This theory does not have a place, however, for the 'entrepreneur' as a cause of economic activity. Suppliers should instead respond to market pressures: if prices rise they should supply more, and if prices fall, less. They should not upset this equilibrium by introducing innovative products or services. Classical economists, and in particular a group in Austria, objected to this absence of entrepreneurialism. One of their students was Joseph Schumpeter, who went to the United States early in his career. He believed that the concept of innovation, described as the use of an invention to create a new commercial product or service, was the key force in creating new demand and thus new wealth. Entrepreneurs were the owner-managers who, in this way, started new businesses to exploit invention. If successful they thus created wealth for themselves and employment for others from their ability and ambition, rather than only from ownership of land or capital (see also Case 1.1 in Chapter 1).

Leibenstein, whose first theoretical observations on entrepreneurship were published in 1968, distinguished between two activities: the activity of the entrepreneur who introduces innovation in product, process or service, and the activity of the manager who establishes or runs a business in traditional ways. Schumpeter argued in 1934, in *The Theory of Economic Development*, that entrepreneurs were different from those who solely managed businesses without innovating, and it was these entrepreneurs who were the key to wealth creation and distribution in capitalism. Innovations create new demand and entrepreneurs bring the innovations to the market. This destroys existing markets and creates new ones, which will in turn be destroyed by even newer products or services. Schumpeter called this process 'creative destruction'. This is a dynamic process, which contrasts sharply with the static equilibrium theory of the neo-classicists. Nevertheless it was the almost scientific appeal of the latter that maintained it as the dominant theory for much of the twentieth century.[39]

Whyte, in his book *The Organisation Man* (1956), suggests that the American experience of the Depression followed by the military training of the Second World War created a belief in, or at least an obedience to, bureaucracies.[40] America had thus become conditioned to believe in the large corporation as the major, and as the preferred, source of employment. In 1967 John Kenneth Galbraith published *The New Industrial State*, in which he highlighted the benefit of economies of scale in production, as evidenced by

Henry Ford's assembly lines.[41] As production organisations become larger, the theory went, greater specialisation of labour and machines was possible, which in turn reduced the unit cost of production. Large firms therefore have lower costs of production than small ones and, as there are no theoretical limits to their size, they will dominate society. Galbraith thus believed that large corporations would work with government and large unions and, based on a shared view of organisation life, they could in effect run the state.

The idea of economies of scale fitted in well with neo-classical economic theory and evidence for their existence appeared to be provided by management information and by plant engineers' calculations. The fact that researchers had difficulty in documenting real examples did not impinge on mainstream economic thought. Big business ruled, and the dominant perception of entrepreneurs was summed up in the saying that 'Entrepreneurs are people who start their own business to avoid getting a job'.[42] It was the results of Birch's economic analysis that helped to change this perception. He concluded that in the United States, in the period between 1969 and 1976, small firms created the majority of the net new jobs, a result that was initially discounted by most economists.[43] While Birch's conclusions have been challenged by some subsequent work, the importance of the entrepreneur and the relevance of Schumpeter's theory were at last established and became accepted by mainstream economists. (See also Case 1.1 in Chapter 1.)

Although this central role of the entrepreneur, and therefore of entrepreneurship, in business and economics is now accepted, this does not now mean that there is a single accepted definition of what an entrepreneur is. On the contrary, there are a range of possible meanings, derived from different ways of looking at the entrepreneur and how he or she operates. Table 2.1 summarises the main approaches (aspects of which are also explored in more detail in Chapter 3).

It is the role of entrepreneurship in economic development that is one of the areas of meaning assigned to 'enterprise'. In this context the words enterprise and entrepreneurship can be synonymous. The word 'enterprise' is also used to mean a unit of business, the processes of business start-up, and the process of being in business and of business growth and development. In other words, it is used to refer to the various elements that contribute directly to economic development and to job creation. These are the 'narrow' meanings of enterprise and of entrepreneurship: they refer to a form of behaviour devoted to the successful development of business.

Enterprise, entrepreneurship and SMEs

As the previous paragraphs indicate, the narrow meaning of enterprise is closely associated with the concept of entrepreneurship and with smaller businesses in particular, often referred to as 'small and medium-sized enterprises' (SMEs). Again, as with enterprise, there is no single generally accepted definition of entrepreneurship but it is not necessarily synonymous with small business, because some take the view that not all small businesses are entrepreneurial and questions are thus asked about the extent to which 'entrepreneurship and SME agendas relate to each other'.[44] Among the definitions and uses of 'entrepreneurship' are:

- 'In this paper we will use the terms business ownership and self employment as equivalent to entrepreneurship.'[45]

Table 2.1 Summary of approaches for describing entrepreneurship

Entrepreneurial model	Central focus or purpose	Assumption	Behaviour and skills	Situation
Great person school	The entrepreneur has an intuitive ability - a sixth sense - and traits and instincts with which he or she is born	Without this 'inborn' intuition, the individual would be like the rest of us mortals, who 'lack what it takes'	Intuition, vigour, energy persistence, and self-esteem	Start-up
Psychological characteristics school	Entrepreneurs have unique values, attitudes and needs that drive them	People behave in accordance with their values; behaviour results from attempts to satisfy needs	Personal values, risk-taking, need for achievement, and others	Start-up
Classical school	The central characteristic of entrepreneurial behaviour is innovation	The critical aspect of entrepreneurship is in the process of doing rather than owning	Innovation, creativity and discovery	Start-up and early growth
Management school	Entrepreneurs are organisers of an economic venture; they are people who organise, own, manage and assume the risk	Entrepreneurs can be developed or trained in the technical functions of management	Production planning, people organising, capitalisation and budgeting	Early growth and maturity
Leadership school	Entrepreneurs are leaders of people; they have the ability to adapt their style to the needs of people	An entrepreneur cannot accomplish his or her goals alone, but depends on others	Motivating, directing and leading	Early growth and maturity
Intrapreneurship school	Entrepreneurial skills can be useful in complex organisations; intrapreneurship is the development of independent units to create, market and expand services	Organisations need to adapt to survive; entrepreneurial activity leads to organisational building and entrepreneurs becoming managers	Alertness to opportunities, maximising decisions	Maturity and change

Source: J. B. Cunningham and J. Lischeron. 'Defining Entrepreneurship,' *Journal of Small Business Management*, 29 January 1991, p.47.

- 'Entrepreneurship has been defined as "any attempt to create a new business enterprise or to expand an existing business by an individual, a team of individuals or an established business"'.[46]

- 'Most definitions of the word "entrepreneur" will take into account the individual aspect, the innovative aspect, the commercial organisation aspect and business behaviour. ... However ... [only] a small fraction of new starters are really innovative [and] if such a criterion is used ... the level of entrepreneurial vitality will be fairly low. ... We use an approach to define entrepreneurs [as] mainly people in the pre-start-up, start-up and early phases of business ownership.'[47]

Therefore if one person or culture uses the word 'enterprise' and another 'entrepreneurship', it should not necessarily be inferred that they are taking about different concepts. It might be that they are just using different language to refer to exactly the same thing.

The broader view of enterprise and entrepreneurship: attributes and resources

'An enterprising individual has a positive, flexible and adaptable disposition towards change, seeing it as normal, and as an opportunity rather than a problem. To see change in this way, an enterprising individual has a security, born of self-confidence, and is at ease when dealing with insecurity, risks, difficulty and the unknown. An enterprising individual has the capacity to initiate creative ideas ... develop them, and see them through into action in a determined manner. An enterprising individual is able, even anxious, to take responsibility and is an effective communicator, negotiator, influencer, planner and organiser. An enterprising individual is active, confident, purposeful, not passive, uncertain and dependent.'

OECD/CERI[48]

The make-up of the entrepreneur has been explored by a number of people. McClelland looked at motives, and identified three underlying ones: the need for achievement, the need for affiliation and the need for power (see also Chapter 3). According to him, the person motivated for high achievement has optimism, wants responsibility, enjoys challenges and novelty, and is a moderate risk-taker.[49] Others have looked at the need for autonomy and the desire for influence. What however is generally being described is a set of attributes that can be used in a number of situations, although often the starting point for identifying these attributes has been the entrepreneur.

Enterprise, claims Gibb, is the exercise of such a set of attributes and the entrepreneur, he suggests, is someone who demonstrates a marked use of these attributes in a particular task or context, usually in business or commerce (and see Table 2.2). If, though, entrepreneurship is defined solely in terms of a form of behaviour related to a set of attributes and skills, it follows that there are entrepreneurs in all kinds of organisations, for these attributes are displayed and developed by a wide

Table 2.2 Entrepreneurial behaviours, attributes, skills, values and beliefs

Entrepreneurial behaviours
Opportunity seeking and grasping
Taking initiatives to make things happen
Solving problems creatively
Managing autonomously
Taking responsibility for, and ownership of, things
Seeing things through
Networking effectively to manage interdependence
Putting things together creatively
Using judgement to take calculated risk

    Entrepreneurial attributes
    Achievement orientation and ambition
    Self-confidence and self-belief
    Perseverance
    High internal locus of control (autonomy)
    Action orientation
    Preference for learning by doing
    Hardworking
    Determination
    Creativity

        Entrepreneurial skills
        Creative problem solving
        Persuading
        Negotiating
        Selling
        Proposing
        Holistically managing business/projects/situations
        Strategic thinking
        Intuitive decision making under uncertainty
        Networking

            Values and beliefs – entrepreneurship is embodied in sets of values and
            beliefs relating to:
            Ways of doing things
            Ways of seeing things
            Ways of feeling things
            Ways of communicating things
            Ways of organising things and, importantly for education:
            Ways of learning things

              But not – Entrepreneurial behaviours, skills and attributes are not
synonymous with interpersonal, transferable or core skills as set out in GNVQ literature. Problem
solving is very different from creative problem solving. Communication, presentation skills,
numeracy and so on underpin entrepreneurial skills but are not identical with them and can be
utilised in 'bureaucratic' occupations. Without clearer thinking it is therefore possible to end up
confusing entrepreneurship with:
              Industrial awareness
              Financial awareness
              Economic awareness
              Business management skills
              Small business management
              Work experience
              Project work in industry
              Start-up simulations
              Transferable skills
              Key skills

Source: Based on *Creating The Leading Edge*, Allan Gibb and Judi Cotton, Durham Business School, 1998.

variety of people working in many different circumstances – these are 'enterprising' people. There is, for example, much scope for entrepreneurial behaviour within bureaucracies, although when this behaviour is frustrated or cannot be contained within the organisation and is regarded as deviant, then job change, or indeed self-employment, may be pursued as a means of exercising these attributes. This is in line with the idea of the entrepreneur as a 'marginal man': put simply, this is someone who does not fit easily into the conventional organisation. Within the conventional employee role, there may be more or less scope for exercise of entrepreneurial attributes, depending on the structure and purpose of the organisation (or parts of it) and the amount of individual freedom. Motivation to develop and exercise entrepreneurial attributes, whatever the nature of the work or location, is important. It is clear that, in some organisations, the exercise of such attributes will be seen as 'desirable'; in others it will be labelled as 'deviant'. The issue of 'desirability' of entrepreneurial behaviour is an important one not confined only to the culture of the work place, but also clearly of importance in terms of society as a whole.[50]

If enterprise, or entrepreneurship, is the exercise of a set of attributes and behaviours then those attributes can also be illustrated by the process by which they might, or might not, be developed. Gibb has analysed and described the relevant attributes, ideas, ambitions and culture and their development utilising a number of diagrams. At almost all stages of life, he believes, there are factors that can influence the development of enterprising/entrepreneurial ideas and some of these are summarised in Table 2.3.

An enterprise culture is generally one in which several influences combine to reinforce the development of enterprise. This is for instance indicated in Figure 2.1

Table 2.3 Influences on the development of entrepreneurial ideas and ambitions at different stages of life

Childhood	Adolescence	Early adulthood	Middle adulthood	Late adulthood
Parental and wider family class and class mobility	Parental/wider family influence on educational choice	Choice of further education/ training	Occupational and class mobility	Class attained and income/wealth achieved
Parental and wider family work situation	Parental and wider family influence on vocational preference	Own class ranking	Nature of work	Family situation
Parental and wider family educational choice	Choices of vocational education available	Friendship and community attachment	Own family and friendship	Communal attachments
Parental and wider family values and 'life goals'	Education as provider of values and goals	Residual family influence	Working relationships	Extra work opportunities
	Friendship and community attachments	Possible own family	Reward systems and job satisfaction	Job satisfaction
		Nature of work	Interactions with environment socially and at work	Pensions and early retirement facilities
			Business training and development	

Source: A. A. Gibb, 'Enterprise Culture: Its Meaning and Implications for Education and Training', *Journal of European Industrial Training* (1987), p.13.

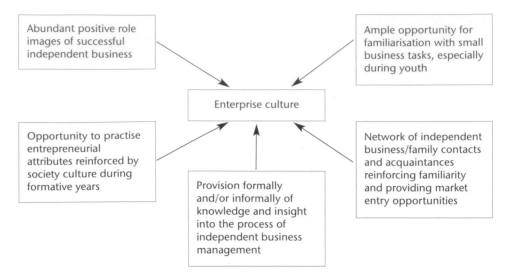

Figure 2.1 The components of enterprise culture

Source: A. A. Gibb, 'Enterprise Culture: Its Meaning and Implications for Education and Training', *Journal of European Industrial Training* (1987) p.14.

although this example presents enterprise somewhat towards its narrower definition.

Youth is the stage of life when people are most susceptible to the influences which might make an enterprise culture. Often, however, the focus of formal education is different from that of enterprise, as Table 2.4 shows.

Later in life also, people are subject to influences that are not enterprising ones. Gibb, for instance, contrasts the values and systems embodied by a corporate and/or bureaucratic approach to those of an entrepreneurial management system (Table 2.5).

The issue of enterprise within business relates both to business-founding owners, who might be expected to have some enterprise, and business managers, who might be more inclined to take the corporatist approach. In the 1950s and 1960s, when markets seemed more stable, many managers saw the efficient utilisation of resources and the perfecting of performance in marketing and production as their primary tasks. They implemented plans, co-ordinated disparate activities and controlled behaviour.

In the relatively more turbulent world of the 1980s this behaviour no longer brought continued success. Rapid changes in knowledge, in markets and in education meant that organisations needed to strive for both efficiency and the customisation of goods or services. Several writers have highlighted the role of managers in energising adaptable employees to use all their skills and knowledge in a flexible manner to provide customers with satisfaction. High-quality customised products provide benefits, but they can only be produced by committed flexible ~~·~~s, not alienated ones maintaining rigid demarcations.[51] Thus, for Sala-~~:~~ essence of management is the ability to enhance the performance of ~~ı~~ates by 'doing the right things, doing things right and then better, or ~~ʒ~~ to do new things'.[52] While new small businesses may play an increasing

Table 2.4 The focus of learning

Education focus on	Entrepreneurial focus on
The past	The future
Critical analysis	Creativity
Knowledge	Insight
Passive understanding	Active learning
Absolute detachment	Emotional involvement
Manipulation of symbols	Manipulation of events
Written communication and neutrality	Personal communication and influence
Concept	Problem or opportunity

Source: A. A. Gibb, 'Enterprise Culture: Its Meaning and Implications for Education and Training', *Journal of European Industrial Training* (1987), p.17.

Table 2.5 Entrepreneurial versus corporatist management – some contrasts

Entrepreneurial management	Corporatist management
Values, beliefs and goals	
Growth by green field management	Growth by acquisition
Short time horizons	Long time horizons
Informal strategic project planning (policy and practice interlinked and changing and emerging)	Formalised planning systems (policy laid before practice)
Failure means missed opportunity	Failure means resource-centred misdemeanour (variance from standard)
Seeks incremental development as a means to reduce risk	Seeks large-scale development with risk reduction by analysis/information
Pursues action strategies with negotiation as and where necessary	Pursues pre-negotiation strategies for decision making (personal risk reduction)
Management evaluation on task completion	Management evaluation as routine aspect of organisation
Status equals success in the market	Status equals control over resources
Avoidance of overhead and risk of obsolescence by high subcontracting	Seeks ownership of all resources with objective of power and control
Pursues effectiveness in the marketplace	Pursues efficiency information to justify control
Organisational contrasts	
Flat organisational structure	Hierarchical organisation structure
Challenge to owner legitimacy	Clear authority
Need to trust others for reward	Clear reward system defined
Organic relationship emerging	Rational/legal structures

Source: A. A. Gibb, 'Enterprise Culture: Its Meaning and Implications for Education and Training', *Journal of European Industrial Training* (1987), pp. 21–2.

role in net job creation, increasing enterprise in established businesses is also critical to at least the continuance of existing jobs.

Within the debate on enterprising attributes and culture, it has been pointed out that the characteristics that are required for the wider application of enterprise are also those needed for the narrower one. It is not possible only to develop attributes in, or for application in, a business context. If someone has these attributes then he or she is liable to use them wherever they appear to be appropriate, whether it be for an economic, a social, a political, an environmental or other purpose. Further, if these attributes are, at least in part, acquired during upbringing and through education then that often happens before career choices are made. To get more enterprise in business it therefore would appear to be necessary to try to develop more enterprise for all contexts.

Other aspects of enterprise

A further development of this debate has taken place more specifically in the context of enterprise as applied to business start-up. The more traditional view of enterprise has been largely that it is a form of behaviour that exists and can be measured and encouraged, but which is not evenly distributed among the population. Some have more of it than others, and it is those with more of it who tend to display enterprising activity such as starting businesses. The implication has been that if more of those individual levels of enterprise could be raised above some sort of implicit enterprise threshold then more enterprise activity and more business start-ups would be the result, yet this view of enterprise does not fit with some of its observable aspects. It is not static, yet the threshold theory makes no provision for the dynamic effects that can be observed when enterprise behaviour snowballs as people are influenced by the example of others. Nor is enterprise a one-way activity: people can move out of it as well as into it. Enterprise is complex and there are many influences on whether an individual displays enterprise activity. Therefore raising levels of enterprise attributes, if that is possible, may be swamped in its effects by other influences.

An alternative view of enterprise, and of enterprising behaviour, is based on the attributes and resources that an individual may possess at any point in time. It is suggested that it is the interaction between these factors which produces a rational response, on the basis of available information, when the opportunity occurs for a business start-up. This view acknowledges however that there is inertia in individual behaviour and that it may take a discontinuity in work, or in life, to trigger a review of an individual's situation. Whether this review will lead to an individual trying his or her own enterprise will depend in turn on the attributes and resources accumulated and on the perception of environmental factors such as the availability of grants and training. (This and other related concepts are developed further in Chapter 3.)

A close examination of what is taught under the name of enterprise reveals, however, that instead of the consensus claimed by leading practitioners, the organisations that are teaching this new culture are all working with different lists of the core skills.

> Part of the confusion stems from the fact that the word 'enterprise' is used in different ways, sometimes referring to an individual ability considered amenable to improvement and at other times to a form of economic activity, usually in small business.
>
> We are not dealing with a tightly defined, agreed and unitary concept but with a farrago of hurrah words such as creativity, initiative, and leadership.
>
> Professor Frank Coffield[53]

Conclusions

As indicated earlier there are many different usages, and therefore definitions, of the word 'enterprise'. These different meanings are related to each other, however. There are not just two or three distinct meanings but instead a spectrum: a range of meanings, each one merging with those close to it but perceptibly different from those far from it. It is not possible to indicate that one particular meaning is the correct one. The word is in practice used in these different ways, and those trying to understand it need to be aware of what it means to whoever is using it.

It can be observed that the UK government, however, has almost always used it in the context of economic growth through (small) business start up and growth. That is what its 'enterprise' schemes are aimed at. Training and enterprise councils, enterprise agencies and similar organisations have had the same usage. Other initiatives, such as Enterprise in Higher Education, have treated enterprise more as a set of behaviour, attitudes and skills that may have a wider application than just the world of business. Its most famous application might be the *Starship Enterprise*, the spacecraft in the *Star Trek* series, which has nothing to do with business and everything to do with a readiness to explore the new.

One end of the spectrum of meaning could be considered to be the 'narrow' definition of enterprise, which could be summarised as:

$$\text{Enterprise} - \text{Entrepreneurship} - \left\{ \begin{array}{l} \text{Starting up a business,} \\ \text{Being in business, and} \\ \text{Growing and developing a business} \end{array} \right.$$
(or = a Business)

The other end of the spectrum could be enterprise as a positive, flexible and adaptable attitude to change. It is the exercise of enterprising behaviour, attitudes and skills. It is a new balance in power between the institution and the individual. In this context it has a far wider application than just business, as such attributes can be applied in all walks of life. It could be summarised as:

Enterprise = The application of innovative attitudes, skills and behaviour

The spectrum analogy is not perfect, however, because a broad meaning can include a narrow one. To get the enterprise that is sought in business, some believe, it is necessary to promote a culture of enterprise that is much broader than business. For them it is all or nothing: you can't only have enterprise in business and not in other fields – you must have both or neither.

The application of enterprise in practice, however, takes more than just an aspiration to be enterprising. For someone to behave in an enterprising way, he or she may need at least some of the right attributes combined with some of the relevant skills and resources with which to apply the attributes. Even then it may take a specific trigger to start it off.

Enterprise in the way people apply the word is undoubtedly very varied. Some further aspects of that variety are now explored in the rest of Part I of this book.

THE KEY POINTS OF CHAPTER 2

- The term 'enterprise' has been attached to a variety of initiatives, and recently 'entrepreneurship' has become a popular label. It has often seemed, though, that they have been used more for the cachet of a supposedly desirable label than because either is the most appropriate word in the particular circumstances.

- The way they are used indicates nevertheless that they now have a wide continuum of meanings. In some cases the use implies a meaning that is limited to a business context, and enterprise can even be used as a synonym for business. Other uses, however, imply a wider meaning, often associated with an attitude to life: of exploring, of developing, of leading and of taking the initiative. Such an attitude can be very helpful in the business context, but it also has much wider applications.

- These different uses have been described as the narrow and broad meanings of 'enterprise'. The narrow meaning regards enterprise as business entrepreneurialism, and in that context the words 'entrepreneurship' and 'enterprise' are usually interchangeable. The broad meaning, on the other hand, regards enterprise or entrepreneurship as a set of attitudes and skills that enable individuals and groups that possess them to be flexible, creative and adaptable in the face of change. These two approaches to enterprise have also been labelled the 'economy school' and the 'education school': at the heart of the latter is the concept of personal development and the development of self-confidence.

- In a business context, the word 'entrepreneurship' is often used in the same way as the word 'enterprise'. Its use can be traced to eighteenth-century France and, with the development of the concept of capitalism, the entrepreneur came to be seen as essential to the process of wealth creation. When very big businesses developed, the entrepreneur seemed to have been supplanted by the manager in business relevance, but the recent demonstrations of the potential and achievements of small businesses has once again highlighted the importance of the entrepreneur.

- Those who have looked at the make-up of the entrepreneur have identified entrepreneurship, or enterprise, as the exercise of a set of attributes. The possession of at least some of these attributes has been particularly helpful in times of change, but their exercise need not only be limited to a business context. There is however no clear agreement on precisely what these attributes, skills and attitudes are.

- Further, the possession of such attributes, skills and attitudes is not necessarily sufficient for a person to act in an enterprising manner, especially when that implies taking the initiative in business formation and development. What is also needed may be the resource with which to act and a trigger to start it off. It is also believed by some that the necessary qualities can be acquired and are not necessarily innate.

- Enterprise and entrepreneurship are therefore varied concepts, both in their application and in their explanation. They remain the subject of considerable interest.

CASE 2.2

Pathfinder initiatives

In Northern Ireland the former Department of Economic Development (now the Department of Enterprise, Trade and Investment) launched its 'Pathfinder' initiative in 1986. Its aim was 'to find new and better ways of building a stronger economy in Northern Ireland ... to find new ways to build on our strengths and to correct our weaknesses'. Among those weaknesses were the 'lack of an enterprising tradition: Northern Ireland is proud of its "work ethic", but this is essentially an employee ethic. As a result there are few role models or mentors for those who wish to enter business and the option of self-employment is novel in many areas.' 'Enterprise', the Pathfinder report defined as: 'the propensity of people to create jobs for themselves and for others by engaging in and creating a legitimate activity which will earn them a living or by developing their existing jobs.'[54]

One of the taskforces in the Pathfinder initiative was the Enterprise Taskforce and the following is a summary of its initial findings:

Brief

To examine the level of enterprise in Northern Ireland, attitudes to enterprise and how these might be changed, whether current arrangements for stimulating business start-up are adequate and how the community can be involved more fully in economic development.

Background

- 'Enterprise' was defined as the propensity of people to create jobs, for themselves and others, by engaging in and developing a legitimate activity which will earn them a living or by developing their existing jobs.

Attitudes

- There is a general attitude in Northern Ireland that working for oneself rather than for an established company is somehow second best.
- Self-employment is often seen as impractical or excessively risky: not as legitimate or socially desirable as other employment.

Support currently available

A wide range of support is currently available to those wishing to establish or develop a business:

- Finance, in the form of enterprise grants (from the Local Enterprise Development Unit) and enterprise allowances (from the Department), supplements commercial and voluntary sources of business finance.
- Training, ranging from brief seminars for enterprise allowance participants to courses such as the graduate enterprise programmes, provides information and skills which are important to small business growth and development.
- Advice, ranging from informal counselling to the inputs of professional advisers such as accountants, is also an important part of a small business and enterprise support system.

Conclusions

- There is a need to generate a more positive attitude to enterprise throughout the community.
- Northern Ireland needs to generate greater self-confidence and skills among those who may wish to start a business so that they can identify and respond to challenging business opportunities.
- A restructuring of assistance is required to ensure that all types of assistance are made available in a co-ordinated way, both in terms of those eligible for assistance, and in terms of measures which should be complementary.
- Particular attention should be paid to the development of supportive networks of contacts and advisers.

Source: Department of Economic Development, *Building a Stronger Economy: The Pathfinder Process* (Belfast, Department of Economic Development, 1987). This material should not be taken to reflect the current policy of the Department of Enterprise, Trade and Investment or of Invest Northern Ireland.

Points raised

This example gives an insight into how a UK government department interpreted an 'enterprise' brief in the 1980s.

QUESTIONS, EXERCISES, ESSAY AND DISCUSSION TOPICS

- Distinguish between 'enterprise', 'entrepreneurship' and 'small business'. To what extent do these concepts overlap?
- What is an enterprise culture?
- In what ways can education stimulate entrepreneurship?
- Does the Scottish Institute for Enterprise (see Case 2.1) try to teach enterprise?
- Is it possible to promote enterprise only in its 'narrow' sense?
- How might the brief for a 'Pathfinder Enterprise' initiative (see Case 2.2) be written today?

Suggestions for further reading and information

R. Gavron, M. Cowling, G. Holtham and A. Westall, *The Entrepreneurial Society* (London: Institute for Public Policy Research, 1998).
P. Carr, *The Age of Enterprise* (Dublin: Blackhall, 2000).
www.businesslink.co.uk – Business Links have agendas which overlap those of the former TECs.

References

1. Commission of the European Communities, *Commission Staff Working Paper: Towards Enterprise Europe – Work Programme for Enterprise Policy 2000–2005* (Brussels, 2000), p. 3.
2. Taken from www.europa.eu.int.scadplus.
3. Taken from www.oecd.org (accessed 17 January 2008).
4. In answer to questions during a celebrity lecture in Northern Ireland, May 1993.
5. Howard Davies, *A Review of Enterprise and the Economy in Education* (HM Treasury/HMSO, 2002).
6. http://ncge.wordpress.com/2008/02/06/enterprising-britain, accessed 12 February 2008.
7. *DTI: The Department for Enterprise*, White Paper presented to Parliament, Cm 278 (January 1988), p. 41.
8. Ibid., p. ii.
9. Ibid., pp. 1 and 5.
10. As reported in R. Huggins and N. Williams, *Enterprise and Public Policy: A Review of Labour Government Intervention in the United Kingdom* (The University of Sheffield Management School Discussion Paper No 2007.03, August 2007).
11. Taken from www.scottish-enterprise.com (accessed 17 January 2007).
12. Nottingham Polytechnic, *Enterprising Nottinghamshire Final Evaluation Report* (1991) and personal communication.
13. London Enterprise Agency, *Annual Review* (1992), p. 1.
14. *Business in the Community*, 'A Review of the Enterprise Agency Network', June 1989, p. 5.
15. *The Vision*, Enterprise Northern Ireland, 2007, p. 2.
16. Training Agency (1990).
17. University of Ulster, 'Enterprise in Higher Education', leaflet.
18. www.berr.gov.uk accessed 12 February 2008.
19. www.enterprise.ac.uk accessed 12 February 2008.
20. P. Morgan (Director General, Institute of Directors), speech to Institute of Directors' Convention reported in *Director*, March 1990.
21. J. Ritchie, 'Explaining Enterprise Cultures', paper presented at the Tenth National Small Firms Policy and Research Conference, Cranfield Institute (1987).

22. F. Coffield and R. MacDonald, *Risky Business? Youth and the Enterprise Culture* (Falmer Press, 1991), p. 29.
23. 'Enterprise and Education' – The *Primary Enterprise Package* sponsored by Marks & Spencer.
24. A. L. Zacharakis, W. D. Bygrave and D. A. Shepherd, *Global Entrepreneurship Monitor United States of America 2000 Executive Report* (Kansas City, Mo.: Kauffman Centre for Entrepreneurial Leadership at the Ewing Marion Kauffmann Foundation, 2000), p. 5.
25. S. Shane, *A General Theory of Entrepreneurship* (Cheltenham: Edward Elgar, 2003), p. 4.
26. Reported in H. H. Stevenson 'Intellectual Foundations of Entrepreneurship', in *Entrepreneurship: The Way Ahead*, edited by H. P. Welsch (New York and London: Routledge, 2004), p. 3.
27. *Entrepreneurship and Education Action Plan* (Northern Ireland: DETI, DE and DEL, published in March 2003), p. 5.
28. A. A. Gibb, 'SME Policy, Academic Research and the Growth of Ignorance, Mythical Concepts, Myths, Assumptions, Rituals and Confusions', *International Small Business Journal*, 18(3), 2000, pp. 13–35.
29. Reported by S-M. Mukhtar and J. Redman, in 'Developments in EU/UK Entrepreneurship/Enterprise Education Policy: Current Debate and Implications', a paper presented at the 27th ISBA Conference, Newcastle, November 2004. p. 3.
30. U. Hytti and P. Kuopusjärvi, 'Three Perspectives to Evaluating Entrepreneurship Education: Evaluators, Programme Promoters and Policy Makers', paper presented at the EFMD 34th EISB Conference, Turku 2004, based on Evaluating and Measuring Entrepreneurship and Enterprise Education, Small Business Institute, Turku, Finland, 2004 – from a Leonardo funded project.
31. http://ncge.wordpress.com/about accessed 12 February 2008.
32. Reported in H. H. Stevenson 'Intellectual Foundations of Entrepreneurship', in *Entrepreneurship: The Way Ahead*, edited by H. P. Welsch (New York and London: Routledge, 2004), p. 3.
33. From the crossword, *Independent*, 8 January 1996.
34. 'Towards an "Enterprising" Culture: A Challenge for Education and Training', *OECD/CERI Educational Monograph*, No. 4 (1989), pp. 6–7.
35. 'What Do We Mean by Enterprise?' *Employment Initiatives*, February 1990, pp. 3–4.
36. J. A. Schumpeter, *The Theory of Economic Development* (New York: Oxford University Press – Galaxy, 1961), p. 74.
37. W. K. Bolton and J. L. Thompson, *Entrepreneurs: Talent, Temperament, Technique* (Oxford: Butterworth-Heinemann, 2000) – see p. 261.
38. A. Smith, *An Inquiry into the Nature and Causes of the Wealth of Nations* (New York: Modern Library, 1937) (first published in 1776).
39. J. A. Schumpeter, *The Theory of Economic Development* (Cambridge, Mass.: Harvard University Press, 1951) (first published in 1934).
40. W. H. Whyte, *The Organisation Man* (Garden City: Doubleday Anchor Books, 1957).
41. J. K. Galbraith, *The New Industrial State* (Boston, Mass.: Houghton Mifflin, 1967).
42. B. A. Kirchhoff, personal communication (1993).
43. D. L. Birch, *The Job Generation Process* (Boston, Mass.: MIT study on neighbourhood and regional change, 1982).
44. A. Lundström and L. Stevenson, *Entrepreneurship Policy for the Future*, Stockholm: Swedish Foundation for Small Business Research, 2001), p. 15.
45. I. Verheul, S. Wennekers, D. Audretsch and R. Thurik, *Research Report: An Eclectic Theory of Entrepreneurship: Policies, Institutions and Culture* (Zoetermeer Holland: EIM/Small Business Research and Consultsancy, 1999), p. 9.
46. A. L. Zacharakis, W. D. Bygrave and D. A. Shepherd, *Global Entrepreneurship Monitor National Entrepreneurship Assessment: United States of America* (United States: Kaufamn Centre for Entrepreneurial Leadership, 2000), p. 5.
47. A. Lundström and L. Stevenson, *Entrepreneurship Policy for the Future* (Stockholm: Swedish Foundation for Small Business Research, 2001), p. 18–19.
48. 'Towards an "Enterprising" Culture', quoted in C. Ball, B. Knight and S. Plant, 'New Goals for a Enterprise Culture', *Training for Enterprise* (1990), p. 21.
49. D. C. McClelland and D. G. Winter, *Motivating Economic Achievement* (New York: Free Press, 1969).
50. A. A. Gibb, 'Enterprise Culture: Its Meaning and Implications for Education and Training', *Journal of European Industrial Training* (1987), p. 10.
51. C. Alter and J. Hage, *Organisations Working Together* (Newbury Park, Calif.: Sage, 1993).
52. G. Salaman, *Managing* (Buckingham: Open University Press, 1995), p. 60.
53. F. Coffield, 'Hunting a Heffalump in the World of the Enterprise Industry', *Independent*, 29 August 1990.
54. Department of Economic Development, *Building a Stronger Economy: The Pathfinder Process* (Belfast: Department of Economic Development, 1987).

CHAPTER 3
Enterprise in individuals

Contents

KEY CONCEPTS

This chapter covers:

- Perceptions on the nature of enterprise.
- Economists' views on the role of the entrepreneur in economic systems.
- The different theories about people's internal make-up which have been suggested to explain why some people are more enterprising than others.

- The key points and limitations of these theories.
- The significance of gender and ethnicity in enterprise.

LEARNING OBJECTIVES

By the end of this chapter the reader should:

- Know a range of views on the role of the entrepreneur.
- Have an appreciation of the different theories about people's internal make-up which have been suggested to explain why some are more enterprising than others.
- Understand the key points and limitations of each theory.
- Be able to recognise the key personal traits which distinguish entrepreneurs and enterprising people from other groups in society.
- Have a view on the usefulness of trait theory.
- Be aware of the main points of cognitive theories of entrepreneurial motivation.
- Understand the possible roles played by gender and ethnicity in the enterprise shown by individuals.

Introduction

Chapter 2 showed that the word 'enterprise', in the way it is actually used, has a range of meanings. Some of these overlap, some embrace others and some appear to be very different. Within this range there are two main areas of meaning: those reflecting the 'broad' or 'education' approach, in which enterprise is a type of behaviour that can be exhibited in many contexts, and those representing the 'narrow' or 'economy' application, in which 'enterprise' is sometimes used as a synonym for small business or the process of starting one. The latter use is sufficiently common and important to be explored further in Part II. However there are many aspects of the 'broad' definition worthy of further consideration also.

The broad approach to enterprise considers it to be a type of behaviour demonstrated in the actions of a variety of individuals. These actions are taken as the result of individual decisions, but the factors which are thought to influence these decisions and therefore to influence both enterprise and entrepreneurship are many and varied. They can be categorised in a number of ways but one of the main divisions is probably that between the internal and the external: between those factors which are apparently unique or specific to each individual, whether innate or acquired, and those factors which determine the environment in which individuals operate.

Therefore the internal factors or influences are considered in this chapter and the external influences in Chapter 4. However it should be pointed out that the boundaries are not absolute and there are areas of overlap. Also, for convenience, some of those theories which combine both internal and external influences are considered in Chapter 4, after both sets of factors have been presented.

Enterprising acts

The 'broad' or 'education' approach is largely based on the concept of enterprise as something demonstrated in the actions individual people take: actions that can be enterprising in a variety of situations, not just in business. These actions are in turn due to a considerable extent to the make-up of the individuals concerned: and to what are variously referred to as their behaviours, attributes, competencies, attitudes, skills, ideas and resources. The context in which the individuals operate is also of relevance, because enterprise in some aspects and in some contexts seems to be due more to group and societal dynamics than to individual ones. This chapter, however, explores enterprise largely from the perspective of the individual; the group and societal aspects are considered in Chapter 4.

In looking at the personal aspects of the broad definition of enterprise, it is worth considering how far they apply also to the narrow definition and therefore, by implication, whether the two are inconsistent with each other. The narrow definition regards enterprise as synonymous with business founding, for which the term entrepreneurship is also often used, while the other sees it as the application of an array of adaptable skills to new, unique or complex tasks. Enterprising individuals often initiate and develop projects; they do not sit around and wait for things to happen but take control and see issues through to their conclusion. Although there is an apparent difference between the two aspects of enterprise, the distinction may be more apparent than real. In reality, founding a business can be just as much an enterprising act as any other, and that aspect of enterprise can be seen as one component of a larger domain. The 'narrow' definition is in this case just an example of the 'broad'.

Consider the act of initiating and developing a business venture. In developing a business idea, many potential proprietors will have a futuristic and opportunistic orientation and think creatively about different ways of satisfying human needs. In locating and marshalling necessary resources and suppliers of funds, they will be imaginative and persistent. In recognising and overcoming unique problems they will display proactivity and flexibility. And in keeping going in the face of innumerable setbacks they will draw on all their self-confidence, perseverance and dynamism. However, numerous acts in other environments can be considered as enterprising, such as those of the university dean who successfully introduces a radical way of teaching graduate students, the nurse who revolutionises post-operative care, the community leader who convinces the local authority to care for the homeless or the missionary who improves the conditions of the underprivileged. It might be considered that such actions are specific to their different situations, but they do appear to have many common features. However, before they can all be described as enterprising, it will be helpful to have some idea of what constitutes an enterprising act.

Entrepreneurship has been described as 'the creative extraction of value from environments',[1] which emphasises the outcome as well as the process and is a starting point in considering enterprising acts as enterprising outcomes. In the context of business, few doubt the often enterprising nature of business formation and development. One possible indicator of the degree of enterprise to be found in individuals in a community or in an economy is therefore the number of small firms in existence there. It is relevant to note, however, that business formation rates fluctuate widely, and that many self-employed people and small firms fail each year. How, then, should business failure be regarded? If the act of starting a small business is enterprising, what is a subsequent failure? Does it negate the enterprise of the original act? There are no obvious answers to these questions but they do highlight the complexity of coming to terms with the notion of enterprise.

If it is difficult to say unequivocally whether an action is enterprising in a business context, what are the prospects in other contexts? Consider a welfare officer faced with a serious drug problem among teenagers. The officer has ideas about what might be done. She mobilises parents, community groups, doctors, police and others connected with the problem to take action. She communicates with the teenagers and elicits their views on the issue. She lobbies, deals and harangues to obtain the physical and monetary resources to create a day centre manned by advisers with access to medical personnel. One year after her intervention the drug problem has not gone away, but teenage suicides have decreased in the area, fewer teenage pregnancies are reported and large numbers attend group therapy sessions. Was this an enterprising process? The individual concerned displayed many of the qualities usually associated with the business formation process and the outcome of this project would be regarded by many as reasonably successful, even if the original aim was not achieved. Many therefore would describe the individual concerned as enterprising.

There are innumerable undertakings of this nature in business, social, family and private life that can be described as enterprising and, though it is a relative and not an absolute term, it can be considered appropriate to enumerate the key characteristics of such undertakings. In doing so it can be helpful to distinguish between the nature of the task and the manner in which it is tackled. Broadly, however, the label 'enterprise' might be applied when:

- The task is non-routine.
- The task is somewhat complex.
- The task is goal-directed.
- The goal(s) are demanding but attainable.

Also when:

- The task is tackled in an adventurous manner.
- The task is approached in a determined and dynamic manner.
- The task accomplishes the set goals (or comes near to so doing).

A project has been defined as 'a task requiring considerable or concerted effort'[2] and, in short, it might therefore be considered that an enterprising act is one in which a project is undertaken in an energetic, bold and adaptable manner. This means therefore that there are businesses, and even business start-ups, which would not be considered to be enterprising. This would be the case, for instance, in some family businesses when a second or third generation takes over without making any significant changes, or perhaps in some forms of self-employment.

Defining enterprise in this way can accommodate both the narrow and broad approaches to the subject outlined in Chapter 2, and underpins the importance of newness, change and flexibility for enterprise. This definition also emphasises the relevance of success. Bold, dynamic acts that fail to meet predetermined goals may not always be considered to be enterprising. Those goals, however, need not be economic, and success in enterprise is not just limited to commercial success. In addition actions that appear to be, or indeed are, initially successful and would be regarded as enterprising, but which then subsequently fail, would usually still be regarded as having been enterprising. Enterprising acts take place within a time-frame, and outside it conditions can change radically.

Enterprise and entrepreneurship

As explained in Chapter 2, the term 'entrepreneurship' is frequently, but not exclusively, used in conjunction with issues of business formation and development. Further, the ways in which entrepreneurs are said to act when seeking business opportunities, and in co-ordinating resources to cope with business problems, are very similar to what has been described as enterprise in looking to the future, initiating projects and managing them in a creative and adaptable manner. Entrepreneurship is, in effect, the same thing as enterprise in its narrower sense and so, in this chapter, an analysis of entrepreneurship has also been included in the discussion of the determinants of enterprise.[3]

Invention and innovation

The concepts of creativity, invention and innovation are also closely associated with enterprising outcomes. They cover part, but not all, of the process of generating those outcomes. Invention, it is generally agreed, is the origination of a new concept or idea as the result of a process of creativity. There is less agreement on what innovation is. For some it is the development or adoption of new concepts or ideas, while for others it is the new or adopted ideas themselves. These approaches are linked, however, and there is general agreement that invention precedes innovation and that the latter can be viewed as the successful exploitation of new ideas, but not the origination of the ideas.[4] Creativity is having the idea, and innovation is its application. Creativity is not itself enterprising and neither is invention, because they do not generate change; that does not happen until the innovator takes the idea and does something with it, typically the process of commercialisation.

The place of innovation in commercial success has been illustrated in Figure 3.1, and this can be extended to the successful exploitation of new ideas that leads to any form of increased organisational or social benefit.

What skills are needed by successful innovators? Forehand suggests that innovative behaviour 'includes the development and consideration of novel solutions to ... problems, and evaluation of them in terms of criteria broader than conformity to pre-existing practice', and argues that self-reliant, enquiring, flexible, original and independent people are most likely to engage in innovative behaviour.[5] It will be seen that there is considerable similarity between these attributes and those linked with enterprising behaviour. However, the inclusion of originality and enquiry underline the importance of uncovering new ways of doing things. Moss Kanter considers that innovators must develop a vision of something new, must generate a power base to progress the idea, and must build commitment and systems to sustain the new endeavour.[6] For Moss Kanter, visions emerge from kaleidoscopic thinking. Some people have the capacity to view existing structures and behaviours from a

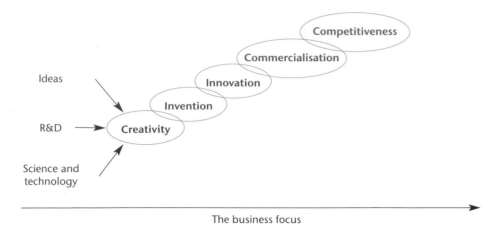

Figure 3.1 The role of innovation

variety of perspectives and, unrestrained by existing assumptions, are able to see useful new combinations of resources. Once envisioned, this new possibility must be enthusiastically and articulately communicated to others.

This is very similar to the language used to describe successful enterprise, and so it would appear that there are many similarities between innovation and enterprise. Both involve extended and concerted effort; enterprise requires boldness because its steps are often new, while innovation employs novel solutions that may take boldness to implement; implementation of both takes place in uncertain conditions and may require consideration of technical, economic, social and political dimensions; and both are likely to draw on change management skills, including networking, for success. However, enterprise is concerned with initiating and managing tasks and projects, and may not involve many new or unique approaches. Innovation, on the other hand, is vitally concerned with novel approaches, new ideas, enquiry and originality, and is the means by which ideas are exploited for competitive advantage.

Enterprising individuals

Enterprising acts, whether in business or in a wider context, and whether incorporating original ideas or not, are generally acts initiated or led by individuals. Those individuals are said to display enterprise. Thus to a considerable extent it can be envisaged that there is something within those individuals that makes them disposed to, and prepared for, such acts. Enterprising acts are defined as such because they have particular characteristics and certain individuals may be predisposed to pursue such activities. Many therefore have seen the individual as important for enterprise, indeed as key to its success. Lord Young suggested that 'the basis for the enterprise culture lies with the restoration of the age of the individual.'[7] This is not necessarily so, however. The completion of an enterprising project often requires the involvement and co-operation of numerous people, but individuals and small groups are the building blocks for community and society, and it therefore seems unlikely that an enterprise culture will develop in the absence of a critical mass of enterprising individuals.

Are entrepreneurs born or made?

Underlying much of the debate about entrepreneurship in individuals is the question of whether entrepreneurs are born or are made (nature or nurture). Many people have assumed that they are born: that is, they have certain inherent characteristics which lead them to be enterprising and therefore if a person is not born with these characteristics they cannot be induced by subsequent upbringing, experience or training. Those who subscribe to the 'born not made' view assume that the internal influences on an individual's behaviour (those covered in this chapter) are the important ones, whereas those who believe that at least a certain amount of 'making' is possible also consider that the external influences (those covered in Chapter 4) can be relevant.

In Chapter 2 the broad definition of enterprise was connected to the possession and use of enterprising or entrepreneurial attributes. Figure 3.2 illustrates two possible models for the distribution in a population of those attributes. There is a tendency to think that the distribution of entrepreneurial attributes amongst people is like that illustrated in Model A, with two distinct groups: those with few attributes and those with many. Actually it is probably more like Model B. A key difference is that, if the first model were correct, it would imply that making incremental changes in the distribution will not have much effect: there will still be few people with many attributes; whereas in the second model an incremental change will have the effect of a significant increase in the number with many attributes or at least with sufficient attributes to act entrepreneurially.

These models of entrepreneurial potential also relate to the born or made debate. Model A is consistent with the view that entrepreneurial potential is essentially innate whereas Model B supports the contention of many that entrepreneurial potential can, to at least some extent, be developed or learnt. Individual capacity is of course variable and, while many 'stellar' entrepreneurs may owe their achievement more to their own innate abilities than to any formal development process they may have been through, that does not mean that efforts at developing attributes will be inappropriate or wasted, in particular for those without the same 'stellar' capacity.

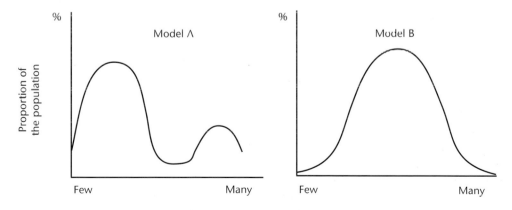

Figure 3.2 Possible models of the distribution of entrepreneurial attributes

The debate

The 'born' or 'made' debate is in some ways a false one, as the views one holds may well depend on the definitions one employs – not least one's definition of an entrepreneur. While some may view any person who owns and runs a business to be an entrepreneur, others may reserve the word for exceptional individuals such as Bill Gates, Michael Dell, Richard Branson and Anita Roddick – often referred to as 'stellar' entrepreneurs. These 'stellar entrepreneurs' are reasonably regarded as the product of their 'genes', or at least of some little understood and certainly not easily reproduced environment in their (early) formative years (or both). If one limits the word 'born' to such exceptional individuals, the 'born' case can readily be made. If all small business owners are considered to be entrepreneurs, however, the case is more difficult to make. Is the self-employed plumber, joiner or refrigeration engineer an entrepreneur? And is the 'born' case quite so strong?

Various writers have developed a range of owner typologies built on the presumption that not all business owners are the same. Most studies have identified three main types of owner, typically labelled artisan, professional manager and entrepreneur (Figure 3.3). Artisan owners run rigid, stable firms, often with few if any employees. Professional manager types grow adaptive firms over time while the entrepreneur creates and develops a firm 'not as an end in itself' but as a mechanism to facilitate invention and the presentation of new products.

This sort of categorisation helps to make the point that not all business owners are equally entrepreneurial or even entrepreneurial at all. For example, an artisan practising the same trade as his/her parents in the same way may start and run a business but may not be entrepreneurial. Work by Miner et al. in the 1990s served to confirm the existence of this tripartite typology.[8] To the extent that most business owners are not 'stellar', is it reasonable to assume that they can be 'made'?

It is suggested by some that where a business owner can succeed on the basis of his or her knowledge and skills in a trade/occupation, and where a higher order of competence (which some call 'talent') is not necessary for survival or growth, then they can 'learn' to be entrepreneurs. Since many people can acquire (and be helped to acquire) the necessary knowledge and skills for business ownership, the supply of entrepreneurs is elastic; in short, more can be created. If, on the other hand, the key to successful business ownership is the possession and display of 'talent' (implying it cannot be acquired easily – or perhaps at all), then the supply of entrepreneurs will be relatively fixed or 'inelastic'. Bolton and Thompson in similar vein, distinguish amongst the terms talent, temperament and technique in seeking to identify the differing requirements for successful entrepreneurship.[9] A possible framework for discussion is presented in Figure 3.4 and see also Illustration 3.1.

It is interesting to contrast the views of two broad schools of thought on the issue of whether and how the supply of entrepreneurs can be increased, exemplified by Jovanovich and Baumol.

Jovanovich argues that the supply can be increased, believing that new business formation is shaped by the nature of prior beliefs held by individuals and that the stronger the beliefs the greater the likelihood of such action.[10] Policies for intervention then should promote individuals' perceptions of the desirability and feasibility of this kind of enterprising action, thus increasing their propensities in such directions; a view supported by Lundstrom and Stevenson.[11]

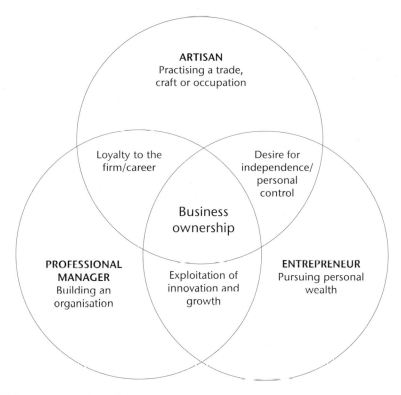

Figure 3.3 Three types of small business owner

Source: R. W. Hornaday, 'Dropping the E-words from Small Business Research', *Journal of Small Business Management*, vol. 28 (1990) pp.22–33.

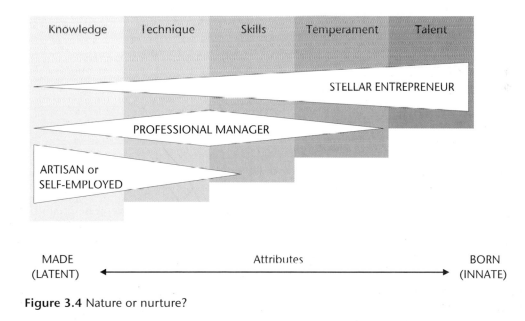

Figure 3.4 Nature or nurture?

Baumol reflects another view which contends that there is no shortage of entre-preneurs.[12] Indeed, he claims almost paradoxically that the supply of them is constant but their distribution across productive, unproductive and destructive activities is affected by institutional arrangements and the structure of social pay-offs. What can happen though is that they utilise their abilities in other ways and in other occupations. The task of policy-makers is to 'set the rules of the game' such that 'productive entrepreneurship' is the 'rational and informed choice for individ-uals with entrepreneurial talent'.[13] It is, he would argue, a waste of time to seek atti-tudinal change since that does not affect the root cause of the problem. Instead 'society should align its incentives (ie taxation and the regulatory framework) to support, legitimate and socially beneficial entrepreneurs.'[14]

In effect, Baumol is saying that there is a plentiful supply of entrepreneurs, the chal-lenge being to activate them and in the desired direction. Issues of whether they are born or made, therefore, become largely irrelevant.

Why are some individuals more entrepreneurial than others?

Identifying what it is that makes some individuals more entrepreneurial than others has been a challenge for a number of researchers. Among the explanatory approaches explored in the study of this question are the following:

- economic approaches
- personality approaches, including
  - psychodynamic theories
  - social-psychological theories
- sociological approaches
- behavioural approaches, including
  - cognitive theories
- integrated approaches.

These approaches are described in more detail below.

Economic approaches

In the work of many writers within the field, the perception of the role of the entre-preneur has changed over time and it is these changes that form this overview of the economists' approaches to the entrepreneur.

- *Introduction.* Essentially the theories cover a process where the entrepreneur can be allocated the role of being directly involved with arbitrage as a natural trader through buying and selling for a profit. An opportunity is spotted and taken advantage of. As we progress, this view is reinforced through the concepts of risk and uncertainty. From this is added ingenuity, innovation and the effective management of resources to create wealth.

ILLUSTRATION 3.1
Talent, temperament and technique

Len Hutton was perhaps the greatest opening batsman that England has ever produced. He had a talent as a batsman that few possess, he was a natural. The coach who took Hutton under his wing when he was 16 years old and taught him the technique of batting commented that 'no instructor was ever blessed with a more voracious learner' – a sure sign of real talent. Yet Hutton rarely gave his talent free rein because of his obsession with batting technique. He was a perfectionist always striving to improve, so that his natural ability was often inhibited.

Temperament was Hutton's area of greatest ambiguity. His ability to focus and concentrate was legendary. He once batted for more than 13 hours to set a world-record individual score of 364. His weakness was his caution and low-risk approach. He found it difficult to cope with stress and believed that 'tension was the root cause of failure and the bane of cricket'. He knew this from bitter experience for in his first match in county cricket and his first at international level he failed to score.

Nature–nurture model

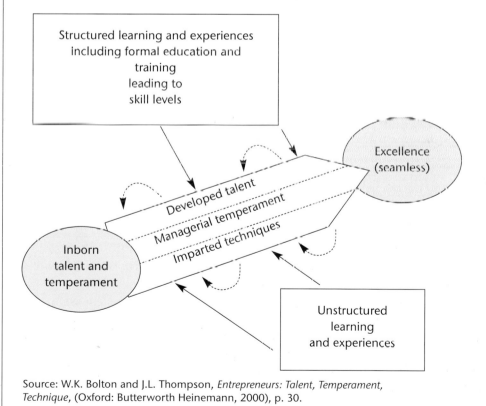

Source: W.K. Bolton and J.L. Thompson, *Entrepreneurs: Talent, Temperament, Technique*, (Oxford: Butterworth Heinemann, 2000), p. 30.

- *The speculative trader.* Cantillon (1680–1734) cites the entrepreneur as any individual who operates under conditions where expenditures are known and certain, but incomes (sales revenues) are unknown and uncertain. The unique characteristic of Cantillon's entrepreneur is foresight and the confidence to operate under conditions of uncertainty. The main qualities of the Cantillon entrepreneur lie in the creation of entrepreneurial income through decision making and risk taking rather than orthodox effort.

- *Managing demand and supply.* In the German-Austrian tradition personified by Mengler and Schumpeter, the entrepreneur is characterised as someone who manages the inputs into the process in such a way that the outcome is higher-level outputs: essentially, trying to manage demand and supply. In this the entrepreneur has to cope with uncertainty and is as a result a risk bearer.

- *Driving the economy through innovation.* Schumpeter saw the role of the entrepreneur as driving through 'innovation'. Innovation will lead to the creation of new firms and to the demise of old firms. The survival of the fittest process detailed by Schumpeter leads to the creation of wealth. Schumpeter believed that only large firms would have the resources to both innovate and prevent the competition from new entrepreneurs threatening them. However, we know that small firms continue to be an engine of innovation in any economy and that these firms are led by entrepreneurs.

- *Acceptor of risk and uncertainty.* The Chicago tradition, outlined in the work of Knight, indicates that the entrepreneur does take risks. This is the fundamental characteristic of the entrepreneur. This is linked to the level of uncertainty that exists within any economy. The entrepreneur needs to be able to deal with uncertainty.

- *More than a business man.* The work of Schultz sought to provide for a bigger role for the entrepreneur in that the entrepreneur should not have a limited role as a business man. This view is also outlined in the work of Mises writing within the modern Austrian tradition.

- *The entrepreneur as the agent of economic change.* The same modern Austrian tradition seeks to portray the entrepreneur as someone who must demonstrate 'great ingenuity' and in so doing reaches the higher level of promoting economic change. This means that the entrepreneur can be someone who can contribute much more to the economy and is much more than just an effective manager.

- *Alert to opportunity.* For Kirzner the entrepreneur is not interested in routine managerial tasks. Kirzner's entrepreneur is concerned to demonstrate qualities of creativity and perception. The entrepreneur is alert to changes in the economy and takes advantage of this.

- *Combining effective management with innovation.* The work of Liebenstein moves towards confirming the more complex profile of the effective entrepreneur. The first is a routine or managerial figure allocating inputs to the production process in a traditional manner. The other is the Schumpeterian entrepreneur who can produce a new product or process through innovation. The effective entrepreneur is one who is capable of playing both roles. Liebenstein observes that such individuals are scarce. This separation moves towards the distinction between entrepreneurial management/organisation, and an alternative organisational form which can be designated as professionally managed.

- *The multi-skilled entrepreneur.* This notion links the work of the classicists and particularly of Say, who perceived the entrepreneur as someone who can effectively manage all of the factors of production such as: materials, labour, finance, land and equipment. For Say the entrepreneur is someone who has mastered the art of administration and superintendence. This type of entrepreneur is a real team player and capable of managing the growth of a larger organisation. Again it can be observed that few entrepreneurs show these capabilities and many have no desire to manage, co-ordinate and combine all of the factors of production.

A number of other economists have considered the role of the entrepreneur. Thünen, for example, recognised the role of the entrepreneur as a risk taker, but also as a problem-solver and innovator. The neo-classical school tended, in the main, to see the role of the entrepreneur as the vehicle for stabilising markets (through entry and exit to eliminate super profits or losses), albeit Marshall recognised the entrepreneur as someone who spotted opportunities and could be innovative in devising new production methods.

In conclusion, it can be noted that economic approaches do not indicate why some people emerge as entrepreneurs and others do not. In addition they consider that entrepreneurs are rational decision makers and play down the role of perception and interpretation in this process.

Personality approaches

Personality approaches to entrepreneurship consider that it is the personality of individuals that explains their actions. The simplest theory suggests that it is the possession by individuals of a trait, or traits, that predisposes them towards entrepreneurial behaviour; the traits most often proposed are achievement motivation, risk-taking propensity or the desire for control. Other personality theories consider combinations of traits. The psychodynamic approach views the entrepreneurial individual as someone who is 'deviant' in society, and the social psychological approach also views the context in which the individual operates.

CASE 3.1
One person's summary of what makes an entrepreneur

It is ironic that one of the biggest academic growth industries in recent years has been the study of what makes entrepreneurs tick. Every university worth its salt has groups of researchers scurrying round the topic. Yet no real entrepreneur actually believes entrepreneurial skills are learnable or transferable. You're either an entrepreneur or you're not. It is a state of being, not a trade or a vocation.

That said, the eggheads do occasionally come up with interesting hypotheses about entrepreneurs. Psychoanalyst Abraham Zaleznik, for instance, the Matsushita

Professor of Leadership at Harvard Business School, says that if you want to understand entrepreneurs, you have to study the psychology of the juvenile delinquent. 'They don't have the same anxiety triggers that we have,' he explains.

Leaving aside the question of whether Zaleznik therefore regards entrepreneurship as a good career move for upwardly aspirant juvenile delinquents, maybe the professor has put his finger on something important.

The textbook definition of an entrepreneur is someone who undertakes the risks of establishing and running a new business in return for profit – and risk takers do tend to be people who, rather than calculating the odds of success or failure in a systematic way, get an adrenaline rush from going out on a limb. They do not avoid anxiety, they embrace it.

Of course, those who go out on a limb often fall off. The ability to do so and survive, according to management writer Charles Handy, is a prime qualification, almost a *sine qua non* for the entrepreneur. Successful entrepreneurs, he calculates, have on average nine failures for every success:

> It is only the successes that you will hear about, the failures they credit to experience. Oil companies expect to drill nine empty wells for every one that flows. Getting it wrong is part of getting it right.

Sacred mushroom

Richard Branson has turned his entrepreneurial flair into a multi-million-pound business by the trick of making those who work for him want to emulate him, be him. Yet he isn't quite sure how he does it:

> 'I never actually set out to see how I could make the most cash,' he told Jeffrey Robinson, author of *The Risk Takers*. 'I've always merely tried to make the figures fit the ideas I've had rather than the other way around. I guess that's doing it backwards.'

Ted Levitt, editor of the *Harvard Business Review*, calls entrepreneurship the 'sacred mushroom of the 1980s' – 'it seemed delusively greater and grander than it was' – but many of his fellow scholars and not a few businesspeople are still mesmerised by it. Finding that entrepreneurs cannot be made, they have come to the conclusion that they can at least be made use of. Hence the advent of the 'intrapreneur', an entrepreneur who works within a big corporation.

Ignoring the fundamental difference between the entrepreneurial and corporate mind-sets, the academics hypothesise that the intrapreneurs, who are encouraged to do things like working out ways to 'sell' their goods and services to other people within the organisation, will somehow spread the entrepreneurial habit like a benevolent virus.

The idea seems to miss the obvious point that no real entrepreneur would be seen dead inside a big corporation; these are clearly only ersatz ones. A version of intrapreneurship did work in the United States for a short time in the 1980s when a number of blue chip corporations set up special enclaves for handfuls of brilliant but anarchic individuals who were encouraged to 'do their own thing' in the hope that they would come up with something marketable. The special units became known as 'skunk works' and, predictably, their inhabitants often behaved like the eponymous animals, hightailing it as soon as they got a good idea.

Maybe the great corporate chieftains could have been taught at least that at business school – that trying to mix the two cultures would be like mixing oil and water.

In his latest book, *Great Myths of Business*, author and self-made millionaire William Davis nominates the idea that entrepreneurship can be taught as one of the great myths of our time. He quotes Anita Roddick, the founder of the Body Shop, to reinforce his point. Roddick, as it happens, sounds uncannily like Harvard's Professor Zaleznik when she gets going. How, she asks, do you teach an obsession?

> There is a fine line between the delinquent mind of an entrepreneur and that of a crazy person. The entrepreneur's dream is almost a kind of madness, and it is almost as isolating. When you see something new, your vision usually isn't shared by others. The difference between a crazy person and the successful entrepreneur is that the latter can convince others to share the vision.

Source: Malcolm Brown, 'Risky Business', *Holland Herald* (the in-flight magazine of KLM). Reproduced with permission of M. Brown and of K. Wilkie, the editor of *Holland Herald*.

Points raised

This is an example of the point of view that entrepreneurs are 'born, not made'. It also summarises some views about the entrepreneur's approach and the essence of entrepreneurship, including its ability to flourish in difficult contexts.

Personal qualities: traits and attributes

There is a considerable literature on those factors or traits that purport to predispose individuals to behave in an enterprising or entrepreneurial fashion. Many commentators consider that entrepreneurs have a strong need to achieve and to control their own destiny, and we can readily see why people with these dispositions might be interested in tackling enterprising tasks.[15] The successful accomplishment of an enterprising task would provide individuals with a strong sense of achievement and confirm their capacity to control their lives. Others consider that risk-taking tendencies are characteristic of entrepreneurs, although there is a general view that they take calculated risks (but are not 'gamblers' in the sense of taking excessively high risks). Stevenson and Gumpert do not define the degree of risk taken, but note that entrepreneurs continuously seek business opportunities without being concerned about the necessary resources.[16] They take a chance on resources, and consider that suitable quantities will be forthcoming. Timmons considers that people with persevering, problem-solving and reliable temperaments will have entrepreneurial tendencies, but his list of traits is long and it is unlikely that many entrepreneurs will exhibit all the traits he mentions.[17]

In addition to these traits there is a plethora of qualities that are purported to predispose people to being enterprising. Such personal qualities include being purposeful, proactive, dynamic, active, positive and able to take the initiative; being able to regard change as an opportunity; being able to identify ideas; being innovative, imaginative, creative, flexible and able to tolerate ambiguity; being adaptable, trusting, moderate risk takers, at ease with risk; being determined, persistent, capable of seeing ideas through to fruition; and being responsible and self-confident. There are numerous variables, but we can see that these attributes are clustered, and research on enterprising tendencies reveals that enterprising people tend to have a strong need for achievement and autonomy, an internal locus of control, are strongly proactive and independent, have a creative tendency, and are moderate risk takers.[18] Others add self-confidence, persistence, an ability to deal with failure, and trust.[19] More recently vision has been added to the list.

These qualities may emerge from traits, life's experiences or the structure of organisations and society, but their antecedents are less important than their link with enterprise.

Some of the main traits or qualities identified are described below.

Achievement motivation

Entrepreneurial people have a strong need for achievement (sometimes referred to as NAch), which stimulates them into action. When they accomplish something they consider to be worthwhile, their self-esteem is enhanced and they are encouraged to seek other demanding assignments. Thus enterprising people are constantly on the lookout for challenges.

Content theories of motivation suggest that individuals have basic needs, and from time to time a particular need is not fulfilled. When this happens the person experiences unease and attempts to satisfy this need. He or she does this by attaining goals that have the capacity to meet the need. Once these are satisfied, the unease or tension diminishes and will not motivate an individual until, once again, the need is not realised. Whether achievement is an innate need like the need for food or is learned, probably during childhood, can be debated. It has been suggested that strong-willed children, with parents who make their expectations known and who provide feedback, become high achievers, although McClelland also argues that NAch can also be developed in adults.[20]

NAch has been widely used as one measure of the entrepreneurial personality but results are not clear-cut. Cromie reviews findings and concludes that whilst NAch shows that entrepreneurs consistently out-score undergraduates, naval officers and civil servants on measures of NAch, other groups such as managers and university professors have equally high scores.[21] However, since professors and managers might also be enterprising, it could be that NAch is a basic attribute of the enterprising.

An interesting point also arises in connection with causality. It is generally assumed that achievement-oriented people become entrepreneurs or enterprising individuals.

However, it is equally plausible that the sense of mastery and achievement that accompanies a successful enterprising project such as establishing a business might create the need to achieve more. Behaviour becomes ingrained in the personality. Some evidence for this social construction of personality is provided recently by Littunen. Her empirical work confirms that 'a change in life (entrepreneurship) shapes to some extent the characteristic of the entrepreneur'.[22]

The importance of NAch for enterprise is not generally in dispute, but how can an individual with a high NAch be recognised? McClelland argues that such a person:

> is more self confident, enjoys taking carefully calculated risks, researches his environment actively, and is very much interested in concrete measures of how well he is doing. Somewhat surprisingly ... he does not seem to be galvanised into activity by the prospect of profit; ... [he] works hard anyway, provided there is an opportunity of achieving something.[23]

High achievers often regard money as a measure of achievement, not an end in itself, but they do need feedback of evidence of their achievement, and money can provide such feedback.

CASE 3.2
An achiever

A business founder, when asked why she created her firm replied: 'the major attraction is self-esteem ... the ah ... carrying a job through from beginning to end ... ah ... I suppose putting my standard on things. I had four children and so all I felt I was good for was being a mum and you don't always get a lot of appreciation for this.'[24]

Point raised

The motivation for achievements is not always obvious.

Risk-taking propensity

Proactive achievers break new ground, but there are considerable risks in this behaviour. Failures can spell disaster for an organisation or a career. The outcomes of enterprising events are less certain than those of conservative ones, and therefore enterprising individuals will need to have the capacity to tolerate risks: to have the psychological make-up and resources to cope with any failure.

While they must be able to countenance risk, that is not to say that enterprising people are high-risk takers. Entrepreneurial research suggests that effective entrepreneurs are moderate risk takers, while others believe that enterprising people take calculated risks. They assess situations thoroughly and do not pursue options which they consider to have a small probability of success. In this vein Drucker argues that successful entrepreneurs 'try to define the risks they have to take and to minimise them as much as possible'.[25] They search for opportunities, give them serious consideration and if promising, capitalise on them. Drucker goes so far as to say that successful entrepreneurs tend to be cautious and are opportunity focused, as opposed to risk focused. For them, 'defending yesterday' rather than 'making tomorrow' is really risky. Chell et al. point out that there are problems in defining risky behaviour.[26] Risk assessment takes place in context and behaviour that appears risky to outsiders may not be perceived as risky by those who are fully cognisant of a situation. Enterprising persons may not perceive a course of action as risky because they fully understand the situation, but this can also arise because of cognitive biases. It is argued that entrepreneurs may not perceive a risk in a risky situation because they are overconfident, because they have the illusion that they are in control of a situation and because they tend to associate with optimistic people who do not dwell on failures.[27] They take mental shortcuts when making decisions with the result that '[low] risk perception, rather than [high] risk propensity, might explain why individuals start ventures.'[28] Simon et al. present evidence that entrepreneurs rely on a narrow range of sources of information and are not exposed to disconcerting facts. This is an interesting development in that it moves the debate on entrepreneurial motivation from the innate drives of individuals to their decision-making processes, and this issue will be explored later in the chapter. It is contended by some entrepreneurs that they 'enjoy the risk', it gives them a 'buzz' and they expect to succeed anyway.

Locus of control

'Locus of control' refers to being in control of events. Enterprising people believe that they personally make things happen in a given situation, and underplay the importance of luck and fate. They make things happen; things do not happen to them. In essence they feel that they exercise considerable control over events in their everyday world. Rotter was instrumental in assessing this aspect of personality, and he designated those who feel in control as 'internals' and those not in control as 'externals'. 'Internal' declarations emphasise the importance of ability, hard work, determination and planning in achieving outcomes, and their outlook is epitomised by the statement 'What happens to me is my own doing.'[29]

Locus of control is often regarded as a crucial indicator of enterprising potential but there are concerns about the construct.[30] The concept was not designed for entrepreneurial settings and has been described as a 'distal' measure:[31] that is, it might explain general behaviour but is of little use in predicting how people will behave in specific situations. In addition, entrepreneurial studies which have used the construct have produced inconclusive results. As Chell et al. point out, perceptions of control will be influenced by many variables, including experience. If individuals have recent successful experience of completing enterprising projects they might consider themselves to be capable of controlling events. If however, they have experienced failure they may blame external factors.

Need for autonomy

'Autonomy' refers to independence from other people, being in control of one's own destiny. This can accompany 'locus of control', which involves control of events beyond the individual, but it is not the same thing. Entrepreneurial people have a strong desire to go it alone. In interviews, enterprising people constantly refer to a need to control their own lives. Phrases such as 'I want to be in control,' and 'I do things my way,' are used regularly.[32] Individuals in many groups, organisations and societies are expected to adhere to the norms, rules and regulations of collective social organisms. Conformity is the price of membership. However, independent people often resent these constraints and regard them as counterproductive in developing innovative proposals. Enterprising people want to reduce barriers to progress, and though they may see some merit in the stabilising impact of rules and behavioural norms, they see more merit in independent thought and action.

People who do their own thing regardless of others or who disregard with impunity rules that constrain them could be considered as disruptive. Dissenters may leave and set up their own ventures. When asked why they wanted to start their own firm, aspiring entrepreneurs in one study most frequently cited autonomy and the need to achieve as the most important factors in their decisions.[33] It should be noted, however, that the experience of entrepreneurship can cause people to want even more autonomy.[34]

Determination

Entrepreneurial people also possess determination. They normally complete projects, and a degree of persistence is necessary for success. If individuals wish to exercise their individuality in meeting 'standards of excellence' then they will need to explore alternatives, overcome difficulties and make their plans work. Being in control is important, as is the freedom to exercise ingenuity, but a determination to see a difficult project through is also vital.

Initiative

The entrepreneurial individual may also need to be proactive. A person may have a strong need to achieve, may possess determination, may welcome the chance to do his or her own thing and to exercise control over his or her environment in pursuit of an assigned project, and may, when presented with an opening, exhibit many enterprising qualities. If, however, he or she does not actively take the initiative and seek openings and opportunities, then the enterprise is limited.

Entrepreneurial people take bold steps and have a propensity to seek new opportunities. The search for newness can often lead to uncharted waters, and proactive people generally seize the openings that present themselves and outdo others.[35]

Research by Ardichvili and Cardozo provides detail on the process by which opportunities are recognised. These authors claim that opportunities are uncovered through recognition rather than through organised searches, and they believe that certain factors facilitate recognition.[36] They feel that entrepreneurs must be alert to surrounding information. Ray and Cardozo define entrepreneurial alertness as 'a propensity to notice and be sensitive to information about objects, incidents and patterns of behaviour in the environment, with special sensitivity to ... problems, unmet needs and interests, and novel combinations of resources'.[37] People pay attention to information that is connected to information they possess already and it is suggested that prior learning creates a 'knowledge corridor' which allows entrepreneurial people to recognise some opportunities but not others.

They will still need to 'act on rather than react to their environments',[38] although they may not go so far as to 'change the environment to create opportunities'.[39]

Creativity

The entrepreneurial person is often concerned with developing new products, processes or markets, but the ability to 'bring something new into being' is not evenly distributed within the population. Such people tend to have more originality than others and are able to produce solutions that fly in the face of established knowledge. They are also inclined to be more adaptable, and are prepared to consider a range of alternative approaches. They challenge the status quo, which can sometimes bring them into conflict with their colleagues.

Entrepreneurial individuals take bold, creative steps but situations encourage creativity. Thompson summarises the situational requirements for creativity succinctly. He feels that creativity is enhanced when people have 'some freedom, but not too much; high internal commitment to the task, but not too high a commitment; a high proportion of intrinsic rewards, but some extrinsic rewards as well; some competition but not winner-take-all competition'.[40] It is, however, important to recognise, as indicated earlier, that an enterprising outcome depends on the process of innovation following creativity, not on the creativity alone.

Self-confidence and trust

It has been argued that entrepreneurial individuals seek out demanding tasks that produce the intrinsic rewards of achievement, that they act on their environments in uncovering these opportunities rather than responding to changes, that they impose their independent authority to explore creative, risky options for problems or opportunities. It is most unlikely that people who lack self-confidence could undertake these tasks. Proactivity, creativity and achievement are not accomplished without major change and, as Gibb has argued, enterprising persons have 'a security borne of self-confidence' in uncertain situations. Self-confidence therefore seems to be indispensable for entrepreneurship.

If, as a result of their endeavours, projects are successfully completed, self-confidence will be reinforced. Success generates more success and may encourage individuals to take on ever more enterprising projects. But what of failure? In such an uncertain environment failure is common and may be viewed as a learning experience, but if failure is repeated then it can dent the confidence of the most self-assured. Continuing enterprise would seem to rely on regular or intermittent success.

Along with self-confidence generally goes trust. Some people consider entrepreneurial individuals to be selfish, exploitative and uncaring, with a short-term, get-rich-quick approach to business. In reality, however, successful enterprise requires the co-ordination of disparate inputs, and a degree of trust. Indeed: 'Studies of entrepreneurs indicate that many are highly ethical and socially responsible compared to the general population.'[41]

Critique of trait theory

Simple trait theory implies that the kind of person you are will influence whether you become an entrepreneur, but this short review of some classic traits suggests that the connection between innate qualities and entrepreneurship is not simple. The traits and qualities described do impact on behaviour but it is accepted that most entrepreneurs do not possess all the enterprise traits identified, and many of the traits are also possessed by those who would not be described as entrepreneurs. However, some authors go further and suggest that trait theory is obsolete. Delmar for instance feels that trait theory has serious limitations.[42] He argues that there is a little consistency in trait research in that there are a large number of traits linked to entrepreneurship, the same traits are operationalised in different ways, and research findings linking predisposition, enterprise and performance are at variance. In effect, a particular combination of traits does not predict a particular form of behaviour. Further difficulties relate to the supposed static nature of entrepreneurial traits and the environments in which enterprise is acted out. In practice traits change over time in individuals, while behaviour itself, however influenced by traits, is conditioned by environments which can and do vary in space and time. Delmar also claims that the bulk of the research on this matter has been based on US samples and feels that some entrepreneurial attributes are culturally dependent. For example the drive and desire to achieve is instilled into American children from an early age. Finally, he claims that 'the theory and methods in use are, in relation to modern psychological research, obsolete.'

However not everyone agrees with Delmar and the trait approach still has its supporters who argue that personality traits play a meaningful role in predicting behaviours.[43] Fagenson argues that it is still important to carry out research 'that can further delineate the fundamental psychological differences between entrepreneurs and non-entrepreneurs' but an examination of some other approaches to the entrepreneurial personality is warranted and this will be done in due course.[44]

Psychodynamic approaches

Psychodynamic approaches are the product of Freud's psychoanalytic theory of personality. Freud considered that individuals have instinctive drives (the id), and that a part of the personality seeks instant gratification for these desires. However, the pursuit of instant gratification can get people into trouble and as people develop their ego emerges to constrain instinctive behaviour. This controlling mechanism protects the individual from the unpleasant consequences of pursuing innate desires. With further development the individual realises that behaviour can meet with the approval or disapproval of significant others and a superego develops to limit behaviour to that which is in keeping with the moral code of parents and society. Freud argues that there are many conflicts between these forces, and that the resolution of these conflicts is instrumental in creating the personality. If instinctive behaviour is severely constrained then it can lead to frustration, and psychodynamic approaches to entrepreneurship consider that this frustration is the source of much entrepreneurial motivation.

Psychodynamic approaches are based on three basic premises: that most behaviour is goal-directed and is caused by a force within the person, that much behaviour originates from the unconscious mind, and that early childhood experiences are crucial in the development of the personality. One of the leading advocates of this approach in the entrepreneurial field is Kets de Vries, who suggests that early frustrations are the product of unhappy family backgrounds.[45] Fathers, in particular, are seen as controllers and manipulators who are remote. In addition they are often seen as deserters who place an unwarranted burden on heroic mothers. These negative images of fathers may have little basis in reality, but perception is all-important. As a result of these experiences or perceptions, individuals develop an intense dislike of authority figures and develop suppressed aggressive tendencies towards persons in control.

These unconscious motives impact adversely on careers. Rejection of controlling others in organisations leads these individuals to be classified as 'deviant' or 'marginal' people, with the result that they change jobs on a regular basis. While they cannot tolerate direction and control in organisations, the variety of job experiences provides them with a range of skills that are indispensable for running a business. As a consequence of their behaviour these individuals make a determined effort to start their own businesses. In this milieu they are in control, are answerable to no one and are 'at the centre of action'.

Psychodynamic theories have, in general, been criticised because of their subjective nature and the lack of empirical evidence. Their ability to explain enterprise, especially in the context of entrepreneurship, has been found wanting because they do not cover all situations, such as a business start prompted through unemployment; because not all deviants start businesses and many characteristics associated with deviancy are not typical of successful entrepreneurs; and because entrepreneurs tend to create their ventures in their thirties or later when many of life's experiences, not merely childhood ones, will influence their behaviour.[46]

Delmar supports these general contentions and points out that Kets de Vries work is useful in that it does not present the entrepreneur as an exceptional person with superhuman capabilities.[47] Entrepreneurs have problems like everyone else and they are not immune to failure when creating an enterprise.

Social-psychological approaches

Trait approaches depict behaviour as being determined by innate qualities but it is widely recognised by social psychologists that behaviour is constrained by contextual factors. Behaviour is influenced by social realities and is also interpreted in a given context. The work of Chell and her colleagues, already mentioned, notes that behaviour which is classified as risky and innovative can only be categorised as such in a given context. Those who observe entrepreneurial individuals, and indeed the entrepreneurs themselves, classify given behaviour as entrepreneurial only in certain circumstances.

Chell and her colleagues, following the procedures suggested by Hampson,[48] developed a holistic classification system for business owners. To classify business owners, these researchers identified defining characteristics of prototypical entrepreneurs and their associated behaviours. An entrepreneur was considered to be 'alert to business opportunities, proactive, innovative, a utiliser of a variety of sources of finance, a high profile image maker, restless, adventurous, an ideas person and an agent of change'. To classify individuals, Chell et al. presented their subjects with certain critical incidents and asked them to describe their likely behaviour in these situations. The researchers noted how often and how consistently behaviours were exhibited before classifying them as prototypically entrepreneurial. They also took into account the growth orientation and stage of development of the subjects' businesses and considered that, compared with other types of business owner, entrepreneurs are more likely to own growth-oriented businesses. Some business owners had all of the characteristics mentioned above, some had none and others were in between. A hierarchical model was conceived therefore with four categories of owner: the entrepreneur, the quasi-entrepreneur, the administrator and the caretaker.

Content is important and some writers argue that individuals who find it difficult to make progress in mainstream careers become marginalised and turn to entrepreneurship as a means of escape.[49] This is an interesting debate and it has been used to explain the emergence of women and ethnic entrepreneurs in Britain – two topics which will be examined later in the chapter.

In summary, while Chell et al's theory is based on quite a narrow sample and does not yet appear to have been validated by other researchers, it is nonetheless useful in pointing to the influence of context on behaviour. It also points out that there is not one entrepreneur but several types and that traits 'co-occur' to create an entrepreneurial profile.

Sociological approaches

Psychological and economic approaches to entrepreneurship emphasise the degree of choice exhibited by individual potential entrepreneurs, but some sociologists consider that individuals are seriously constrained in making career choices. They argue that choices are limited by the experience and expectations that individuals face in the social world. Indeed, Roberts goes so far as to say that careers follow patterns that are 'dictated by the opportunity structure to which individuals are exposed first in education, and subsequently in employment'.[50] He contends that ambition is moulded by 'the structures through which' people pass. Others, who would not deny that individual choice plays a part in career decisions, still emphasise contextual awareness. Opportunity structures vary from person to person, and different structures will lead similar individuals towards the development of different levels of knowledge, skill and drive.

Different opportunity structures expose people not only to different possibilities but also to different expectations from other people. Individuals are socialised to behave in ways that meet with the approval of their role set. For example, a young person with a business-owning parent may well be expected to join the family business, and not to do so would create a vacuum in the business. The son of an unemployed labourer may well be socialised quite differently. The dominant values of close associates will translate into expectations which strongly influence individual behaviour.

Some sociologists emphasise the importance of entrepreneurial opportunity in the entrepreneurial process. For example, it is suggested that the decision to seize opportunities is made when the opportunities present themselves. It has been argued that enterprising individuals do not just sit around and wait for opportunities to emerge; if a society does present numerous opportunities, however, this will quite clearly act as a catalyst for entrepreneurship.

If it is accepted that entrepreneurs require ideas, opportunities, resources, skills and motivation for success, then the social structures and situations to which they are exposed will impact on the choice process. It could well be, for example, that socioeconomic factors such as social class, family composition and background and parental occupation will strongly influence entrepreneurial decision making. In the

UK at least, it appears, for instance, that individuals whose parents or other close relations have had their own business appear generally much more likely to have businesses themselves, and certain social groupings, such as ethnic minorities, produce proportionately more entrepreneurs than others. As evidence of parental influence, Stanworth and Gray describe research findings for persons employed in selected service sectors:

> Overall some 43.5 per cent ... had fathers and/or mothers who had been self-employed ranging from 56 per cent for the owners of free houses, wine bars and restaurants down to 33.3 per cent for the owners of both advertising, marketing and design companies and computer services business. This finding thus strongly supports the contention that parental experience of self-employment in general, and small business ownership in particular, is the best single predictor of the propensity to enter into small business ownership, although this propensity will clearly differ across different types of small enterprise.[51]

Localities that allow individuals to develop problem-solving and marketing skills, which contain institutions geared to the support of small businesses and that are favourably disposed to the notion of entrepreneurship, are likely to encourage and sustain more entrepreneurship than other regions.[52] Such localities might be said to have an enterprise culture, which is defined by Gibb as 'a set of values, attitudes and beliefs supporting the exercise in the community of independent entrepreneurial behaviour in a business context'.[53] Gibb has illustrated (see Table 2.5) the difference between 'entrepreneurial management' and the more traditional corporate or bureaucratic management by looking at their respective values, beliefs and goals.

The implication of this approach is that enterprising individuals differ from others in at least some of their values and beliefs and these are derived from many sources, including the family, peers, community activists and the media.

Cognitive approaches

Trait theories are concerned with the innate qualities which motivate individuals to act in certain ways, and social psychological and sociological approaches emphasise the impact of social structures on behaviour. However, another approach has found favour recently: that of cognitive psychology.

Cognitive approaches consider that whilst the personal characteristics of individuals may play a part in determining who becomes an entrepreneur it is more important to examine the decision-making process by which individuals choose to act entrepreneurially. Cognitive theorists argue that decisions are made not on the basis of reality, but on the basis of perceived reality: entrepreneurs in other words perceive things differently. Delmar argues that entrepreneurship, and other career choices, have a major interpretative element and that behaviour 'is heavily based on how individuals perceive the situation or environment and how it is presented to them'.[54] For a person to decide to become an entrepreneur he or she will have to believe that this is a viable career option. The intending entrepreneur will form an opinion about the 'job' – the requisite attributes, knowledge, skills and resources needed for success – and about self: the perceived attributes, knowledge, skills and resources that are possessed by the person before expending energy in the pursuit of this career. The personal background of the prospective entrepreneur will also be an issue. The individual, on the basis of these assessments, which may not be worked out in a precise manner, will decide on his or her level of potential. However, it has been suggested that potential will only be realised if individuals have:

- a certain specific ability and sensitivity
- environmental possibilities
- social support.[55]

Delmar has produced a useful analysis of cognitive models of entrepreneurship and his main ideas will be summarised in this section. Delmar first explores attitude-based models of motivation. As mentioned above, a potential entrepreneur must believe that this 'career' is a viable option and if this is so he or she will tend to adopt a positive attitude towards entrepreneurship. Whilst there is some debate about the impact of attitudes on behaviour, it is suggested that they can be influential in certain circumstances. Furthermore attitudes are more specific or 'proximal' than 'distal' traits, and are more easily influenced than personality traits. However, while attitudes can influence choice they tell us little about how much effort will be expended in pursuing a course of action.[56]

Beliefs and attitudes can influence behaviour but it is suggested that the link between these variables is mediated by intentions. Boyd and Vozikis argue that intentions are indicative of a person's willingness to engage in a behaviour and are influenced by personal factors such as personality, experience and perceived ability, and by contextual factors such as social and economic structures.[57] Intentions are moulded further by analytic and holistic thought processes. These ideas lead to be development of a theory of planned behaviour which illustrates how people behave in situations that are not entirely within their control. This is the situation facing the intending entrepreneur who cannot control how external backers and other interested parties will behave.

Behaviour is influenced by intentions which are themselves dependent on attitudes, but Delmar argues that more is needed to elicit planned behaviour. A second condition is that perceived social norms must be supportive of the intended behaviour. In other words the potential entrepreneur must believe that significant others will approve of the chosen course of action. However, supportive attitudes and societal norms are necessary but not sufficient conditions. Unless individuals feel in control of key factors which can create a successful outcome, intentions will not be converted into actual behaviour. If people are positive about their ability they are said to have perceived behavioural control, and this will be influenced by issues such as experience, perceived aptitudes and favourable economic conditions. The belief by a person that he or she has the capability to succeed will strongly influence behaviour; indeed it is suggested that this factor is much more important than either supportive attitudes or encouraging societal norms. The concept of 'self-efficacy' is defined by Boyd and Vozikis as 'a person's belief in his or her capability to perform a given task'.[58] These authors argue that self efficacy is crucial in determining whether a person will pursue a goal and is equally important in maintaining motivation once action is taken. In short, if people firmly believe that they have what it takes to set up and complete enterprising projects, this will strongly influence their intentions to attain this outcome. However, if a person has low self-efficacy, he or she is unlikely to pursue a given goal even if it is regarded as important by self, others and society. Self-efficacy develops over time and may develop into a self-fulfilling prophecy. A probable course of events is: I believe I can do, I aspire to achieve, I achieve, and consequently I believe that I can accomplish more. Failure to achieve may produce negative reinforcement.

Favourable attitudes and social support, perceived behavioural control and high self-efficacy can encourage entrepreneurship, but Delmar introduces an additional concept to the debate: the notion of intrinsic motivation. People are intrinsically motivated when they carry out an act simply because they enjoy it. Activities are undertaken for their innate attractiveness and Bandura points out that intrinsic motivation improves perceived self-efficacy, which in turn increases intrinsic motivation.[59] If people are intrinsically motivated they are interested in an activity, whilst their attitudes reflect the importance attributed to events. Taken together these issues influence the manner by which individuals choose between alternatives when making decisions. Interests influence what people pay attention to and consequently have an impact on how they interpret and perceive events. Interests, together with a strong sense of self-efficacy, also play a part in achievement. Achievers are interested in goals which are demanding but attainable, and once they achieve them self-efficacy is increased. Interests are also related to other important entrepreneurial concepts such as autonomy and creativity. If a person finds aspects of the entrepreneurial process attractive he or she will set goals which are capable of attaining desired outcomes and strive hard to achieve such goals. An important entrepreneurial goal may be business growth, and if individuals find such a goal to be attractive Delmar argues that there is a strong possibility that they will succeed in expanding their ventures. Furthermore his research reveals that 'job interests have been shown to predict entrepreneurial behaviour (measured as business growth and profitability) and how it is manifested.'[60] In general, 'interest leads to higher attention, better decision-making and a feeling of enjoyment,' If interest is accompanied by perceived self-efficacy a mutually reinforcing cycle of behaviour will emerge and enhance entrepreneurship.

Delmar argues that this approach is more useful than trait theories in that it more clearly reflects the complexity of the entrepreneurial decision-making process. It also highlights some factors which are amenable to change through intervention. However, he concedes that the connection 'between intentions and actual behaviour is still an uncharted area'.[61] This link between intentions, norms and actual behaviour is also reflected in Krueger's model, discussed below.

Overall the cognitive concepts reviewed by Delmar are useful in understanding the process of business formation and growth. They are less concerned with the way people are and place greater emphasis on how people interpret events, perceive issues and make decisions. They bring the following issues to the forefront of the entrepreneurial debate:

- the role of attitudes in determining what is considered important
- the impact of attitudes on intentions
- the role of perceived social support for activities
- the impact of perceived behavioural control on decision making and outcomes

- the specific and important role of perceived self-efficacy on choice and action
- the way in which interest and the emotional matter of enjoyment impact on attention, perception and achievement.

These models more readily reflect the complexity of the entrepreneurial process than trait theories, and they lend themselves to empirical testing. Concepts such as self-efficacy are also more 'proximal' than 'distal' constructs like locus of control and, because they relate to thinking processes, perception and decision making, they are more amenable to manipulation through intervention.

Behavioural theories

Cognitive theories emphasise the individual decision-making process and the impact of perceived competence in the decision to become an entrepreneur. The context, or at least the manner in which it is interpreted, is regarded as important.

The behavioural approach to studying enterprise also views an enterprising act in the context in which it happens, a context that is often complex. The study of the enterprise of individuals should focus therefore on the behaviours they display in this context, rather than on what they themselves are. One approach with particular relevance to this theory is the examination of individual 'competencies' relevant to a specific event.

Competencies

Cognitive approaches have been highlighted by psychologists but other writers have also commented on the role played by competencies, attributes and resources: ideas that are closely linked with issues such as perceived behavioural control and self-efficacy in the entrepreneurial decision-making process.

An individual will not be in control of an enterprising event if he or she is not competent, and there is now considerable interest in enumerating the key competencies of successful entrepreneurs. Competence has been described as the modern terminology for ability. However, there is still considerable confusion around the concept, in particular with regard to what the term 'competency' actually means. There are two broad approaches to the question. Boyatzis considers that competency relates to the 'personal characteristics' of individuals, while the Management Charter Initiative in the UK adopts a work-functions approach. The former focuses on the person and on the characteristics that make people competent, while the latter looks at the job and details those job functions that competent people can perform effectively.[62]

Most work in the area is devoted to managerial competency, but Caird has explored some competencies for enterprise.[63] She concludes that there are four aspects of competency – knowledge, performance, skill and psychological variables – which specifically relate to a field of expertise.[64] Her model is presented in Figure 3.5 and it includes variables examined by both trait and cognitive theorists.

Caird argues that, while the requisite knowledge and skill is contextual, the underlying psychological variables may be more generic. She points out also that it is important to distinguish between the everyday aspects of competency and those aspects that are critical in separating very enterprising people from the only adequately enterprising.

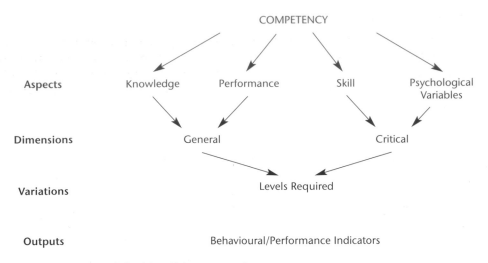

Figure 3.5 Framework for identifying enterprise competency

Source: Reprinted by permission of Sage Publications from S. Caird, 'Problems With the Identification of Enterprise Competencies and the Implications for Assessment and Development', *Management Education and Development*, vol. 23 (1992) p.16. © Sage Publications.

The former can cope with complex and variable situations, while the latter may not. In addition, different levels of competency are required in different jobs and business ventures. Caird's work is useful in clarifying concepts, but she notes that there still 'is no clear understanding of what enterprise competency means', with the result that the concept 'runs the risk of meaning everything and nothing'.[65]

There are a number of lists of possible enterprise competencies that overlap but do not coincide, and the lists of enterprise competencies also overlap with lists of enterprise traits or attributes. The following are some of the enterprise competencies frequently cited:

Dedication	Creativity	Technical competencies
Decision making	Confidence	Sensitivity to changes
Goal setting	Innovation	Networking and contacts
Planning	Risk taking	Developing relationships
Responsibility	Insight	Project management

It can be seen that these competencies include personal qualities set alongside skills and individual orientations.

In general, a major problem with the competency approach, as with some other approaches, is that it is not definitive. There appears to be no competency that is possessed by all entrepreneurs, and many examples exist of non-entrepreneurs who appear to possess more entrepreneurial competencies than do some people who clearly are entrepreneurs. Lists of competencies are more general than domain specific concepts such as self-efficacy. However, if individuals could be convinced of their self-efficacy with respect to key entrepreneurial competencies this would increase their motivation to become an entrepreneur.

Integrated approaches

Each of the theories so far considered has drawbacks, in particular because no single theory seems to cover all aspects of enterprise. Therefore attempts have been made to amalgamate parts of two or more theories to produce an integrated approach with more general application. One such attempt is the Krueger model which is considered below, followed by the attributes and resources approach which is similar.

Krueger's model

Krueger produced a model of entrepreneurial potential (see Figure 3.6), which argues that intentions to act entrepreneurially are underpinned by the development of potential, which is in turn built upon credibility.[66]

Krueger contends that to be credible to oneself and to others, entrepreneurs must both perceive the probable outcome of their endeavours in a favourable light and believe that they have the wherewithal to succeed. Perception is all-important in this process; indeed it may be more important than reality. This favourable light is a product of personal preference and social approval for entrepreneurship, and the wherewithal comes from experience, from innate and learned attributes that might enhance enterprising propensity, and from skills, knowledge and resources that increase self-efficacy. That light and that wherewithal alone, however, are not necessarily sufficient. A trigger or key event (a situational context) may be necessary to start the individual on an enterprising course of action. (The model shown in Figure 3.6 is used to explore issues surrounding gender and entrepreneurship.) It can be seen that this model draws on ideas from trait, cognitive, sociological and behavioural approaches and neatly summarises a range of relevant variables.

Delmar has however suggested that what stands out among these sorts of influences is whether people feel that entrepreneurship is a feasible option for themselves.[67] He

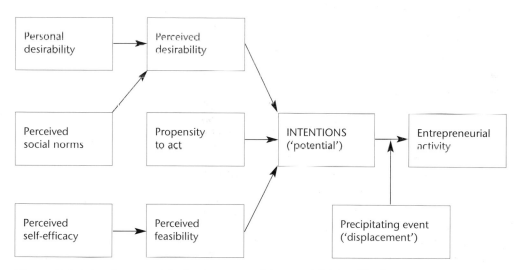

Figure 3.6 Intentions model of entrepreneurial potential (simplified)

Source: N. F. Krueger, *Prescription for Opportunity: How Communities Can Create Potential for Entrepreneurs* (Washington, DC: Small Business Foundation of America, Working Paper 93-03, 1995), p.10.

cites for instance the work of Davidsson who explored intentions to start a business in Sweden and found that, while men and women differed little in their attitudes to enterprise, women were low on perceived behavioural control, which could explain why they were under-represented amongst entrepreneurs there.[68] They did not have enough confidence in their own ability and know-how to start and operate a business and therefore abstained from doing so.

It may also be relevant to point out that simply because a person took an enterprising decision at one time it does not necessarily mean that he or she would automatically do it again. For instance an owner's motivation to expand a business may decline once that business produces a satisfactory level of income or if their personal circumstances change. This can be explained as a change in personal desirability and shows the need to take into consideration more than factors such as attributes and traits.[69]

Attributes and resources

Similar to the Krueger model, the attributes and resources approach offers perceived self-efficacy as an important aspect of cognitive models. It corresponds with a view of enterprise, and of enterprising behaviour, that is based on the attributes and resources an individual may possess at any point in time. Attributes may include self-confidence, diligence, perseverance, interpersonal skills and innovative behaviour. Resources may include finance, experience, knowledge, skills, a network and a track record. It is suggested that it is the interaction between these factors that produces a rational response, on the basis of available information, when the opportunity occurs for a business start-up.

This view, however, also acknowledges that there is inertia in individual behaviour and that it may take a discontinuity in work, or in life, to trigger a review of an individual's situation. Whether this review will lead to individuals trying their own enterprises will then depend on the attributes and resources they have accumulated, together with their perception of environmental factors such as the availability of encouragement, and support such as advice, grants and training. This is illustrated in Figure 3.7.

The implications of this view are that the start-up decision will be affected by the

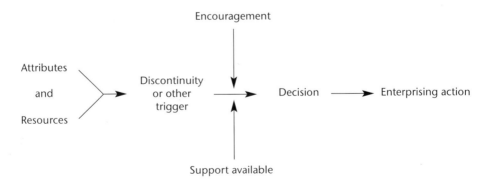

Figure 3.7 Attributes and resources model

Table 3.1 Attributes and resources, and how they are acquired

Attributes	Resources
Attitude	Ideas
Self-confidence	Technical skills
Enthusiasm	Interpersonal and communication skills
Diligence and perseverance	Information, and access to it
Initiative	Network
Independence	Finance
Persuasiveness	Experience, e.g. of small business, of marketing and of planning
Positive outlook	Track record and credibility
Perception	
Attitude to risk	
Direction	

How acquired	
Attributes can be acquired from both nature and nurture. The nurture influences can include family, education, culture, work experience, role models, peers, economic structure lifestyle and stages of life.	Resources are acquired through many of the processes of working and living. They will be more readily acquired if this acquisition is planned and targeted.

attributes and resources acquired prior to the trigger for taking the decision, and that there is scope for initiatives to enhance the acquisition of those attributes and resources. (For a list of possible attributes and resources, and how they are acquired, see Table 3.1.) It does not deny that, at the time of the decision, the availability of support such as grants and training is influential on that decision. It does, however, indicate that, whether or not grants and training are available, more people are likely to decide to try a business start-up, and with more chance of success, if they are in possession of the relevant attributes and resources. There should therefore be economic benefits to be gained from enhancing relevant individual attributes and resources.

Perceived behavioural control, self-efficacy, integrated competencies and attributes, and resources models of enterprise and entrepreneurship are extremely useful from a policy perspective. This is because constructs such as self-efficacy, though quite stable, are amenable to change through intervention. Furthermore, interventions can focus on the micro level of the individual or on the macro level of the community.

Entrepreneurial profiling and enterprise prediction

One particular application to which the different theories of enterprising behaviour have been put has been to try to construct a profile of an enterprising person. This has been done primarily in the field of entrepreneurship with the objective of predicting who is most likely to succeed as an entrepreneur. However, with a lack of consensus on the definition of 'enterprise' and of an 'entrepreneur', and in the absence of a single accepted model of enterprise/ entrepreneurship, this approach has so far had little success.

CASE 3.3
An entrepreneur

Alex Hunter is a young single man who had an interest in having his own business. He had always 'messed about with motors', repairing and tuning them. He took several 'O' levels and joined an engineering firm as an apprentice. However, he did not like the atmosphere in this very large organisation, so he left before his apprenticeship was completed. He joined a small local engineering company and sold their products. He loved his job and worked enthusiastically for the company. After three years employment he became a manager and began to learn about the administrative as well as the technical side of the business. However, his attitude towards the company changed dramatically after a serious industrial injury. He spent some time in hospital and on returning to work found that the firm had appointed a new sales manager and that he had no 'real' job. As a result he decided to have his own firm.

Alex had an eye for business and had been running a little part-time firm, which repaired damaged machine-tool equipment. On the advice of his bank manager he did considerable market research and established that there appeared to be a big demand for this kind of service. Alex left the engineering company, joined a business start-up training programme and prepared for the launch of his own business. His principal motives for founding a firm were the desire for autonomy, achievement, increased personal satisfaction and a desire to make lots of money. He felt strongly about the impossibility of ever getting rich working for someone else.

In spite of his youth Alex was quite well prepared for managing a business. He had developed important technical skills, had one year's managerial experience, had always dabbled in small businesses, and had a good business brain which he subsequently used to employ 50 workers.

Points raised

Such cases, which are typical of small business entrepreneurs, show both push (no real job) and pull (a desire for autonomy) influences. They also show the relevance of attributes (such as self-confidence) and resources (such as technical skills) together with a trigger.

Gender and ethnicity

Two other prominent aspects of individuals are also perceived, at least in some circumstances, to be relevant to the extent to which people engage in entrepreneurship or in wider aspects of enterprise. They are the individual's gender and ethnicity.

Female enterprise and entrepreneurship

While it might be supposed that gender would have little or no effect on whether a person was enterprising, the specific example of gender in the business context shows that this may not be the case. Historically most entrepreneurs have been men and those businesses which have been created by women have generally been in a limited range of business sectors. However in the 1980s and 1990s this picture began to change:

- The National Women's Business Council in the United States reported that in 1993 a third of all businesses were owned by women.[70] They also estimated that the number of firms with female proprietors was growing twice as fast as firms in total, and that 11 million people were employed in female-owned businesses. Figures provided by the Small Business Administration on the number of women-owned firms in 1980 and 1993 indicate that the proportion of increased from 26 per cent to 33 per cent of all firms in this period.[71] A more recent study by Carter suggests that the figure approaches 38 per cent.[72]

- Research in Scandinavia also found that around 20 per cent of new firms are now founded by women and that 25 per cent of all private firms in Sweden are female owned.[73]

- Figures from Britain are in line with those in Scandinavia and the United States. Carter reported that between '1979 and 1997 the number of self-employed women in the UK increased by 163 per cent from 319,000 to 840,000. In the same period the number of self-employed males increased by 67 per cent, from 1,449,000 to 2,421,000.'[74]* Similarly the Equal Opportunities Commission report that the 1980s and 1990s have seen a large increase in the percentage of self-employed females from a little 'over 3 per cent of the female workforce in 1979 to nearly 7 per cent in 1997. In 1999, 26 per cent of all those running their own businesses were women.'[75]

Therefore, while the proportion of female entrepreneurs is increasing, it is still in most areas significantly less than the proportion of male entrepreneurs. The reasons advanced for this include the patriarchal attitudes that existed until recently in countries like Britain, where not so long ago women were required to give up their jobs when they got married or, as exemplified by the airline industry, when they reached the 'advanced' age of 27. Barriers such as this prevented enterprising women from acquiring the essential business knowledge and skills so necessary for a successful business launch. Also the recent increases in the proportion of female entrepreneurs could reflect changes in the labour market. Many more women are economically active nowadays. In Britain between 1984 and 1999 women's activity rates increased from 66 to 72 per cent, and some of this increased number are likely to opt for self-employment.

However the reasons why entrepreneurship has remained a largely male preserve are probably more complex than that and some of the factors which appear to be involved are presented below.

Motivation to create a venture

Krueger's model of entrepreneurial potential, presented earlier in this chapter, seeks to integrate various theories of entrepreneurial intentions and it seems logical therefore to explore the extent to which the various factors in this model apply differently to women than to men.

---

* However, as pointed out also in Chapter 12, Sara Carter also adds that 'the absolute rise in female self-employment appears to have been largely caused by the overall increase in the number of women in the labour market as a whole.'

Personal desirability

Individuals have needs and they engage in activities which should fulfil those needs. Since women and men have historically had a differential attraction to entrepreneurship it might be that women and men's needs differ, and much of the early research on female entrepreneurs explored their motivation to start a firm.

Chell and Baines argue that some feminist literature depicts women and men as biologically different and this might result in different social and economic roles for the sexes.[76] Others argue that biological differences are small and conclude that different socio-economic roles arise from social constrictions imposed on entrepreneurial choice by factors such as family, cultural, political and industrial structures. These factors create and are reinforced by a strongly segregated labour market and occupational structure. These factors suggest that women and men's experiences of occupational choice are different and may explain women's under-representation amongst entrepreneurs.

Despite these and other factors which could account for different motivations of male and female entrepreneurs, many early studies of female entrepreneurs seemed to depict the male experience as the norm, and this may have led to the conclusion that 'women act from similar motivations and look for similar rewards from entrepreneurship as their male counterparts.'[77] In support of this view, Carter notes that early studies of the stated reasons for business founding reported by women were quite similar to those mentioned by men. Men and women were depicting those outcomes of business formation which stimulated them into action and many of the reasons were similar. From an 11-country study of motivations for starting a business, three broad categories for both genders were identified: challenge, wealth and autonomy.[78] Those studies which used psychological instruments to assess the personal traits of male and female entrepreneurs also found few differences between the genders.[79] However a study by Goffee and Scase did indicate that female entrepreneurs were not a homogeneous group and could be classified according to their attachment to entrepreneurial ideals and conventional female roles.[80] Those women with a strong attachment to both were called 'conventionals'. They accommodated business aspirations and female roles by using flexible working schedules and locations. 'Innovative' women were strongly committed to entrepreneurial ideas such as autonomy and played down conventional female 'responsibilities'. 'Domestics' organised their business ventures around the needs of the family, whilst 'radical' women had low attachments to entrepreneurial and traditional female roles. They rejected conventional business and gender-related norms and were keen on radical change in society. This model and a similar one developed by Cromie and Hayes were criticised on a number of counts, but Carter notes that early research on the female entrepreneur did bring the issue of women entrepreneurs into the public domain and did point to some of the tension experienced by female business founders. However, it should be pointed out that men who own firms also experience tension between meeting economic and family needs.

A recent review of the literature by Ljunggren and Kolvereid suggests that there may well be differences in men's and women's motives.[81] Women seek economic outcomes such as profit and growth but they also seek social and relationship goals. Furthermore, Holmquist and Sundin conclude that women often start a firm to allow them to create their own workplaces.[82] This allows them to meet both business and family demands. Ljunggren and Kolvereid do report however that there is no consistency in findings about the association between gender and motivation across countries. For example in Norway men were more likely than women to be motivated by a desire to continue a family tradition and to remain at the forefront of innovative technological developments.

Perceived social norms

Individuals have different needs and therefore some entrepreneurial outcomes will motivate one person but not another. However, Krueger points out that societal norms can also influence the perceived allure of an outcome. If entrepreneurs are revered in a society and if the perceived outcomes of this process are attractive to individuals, this will encourage entrepreneurship. But does society respect female entrepreneurs? In many parts of the world it is assumed that a woman's role is to manage the households and to raise children. Also it is assumed that this requires the so-called feminine qualities such as tenderness and relatedness, and these are respected less than supposed masculine characteristics of material success, competition and ruthlessness.

While societal norms may not encourage women to be entrepreneurs to the same extent as men, that does not mean that men are universally encouraged. Indeed there would still seem to be elements of society, even in the 'enterprise' culture of the UK at the end of the twenty-first century, which say that starting a business is something only done by people who couldn't get 'a proper job'. Also there is some evidence that women entrepreneurs do tend to have strong supporters, especially from within their families. Ljunggren and Kolvereid investigated the extent to which close family members, work colleagues, entrepreneurial acquaintances and important contacts in the local community supported male and female entrepreneurs in their decision to start a venture.[83] They also asked their respondents whether they cared about what their families thought about their decision to start a venture. The results showed that women perceived significantly stronger social support than men but they do not feel any more compelled than men to comply with external pressure to start a firm. Ljunggren and Kolvereid surmise that women are less willing to start a firm until they have a support network in place. This might be because the life and occupational experiences of women have not equipped them for entrepreneurship. They need to compensate for limited knowledge and experience by marshalling support.

Anna et al. have also completed some empirical work on support for female entrepreneurs.[84] They argue that social persuasion can be important in encouraging would-be entrepreneurs to pursue this career. This persuasion can range from positive encouragement from significant others to professional advice from a variety of sources. Research reveals that women tend to have strong support from a network of contacts who provide pertinent information about markets, sources of finance and likely suppliers.

Strong social support can positively influence the attitudes of prospective entrepreneurs; it can encourage women to have self-confidence. Anna et al. studied female entrepreneurs in business areas traditionally associated with women and in 'non-traditional' areas and hypothesised that those in non-traditional areas would find it more difficult to gain access to emotional, financial or operational support systems.

The results were inconclusive with respect to operational support but women in non-traditional areas found it more difficult to obtain emotional and financial support than those in traditional sectors and women moving into non-traditional areas perceived that support was harder to come by. The 'non-traditional' women described their frustration in trying to secure loans and venture capital from banks and other organisations.

Perceived self-efficacy

To start and run a business an individual needs to be motivated, needs to have a viable business idea and needs relevant knowledge, experience, skills and resources. That person must believe that he or she has the wherewithal to succeed. This, in Krueger's terms, is self-efficacy, which can be described as a contextual judgement by individuals about the appropriateness of their skills and abilities for achieving a given goal.

Anna et al. argue that beliefs influence subsequent behaviour through the intervening variable of intentions. People form attitudes about doing things. For example, they might develop a positive attitude towards starting a business but this attitude will be strongly influenced by an individual's belief that by performing certain acts the goal of entrepreneurship can be attained.

Perceived self-efficacy leads to intentions which ultimately lead to behaviour. The notion of self-efficacy has been used since about 1980 in examining occupational choice. If individuals do not have a strong perception of self-efficacy then they will fail to realise their career potential, and Hackett and Betz claimed in 1981 that this is why many women 'fail to fully realise their capabilities and talents in career pursuits'.[85]

Successful business formulation and management requires multiple competencies, and Milne and Lewis suggest that entrepreneurs rapidly develop 'a portfolio of knowledge in two fields: first, the product or service techniques and technologies appropriate to their business, and second the business of being a businessman'.[86] They need technical, business and managerial knowledge and skill, and they get these largely through employment experience and/or educational exposure; it is also suggested that entrepreneurial learning can be gained most effectively from previous entrepreneurial experience, previous experience in the same or similar sector as that of a new enterprise, in smaller and entrepreneurial incubator organisations, from a family business and from appropriate educational experience. In the case of the latter, management education used to be a male preserve but in the past 20 years women have increasingly taken courses in business and management studies.

However in the case of employment experience there is a key issue. The labour markets in Britain, the United States and many other countries exhibit pronounced gender segregation. Blau reported in 1978 that the women in the United States who had flocked into the labour force in the 1970s were crowded into an extremely narrow range of industrial sectors and occupations.[87] They were not absorbed 'through an across-the-board expansion of employment opportunities'. The Equal Opportunities Commission reported in 2001 that in Britain the 'most significant differences between the sexes is the pronounced pattern of gender segregation in different industrial groupings and occupations'.[88]

This gender segregation means that women 'are concentrated in lower skilled and lower paid jobs with less access to vocational training and education'.[89] Carter reports that early research from the UK and the United States found that women were pressurised to start businesses in the service and retail areas and that they often lacked the knowledge and managerial experience needed to start elsewhere. However the relative lack of employment opportunities for women may encourage more of them to take the risks of self-employment. Allen and Truman[90] suggested that quite often 'women enter self -employment because they have no alternative means of earning a living', and a recent study of self-employed women in Northern Ireland by Borooah et al. suggest that the precariousness of the female labour market coupled with low pay encouraged women to seek self-employment 'to gain some form of economic independence'.[91]

These studies suggest that the employment experience of women may mean that they are relatively less well prepared for entrepreneurship. However studies of perceived self-efficacy, such as that by Ljunggren and Kolvereid, investigated the perceived behavioural control and entrepreneurial ability of emerging male and female entrepreneurs.[92] They found that there were no differences between the genders in their ability to detect entrepreneurial opportunities and surmised that this might occur because women, recognising their lack of skill and the risks involved, engage in considerable self analysis before starting a firm: they prepare thoroughly.

(Further information about women in business is included in Chapter 7.)

Enterprise and entrepreneurship in ethnic groups

Issues of ethnicity in enterprise arise not so much in the ethnic homeland, where these are also matters of politics and culture (and which are considered in the next chapter), but where there are minority ethnic groups in other countries. Again, as with women, the studies of enterprise among these groups in a number of countries have tended to look specifically at the practice of enterprise in a business start context. They have found that two issues predominate in the initial decision to create an ethnic business: structural matters such as the inhospitality of the environment in which ethnic groups are embedded, and the advantage conferred on ethnic business by the ethnic resources at their disposal. A sub-set of the latter is the cultural issue of the relative propensity of certain ethnic groups to become entrepreneurs.[93]

Inhospitality takes many forms but two broad theoretical approaches to ethnic entrepreneurship – middleman minority and ethnic enclave theories – highlight discrimination in the labour market 'exhibited in a denial of access to majority-controlled paths of economic advancement' as a major cause of business formation.[94] Ram and his colleagues are aware of supposed ethnic resources but place more emphasis on the restricted opportunity structures and straightforward racism faced by ethnic minorities in Britain.[95] In addition, Phizacklea and Ram argue that social marginalisation due to the absence of satisfactory work in mainstream employment and unemployment were by far the most often stated reasons 'for creating a business in both Lyon and Birmingham'.[96] Ram recognises that other researchers in Britain have reached different conclusions. Other studies conclude that positive issues, such as the desire to achieve, motivate ethnic entrepreneurs but it is possible that the upward mobility of second-generation immigrants can account for this outcome.[97]

Resource-based explanations of start-up focus on the advantages accruing to those belonging to and strongly connected to an ethnic group. Greene argues that ethnic entrepreneurs are influenced by the cultural context within which they function. Many ethnic communities have their particular value systems, transactions are often conducted on the basis of reciprocity, groups often have a sense of belonging and solidarity, and relationships are based on trust. These values and expectations can be a source of social capital, not merely in the more tangible form of 'protected markets', sources of labour and financial support but also in the form of intangibles such as values, traditions, ties to one another, group solidarity and networks of information. For example, group solidarity can provide a source of stability for firms as they are established and develop, and those communities with a strong proclivity for entrepreneurship will have visible role models and an atmosphere generally supportive of business formation. The success of business ventures can be a source of pride throughout the ethnic group. Networks which assist in gaining access to information, capital and support and tradition can also be a source of stability in a difficult world. Not all ethnic communities however use such resources to the same extent. Resources only contribute to value when they are utilised, and ethnic communities vary in the extent to which resources are used.

An important resource for business start-up is finance. Many small businesses rely on personal savings and informal financial assistance from friends but Fadahunsi et al. argue that these sources, with additional help from co-ethnics, are particularly important for ethnic entrepreneurs.[98] Networks of contacts were used by some owners to get introductions to bankers and other providers of finance, although the procedure was used much more by Pakistani and Indian Sikh groups than by Nigerians or West Indians. The latter groups also used informal personal networks to raise money in the form of gifts but more usually in the form of loans, which were offered on the basis of trust between borrower and lender. In this context, Fadahunsi and his colleagues quote the example of a Somali business owner who borrowed £7000 as an interest-free loan from 25 co-ethnics. Clusters of trusting co-ethnics who provide finance are an important feature of the start-up process amongst several socio-cultural groups. (Further information about ethnic businesses is included in Chapter 7.)

ILLUSTRATION 3.2
Ethnic community support

In the United States, Greene compared official and community-sponsored support programmes and concluded that community sponsorship was much more powerful than general sponsorship. She used a case study of community support for Ismaili-Pakistani immigrants in the Southwest United States to support her argument.[99]

She interviewed 82 family members in this community and found that Ismaili groups have a long history of business formation and that religious leaders have long promoted self-help, community involvement and business venturing. She also discovered that there is a recognisable route from entry into the community to business founding. New immigrants are attached to sponsors who arrange employment and tutoring in English and American business practices. In return new entrants are expected to accumulate savings. Once assimilated, immigrants are assisted in seeking and evaluating business opportunities and if a suitable prospect emerges they can borrow from a substantial community investment fund. Successful business founders meet regularly with their peers and a variety of support is made available to business associates.

Greene compares this community sponsorship programme with general sponsorship in Table 3.2, and it can be seen that the community programme is likely to offer much more sustained competitive advantage than the general programme.

It is special in that there is a semi-formal process to the sponsorship and it provides tangible resources such as capital, and intangibles like an entrepreneurial culture. Furthermore these resources are only available to insiders. Trust is also an issue. Funds are provided in the expectation of reciprocity and on the assumption that resources will not be used to exploit co-ethnics.

It is unlikely that any official sponsorship programme can compete with a scheme like the Ismaili-Pakistani one, but not all community support schemes are so well endowed or actively utilised.

Table 3.2 Ethnic sponsorship as a sustainable competitive advantage (SCA)

SCA Principles	General Sponsorship	Ethnic Community	Ismaili/Pakistani Community Example
Valuable	Valuable over the short term	Valuable indefinitely	Ethnic capital fund Assistance in opportunity search Provision of business information Expressive and instrumental support
Rare	Not particularly rare	Increased rarity for members of minority groups	Found only in certain minority groups
Imperfectly imitable unique historic	Unique historic conditions	Unique historic conditions	Recent immigrants
Causally ambiguous	Causally ambiguous	Causally ambiguous	
Socially complex	Socially complex	Socially complex	Confounded with cultural and religious norms
Lack of strategically equivalent substitutes	May provide unsubstitutable resources over the short term	Provide unsubstitutable resources over the short term	Resource mix available indefinitely to members of the community

Source: P. G. Greene, 'A resource based approach to ethnic business sponsorship - a consideration of Ismaili-Pakistani immigrants', *Journal of Small Business Management*, Vol. 35 (1997) p. 66. This table was developed from J. Barney, 'Firm resources and sustained competitive advantage', *Journal of Management*, Vol. 17 (1991) pp. 99-120 and D. M. Flynn, 'Sponsorship and the Survival of New Organisations', *Journal of Small Business Management*, Vol. 31 (1993) pp. 51–62. Reproduced with the permission of Blackwell Publishing Ltd.

Postscript

This brief review of some of the forces that impel individuals to act, or constrain them from acting, in an enterprising fashion has indicated that there is a broad range of variables in any model of entrepreneurial choice and behaviour. Not all variables will impact on all enterprise, but many of these factors will be considered, implicitly or explicitly, by those taking enterprising actions, and will help to determine whether an individual does or does not become an entrepreneur. It is important to note, though, that enterprising individuals are not homogeneous and that therefore different approaches looking at different groups at different stages of organisational development will result in a complex picture. In general there are many variables that can impact on enterprise but, in spite of calls to develop multidimensional models, few have taken up the challenge to do so. The complexity of such models, and the enormous difficulty of using multivariate analysis with so many variables that are difficult to measure, have daunted researchers.

However, the development of cognitive models of entrepreneurial motivation may offer more promise. They focus on the decision-making process, and whilst they incorporate 'soft' behavioural matters such as perception, the social construction of reality, attitudes and emotions, it has been suggested that they are easier to construct and operationalise than other complex models in this area. It could be said therefore that the study of entrepreneurship requires the study of people much more than the study of the businesses they create.

THE KEY POINTS OF CHAPTER 3

- Enterprise is generally recognised in the outcomes of acts by enterprising individuals. They can be called enterprising outcomes. They can be seen in the narrower definition of enterprise synonymous with entrepreneurship, or small business formation, and in the wider approach of enterprise, which applies to any task that is non-routine and goal-directed and is accomplished in a determined and adventurous manner.

- Enterprise activity is dependent on enterprising individuals. There have been many studies and approaches to analysing what makes some individuals more enterprising than others. They include:

  - economic theories (and see also Chapter 4)

  - personality theories considering traits in individuals that predispose them to enterprise, psychodynamic approaches that look at the enterprising personality, social psychological approaches that take into account the context in which an individual operates

  - sociological approaches which consider the opportunities for and constraints on career choices

  - cognitive approaches which suggest that decisions are made on the basis of perceived reality, which is in turn affected by attitudes and behaviour

  - behavioural theories, including the competencies approach

- integrated approaches, such as that advanced by Krueger, which combine a number of different factors.

- All of these approaches offer some insight into what makes an individual act in an enterprising way. The integrated approaches offer potentially the most useful models for examining the process of enterprise. None however has yet proved to be helpful in predicting future enterprise or entrepreneurial success although recent work on entrepreneurial self-efficacy may hold promise.

- Two other aspects of individuals which are perceived to have some influence on their enterprise are their gender and ethnicity.

CASE 3.4
Two enterprising people?

Helen

Helen was born and reared in a rural community in Scotland by middle-class parents who had no connection with any small business. When she left school she was sponsored by a large organisation to take a business studies degree and worked for them for a year after graduation.

However, she was not content with the routine nature of the work and left to study for a PhD in finance. After graduating she worked as a research assistant in a university department but soon left to take up a post in a commercial research team. The job did not live up to her expectations: she found little challenge in it and did not respond well to taking orders from her boss. She found that she was not in control and disliked being told to do things. It was around this time that she married a university lecturer.

Helen left this job and returned for a short time to a university research post but was head-hunted and offered a senior position in the small business unit of a consultancy firm. She imagined that she would have lots of freedom in this post, but much of the job was in running pre-planned courses with little non-recurring, innovative work. She also disagreed with her superiors about the kind of contracts that they sought.

Throughout her work history Helen had always tried to be successful and she discovered that she did not like taking orders from anyone. She also found out that her boredom threshold was low: she was always on the lookout for new challenges. She therefore began to think about having her own enterprise. Then things happened very quickly; she wrote a business plan, contacted bank managers, sought clients and copyrights on some of her material and disengaged from her employment. Her main stimulus for starting the business was a realisation that she was very bad at accepting orders from authority figures, and her stated motives were: frustration over not being able to do the things she wanted to; the desire to do something worthwhile and earn more money at the same time; and the wish to get back to the 'sharp end' of finance where the excitement was.

Helen created an innovative financial services business with clients throughout the British Isles. She had developed both the technical and the managerial skills needed for this business through past experience. However her perception of the entrepreneurial role was not clear and she fully recognised that this might cause a problem. She predicted that her life would be a rather lonely one and she was not looking forward to the isolation. She did have a long discussion with a friend who owned his own enterprise, and his advice was not to 'go for all the trimmings; just to have a go and meet the problems as they arise'.

John

John came from a Northern Irish lower-middle-class family which had a long association with a number of small entrepreneurial ventures. He left school without formal qualifications and trained as a caterer but, due to the awkward hours and poor payment, he soon left. His next job was as a bricklayer, a job he thoroughly enjoyed. He was paid an efficiency bonus and felt that he was rewarded for effort. However he fell and sustained injuries which effectively ended his bricklaying days. Next, he attended college, took some 'O' levels and was offered a place on an HND course in business studies, but declined the offer. After this he took clerical and junior administrative jobs in two engineering companies but he could not settle into the required routine.

Around this time John got involved with a number of part-time entrepreneurial ventures, including a disco, window cleaning, selling fruit and vegetables, and painting and decorating. He always had a desire to have his own business and his first major venture was a small catering enterprise. He was employed by a catering firm for a time but he and a partner started their own firm. The venture did not last: John accused the partner of incompetence and they broke up on acrimonious terms. While working in the catering firm he got married and the lack of security in running a venture concerned him, so for the next six years he got involved in selling. He worked for a number of companies and eventually achieved the position of sales manager. However his final employer 'did the dirty on him' so he left. He was scathing about the whole business of selling.

In reviewing his work history he said that he always was rebellious and thought that he had been held back a lot because he was too young. He felt that his working life had been a failure in that he had numerous goals but none of them were really fulfilled. He had little time for authority figures and often felt that others had let him down. He was resentful about his lack of career progress and saw entrepreneurship as a possible way out of his dilemma.

He wanted to be an entrepreneur but had no business idea. Therefore he searched through various catalogues in pursuit of one. He came across an idea for repairing damaged motor vehicles and, because it was already patented by an American, he spent a long time negotiating over patent rights. He negotiated a deal and then set about building prototypes and conducting market research in an attempt to launch his enterprise.

John's motives for founding a business were above all a desire for autonomy, followed by achievement and a desire to make money. His scores on key entrepre-neurial characteristics were all high and this, together with his background and job history, might be thought to mark him out as a 'natural' entrepreneur. However he had no previous experience of the motor trade and no knowledge of the motor insurance business. His prior entrepreneurial experience might help with the running of the business but will that be enough?

Points raised

Like the subject of Case 2.3, these are typical entrepreneurs, but the examples suggest that not every entrepreneur is perfectly suited and prepared for that role. The desire to have one's own business does not guarantee success; other attributes and resources are necessary

QUESTIONS, EXERCISES, ESSAY AND DISCUSSION TOPICS

- Critically evaluate the usefulness of trait theory in predicting who will become an entrepreneur.
- Critically evaluate the usefulness of cognitive theories of motivation for those persons charged with increasing the degree of enterprise in a community.
- Comment on the views expressed in Case 3.1.
- According to Case 3.1, 'enterprise can't be taught'. So what is the role of academic schools of enterprise and entrepreneurship?
- Based on Krueger's model, what would you do to encourage more entrepreneurial activity? How would this differ from an approach based on the attributes and resources model?
- Using either Krueger's model or the attributes and resources approach, suggest a programme to help individuals to prepare themselves for eventual self-employment.
- Entrepreneurs need motivation, skills, resources and ideas to start businesses, and women are just as capable as men of making a success of a business venture. Discuss.
- Compare the motivations of ethnic entrepreneurs with those of indigenous entrepreneurs.
- If you can run a family, you can run a business. Discuss with reference to Case 3.2.
- Are entrepreneurs 'born' or 'made'? Discuss with reference to Cases 3.1, 3.3 and 3.4.
- Study the short profiles of Helen and John in Case 3.4. Which person is the more likely to run a successful firm? Give reasons for your choice.
- Which theories best explain the examples in Cases 3.3 and 3.4?

Suggestions for further reading and information

W. K. Bolton and J. L. Thompson, *Entrepreneurs: Talent, Temperament, Techniques* (Oxford: Butterworth-Heinemann, 2000).

E. Chell, *Entrepreneurship: Globalisation, Innovation and Development* (London: Thompson Learning, 2000).

S. Carter and D. Jones-Evans, *Enterprise and Small Business* (London: Pearson Education, 2nd edn, 2005) Chapters 8, 10 and 11.

R. Branson, *Losing My Virginity* (Virgin Publishing, 1999).

A. Roddick, *Body and Soul* (Vermillion, 1991) and *Business as Usual* (HarperCollins, 2000).

www.dyson.com – the website for James Dyson and the innovatory Dyson appliances.

www.eoc.org.uk – the website for the Equal Opportunities Commission.

References

1. M. Scott, A. Fadahunsi and S. Kodithuwakku, 'Mastering Enterprise, no. 7', *Financial Times*, 13 January 1997, p. 6.
2. *New Collins Dictionary* (Glasgow: HarperCollins, 1992).
3. A. A. Gibb, 'The Enterprise Culture and Education', *International Small Business Journal*, Vol. 11 (1993), pp. 11—34.
4. W. G. Biemans, *Managing Innovation Within Networks* (London: Routledge, 1992).
5. G. A. Forehand, 'Assessment of Innovative Behaviour: Partial Criteria for the Assessment of Executive Performance', *Journal of Applied Psychology*, Vol. 47 (1963), pp. 206–13.
6. R. M. Kanter, 'Change Master Skills', in *Managing Innovation*, edited by J. Henry and D. Walker (London: Sage, 1991), pp. 54–61.
7. Lord Young of Graffan cited in A. Tate, 'A Strategy for Enterprise in the University of Ulster', *Journal of Irish Business and Administrative Research*, Vol. 14 (1993), pp. 1–11, p. 1.
8. J. B. Miner, N. R. Smith and J. S. Bracker, 'Defining the Inventor-Entrepreneur in the Context of Established Typologies', *Journal of Business Venturing*, 7 (1992), pp.103–13
9. W. K. Bolton and J. L. Thompson, *Entrepreneurs: Talent, Temperament, Technique* (Butterworth-Hennemann: Oxford, 2000).
10. B. Jovanovich, 'Selection and Evolution of Industry', *Econometrica*, 50(3) (1982), pp. 647–70
11. A. Lundstrom and L. Stevenson, *Entrepreneurship Policy: Theory and Practice* (New York: Springer Science+Business Media, 2005).
12. Baumol, W. J. 'Entrepreneurship: Productive, Unproductive and Destructive', *Journal of Political Economy*, 98(5) (1990), pp. 893–921
13. F. J. Greene, K. F. Mole, and D. J. Storey, *Three Decades of Enterprise Culture* (Basingstoke: Palgrave, 2008), p. 247.
14. Ibid., p. 14.
15. See D. McClelland, *The Achieving Society* (Princeton, New Jersey: Van Nostrand, 1961), and J. Rotter, 'Generalised Expectancies for Internal Versus External Control of Reinforcement', *Psychological Monographs*, Vol. 80 (1966), pp. 1—27; see McKenna also for a discussion on psychoanalytical approaches to personality.
16. H. H. Stevenson and D. E. Gumpert, 'The Heart of Entrepreneurship', in *The Entrepreneurial Venture*, edited by W. A. Sahlman and H. H. Stevenson (Boston, Massachusetts: Harvard Business School, 1992).
17. J. A. Timmons, *The Entrepreneurial Mind* (Andover: Brick House, 1989).
18. S. Caird, *A Review of Methods of Measuring Enterprising Attributes* (Durham University Business School, 1988).
19. Timmons, op. cit.
20. D. C. McClelland, 'Achievement Motivation Can be Developed', *Harvard Business Review*, November-December (1965), pp. 6–24.
21. S. Cromie, 'Assessing Entrepreneurial Inclinations: Some Approaches and Empirical Evidence,' *European Journal of Work and Organisational Psychology*, Vol. 9 (2000), pp. 7–30.
22. H. Lithunen, 'Entrepreneurship and the Characteristics of the Personality', *International Journal of Entrepreneurial Behaviour and Research*, Vol. 6 (2000), pp. 295–309. Quotation on p. 301.

23. D. C. McClelland (1965) op. cit. p. 7.
24. See this comment by an interviewee in S. Cromie, 'Motivation of Aspiring Male and Female Entrepreneurs', *Journal of Organisational Behaviour*, Vol. 8 (1987), pp. 251—61.
25. P. F. Drucker, *Innovation and Entrepreneurship* (London: Heinemann, 1985), p. 128.
26. E. Chell, J. Haworth and S. Brearley, *The Entrepreneurial Personality: Concepts, Cases, and Categories* (London: Routledge, 1991).
27. M. Simon, S. M. Houghton and K. Aquino, 'Cognitive Biases, Risk Perception and Venture Formation: How Individuals Decided to Start Companies', *Journal of Business Venturing*, Vol. 15 (1999), pp. 113–34.
28. Ibid p. 116.
29. One of the statements used in a questionnaire designed by Rotter, op. cit.
30. See Cromie (2000), op. cit. for a recent review of research on locus of control.
31. See Delmar (2000), op. cit. for a discussion on this concept.
32. See comments by respondents in Cromie (1987), op. cit.
33. Cromie (1987), op. cit.
34. See Cromie (1987), op. cit.
35. D. Miller, 'Strategy Making and Structure: Analysis and Implications for Performance', *Academy of Management Journal*, Vol. 38 (1987), pp. 7–32. See p. 32 for a scale to measure proactivty.
36. A. Ardichvili and R. N. Cardozo, 'A Model of the Entrepreneurial Opportunity Recognition Process', *Journal of Enterprise Culture*, Vol. 8 (2000), pp. 103–19.
37. S. Roy and R. N. Cardozo, 'Sensitivity and Creativity in Entrepreneurial Opportunity Recognition: A Framework for Empirical Investigation', Proceedings of the PDMA Conference, 1995, p. 105.
38. Miller, op. cit. p. 10.
39. M. D. Ensley, J. W. Carland and J. C. Carland, 'Investigating the Existence of the Lead Entrepreneur', *Journal of Small Business Management*, Vol. 38 (2000), pp. 59–77. Quotation on p. 61.
40. See V. Thompson, *Bureaucracy and Innovation* (Alabama: Alabama University Press, 1969) for a discussion on creativity. Thompson's quotation is from page 11.
41. J. B. Cunningham and H. Lischeron, 'Defining Entrepreneurship', *Journal of Small Business Management*, Vol. 29 (1991), pp. 45–60, p. 47.
42. Delmar (2000), op. cit.
43. I. J. Deary and G. Matthews, 'Personality Traits Are Alive and Well', *The Psychologist*, July 1993, p. 299
44. E. A. Fagenson, 'Personal Value Systems of Men and Women Entrepreneurs Versus Managers', *Journal of Business Venturing*, Vol. 8 (1993), pp. 409–30. Quotation on p. 424.
45. M. Kets de Vries, 'The Entrepreneurial Personality: A Person at the Crossroads', *Journal of Management Studies*, Vol. 14 (1977), pp. 34–57.
46. A. Mac Nabb, *Entrepreneurial Profiling* (Belfast: Institute for Enterprise Strategies, 1993).
47. Delmar (2000), op. cit.
48. See Chell et al, op. cit. and S. E. Hampton, *The Construction of Personality* (London: Routledge, 1988).
49. M. J. K. Stanworth and J. Curran, 'Growth and the Small Firm: An Alternative View', *Journal of Management Studies*, Vol. 13 (1976), pp. 95–110.
50. A. K. Roberts, 'The Social Conditions, Consequences and Limitations of Careers Guidance', *British Journal of Guidance and Counselling*, Vol. 5 (1977), pp. 1 9, p. 7.
51. J. Stanworth and C. Gray (eds), *Bolton 20 Years On: The Small Firm in the 1990s* (London: Paul Chapman, 1991), p. 174.
52. J. Curran and R. A. Blackburn, 'Introduction', in J. Curran and R. A. Blackburn, *Paths of Enterprise* (London: Routledge, 1991).
53. A. A. Gibb, 'Enterprise Culture: Its Meaning and Implications for Education and Training', *Journal of European Industrial Training*, Vol. 11 (1987), p. 11.
54. Delmar (2000), op. cit. p. 139.
55. Delmar (2000), op. cit. p. 139.
56. E. A. Locke, 'The Motivation Sequence, the Motivation Hub and Motivation Core', *Organisational Behaviour and Human Decision Processes*, Vol. 50 (1991), pp. 288–99.
57. N. C. Boyd and G. S. Vozikis, 'The Influence of Self-efficacy on the Development of Entrepreneurial Intentions and Actions', *Entrepreneurship: Theory and Practice*, Vol. 18 (1994), pp. 63–78.
58. Ibid., p. 67.
59. A. Bandura, 'Perceived Self-efficacy', in *The Blackwell Encyclopaedia of Social Psychology*, edited by A. S. R. Manstead and M. Hewstone (eds.) (Oxford, Blackwood Publishers, 1995).
60. Delmar (2000), op. cit. p. 152.

61. Delmar (2000), op. cit. p. 147.

62. See R. Boyatzis, *The Competent Manager* (New York: Wiley, 1982) and *Management Charter Initiative, Management Standards Implementation Pack* (London: MCI, 1991).

63. S. Caird, 'Problems With the Identification of Enterprise Competencies and the Implications for Assessment and Development', *Management Education and Development*, Vol. 23 (1992), pp. 6–17.

64. Ibid. p. 14.

65. Ibid. p. 16.

66. N. F. Krueger, *Prescription for Opportunity: How Communities Can Create Potential for Entrepreneurs* (Washington, DC: Small Business Foundation of America, Working Paper 93–03, 1995).

67. F. Delmar, 'The Psychology of the Entrepreneur', in S. Carter and D. Jones-Evans, *Enterprise and Small Business* (London: Pearson, 2000), p. 148.

68. P. Davidson, 'Determinants of Entrepreneurial Intentions', Paper presented at the Rent IX Conference, Piacenza, Italy, November 1995.

69. See for instance D. Smallbone and P. Wyer, 'Growth and Development in the Small Firm', in S. Carter and D. Jones-Evans, op. cit. p. 413

70. National Women's Business Council, *Expanding Business Opportunities for Women* (Washington, D.C: National Women's Business Council, 1996).

71. R. K. Z. Heck and E. S. Trent, 'The Prevalence of Family Business from a Household Perspective', *Family Business Review*, Vol. 12 (1999), pp. 209–20.

72. S. Carter, 'Improving the Number and Performance of Women-owned Businesses: Some Implications for Training and Advisory Services', *Evaluation and Training*, Vol. 42 (2001), pp. 326–34.

73. E. Ljunggren and L. Kolvereid, 'New Business Formation: Does Gender Make a Difference?' *Women in Management Review*, Vol. 11 (1996), pp. 3–12.

74. S. Carter, 'Gender and Enterprise', in S. Carter and D. Jones-Evans (eds), op. cit., p. 167.

75. *The Labour Market, Women and Men in Britain* (London: Equal Opportunities Commission, 2001), p. 3.

76. E. Chell and S. Baines, 'Does Gender Affect Business Performance? A Study of Microbusinesses in Business Services in the UK', *Entrepreneurship and Regional Development*, Vol. 10 (1998), pp. 117–35.

77. S. Marlow and A. Strange, 'Female Entrepreneurs: Success by Whose Standards?' in *Women in Management: A Developing Presence*, edited by N. Tanton (London: Routledge, 1994), p. 173. Cited in E. Chell and S. Baines, op. cit.

78. S. Scheinberg and I. C. MacMillan, 'An 11 Country Study of Motivations to Start a Business', in *Frontiers of Entrepreneurship Research*, edited by B. A. Kirchoff, W. A. Long, W. E. McMullan, K. H. Vesper and W. E. Wetzel (Wellesley, Mass.: Babson College, 1988).

79. Cromie (1987) op. cit., pp. 251–61.

80. R. Goffee and R. Scase, *Women in Charge* (London: Allen and Unwin, 1985).

81. Ljunggren and Kolvereid, op. cit.

82. C. Holmquist and E. Sundin, 'The Growth of Women's Entrepreneurship: Push or Pull Factors?' Paper presented to the EIASM Conference on Small Business, Durham Business School, 1989.

83. Ljunggren and Kolvereid, op. cit.

84. A. L. Anna, G. N. Chandler, E. Jansen and N. P. Mero, 'Women Business Owners in Traditional and Non Traditional Industries', *Journal of Business Venturing*, Vol. 15 (1999), pp. 279–303.

85. G. Hackett and N. E. Betz, 'A Self-efficacy Approach to the Career Development of Women', *Journal of Vocational Behaviour*, Vol. 18 (1981), pp. 326–39.

86. T. Milne and J. Lewis, 'Models and Approaches to Teaching Entrepreneurship', in *Small Business Research*, edited by T. Webb, T. Quince and D. Watkins (Aldershot, Gower, 1983), p. 69.

87. F. D. Blau, 'The Data on Women Workers, Past, Present and Future', in *Women Working*, edited by A. H. Stromberg and S. Harkness (Palo Alto, Calif.: Mayfield, 1978), p. 44.

88. The Equal Opportunities Commission, op. cit., p. 1

89. Ibid., p. 1

90. S. Allen and C. Truman, 'Women in Business', in *Paths of Enterprise*, edited by J. Curran and R. Blackburn (London: Routledge, 1991), p. 117.

91. V. K. Borooah, G. Collins, M. Hart and A. McNabb, 'Women and Self Employment', in *Small Firms: Entrepreneurship in the Nineties*, edited by D. Deakins, P. Jennings and C. Mason (London: Paul Chapman, 1997), p. 78.

92. Ljunggren and Kolvereid, op. cit.

93. M. Ram and D. Smallbone, *Ethnic Minority Enterprise: Policy and practice* (London: DTI, the Small Business Service and Kingston University Small Business Research Centre SME Seminar Series, 2001).

94. P. G. Greene, 'A Resource Based Approach to Ethnic Business Sponsorship: A Consideration of Ismaili-Pakistani Immigrants', *Journal of Small Business Management*, Vol. 35 (1997), pp. 57–71. Quotation on p. 58.

95. M. Ram and G. Barrett, 'Ethnicity and Enterprise', in *Enterprise and Small Business*, edited by S. Carter and D. Jones-Evans (London: Pearson Education, 2000).

96. A. Phizacklea and M. Ram, 'Ethnic Entrepreneurship in Comparative Perspective', *International Journal of Entrepreneurial Behaviour and Research*, Vol. 1 (1995), pp. 48–58. Quotation on p. 50.

97. Phizacklea and Ram, op.cit. p. 50 for the quotation. For positive motivation among ethnic entrepreneurs see J. Curran and R. Blackburn, *Ethnic Enterprise and the High Street Banks: A Survey of Ethnic Businesses in Two Localities* (Kingston Upon Thames University: Small Business Research Centre, 1993).

98. A. Fadahunsi, D. Smallbone and S. Supri, 'Networking and Ethnic Minority Enterprise Development: Insights from a North London Study', *Journal of Small Business and Enterprise Development*, Vol. 7 (2000), pp. 228–40.

99. P. G. Greene, op. cit.

CHAPTER 4

Enterprise: the external influences

Contents

KEY CONCEPTS

This chapter covers:

- The various environmental factors, external to the individual, which have been identified as having some influence on the extent of enterprise and entrepreneurship. They include:

    - cultural, political and economic conditions

    - social capital

    - demand factors

    - supply factors

    - government and other interventions

    - equilibrium rates.

- Theories, and investigations, which attempt to link some or all of these factors, and the internal factors considered in the previous chapter, into one model to explain the different rates of enterprise and entrepreneurship observed in different contexts.

LEARNING OBJECTIVES

By the end of this chapter the reader should:

- Know what are thought to be the main external sources of influence on the extent of enterprising behaviour and entrepreneurship.
- Understand how these factors are thought to influence enterprise and entrepreneurship and the differences they are believed to make.
- Be able to describe how these factors, in combination with internal factors, might explain why there are different rates of enterprise in different contexts.

Introduction

Chapter 3 looked at those factors internal to people, or at least with an internal component, which are thought to influence enterprise. Its starting point was that enterprise is recognised in enterprising acts performed by individuals. It therefore considered the attributes possessed by those individuals that dispose them towards acting in an enterprising manner. It also looked at Krueger's model which suggests how the various possible factors might combine to influence an individual to engage in enterprising activity. Amongst the components of Krueger's model are social norms and perceived feasibility, which are not, however, issues only or mainly internal to the individual.

It is a complex task to understand the linkage between individual attributes which are innate or acquired and attributes determined by the society in which those individuals grew up, and our knowledge about it is still evolving. There is undoubtedly considerable feedback between those attributes which are perceived as innate or acquired and developed early in life (and so may be referred to as being 'born') and those perceived to be attributable to environmental 'conditioning' (often referred to as 'made'). Chapter 3 concentrated on the issues which are considered to be largely internal to the individual. But there are other influences external to the individual, such as societal culture and the 'pull' or demand factor of opportunity, which are also thought to have an impact. In the search for an explanation of why different groups of individuals show different levels of enterprise, many external factors have been suggested. As well as economic and political conditions, cultural and demand factors, external supply factors, external intervention and equilibrium rates have all been proposed. This list of issues which might have an impact on the level of enterprise in individuals, and thus on the level of entrepreneurship and on their businesses, is summarised in Figure 4.1 and it is these issues which are considered in this chapter.

Listing the issues separately, however, does not mean that the issues themselves can

National and societal culture

Economic conditions
including: equilibrium
rates of enterprise

Political conditions
including: government
influence and enterprise
support

*The individual entrepreneur,
with his or her attributes,
resources and beliefs, and
his or her business*

'Demand' factors
such as: economic,
political, technical and
industry issues

'Supply' factors
such as: participation
rates, income levels and
population growth

Social capital

Figure 4.1 Suggested influences on the level of enterprise in people and their businesses

be completely separated from each other. And, just as the various influences on enterprise, innate and acquired, individual and environmental, are not clearly delineated, so the categories used in this chapter are not absolute and indivisible. They are used as a way of presenting the issues, not as an indication of clear distinctions.

How then do ideas of enterprise based on individual attributes and perceptions

---

ILLUSTRATION 4.1
The importance of context

The importance of context is highlighted by a study carried out by the University of Groningen, covering nine countries (Brazil, Cameroon, Colombia, Indonesia, Japan, Kenya, the Netherlands, the UK and West Germany) and almost 2700 entrepreneurs. It gave some interesting indications into the values and motivations that differ between Western and Eastern countries and those that differ between the industrialised and the less developed countries. Among the findings were:

- Entrepreneurs in the industrialised countries more often started their businesses due to dissatisfaction (push factors) rather than ambition (pull factors). The reverse was the case in less developed countries.

- When determining choice of business activity, personal initiative plays a significant role in the highly individualistic West. Allowing oneself to be guided by the insight and initiative of someone else is very important in highly collectivist countries such as Japan and Indonesia.

- Entrepreneurs in less developed countries ascribe more importance to the business firm as a family institution. In the West, the firm is seen as the institutionalisation of work.

- In collectivist cultures, receptiveness to help and support the environment is greater.
- Entrepreneurs in European countries are the most individualistic and display self-confidence in their entrepreneurial ability. Japan and Indonesia are the least individualistic (suggesting that individualistic and entrepreneurial behaviours are not, in this context, synonymous).

Other problems of cross-cultural interpretation are revealed by this study, in particular in ascribing variations in entrepreneurship to different cultural, political or economic environments. The authors commented that it is very difficult to disentangle the relative importance of the 'two environments, which, while they may be distinguished from one another, are interdependent'. They went on to say, however, that 'evidence is building' which suggests that entrepreneurship is primarily influenced by the politico-economic environment, which is, 'on the whole', more important than the cultural environment.

This is illustrated by considering the consequences for entrepreneurial behaviour in a less developed country, which may, typically, have an unstable and unpredictable environment. A business functioning successfully one moment can be faced with insurmountable problems the next. Businesses can be viewed as 'temporary projects', with people working on them and earning money in them as long as possible until a more attractive 'project' appears. In more economically stable countries, the continuity of the business, spanning many generations, can be of primary importance to the entrepreneur, and the motivation is not limited just to earning a living. Therefore it is argued that the concept of entrepreneurship acquires an entirely different meaning. 'The term "business" must, under these conditions be interpreted as a "project", and "entrepreneur" must be seen as someone who, perhaps temporarily or part-time, provides leadership for a project.'

It is not surprising, therefore, when the studies show that in less developed countries:

- The birth rate of businesses is higher than in developed countries.
- More businesses are started by entrepreneurs than are bought or inherited.
- More entrepreneurs have had more than one business.
- Risk-avoidance behaviour is more pronounced (for example, 'sell out today – who knows what tomorrow holds?').

These are characteristics which might be thought to be culturally determined but in this context can be shown to have their roots in the economic facts of life.

Source: Based on H. Pompe, M. Bruyn and J. Koek, 'Entrepreneurs in Small Business in International Comparative Perspective', Paper presented at the 13th International Small Business Congress, London, 1986.

relate to the idea of the influence of an enterprise culture? Do they offer contradictory or complementary notions? If plants grow well is that due to the genes in the seeds, or the growing culture in which they have germinated? If there is such a thing as an enterprise culture, is it something more than just a collection of individuals who are themselves enterprising, or can the culture of a group, or society, itself be enterprising or influence the enterprise shown by its members? Take for instance the example of the 'tiger' economies of the Pacific Rim. They are thought by many to be very enterprising but they do not in general have a culture based on the individual, and their success is seen to come from aspects of their society as a whole. They provide therefore a *prima facie* case for saying that an understanding of enterprise must include a view as to its wider context beyond the individual.

In exploring these issues this chapter includes theories which attempt to combine a number of possible influences, both internal and external, to give a more complete view of why enterprise, especially in the context of entrepreneurship, occurs when it does. There is more than one such theory and they do not all include the same factors but that does not mean that some have to be wrong. Essentially these theories are looking at the same issue but from somewhat different perspectives. Therefore they include many of the same components, although not always under the same names, but they present somewhat different aspects, each of which is only one possible view of part of a complex, and not completely understood, whole.

ILLUSTRATION 4.2
From *An Eclectic Theory of Entrepreneurship*

The process by which the actual rate of entrepreneurship is established involves both macro and micro components. On the demand side, entrepreneurial opportunities are created by the market demand for goods and services, whereas the supply side generates (potential) entrepreneurs who can seize the opportunities provided they have the resources, abilities and preferences to do so. Moreover, personality characteristics need to be in line with the entrepreneurial opportunity. The entrepreneurial decision, i.e. occupational choice, is made at the individual level, taking into account entrepreneurial opportunities and resources, abilities, personality traits and preferences of the individual.

An individual's risk–reward profile represents the process of weighing alternative types of employment and is based on opportunities (environmental characteristics, resources, abilities, personality traits and preferences). The occupational choices of individuals are made on the basis of their risk–reward profile of entrepreneurship versus that of other types of employment.

Source: I. Verheul, A. R. M. Wennekers, D. B. Audretsch and A. R Thurik, *Research Report – An Eclectic Theory of Entrepreneurship: Policies, Institutions and Culture* (Zoetermeer Holland, EIM/Small Business Research and Consultancy, 1999), pp. 67–9; subsequently published as Chapter 2 in D. Audretsch, R. Thurik, I. Verheul and S. Wennekers (eds), *Entrepreneurship: Determinants and Policy in a European–US Comparison* (Dordrecht, the Netherlands and Norwell, Mass.: Kluwer Academic Publishers, 2000), p. 19. Reproduced with the permission of Kluwer Academic Publishers.

Cultural, political and economic conditions

Cultural, political and economic conditions are interlinked and there is little doubt that the disposition towards, and triggers for, enterprise are found along a continuum from inborn attributes of individuals to complex interrelationships amongst often changing cultural, political and economic conditions at national, regional and local levels. Further evidence of these interrelationships is provided by, *inter alia*, Hofstede,[1] Morrison[2] and Garrison[3] as they seek to understand the factors which contribute to or stifle enterprise and entrepreneurship initiation. Hofstede, for example, while concentrating on the importance of cultural influences on development, states the need for a 'market' and a 'political condition' that allow development. He notes that the market circumstances for growth of the 'dragon' economies began only in the mid-1950s as world markets freed up:

> The need for a supportive political context was met in all 'dragon' countries but in very different ways ... with the role of government varying from active support to laissez faire. Labour unions were weak and company-orientated in all the countries and a relatively egalitarian income distribution meant that support for revolutionary social changes was weak.[4]

A representation of these categories of influence on enterprise and their interrelationship can be seen in Figure 4.2.

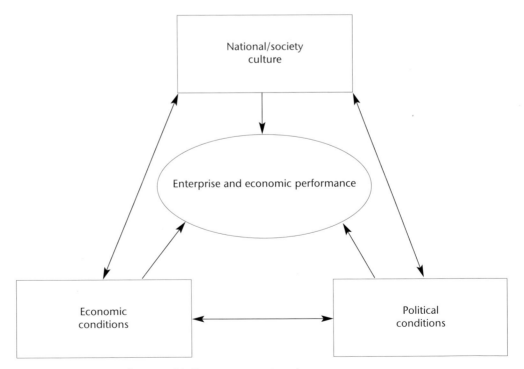

Figure 4.2 Impact of external influences on enterprise

National and societal culture

It is argued by some that nations should not be equated to societies, as 'societies are organically developed forms of social organisation, and the concept of a common culture applies, strictly speaking, more to societies than to nations.'[5] The nation is a relatively recent phenomenon in human history and can incorporate plural cultures and layers of sub-cultures. Nevertheless, the nation or country is seen as a feasible proxy for a single organisational unit in 'humanity's organisation of the world today'.[6]

Tayeb defined culture as 'a set of historically evolved learned values, attitudes and meanings shared by the members of a given community that influence their material and non-material way of life'.[7] Members of the community learn these shared characteristics, she claims, 'through different stages of the socialisation processes of their lives in institutions, such as family, religion, formal education and society as a whole'.

Hofstede, noting that 'culture in the form of certain dominant values is a necessary but not a sufficient condition for economic achievement',[8] defined culture similarly. It is the 'shared values that typify a society' and 'the collective programming of the mind which distinguishes the members of one group or category from another'. Hofstede further explains that, as almost everyone belongs to a number of different groups and categories of people at the same time, he or she will unavoidably carry several layers of what he calls 'mental programming' within himself or herself corresponding to different levels of culture.[9]

ILLUSTRATION 4.3
Mental programming

Few will doubt the importance of the formal education system in shaping the attitudes and behaviours of individuals and groups, but in attempting to understand another country or culture it is difficult at times to question one's basic assumptions – deeply ingrained consciously or unconsciously over the years. The purpose of education is perceived differently from society to society. An individualist society aims at preparing the individual for a place in the society of other individuals. This means learning to cope with new, unknown and unforeseen situations. ... [T]he purpose of learning is less to know how to do as to know how to learn. ... In the collectivist society there is a stress on adaptation to the skills and virtues necessary to be an acceptable group member. This leads to a premium on the products of tradition. ... [T]he young have to learn how to do things in order to participate in society.

Hofstede[10]

Culture is recognised as a complex phenomenon. Garrison suggests that:

attempts at definition are problematic due to culture's amorphous, shifting nature. This is further compounded by its multiple representation within such elements as:

- different levels (national, regional, business, individual);
- layers of society (gender, age, social class, occupation, family, religion);
- varying context of life (individual, group, community).[11]

Hofstede identifies and analyses five dimensions by which cultures can be described:

- *Power distance*: expresses dependence relationships in a country. It defines the extent to which the less powerful members of institutions and organisations expect and accept that power will be distributed unequally. For instance, there is only a small power distance in situations where subordinates would expect to participate in decision making with superiors.
- *Individualistic/collectivist*: reflects the extent to which it is the interest of the individual or the interest of the group that prevails.
- *Masculinity/femininity tendencies*: defines the extent to which social gender roles in the society are clearly distinct. In masculine societies, men are supposed to be tough, assertive and focused on material success, and women to be more modest, tender and concerned with the quality of life. Femininity pertains to societies where the social gender roles overlap.
- *Uncertainty avoidance*: defines the extent to which the members of a culture feel threatened by uncertain or unknown situations. This feeling is expressed through nervous stress and in a need for predictability (including a need for written and unwritten rules).
- *Long-term orientation*: defines a country in terms of its trade-off between short-term and long-term gratification of needs. (Long-term orientation emphasises values such as perseverance and thrift.)

Ultimately these dimensions reveal themselves in individual and group values, preferences and behaviour which have been acquired in the context of family, school and occupation. They are a measure of what we call national culture and which many perceive to be a key determinant of the degree of enterprise in a country.

They pose interesting questions such as whether a 'large power-distance' country is likely to be enterprising. In such a country, subordinates in organisations are more likely to accept inequality and hierarchy and, it could be argued, acquire attitudes inimical to entrepreneurial endeavour. Where individualism is counter-cultural, as in Japan (and children think of 'we' not 'I'), is enterprising behaviour inhibited – or can groups be as enterprising as individuals? It has traditionally been common to view attributes of the feminine gender as inherently less likely to lead to enterprising behaviour. Similarly, if a culture is uncomfortable with uncertainty and ambiguity, one might question if it can be as entrepreneurial as one that is comfortable coping in such situations. Equally, taking a long-term view may be felt likely to lead to caution and conservative behaviour. Intriguingly, little is known of how these different dimensions interact to reinforce or negate each other. Hofstede's work reveals that successful nations (in economic terms) can exhibit significantly different scores on each of the dimensions he describes, suggesting that there are no easily defined 'right' or 'wrong' cultural conditions. Positive economic outcomes can emerge from a wide range of contexts.

ILLUSTRATION 4.4
Culture and learning

A Japanese friend once said that he could never ask a question in a class or lecture room unless, by so doing, he was obviously advancing everyone else's knowledge and understanding. Otherwise, he should not waste the teacher's or his fellow students' time. He believed that problems of learning should be handled outside the group.

In the context of modern Western educational practice, such failure to participate and generate teacher feedback would be considered reticent and unenterprising.

Another approach which has been used to develop a model which seeks to identify, categorise and analyse the key features associated with 'entrepreneurship initiation' in society is that of Morrison.[12] Her summary of the influences upon entrepreneurial behaviour as derived from her cross-country research and review of relevant literature is shown in Figure 4.3.

The initiation of entrepreneurship starts, she suggests, at the 'grass roots' level where 'a range of inputs commences the mental and social conditioning of the populace'. These inputs include religion, education, politics, family history, role models and personal characteristics (that is, external and internal influences).

The 'socially developed entrepreneur' is further surrounded by social, economic and institutional constructs within which entrepreneurs may exercise their judgement as to whether 'they are sufficiently robust to support the initiation of entrepreneurship'. These constructs include policy, the economy, employment, industry, corporations and networks. They embrace matters such as: the extent to which policy frameworks and conditions are encouraged in which the individual (as opposed to the state) can flourish; the small firm sector is supported; large corporations offer entrepreneurial opportunities through delayering, outsourcing and re-engineering; and strong formal and informal networks exist and grow.

'Inputs' and 'social constructs' combine 'to provide the evidence, negative and/or positive, of entrepreneurial behaviour' and impact upon the extent to which a society values and nurtures or stifles such behaviour.

The outcome is evidenced through a range of factors such as:

- *Ideologies*: particularly in relation to attitudes towards unsuccessful endeavour and a regard for entrepreneurial behaviour generally.

- *Social consequences*: the extent to which it is believed that entrepreneurship has the potential for beneficial outcomes for society as a whole.

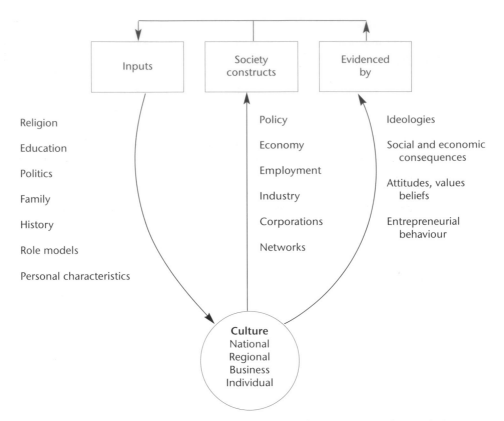

Figure 4.3 Summary model: key features associated with entrepreneurship initiation

Source: A. Morrison, 'Initiating Entrepreneurship', in S. Carter and D. Jones-Evans (eds), *Enterprise and Small Business: Principles, Practice and Policy* (London: Financial Times/Prentice-Hall, 2000), p.106. Reproduced with the permission of Pearson Education Ltd.

- *Economic consequences*: the extent to which entrepreneurial endeavour is seen to be a key driver in generating economic benefits at the level of the individual and business, regionally and nationally.

- *Attitudes, values and beliefs*: whether the dominant value system of a population is communal or individualistic, and the extent to which entrepreneurship is consistent with such a value system.

- *Entrepreneurial behaviour*: its development or otherwise will be influenced by a combination of the above factors which react to determine the fertility of the soil for such endeavour and sow the seeds for future propagation.

The work of McClelland, who built a reputation for pioneering investigation in the field of achievement motivation, also helps to relate enterprise to culture. His is essentially a Western, individualistic view of motivation, the person being largely his unit of investigation. He points out that persons who are viewed as having engaged in 'outstanding' activities may be motivated by the need for power and/or the need for achievement. He demonstrates that the need for achievement, its frequency in the popular literature of a country, and national economic growth, all correlate:

ILLUSTRATION 4.5
Cultural reinforcement

McClelland provides interesting insights and, as noted in Chapter 3, he links enterprise to the urge to achieve: 'Most people in this world can be divided into two broad groups. There is that minority which is challenged by opportunity and willing to work hard to achieve something, and the majority which really does not care all that much.'[13] He asks, 'Is the need to achieve an accident, or is it hereditary, or is it the result of the environment?' And further, 'Is there some technique that could give this will to achieve to people, even whole societies?'[14]

The importance of cultural reinforcement is seen in a study by McClelland in which he attempted to increase the achievement motivation of bright 14-year-old boys.

Boys from lower-income groups did not maintain their improvements. Possibly it was because they moved back into an environment in which neither parents nor friends encouraged achievement or upward mobility. 'Negroes seeking to improve their condition frequently confront this problem faced by scepticism at home and suspicion on the job,' claimed McClelland on the basis of his work in the United States.[15]

An interesting contrast to the Negro situation may be the entrepreneurialism displayed by some immigrant groups, such as Hong Kong Chinese or Indians. If, and it is not always the case, immigrants are moving to seek betterment of their condition, it is also likely that entrepreneurial behaviour by members of their community will receive positive reinforcement.

A nation which is thinking about doing better all the time (as shown in its popular literature) actually does do better economically speaking. Careful quantitative studies have shown this to be true in Ancient Greece, in Spain in the Middle Ages and in England from 1400–1800, as well as among contemporary nations, whether capitalist or communist, developed or underdeveloped.[16]

It is worth noting that it is not a question of some people being motivated and others not being motivated, but that some are motivated by one goal and others by another. Overall, McClelland has found that while it is possible to change an individual's motivation (and performance), motivational change by itself is not enough if the environment in which he or she lives doesn't support, to at least some degree, his or her new efforts. This recognises the influence of the cultural and societal context of values and behaviour. In short enterprise and entrepreneurship happen in all societies. The form in which they happen, however, varies from society to society.

It is appropriate, therefore, to examine societal culture and to consider how the concept of enterprise fits into it. Without such understanding, interventions to promote enterprise cross-culturally will, it is reasonable to deduce, be less effective, if not actually counter-productive. Interesting issues are raised by exploring the meaning and nature of enterprise in the context of cultural dimensions.

Redding notes that:

> other features older and deeper than modern policies have helped large Japanese and Korean organisations to ... take a huge chunk of the world market. ... These extra features include societal norms supporting acceptance of authority and discipline, a sense of the importance of the organisation in one's life and a consequent wish to belong to it, association of individuals with the collective good of the group, and intense competitiveness on behalf of the nation via the company.[17]

He adds that another societal feature critical to economic efficiency is the 'notion of trust', which explains 'why the Japanese and Koreans can handle very large scale organisations efficiently', the well-publicised problems faced by some of Korea's leading conglomerates in relatively recent times notwithstanding.

That some nations have achieved significant economic growth without exhibiting preconceived Western notions on the appropriate cultural dimensions should not therefore be surprising. Those Western definitions of entrepreneurial characteristics are themselves culturally biased, as indeed may be the conventional definitions of enterprise and their association with economic success.

ILLUSTRATION 4.6
Entrepreneurship and culture

At the top of Maslow's hierarchy ... there is the motive of self actualisation: realising to the fullest possible extent the creative potential present within the individual. This means 'doing one's own thing' [and] this can only be the supreme motivation in an individualistic society. In a collectivist culture, what will be actualised is the interest and honour of the in-group which may very well ask for self-effacement from many of the in-group members. As the interpreter for a group of American visitors to China remarked, the idea of 'doing your own thing' is not translatable into Chinese ... the Chinese language has no equivalent for 'personality' in the Western sense. Personality in the West is a separate entity, distinct from society and culture: an attribute of the individual. The closest translation into Chinese is *Jen* ... which includes not only the individual but also his or her intimate societal and cultural environment which makes his or her existence meaningful.

Hofstede[18]

The collectivist tradition and culture is about subordinating personal to group interests, sharing, co-operation and group harmony (see Table 4.1). Is entrepreneurial behaviour, therefore, exhibited by the group itself, by individuals working through the group or by breaking group norms? Or does the concept of 'entrepreneurial behaviour' need to be redefined in different cultural contexts?

Table 4.1 Key differences between collectivist and individualist societies

Collectivist	Individualist
Collective interests prevail over individual interests	Individual interests prevail over collective interests
Private life is invaded by groups	Everyone has a right to privacy
Opinions are predetermined by group membership	Everyone is expected to have a private opinion
Economy based on collective interests	Economy based on individual interests
Ideologies of equality prevail over ideologies of individual freedom	Ideologies of individual freedom prevail over ideologies of equality
Harmony and consensus in society are ultimate goals	Self-actualisation by every individual is an ultimate goal
People are born into extended families or other in groups which continue to protect them in exchange for loyalty	Everyone grows up to look after him/herself and his/her immediate (nuclear) family only
Identity is based in the social network to which one belongs	Identity is based in the individual
Children learn to think in terms of 'we'	Children learn to think in terms of 'I'
Harmony should always be maintained and direct confrontations avoided	Speaking one's mind is a characteristic of an honest person
Purpose of education is learning how to do	Purpose of education is learning how to learn
Relationships between employer and employee are perceived in moral terms, like a family link	Relationships between employer and employee are a contract supposedly based on mutual advantage
Hiring and promotion decisions take employees' in-group into account	Hiring and promotion decisions are supposed to be based on skills and rules only
Management is management of groups	Management is management of individuals
Relationship prevails over task	Task prevails over relationship

Source: G. Hofstede, *Cultures and Organisations* (London: HarperCollins, 1994) pp.67 and 73.

Given the wide variations in societal understanding, perceptions, attitudes and behaviours, a unicultural interpretation of the meaning of enterprise and its development presents many dangers. Without recognition of such differences, there will be difficulty in gaining global acceptance of enterprise as a positive concept. It will also be more difficult for business leaders to function effectively in other cultures as the drive towards globalisation continues. It is however clear that a supportive cultural environment for actions and policies to promote enterprise development and business start-up and growth is important, and that it can take many forms.

Social enterprise

So far in this book, in looking at the influences of culture on enterprise, the enterprise being influenced has primarily been enterprise as it is manifested in private sector business. Therefore the influences on enterprise have been considered in terms of the effects they may have had on business formation and success. This was done primarily because that is the aspect of enterprise that has been most studied and it is therefore the easiest to analyse. However enterprise can be manifest in other ways: for instance in leisure, in cultural activities and in community enterprise.

CASE 4.1
Different structures for enterprise

Not only are ways of doing business in Asia subtly different from those of the West but they are also different within the region itself. ... The past 30 golden years have seen the emergence of three powerful systems of business, each represented by a particular kind of organisation:

- in Japan the large complex networked business, known as the *kaisha*
- in South Korea the now internationalising *chaebol*
- elsewhere, in areas where business needs strong local knowledge and connections, the Chinese family business – that most unobtrusive and little understood instrument of wealth creation and progress.

Each of these instruments for bringing together the components of economic behaviour has emerged as a distinct response to its circumstances. They are embedded in the cultures and development histories of their societies. They are not copies of Western forms and their behaviour does not follow Western rules or ideals. In simple terms, they exist for different reasons.

The main reason for the existence and driving logic of the large American corporation is return to shareholders, but that of the *kaisha* is to employ people. The *chaebol* has derived much of its dynamism from its contribution to the national development goals of Korea. The Chinese family business exists primarily to create and sustain family fortunes.

The outcome of these different routes to modern capitalism is that the Japanese firm is a large, professionally managed and highly complex enterprise with wide ownership; the Korean is a huge family business run like a regiment; and the Chinese is a small family business networking to escape the limitations of its size and doing so successfully.

These different organisations compete on equal terms in world markets. Asia today contains some of the world's most competitive forms of enterprise, which are able to hammer each other in world markets on equal terms. In doing so however, there is no logic which says they all have to have the same book of rules.

Redding[19]

Points raised

This example shows that the Western model of enterprise is not the only one and that different cultures are likely to produce different working models better suited to their group values and beliefs.

Even business formation and entrepreneurship do not always have profit for individuals as a major motivation. Businesses can be started for other reasons such as social, family, community or cultural development. Also, businesses need not be started by individuals but can be started by groups. Much enterprise behaviour by groups has been variously known as 'social enterprise', 'community enterprise' or 'social entrepreneurship' and these concepts are explored in more depth in Chapter 5.

CASE 4.2
A history of regional difference

To understand the reasons for differences in enterprise and economic regeneration between different areas in England, Dodd suggests, it is necessary to examine the relevant social history of the areas over many hundreds of years.[20]

Compared with the North East, the Black Country recovered well from major job losses and (in 1990) still has 50 per cent of its workforce in manufacturing. 'There is still plenty of metal-bashing and lots of foundries and it is still easy to get into all sorts of trades like pickling zinc.' Its history has a number of curious features. It was never conquered by the Romans because it was marshy, inhospitable and easily bypassed. From the thirteenth century rich seams of coal near the surface gave the region its character. For several centuries mining was carried on by groups of families. By 1665 there were 20,000 smiths within a ten-mile radius of Dudley, and an industrial culture appears to have been in full swing before the Industrial Revolution proper arrived.

It was observed that 'the Black Country was born, not as one area, but as a collection of separate entities of often fierce independence brought together on and about a unique coalfield, heaven-sent complete with an abundance of ironstone, limestone and clay.'

In contrast, Tyneside in the North East also had coal mining but there that industry had a feudal feel about it, with enormous gaps between owners and workers, a relationship which might have been a carry-over from the employer and employee relationship that had existed in agriculture and tin and lead mining. The process of industrialisation in the North gave rise to relatively few small firm operations in manufacturing and engendered attitudes incompatible with entrepreneurial behaviour. The high unemployment of the early 1980s, following the disappearance of many of the big manufacturing operations, was not therefore relieved by smaller operations, as happened in the Black Country, and self-employment is still below the national average.

Points raised

This example too shows that, even within the same country, the different social histories of different communities appear to have an impact on the levels of enterprise. It was originally published in 1990 and it is interesting to note that Greene et al, writing in 2008, report that, despite 'huge resources ... devoted to initiatives to increase the entrepreneurial capacity and propensity of the area', Teesside was still 'a deep pocket of economic deprivation located within the least entrepreneurial region of England'.[21]

ILLUSTRATION 4.7
Ethnic or social networks

Mary Waters sheds some light on the issue of ethnic enterprise in a review of five American books on ethnicity and entrepreneurship in the urban United States.[22] The books examine entrepreneurship amongst various ethnic groups in several cities but Waters concludes that they point to the overwhelming importance of social networks and ties in entrepreneurship, and they all explode simple ideas that there are personality characteristics such as risk taking or rugged individualism that explain specialisation as an entrepreneur.[23] In general the choice of entrepreneurship by specific groups is supported by the existence of 'class resources' such as education and so forth and by 'ethnic resources' such as ties to one another, ethnic solidarity and ethnic connections. More specifically Waters argues that Korean-Americans were channelled into small businesses because they had middle-class ambitions and savings, together with 'intact families where members could save some additional capital', and because they were blocked in mainstream jobs. Many ethnic groups collectively enter new industries and occupations but there is widespread gloom about the prospects of African-Americans in America entering entrepreneurship in large numbers. This is in part because of the low level of skills attained by this group but also because of the persistence of a Black Nationalist ideology in American cities which focuses on community and economic control.

Localities that allow individuals to develop problem-solving and marketing skills, that contain institutions geared to the support of small businesses and that are favourably disposed to the notion of entrepreneurship, are likely to encourage and sustain more entrepreneurship than other regions.[24] These and other related matters are important aspects of the cultural dimension of entrepreneurship.

In general, sociological approaches recognise the importance of social structures on individual decision making and are a counter to those who might extol the virtues of rugged individualism as the sole determinant of entrepreneurship. However, while they do tell us quite a lot about the kind of people who become entrepreneurs, they do not tell us much about the process by which social factors actually influence decision making.

Political conditions

As explained earlier, political and economic conditions are closely linked with cultural conditions and therefore, in considering the cultural influences above, political and economic influences have also been introduced. Political conditions are often very hard to separate from economic conditions and therefore their contribution to the total effect is hard to determine. However Case 4.3 presents an example where this seems to be possible and shows that differences in political policies may at least appear to contribute to differences in enterprise behaviour.

CASE 4.3
A study of political conditions

While it is generally impossible to separate the influences of political conditions from the other influences of economics and culture, the island of Saint Martin in the Lesser Antilles does offer one example of a contrast in political styles and of the different effects they appear to have on business enterprise.[25]

The island is the smallest land mass in the world that is shared by two governments. It is only 37 square miles in area, but it is divided into two legal entities: Dutch Sint Maarten and French Saint Martin. Sint Maarten is 16 square miles in area and its capital is Philipsburg. It has a Netherlands Antilles constitution and has been self-governing since 1954. Saint Martin is 21 square miles in area; its capital is Marigot but the real administrative centre is Basse Terre on Guadeloupe. Guadeloupe is an overseas department of France and therefore Saint Martin is governed as an integral part of France.

In Sint Maarten there is relatively little government regulation of business. Starting a small business, for instance, is very easy: there is no need for a licence to do so and incorporation is simple, requiring only the assistance of a lawyer specifically appointed to pass deeds. There is no exchange control on currencies imported or exported, and bank accounts may be opened in any currency. There are no import duties and taxes generally are low, with tax holidays and other benefits in certain circumstances. There is an international airport with a 2000-metre runway which accommodates daily international flights and helps to boost the tourist industry. Further, to enhance tourism a number of casinos have been opened. The absence of all customs formalities makes Sint Maarten in essence a free port.

In contrast Saint Martin, the French part of the island, has inherited an abundance of regulations from its mother country. Rules made in France for France must be obeyed in Saint Martin. Some prices, as well as wages, are regulated. A new business venture must involve local participation. Foreigners staying for over 21 days must provide proof of departure as well as proof of citizenship (even though there is no longer any physical barrier, or even a border checkpoint, between the two sides of the island). The airport is tiny, virtually deserted and, because of red tape, there are no casinos.

The contrast between the two parts of the island is striking. Dutch Sint Maarten is a thriving business community with significant entrepreneurial activity, while French Saint Martin is largely rural and agricultural. Sint Maarten has not only achieved full employment for itself, but employs many workers from French Saint Martin and from other neighbouring islands such as the Dominican Republic.

These differences have been ascribed to the different government policies applied to the two parts of the island. On the Dutch side the attitude taken appears to be that it is dangerous to have the government in business and that government can best help business by staying out of it and by being a facilitator rather than a regulator. On the French side the attitude appears to be that government should intervene in the business sector for the purpose of keeping out potential danger.

Rules are therefore established to protect business even if to some extent they hinder entrepreneurial activity.

Both sides of the island share a common history. The island was originally populated by Arawak Indians, who survived on local vegetation and seafood. They were then invaded by the more violent Carib tribes migrating from the Amazon basin, who were in turn followed by conquests from Spain, France, Britain and the Netherlands. As the Indians were wiped out the island was populated by slaves imported from areas such as Togo and Ghana in Africa.

Now, however, there are distinct differences in enterprise and economic performance between the two parts of the island. The reason for this appears to be the different political agendas: one side follows a policy of minimal economic intervention and minimal regulation, while the other has a policy of relatively heavy intervention and rules designed to protect business.

Points raised

In this example it is the different political approaches that appear to explain the difference in the level of enterprise.

Government influence

There are a number of things that governments do, or could do, which can or might have an influence on the level of enterprise. Governments, and sometimes other organisations such as enterprise agencies, do intervene to promote more enterprise and they do so on the presumption that they will have an effect. Their interventions therefore must be considered among the factors which influence enterprise. The motivations and methods for, and the effectiveness of, these interventions are considered further in Part III of this book. Government influence in the area of enterprise can be considered to fall into two categories: setting the conditions, and intervening to support the process.

Regulations and fiscal policy

Governments set many of the conditions for enterprise. Government-imposed regulations, such the registration requirements for new businesses, can have a considerable influence on how easy or hard it is to start a business, and government fiscal policy can significantly affect the potential for legitimate profitability, and therefore the attractiveness, of a business enterprise.

Enterprise support

Governments and other organisations often intervene to try to promote more enterprise through either more business start-ups or more business growth, or both. Such support interventions include encouraging entrepreneurship education schemes, subsidising enterprise advice and training, and the provision of financial support schemes and incubation workspace.

Economic conditions

For examples of the differences that economic conditions can make it may be illustrative to look at the transition economic conditions of the former Warsaw Pact or communist countries in Europe. From the 1950s to the late 1980s these countries shared a common economic system: one of central planning based on a communist ideal. Before that system was imposed, however, there had been considerable differences amongst their economies. A number of them had been quite enterprising, with countries like the former Czechoslovakia and Hungary being fully part of central European economic life.

When they became part of the Soviet Bloc and its economic system, the attitude to enterprise and entrepreneurship in all these countries changed. To a greater or lesser extent entrepreneurial behaviour was viewed with considerable suspicion; successful entrepreneurs were seen as antisocial and self-seeking, and frequently as acting unethically, if not illegally. Disparities in income and wealth (and so behaviour likely to generate such disparities) made many reasonable people feel uncomfortable about enterprise and see it as a destabilising force in society, once they had grown accustomed to, and comfortable with, an equality that is unusual in non-socialist countries.

ILLUSTRATION 4.8
Employment: the system and the individual

To comprehend the nature of the employment contract in 'communist' Eastern Europe it was claimed by some that you had to understand two 'facts'. The first 'fact' was that the system owed the individual a job. It was the system's clear obligation to provide paid employment for everyone. The second 'fact' was that it was the individual's duty to better him or herself, not by hard work, which would return no direct benefits, but by doing as little as possible for the salary which was his or her right.

It has been argued that the collapse of the Iron Curtain came, at least in part, because the disparity between the economic benefits of the 'market' economies on one side and the central 'socialist' economies on the other could no longer be disguised. When it went, there was a desire by many on its former Eastern side to catch up with the West. Based on the perception that enterprise and an enterprise culture were preconditions for a successful market economy, attempts were made to introduce and encourage them. The political imperative of creating wealth in these transition economies, not least through attempts to inculcate such enterprise into them, has however had another effect. It has brought into greater focus the issue of the cultural context of enterprise. Given the different nature of these nations after almost two generations of a particular political and economic system, one cannot ignore the differences in individual and group values, priorities and goals as compared with those in countries with different histories.

The Western cultural traditions they are trying to emulate have been rooted in individualism and, as Chapter 3 and Table 4.1 above indicate, definitions of entrepreneurial characteristics emphasise individuality – founding by a single person, personal innovation, risk taking, proactivity, persistence and creativity. Individualism is concerned with self-sufficiency, difficulty in coping with a structured pursuit of goals, personal goals that may conflict with those of one's group, a willingness to confront members of the group one belongs to, a suspicion of the world around. It is a culture where a person derives pride from his or her own achievements coupled with a desire for recognition. In contrast, as already noted, the more collectivist tradition and culture involve subordination of personal to group interests, sharing, co-operation and group harmony and, to that extent, an emphasis on the individual is counter-cultural.

ILLUSTRATION 4.9
Unwelcome aspects of enterprise

When the Central and Eastern European system was beginning to change in the early 1990s it was asked if this meant that the entrepreneur was now in the economic driver's seat. One reply from Poland, one of the first of these countries to move towards a market economy, said that the answer was 'yes, the entrepreneur was driving'; however, he or she had no driving licence, had no brakes, had no airbag, had not enough petrol to complete the journey and found the road ahead was filled by a big empty truck driven by a blindfolded union legislator.

In Hungary, in the late 1990s, a comment passed at an entrepreneurship seminar was that Hungarian entrepreneurs very much liked the possibilities they now had for enterprise success, but they thought that the associated concept of being allowed to fail was not at all desirable.

Although there were and are considerable differences amongst countries in Central and Eastern Europe, and although they had not all been centralised, socialised or collectivised to the same extent, it would seem that the economic system did affect enterprise and the attitudes it engendered are themselves affecting attempts to reintroduce enterprise. The extent to which an economy has an enterprise culture has assumed a particular importance in understanding the prospects for the development of that economy. However, attempts to understand what an enterprise culture means and the process by which a culture develops has to be done in the context of the socio-economic conditions of the region under investigation.

Equilibrium levels of entrepreneurship?

It has been suggested (see section on GEM later in this chapter) that different stages of economic development are characterised by different levels of entrepreneurship. This has led to the suggestion that there will be an equilibrium level of entrepreneurship, determined by the stage of development of an economy. That has the implication that deviations in practice from that equilibrium level might, other things being equal, tend to be accompanied by a correcting influence.

In 1999 Carree, van Stel, Thurik and Wennekers produced a report of an empirical investigation into the relationship between the extent of business ownership and economic growth.[26] They investigated:

- 'Whether there is a long-term relationship between the numbers of business owners and the stage of economic development. This arises from scrutinising empirical and theoretical work in this area. The relation is hypothesised to be a decreasing function of economic development in that the self-employment rate is high in low developed economies whereas there is a later phase where mass production and scale economies thrive. A vast literature points at a still later phase of economic development where the business ownership rate is increasing again. This phase is characterised by "the reversal of the trend" towards increasing economies of scale and scope. However, it is still unclear to what extent this reversal will be structural. Therefore both a U-shaped as well and an L-shaped equilibrium relation were tested.

- Whether there exists a correction mechanism when the rate of business ownership is out of equilibrium and what the speed of convergence is. Out of equilibrium situations can occur due to exogenous shocks and institutional divergences (for instance, from government regulation of market activity).

- Whether deviating from the equilibrium rate of business ownership leads to lower economic growth.'

These three aspects were tested using a data panel of 23 OECD countries. The investigations showed that:

> both the U-shaped and the L-shaped relation between the number of business owners and the stage of economic development produce satisfactory results, that a statistical discrimination cannot be made since 'the reversal of the trend' is of a recent date only and that the minimum of the U-shaped equilibrium relation is within the range of observations of economic development. The assumption of a U-shaped curve would imply that modern economies are now in a phase where the rate of business ownership is likely to increase structurally. The rate of business ownership is shown to influence economic growth through deviations from the equilibrium rate. As a consequence, economies can have both too few or too many business owners and both situations lead to lower growth rates. By and large, a five per cent point deviation generates a growth loss of between one and three per cent over a period of four years. In particular, the fact that economic development may be hampered by a number of business owners being too high considering an economy's stage of development may come as a surprise for European politicians who see self-employment as a forceful weapon when fighting unemployment and stagnating growth. Different economic stages call for different development and stimulation programs. An error-correcting mechanism exists between the real rate of business ownership and the equilibrium rate. Lagged unemployment appears to be a significant push factor of business ownership whereas a high lagged labour income quota appears to decrease business ownership rates indicating the effect of low business profitability.

Social capital

Whatever the cultural, economic or political conditions, the extent and type of relationships between people involved in enterprise and between those who might start enterprises and those might help or hinder them is considered by many to be particularly important. Fukuyama, for example, has identified trust beyond that in family relationships as a key factor in economic development. He suggested that trust is needed for enterprises to develop and that 'it would appear to be no accident that three high-trust societies, Japan, Germany and the United States, pioneered the development of large-scale, professionally managed enterprises.'[27] Harford, taking Cameroon as an example of a country with a very under-developed economy, observes that:

> We still don't have a good word to describe what is missing ... but we are starting to understand what it is. Some people call it 'social capital', or maybe 'trust'. Others call it 'the rule of law', or 'institutions'. But these are just labels. The problem is that Cameroon, like other poor countries, is a topsy-turvy world in which it's in most people's interest to take action that directly or indirectly damages everyone else.'[28]

Increasingly what is often now referred to as social capital is being recognised as an essential requirement for a successful enterprise. Few writers have done more to boost the status of social capital, in the West at least, than Robert Putman. His early definition referred to it as 'the networks, norms and trust that enable participants to act together to effectively pursue shared objectives'.[29] It has often been referred to in the context of social enterprises but it has a much wider application. In 2007, for instance, the *International Small Business Journal* dedicated an entire edition (Vol. 25, No. 3) to the connection between social capital and entrepreneurship. In particular, the contributions to the journal valued the quality of networks and relationships as a resource and asset which could help to explain the performance of entrepreneurs.

Social capital involves social interaction and would appear to reside in and between connections to others. It could even be regarded as representing 'networking capital' since, in essence, it is really a relational phenomenon and a term that actually refers to the social connections entrepreneurs use to obtain resources they would otherwise acquire through expending their human or financial capital.[30] Anderson et al. saw social capital as 'a relational artefact, produced in interactions, but that resides within a network. Individuals may have a high or low propensity to develop social capital, but they can only do so within social interactions'.[31] Casson and Della Giusta argued that different types of networks are needed to support entrepreneurship at different stages of development and these are evident at the local, regional, national or global level.[32]

As well as trust and information networks, having enterprising role models as examples to follow can also be an aspect of social capital. Gibb has identified 'abundant positive role images of successful independent businesses' as a key aspect of an enterprise culture (see Figure 2.1) and Krueger has suggested that 'perceived social norms' are a key influence on entrepreneurship (see Figure 3.6). Relationships clearly matter to entrepreneurs, but understanding how they function requires an appreciation of social capital, and its presence or absence is likely to influence the very nature of the entrepreneurial venture.

Thus, although there is no single widely accepted definition of it or even agreement on just what it entails, social capital nevertheless is increasingly being recognised as an important factor in enterprise development.

Demand and supply factors

Demand and supply factors, as the use of economic terminology implies, are most easily identified in entrepreneurship, rather than in the wider non-business aspects of enterprise.

Demand factors

The demand factors are those aspects which create entrepreneurial opportunities through the market demand for goods and services, whereas the supply factors stimulate a supply of entrepreneurs to take advantage of those opportunities. The demand for entrepreneurship is affected by issues such as the stage of economic development, globalisation and the stage of technological development, as illustrated in Figure 4.4.

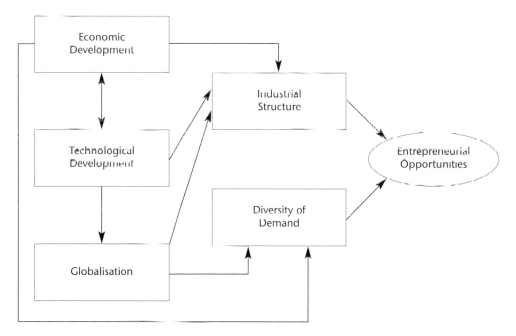

Figure 4.4 Demand side determinants of entrepreneurship

Source: D. Audretsch, R. Thurik, I. Verheul and S. Wennekers, (eds) *Entrepreneurship: Determinants and Policy in a European-US Comparison* (Dordrecht, The Netherlands and Norwell, MA, USA: Kluwer Academic Publishers, 2000), p. 23. Reproduced with the permission of Kluwer Academic Publishers.

Economic development

The impact of economic development on entrepreneurship has not been clear. For instance, economic development tends to raise wage rates and higher wages can discourage people from trying self-employment as there is more for them to lose. However 'it is an observed fact that, since the 1970s, per capita income has had a positive impact on the self-employment rate, at least in developed countries.'[33]

Technological development

Technology led to the Industrial Revolution but technology does not always favour the bigger business. In recent years the speed of technological development, which places a premium on responsiveness, and in particular developments such as information and communications technology, which reduces the advantages of scale, have enhanced the opportunities for entrepreneurs.

Globalisation

Globalisation, involving as it does the integration of world markets, favours the larger business able to supply world markets. At the same time, it makes people more aware of the diverse range of goods and services available elsewhere and stimulates a demand for them, a demand which can often be satisfied locally by small businesses able to compete in niche markets. For instance the greater awareness across the world of the cuisine of other countries has stimulated a demand for local ethnic restaurants, many of which are small businesses.

Industrial structure and clustering

It is clear that different stages of economic development have been characterised by different levels of self-employment. Agricultural economies have high levels of self-employment but industrial economies favour bigger businesses. The break-up of monopolies, monopolistic practices and protectionism has offered further opportunities, for instance in telecommunications, pharmaceuticals and transportation. Service economies favour small businesses also. Other trends, such as outsourcing and clustering, have also created opportunities for small businesses to service bigger ones.

Supply factors

Various factors may, as indicated below, have had the effect of either increasing or decreasing the supply of entrepreneurs.

Population growth and density

Expanding populations do not just mean extra demand for goods and services but also more people looking for employment. Especially in conditions of population density, such as in urban areas, the local availability of markets and business role models means that many people are likely to consider self-employment as a means of securing an income.

Age structure

Entrepreneurial attitudes, skills and resources are acquired over time, and consequently age has an impact on entrepreneurship. It has been suggested, for example, that many people in their twenties may not have acquired sufficient organisational experience or social capital, while those aged 45 or more may no longer possess the required energy. However changes in the real value of state pension provisions and the collapse or reduction of some final salary pension schemes have had the result that the only group of people in the UK recently to have an increased proportion who are self-employed is the over 55s. But, for whatever reasons, if there is a best age band in which to start a business, the age structure of a population will determine how many people there are it.

Immigration

Immigrants need work but are not in established job networks or may lack the communication skills needed to access existing jobs. Therefore they may, perforce, try self-employment. However, in some cases the identification of immigrants with self-employment is sufficiently well established to suggest to many that their indigenous culture suits them specifically for it. This is especially the case when the immigrants are ethnically different from the native population, when issues of ethnicity, which were considered at the end of Chapter 3, will also apply.

Participation

Increased participation in the labour market, especially by women (see Figure 4.5) has also increased the number of people seeking economic activity in the form of self-employment. If they are not the sole income earners in their families that also means that they can afford to be relatively less risk-averse, which can also help when contemplating self-employment.

Income levels and unemployment

High income levels can, as suggested above, mean that people have more to lose when they leave jobs. Unemployment, on the other hand, or very low income, mean that there is no job or little to lose and therefore, apart from benefit entitlement, little to

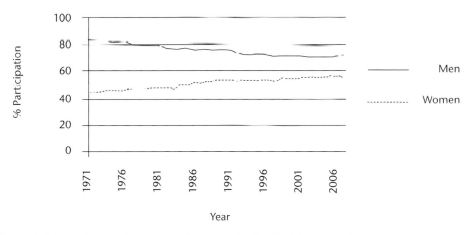

Figure 4.5 Participation by men and women in the UK labour market

Source: Labour Market Statistics on www.statistics.gov.uk (accessed 18 January 2008).

risk and an income to gain in trying a self-employment venture. It has also been argued that low levels of unemployment mean a thriving economy which can be a stimulant to entrepreneurship.

Comment on supply and demand factors

In looking at the possible supply and demand factors identified, it would appear that in many cases the result of the influence is uncertain as the factors in question may have both positive and negative features in respect of enterprise. However the issue is whether or not there is an influence to be considered, and in all cases it is suggested that there is. The uncertainty of the direction of the effect is not a reason for denying the effect; it just adds to the complexity of the subject. (The Global Entrepreneurship Monitor project, which is summarised later in this chapter, has tried to examine some of the factors suggested as possible causal mechanisms affecting national economies, but so far without apparently finding conclusive answers. Nevertheless a currently popular example of a policy approach based on factors thought to have an impact on entrepreneurship is also given in Chapter 12 in Illustration 12.4.)

A summary of the demand and supply-side influences on the development of the SME sector (including entrepreneurship generally) is given in Table 1.3 in Chapter 1.

Integrated theory

As well as the theories which relate entrepreneurship to various demand or supply factors, some of which have been described above, there are also some theories which have been advanced that attempt to link together some or all of these factors, and the internal factors considered in Chapter 3, into a single model. Such a model seeks to explain the different rates of entrepreneurship found in different contexts. Verheul et al., for instance, postulate a theory of entrepreneurship which brings together the multiplicity of influences identified in Figure 4.1 and elsewhere, and reflect upon the different levels of entrepreneurship – macro, meso and micro – each of which needs to be understood in its own right as well as in its interaction with the other two levels.[34] However, as they explain, 'entrepreneurship is a multi-faceted phenomenon' and:

> this may explain why research on entrepreneurship spans so many academic fields under many disparate guises. At its best, the subject has generated a diversity of approaches and perspectives. At its worst, it has a Tower of Babel nature, where each academic discipline speaks its own distinct language with its own methodology, impenetrable by outsiders.[35]

The Global Entrepreneurship Monitor

A potentially significant development in the field of entrepreneurship research was the creation in 1999 of the Global Entrepreneurship Monitor (GEM). It was a joint initiative by Babson College, Massachusetts, United States, and the London Business

School, UK, and is concerned with 'improving our understanding of the relationships between perceptions of entrepreneurship, entrepreneurial activity and national economic growth'.[36] GEM was designed as a long-term longitudinal research study involving international comparisons between the G7 countries (Canada, France, Germany, Italy, Japan, the UK and the United States) and initially three others (Denmark, Finland and Israel). Further additions raised the total number of countries involved to 42 by the year 2007.

For the purposes of the GEM study, entrepreneurship was defined as 'any attempt to create a new business enterprise or to expand an existing business by an individual, a team of individuals or an established business' and GEM initially planned to explore three questions about it:[37]

1. Does the level of entrepreneurial activity vary amongst countries and, if so, to what extent?
2. Does the level of entrepreneurial activity affect a country's rate of economic growth and prosperity?
3. What makes a country entrepreneurial?

Over time, however, GEM has changed these questions and, in the2007 report, it stated that the three main objectives on which it focused were:[38]
The following paragraphs present a summary of GEM's responses to its original three questions.

1. To measure differences in the level of entrepreneurial activity between counties.
2. To uncover factors determining national levels of entrepreneurial activity.
3. To identify policies that may enhance national level [sic] of entrepreneurial activity.

Levels of entrepreneurial activity

To indicate differences in levels of entrepreneurial activity amongst countries, GEM developed a measure called the Total Entrepreneurial Activity (TEA) index. The index value shows for each country the percentage of the adult population who have taken some action towards creating a new business in the past year or who are the owner/managers of an active business less than 42 months old. This value is therefore made up of two measures:

- the nascent start-up rate (those in the process of creating a business)
- the new firm rate (those actually running early stage businesses).

The range of TEA values indicated in the 2006 survey is shown in Figure 4.6

In 2001 the GEM study was widened to explore two sub-sets within entrepreneurship: opportunity entrepreneurs and necessity entrepreneurs. As the 2006 report stated:[39]

The GEM study allows for differentiation according to the reasons that motivate entrepreneurial behaviour. In the GEM framework, individuals start a business for two main reasons:

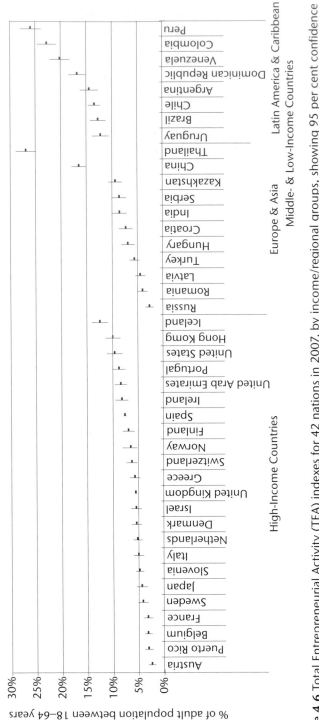

Figure 4.6 Total Entrepreneurial Activity (TEA) indexes for 42 nations in 2007, by income/regional groups, showing 95 per cent confidence intervals.

Source: GEM Adult Population Survey (APS).

- They want to exploit a perceived business opportunity (opportunity entre-preneurs).
- They are pushed into entrepreneurship because all other options for work are either absent or unsatisfactory (necessity entrepreneurs).

However the usefulness of categorising entrepreneurship as either necessity or oppor-tunity has been questioned. Peter Rosa et al., for instance, looked at Uganda and Sri Lanka and found that there the '"necessity theory" as conceptualised by GEM researchers is not supported by the empirical evidence' of their study.[40] It may be rele-vant therefore that GEM itself became possibly less dogmatic on this issue, and in later reports indicated that some people might fall into both categories before, for the 2007 report, it refined its calculation methods.

The relationship between the level of entrepreneurial activity in a country and its rate of economic growth

In the first three years of its work the GEM reports indicated that a statistically significant association had been found between entrepreneurial activity and national economic growth (as indicated by a growth in GDP) although 'the strength of the association tends to vary depending on the countries included ... and the nature of the entrepreneurial activity.'[41] In 2001, when GEM for the first time looked separately at opportunity and necessity entrepreneurship, it reported that 'the prevalence rate of necessity entrepreneurship was positively associated with national economic growth and that this association was strongest when countries highly dependent on international trade (Belgium, Hungary, Ireland, the Netherlands, and Singapore) were excluded,' but that 'the prevalence rate of opportunity entrepreneurship was not associated with any measure of national economic growth.'[42]

Since 2004 GEM has been reporting a different relationship (the 2007 version is shown in Figure 4.7). This is essentially a U shape in which:

- For low/middle-income countries the level of entrepreneurship is relatively high but it reduces as income levels rise.
- For high-income countries necessity entrepreneurship is low but opportunity entrepreneurship starts to increase as income levels rise.

GEM does caution however that this approach does not imply any specific causal relationship between entrepreneurial activity and economic development.

The factors that make a country entrepreneurial

The GEM research programme was derived from a conceptual model summarising the major causal mechanisms thought to affect national economies. This model is illustrated by Figure 4.8 and the components of the model are interpreted in Table 4.2.

The issue of what makes a country entrepreneurial appears to be the original ques-tion on which GEM now says least. Indeed this question in its original form has been dropped and the objectives of uncovering the factors determining the levels of entre-preneurial activity and identifying policies that may enhance the level of entrepreneurial activity have been assumed instead. Nevertheless successive GEM

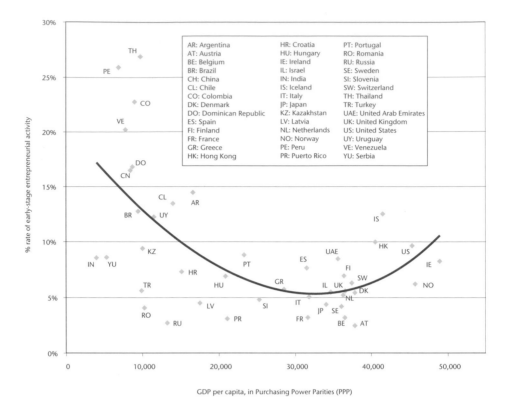

Figure 4.7 Early-stage entrepreneurial activity rates and per capita GDP, 2007

Source: GEM Adult Population Survey (APS) and IMF.

reports have said little directly about these objectives. The 2007 report, for instance, looks at different aspects of entrepreneurial activity across the globe, at the characteristics of that activity, at perceptions about entrepreneurship and the link with entrepreneurial activity, and at global economic institutions and national regulation. It indicates that different countries have different rates of entrepreneurship but it says little to indicate why, or how lower rates of entrepreneurship might be raised.

GEM conclusions

GEM set out to explore a number of questions which are very relevant to the wider study of entrepreneurship and how to promote it, but it has not answered all of them. GEM has assembled a considerable amount of data about entrepreneurship in a wide range of countries and its studies to date do indicate that the level of entrepreneurship does differ considerably across countries. However GEM is not claiming to have found any causal relationship between the level of entrepreneurship and the level of, or rate of increase in, a country's GDP or per capita income. GEM is also refraining from suggesting what might determine the level of entrepreneurship in a country. Despite the apparent relevance of its initial questions to entrepreneurship policy, GEM does not now seem to offer much policy advice.

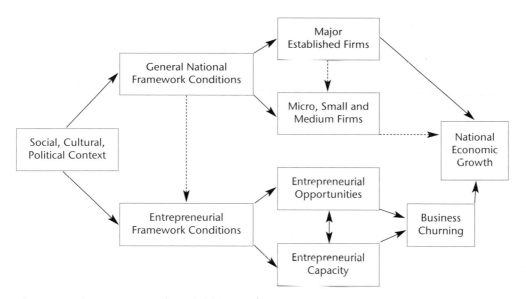

Figure 4.8 GEM conceptual model (the total process)

Source: A. L. Zacharakis, W. D. Bygrave and D. A. Shepherd, *Global Entrepreneurship Monitor National Entrepreneurship Assessment: United States of America, 2000 Executive Report* (Kansas City, Mo.: Kauffman Centre for Entrepreneurial Leadership, 2000), p.6.

Conclusions

It has been said that, when decisions about potential enterprise actions have to be taken, a number of influences are at work. Krueger's model of these influences (see Chapter 3) includes, for an individual or team:

- the perception of the attractiveness of the outcome of an action
- the perceived opinion of family, friends and peer group
- the individual's or team's views of their own competency
- the perception of the environment in which they operate, especially its support for and receptiveness to the proposed actions and their likely outcomes.

Some of these influences are due to internal factors but others are due to external conditions. Broadly speaking, the external influences can be ascribed to the cultural, political or economic environments, although the effects of all three are interlinked. Studies of enterprise in different countries show that they can all have an impact on enterprise.

This chapter seeks to identify some of the key features necessary in understanding the intricate and complex manner 'in which entrepreneurship, culture, politics, society, the economy and business development and management are interwoven within the institutional structure of society'.[43] Cultural variations exist across countries and the cultural context in which people are embedded and develop influences their beliefs, attitudes and behaviour in many spheres of activity, including their disposition towards enterprising behaviour. Policy-makers in many countries actively

Table 4.2 Interpretation of components of the GEM conceptual model

Variable	Interpretation
Social cultural and political context	Factors shown to play an important role in shaping a country's national framework conditions, such as demographics, investment in education, social norms and attitudes as they relate to, for example, independence and entrepreneurs
General national framework (GNF) conditions	Role of government institutions, R&D, physical infrastructure, labour market efficiency, legal and social institutions
Entrepreneurial framework (EF) conditions	Comprise factors believed to be more volatile than GNF conditions and reflect intermediate variables in the overall causal sequence. They include: • financial support: the availability of financial resources, equity and debt, for new and growing firms including grants and subsidies; • government policies: the extent to which government policies concerning taxes, regulations and their application are size neutral and/or whether these policies discourage or encourage new and growing firms; • government programmes: the presence of direct programmes to assist new and growing firms at all levels of government - national, regional, and municipal; • education and training: the extent to which training in starting or managing small, new, or growing businesses features in the educational and training system, and the quality, relevance and depth of such education and training in creating or managing small, new or growing businesses; • research and development transfer: the extent to which national research and development leads to new commercial opportunities, and whether or not R & D is available for new, small and growing firms; • commercial and professional infrastructure: the influence of commercial, accounting, and other legal services and institutions that allow or promote new, small or growing businesses; • market openness / barriers to entry: the extent to which commercial arrangements are prevented from undergoing constant change and redeployment, preventing new and growing firms from competing and replacing existing suppliers, subcontractors, and consultants; • access to physical infrastructure: the access to physical resources - communication, utilities, transportation, land or space, at a price that does not discriminate against new, small, or growing firms; • cultural and social norms: the extent to which existing social and cultural norms encourage, or do not discourage, individual actions that may lead to new ways of conducting business or economic activities and, in turn, lead to greater dispersion in wealth and income.
Entrepreneurial opportunities	The perception as well as the reality of market opportunities
Entrepreneurial capacity	Attitudes and resources of potential entrepreneurs
Business churning	The processes which lead to birth, death, expansion and contraction of businesses
National economic growth	Subsumes a variety of common economic measures such as growth in GDP, employment and per capita income

strive to strengthen those cultural factors which facilitate enterprising intent and minimise those which inhibit it, while at the same time creating the political and economic conditions which not only reinforce such intent but provide the opportunities for it to find expression. Efforts have had variable success within and across countries, and such imperfect results are likely to continue until there is a better understanding of the wide range of factors at work in society and the economy which influence enterprising behaviour.

Trying to identify the factors which influence the development of enterprise might not be unlike searching for the factors which influence the growth of plants. Plants too can be subject to internal inherited factors in their genes which might predispose them to stronger growth than other plants, but all plants, whatever their genes, are affected by the external culture and environment in which their seeds germinated and/or in which they are now growing. Factors such as the soil structure, available nutrients and drainage, and other aspects of the environment, such as additional fertiliser, water and sunlight, are all potentially relevant. However our knowledge about this process is still not complete. For instance it used to be thought that it was environmental factors, such as more sunlight, warmer days, or more rainfall, which provided the stimulus that plants needed to resume growth after dormant periods, but recent research has indicated that plants have growth restrainers which need to be countered before growth can take place. Those growth restrainers serve the useful purpose of preventing plants, when stimulated by rain or sun, from growing too fast in otherwise adverse conditions which could not support larger plants in the longer term.[44] Nevertheless these restrainers mean that the application of supposed growth factors does not always lead to growth, which is a situation that is also found in enterprise.

It is clear that, like our understanding of plants, our understanding of the conditions which encourage the development of enterprise is also incomplete. Indeed it seems likely that there is no single economic, political or cultural condition that universally best promotes and supports enterprise. Methods of increasing enterprise which work in one situation therefore may not transfer successfully to other situations or to other societies.

THE KEY POINTS OF CHAPTER 4

- Chapter 3 looked at the factors internal to people which are thought to influence enterprise. This chapter has looked at various factors external to the individual which have been identified as having some influence on the extent of enterprise practice both in its broad sense and, particularly, in the context of entrepreneurship.

- Considerable variations are found in the levels of enterprise and the rate of emergence of entrepreneurs in different countries and cultures. There are theories which attempt to combine a number of possible influences, both internal and external, to provide a more complete view of why enterprise, especially in the context of entrepreneurship, occurs when it does.

- Among the factors which have been identified as influencing enterprise are:

- national and societal culture
- economic conditions, such as a 'market' economy
- political conditions, such as government administrative and regulatory regimes
- demand-side factors, such as technological development, globalisation, economic development and industrial structure
- supply-side factors, such as population growth and density, age structure, immigration, participation rates, income levels and unemployment
- interventions by government, or other agencies
- equilibrium rates of enterprise
- other influences, including social and cultural enterprise.

- Integrated theories are being advanced to explain the influence of such factors, and those 'internal' factors considered in the previous chapter.

- A potentially significant development in the field of enterprise research has been the work of the Global Enterprise Monitor which has explored the extent of entrepreneurship in many different countries and its relationship with national economic conditions. However, although it has assembled a considerable amount of data about entrepreneurship in a wide range of countries, it does not yet seem to have produced any clear conclusions about the factors which cause or influence it.

CASE 4.4
Enterprise in Wales

Research conducted in 2000 for a regional enterprise strategy for Wales found that:[45]

- Wales had the second lowest weekly earnings of any region in the UK.
- Only a third of the growth in the national income of Wales was due to entrepreneurial activity.
- The birth rate of new businesses in Wales as a proportion of the existing stock was at least 30 per cent behind the UK average and was lower than it had been two decades previously.
- Wales was losing businesses at a faster rate than the UK average. Between 1994 and 1998 Wales lost 4700 businesses while the UK gained 51,100 overall.
- Only 4 per cent of adults in a recent poll described themselves as entrepreneurs.
- Only one in eight adults in Wales knew an entrepreneur personally, and only 1 per cent, when asked to name famous entrepreneurs, named a Welsh person.
- One in five Welsh people said that they would like to be an entrepreneur. The reasons the others gave for not wanting to be an entrepreneur included 'I'm too old,' 'It's too stressful,' and 'I'm not made that way.'

- Groups such as Welsh speakers, women, young people and third-age people are under-represented in enterprise creation.
- Many entrepreneurs leave Wales to become successful, and do not return.
- Wales is too heavily dependent on slow growth markets and has too small a share of fast growth sectors.

Points raised

This example quotes some findings which might help to present a more complete picture of the level of entrepreneurial potential in Wales than merely using business start-up rates.

QUESTIONS, EXERCISES, ESSAY AND DISCUSSION TOPICS

- Are entrepreneurs born or made?
- Which is the more important influence on enterprise in individuals: their attributes and resources or the environment in which they operate?
- To what extent is a person's cultural background likely to affect his or her entrepreneurial behaviour?
- Using examples from your own experience (family, friends and so on), illustrate which of the factors described have had an influence on your disposition towards starting your own business.
- If the factors in Figure 4.1 explain the extent of enterprise, what role does personal choice play?
- Describe the main demand-side and supply-side factors which influence the level of entrepreneurship in GEM participating countries.
- To what extent are any of the models of the influences on enterprise consistent with the reported facts on Welsh enterprise?
- How would you rate your own region on a scale of entrepreneurial activity?

Suggestions for further reading and information

R. Burrows (ed.), *Deciphering the Enterprise Culture: Entrepreneurship, Petty Capitalism and the Re-Structuring of Britain* (London: Routledge, 1991).
B. Deacon, *The New Eastern Europe* (London: Sage, 1992).
T. Garrison, *International Business Culture* (Huntingdon: ELM Publications, 1996).
G. Hofstede, *Cultures and Organisations* (London: HarperCollins, 2001).
A. Lundström and L. Stevenson, *Entrepreneurship Policy for the Future, Volume 1 of the Entrepreneurship for the Future series* (Stockholm: Swedish Foundation for Small Business Research, 2000).
For information on the Global Entrepreneurship Monitor see www.gemconsortium.org.

References

1. G. Hofstede, *Cultures and Organisations* (London: HarperCollins, 1994).
2. A. Morrison (ed.), *Entrepreneurship: An International Perspective* (Oxford: Butterworth Heinemann, 1998).
3. T. Garrison, *International Business Culture* (Huntingdon: ELM Publications, 1996).
4. Ibid., p. 169.
5. S. Carter and D. Jones-Evans (eds), *Enterprise and Small Business: Principles, Practice and Policy* (London: Financial Times/Prentice-Hall, 2000), p. 105.
6. Hofstede (1994), op. cit., p. 105.
7. M. H. Tayeb, *Organisations and National Culture* (London: Sage 1988), quoted in S. Carter and D. Jones-Evans (eds), op. cit., p. 99.
8. Ibid., p. 169.
9. G. Hofstede, *Culture and Organisations: Software of the Mind* (London: McGraw-Hill, 1991), p. 5.
10. Hofstede (1994), op. cit., p. 63.
11. T. Garrison, *International Business Culture* (Huntingdon: ELM Publications, 1996), quoted in S. Carter and D. Jones-Evans (eds), op. cit., p. 99.
12. A. Morrison, 'Initiating Entrepreneurship', in S. Carter and D. Jones-Evans (eds), op. cit., pp. 105–13.
13. D. McClelland, 'That Urge to Achieve', *THINK* (IBM, 1966), p. 111.
14. Ibid., p. 111.
15. Ibid., p. 117.
16. Ibid., p. 114.
17. G. Redding, 'Three Styles of Asian Capitalism', in 'Mastering Enterprise', No. 7, *Financial Times*, January 1997, p. 10.
18. Hofstede (1994), op. cit., pp. 73, 74.
19. Redding, op. cit., p. 10.
20. P. Dodd, *The Influence of Culture on Enterprise*, Theme pamphlet (London: Industrial Christian Fellowship, 1990), pp. 2–5.
21. F. J. Greene, K. F. Mole and D. J. Storey, *Three Decades of Enterprise Culture* (Basingstoke: Palgrave, 2008), pp. 3–4.
22. M. C. Waters, 'Immigrant Dreams and American Realities: The Causes and Consequences of the Ethnic Labour Market in American Cities', *Work and Occupations*, 26 (1999), pp. 352–64.
23. Waters (1999), op. cit., p. 352.
24. J. Curran and R. A. Blackburn, 'Introduction', in *Paths of Enterprise*, edited by J. Curran and R. A. Blackburn (London: Routledge, 1991).
25. Excerpts from L. Dane, 'Contrasting Models of Policy Governing Small Business: Does Heavy Regulation Really Hinder the Small Business Sector?' Unpublished paper.
26. M. Carree, A. van Stel, R. Thurik and S. Wennekers, *Research Report 9809/E-Business Ownership and Economic Growth* (Zoetermeer, the Netherlands: EIM Small Business Research and Consultancy, 1999), pp. 47–9. Subsequently published in *Small Business Economics*, 18 (2002).
27. F. Fukuyama, *Trust* (London: Hamish Hamilton, 1995), p. 338.
28. T. Harford, *The Undercover Economist* (London: Little Brown, 2006), p. 201.
29. Putnam, R. (2007) E Pluribus Unum: Diversity and Community in the Twenty-first Century. The 2006 Johan Skytte Prize Lecture, *Scandinavian Political Studies*, 30(2), pp. 137–74.
30. J. Cope, S. Jack and M. Rose, 'Social Capital and Entrepreneurship: An Introduction', *International Small Business Journal*, 25(3) (2007), pp. 213–19.
31. A. Anderson, J. Park, and S. Jack, 'Entrepreneurial Social Capital', *International Small Business Journal*, 25(3) (2007), pp. 245–72.
32. M. Casson, and M. Della Giusta, 'Entrepreneurship and Social Capital: Analysing the Impact of Social Networks on Entrepreneurial Activity from a Rational Action Perspective', *International Small Business Journal*, 25(3) (2007), pp. 220–44.
33. I. Verheul, S. Wennekers, D. Audretsch and R. Thurik, *Research Report: An Eclectic Theory of Entrepreneurship: Policies, Institutions and Culture* (Zoetermeer, the Netherlands: EIM Small Business Research and Consultancy, 1999), p. 22. Subsequently published as Chapter 2 in *Entrepreneurship: Determinants and Policy in a European–US Comparison*, edited by D. Audretsch, R. Thurik, I. Verheul and S. Wennekers (Boston, Mass. and Dordrecht: Kluwer, 2002).
34. I. Verheul et al., op. cit., pp. 67–9.
35. D. Audretsch, R. Thurik, I. Verheul and S. Wennekers (eds), *Entrepreneurship: Determinants and Policy*

in a European-US Comparison (Dordrecht, the Netherlands and Norwell, Mass.: Kluwer Academic Publishers 2002), Chapter 2.

36. N. Bosma, K. Jones, E. Autio and J. Levie, *Global Entrepreneurship Monitor 2007 Executive Report* (Babson College and London Business School, 2007), p. 4.

37. A. L. Zacharakis, W. D. Bygrave and D. A. Shepherd, *Global Entrepreneurship Monitor United States of America 2000 Executive Report* (Kansas City, Mo.: Kauffman Centre for Entrepreneurial Leadership at the Ewing Marion Kauffman Foundation, 2000), p. 5.

38. N. Bosma, K. Jones, E. Autio and J. Levie, *Global Entrepreneurship Monitor 2007 Executive Report* (Babson College and London Business School, 2007), p. 8.

39. N. Bosma and R. Harding, *GEM 2006 Results* (Babson College and London Business School, 2006), p. 18.

40. P. Rosa, S. Kodithuwakku and W. Bakunywa, 'Reassessing Necessity Entrepreneurship in Developing Countries', paper presented at the 29th ISBE Conference, Cardiff 2006. p. 12.

41. P. R. Reynolds, S. M. Camp, W. D. Bygrave, E. Autio and M. Hay, *Global Entrepreneurship Monitor: 2001 Executive Report* (Kansas City, Mo.: Kauffman Centre for Entrepreneurial Leadership at the Ewing Marion Kauffman Foundation, 2001), p. 12.

42. Ibid., p. 5.

43. S. Carter and D. Jones-Evans (eds), op. cit., p. 113.

44. See, for instance, N. Harberd, *Seed to Seed* (London: Bloomsbury, 2007), pp. 264–5.

45. D. Jones-Evans, 'Creating a Regional Enterprise Strategy for Wales', Paper prepared for the European Small Business Seminar, Dublin, September 2001.

CHAPTER 5
Other aspects of enterprise

Contents

KEY CONCEPTS

This chapter covers:

- Some of the other agenda, perceptions and connotations which have been associated with enterprise.
- The potential advantages and disadvantages associated with enterprise.
- Future trends which may have an impact on enterprise.
- Social enterprise and the social economy, community enterprises and social capital.

LEARNING OBJECTIVES

By the end of this chapter the reader should:

- Recognise that enterprise is a value-laden concept.
- Have an understanding of the agenda sometimes associated with enterprise.
- Have an appreciation of the potential advantages and disadvantages sometimes ascribed to enterprise.
- Understand some of the issues which may impact on the future of enterprise.
- Understand the concept of a social enterprise and of the social economy.

Introduction

So far Part I of this book has looked at the ways in which the terms 'enterprise' and 'entrepreneurship' have been used in order to ascertain what people actually mean when they use the words, rather than just what a dictionary suggests they should mean. Entrepreneurship was at one time used in a narrower context than enterprise but this exploration has shown that, rather than having limited narrow definitions, the word 'enterprise', and now the word 'entrepreneurship' also, can have a whole range of meanings, although these can often be grouped either into a narrow definitional range or a broader meaning. In the former, enterprise basically means business, and especially small business, and entrepreneurship means the process of business formation or growth; in the latter, either word can refer to the set of attributes that enable those who possess them to be creative, adaptable, proactive, innovative and responsive to change.

Such individual attributes were explored further in Chapter 3, which examined those factors largely internal to people which influence the extent to which they are enterprising. Enterprise and entrepreneurship, however, are also influenced by the external environment in which individuals operate, and these influences were considered in Chapter 4.

There are some other factors moreover which might be considered to relate to these chapters, and some other aspects of enterprise and entrepreneurship and implications of the ways in which the terms are used which have not yet been covered. Therefore before Part II, in which enterprise is considered specifically in the context of business, this chapter attempts to complete the picture by looking at some of these other aspects. First it considers some of the perceptions people may have about enterprise and entrepreneurship and the connotations these terms can have; it examines the potential and real disadvantages of enterprise; and it reviews some of the forces that may influence its future. Then, in the second part of the chapter, it looks at that part of economic activity that is now often referred to as social enterprise.

Some perceptions of enterprise

A number of judgements are sometimes made about enterprise. While many people might agree with them they should not go unexplored. They include:

- Enterprise is a relative concept.
- Enterprise is a good thing.
- Enterprise is essential for economic advancement.
- Enterprise has strong political and social connotations.

Enterprise is a relative concept

At any particular time some societies and some individuals are seen as more enterprising than others. For much of the second half of the twentieth century, the 'tiger' economies of the Pacific Rim were seen to be more enterprising than most Western economies, and they in turn were more enterprising than the communist Bloc countries. Whether the Western economies were considered to be enterprising therefore depended upon that with which they were compared. Thus the assessment of their level of enterprise was relative.

Comparisons of relative enterprise are still frequently made. For example it is claimed that 'Britain is not as enterprising as it was in the nineteenth century'; that 'the European Union countries demonstrate much less enterprise than the United States'; and that 'more enterprise is to be found in the informal (black) economy than in the formal economy.' Whether such statements are true is a different matter. As indicated in the previous chapter, this relative nature of enterprise has also been given clear expression in the reporting of the Global Entrepreneurship Monitor, which positions countries in league tables according to assumed indicators of entrepreneurial activity.[1] There is however also evidence that enterprise is not spread evenly across countries, and within countries with an apparently high level of enterprise there can be areas and groups with much less enterprise than the national average.

Individuals can be judged to be enterprising or not be enterprising, which implies some sort of absolute judgement, depending on whether or not they engage in enterprising acts. In reality, we are making comparisons of one individual against another or against some notion of a 'standard' level of enterprise activity, although that standard will change over time and place. However, even in a so-called enterprising society, not every individual will be considered enterprising, yet the society as a whole may be judged to be so. Although as more individuals demonstrate enterprise then the society could be said to be more enterprising.

In short there are no objective benchmarks for what constitutes a high, low or normal level of enterprise.

Enterprise is a good thing

More enterprise is deemed to be preferable to less. This perception seems often to be based on the assumptions that a more enterprising person creates more utility, pleasure or social welfare, or any combination of these, than a less enterprising one. The same views exist in respect of nations and societies. Enterprising nations are often viewed as being in a superior condition or moving towards a superior condition (however defined) than less enterprising ones. Why that should be is not always clear, but it appears to be connected with the view that enterprise leads to a higher standard of living or to a greater ability to influence one's own destiny. Indeed, enterprising people and enterprising economies have become synonymous with successful people and successful economies.

The link between enterprise and material reward is one which is often presented. If however happiness is perceived to be more reliant on spiritual or emotional fulfilment than material possessions then there might be a lesser association between enterprise and the success on which happiness depends.

CASE 5.1
However ...

A visitor to a Mediterranean country, impressed by the climate and its potential, got into a discussion with a local farmer who was sitting at the side of the road enjoying the sunshine and admiring the view. 'Why', he asked the local, 'are you sitting here, when, with a little effort, this farm could be so much more successful? You could grow such a variety of crops here'. 'Why', the farmer replied, 'should I want to do that?' 'Because you could invest in more land, grow even more crops and soon you could afford a large house with lots of features such as a terrace and swimming pool.' 'Why would I want that?' 'Because you could then relax and enjoy yourself sitting on the terrace and enjoying the sun and the view.' 'And what do you think I am doing now?'

Points raised

Sometimes we can forget why we engage in enterprise. There may be other ways to achieve the same fulfilment.

Enterprise is essential for economic advancement

Enterprise may create happiness or a superior condition, but the means or process whereby this happens is rarely clearly articulated. It would appear that what is envisaged is that enterprise leads to economic growth, which in turn engenders more happiness. Whether economic growth does produce more happiness can be debated, but is beyond the scope of this book. It is nevertheless worth considering here the link between enterprise and economic growth.

There is a correlation between the nations that are generally regarded as enterprising and those that achieve significant growth (albeit often at a social cost). Hong Kong has demonstrated a capacity for economic growth, and is regarded as being enterprising by virtue of its thriving business activity, international trading links and considerable entrepreneurial activity. But what is the process by which enterprising behaviour leads to enhanced economic growth? One possible route is that enterprise generates innovation and entrepreneurialism, which produce new and growing businesses, which in turn lead to economic growth.

It is possible, presumably, for a nation to be enterprising but not to achieve economic growth if that enterprise finds outlets that are independent of economic achievement. It is also presumably possible to achieve economic growth without enterprise, at least in the short term, through for example the exploitation of mineral and other natural resources or inward investment. Neither of these two conditions appears to be common. That leads to the conclusion that enterprise and economic growth are linked, and that the mechanism for this is that enterprise produces entrepreneurship, which in turn expands the economy. The link between entrepreneurialism and economic development has been assessed by the Global Entrepreneurship Monitor (see Chapter 4), and the additional link to enterprise also needs to be considered when the creation of an enterprise culture, or the promotion of enterprise and an enterprising society, become part of public policy. This is not least the case when the concept is perceived as ideologically based. All are agreed, however, that the concept of enterprise has a variety of connotations – not just political and economic, but also social and cultural.

Enterprise has strong political and social connotations

The term 'enterprise' has been applied and used to indicate aspects of a wider culture or value system as well as to describe the way an individual performs. Within Europe, for a significant part of the twentieth century, the governments of the Central and Eastern countries were called communist. The economies of these countries were centrally planned in contrast to the market economies of the rest of Europe. The latter economies, with those of many other countries (most notably the United States), were often referred to as 'free enterprise' (see also next section), and in this way the word 'enterprise' has acquired a political association. Such references to enterprise convey notions of freedom, liberalism, the dominance of markets and individual action and choice, for good or ill. Indeed, the concept of the 'enterprise culture' has been used politically in Britain (like 'Thatcherism') as a sort of independent variable which 'has had a considerable impact upon a range of other dependent variables: small business, self-employment, trade unions, manufacturing industry, the public sector, education, welfare and so on'.[2]

This may be a gross distortion of cause and effect, and an unduly simplified political analysis, but it is a view nevertheless propagated, at least in part, by some people. However, the restructuring of Britain in the 1970s and 1980s has been attributable to changes to which it has been convenient to attach such a handy label or slogan. In the process, the concept of an enterprise culture has assumed meanings that incorporate dimensions such as 'individualism, independence, flexibility, anti-collectivism, privatism, self-help and so on'.[3] Consequently, it has been argued that the former communist countries, if they wish to achieve economic growth, should restructure and develop these characteristics, which have social as well as politico-economic implications.

ILLUSTRATION 5.1
Devalued enterprise

This is what angers people about the highly simplistic and distorted ways in which enterprise and the enterprise culture have sometimes been promoted and practised. They miss the human and social justice imperatives entirely. They turn 'enterprise' into a good-for-some part of a political and economic philosophy which is uncaring and divisive, synonymous with greed and self-interest, and a subtle justification of the seeming inevitability of the coexistence of success and failure, richness and poverty, privilege and underprivilege. Others abhor this, and would point out that without social care, justice and cohesiveness, there can be no truly enterprising culture.

'Enterprise' has become one of the most devalued terms in the English language. A word that should embody all the complexities of risk taking has come to stand as the legitimator of tax cuts, breaking trade unions and denying there is any case for examining how companies are owned and managed.

By this definition, the genius of enterprise is essentially about individuals pitting their wits against the market. It is an individual who develops a new product, grows a company or cuts a deal. The structure and culture of the organisations in which these individuals strut their stuff are ignored. It is low-taxed, lightly-regulated, have-won-the-right-to-manage individuals who make the capitalist system tick ...

Enterprise is in part an economic, in part an individual and in part a moral act. Companies have to reconcile the claims of individuals as social beings as much as assert the iron laws of the balance sheet – and these iron laws themselves change in different cultures and value systems. Enterprise is culturally determined.

Enterprise is as much a social and moral act as economic – but, until this is widely understood, economic success will be elusive. Early accounts of the rise of capitalism ... stressed the congruence between Protestant values and those of successful capitalism. Religious non-conformism compelled the early capitalists to invest and not to dissipate their profits in consumption. The early Protestant sects were earning a place in heaven by their acts in the world, and so launching early capitalism.

Will Hutton[4]

Other enterprise connotations

The word 'enterprise' has a number of other connotations. People talk of free enterprise, of enterprise as being the opposite of dependency, and of enterprise occurring in clusters.

Free enterprise

Economic enterprise is said to thrive in a free, or market, economy. It was Adam Smith in *The Wealth of Nations* in 1776 who argued that the enormously complex task of deciding which goods and services to produce in an economy should not be carried out by a central authority but should be delegated to individual buyers and sellers.[5] He did recognise that government nevertheless had a role in such a free market. It had the responsibility for the framework of laws to protect the right of individuals involved in the market and for mechanisms to maintain social stability.

Others more recently have been equally enthusiastic about the workings of the free market. Hayek argues persuasively in *The Road to Serfdom* that socialist planning restricts individual decision making and is invariably inefficient.[6] Neither innovative technological changes nor changes in consumer preferences can be predicted with any accuracy, and consequently attempts to plan such matters are doomed to failure. The free market is the most flexible and responsive of economic systems and is always more efficient than deliberate economic decision making by the state. Free enterprise systems can lead to inequality, but it is argued that those with the best economic judgements of events reap the greatest rewards. Hayek deplores any attempt by centralised decision makers to legislate for equality, because it would restrict liberty and ultimately be ineffective.

These are the principal proponents of the line of economic thought that puts the emphasis on the individual in a system that is regarded as highly flexible and responsive to change and that provides the freedom to choose. This free enterprise economy, with its market-driven changes, is thus an attractive milieu for enterprising individuals to spot economic opportunities and exercise skill and judgement in the pursuit of economic rewards. By way of contrast, it can be seen that individual enterprise would be severely constrained in a command economy.

Much of the rivalry in the last century between the so-called 'East' and 'West', between the first two 'worlds', can therefore be seen in terms of a conflict between the relative advantages of a market versus a command economy. Capitalism, as practised in the nineteenth century, had been thought by Marx and others to promote the advance of the few and the economic enslavement of the many. Communism was the alternative that promised to end this inequality and to promote the benefit of the many. 'Bourgeois and Proletarians' is the heading of the first section of the Communist Manifesto and a note by Engels explains that by 'bourgeoisie' is meant the class of modern capitalists, owners of the means of social production and employers of wage labour, and by 'proletariat' is meant the class of modern wage-labourers who, having no means of production of their own, are reduced to selling their labour power in order to live. The Communist Manifesto specifically advocates the ending of the capitalist market, and those states that have subsequently claimed to be based on a Marxist ideal have by and large had centrally planned, rather than market, economies. The apparent failure of this approach, and the abandonment of central planning in favour of the reintroduction of market forces, have been seen as a victory of 'free enterprise' over communism and as proof therefore of the superiority and rightness of the market approach.

That superiority may not always be so obvious, and it is not always so easy to replace a command economy with a free one. The post-1989 apparent degeneration of the Russian economy into a 'mafia'-dominated confusion indicates that the much-heralded victory of Western market-dominated economics is not everywhere so clearly beneficial to the majority of the population as may have been claimed initially.

The market approach has been identified with enterprise in this way and criticisms of a market economy approach have been portrayed as attacks on the ideas of enterprise. However, there are many variations of the market economy and much of the criticism of one variation is also intended to promote another. Nevertheless, some of this debate has been seen to be anti-enterprise. To see whether it is or not, it is necessary to distinguish between some different models of the market economy and their advantages and disadvantages.

The outward micro-economic manifestation of free-market thinking and behaviour is the perfectly competitive model. In this economic model there are very many firms in each industry producing largely homogeneous goods. No firm is large enough to influence the industry's price; firms and consumers have perfect knowledge; and firms will expand production until the cost of producing an additional item equals the revenue obtained from selling it. Under these conditions there is an optimal distribution of resources among competing ends. When markets are not in equilibrium, the price mechanism comes into play to restore the balance.

Among the criticisms of this model are the claims that in reality there are many matters that create and sustain imperfections in the model. Advertising allows firms to differentiate products, monopolistic firms dominate markets, labour markets do not 'clear' the unemployed, and inflation persists. According to one commentator, 'the major tenet of free market economics – that unregulated markets will of their own accord find unimprovable results for all participants – is now proved to be nonsense. It does not hold in theory. It is not true.'[7]

In spite of the claims that economic development in the United States is the 'product of the initiative and drive of individuals co-operating through the free market',[8] governments (the Kennedy and Johnson administrations are examples) have intervened to produce variations on the capitalist theme and federal tax policies have been a major weapon in the drive for new jobs. Thomas cites Keegan in concluding that there are at least three versions of capitalism: the American or liberal model, which draws heavily on the views of Smith and Hayek; continental European capitalism, which has active government involvement and embraces important interest groups that run the economy conjointly; and Japanese capitalism, with strong state involvement, partnership and a focus on manufacturing prowess. In the European and Japanese versions, Keegan reports, the notion of 'community' is not seen as injurious to creativity or to the 'incentive to work'. He considers that the Japanese model, which emphasises loyalty and 'the value of long-term relationships between companies, their customers and suppliers, and within companies between the organisation, the employees, and the senior executives', is worthy of consideration.[9] Enterprise, in or through a more collaborative German or Japanese model, can indeed flourish in non-liberal (in the US sense) capitalist economies.

The economically sensitive, responsive, American-style capitalism presents many opportunities for enterprising individuals, but setting up and managing projects requires collaboration. Therefore the European and Japanese versions of capitalism can offer opportunities to do new things and to do so with the assistance of others. 'Markets, whether we like it or not', says Hutton, 'are embedded in a country's social system and values.'[10] Thus deviations from the perfectly competitive model of 'free enterprise' are not necessarily inherently contrary to enterprise. They may simply be adjustments to produce a system that promotes the benefits of enterprise in a way that works in reality.

Enterprise and dependency

It has not been only under communism that economic systems have discouraged enterprise, or at least discouraged what are perceived as some of the more beneficial sorts of enterprise. One way of defining enterprise is to describe it as the opposite of dependency; and yet dependency, it is argued, has been the result of some well-meaning attempts at economic stimulation. While governments have naturally been keen to ensure that their efforts benefit the worst-off in society, as well as, if not even more than, those who are more advantaged, their efforts have not always been as effective as they might have wished.

One reason for this is encapsulated in the saying, 'Give people fish and you feed them for a day; teach them to fish and they can be fed for life.' In economic terms, however, it is often argued that teaching someone to fish is no help if there are no fish in the immediate area and that, in any case, it is a long-term strategy. What is often first needed is short-term relief, and governments often seem to have the resources to buy in fish in the short term. However, economies are said to work when they create wealth and, if poorer regions are not creating wealth, then just putting in money, which is often the main resource to which governments can resort, is unlikely to change things.

Although governments do not like admitting to wasting resources, there is evidence that, even if economic development assistance appears to be carefully used, the result can be to build an attitude of dependency, not of enterprise. In Northern Ireland, for instance, studies in the late 1980s showed that the effect of years of grant support for businesses, ostensibly to help those businesses offset a variety of factors reducing their competitiveness, had had the effect instead of making them 'at least as profitable as their (foreign) counterparts' while remaining less productive.[11] In other words an overall effect of the grants was to underwrite a lack of competitiveness. What could be said to be happening was that individual business owners were learning to be enterprising not in improving business worth by superior competitiveness, but in improving business worth by becoming better at accessing grants. That is enterprise, but like the stories of individuals in the so-called communist systems who became expert at getting the most out of the system while putting in the least, it is not the sort of enterprise that helps an economy to grow.

It can also be argued that strong government support of that kind can do more than just promote the rise of opportunistic 'grantrepreneurship'. It can also build a real dependency on that support. If there is a feeling that the economic situation is poor and that government ought to do something, and government then does intervene to do something, it reinforces the belief that sorting out the problem is the duty of government and should be left to it. Often the solution sought is inward investment: the attracting into the poorer regions of large industrial projects from elsewhere to provide employment. That employment, however, is then dependent on the continuation of those projects and they are often the first to be closed by their parent companies in periods of economic retrenchment, particularly if they do not include any 'head office' functions such as R&D or marketing. Meanwhile, established local businesses and prospective new businesses, having become used to the availability of grants, tend to develop the attitude that if there isn't a grant for something then they won't do it. And even in local economic development initiatives, local businesses and organisations become dependent on government for ideas and drive. It can be like a patient being put on a life-support machine who, if the basic illness is not treated, becomes dependent on that machine for continued life. Enterprise, it could be argued, should be about taking your own initiative to improve your circumstances, not being dependent on others to do it for you.

ILLUSTRATION 5.2
Learned helplessness

Learned helplessness is a recognised healthcare problem in which patients learn to become dependent on external assistance and cannot do without it even when their original complaint is cured. Businesses, it would seem, can suffer from similar problems.

Clusters and competitiveness

What then does actually promote industrial competitiveness? One answer comes from Michael Porter who, in his book *The Competitive Advantage of Nations*, seeks to overturn the traditional view on this subject. The prevailing theory, he suggests, had been that economies of scale, labour costs, and interest and exchange rates were the strongest factors in determining competitiveness. He argues, however, that it is domestic rivalry and geographic concentration that provide the conditions necessary to build the expertise and innovation that really produce competitiveness. 'The presence of strong local rivals is a ... powerful stimulus to the creation and persistence of competitive advantage,'[12] and again, 'Nations succeed in particular industries because their home environment is the most forward-looking, dynamic, and challenging.'[13]

Companies achieve competitive advantage through innovation, including innovation in technology, in new ways of doing things, and in perceiving new markets or new opportunities in existing markets, and these are all aspects of entrepreneurship. Innovation is, however, linked to change and change is often unnatural. Conventional wisdom had argued that domestic competition was wasteful: that it led to duplication of effort and reduced the potential for economies of scale. Porter suggests, on the contrary, that it is domestic competition that provides the stimulus for innovation and that it is domestic competition that ultimately both forces domestic companies to look at export markets for their expansion and toughens them to succeed in them. When that domestic environment includes demanding customers and strong competition, together with appropriate support industries and the factors of production, there is the basis for international competitiveness. This is termed the 'cluster theory', because it suggests that these are the factors which have led, in different parts of the world, to clusters of internationally competitive businesses.

Porter's views are not primarily about the promotion of enterprise per se, but they argue against the once conventional wisdom that economic prosperity is linked primarily to big businesses. If he is right then the conditions and attitudes that will give a nation a competitive advantage are those of an enterprise culture. National competitiveness and enterprise will be linked.

ILLUSTRATION 5.3
Network capitalism

While the examples of 'Third Italy' and Silicon Valley in the United States are often quoted as classic examples of clusters, equally impressive are the achievements of ethnic Chinese family businesses in many countries of the Association of South East Asian Nations (ASEAN). The ethnic Chinese have developed a formula for business which appears to have turned them into strong competitors on a world stage. Redding, writing of 'network capitalism', claims that:

> their domains are OEM (original equipment manufacture) production, property, services, retailing, trading. ... This network capitalism of the ethnic Chinese is designed to respond to markets which companies from advanced economies would consider disorderly, volatile and very difficult to cope with.[14]

The advantages and disadvantages of enterprise

> All that glisters is not gold.
> Shakespeare, *The Merchant of Venice.*

There is, in many places, a prevailing desire to promote enterprise and entrepreneurship, which is in turn based on the assumption that enterprise is essentially something of value and that it and entrepreneurship are good things. It may therefore be necessary to temper this implication by looking at some of the disadvantages of enterprise and entrepreneurship as well as their advantages, and by pointing out some of the problems and the downside. These can lie in the results of the practice of enterprising behaviour, in the way that a label of enterprise can appear to justify otherwise undesirable practices, and in the assumption that true enterprising behaviour is what should always be encouraged.

Enterprise can get things done, it can change things, it can give rein to creativity and innovation. In the context of business entrepreneurship it can provide people with financial returns, with greater freedom, with a greater sense of achievement and with more enjoyment. However enterprise, it has been said, is spelt R-I-S-K. It is important therefore, when promoting enterprise, to remember that, inherent in enterprise and especially in enterprise in the business context, is risk: the risk of loss of career and of livelihood, of loss of money and resource, and of loss of reputation. While in an enterprising culture it may be expected that many new ventures will work and that as a result, on average, things will progress, it must be remembered that individual initiatives, and the individual people behind them, will not all follow that average path. Some will fail. If however no one is prepared to risk that failure, which is a necessary condition for any venture, then little will progress. An economy is like an ecosystem in nature: organisms in it cannot stand still and survive, at least not for long. In a healthy environment there are both births and deaths. If a living organisation does not continue to renew itself it will die, but not all renewal initiatives will work.

Just as enterprise and entrepreneurship do not ensure success, neither is either of them a magic cure-all. They can be an important element in economic, or other, improvement. Despite this, the ways in which they are promoted can be both highly distorting and distorted. They can suggest that enterprise is itself sufficient and can highlight selfish aspects only, as if they alone were what mattered.

If enterprise and entrepreneurship can be misused in this way, do we want them at all? Are they a force for good, or for bad, or are they actually neutral with the potential goodness or badness lying in the way they are used? Some resist them because they see them as replacing clearer positive values with something that is at best only neutral. Attempts to introduce enterprise education into schools have been seen by its proponents as a long-needed attempt to help schools educate their students for a life in the 'real world'. Others, however, have resisted these attempts as propaganda and as a preparation only for the 'nasty' commercial world of business without introducing any positive elements such as consideration, tolerance or generosity. 'Do we really want our nine-year-olds to be adopting such a hard-nosed attitude – shouldn't they, during their ever-shrinking childhood, be thinking about saving the whale, rather than contracting to sell apples in the school tuck shop?'[15] While it can be pointed out that attempting to save the whale will itself require enterprise, there is still the potential danger that the application of commercial considerations will have the opposite effect.

Business failure

One area in which the drawbacks of enterprise and entrepreneurship are most obvious is that of business failure. In the world of business, failure is not uncommon, but it is often not possible to quantify it. Storey points out that, in the UK, statistics on business failure are bedevilled with problems over definitions and the choice of variables to be used in their measurement.[16] Terms such as bankruptcy, insolvency, failure, ceasing to trade and closure are used at the level of the individual, the plant and the company; and in any case, ceasing to trade and closure may not actually be failures.

(See also 'Business failure' in Chapter 7.) Storey concludes that we do not really know how many firms go out of business each year because failure is measured by recording compulsory liquidations, individual bankruptcies, company de-registrations, self-employment termination and VAT de-registrations, and we do not know how many of these might actually be for positive reasons.

Differences in failure rates amongst different types of ownership have been explored and, for instance, there is some *a priori* evidence that businesses run by women do not survive as long as male-owned firms. In the United States Boden and Nucci argue that women, because of their work and life experiences, do not accumulate as much human and financial capital as men.[17] They are less likely than men to acquire the knowledge, skill and financial resources needed to run a viable business. In contrast some recent work in Britain by Chell and Baines points to numerous contradictions in research findings in this area and to the lack of sophistication in research methods.[18] Furthermore, empirical research by Chell and Baines on the performance of micro-businesses shows that there are no significant differences between that of male-owned and female-owned firms.

However, in spite of the lack of clarity over the extent of failure rates, businesses do fail and indications of this in the UK are to be found in the types of statistics discussed below.

VAT de-registrations

Burns considers that VAT data offer the best guide to the changing structure of the SME sector.[19] In 2005 in the UK, although there were 177,900 VAT registrations there were also 152,900 de-registrations leaving a net increase of only 25,000 registrations and a total, at the start of 2006, of 1,917,615 business registrations.[20] However, not every VAT deregistration necessarily indicates a business failure. For instance a business changing its form, such as a sole trader establishing a limited company, will involve a deregistration of the original business and a re-registration of the new one.

Insolvency figures

A company or person with debts which they cannot pay is said to be insolvent. When it becomes necessary to terminate a company's existence, whether owing to insolvency or for some other reason, the process is called 'winding up'. In England and Wales in 2005, there were about 12,000 company winding-up petitions, about 20,000 creditors' bankruptcy petitions and about 37,000 debtors' bankruptcy petitions.[21]

The consequences of failure

If a business fails employees lose their jobs, shareholders lose their investments, 'creditors suffer through exceedingly long and potentially expensive legal avenues of debt collection; and managers may lose credibility and reputation, effectively precluding them from future jobs.'[22] Since liquidations are most common among firms which have large capital requirements, the potential financial losses can be severe. Furthermore, the stigma attached to failure can be powerful and may limit the likelihood of failed owners getting another chance.

Being an owner-manager is a risky form of enterprise and if an individual is forced out of business the costs can be considerable. Self-employed people in particular tend to create ventures in sectors with few barriers to entry, and competition in these crowded areas is severe. Even if they do not actually fail, they may make little money. They may not accumulate pension funds or savings, with the result they have little financial security, and if they do lose their businesses, their financial prospects can be bleak, especially if they become bankrupt as a consequence.[23] They (and possibly their families) may lose all their assets and they may not be in a position to avail themselves of the protection afforded to bankrupts.[24] Self-employment for some can therefore be the route to impoverishment, not to success.

Learning from failure

> Wisdom is meaningless until our own experience has given it meaning.
>
> Bergen Evans

Despite its harmful consequences, an element of failure is an inevitable, and even an essential, ingredient of an enterprising economy. Indeed a high start-up rate and a consequent high rate of mortality among firms are often seen as indicative of a vibrant economy. Attempting a business formation which fails can also be a very useful learning experience. Entrepreneurship is a multi-skilled job and it is difficult to learn all about it only through education and training. Learning from experience is vital and much can be learned from 'intelligent failure'. Indeed it has been shown that an impressive array of British entrepreneurs, including Mike Gooley, owner of Trailfinders travel firm, Katherine Hamnet, the designer of clothes for the trendy, and Theo Fennell, a bespoke jeweller, have all had their business failures.[25] Fennell's jewellery firm went into voluntary liquidation in 1986 and the mistake cost him almost everything. However, he learned a lot and this helped him to do things differently with his other ventures.

Failure can be a good learning experience, particularly if the individual who fails is motivated to find out why, prior to trying again. McGrath considers that an intelligent analysis of the cause(s) of failure is necessary if learning is to occur and suggests that entrepreneurs should adopt some of the procedures adopted by academic researchers when seeking explanations for failure.[26] Entrepreneurship is a complex task, and action does not always produce expected outcomes. Therefore entrepreneurs should develop hypotheses or sets of assumptions about the likelihood of achieving specific outcomes. If actual outcomes are at variance with expected ones, this information can be used to reformulate assumptions. A mindset which considers deviations between actual and expected outcomes as 'vehicles for testing assumptions rather than as failures' can facilitate the discontinuance of, or the alteration of resource flows to, an entrepreneurial project.[27] McGrath suggests that an experimental approach to entrepreneurial action and the conduct of intelligent post-mortems can help promote a step-by-step approach to the development of entrepreneurial projects. In this way entrepreneurs learn from experience and only commit resources when assumptions have been tested. This helps avoid the financial losses that can occur when 'huge, irreversible investments' are made 'as single attempts at innovation'.[28] Wisdom, it has been said, comes from the sum of our failures.

The future of enterprise

Forecasting is difficult – especially when it concerns the future.

Groucho Marx

This book was written in response to an increasing emphasis in recent years on enterprise in many areas of life but especially in the economic field. It is therefore relevant to consider whether that emphasis is likely to continue and whether the concept of enterprise, as described here, is likely to continue to be relevant. The following are some of the trends, ideas and concepts which may influence the future of enterprise.

Technology

The rate of development of technology shows no sign of slowing. One obvious result is to make older technologies obsolete and the industries dependent on them expendable. If technology changes, then businesses dependent on it must change too in order to remain competitive. Nowhere is this more so than in the computer and telecommunications industries. The technological changes have been profound, and this has assisted firms in their search for ever more flexible but cost-effective production methods. However, the impact of computers, assisted by fibre-optic capability, has been even more profound in revolutionising information processing. Personal computers, electronic mail, fax machines, mobile telephones and the Internet have transformed the provision of services such as market research, industrial design and advertising. Knowledge-based industries rely on information-processing ability to confer competitive advantage. Therefore, the combination of computing capacity, a focus on knowledge and fibre optics has, and will continue to have, a marked impact on the way we work.

No longer is it necessary to work in a fixed location under the direct supervision of a manager. The communications revolution has brought the possibility of global teleworking, reducing the problems of distance and the need for sales premises within easy reach of the customer. Even small businesses can join in and offer something on a worldwide basis. Improved communications provide the opportunity for improved services with faster turn-round times, but faster responses also require more flexible organisations. Small businesses are then not only able to join in but can do so at an advantage with respect to their bigger rivals. While many of the initial dot.com ventures which tried to take advantage of enhanced information and communication technology (ICT) may have failed because they were far too optimistic in their projections, nevertheless e-business, with its advantages for small businesses, is a reality and is continuing to grow.

Advances in biotechnology are also having a major impact on our daily lives. Not only can food now be grown in formerly inhospitable areas, but microbes are being developed that destroy waste and toxins, and medical advances are taking place on many fronts. Consequently people will be able to live longer in most parts of the world, which will have profound social and economic consequences. However some biotechnology innovations, such as genetically modified crops (GM), have led to adverse market reactions and consumer preference has instead stimulated a dramatic rise in the availability of organic produce in supermarkets.

Flexibility and service

The possibility of, and the demand for, flexible production and service are increasing. Large, inflexible production lines with their economies of scale, but also with their associated limitation that 'you can have any colour you like as long as it's black', are no longer the only way to meet customer demands. Customers can have, and now expect, variety as well as relative cheapness. Production must change to provide what customers want to buy, not what the business wants to supply. Businesses compete on flexibility and speed of response as well as on price.

Smaller businesses can be more flexible in their approach and quicker to change to meet new conditions. Service industry, where flexibility, quality and speed of response are of primary importance, has a high proportion of small businesses. These combine organic, flexible structures with the decentralisation of decision making to those with knowledge and expertise. In addition, the need to solve specific client problems, or to customise products for market niches, will entail the use of temporary project groups to meet customer needs. The equipment used by problem-solving work groups will tend to be sophisticated, but employees will exercise a good deal of discretion in utilising it effectively. The organisations doing this will therefore tend to be smaller, more responsive, quality conscious and much less bureaucratic than formerly. They may well employ a small number of core professional staff and contract out work that is very specialised or for which demand is uneven. They will both be enterprising themselves and also create the opportunity for the enterprise of others.

Changing lifestyles

It is not only the demands of the world of work that are changing, but also the way people feel that they can live their lives. It used to be the case that people expected to work for as long as they could and not to survive very long after that. Now, though, changed work expectations, combined with longer lifespans, mean that more people are planning for what amount to second lives in which their styles of living will be significantly different from those of their first lives. They are no longer planning on the basis of lifetime careers in one organisation, but are increasingly likely to have a second career in which they will be dependent on their own enterprise for their work and income.

Market changes

Markets are also changing. Consumers want not only improved products and services but also improved by-products from those processes. Consumer influence is particularly noticeable, for instance, in the field of environmental issues and a concern for global warning, which has been influenced by Presidential candidate Al Gore's Oscar-winning film *An Inconvenient Truth*. Businesses now have to consider the social, as well as the economic, consequence of their actions. Those that cannot adapt will fail. Consequently there will be openings for new businesses that can adapt and for service businesses to help the others to address, reduce or deal with the unwanted consequences of their actions.

Markets are also becoming more international. In a global environment in which businesses increasingly seek, and are encouraged, to establish overseas subsidiaries, who should adapt to whose culture? Should it be the business which wants to sell or the host country which wants the inward investment? There will be a need to think globally but act locally. That too will require enterprise.

Results

The result of all these, and of other, developments is change. Charles Handy among others has pointed out that organisations can normally cope effectively with rapid change so long as the change is incremental and developmental.[29] Organisations have much more difficulty in coping with discontinuous change, but this, according to Handy, is precisely what is happening in today's world. With this type of change, old ways of thinking and functioning are inappropriate and radical new reasoning is required.

In the economic sphere many of the more developed countries will continue to reduce their reliance on the mass production of consumer durables in favour of high-quality, high-volume, customised goods and services. In essence they can no longer compete in labour-intensive or skill-intensive sectors and must move to knowledge-intensive business. Added value will come from the innovation and knowledge base of people in organisations, not from their physical labour. Changes in markets require firms nowadays to offer 'quality, flexibility and innovativeness' along with the 'customisation of products' rather than low-cost, high-volume, standard products.[30]

For these reasons, and for others possibly including the management fashion for 'downsizing', many larger businesses have been actively reducing their direct manpower requirements. Charles Handy has spoken of the 'shamrock organisation' (see also Chapter 1): a structure with three parts, each of which has different expectations, management systems and methods of payment. One part is the professional core essential to the survival of the organisation; the second part consists of the subcontractors who will actually do much of the work; and the third leaf is the growing number of flexible and temporary workers and consultants who are hired for specific jobs as the need arises.

As a consequence, the traditional notion of the career is increasingly a thing of the past. Those in the core, with a 'normal' full-time career, will be encouraged to work very hard indeed and face the likelihood of burnout by their forties. It did seem at one time that many of these people would have been able to retire in their early to late fifties and leave their intensive brainwork to a younger generation. However the strain on the pension system of people living longer has put this under threat, with many people now likely to have to work much later than anticipated. They can expect to live for 30 more years, but their source of income will have to change. A large number of people will have job histories characterised by part-time or temporary work assignments. Their earning power will be less than that of full-time careerists, and they will lack job security.

Other changes may incidentally help with the process of mid-career readjustment. There will be the subcontracting opportunities for those who want to take them up and, if individuals have the right mental preparation, then some of them may find that the necessary resources are provided by others. Redundancy payments are one obvious source of investment for new business ventures, and, in countries that have enjoyed a high standard of living for a period, inheritance of the assets accumulated by parents is an increasing factor. Also, it has been suggested that a contributory factor in the recent considerable increase in the number of businesses started by women in some parts of the United States is the life-change occasioned by divorce, combined with the opportunity provided by alimony payments.

Rapid and discontinuous change therefore seems likely to go on having a major impact on the lives of people, organisations and society. Successful individuals in the world of tomorrow will need to be flexible in their attitudes, their acquisition of skills and their knowledge base. Faced with ever faster environmental changes, organisations must respond, and people – their most flexible of resources – must be equally responsive. Specific knowledge is important for specific roles, but problem solving, information search and analysis, and decision making will be crucial skills. People must be adaptable and be able to learn continuously. They must espouse a 'spirit of inquiry' and develop value systems that encourage 'inquiry, examination, diagnosis and experimentation'.[31] In short, they must be enterprising.

In a situation of discontinuous change, individuals, organisations and nations must develop the capacity to cope. In doing this, people who display enterprising attitudes, attributes and behaviours will be particularly useful. Individuals, organisations and countries must become more flexible, responsive, knowledgeable, mobile and proactive; and people who possess enterprising attributes such as boldness, innovation and confidence will not only profit themselves but will lead society in its drive to make necessary changes. The future, or at least a significant part of it, is therefore likely to be made by, and to belong to, the enterprising.

Social enterprise and the social economy

One aspect of economic activity which has been the subject of increasing interest in recent years is that part of the economy which is classified as being in neither the public nor the private sector. The organisations in it are many and varied including, for instance, charities and churches, associations and amateur dramatic clubs, foundations and fair trade companies, co-operatives and community bodies, mutuals and trades unions, voluntary organisations and professional bodies. Although many of them are enterprises, because they generally are not formed primarily to make a profit for their members and/or founders they are not considered to be in the private sector. And although many of them have social purposes, because they are not part of the government system and paid for by taxes, they are not considered to be in the public sector. Being therefore in neither of the two sectors traditionally ascribed to an economy, they are sometimes referred to collectively as the third sector.

As enterprises with a social purpose, many of these organisations are often referred to as social enterprises and are said to form part of the social economy. Some of them may also be referred to as community enterprises and be considered to be in the community or voluntary sector.

The emergence of the social economy

From the time that the private and public sectors first emerged as separate parts of an economy, there have been organisations which belonged to neither of those sectors. Churches are obvious early examples, and also the first schools and hospitals which were often based on religious bodies. But in England in the thirteenth century, schools and university colleges were being founded which were secular both in their purpose and their governance. While much education and medicine has since then been taken over by the state and now lies within the public sector, some of the early education bodies still survive and are among the oldest surviving non-governmental organisations.

To some extent this part of the economy has been overlooked, not least because there has not been a suitable vocabulary with which to refer it. However in 1830 the term *économie sociale* was first used by the French economist Charles Dunoyer and this was the origin of the term social economy. It has been suggested that the emergence of the social economy as a specific concept, in France and at that time, was the result of institutionalisation and a theoretical assessment of practical experiences.[32] Those experiences might be said to have had their roots in aspects of Egyptian, Greek and Roman life, and later in the guilds that appeared in north-west Europe in medieval times when a rich associative life was evident. This was the case in other parts of the world also, including medieval Byzantium, Muslim countries and India, in which 'associations' were formed in order to organise and protect communities of interest.

Moulaert and Ailenei, in a study of the social economy, quote several authors who contend that the social economy has a history of emergence and re-emergence linked to a series of economic and social crises.[33] Many of the guilds and other associations, they suggest, were created to provide assistance, mutual support and charity in the uncertain times of the early Middle Ages. The changes later brought about by the Industrial Revolution led to a decline in craft-co-operatives and created renewed interests in 'utopian socialism' and the values of co-operation and mutual support. The French Revolution, it has been argued, fostered political equality but not material equality and, because material inequalities remained, mutual support organisations (*mutuelles*) appeared in the middle of the nineteenth century. In the last quarter of that century, agricultural and savings co-operatives were formed in response to the needs of small producers affected by increasing accumulation and the economic power of the bigger businesses thus created. In France, it might be said, republican ideals generated distinctive interests in associations as a buffer between individuals and the state, whereas in England, ideas around communitarianism strongly influenced the co-operative movement.

Although the social economy may have been first conceptualised in the nineteenth century there have been crises since then which have further stimulated its development. In the twentieth century, the economic collapse of 1929–32 led to the formation of consumption co-operatives for food and housing[34] and further initiatives in 1970s

Europe have been seen, on the one hand, to be a reaction to crises in the mass production system and, on the other hand, to be a response to the overburdening of the welfare state.[35] Indeed Amin et al. trace the most recent interest in the social economy to the end of full employment and the crisis in welfare provision which started in the 1970s. This 'post-Fordist' environment, they suggest, was characterised by:

- rising global energy prices
- rising imports from low-wage counties and flexibly organised new economies
- wage drift and sustained opposition from organised labour
- decreasing return on sunk capital
- growth of new technologies and organised principles no longer dependent on economies of scale
- falling demand for mass-produced goods and the rise of customised consumption
- waning support for mass representative democracy
- strains on government to provide expensive welfare services and the rise of new-right market ideas on the management of the relationship between the state and economy.[36]

But this crisis, Amin et al. suggest, simultaneously renewed interest in the potential of the social economy as a place of work and provider of welfare services. For instance the European Commission established its Social Economy Unit, within DGXXIII, in 1989, and the importance of the social economy was formally recognised by the European Union in its 1994 White Paper on *Growth, Competitiveness and Employment*. This paper indicated that the EU saw the 'third sector' as a potentially important contributor to the growth of employment and as means of avoiding dual labour markets, twin-speed societies and urban segregation. By the end of the 1990s attention was being paid to the social economy in many of the EU member states, including the UK, and it would seem that this re-emergence of the social economy as a subject of interest can be linked to economic and social change resulting, at least in Western Europe, from the late-twentieth-century 'post-Fordist' changes to manufacturing strength and the welfare state environment. From different shades of political opinion the social economy is, in many quarters, now attracting considerable attention.

Issues of terminology

In France the concept of *l'économie sociale* came to be seen as encompassing specifically co-operatives, *mutuelles* (mutuals) and associations. The classification *économie sociale* used in some EU member states has specifically included those three categories of organisation, and was expanded in the early 1990s to include foundations also. (These categories are sometimes referred to as CMAFs: co-operatives, mutuals, associations and foundations.)

The social economy is often not so closely defined. In the UK a government report suggested that 'the social economy is an imprecise term – but in general can be thought of as those organisations who [sic] are independent of the state and provide services, goods and trade for a social purpose and are not profit distributing.'[37] The European Commission also does not formally define the social economy, but, presumably based on the *économie sociale* classification, has indicated that:

The so-called social economy, including co-operatives, mutual societies, non-profit associations, foundations and social enterprises provides a wide range of products and services across Europe, and generates millions of jobs.[38]

and that:

The importance to the European economy of co-operatives, mutual societies, associations, foundations and social enterprises (which together are sometimes referred to as the Social Economy) is now receiving greater recognition.[39]

These approaches to the social economy are based on including only certain categories of organisation which have a number of shared characteristics. There are however many organisations which, while not belonging to either the public or private sectors, do not share all these characteristics. Therefore, while the term social economy is sometimes used to refer to the whole of the third sector, it is clear that it sometimes refers only to a part of that sector. Alternatively, if it is indeed a sector in its own right, then there must also be a fourth sector.

Other terms which have been used in a similar context are the third system and the third way, the non-profit or the not-for-profit sector, the voluntary sector and the voluntary and community sector, the community sector or the community economy. Not only have many of these terms at some time been used more or less interchangeably with one or more of the others terms, but they also have sometimes been used to refer to a sub-sector and sometimes to the sector overall. The result is that this is often an area in which the terminology can be confusing because there is no accepted standard practice, as the following examples illustrate (italics added):

In 2003, the *voluntary, third* or *non-profit* sector occupies centre stage in public policy discussions in the UK.[40]

In what might be called the 'community era' we talked of community action, *community enterprise*, and *community business*. Today, in the contemporary 'social era', we are more likely to talk of *social entrepreneurs, social enterprise* and *social business*. Is there some serious significance in this shift in vocabulary from community to social? Does it matter?[41]

Social economy refers to a *third sector* in economics between the private sector ... and the public sector.[42]

The *third sector* can be broken down into three sub-sectors: the *community sector*, the *voluntary sector* and the *social enterprise sector*.[43]

What is the social economy?

Basing descriptions of the social economy on objective assessments of what is in it might appear to be logical, but it is not the sequence that often appears to be followed. Instead assessments of what is considered to be in the social economy are, in effect, based on definitions subjectively derived from the function that it is expected, or hoped, that the social economy will serve.

One of the reasons advanced for the lack of a single, generally accepted, definition of the social economy is that it is due, at least in part, to the various different traditions and policy emphasis that exist. Amin et al., for instance, have identified 'considerable international differences in the ways in which the social economy and its relationship to market, state and civil society are envisioned'. In the United States, they suggest, which compared with many European countries has a weak welfare state playing a largely residual role, the sector is shaped by 'bottom-up' community development processes fronted by a voluntary sector that is now only loosely connected with political activism. In Western Europe, the tendency towards a withdrawal of state funding has encouraged stronger community economic development and enterprise linked to an expanded role for the third sector more generally. France could be seen perhaps as the paradigmatic model of a state-supported social economy in which the social enterprise has been accorded a specific legal status. But within Europe there are significant variations between a French-German-Belgian tradition of strong social economy providers recognised and regulated by national governments and a weaker Mediterranean model where formal recognition and development of a social economy distinct from strong charities is, at best, embryonic. The Anglo-Saxon model has a particular emphasis on tackling social exclusion, has become strongly spatialised and, in the UK, has been closely connected to the New Labour ideas of building a Third Way between the market and the public sector. Amin et al. also find potential in Nordic interpretations of the social economy, as there the presence of large public sectors and comparatively strong welfare systems create the conditions for the social economy to play a strong role in the progressive politics of redistribution.[44]

The different roles that social enterprises in these different traditions have played, or are expected to play, not only lead to different definitions reflecting those different roles but also cause some people to focus on the social economy and some on social enterprises. Peter Lloyd, for instance, has identified two very different schools of thought, one of which he identifies as a US/UK, approach and the other as a European approach. The European approach, he suggests, is a social economy approach which does not hold back from offering a challenge to the post-1980s hegemony of liberal market forces as the only grand narrative and takes a whole society perspective instead of just a business-focused one. In contrast the US/UK approach is a social enterprise approach as it starts with the enterprises of which the social economy is composed, and defines them as businesses operating in a market context but using surpluses to achieve social objectives. Lloyd suggests that this difference reflects a fundamental difference in paradigms between a European political economy approach and the narrow market-based approach arising from Anglo-Saxon neo-liberal traditions.[45]

What is a social enterprise?

The different models of the social economy which are summarised above seem to treat social enterprises differently. The European approach starts with the social economy which, the EU indicates, includes co-operatives, mutual societies, associations, foundations and social enterprises. Thus, by specifying social enterprises alongside co-operatives, mutual societies, associations, foundations, it suggests that organisations in the latter categories, while being at the core of the social economy, are not themselves social enterprises. The US/UK approach, however, in effect starts with social enterprises and seems to imply that the social economy amounts to the sum of all the social enterprises within it, which implies that co-operatives, mutual societies, associations, foundations are social enterprises because they are in the social economy.

One way of avoiding the issue of whether social enterprises include co-operatives, mutual societies, associations and foundations is to talk instead about social economy enterprises as a generic term. The European Commission, for instance, under the heading of social economy enterprises, indicates that there are certain common characteristics shared by what it then calls social economy entities:

- Their primary purpose is not to obtain a return on capital. They are, by nature, part of a stakeholder economy, whose enterprises are created by and for those with common needs, and accountable to those they are meant to serve.

- They are generally managed in accordance with the principle of 'one member, one vote'.

- They are flexible and innovative – social economy enterprises are being created to meet changing social and economic circumstances.

- Most are based on voluntary participation, membership and commitment.[46]

In 1997 the European Network for Economic Self Help and Local Development analysed the variety of social enterprises in European countries and identified some common principles, which in turn led to working definitions of social enterprises. The common principles were:[47]

- They seek to tackle specific *social aims by engaging in economic and trading activities*.

- They are *not-for-profit organisations*, in the sense that all surplus profits generated are either re-invested in the economic activities of the enterprise or are used in other ways to tackle the stated social aims of the enterprise.

- Their legal structures are such that all assets and accumulated wealth of the enterprise do not belong to any individuals but are held in trust to be used *for the benefit of these persons or areas* that are the intended beneficiaries of the enterprise's social aims.

- Their organisational structures are such that the full participation of members is encouraged on *a co-operative basis* with rights accorded to all members.

- It is a further characteristic of the social enterprise that it encourages *mutual co-operation* between social enterprises and with other organisations in the wider economy.

A shorter definition of a social enterprise is one from the UK government:

A social enterprise is a business with primary social objectives whose surpluses are principally reinvested for that purpose in the business or in the community, rather than being driven by the need to maximise profit for shareholders and owners.[48]

Key aspects of social enterprises

There is really no definitive boundary between many social enterprises and other small businesses. Small businesses are not all driven principally or exclusively by the desire to maximise profits; often they are started to provide benefits to their founders, and those benefits can include social as well as financial returns. Running social enterprises is however not without its problems, and is frequently a more complex task than that of running other businesses. There is the same need to secure income, without which even survival is not possible, but the income generation is not the end in itself and has to be balanced with achieving the delivery of the social purpose. Nevertheless social enterprises do have some particular characteristics and these are to be found, for instance, in:

- *Their founders and their motivations*: Like the founders of private sector organisations, the founders of social enterprises reveal great heterogeneity, but very often social enterprise are promoted, established and/or directed by groups of people, rather than by individuals.

- *The variety of organisational aims*: Social aims are typically either the primary aims, or are among the primary aims, of social enterprises in what is often referred to as 'the triple bottom line': alluding to social and environmental objectives as well as, and underpinned by, financial objectives. Sometimes an ethical objective is also added, thus making a 'quadruple bottom line'.

- *The possible legal structures*: Third sector organisations have developed differently in different countries, often because of the different regulatory frameworks that exist and the different forms of legal entity that are available. So it is important to recognise that third sector organisations, including social enterprises, are not typically defined by their legal status. A third sector organisation, depending on what sort of organisation it is, may operate as a trust, an industrial and provident society, a co-operative, a company limited by shares, a company limited by guarantee, a public limited company, an unlimited company or a partnership.

- *The concept of ownership*: The concept of ownership of many social enterprises is not straightforward. In the case of a company limited by shares it is clear that the shareholders are the company's owners with the extent of their ownership being determined by the number (and type) of shares they hold. In the case of a company limited by guarantee, the ultimate authority in the company is its members and it is they who elect its directors, usually on the basis of one vote per member. Those members, while they may control the company in that way, are precluded from selling off the company and/or its assets and keeping the proceeds. In that sense they are not its owners, but then neither is anyone else. Often, however, the people who control social enterprises may be community based. They may be individuals appointed from within the relevant community, elected community representatives, or representatives of other community bodies.

- *Their employment profiles*: There can be a perception that jobs in social enterprises are 'low quality' but the meaning of 'low quality' in this context often seems to lack precision. It appears generally to reflect a perception that many jobs in the third sector have low remuneration and are relatively unskilled, temporary and/or part time. There is, however, a lack of reliable data upon which to substantiate or refute such assertions, and it can also be relevant to ask what a 'quality' job is in this context. An indication of a high-quality job might also be a low employee turnover rate, which might indicate that the people concerned liked their jobs or at least preferred them to alternatives available.

- *Their profitability*: The essence of social enterprises is that they have been established for social purposes and not, or not primarily, to maximise financial returns to their investors. However they all survive by securing income for the services they provide. Describing these organisations as 'not-for-profit', though, can be misleading. Many of them are actually 'not for profit distribution to individuals' (although co-operatives can remit profits to their members). But they need to make a profit, or at least to break even over the longer term, to survive, and the widespread use of the term 'not-for-profit' may have encouraged some groups to forget this and to concentrate instead on the social purpose: a strategy which has on occasion been fatal to the organisation, as the resultant losses meant that it collapsed. On the other hand there are some organisations in which so much emphasis is placed on achieving financial viability that the overall purpose for which the financial viability is sought gets neglected. Nevertheless the longevity of some social enterprises shows that problems of viability can be overcome.

- *Their financing*: Social enterprises, like other enterprises, need access to money to start, develop and grow, but their inability to distribute profits to investors precludes them from some forms of finance. There are though various ways in which they can access financial support, including grants, endowments and commercial loans, and recently there has been a growth in the sophistication of financial supports for the sector.

- *Their reporting task*: Because of their multiple 'bottom lines' social enterprises often face a complex task in reporting to their stakeholders on their effectiveness and on the success, or otherwise, of their efforts to achieve their aims.

Social capital

Social capital is mentioned in Chapter 4 as a necessary factor for all enterprises. However social capital seems sometimes to be associated particularly with social enterprises and the social economy, along with suggestions that the social economy has a particular potential to help disadvantaged communities. This claim appears to reduce to the two assumptions that for disadvantaged communities the key lack is often social capital and that social enterprises create social capital. From these assumptions the conclusion is then drawn that social enterprises will help disadvantaged communities. However, while there are grounds for saying that there is something which is often referred to as social capital which is lacking in disadvantaged communities, whether it alone can effect improvement is much less certain and whether social enterprises necessarily create social capital is also debatable. Indeed a counter-argument is that, just as financial capital is needed to start businesses, so too is social capital needed to start enterprises, including social enterprises and, as disadvantaged communities often lack social capital, they are not good places in which to start social enterprises.

Community enterprise

Despite this often enterprises are started to try to help particular communities, and may then be referred to as community enterprises. For some communities the low levels of economic activity they have experienced, associated with high rates of unemployment, often result in a lack of confidence, a lack of relevant skills, a lack of resources and a lack of infrastructure. This can be a vicious circle of deprivation: there is a lack of business tradition, little enterprise and an absence of entrepreneurs. There are therefore no role models and a lack of confidence is reinforced. That is the antithesis of an enterprise culture and it is sometimes thought that community enterprises can help to counter it.

A community enterprise, however, can relate to any community, not just a disadvantaged one. Community enterprise, if it is distinguished from social enterprise, seems generally to be enterprise which, while fitting a social enterprise definition, is specifically run for the benefit of a particular community, and often by a group of people from that community. Sometimes individuals acting together as a team or group can demonstrate qualities, command resources and engage in enterprising behaviour in a way that acting individually they would not. Quite often, though, the catalyst for effective community group action is an outsider or enterprising community member who mobilises and releases the latent enterprise in others. Such an individual is often referred to as a community entrepreneur.

Community and social entrepreneurship

Various attempts have been made to define the concept of the community entrepreneur, and there is general agreement that it is about the use of personal networking, facilitation and resource-accessing skills (that is to say enterprise skills) so as to improve a local community in both social and economic areas. Community entrepreneurs facilitate community enterprise in the way that the more traditional entrepreneurs facilitate business development, although, while enterprise in the context of business is often seen in the start-up of new businesses, community enterprise is not generally applied to the start-up of new communities but to the revitalisation of old ones.

Community entrepreneurship is therefore a form of social entrepreneurship, in which the act of forming or growing a social enterprise is applied in the context of a community. The description of community entrepreneurs, given in comparison with private sector entrepreneurs in Table 5.1, thus also applies to social entrepreneurs, except that their social purpose may not be related specifically to the needs of a particular community.

Government interest in the social economy

Because of their focus on issues wider than just enriching their backers, social enterprises and the social economy are seen as having the ability to provide a variety of benefits, including:

Table 5.1 Autonomous and community entrepreneurs compared

Autonomous entrepreneurs	Community entrepreneurs
Aim for the growth of personal resources as the main personal goal	Aim for the development of the community as the main personal goal
Enhance own self-competence	Help to build the self-respect and competence of others
Mobilise resources to build their own enterprises	Inspire others to start their own enterprises
Put themselves at the top of the organisation	Regard themselves as the coordinator in a loose federation
See authority and society interest groups as hindrances	See authority and society interest groups as potential supporters and resource providers

Source: Adapted from B. Johannisson and A. Nilsson, 'Community Entrepreneurs: Networking for Local Development', *Entrepreneurship and Regional Development* (1989), 1, p.5. Reproduced by kind permission of Taylor & Francis, Publishers. Consultwww.tandf.co.uk/journals.

- The provision of goods, services and social benefits which the public sector doesn't adequately provide, and a means for addressing some problems of the welfare state.
- The provision of jobs for people who might not otherwise be employed.
- The fostering of enterprise and economic competitiveness.
- The promotion of environmental sustainability, or ethical operations.
- The creation of social capital and social cohesion. This is sometimes seen as giving it the ability to reach parts that other initiatives cannot reach, in particular when trying to tackle disadvantage through urban and rural regeneration projects (but see note on social capital above).

Many of these benefits, if not all of them, are of interest to governments. As a result, many governments have shown an interest in promoting the social economy and social enterprises. They are prepared to intervene to promote the sector and to encourage and support its establishment and development.

THE KEY POINTS OF CHAPTER 5

- A number of judgements are sometimes made about enterprise. While many people might agree with them they should not go unexplored. They include:
  - Enterprise is a relative concept. Whether an individual or society is enterprising or not may depend on with what it is compared.
  - Enterprise is a good thing. Enterprising people and economies have become synonymous with successful people and economies.
  - Enterprise is essential for economic advancement. There appears to be a correlation between enterprise and economic growth, but the mechanism may need to be understood better.

- Enterprise has strong political and social connotations. Enterprise has come to convey notions of freedom, of market choice and of liberalism and has been used as a label for political changes.

- A number of concepts have been attached in some situations to the word 'enterprise'. These associations include:

  - Free enterprise: Capitalism, and particularly American-style capitalism, has been given the title 'free enterprise', and it has been hailed as the victor in the economic side of the 'cold war' between the Western alliance and the Soviet Bloc. However, there are other forms of capitalism than the American one, and enterprise flourishes in many of them.

  - Dependency: There is a danger that, in trying to promote enterprise, initiatives which use means such as grants have instead promoted dependency. Learned helplessness is a recognised medical problem in which patients learn to become dependent on external assistance and cannot do without it even when their original complaint is cured. Business can suffer from similar problems.

  - Clusters and competitiveness: Michael Porter has shown that clusters of strong competing domestic rivals can develop strong international competitiveness. It is a truly enterprising culture that gives the clusters their effectiveness.

- Social enterprises are organisations whose aims include both economic and social purposes. They, and the social economy to which they contribute, are concepts that challenge the traditional division of organisational activity into either economic or social categories. Social enterprises include community enterprises in which enterprise is applied specifically for community benefit.

- Enterprise is frequently promoted as something positive. It does however have a number of real or potential drawbacks. Enterprise involves risk; there can be no guarantee that an enterprising act will succeed, and when it fails there will be some loss. Enterprise is not the magic cure-all some people seem to want it to be. In the business context in particular some failure is to be expected. It can be minimised and it can produce useful lessons, but it can have unfortunate consequences for those involved. Enterprise can be an important element in economic improvement, but a distorted view of it and its benefits is sometimes presented, with the result that enterprise promotion is seen by some as just propaganda for a nasty world of shady commercial dealing.

- Enterprise does however have a future. The pattern of work and business is changing. More or different people will be working in and/or establishing their own small businesses. The reasons for this include technological developments, an increasing demand for flexibility and service, changing life styles and changes in markets. The result is that the future, or at least a significant part of it, is likely to belong to the enterprising.

QUESTIONS, ESSAY AND DISCUSSION TOPICS

- Do we need more enterprise?
- Can enterprise flourish only under capitalism and, if so, what sort of capitalism?
- 'A social enterprise is not a real enterprise and does not require the same discipline and purpose.' Discuss.
- In enterprise the risk of failure is often underrated. For many people the potential rewards are too few and the risks too great to justify entry into business. Is this true?
- Should we intervene to help failing businesses or failed entrepreneurs?
- Is small business the wealth-creating model for the future?
- Where would you strike the balance between earning and living (see Case 5.1)?

Suggestions for further reading and information

S. Carter and D. Jones-Evans (eds), *Enterprise and Small Business Development* (London: Financial Times/Prentice-Hall, 2000), Chapter 3.

W. K. Bolton and J. L. Thompson, *Entrepreneurs: Talent, Temperament, Techniques* (Oxford: Butterworth-Heinemann, 2000), Chapter 10.

C. Handy, 'Tocqueville Revisited: The Meaning of American Prosperity', *Harvard Business Review*, 79 (2001), pp. 57–63.

C. Whyley, *Risky Business: The Personal and Financial Costs of Small Business Failure* (London: Policy Studies Institute, 1998).

S. Bridge, B. Murtagh and K. O'Neill, *Understanding the Social Economy and the Third Sector* (Basingstoke: Palgrave, 2008).

References

1. P. D. Reynolds, M. Hay, W. D. Bygrave, S. M. Camp and E. Autio, *Global Entrepreneurship Monitor 2000 Executive Report* (Kansas City, Mo.: Kauffman Centre for Entrepreneurial Leadership at the Ewing Marion Kauffman Foundation, 2001).
2. R. Burrows, *Deciphering the Enterprise Culture: Entrepreneurship, Petty Capitalism and the Restructuring of Britain* (London: Routledge, 1991), p. 5.
3. Ibid., p. 9.
4. W. Hutton, 'Ethics Man Finds No Place In the New Enterprise Era', *Guardian* ©, 21 March 1994.
5. A. Smith, *An Enquiry into the Nature and Causes of the Wealth of Nations* (Edinburgh: Adam and Charles Black, 1882; first published in 1776).
6. For a discussion of Smith's and Hayek's contribution to economic theory, see D. King, *The New Right* (Basingstoke: Macmillan (now Palgrave Macmillan), 1987), pp. 70–90.
7. W. Hutton, *The State We're In* (London: Vintage, 1996), p. 237.
8. M. Friedman, *Capitalism and Freedom* (Chicago: University of Chicago Press, 1962), p. 200.
9. W. Keegan, *The Spectre of Capitalism* (London: Random House, 1992), p. 106, cited in M. Thomas, 'Marketing: In Chaos or Transition?' *European Journal of Marketing*, 28 (1994), pp. 55–62.
10. Hutton (1996), op. cit., p. xxviii.
11. Department of Economic Development, *Competing in the 1990s: The Key to Growth* (Belfast: Department of Economic Development), p. 44.

12. M. Porter, 'The Competitive Advantage of Nations', *Harvard Business Review*, March-April (1990), pp. 82.
13. Ibid., p. 74.
14. G. Redding, 'Three Styles of Asian Capitalism', in 'Mastering Enterprise', No. 7, *Financial Times*, 13 January 1997, p. 11.
15. K. Gold, 'Must We Buy Schooling from Marks and Spencer?' *The Observer*, 21 January 1990.
16. D. Storey, *Understanding the Small Business Sector* (London: Routledge, 1994).
17. R. T. Boden and A. R. Nucci, 'On the Survival Prospects of Men's and Women's New Business Ventures', *Journal of Business Venturing*, 15 (2000), pp. 347–62.
18. E. Chell and S. Baines, 'Does Gender Affect Business Performance? A Study of Micro-Businesses in Business Services in the UK', *Entrepreneurship and Regional Development*, 10 (1998), pp. 117–35.
19. P Burns, *Entrepreneurship and Small Business* (London: Palgrave (now Palgrave Macmillan), 2001).
20. Figures from http://stats.berr.gov.uk (accessed 18 January 2007).
21. Statistics from www.dcs.gov.uk/statistics (accessed 18 January 2008).
22. Z. J. Acs and D. A. Gerlowski, *Managerial Economics and Organisation* (Englewood Cliffs, NJ: Prentice-Hall, 1996), p. 249.
23. N. Meager, 'Does Unemployment Lead to Self-Employment?' *Small Business Economics*, 4 (1992), pp. 87–103.
24. D. Brooksbank, 'Self-Employment and Small Firms', in *Enterprise and Small Business*, edited by S. Carter and D. Jones-Evans, (London: Financial Times/Prentice-Hall, 2000), pp. 7–31.
25. R. Rigby, 'There's No Disgrace in an Honest Business Failure', *Management Today*, July (2001), pp. 74–6.
26. R. G. McGrath, 'Falling Forward : Real Options Reasoning and Entrepreneurial Failure', *Academy of Management Review*, 24 (1999). pp. 13–31.
27. McGrath, op. cit., pp. 23.
28. McGrath, op. cit. , pp. 24.
29. C. Handy, *The Age of Unreason* (London: Arrow, 1990).
30. C. Alter and J. Hage, *Organisations Working Together* (Newbury Park, Calif.: Sage, 1993), p. 14.
31. E. H. Schein and W. G. Bennis, *Personal and Organisation Change Through Group Methods* (New York: Wiley, 1965), p. 7.
32. F. Moulaert and O. Ailenei, 'Social Economy, Third Sector and Solidarity Relations: A Conceptual Synthesis from History to Present', *Urban Studies*, 42(11), pp. 2037–53.
33. Ibid.
34. Ibid.
35. Ibid.
36. A. Amin, A. Cameron and R. Hudson, *Placing the Social Economy* (London: Routledge, 2002), pp. 3–4.
37. Policy Action Team 3, *HM Treasury, Enterprise and Social Exclusion*, 1999 (www.hm-treasury.gov.uk/docs/1999/pat3.html, accessed 1 March 2000), paragraph 5.2.
38. http://ec.europa.eu/enterprise/entrepreneurship/social_economy.htm, accessed 3 August 2007.
39. http://ec.europa.eu/enterprise/entrepreneurship/coop/index.htm, accessed 3 August 2007.
40. J. Kendall, *The Voluntary Sector* (London: Routledge, 2003), p. 1.
41. J. Pearce, *Social Enterprise in Anytown* (London: Calouste Gulbenkian Foundation, 2003), p. 66.
42. From the wikipedia entry on social economy (en.wikipedia.org accessed July 2006).
43. www.wikipedia.org/wiki/Social_Economy, accessed 7 December 2006.
44. Amin, A. et al., op. cit., pp. 9–11.
45. P. Lloyd, in *Rethinking the Social Economy*, CU2 Contested Cities – Urban Universities, Queen's University Belfast, 2006.
46. http://ec.europa.eu/enterprise/entrepreneurship/coop/index.htm accessed 28 March 2007.
47. European Network for Economic Self Help and Local Development (1997) *Key Values and Structures of Social Enterprise in Western Europe: Concepts and Principles for the New Economy* (Berlin: Technologie-Netwzwerk with 47 European Network for Economic Self Help and Local Development).
48. Cabinet Office/Office of the Third Sector, *Social Enterprise Action Plan: Scaling New Heights*, November 2006, p. 10.

Enterprise and small business

Introduction

Part II of this book explores the concepts of enterprise and entrepreneurship and why they are the subject of interest. It shows that the word 'enterprise', and now also the word 'entrepreneurship', have a range of meanings: from the narrow meaning of enterprise, referring to small businesses and the act of starting them, to the broad meaning of enterprise as a set of personal attributes and behaviours that can be demonstrated in a wide variety of different situations and contexts.

The use of the word 'enterprise' to relate specifically to small business is, however, very widespread, and it is the economic and social benefits that small businesses are adjudged to bring that are the prime reasons for the wide interest in enterprise. Part II therefore looks at this aspect of enterprise in more detail.

The specific aspect of small businesses that distinguishes them from other businesses is obviously their size. Because of this they tend to have some features in common, but they are by no means all identical. There are many varieties of small business, which differ for instance in their stage of development, in their business sector, or in the attitudes and aptitudes of their owners. Small businesses are not however just smaller versions of big businesses. They have a number of distinctive features that are not always obvious to the untutored observer. Those who wish to understand small businesses therefore need insight into the specific nature of such organisations. The distinctive features of small business are explored in Chapter 6.

Chapter 7 looks at business development issues at the pre-start and start-up stages, and at the key role of the entrepreneur in this. For those who wish to see more business start-ups, understanding what influences them is important.

Chapter 8 looks at the post start-up stages of business development. If small businesses are popular because they provide employment potential, growth businesses are particularly desirable because they are fewer in number and create disproportionately more jobs. But businesses also stay static, decline and/or terminate, and businesses at each of these stages have particular issues to address.

Although the aim of small business growth policy has been to encourage small businesses to get bigger, the terms 'enterprise' and 'small business' still tend to be used synonymously and, from the perspective of the bigger business, some aspects of 'small' can still seem to be 'beautiful'. Chapter 9 therefore looks at the advantages of small size from this perspective. It considers attempts by bigger organisations to continue to be entrepreneurial, a process often known as 'corporate entrepreneurship' or 'intrapreneurship', and at situations where it really does seem to be an advantage to be small. An alternative view of this is the interest in the profile of an entrepreneurial organisation developed out of the entrepreneurial venture.

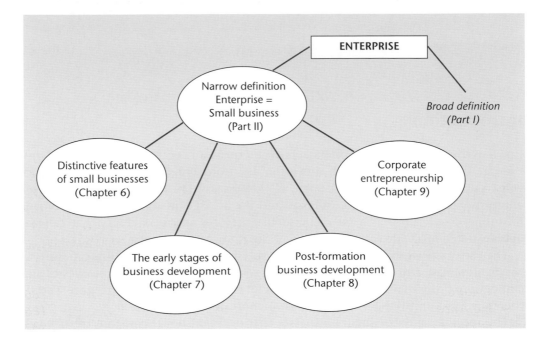

CHAPTER 6
Small business: definitions, characteristics and needs

Contents

KEY CONCEPTS

This chapter covers:

- The definitions of a small business.
- The different perspectives provided by taking the entrepreneur and the business as the core unit of study.

- The key areas of difference between small and big business.
- Other variations in small businesses, including family firms, and the different issues relevant to them.
- The implications of being small.
- The statistics on job creation by small businesses.

LEARNING OBJECTIVES

By the end of this chapter the reader should:

- Know the main definitions of a small business.
- Be aware of the major changes in SME numbers and employment in the UK.
- Understand the different perspectives produced by taking either the business or the entrepreneur as the unit of study.
- Appreciate the differences in types of small business.
- Understand other variations in the types of small businesses and the different issues relevant to them.
- Understand some of the problems in interpreting statistics on the role of small businesses in job creation.

Introduction

This chapter seeks to explore further what is meant by the term 'small business'. Small businesses are not just small versions of big businesses. They have a number of distinctive features which are not always obvious to the untutored observer. Nevertheless they are, in many other respects, heterogeneous rather than homogeneous. This chapter therefore considers some of the many different definitions of a small business. It considers small businesses at different stages of their development, in different sectors and under different types of ownership. It seeks to establish what they have in common, as well as the range of their diversity. It also looks at their job creation potential, as this is of interest to many people.

Definitions

ILLUSTRATION 6.1
Some official definitions of a small business

United Kingdom

In the UK, for statistical purposes, the Department for Business, Enterprise and Regulatory Reform (BERR), and the Department for Trade and Industry (DTI) before it, have used the following definitions (at the time of writing, November 2007):

- micro-firm: up to nine employees
- small firm: up to 49 employees (includes micro)
- medium firm: 50–249 employees
- large firm: 250 employees and over.

Companies Act

Section 249 of the Companies Act of 1985 states that a company is 'small' if it satisfies at least two of the following criteria:

- a turnover of not more than £2.8 million
- a balance sheet total of not more than £1.4 million
- not more than 50 employees.

A medium-sized company must satisfy at least two of the following criteria:

- a turnover of not more than £11.2 million
- a balance sheet total of not more than £5.6 million
- not more than 250 employees.

Value added tax

In the UK the VAT registration threshold is a turnover of £67,000 and the deregistration limit is a turnover of £65,000.

Small Firms Loan Guarantee Scheme

The Small Firms Loan Guarantee scheme applies to businesses with fewer than 200 employees and with a turnover of not more than £5.6 million. The lending limit to all SMEs is now £250,000 and the scheme covers 75 per cent of the loan.

Corporation tax

The Small Companies Rate of corporation tax applies to businesses with taxable profits of up to £300,000 and a marginal rate applied to profits between £300,000 and £1,500,000. Over that the full rate applies. The SME tax rate is 19 per cent and the full rate is 30 per cent.

British Bankers' Association (BBA)

For BBA statistical purposes, small businesses are defined as those having an annual debit account turnover of up to £1 million per year.

European Commission

In 1996 the European Commission adopted the following definitions of SMEs:

Maximum	Micro-enterprise	Small	Medium-sized
Number of employees	10	50	250
Turnover (€ million)	N/a	7	40
Balance sheet total (€ million)	N/a	5	27
Independence criterion*	N/a	25%	25%

* The independence criterion refers to the maximum percentage that may be owned by one, or jointly owned by several, enterprises not satisfying the same criteria.

To qualify as an SME both the number of employees and the independence criteria must be met, and either of the turnover or the balance sheet total criteria.

The Bolton Report in 1971 was very significant in developing the understanding of small businesses in the UK. It defined a small business by reference to an ideal type:

> First, in economic terms, a small firm is one that has a relatively small share of its market. Secondly an essential characteristic of a small firm is that it is managed by its owners or part-owners in a personalised way, and not through the medium of a formalised management structure. Thirdly, it is also independent in the sense that it does not form part of a larger enterprise and that the owner-managers should be free from outside control in taking their principal decisions.[1]

This summary of definitions indicates that, although small businesses have been the subject of considerable interest since the Bolton Report, today there is still no single, clear, precise and widely accepted definition of what is a small business. Different definitions exist, often for different purposes such as the application of support policy, taxation or legislation. Many people, however, feel that they know what is meant by a 'small business'. It is one that has few employees, a low turnover, little or no formal structure and is usually managed by one person, who is also the business owner. It is these characteristics that make a small business behave in the way it does, and many feel that the key point at which a growing business ceases to be small is when it has to change its organisational and control system, from the loose and informal to the structured and formal, if it is to continue to be effective. However, most definitions use the size of the business as its distinguishing feature, presumably because that is easier to measure. Definitions vary widely in the way they measure the size of a small business. Some use turnover, which can change over time with inflation, but most go for employment, which, as already indicated, also happens to be the benefit which very often provides the rationale for small business support. Even when employment is used there are different definitions. The EU definition of an SME* used to be one that had fewer than 500 employees, but the limit is now 250. (See Illustration 6.1.) The US Small Business Administration uses 500 as the limit for its remit. Elsewhere the limit is

---

* The term 'small business' is, on occasion, used to embrace medium-sized businesses also. To avoid confusion, however, the now ubiquitous term 'SME' (small and/or medium-sized enterprise) has entered the language, particularly that of policy-makers.

often set at 200, which many take as being closer to the size that forces a change in organisational structure. Some use 100 as the limit, and there are some small business agencies which use 50.

The above definitions are almost entirely quantitative, but there are qualitative ones. Small businesses tend to share a number of qualities. They are generally businesses that serve only local customers and have only a very limited share of the available market; that are owned by one person, or by a small group of people; and are managed by their owners, who deal with all management issues, usually with little other help; and they are independent businesses, not parts of, or owned by, larger companies.

A definition based on only one of these qualities would be in danger of excluding some businesses that others would regard as small. A number of qualitative characteristics should therefore be included. One attempt to do so has been to define a small business as one which possesses at least two of the following four characteristics:

- Management of the business is independent. Usually the managers are also the owners.
- Capital and ownership are provided by an individual or a small group.
- The areas of operation are mainly local, with the workers and owners living in one home community. However the market need not be local.
- The relative size of the business within its industry must be small when compared with the biggest units in the field. This measure can be in terms of sales volume, number of employees or other significant comparisons.[2]

Most of the definitions of a small business given above are, however, in effect only attempts to provide a proxy for what is the essence of 'smallness' in business units. Smallness is about being autonomous yet having limited resources of manpower, time, skills, expertise and finance, and therefore having to be dependent on external support. It is about having to cope with greater uncertainty and about carrying greater risk while having few opportunities for risk spreading. It is also about:

- the influence of ownership on entrepreneurial behaviour
- having greater individual authority
- managing a total activity and carrying total responsibility; being closer to customers, and being potentially more flexible and adaptable; managing networks of suppliers, customers, and financiers
- paying greater attention to business opportunities
- taking a strategic approach while also having close and informal control structures and communication channels
- embracing a 'can-do' culture.

These are the things that being small means and that present challenges and opportunities different from those in larger businesses.

Some UK SME statistics

Table 6.1 provides a statistical profile of business enterprises in the UK at the start of 2006. The importance of SMEs can be seen from the figures that indicate that SMEs

Table 6.1 A recent statistical profile of business enterprises in the UK

Number of enterprises, employment and turnover in the whole economy by number of employees, UK, start 2006

	Number				Percent		
	Enterprises	Employment (/1,000)	Employees (/1,000)	Turnover (/£ million)	Enterprises	Employment	Employees	Turnover
All enterprises	4,550,930	29,331	25,460	2,820,025	100.0	100.0	100.0	100.0
With no employees	3,270,105	3,570	440	207,617	71.9	12.2	1.7	7.4
All employers	1,280,830	25,761	25,020	2,612,408	28.1	87.8	98.3	92.6
1-4	845,375	2,376	1,845	232,507	18.6	8.1	7.2	8.2
5-9	218,795	1,530	1,429	161,726	4.8	5.2	5.6	5.7
10-19	118,120	1,638	1,584	173,370	2.6	5.6	6.2	6.1
20-49	60,575	1,874	1,840	217,197	1.3	6.4	7.2	7.7
50-99	18,925	1,316	1,308	164,223	0.4	4.5	5.1	5.8
100-199	9,120	1,271	1,267	170,404	0.2	4.3	5.0	6.0
200-249	1,810	404	403	66,932	0.0	1.4	1.6	2.4
250-499	3,700	1,287	1,285	211,081	0.1	4.4	5.0	7.5
500 or more	4,415	14,065	14,058	1,214,967	0.1	48.0	55.2	43.1

Source: BERR Enterprise Directorate Analytical Unit.

together (0–249 employees) accounted for nearly half of the employment (47.6 per cent) and turnover (49.4 per cent) in the UK economy. Small enterprises alone (0 to 49 employees) accounted for 37.4 per cent of employment and 35.2 per cent of turnover. Small businesses are clearly important to the economy, but so too are larger businesses.

The change in some of the statistics over the previous years is of interest. In 2000 the number of 'all enterprises' was about 3.8 million. In 2003 it was just over 4 million and, as shown above, for 2006 it has increased to over 4.5 million, a 20 per cent increase in six years. The number of businesses with no employees was 2.6 million in 2000 but had increased to nearly 3.3 million in 2006: an increase of 25 per cent. These were the highest levels of 'all enterprises', and incidentally of businesses with no employees (self-employed people), since the time series began in 1994. The increase in the numbers of self-employed people is in the context of a growing labour market which might imply that people are being pulled into entrepreneurship rather than being pushed.

(NB: In the statistics shown in Table 6.1 the 'employment' figures given include every person employed by the business, including the business owner-manager(s), and the 'employees' figures do not include the owner-manager(s). A full review of UK business statistics, including survival rates, is available on the BERR web site: www.berr.gov.uk.)

The entrepreneur or the business

The previous section gives some definitions of a small business and information on the number of small businesses in the UK. However, before going on to explore other aspects of the concept of a small business, another issue should be highlighted. So far the emphasis has been on the firm, on the enterprise or business created, and that tends to imply that it is that entity which is the primary unit of analysis. It is easy to see why there should be such a focus. It is the business which can be seen to start or to end, it is the business which has the turnover or employment which can be measured, and it is the business which delivers things people want such as jobs and economic growth.

This existence of the business as a potential subject for consideration is clearest when the business is a separate legal entity, such as a limited company, and is least clear when the business is the activity of an individual operating as a 'sole trader'. The assumption may have been that the sole trader should be seen as an embryonic limited company which has not yet made it, but nevertheless the lack of a clear distinction between a sole trader and his or her business points to an important consideration. The business is not only the creation of the person but is also the expression of the person, even when the business is legally separate from that person. A person may start up and close down a business but the person will still continue to exist. The closure of the business is not therefore the end of the matter. It might, as in the case of a 'habitual entrepreneur' (see below), be followed by the start-up of another business and the reason for the closure may lie with the entrepreneur rather than with the business. To make sense of the totality of the entrepreneurial process it is therefore necessary to take the entrepreneur as the focus and unit of investigation, not the business.

Analysing the small business process from this different perspective also reveals another potentially useful focus: that of the group, or cluster, of businesses linked together in some way through common ownership and management by an entrepreneur or entrepreneurial team.[3] Measured on the performance of their latest venture, habitual entrepreneurs may seem to perform no better than novice entrepreneurs, whereas if the performance is measured across the cluster it has been found to be considerably better. Indeed is it quite likely that new firm formation within a cluster is a growth mechanism and therefore that, while individual firms in a cluster may not grow, the cluster does.[4] It may also be relevant to realise that the individual businesses in such a cluster may not, at least under the EU definition, be considered to be SMEs because they do not satisfy the ownership criterion.

Another relatively common form of very small business is the part-time business. Here, looked at from the perspective of the business, a part-time business may seem to indicate a lack of seriousness, but from the point of view of the person it may be a very sensible arrangement. Therefore, in exploring many aspects of the subject of business development, the fundamental unit should be the entrepreneur, not the firm.

Novice and habitual entrepreneurs, serial and portfolio entrepreneurs

There are entrepreneurs who start just one business and those who start more than one. The term 'habitual entrepreneur' was coined to describe a person who is not satisfied with starting just one business but who goes on to start others also, either in sequence or simultaneously. He or she was considered to be a special type of entrepreneur, different from the supposedly more common 'novice entrepreneur'. Research, for instance by Scott and Rosa, has indicated that multiple business ownership is more common than had been suspected and has more variety.[5] Habitual entrepreneurs have been subdivided therefore into 'serial entrepreneurs', who start a succession of businesses but only manage one at a time, and 'portfolio entrepreneurs', who start a succession of businesses and keep some or all of them going at the same time.[6]

Scott and Rosa have studied the process of multiple business ownership, considering it to be 'fundamental to understanding the process of capital accumulation in a free enterprise capitalist economy'.[7] Their work on the diversity of business foundations revealed many differences between entrepreneurs as regards the kind of ventures they started, the strategies they followed and the management practices they adopted which, due to the considerable heterogeneity of individual entrepreneurs, could only be categorised on very broad criteria (see Table 6.2).

Once it is recognised and looked for, habitual entrepreneurship appears to be very common. Rosa and Scott looked at the extent of habitual entrepreneurship in Scotland and found that up to 40 per cent of new limited companies had multiple-ownership and/or cross-linkages with other firms.[8] Others have explored the implications this has for the businesses concerned. Research by Westhead et al. into habitual entrepreneurs in Scotland, yielded information on business performance in 2001 which indicated that the average sales revenues reported by portfolio entrepreneurs were higher than those reported by serial entrepreneurs by a factor of three times, and higher than those reported by novice entrepreneurs by a factor of five times.[9] Marked differences in employment patterns were also detected. In 2001, in

Table 6.2 Three dimensions of habitual entrepreneurship

Dimension 1: The background and nature of the habitual entrepreneur

- Multiple venture founders from corporate backgrounds, who tended to be more deliberate in their formation of business clusters and who used more formal management practices in their new ventures

- Multiple venture founders from financial and consultancy backgrounds, who tended to start their careers as management consultants or financial advisers, as well as high-technology engineers founding new firms with limited managerial experience

- Multiple venture founders from non-corporate backgrounds (mostly associated with traditional family businesses), who were especially creative in reacting to new opportunities but who often lacked the resources or capability to take full advantage of them

- Non-entrepreneurial habitual founders, who were involved in several businesses but as a partner of the true driving entrepreneur

Dimension 2: The nature of ventures founded

- Related diversifications: by far the most common form of new venture

- New types of mainstream venture: a complete change of direction (rare)

- Pilot businesses: 'suck-it-and-see' experimental businesses

- Phantom businesses: non trading ventures set up to trade but which never got off the ground

- Financial management businesses: businesses set up to manage the funds flowing from other businesses

- Buyouts, mergers and acquisitions

- Holding companies

Dimension 3: The strategies used to create and manage ventures

- Competitive efficiency: many new ventures did appear to some respondents to have resulted in some operational advantage

- Serendipity: entrepreneurial opportunism can appear to be an unplanned and serendipitous process

- Strategic accommodation of serendipity: small business owners can have a high degree of strategic awareness

- Strategic management of adversity: the tendency of most entrepreneurs when faced with recession or financial difficulty is to 'pull in their horns' and reduce or eliminate the formation of new ventures

Source: Based on P. Rosa, 'Entrepreneurial Process of Business Cluster Formation and Growth by "Habitual Entrepreneurs"', *Entrepreneurship Theory and Practice* (1998), 22, pp.48–51. Reprinted with the permission of Baylor University, the publisher of *Entrepreneurship Theory and Practice*.

terms of total employment, portfolio entrepreneur firms were on average about three times larger than serial entrepreneur firms and about four times larger than novice entrepreneur firms. The authors of the study suggested that such findings highlighted the need for policy-makers and practitioners to target policies towards the varying needs of each type of entrepreneur rather than provide broad 'blanket' policies to all types of entrepreneur.

In contrast, however, a study of the changing nature of entrepreneurship over a 30-year period (the 1970s,1980s and 1990s) in the 'low' enterprise area of Teesside found that 'portfolio entrepreneurs performed no better than others who did not own another business' and that 'the performance of serial entrepreneurs was even worse.'[10] The apparent difference between these findings and those of Westhead et al. may be due to the nature of the sample used. Teesside is associated with a decline in heavy manufacturing and subsequent rates of high unemployment whereas the Scottish study relates to a larger area of the country with a more diverse economic performance and used a different array of research methods. Nevertheless the different findings do suggest that local factors may be important and that the conclusions of such studies might therefore have limited application outside areas studied.

The importance of location is further supported in a study of rural farmers in a specific area of England (East Anglia) which had, at the time of the study, the fastest growing population of any region of the UK, the lowest levels of unemployment and the highest levels of self-employment.[11] The study demonstrated that there is a core of farmers who have multiple business interests and that these additional business activities made a substantial contribution to both the number of enterprises and employment creation. In presenting these conclusions, Carter commented that within small business studies the conventional use of the firm as the sole unit of analysis appears to have obscured not only the range of activities of individual entrepreneurs, but also their wider economic contribution.[12]

Owners' motivation

As Elizabeth Chell and her colleagues reported (see Chapter 3) there are different types of entrepreneur with different clusters of traits and behaviours. Different types will have different motivations and these can affect their businesses. There will be a lot of difference between a business developed by a sole owner who wants enough income to support his or her lifestyle and a business currently of the same size developed by a group of investors with a view to maximising its future value.

Owners' motivations (see also Chapter 8) have been divided into three broad categories:

- *Lifestyle*: This is the description often given to a business run by an individual because it not only facilitates, but is also part of, the lifestyle that individual wants to have. Examples of lifestyle businesses are frequently to be found in art or craft businesses where the owner lives to practise that craft rather than only practising that craft in order to live.

- *Comfort-zone*: A comfort-zone business is typically one that provides its owner with sufficient returns for the level of comfort he or she wants in life. Unlike in the case of the lifestyle business, the basis of the business is less important than the level of benefit it can provide in return for a reasonable amount of effort. In some places the comfort-zone business has been characterised as the 'BMW syndrome'. This is where the level of comfort desired includes the possession of recognised symbols of success. Once that level of comfort is reached, however, there is little incentive to build the business further.

- *Growth*: The 'growth' business is the one that approaches closest to what to many is the ideal business, namely one where the owner wishes to manage the business to maximise its earning potential, especially for the future.

It is the influence of the owner, in whatever category his or her motivations may fall, that is a major determinant of how a business behaves, and the particular ways in which small businesses behave is considered further in the next chapter.

Distinctive characteristics of small businesses

The section above highlighted the importance of recognising the influence of the entrepreneur behind the business. Nevertheless the more traditional approach to considering small businesses, and the one used in most research and writing about enterprise, has been to take the business as the key unit of analysis. Both approaches can have their uses but this chapter is primarily concerned with businesses and so the remaining sections generally take the business-centred approach.

> The differences in the administrative structure of the very small and the very large firms are so great that in many ways it is hard to see that the two species are of the same genus. ... We cannot define a caterpillar and then use the same definition for a butterfly.
>
> Dame Edith Penrose[13]

Many commentators, including Gibb, have identified differences between the behaviour of small and big businesses, differences manifest in a range of characteristics.[14] Some of these have already been indicated in Chapter 2, where the meaning of 'enterprise' was explored. Others significant differences include those discussed below.

An absence of functional managers
Often the management of a small business resides with one person. The advantage of this can be that an overall view of management, including production, finance and marketing, is taken instead of there being a conflict between the different functions. On the other hand, knowledge of such functions may not be evenly developed and in some areas may be severely lacking.

On the job learning
Many small business owner-managers have acquired most of their business knowledge on the job. They will often have been in the job a long time and may therefore have a deep experience, but not necessarily a broad one or an objective and informed view. The business systems employed are likely to be of their own devising, based on experience, and are unlikely to be changed unless experience also suggests it is necessary.

Investment and resources
Money invested in the business is often personal money, not that of impersonal investors. There can therefore be a reluctance to spend this money on anything except the bare essentials, for short-term obvious returns. More formal investment appraisal methods are not seen as being as useful as a 'feel' for what is right. Similarly, the time needed for formal 'training' or review is seen as both an unaffordable distraction from the real work of the business and as earning a return that is more theoretical than practical. Change, where it occurs, is likely to be the response to short-term need rather than the result of long-term strategy.

Discontinuities

There are thresholds and discontinuities in a small business that do not occur in a bigger one. In a bigger business, for instance, increasing capacity by 10 per cent in a key department to cope with a 10 per cent increase in turnover may be relatively straightforward. In a small business however there may be only two people in the department, who are already fully loaded. Extra capacity is still needed, but taking on an extra person would be a 50 per cent increase and may not be justified by the likely extra return. This is also true of getting a second machine when one is only just unable to cope.

Informal systems and procedures

Many businesses start with one person, for whom formal systems and procedures will seem unnecessary. They will grow by taking on new employees in ones and twos and, again, it would seem strange to introduce formal systems for just a few people, who will learn what is going on quickly enough through their direct involvement in the small team. In any case the owner-manager is probably too busy to introduce more formal systems for running the business. This state of affairs is likely to continue until a crisis arises because the business has grown too big to be run informally. As many small businesses never get to that stage, informality in systems and procedures is a characteristic that they share.

Control and organisation in small businesses

Top-down

In a small business the dominant position of the entrepreneur can create a person-centred culture. Consequently the strategy, or absence of one, of the business will correspond to that of the entrepreneur. This top-down approach can be attractive in a stable environment, if the entrepreneur articulates a vision that motivates others. Increasingly, however, even in small businesses, it is often the intelligent employees, more than the entrepreneur, who are in touch with the latest technological, economic and sociological developments. Considerable decision-making discretion, even at the strategic level, may have to be delegated to these individuals, but entrepreneurs are notoriously reluctant to share their power. In a world of discontinuous change that is a drawback.[15]

Decision making

In general, the decision-making process in small businesses will be less formal and more personalised than in larger ventures. In a rational approach, objectives are set, alternatives are investigated and economic evaluations are made of alternatives. In a large business the distance from top to bottom, and the consequent number of layers and communication steps, may mean that the message and the rationale behind it can be distorted. In small businesses the omnipresence of the owners can mean that everyone in the business can hear a clear articulation of the goals and objectives. However, the smallness of the business, and the lack of managerial skills of its owner, can also mean that goals are not articulated at all. Clear objectives facilitate rationality, but rational economic decisions often depend on having access to large amounts of information and the employment of sophisticated quantitative techniques to make sense of it. The lack of resource in small businesses, and their heavy reliance on information gleaned from personal contacts, are unlikely to encourage rational evaluations of alternatives. The information available to decision makers in small businesses will be even more inaccurate, incomplete and time-bounded than in other organisations.[16] In the same way, time horizons for planning, whether formal or informal, will tend to be much shorter than in larger businesses. Moreover, decisions are much more likely to be influenced by an owner-manager's emotions and personal interests than by objective analysis.

Organisational structures

Most work in large organisations is highly specialised, and much of the brainwork is removed from operational tasks. However, an extensive division of tasks, especially at management level, only makes sense when there is a large volume of work; it is no use employing experts if they are underemployed. By definition, a small business does not have a large volume of output and the work must often be done by generalists. Furthermore, organisations tend to perpetuate the fruits of their learning and standardise regularly recurring activities; however, this is sensible only when environmental conditions are stable. In the turbulent environment so characteristic of the small business, change is the order of the day and problem solving is a higher requirement of organisations than efficiency.[17] As a result of these factors, small firms tend to have simple, flexible, non-differentiated structures and flexible work practices, to possess general-purpose rather than specialised machines, and to exhibit few of the features so characteristic of bureaucracies. The general nature of employee skills and flexible production capabilities means that much more of the creative aspects of production can be easily delegated to operators. Faced with an order from a customer, operators and their managers are more likely to plan operations jointly.

Control

If the all-pervasive control mechanisms of large organisations are absent, how do managers in small businesses exercise control? Decision making can be considered to take place at three levels: strategic, administrative and operational. In the bigger business these will each happen at different levels of the organisation and involve different people. In small businesses they are, as often as not, all done by the same person with no formal or recognised boundaries or hierarchical split amongst them. There is therefore a lack of clarity about the type of decision being taken, with little distinction in thought between strategic and tactical decisions. Once a decision is taken, control through standardisation, performance measurement and bureaucratic structures is often absent in small businesses. Instead the presence of the owners, or their representatives, will mean that control is exercised by direct supervision. These individuals are never far away, and the numerous work-related discussions that take place will confirm the position of managers in an overseeing role. Yet this often leads to much speedier decision making and shorter reaction times, which in turn can mean an improved competitive edge.[18]

A lack of objectivity

Another key feature of small businesses is the inability, or unwillingness, of their owners to be objective about them. Instead they frequently identify closely with their businesses, seeing them almost as extensions of themselves. This, and its implications, are considered in more detail later in the chapter.

The implications of being small

Small businesses have assumed an importance in many people's minds, largely, it would seem because of their employment creation and innovation potential. They are classified as small by their size, whether that is measured in terms of their worth, their turnover or their employment. There are, however, many differences amongst the businesses in those size categories, and there are many aspects, apart from just their size, that small businesses tend to have in common and where they differ from big businesses. It is for these reasons that they often need to be treated differently.

Some aspects of small businesses that require particular insight if misunderstandings are not to occur are considered in the next chapter. It is, nevertheless, relevant to consider here some of the aspects of small businesses that make them different. These differences can be grouped under the headings of culture, influence, resources and ambition. They encompass some of the crucial differences between small and big businesses for which distinctions by size are only a proxy. They are the reason for a separate analysis and consideration of small businesses as a category distinct from big business.

Culture

The culture of a small business is tied in with the needs, desires and abilities of its owner. He or she tends to focus on independence; flexibility, both from preference and necessity; closeness to the customer and supplier; individual and personal, rather than system, control; working with networks of contractors; tolerating uncertainty; and the shorter-term view rather than the longer one. There can be different types of owner with different needs and desires. (See also Figure 3.3 in Chapter 3.)

For many people however the culture of a small business epitomises enterprise. It can, nevertheless, be argued that, while starting a small business may be enterprising, running it need not be. In the case, for instance, of an inherited family business, running it may be what the person concerned has been expecting and preparing to do, possibly from a young age, and involves little that is new or innovatory. Nevertheless, businesses, and particularly small businesses, are frequently referred to as enterprises, which emphasises this aspect of their culture.

Influence

Small businesses have very little influence over their environments or their markets. Their small size may enable them to respond more quickly to changes in those environments or markets but, unlike their bigger counterparts, they have little influence on these changes. Their job creation potential, especially when combined with groupings to promote combined lobbying, may give them some political influence, but it is unrealistic to assume that they will individually be able to change their markets in the ways they might wish.

As well as their final markets, the intermediate markets or distribution channels of small businesses are also beyond their control. Again, bigger businesses may be able to dictate terms to distributors, or may be able to acquire their own distribution channels through 'vertical integration'. But not the small businesses: they are at the mercy of their distributors, and also their suppliers, to a very considerable extent.

Resources

It is almost invariably the case that small businesses lack sufficient resources. Most of them are started on a financial shoestring and few get cash-rich subsequently. Most therefore do not have easy access to the financial reserves necessary to carry them through a lean period or to utilise a sudden opportunity for expansion.

But it is not just finance which they lack. They are usually short of both management time and management skills. As has already been mentioned, there is often only one person, the owner, in a management role, and this role will embrace all aspects of managing the business. This means both that the amount of management time that can be focused on a problem is very limited and that aspects of management expertise are also likely to be missing, because the single manager is unlikely to be fully conversant with marketing, production, financial, technical, legal and human resource aspects of business.

In the business world, therefore, small may mean poor, but not always. There are examples of small businesses that do make very large profits, and others that, if not wealthy in themselves, have, by virtue of their technology, markets or other intangible assets, been very attractive propositions for prospective investors.

Ambition

In terms of their behaviour, however, the biggest difference between small and big businesses is likely to be that which results from the ambition and goals of their owners and managers. As indicated above, the larger the business, the more likely it is to be run by a professional management trying to maximise its financial value. The converse is that the smaller the business, the more likely it is that it will be run by an owner-manager with an aim based on personal values.

The varieties of small businesses

The stage of development of the business may be the consideration most used for distinguishing different types of business, but there are many others that, although sometimes bewildering in their variety, can help to define the distinctions between different types of businesses and their characteristics.

Industry sector

The average size of businesses can differ widely in different industry sectors. Where the purpose of classifying a business as small or large is in relation to its place in its industry and the influence it might have on that industry, it is important to pick a definition that recognises the average size of businesses in the relevant sector. For instance, in relation to other businesses in the same sector, a ten-person window cleaning business would be very large, while a 100-person car manufacturer would be very small. Examples from Europe show some of the ranges: thus in 1995 the average employment in a coalmining business was 924, in a railway business 996, and in a communications business 376; but in a travel agency 12, in a retail business four and in an estate agency two.[19]

Legal structure

In the UK a number of terms are encountered describing possible forms of business structure:

- *Sole trader*: Operating as a sole trader is the simplest form of business. An individual can start a business in this way with the minimum of fuss. In this situation, however, there is no legal distinction between the assets of the business and those of its owner. Such people are 'self-employed' and subject to income tax.

- *Partnership*: A business can be established as a partnership of a group of individuals doing business together. However, the business does not have a separate legal identity, and each partner is jointly and severally liable for any liability incurred by the partners acting for the business. The liability of the partners is unlimited, except in the case of the less common (in the UK) 'limited partnership'.

- *Company*: A business can be established as a company. The company then has its own separate legal existence independent of that of its owners. If it is a limited company, this limits the liability of its owners. This limit can be achieved by shares, in which case the business has shareholders who together own the business and can receive dividends from its profits in proportion to the number and type of shares they hold, or the limit can be by guarantee. A business limited by guarantee is controlled by its members, who each agree to guarantee its liabilities up to an agreed amount (often £1 each) but who cannot benefit from the distribution of the profits of the business. A company limited by shares can be a public or a private company depending on whether the invitation to subscribe for the shares is open to the public or restricted in certain ways.

- *Co-operative*: Co-operative businesses are governed by different legislation from companies. They have to be registered as co-operatives and they have the benefit of limited liability. A co-operative is owned and controlled by its members, who may for instance be a group of workers or people living in a local community, who want to use the business for the benefit of themselves and/or the community. This can be reflected in the memorandum and articles of association of the business. A workers' co-operative is a business owned and controlled by the people working in it, an approach which can lead to greater involvement and responsibility.

- *Social enterprise*: A form of business also sometimes encountered is the social enterprise or community business. This, however, is not a distinct legal form of business but an intention of the owners of the business to use the returns from the business for the benefit of the community in which the business operates. Many co-operatives are social enterprises. (See also 'Social Enterprise' in Chapter 5.)

There were an estimated 2.8 million sole proprietorships in the UK at the start of 2006, of which just 11 per cent had employees. In that year there were also an estimated

500,000 partnerships of which 37 per cent had employees and about 1.1 million companies of which 60 per cent had employees.

Family businesses

One distinct type of business that is often small is the family business. In the days when craft businesses and farms were virtually the only businesses in existence, it was almost the universal practice for them to be passed on through generations of the same family. It is now widely accepted that family businesses still make a major contribution to many economies and their particular characteristics are therefore worth considering.[20] Recent research suggests that in the United States one household in ten has a family business.[21] Of the 22 million firms in America, between 4 million and 20 million of them (depending on the definition used and the survey carried out) are said to be family businesses, making a contribution to GDP of between 12 and 49 per cent.[22] Most of them are small, with more than 90 per cent of them employing fewer than 20 people; they operate mainly in the service, retail, construction and agricultural sectors; 55 per cent had a turnover of less than $100,000, and three-quarters are run by men. One of the early studies of family businesses in the UK found that, of its sample, 52 per cent operated in the service sector, 44 per cent employed 100 or fewer people, 83 per cent had a turnover in the range £2 million to £50 million, and only 25 per cent of family firms achieved growth rates exceeding 20 per cent per annum.[23] In general, family businesses are smaller and less likely to grow than non-family businesses. However, the UK study was based on the top 6000 UK private companies and all 2000 companies quoted on the London Stock Exchange, and consequently it represents the larger and more prosperous stock of UK family firms. A more realistic representation of the typical British family business is presented by Cromie et al.[24] They found that approximately 45 per cent of their sample traded in the service sector and a similar proportion in manufacturing; that 31 per cent had fewer than ten full-time employees and 81 per cent had fewer than 50; that annual turnover was less than £1 million for half of the sample and less than £5 million for almost 90 per cent. These businesses were therefore typically small; but there are some very large firms amongst them.

One of the problems of identifying and describing family businesses is the variety of definitions. One researcher identified more than 20 different definitions[25] but there are a number of common themes. Table 6.3 is an attempt to summarise a recent review of definitions used in US research on the matter which shows that ownership and control by family members, the degree of family involvement in a business, and the intention or practice of transferring ownership and/or control from generation to generation are for many people the key issues in characterising family businesses.[26]

Some of the confusion arises because there are various types of family business.[27] It is unlikely, for example, that a micro-business run just by a husband and wife, on the one hand, and on the other the Ahlstrom Corporation in Finland, which has 200 family members, will display similar characteristics of ownership, control, family-to-business interaction and intergenerational transfers. Issues of age, size and numbers of founders and whether family involvement is increasing, stable or declining will influence the business and they way it behaves.

Broader definitions allow for a developmental, flexible approach to family businesses, but most family business research seems to have focused on the firm and to

Table 6.3 Different criteria by which family businesses have been defined

Ownership and management	Family involvement in the business	Generational transfer
Ownership and control by a family unit	Transactions and interaction between two systems: the business and the family	The actual transfer of ownership and control from one generation to another
One family member has to own and manage the business	Interactions involve lots of family members	The intentions to continue transfers between generations
Two or more family members must own and manage the business	Specific family involvement in business decisions and actions	

Source: Based on R. K. Z. Heck and E. Scannell-Trent, 'The Prevalence of Family Businesses from a Household Sample', *Family Business Review* (1999), 12, pp.210–11.

have considered that family matters are merely an adjunct to that.[28] In line with the suggestion above that often a focus on the entrepreneur provides a better perspective on business development, it has been argued that for family businesses the focus of interest should be on households and that the two-way interaction between business and family dynamics has been neglected in family business research.[29]

Much of the traditional research into the family firm, however, has often been based on a frame of reference in which the family business was regarded as the core system and the family itself was viewed 'only as a component of the business environment'.[30] Other models however recognise that businesses and families are independent systems with each having resources, processes and goals. In a family business context there are interactions between these systems but 'family issues are seen as disabling the effective working of the (business) system'.[31] As a result it is often argued that it is good practice to keep family and business affairs separate. Family business researchers have often used a model of family businesses which sees them as rational units which pursue economic goals. The assumption is then made that family feelings, values and dynamics have a detrimental influence on the business.[32]

This line of reasoning leads to conclusions that family businesses are less efficient than non-family business. Nevertheless, family businesses are reported to be relatively long-lived, with 60 per cent of the family firms in one survey[33] having been established for over 30 years, compared with only 35 per cent of their non-family counterparts. And their managements had longer tenure: over two-thirds of the family businesses had been under the same management for eight years compared with only one-third of non-family businesses.

The problems of family firms

Cromie et al. found that families are very keen to control the issue of shares and are not keen on selling shares to raise finance for growth, that family members dominate boards and senior management positions, and that families are not keen on using outside advisers. In addition conflicts often arise between parents and their offspring, between siblings and between family and non-family personnel. Furthermore, managerial succession is fraught with difficulties with the result that, while there is an impression of stable, conservative, family-dominated institutions, they are often riddled with conflict. The stereotypical image of the family firm is of a rather dismal working environment which offers little opportunity to non-family personnel and which 'becomes sterile and eventually fails'.[34]

The pre-eminence of the controlling family, centralised decision making and long-standing management teams can also result in static thinking. It can make it less likely that new ideas which are essential for long-term development will emerge, and family businesses are often reluctant to use outside advisers, preferring instead the counsel of the family when exploring business matters.

Another difficulty in family businesses can be the conflict that often emerges between family members, in particular founders and their children. The founders often recognise that they have to let go of the reins and develop their successor, but the business is such an important feature of their lives that they fear that the 'loss' of it will damage their self-image and bring their competency into question. Such behaviour can be resented, and tension can build as a result.

Rivalry between siblings is another common source of difficulties. This conflict can reach such a level of seriousness that it has an impact on 'every management decision and magnifies the jockeying for power that goes on in all organisations'.[35] Where multiple family members have an interest in the business they may all expect equal treatment but, in the nature of things, this is rarely possible. Also, they may have different expectations such as short-term riches or long-term growth. As a consequence, various family members may set about gaining power and influence by means of internecine warfare that is often to the detriment of the business.

Conflict is inevitable in organisations, and it must be managed, but its management presents special problems for family-run businesses. Because the conflict can be intense, and because it is transposed from the business to the personal or family arena, it is often suppressed and not resolved. Therefore open discussion and the challenge of ideas, which can help progress in a changing world, may be avoided. In addition, when disputes do occur, the anger and resentment that occurs may also be transferred to family life, and this makes it difficult for family members to break out of a self-defeating cycle of conflict. All this can make rational business decision making exceedingly difficult. In family businesses there are often family concerns that override business sensibilities. Incompetent family members may be retained in post as a favour to shore up deteriorating family relationships, and promotion for otherwise eligible non-family managers may be blocked as a result. Business logic and rationale may thus take a back seat in favour of family preference. There is some evidence that this is especially likely in second-generation family businesses. Attempts to improve the business by recruiting professional managers bring other problems: such managers may find that they can never achieve the measure of recognition, such as promotion to the board, and control that their expertise and contribution merit.

Managing the transition of power and control can often be a difficulty in family businesses, especially the transition from one chief executive to another. There is evidence that this is rarely planned in family firms, and that the transition is, as a result, frequently traumatic. This may contribute to the failure of many family businesses to survive to the second or third generation. This seemingly unprofessional behaviour can come about because owners:

- will not face up to their limited lifespan
- may unconsciously care little about what happens when they are gone
- may resent their successor
- may have an aversion to planning.[36]

Many of the difficulties found in family businesses can be attributed to non-rational behaviour and this view is supported by the traditional approach to family business research. However it has been pointed out that values and perceptions play a key part in the succession process and that concepts from behavioural economics can offer insights into the process. The 'endowment effect' can mean that the person handing over control in a family firm's transition 'is likely to place greater value on the business than is the new leader'.[37] This may well explain why succeeding generations sometimes take risks with or dispose of a business they inherit, and not much can be done about it. However, drawing on notions of 'sunk costs' and 'windfall gains', it is suggested that the more it costs a successor in terms of money, time and effort to buy into a new business, the more highly he or she will value the business and the more likely he or she is to behave in a conservative manner.

It is argued that when people gain assets easily they will not value them highly and will be prepared to gamble with them. In a family business context if a successor is required to display superior performance before succeeding to a position of control, the business will be highly valued and will be treated with discernment. If the succession process is structured in a way which requires successors to invest money and time in the business and to prove themselves before they are handed the reins, they will assume that the business is worth having. Decision making is influenced by rational considerations but values also play an important part.

Advantages of family businesses

There may be drawbacks to family businesses but there are advantages too. When a family group strongly influences management and control, a permanent, solid atmosphere and an esprit de corps can develop. This can often encourage both a closeness among staff and long-lasting relationships with customers, suppliers and other contacts. Family businesses can as a result often build a reputation for dependability and for excellent service.

Staff in family businesses can have a sense of belonging and strong commitment to the goals of the organisation. When the owning family are justly proud of their venture, their enthusiasm and commitment can enthuse non-family staff. This sense of togetherness is a powerful asset in that it can focus the energies of all involved on customers and on the need to serve them.

This commitment can produce a flexibility in terms of working practices, working hours and remuneration. Family members do what is necessary to get a job done. There is little demarcation of duties, and many family members are reluctant to take money out of the business. Some of this flexibility rubs off on non-family members, and this can allow the family business to respond rapidly to changing technological, sociological and economic conditions.

Family businesses are normally free from stock market pressure to produce quick results, since they are not quoted on the market and have no institutional shareholders.

They can, as a result, often take a longer-term view. They are not forced to vacillate, and can pursue a consistent long-term strategy. This long view is reinforced by the permanent nature of their management teams. Permanence of management tends to allow behavioural norms to emerge and a recognised way of doing things to develop.

Family businesses therefore have both advantages and disadvantages, and these are summarised by Kets de Vries in Table 6.4

Family business performance

The result of this combination of advantages and disadvantages can be a business that has staying potential, but which does not usually last beyond the tenure of the founder. For instance, UK data suggest that:[38]

- Fewer than 14 per cent of established family businesses will last until the third generation.

- Fewer than 24 per cent will make it to the second generation.

- The majority of businesses will fail in the first five years.

There is however no conclusive evidence about the performance of family versus non-family businesses. Barbara Dunn, drawing on work in the UK and in the United States, argued that publicly quoted family firms were more profitable than non-family businesses in the 1970s and 1980s.[39] Anecdotal evidence from Finland supports this point of view, where it has been suggested that the $3.3 billion Ahlstrom Corporation prospered

Table 6.4 Advantages and disadvantages of family-controlled businesses

Advantages	Disadvantages

• Long-term orientation
• Greater independence of action
  – less (or no) pressure from stock market
  – less (or no) takeover risk
• Family culture as a source of pride
  – stability
  – strong identification/commitment/motivation continuity in leadership
• Greater resilience in hard times
  – willing to plough back profits
• Less bureaucratic and impersonal
  – greater flexibility
  – quicker decision-making
• Financial benefits
  – possibility of great success
• Knowing the business
  – early training for family members
	• Less access to capital markets may curtail growth
	• Confusing organisation
	  – Messy structure
	  – No clear division of tasks
	• Nepotism
	  – tolerance of inept family members as managers
	  – inequitable reward systems
	  – greater difficulties in attracting professional management
	• Spoiled kid syndrome
	• Internecine strife
	  – family disputes overflow into business
	• Paternalistic/autocratic rule
	  – resistance to change
	  – secrecy
	  – attraction of dependent personalities
	• Financial strain
	  – family members milking the business
	  – disequilibrium between contribution and compensation
	• Succession dramas

by combining the benefits of family involvement with the pursuit of sound business principles.[40] However other British researchers have reported no differences 'in the performance and effectiveness of family and non-family firms'.[41] Inconclusive results can emerge for many reasons but problems with definitions have been alluded to. Definitions are sometimes the product of the working model employed by researchers, and it is noted above that some alternatives to the traditional approach have been proposed recently.

Family business models

It has been suggested that traditional models play down the role of the family in family businesses because they consider family interpersonal and intergenerational relations and processes to be an aspect of the business environment, not of the business. In contrast, Stafford et al. combine a model of family functioning with one of business prosperity to 'yield a model of family business sustainability'.[42] The latter is the product of family and business attainments, together with transactions between the two entities. In this model the family is afforded much more prominence than formerly. It is regarded as a goal-directed system which utilises resources and manages constraints in making transactions which contribute towards desirable goals. If goals are attained a strong sense of achievement results. The achievements can be objective and include such variables as the standard of living. They can also be subjective as represented by such outcomes as satisfaction and successful socialisation. Family resources include physical capital such as property and money, and human capital such as knowledge and effective co-operation. Constraints include such variables as the law, economic realities and societal norms. Families use and combine resources by means of various transactions to achieve desirable goals. Like businesses, families structure their relationships and tasks in various ways to attain their goals.

Stafford et al. present a similar model for businesses. Systems models of organisations are quite common and that of Stafford et al. contains many commonly reported elements but they do point out that the criteria by which success is measured include both objective matters and more subjective issues such as providing a way of life for the family. Business transactions include both resource and interpersonal transformations to reflect both the task-related and emotional transactions in a business.

In a family business there will be regular transactions from family to business and vice versa. Family labour and money might be used by the business, business decisions will reflect the needs of the family, business resources and assets may be used by the family in the pursuit of their objectives, and business managers might allocate time to family needs while at work. In addition to the normal transactions the model includes responses and adjustments by both the family and the business to major changes within either system. In the model, which is reproduced in Figure 6.1, the business and family systems overlap and a sustainable family business is one in which consideration is given to 'the ability of the family and business to co-operate in responding to disruptions in a way that does not impede the success of both'.[43]

The model supports the view that there are different kinds of family business. In some cases the overlap between the systems will be small, and business and family issues will be kept separate. In others there will be a large overlap with lots of transactions and responses between the two systems. An important feature of the model is the attention it devotes to the family, the interaction between family and business, and the introduction

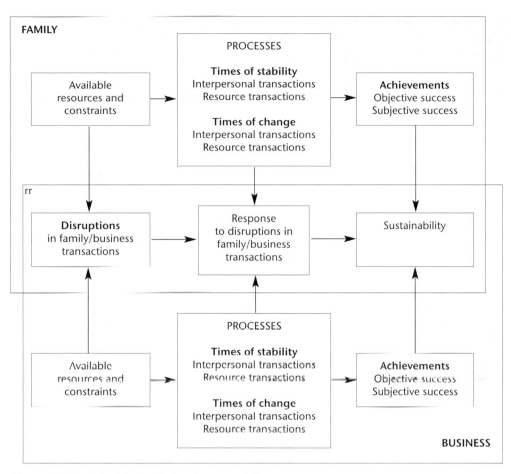

Figure 6.1 Sustainable family business model

Source: K. Stafford, K. A. Duncan, S. Dane and M. Winter, 'A Research Model of Sustainable Family Business', *Family Business Review* (1999), 12, pp.197–208. Reprinted with permission from the Family Firm Institute Inc. All rights reserved.

of the issue of family firm sustainability and its adaptability. It is suggested that the family business is a continuous concept with completely separate and completely embroiled systems only to be found at the extremities of a continuum. However, even where the spheres are kept separate, the family still exerts an influence on the business. The family element makes family businesses unique. To accommodate this reality some American researchers advocate using a household sampling frame rather than a sample composed of firms and they have produced some interesting work on the adjustments that families and businesses make in turbulent times. Both make adjustments but the family accommodates the business more often than conversely.

Women-owned businesses

Another aspect of business ownership which might be expected to have an influence on the business is the gender of the owner. In the UK, there are approximately

1 million self-employed women (7.6 per cent of women in employment) in comparison to 2.7 million self-employed men (17.4 per cent of men in employment). Carter and Shaw point out that there are three main socio-economic issues that influence women's abilities and prospects as business owners:[44] firstly the gender pay-gap; secondly occupational segregation and unequal employment opportunities; and finally work–life balance issues. It is their view that one of the key differences between male and female start-ups is the lower levels of capital that are available to female entrepreneurs. For example, women working in a full-time capacity in the UK earn 17 per cent less than men. This reduced ability to accumulate capital both restricts the type of business that women can start and can restrict future business growth and development. Businesses in fields with low barriers to entry may often have poor growth potential; this restricts the performance of these businesses and could be a factor in the reported incidence of a faster rate of female business exit. As Carter and Shaw (2000) point out, this does not mean that female-owned businesses perform any less well than male businesses; they simply lack the initial resources. This lack of resources is a clear characteristic of female-owned businesses.

Cromie however examined the problems experienced by male and female-owned young businesses and discovered that the problems experienced did not really vary by gender.[45] His sample faced a diverse set of personal problems, including lack of time, having to perform a myriad of duties, working too hard, selling oneself, being too conservative, lacking interpersonal skills, and not being taken seriously. Men and women both experienced personal problems but women recorded more difficulties. This is especially true with respect to a lack of self-confidence and not being taken seriously which, when applied by providers of funds, has led to the under-capitalisation of their businesses. However, women respondents did say that once it was clear that they were committed to making a success of their businesses these problems disappeared.

Carter argues that certain problems were perceived by women to be gender related. These include the 'late payment of bills; a tendency to undercharge; getting business and finding clients; and... the effect of proprietorship upon personal and domestic circumstances'.[46]

Access to business finance

In Britain, Carter reviewed recent work on the financing of women-owned firms and suggested that there have been four recurring problems:[47]

- They have difficulty in obtaining start-up finance.
- They are required to provide guarantees when seeking external finance and they are sometimes unable to provide the requisite collateral.
- They find it more difficult to obtain ongoing finance.
- Bankers tend to have negative stereotypes of women entrepreneurs and discriminate against them.

Results from a study by Carter and Rosa indicate that there is support for some of these propositions but that some differences are accounted for by factors such as firm size and industrial sector.[48] Women do have less start-up finance than men but they use the same sources: personal money, overdrafts and bank loans. There are also gender differences in the use of ongoing finance: women are more likely to use loans while men are more likely to use overdrafts and supplier credit. Carter and Rosa found no support for the propositions about the need for guarantees nor the supposed negative stereotypical images of women among bankers. In general there appears to be little evidence of deliberate discrimination against women.

Ethnic businesses

Another type of small business ownership with distinctive features is the ethnic or minority community-owned business. Immigrants come to their adopted country for a number of reasons. In Britain after the Second World War, immigrants came from the Caribbean, South Asia and other areas to work in various industries which were short of labour, but their intention was often to earn money to send back home and eventually to return home themselves. However, in 1962 entry to the UK from the British Commonwealth was severely restricted and immigrant workers already in Britain's urban areas decided to remain and to bring their families there as well. This led to the development of large ethnic enclaves in inner city areas where, it has been suggested, due to the decline in large-scale industrial employment, to the racism and discrimination they faced in the labour market, and to the revival of the SME sector in the 1980s, people were encouraged to create their own firms.[49]

Ethnic entrepreneurs are considered in Chapter 3, but what, if anything, distinguishes an ethnic business from a small business which happens to be run by someone from an immigrant community? Among the answers suggested are the following:

- A business which draws heavily on a group 'that is socially distinguished (by others or itself) by characteristics of cultural or national origin' for tangible and intangible resources, markets and support constitutes a special kind of small business.[50] Ethnic businesses also develop 'connections and regular patterns of interaction' among people from particular cultural backgrounds.[51] Such ethnic enterprises are commonplace in many parts of the world, but problems with definitions and the sheer diversity of these ventures present difficulties for those who try to quantify the phenomenon.

- Ethnic entrepreneurs in different countries may be from different backgrounds. In Britain Pakistanis, Indian Sikhs, Nigerians, West Indians and East African refugees are common, whereas in the United States, Koreans, Mexicans and Vietnamese are found in large numbers. Nevertheless there is some uniformity in their choice of business activity. For example in North America studies have revealed that ethnic businesses predominate in the wholesale, retail and service sectors, with some presence in light manufacturing.[52] a recent study in Britain of 82 ethnic minority businesses supports the American finding.[53] However, there were variations amongst the different groups of ethnic business and these can be explained partly by the cultural backgrounds of the respondents, their educational backgrounds and the length of time they have been in the country.

- Educational attainment is another factor in the rate of ethnic enterprise and in the nature of the businesses operated. Li identified that amongst the most poorly qualified (with little formal qualifications) it was the Chinese men (34 per cent) and Chinese women (21 per cent) who were most likely to be self-employed, whereas amongst the best qualified, namely those with a first degree or above, it was the Indian and Pakistani/Bangladeshi men who were the most likely to be self-employed.[54] The

Chinese tend to operate predominately micro-businesses whereas the Indian and Pakistani sample tended to operate small to medium-sized enterprises. It was also noted by Li that Black Africans tended to feature amongst the most qualified but showed the lowest incidence of entrepreneurship. Yet this same group, when they did start a business, tended to be amongst the biggest employers, with 25 per cent of Black African businesses employing more than 25 people.

- Two aspects of business in which ethnic businesses rely particularly heavily on others from the same ethnic group are in finding customers and in obtaining labour. Successful businesses must find customers and it is sometimes argued that firms which fully understand the special needs of ethnic groups, and can thus deliver more appropriate benefits, have a competitive advantage. In addition, co-ethnic customers may patronise a particular firm because of a sense of ethnic solidarity with the owner. These factors may confer initial competitive advantage, but it has been argued that sustained competitive advantage will only arise when a business has a strategy which no other business is following and when other businesses cannot duplicate the benefits on offer. However, for ethnic businesses located in service and retail areas where barriers to entry are low, there are many competitors who can follow the same strategy and offer similar benefits. In Britain, therefore, the outcome is increasingly 'a mass of ethnic small business owners trapped in a hostile trading milieu'.[55]

- Labour requirements for small ethnic businesses also come largely from co-ethnics in the community and from the extended family. At start-up, having a supply of part-time labour allows firms to adjust to the ebb and flow of initial workloads and in a way that is cheap and easy to organise. Many of the jobs on offer in the start-up phase are offered to co-ethnics on an informal basis. Indeed, the most noticeable feature of the labour force amongst ethnic businesses is the widespread use of family labour. It is argued that family labour seems attractive in that it helps avoid obstacles to recruitment in the open market, it is flexible and cheap, and problems with the supervision of staff can be avoided.[56] Family members can be loyal and committed to the firm and consequently confer advantages on the firm. There is, however, another side to the employment of family members which is more contentious. In many ethnic businesses women manage the production processes as well as attending to the administrative and financial aspects of the business. Men tend to handle external relationships whilst women manage the workflow. This division of labour by gender could be a source of competitive advantage but there is often an exploitative element in the hiring of women. Women manage the work processes and domestic affairs but get little financial or social reward for their endeavours. Men are the official managers, even though women often play 'critical *de facto* managerial roles in running the business'.[57] The domestic subordination of women is reinforced in the workplace in many ethnic businesses.

The lack of prestige afforded to women who manage ethnic family businesses could well have a detrimental effect on economic performance. Another feature of family involvement which is also problematic is the reluctance, also found in non-ethnic family businesses, to recruit non-family managers even when incumbent family managers are less than competent. Family members can be important to ethnic businesses as a means of overcoming the disadvantages of racism and of providing a flexible source of labour, but their over-reliance on the family can also be a source of disadvantage.

Other categorisations of small business

In a population as heterogeneous as that of small businesses there will be many different ways in which firms can be categorised, and it is neither practicable nor appropriate to try to list them all here. However there are some which get quite frequent mention, even if only by policy-makers seeking to target assistance appropriately. Among them are the following.

High-tech/low-tech

High-tech is a category of businesses often favoured by those promoting small business because of an assumption that high-tech businesses contribute most to an economy. This depends however on what is meant by a high-tech business. Often the definition seems to be that of a business based on a new and relatively hard-to-acquire technology and which is, as a consequence, likely to be less vulnerable to competition and therefore able to earn more, to export more and to survive longer than businesses based on older technologies. However there is more to business success than the technology on which it is based and therefore, while high-tech businesses may have the newness of their technology in common, there is no guarantee that they share the same level of profitability, of exports or of success. They are studied nevertheless as a category because of issues that they are perceived to have in common, such as longer lead times to market, greater difficulty in communicating their potential to other people and needing greater financial resources in order to get started.

Urban/rural

In places like England and Wales, where only 7 per cent of the population live in completely rural areas, it might be expected that the urban business is the norm. Yet there is evidence that in recent years many people have left the city and moved to the country, sometimes to start small businesses. Those businesses are often set up in rural areas for environmental and lifestyle reasons and they would be classed as rural businesses because they are located in a rural area.[58] However that is often in practice the only rural thing about them: they benefit from cheaper property costs and overheads and they have greater distances to go to market, but in other aspects they are just urban businesses which happen to be in a rural setting. Businesses which would have better claims to be rural would be farms and farm diversifications, other primary food producers and rural tourism initiatives.

A distinction is sometimes made between 'accessible' and 'remote' rural areas. Storey points out that 'accessible' rural areas have generally been amongst the most prosperous parts of the United Kingdom and quotes research showing that many businesses there are arts and craft-based and are started by relatively highly educated individuals who are in-migrants to the area seeking a higher quality of life.[59] It is businesses in the 'accessible' areas that outperform comparable firms in urban areas, whereas firms set up in 'remote' rural areas do not appear to perform as well.

Apart from these distinctions there seems to be little evidence that rural businesses are in general significantly distinct from urban businesses, although some research has indicated that a few differences may be discernible. Storey reports a finding that owners of rural businesses are more reluctant to move out of their existing town or village than urban owners and have a commitment to a particular location, even though the opportunities for expansion there might be limited.[60] Another survey in England which was conducted in 1991 found that:[61]

- Rural and small-town firms were younger than conurbation firms and that southern firms were frequently young new enterprises set up in the 1980s.
- There were differences in workforce skill composition between northern and rural firms on the one hand, and southern and conurbation firms on the other. The former employed significantly higher proportions of semi-skilled, unskilled and skilled manual workers, while the latter had higher proportions of clerical and administrative staff, higher professionals and technologists, and managers.
- Urban/rural differences in innovation activity were striking, with higher innovation rates in rural firms compared with conurbation firms.
- There is also a consistent urban/rural gradient in employment growth, with the most rapid employment expansion reported in rural firms and the least rapid in conurbation firms.

'Third age' businesses

Age distributions of self-employed people generally show that self-employment becomes increasingly common as middle age approaches and that it does not cease at the normal retirement age. The reasons given for these features are that middle age may be a time when capital or knowledge assets have been accumulated, and commitments may be reducing, so a start-up can be attempted. Alternatively it might be a time when people are particularly vulnerable to redundancy or attracted by early retirement offers. Self-employment may persist into the sixties and longer because of a reluctance to let go, although hours can be adjusted to allow for age, and there is no statutory retirement age for the self-employed. Alternatively it may continue because some of those in self- employment may not have adequate pension arrangements.[62]

Craft businesses

A further classification often used to distinguish among categories of business is that of craft, manufacture, service, technology or agricultural. However, while these categories are in common use, there are no fixed definitions of them. Confusion can therefore arise in their use. For instance the distinction between 'craft' and 'manufacturing' is not clear, and there would appear to be some overlap. Indeed in mainland Europe the category 'craft business' depends more on size and ownership than on the type of hand-crafted manufacturing associated with the concept of a UK craft business.

Small businesses and job creation

One aspect of small businesses in which there has been considerable interest in recent years has been their role in job creation. Two questions in particular have been raised:

first, what is the extent of the overall contribution of small businesses to job creation; and second, does this contribution come, in the main, from all small businesses or from only a few of them? The questions are very relevant to the targeting of government intervention to promote employment, but the answers are not always clear. The first is about the validity of Birch's work and its application to other countries such as the UK, and the second is about which small businesses create most jobs. Exploring issues such as these highlights a number of problems in small business statistics, which may require some insight if they are to be interpreted properly.

A note of caution

Before looking at these questions in more detail it is important to emphasise that a key problem in studying entrepreneurship and small businesses quantitatively is the availability of appropriate data. There is often a distinct difference between the data which are desired and those that are available. Frequently therefore the data used are borrowed from other sources. For instance, in order to explore the issue of entrepreneurship in the UK, many people would like to know how many small businesses there are and the rate at which new ones are started and others terminate. However the data source often used to indicate this is that of business VAT registrations and many businesses do not register for VAT because their turnover is below the threshold; and many businesses de-register, not because they are terminating, but because their turnover has fallen below the threshold. VAT statistics do not provide good small business data because they cover neither only small businesses nor every small business. Nevertheless they are used because they are the best that are available. Another problem is that the data borrowed may record the right subject but use a different definition in a different context. For instance when researching the characteristics of fast-growth small business, which is a popular area for intervention, making comparisons between different studies is often problematic because of significant variations in the definitions of 'fast growth'. The terms 'small businesses', 'start-ups', 'self-employment', 'owner-managers', 'entrepreneurs' and 'SMEs' are all frequently used, often apparently interchangeably, but they are not the same and to explore each fully would require different datasets in each case. Often however these are not readily available and therefore in many cases the distinction is lost in those data which are used.

The validity of Birch

Birch first indicated in 1979 the significant role that small businesses play in the creation of employment. His original work concluded that 81.5 per cent of all net new jobs formed in the United States between 1969 and 1976 were formed by firms with fewer than 100 employees. Armington and Odle, on the other hand, subsequently looked at job creation results for 1978–80 using a database specially created by the US Small Business Administration (SBA) and found that less than 40 per cent of net new jobs were created by businesses with fewer than 100 employees.[63] They had no explanation for the difference as against Birch's figures, but speculated that Birch may have made errors. Subsequently, Armington and Odle have been cited as experts who found Birch to be in error but, according to Kirchhoff, what is less commented on is that their subsequent research validated Birch and showed that percentages calculated in their way were cyclical.[64]

Sixteen years after Birch, Kirchhoff stated that 'It seems safe to say that, on average, firms with less than 100 employees create the majority of net new jobs in the US economy.'[65] Others however still disagree. Davis et al., in their book *Job Creation and Destruction*, based on the Longitudinal Research Database constructed by the US Census Bureau, state that they 'found no strong, systematic relationship between employer size and net job growth rates'.[66] There is therefore no single agreed verdict on the validity of Birch, who was in any case only looking at the situation in the United States. Nevertheless, right or not, his work was, to a very large extent, the trigger for much current interest in small businesses. Subsequent careful work in both improving and examining the SBA's database appears to have shown that fluctuations in the economy of the United States reveal themselves mainly through job changes in larger firms and that small businesses are consistent net creators of jobs. Taking the period 1976–88 as a whole, it is now estimated that businesses with fewer than 20 employees provided 19.4 per cent of total employment, but about 37 per cent of net new jobs. In the UK a similar analysis has been carried out with broadly similar results. One analysis indicated 'that during the 1987–9 period, 54 per cent of the increase in employment was in firms with fewer than 20 workers'.[67] In the UK, however, all components of employment change are of lower magnitude than in the United States, and job change in the latter is more strongly influenced by births and deaths, especially of large businesses, whereas in the UK job change 'is more influenced by expansions and contractions'.[68] Nevertheless in both countries there are arguments that small businesses do indeed make a disproportionately large contribution to net job creation. Studies of European, Japanese and Australian businesses, as well as American ones, have also found that firms with fewer than 100 employees are net contributors to employment growth, contributing as much as 75 per cent of new jobs.[69]

Which small businesses create jobs?

If small businesses do create significant proportions of net new jobs then governments and others trying to increase employment will be particularly interested in them. However, there are very many small businesses, and support would be spread thinly if it went to all of them. Indications that within the small business population it is a relatively small proportion of each year's cohort of businesses that create a disproportionate share of the jobs over time have had a particular appeal. In the UK, Storey has asserted that 'out of every 100 small firms, the fastest growing four firms will create 50 per cent of the jobs in the group over a decade.'[70] The implication of this was that, if support could be focused on those four businesses, or on the few businesses that had the potential for such growth, it would be applied much more effectively than if all 100 businesses were to be supported. These high-growth businesses are the sort of businesses that Birch called 'gazelles'.

Storey's statement needs to be examined with some care, however. He himself points out that the data it is based on are rather old, but he does indicate that other data, in particular from Northern Ireland, produce fairly similar results. He also acknowledges that the data refer only to manufacturing businesses and then only to new ones.

There is also another issue. Despite the way it is sometimes interpreted, Storey's statement does not mean that 4 per cent of small businesses create 50 per cent of the jobs. What Storey says is that if 100 businesses are started in year t, in the year t + 10 only 40 of those businesses may have survived and just four of those surviving businesses will between them employ as many people as are employed by all the other survivors put together. However, that also means that half of the employment in the survivors will not be in those four businesses, nor will the employment during the intervening ten years in the 60 businesses that did not survive to the end of the period. Storey's own table indicates that all of the four high-growth businesses at the end of ten years employ more than 25 people (one employs 25 to 49, two employ 50 to 99, and one employs over 100);[71] yet he also indicates that businesses with fewer than 20 employees created 'between 78 per cent (1985–7) and 85 per cent of total new employment' from small businesses.[72] It is very hard to compare these figures directly with the ten-year cohort figures and to say how many of them are due to the early stages of growth of the 4 per cent of high-growth businesses. For instance in any one year there will be the following:

Jobs in Storey's 4 per cent of the businesses which started ten years earlier

plus

An equal number of jobs in the other surviving businesses which started ten years earlier

plus

Jobs in businesses which started fewer than ten years earlier (not all of which will survive the ten years but are nevertheless employing people in the interim)

plus

Jobs in businesses started more than ten years ago (some of which will be the 4 per cent of businesses from the earlier cohorts but some of which will also be the other businesses which are nevertheless growing).

Without comparable figures for all these groups, comparisons cannot be made. It would be expected from a Pareto analysis that a relatively small proportion of small businesses that grow significantly would have a disproportionate share of the total employment over time. Nevertheless, the major part of the employment in small businesses appears to come from the other small businesses employing fewer than 20 people, not from the fastest-growing 4 per cent.

Recent analysis has also confirmed a link between small business start-up rates and employment. A model produced by van Stel et al. using data for the period 1980 to 1998 shows that in Britain business start-up activity in the late 1980s had a direct positive effect on subsequent employment change, whereas in the early 1980s start-up activity contributed to growth only after a number of years.[73]

A further factor in small business employment which should not be ignored is that most small businesses are in the service sector, which is labour intensive and for which output can often only be increased by taking on new staff. These staff frequently come from the secondary labour market and may be prepared to work for relatively low wages. Expansion of these businesses will therefore increase employment, and consequently reduce unemployment payments, without causing inflation. This is very attractive to governments.

Dynamic versus static analysis

One of the reasons why Birch's original findings were surprising was that they were contrary to previous research and thinking on job creation. They were also based on a dynamic analysis, while the previous research was carried out using static analysis. Such static analysis is carried out using classified data in the form published by government statistics agencies. Those publications will, for instance, list the number of businesses in given size ranges and the number of jobs in them at the end of each period. However, for a given business size range, the difference between the number of jobs at the end of one period and the number at the end of the previous period does not give the number of jobs created in that period by businesses in that size range. The reason may be illustrated by considering a business employing 70 people which over a period grows by 50 per cent and therefore at the end employs 105 people. At the beginning it would have been classified in the 1–100-employee size range, but at the end it is in the 100-plus size range. The effect is thus to reduce by 70 the number of jobs in businesses in the 1–100 size range, and increase by 105 the number of jobs in businesses in the higher size range. The static statistics will therefore show a reduction of jobs in businesses in the lower size range and an increase in the higher size range. The reality however is that the net increase came from a business that was in the lower size range. In the reverse situation, however, the shrinkage of a business initially in a higher size range will appear at the end of the period as a reduction in that size range, because either the business will still be in the size range but with fewer jobs or it will have left the size range and all its jobs will appear to have gone. A lower size range will then correspondingly appear to have grown. Static analysis assumes implicitly that the net inter-class movement of businesses is negligible, which may not be the case.

Cohort analysis

Cohort, or dynamic, analysis, in which a class of subjects is tracked as it changes over time, will avoid the problem of static research analysis. It will also reveal other interesting features of growth. Dynamic analysis of US small businesses has, for instance, indicated that survival rates of businesses improve exponentially with, for a group founded at the same time, a smaller proportion of the original number terminating in each successive year. It has also shown that less than half of the surviving businesses show any growth in the first six years, but that at between six and eight years of age the number of businesses that show growth leaps increases significantly: a result that confirms suggestions of the 'seven lean years' of business development and indicates that observing business survival and growth over a lesser period may be misleading. In taking only new business starts and looking at their employment after ten years, Storey may therefore be missing from his 'high-growth' business those businesses that do not start to grow until after seven years or more.

Another factor which might usefully be taken into consideration when looking for growth is highlighted in the work of Rosa and Scott, already mentioned in Chapter 6, on multiple business ownership. They suggest that if the unit of analysis is the business, which it often is, then this will not provide a full picture. Instead they suggest that the unit of analysis should be the entrepreneur, or team of entrepreneurs, who may start several businesses. They talk of clusters of businesses with linked ownership in which 'diversifying into additional businesses may not only be common but may also be associated with positive growth strategies.'[74] This means that growth from an entrepreneur already in business can occur through new business creation rather than through the growth of already established businesses, and that would not be picked up by an analysis with a business unit focus.

Summary

It would appear that there is now clear evidence that small businesses do create a disproportionate amount of new employment. However, different researchers vary in their estimates of how much, and there do appear to be variations over time and across countries. It is not yet clear whether this employment is mainly due to only a small proportion of that small business population or to all of it. This lack of clarity may be due to different researchers measuring different things and to their findings being misinterpreted or misrepresented, but overall it would appear that most of those new jobs at a particular point in time come from the very small businesses in the smallest size ranges and not from Birch's 'gazelles'. The impact of the 'gazelles' is seen when following the job creation activity of a cohort of businesses over time. It is also important to be aware that, while on average net new jobs may come from small businesses, the performance of the large firms sector and the fluctuations in its employment will also have a significant impact on the overall employment position.

Conclusions

Although their size distinguishes small businesses from their larger counterparts, there are other features which many of them have in common. Nevertheless small businesses are very diverse, and this chapter has looked not only at their common features but also at their variety by examining them under a number of different classifications. There is no one best way of classifying the different types of small business. Which is most appropriate in a particular circumstance will depend on what form of analysis or prescription one is engaged in.

THE KEY POINTS OF CHAPTER 6

- There is no single definition of what is a small business. Most definitions use the size of the business as the distinguishing feature, as indicated by either asset value or turnover, or, more commonly, by employment. The upper limit in employment terms can however vary from 50 people to, in the case of American

SMEs, 500. It is, however, important to remember that 'small' is often used as a relative term, and what is relatively small in one industry may be relatively large in another.

- In examining small businesses the focus of the analysis has often been the business. However, if the primary unit of analysis is instead taken as the entrepreneur, a different perspective often emerges, which can explain many features of small businesses and which throws light on the process of capital accumulation and entrepreneurship.

- The variety of small businesses is not just due to their different stages of development. Different industry sectors and different legal structures, family ownership and other considerations can all make a difference.

- There is also variety between entrepreneurs, who can, for instance, be categorised as novice or habitual and, if habitual, as serial or portfolio.

- Nevertheless, despite the many differences between different types, stages or ownership of small businesses, they do have a number of key aspects in common, and many of these aspects distinguish them from big businesses. These aspects include issues of culture, influence, resources and ambition. For many commentators it is these aspects that represent the crucial difference associated with size, and even the description 'small' is only a convenient distinction to serve as a proxy for these real differences.

- One other aspect of small businesses which is of considerable interest to many people is their contribution to job creation. The statistics on this need to be interpreted with some care but they do indicate that significant numbers of jobs are created by small businesses, but not by all small businesses.

QUESTIONS, ESSAY AND DISCUSSION TOPICS

- Are definitions based on size meaningful when there is such a variety of small businesses?
- In the absence of a single universally accepted definition how would you summarise the essence of a small business?
- Is the entrepreneur or the business the more enlightening unit of study in seeking to understand business development and wealth creation?
- In what ways do family businesses differ from non-family businesses?
- What are the implications of studying family businesses from the perspective of the family instead of focusing just on the business?
- Apart from a lack of accumulated capital is there really any real argument for saying female businesses are any different from male businesses and should be treated differently?

- How important is formal education in the development of a successful business enterprise?
- Do small businesses create the majority of jobs in your area?

Suggestions for further reading and information

P. Burns, *Entrepreneurship and Small Business*, 2nd edn (Basingstoke: Palgrave Macmillan, 2007).
The BDO Stoy Hayward Centre for Family Business: The Family Business Management Series: Succession management in family companies (2007) www.bdo.co.uk.
Global Entrepreneurship Monitor: www.entreworld.org.

References

1. *The Report of the Committee of Enquiry on Small Firms* (The Bolton Report) (London: HMSO, 1971).
2. D. Carson and S. Cromie, 'Marketing Planning in Small Enterprises: A Model and Some Empirical Evidence', *Journal of Marketing Management*, 5 (1989), pp. 33–50.
3. P. Rosa and M. Scott, 'Entrepreneurial Diversification, Business-Cluster Formation, and Growth', *Government and Policy*, 17 (1999), pp. 527–47, p. 530.
4. P. Rosa and M. Scott, 'The Prevalence of Multiple Owners and Directors in the SME Sector: Implications For Our Understanding of Start-Up and Growth', *Entrepreneurship and Regional Development*, 11 (1999), pp. 21–37, at p. 34.
5. M. Scott and P. Rosa, 'Has Firm Level Analysis Reached its Limits? Time for a Rethink', *International Small Business Journal*, 14 (1996), pp. 81–9.
6. P. Westhead and M. Wright, 'Novice, Portfolio and Serial Founders: Are They Different?' *Journal of Business Venturing*, 13 (1998), pp. 173–204.
7. Scott and Rosa, op.cit., p. 81.
8. Rosa and Scott (1999), op. cit., p. 21.
9. P. Westhead, D. Ucbasaran, M. Wright and F. Martin, *Habitual Entrepreneurs in Scotland* (Scottish Enterprise, 2003).
10. F. J. Greene, K. F. Mole, and D. J. Storey, *Three Decades of Enterprise Culture* (Basingstoke: Palgrave, 2008) p. 238.
11. S. Carter, 'The Economic Potential of Portfolio Entrepreneurship: Enterprise and Employment Contributions of Multiple Business Ownership', *Journal of Small Business and Enterprise Development*, 5(4) (1998), pp. 297–307.
12. Carter, op. cit., p. 297.
13. E. T. Penrose, *The Theory of the Growth of the Firm* (Oxford: Basil Blackwell, 1959).
14. A. A. Gibb, 'Towards the Building of Entrepreneurial Models of Support for Small Business', The 11th (UK) National Small Firms Policy and Research Conference (Cardiff, 1988), pp. 12–15.
15. C. Handy, *The Age of Unreason* (London: Arrow Books, 1990).
16. See A. Minkes, *The Entrepreneurial Manager* (Harmondsworth: Penguin, 1987) for a discussion of entrepreneurial decision-making.
17. H. Mintzberg, *The Structuring of Organisations* (Englewood Cliffs, NJ: Prentice-Hall, 1979), pp. 305–13.
18. R. Goffee and R. Scase, 'Proprietorial Control In Family Firms', *Journal of Management Studies*, 22 (1985), pp. 53–68.
19. *The Third Annual Report of the European Observatory for SMEs* (Zoetermeer, the Netherlands: EIM Small Business Research and Consultancy, 1995), pp. 50–1.
20. Stoy Hayward, *The Stoy Hayward/BBC Family Business Index* (London: Stoy Hayward, 1992).
21. R. K. Z. Heck and E. Scannell-Trent, 'The Prevalence of Family Business From a Household Sample', *Family Business Review*, 12 (1999), pp. 209–24.
22. M. C. Shanker and J. H. Astrachan, 'Myths and Realities: Family Business Contributions to the US Economy: A Framework for Assessing Family Business Statistics', *Family Business Review*, 9 (1996), pp.

107–23.

23. Stoy Hayward, *Managing the Family Business in the UK* (London: Stoy Hayward, 1990).
24. S. Cromie, B. Stephenson and D. Monteith, 'Managing Family Firms: An Empirical Investigation', *International Small Business Journal*, 13 (1995), pp. 11—34.
25. M. S. Wortman, 'Critical Issues in Family Business: An International Perspective of Practice and Research', Proceedings of the ICSB 40th World Conference (1995), pp. 53–76.
26. Heck and Scannell-Trent, op. cit., pp. 209–20, base their model of family firms definitions on W. C. Handler, 'Methodological Issues and Considerations in Studying Family Businesses,' *Family Business Review*, 2 (1989), pp. 257–76.
27. D. Fletcher, 'Family and Enterprise' in *Enterprise and Small Business*, edited by S. Carter and D. Jones-Evans, (London: Financial Times/Prentice-Hall, 2000), pp. 155–65.
28. K. Stafford, K. A. Duncan, S. Dane and M. Winter, 'A Research Model of Sustainable Family Business', *Family Business Review*, 12 (1999), pp. 197–208.
29. Heck and Scannell-Trent, op. cit., p. 212.
30. Stafford et al., op. cit.: 203.
31. Fletcher, op. cit., p. 160.
32. S. Birley, D. Ng and A. Godfrey, 'The Family and the Business', *Long Range Planning*, 32 (1999), pp. 598–608.
33. Stoy Hayward (1990), op. cit.
34. Birley et al., op. cit., p. 598.
35. H. Levinson, 'Conflicts That Plague the Family Business', *Harvard Business Review*, March–April (1971), pp. 53–62.
36. H. Levinson, 'Don't Choose Your Own Successor', *Harvard Business Review*, November-December (1974), pp. 53–62.
37. A. Shepherd and A. Zacharakis, 'Structuring Family Business Succession: An Analysis of the Future Leader's Decision Making', *Entrepreneurship Theory and Practice*, 25 (2000), pp. 25–39.
38. BDO Stoy Hayward, *Across the Generations: Insights from 100 Year Old Family Businesses* (2004).
39. B. Dunn, 'Success Themes in Scottish Family Enterprises: Philosophies and Practices Through the Generations', *Family Business Review*, 8 (1995), pp. 8: 17–28.
40. J. Magretta, 'Governing the Family-Owned Enterprise: An Interview With Finland's Krister Ahlstrom', *Harvard Business Review*, January-February (1998), pp. 113–23.
41. Fletcher, op. cit., p. 157.
42. Stafford et al, op. cit.: 203.
43. Ibid.: 205.
44. S. Carter and E. Shaw, 'Women's Business Ownership: Recent Research and Policy Developments', Report to the Small Business Service, November 2000.
45. S. Cromie, 'The Problems Experienced by Young Firms', *International Small Business Journal*, 9 (1991), pp. 43–67.
46. S. Carter, 'Gender and Enterprise', in *Enterprise and Small Business*, edited by S. Carter and D. Jones-Evans (Harlow: Pearson Education, 2000), p. 172.
47. Ibid., p. 167.
48. S. Carter and P. Rosa, 'The Financing of Male- and Female-Owned Businesses', *Entrepreneurship and Regional Development*, 10 (1998), pp. 225–41.
49. A. Phizacklea and M. Ram, 'Ethnic Entrepreneurship In Comparative Perspective', *International Journal of Entrepreneurial Behaviour and Research*, 1 (1995), pp. 48–58.
50. L. M. Dyer and C. A. Ross, 'Ethnic Enterprises and their Clientele', *Journal of Small Business Management*, 38 (2000), pp. 48–60.
51. R. Waldinger, H. E. Aldrich and R. Ward, *Ethnic Entrepreneurs: Immigrant Businesses in Industrial Societies* (Newbury Park, Calif.: Sage, 1990), p. 33.
52. V. C. Vincent, 'Decision-Making Policies Among Mexican-American Small Business Entrepreneurs', *Journal of Small Business Management*, 34 (1996), pp. 1—13; Dyer and Ross, op.cit.; P. G. Greene, 'A Resource Based Approach to Ethnic Business Sponsorship: A Consideration of Ismaili-Pakistani Immigrants', *Journal of Small Business Management*, 35 (1997), pp. 57–71.
53. A. Fadahunsi, D. Smallbone and S. Supri, 'Networking and Ethnic Minority Enterprise Development: Insights From a North London Study', *Journal of Small Business and Enterprise Development*, 7 (2000), pp. 228–40.
54. Y. Li, 'Assessing data needs and gaps for studying ethnic entrepreneurship in Britain: A review paper', ESRC (URN 07/1052), March 2007.

55. D. Storey, *Understanding the Small Business Sector* (London: Routledge, 1994), pp. 272–3.

56. M. Ram, 'Unravelling Social Networks In Ethnic Minority Firms', *International Small Business Journal*, 12(3) (1994), pp. 42–53, at p. 44.

57. Ibid., p. 51.

58. Economic and Social Research Council, *Characteristics of the Founders of Small Rural Businesses* (Swindon: The Council, 1989).

59. D. Storey, *Understanding the Small Business Sector* (London: Routledge, 1994), pp. 272–3.

60. Storey, op.cit., p. 273, quoting D. Smallbone, D. North and R. Leigh, 'The Use of External Assistance by Mature SMEs in the UK: Some Policy Implications', *Entrepreneurship and Regional Development*, 5 (1993), pp. 279–95.

61. Economic and Social Research Council, *The State of British Enterprise* (Swindon: The Council, 1992).

62. D. Brooksbank, 'Self-Employment and Small Firms', in *Enterprise and Small Business*, edited by S. Carter and D. Jones-Evans, (London: Financial Times/Prentice-Hall, 2000), pp. 15–16.

63. C. Armington and M. Odle, 'Small Businesses – How Many Jobs?' *Brookings Review* 20, Winter 1982.

64. B. Kirchhoff, 'Twenty Years of Job Creation Research: What Have We Learned?' The 40th Conference of the International Council for Small Business, 1995, pp. 201–2.

65. Ibid., p. 202.

66. S. J. Davis, J. C. Haltiwanger and S. Schuh, *Job Creation and Destruction* (Cambridge, Mass.: MIT Press, 1996), p. 170.

67. Storey, op.cit., p. 165.

68. Ibid., p. 168.

69. OECD, *Globalisation and Small and Medium Enterprises, Synthesis Report, Vol. 1* (Paris: OECD, 1997), p. 122.

70. Ibid., p. 113.

71. Ibid., p. 114.

72. Ibid., p. 168.

73. A. van Stel, S. Dielbandhoesing, W. van den Heuvel and D. Storey, 'Entrepreneurial Growth in Great Britain: British Regions In the Period 1980–1998', personal correspondence relating to a not yet published paper.

74. P. Rosa and M. Scott, 'Entrepreneurial Diversification, Business-Cluster Formation and Growth', *Government and Policy*, 17 (1999), pp. 527–47, at p. 527.

CHAPTER 7
The process of business formation

Contents

KEY CONCEPTS

This chapter covers:

- Models of the possible stages of the development of a business.
- The process of business start-up and the supply of entrepreneurs.
- The connection between the business idea and the business opportunity.
- The role and importance of a business plan.

- The nature of start-up finance.
- The many facets of entrepreneurship in relation to types of business start-up.

LEARNING OBJECTIVES

By the end of this chapter the reader should:

- Be aware of the possible development paths for a business.
- Have an understanding of the process of moving from idea to opportunity, and the nature of opportunity development and evaluation.
- Have an appreciation of the relevance of the business plan.
- Have an understanding of the different sources of start-up finance.
- Have an understanding of what constitutes small business success and failure.
- Be aware of the many varied reasons and attitudes behind different types of business start-up.

Introduction

Chapter 6 introduced small business by looking at how they are sometimes defined and by exploring some of their distinctive features. This chapter looks at how they are formed and developed through the entrepreneurial process. In a general sense the emphasis in business development, and in writing about enterprise, has been to look primarily at the business but, as explained in Chapter 6, it can be more helpful to take the entrepreneur as the fundamental unit of analysis. This chapter therefore looks at aspects of business development and start-up and, in particular, at the role in this played by the entrepreneur. It also considers a number of aspects of small business entrepreneurship.

The stages of business development

It is customary to see business formation as consisting of one or more stages in the development of businesses. However, it is important to recognise that the use of the term 'stage' in relation to the business development process does not mean that businesses develop in discrete phases with clear boundaries between them. Separating the development process into stages is rather like dividing the spectrum of visible light into colours. Traditionally there are said to be seven, but in reality there are not seven distinct colours but a continuing gradation through the colours. We can say that one area is green compared with another area which is yellow, but we cannot say precisely where one changes to the other. Dividing the business development process into stages is helpful, in that there are issues at the heart of each stage that differ from the issues central to other stages; but, while we can indicate broadly the stage of development of a business, we cannot say precisely when it moves from one stage to another.

Like the number of colours in the spectrum, the number of areas ascribed to the process is a matter of interpretation. However, unlike the colour spectrum, the order of the areas is not necessarily fixed. While a 'pre-start' stage cannot follow 'start-up', and 'termination' has to be the end, businesses do not have to progress through every possible stage between; they can be static, they can grow and they can decline in any order, they can do these things more than once, and they can reverse their steps. There are many models of the different stages and the sequence in which they occur, but the reality is that very few businesses actually follow the models. Many of the models, in the way they are presented, imply steady growth, for instance by presenting a steadily rising line on a plot with axes of size and time. Growth, however, is not the norm, and where there is growth it is generally achieved through a number of discrete steps rather than by a steady, even progression. It is also important to recognise that these models do not explain what is happening inside a business; they only describe its situation, and they present symptoms not causes. Therefore they do not help in predicting what will happen next to a business.

Nevertheless some models are presented here to provide a context in which to consider different aspects of business formation. One of the simplest, and one of the most used, models has been that of Churchill and Lewis which suggests that there can be five stages from early business existence to eventual maturity (see Table 7.1).

Other models, however, have additional stages that come either before or after the Churchill and Lewis stages, or show additional features in a progression through the stages. While stages which come before the formation of a business are not strictly stages in the development of that particular business, they are nevertheless relevant to the development of the entrepreneur and to an understanding of the inception of the business. These prior-to-business-start stages can include the following.

- *Culture*. People are more likely to think of starting a business, and that business is more likely to survive, if the underlying culture is one that will help to nurture awareness and interest as well as ideas and embryonic businesses.

- *The idea*: Before they can proceed to start-up, people need to have both the notion they can start a business and a product or service idea around which the business can be formed. This is the stage where they are not only aware that business start is possible, but must feel that it might be appropriate for them and that they can do it.

- *The pre-start phase*: This is the process whereby those thinking of starting a business progress from the business idea to the stage of actually starting the business.

Table 7.1 The five stages of business growth

- Existence: staying alive by finding products or services and customers
- Survival: establishing the customer base, demonstrating viability
- Success: confidence in its market position, options for further growth
- Take-off: opting to go for growth
- Maturity: the characteristics of a larger, stable company

Source: N. C. Churchill and V. L. Lewis, 'Growing Concerns: The Five Stages of Small Firm Growth', *Harvard Business Review* (1983) May–June, pp.31, 32, 34, 40.

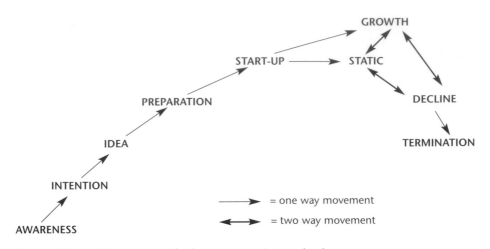

Figure 7.1 Small business paths from conception to death

There are also stages at the end of a businesses life when it declines and terminates. A fuller list of stages might therefore include the following sequence (which is also presented diagrammatically in Figure 7.1):

- culture and awareness
- intention – the notion and intention to start a business
- idea – a product/service idea for the business
- pre-start/preparation
- start-up/inception
- growth and expansion
- static – including survival, consolidation, comfort and maturity
- decline
- termination.

As well as showing both pre-start and termination phases, this model also recognises the dynamics of business development. Despite the straight lines of most models, businesses very rarely progress steadily onwards and upwards. Figure 7.2 recognises this by showing possible paths for a business, not only in steady growth, but also in a phase of growth reversal, in stability with possible oscillation, in a merger with another business and in early failure. This model therefore suggests that there can be problems to be faced by a business as it grows which are elaborated further in Greiner's model in Figure 7.3. These models therefore, in effect, present the precursors or stimulators of change, rather than the change itself. These precursors or stimulators are, however, very hard to measure compared with qualities such as turnover or numbers of employees, and are therefore much harder in practice to use to describe the extent of the development of a business. Nevertheless, their presentation can provide useful insights.

While the stage model approach may have its drawbacks, it helps nevertheless to divide small businesses into different categories to make them easier to examine.

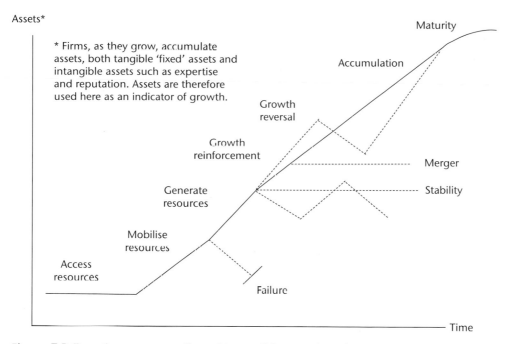

Figure 7.2 Growth process as reflected in possible growth paths

Source: E. Garnsey, 'A New Theory of the Growth of the Firm', Paper presented to the ICSB 41st World Conference, Stockholm, June 1996, p.4.

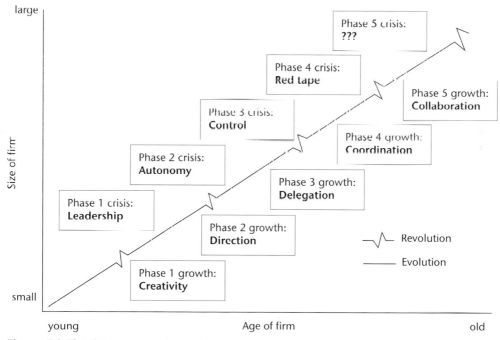

Figure 7.3 The Greiner growth model

Source: L. E. Greiner, 'Evolution and Revolution as Organisations Grow', *Harvard Business Review*, July/August 1972 quoted in P. Burns, *Entrepreneurship and Small Business*, (Basingstoke: Palgrave, 2007) p.211.

Preparing for business start-up

The entrepreneur and the opportunity

Shane has suggested that the components needed for entrepreneurial outcomes are individuals and opportunities:

> The entrepreneurial process begins with the perception of the existence of opportunities or situations in which resources can be recombined for a potential profit. Alert individuals, called entrepreneurs, discover these opportunities, and develop ideas for how to pursue them, including the development of a product or service that will be provided to customers. These individuals then obtain resources, design organisations or other modes of opportunity exploitation or develop a strategy to exploit the opportunity.[1]

The supply of entrepreneurs: the culture stage

What all the listed stages of business development, apart from culture and awareness, have in common is that they are all concerned with people who might be or already are in business. To use a horticultural analogy, they all deal with plants: with sowing the seeds of plants, with growing plants, with pruning plants, with plants flowering and even with plants dying. The culture and awareness stage, however, deals with the preparation of the ground: the preparation of a medium which will encourage, feed and support the seeds and growing plants. Chapter 4 has shown that the surrounding human society or culture is important for business growth, just as the condition and type of the soil are important for plants.

The influences on new firm formation can be many and varied. Krueger's model of entrepreneurial potential, described in Chapter 3, and other cognitive approaches, illustrate some of the antecedent influences on enterprise. An alternative presentation, which represents the same framework but also highlights some of the specific factors that may be influential in a business context, is shown in Figure 7.4.

This approach illustrates the variety of possible antecedent factors that may be relevant to the 'culture' or 'awareness' stage. This stage can be sub-divided to show the progression from no particular interest in enterprise, through awareness and potential interest, to actual new business formation.

The supply of opportunities

A distinction has been made between a small business opportunity and an entrepreneurial business opportunity. As Bolton and Thompson indicate, small business people typically spot an opportunity to do something they can do, but which does not necessarily have any real growth potential.[2] Entrepreneurial opportunities however are opportunities that offer something new and different to the market: where there is a degree of innovation and therefore growth potential.

In a World Bank study, Klapper et al. indicated that there is a clear split between the industrialised countries and the developing countries in the sectors on which entrepreneurs typically tend to focus their efforts.[3] Entrepreneurs in developing

Influences upon the entrepreneurial decision

Antecedent influences upon entrepreneur

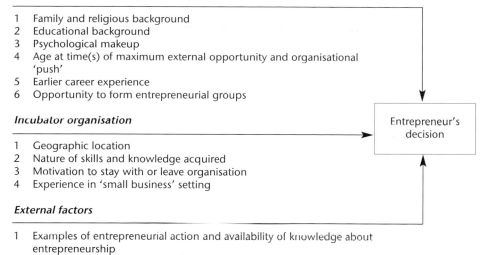

1   Family and religious background
2   Educational background
3   Psychological makeup
4   Age at time(s) of maximum external opportunity and organisational 'push'
5   Earlier career experience
6   Opportunity to form entrepreneurial groups

Incubator organisation

1   Geographic location
2   Nature of skills and knowledge acquired
3   Motivation to stay with or leave organisation
4   Experience in 'small business' setting

External factors

1   Examples of entrepreneurial action and availability of knowledge about entrepreneurship
2   Societal attitudes toward entrepreneurship
3   Ability to save 'seed capital'
4   Accessibility and availability of venture capital
5   Availability of personnel and supporting services; accessibility to customers; accessibility to university
6   Opportunities for interim consulting
7   Economic conditions

Figure 7.4 Model of new enterprise formation

Source: Arnold C. Cooper, 'Technical Entrepreneurship', *R & D Management*, vol. 3 (1973) pp. 59–64.

countries tend to focus their start-up intentions in the retail trade sector because of the lower requirements of investment, human resources, knowledge and capital; whereas in the industrialised nations it is the services and industry sectors that dominate.

According to Wickham[4] a business opportunity is a gap in the market which presents the possibility of new value being created, and according to Bolton and Thompson[5] opportunities are ideas that have commercial potential and can be realised. The assertion here is that opportunities are ideas that exploit unmet, and sometimes unrealised, customer needs. Drucker suggests that change often provides the opportunity for the new and the different.[6] Therefore, given the rapid pace of change in, amongst other things, consumer tastes and technology, these are areas where there should be business opportunities to exploit. Table 7.2 provides examples of the quickening pace of change in the introduction of new technology but, as well as opportunity, new technology also involves risk. Many businesses described as being based on 'cutting edge' (i.e. does not yet work!) technology are often found to be based on under-developed technology that runs away with resources and leads to high failure rates. Illustration 7.1, however, provides an example of a technology which offered the potential for a business opportunity and of a business which has capitalised on that potential.

Table 7.2 New technology adoption rate

The time it has taken for new technology to reach 25 per cent of the US population. For example household electricity was first made available in 1873 and it took 46 years for 25 per cent of the US population to get electricity.

The Technology	Time in Years
Household electricity (1873)	46
Telephone (1875)	35
Automobile (1885)	55
Airplane travel	54
Radio (1906)	22
Television (1925)	26
Video recorder (1952)	34
Personal computer (1975)	15
Cellular phone	13
www (1991)	Less than 10 (estimate)

Source: *Wall Street Journal*, June 1997 in B. Bygrave, 'Building an Entrepreneurial Economy: Lessons from the United States', *Business Strategy Review* (1998), 9(2), p.11.

ILLUSTRATION 7.1
Business opportunities in technology

The technology: text messaging in the UK

In the UK, text messaging reached 4 billion messages a month for the first time in December 2006, according to figures announced by the Mobile Data Association (MDA). December's remarkable total of 4.3 billion took the overall figure for 2006 to 41.8 billion, surpassing the MDA's prediction of 40 billion and giving a daily average for the year of 114 million.

Person-to-person texts sent across the UK GSM network operators throughout the last month of the year showed a growth of 38 per cent on the December 2005 figure of 3.1 billion, representing an average of 138 million messages per day. On Christmas Day this leapt to 205 million texts, an average of 8 million per hour, with the figure for New Year's Day 2007 even higher, reaching a record breaking 214 million, the highest daily total ever recorded by the MDA.

When compared to the mere 42 million messages sent per day five years ago throughout December 2001, it becomes clear just how far the nation has come in embracing text messaging technology which has emerged from a popular craze to becoming an essential communication tool, inclusive to all age groups. The number of mobile phone users accessing the Internet on their handsets is also rising. According to figures announced today by the Mobile Data Association (MDA), a total of 40.7 million users were recorded as having used their phones for downloads and browsing the mobile Internet in the UK during the third quarter of 2006. The total number of users recorded in July 2006 was 13 million, which had increased to 14 million by September.

Source: Mobile Data Association, January 2007.

The opportunity: an SMS reminder service

The growth in text messaging in the UK described above represents an opportunity, and one of the first text messaging business ideas has been used by the National Health Service.

In December 2005 an innovative NHS appointment text messaging service was rolled out to six London-based primary care trusts. The messaging service uses software that is designed to access NHS patient databases and send reminders of appointments. Patients can also be contacted if they are deemed to be 'at risk', and can send confirmation back by SMS.

Toby Gockel, business development manager for iPlato, which supplies the software the messaging service uses, said:

> We extract the relevant information – the mobile phone number, the date and time of the appointment – from each client's site.
>
> Clients could be hospital trusts, surgeries, any independent unit that arranges appointments. We then send the information via a TCP/IP encrypted connection from our server, which enables automatic text messaging. The server generates an appointment reminder message, which is sent via the Orange SMS gateway to every mobile phone.

Source: www.silicon.com (19 December 2005).

Pre-start preparation

Businesses do not arise fully fledged from even the most positive of enterprise cultures. A time of preparation is still needed first. The preparation may include identifying a suitable opportunity (stemming from the idea), acquiring the necessary knowledge and skills, and locating the contacts who will help. Continuing the horticultural analogy, it is the stage of planting and germination of seeds. The growing medium is important, but seeds are also needed to produce plants and those seeds have to have the ability to take root and to put out leaves. In business terms, negotiating this stage requires both a willingness to start it and some ideas about what might best be done in it.

Krueger (see Chapter 3) has argued that a willingness to start comes from the credibility gained for the proposed action because of its perceived desirability and perceived feasibility; in other words from a recognition that there are rewards that can be gained from starting a business and a desire for those rewards, together with a belief that the rewards (not necessarily financial) can be achieved. It may also be relevant to add that this presupposes that the possibility of engaging in the action in question has already occurred to the person concerned.

If these conditions are met and there is a desire to proceed then it is important to know how to do so. Various suggestions have been made about the key components of the ideal pre-start process. The formula produced by Peterson and Rondstadt (Figure 7.5) summarises some of the key components that are needed for start-up success,

Entrepreneurial success   = New venture idea

   + Entrepreneurial know-how

   + Entrepreneurial know-who

Figure 7.5 Entrepreneurial success

Source: R. Peterson and R. Rondstadt, 'A Silent Strength: Entrepreneurial KnowWho', *The 16th ESBS/EFMD/IMD Report*, 86(4), p.11.

components that by implication might then be assembled in the pre-start stage.[7] It is also important to recognise that the pre-start process can be very long.

The pre-start stage can be defined as ending when a business starts, and beginning when there is an intention at some time to prepare for that eventuality.

A traditional view of enterprise has been based on the assumption that some individuals are inherently more enterprising than others. Because of that predisposition towards enterprise, it was assumed that, given the right stimulus, such individuals were more likely to try starting a business. There could then be virtually no pre-start stage in the sense defined above. Another view of enterprise, and of enterprising behaviour, is considered in Chapter 3. It is based on the attributes and resources that individuals may possess, or may believe they possess. Attributes may include self-confidence, diligence, perseverance, interpersonal skills and innovative behaviour. Resources may include finance, experience, knowledge, skills, a network and a track record. It is suggested then that it is the interaction amongst these factors that produces a rational response, on the basis of available information, when the possibility occurs of a business start-up. Illustration 7.2 brings this situation together under a Six Phases of Start-up model.

It is acknowledged that there is inertia in individual behaviour and that it may take a discontinuity in work or in life to trigger a review of an individual's situation. Whether this review will lead to individuals trying to start their own enterprise will then depend on the attributes and resources they have accumulated and their perception of the opportunity and of environmental factors such as the availability of grants. The acquisition of those attributes and resources, if it is done with a view to a possible business start, is the pre-start stage. It is generally perceived as a stage of individual, or small team, preparation. If the culture stage can be seen to relate to the concepts covered in Chapter 4, the pre-start stage relates to the concepts in Chapter 3.

An individual, or a team, can be helped to acquire the components for a start-up. There are many ways in which this can be done, but the following paragraphs illustrate some of the possibilities.

The idea

The 'idea' can cover both the idea of starting a business and the product or service idea for a particular business. The idea of starting a business comes from the issues just

---

ILLUSTRATION 7.2
Starting a business

There are lots of things that it is necessary to do in starting a business. The following list divides them into six phases:

- *Acquiring motivation*: Finding the stimulus and commitment to the notion of starting a business.
- *Finding an idea*: Getting a idea for further investigation. This may involve considering different ways of getting into business, such as franchising or buying a business.
- *Validating the idea*: Testing the proposed product/service, both for technical and functional efficiency and for market acceptance. Also protecting the idea.
- *Identifying the resources needed*: Planning the scale of business entry. Identifying in detail the resources required, the timing, and the other support needed.
- *Negotiating to get into business*: Applying the plan, negotiating for finance, premises and contracts, deciding the type of business (such as limited company, partnership or sole-trader) and registering it.
- *Systems and linkages*: Developing the ongoing business system. Coping with statutory requirements. Establishing ties with customers and suppliers. Developing the workforce.

---

explored and particular business ideas come from the opportunities considered earlier, which may come from a number of sources but usually from the entrepreneur's own experience or from a personal desire. Table 7.3 looks at the self employment business idea spectrum common in small businesses.

Finding an idea can be done either by deliberate search or by unforeseen coincidence. In the deliberate search mode the would-be entrepreneur is deliberately trying to start a business and is actively looking for an idea. This may involve attending business meetings and events of all kinds or getting together with other like-minded individuals to brainstorm ideas. Alternatively, again in deliberate search mode, the entrepreneur, whilst in employment, is looking for a business opportunity which is perhaps not being taken up by his/her present employer. In the unforeseen coincidence mode, however, the idea may actually find the would-be entrepreneur. Often business ideas develop because people find they cannot purchase a product or service and decide to start a business to supply the product or service they could not obtain. Here daily observations are important, as are perhaps hobbies, networking and prior business experience.

Know-how

Know-how covers a number of areas of knowledge and skill, all of which may be needed by the owner-manager of a small business if that business is to be successful.

Table 7.3 The self-employment spectrum

Form or approach	Platform	Springboard
Turning a hobby into a business	Long-standing passion	Personal connections
Becoming a professional consultant/trainer	Specialised knowledge	Professional contacts
Acquiring an existing business	Managerial and marketing skills	Financial resources
Taking on a franchise	Organisational ability	Financial and marketing resources
Creating a business of your own	Enterprising spirit	Marketplace
Matching personal and market potential	Personal knowledge and potential	Knowledge and potential of yourself and others
Developing your vision	Personal charisma and inspiration	Economic and social need/potential

Source: Reprinted by permission of Sage Publications Ltd from R. Lessem, 'Getting Into Self-Employment', *Management Education and Development* (1984), Spring, p.31.

This know-how has been shown to have (at least) four dimensions (see Table 7.4 and Chapter 3).

Small business training is often the means offered for increasing small business know-how. Despite the plethora of courses sometimes offered, it is important to recognise the potential barriers that can make small business owners averse to conventional forms of training, and some of the possible counterbalancing incentives (see Table 7.5).

One skill often overlooked is communication: the ability to relate to and exchange appropriate information with the people who matter to the business, including staff, suppliers, customers, investors and advisers. It has been suggested that the traditional components of pre-start training, namely finance, accounting/bookkeeping, marketing/selling and so forth are secondary skills and that the core skill is communication. Communication is necessary in all aspects of small business development and is of particular relevance in building up and using an appropriate personal network of contacts.

Know-who

The expressions, 'it's not what you know, but whom you know' and 'the old-boy network' reflect a sometimes popular, but essentially negative, perception of certain social networks. Yet those who have examined small firm networking are convinced of its importance for the success of enterprise.

Credibility is established through personal contact and knowledge of the skills, motivation and past performance of the individual – the bankers call this the 'track record'. Since for an embryonic business there is no trading track record, investors must look to their previous relationship with the individual, whether it be commercial or personal. Thus, for example, a previous employer may agree to be the first customer, a friend may allow use of spare office space, or a relative may be prepared to lend money with little real hope of a return in the short or even the medium term.[8]

What used to be referred to as networking has clear links to, or is sometimes now referred to as social capital (see section in Chapter 4). Advice and guidance are often

Table 7.4 The four dimensions of management development

Functional knowledge and skills The technical knowledge and abilities appropriate to the business. The main know-how typically of 'the butcher, the baker and the candlestick maker'	*Generic management knowledge and skills* Planning, organising, managing time, negotiating, coordinating resources, solving problems (not functionally specific)
Business and strategic awareness Understanding the bigger picture, conceptual skills, analysis, synthesis, creativity, opportunity-spotting	*Personal competencies* Results orientation, initiative, interpersonal skills, enthusiasm, perseverance, commitment, leadership

Source: Based on R. E. Boyatzis, *The Competent Manager: A Model for Effective Performance* (New York: Wiley, 1982).

Table 7.5 Barriers and incentives to training

Barriers	*Incentives*
Cost implications	*Value*
• Time is the most valuable and precious resource and time spent on training is considered to be a cost not an investment • Time training is time not working • Much training is not relevant • Much training is not effective	• Courses of real current relevance that require minimal time off the job, and have identified early benefits
	Funding available
	• Grant assistance available to help with the cost
Attitudes	*Content*
• Bad experiences of formal training, e.g. at school • Failure to perceive the need and the potential benefits • A belief that the benefits will not last	• Trainers with business credibility • Training itself promotes further training • Process counselling will be accepted but not expert consultancy
	Promotion
Lack of relevance	• Peer business managers will be believed
• No desire to improve or grow the business • Want solutions to yesterday's problems today • Not prepared to look ahead	• Influencers will be listened to, but not 'officials' • Mail shots don't work • 'It's about increasing profits' • Through networks of contacts
Promotion of training	
• The word 'training' is a turn-off • Suggestions of paternalism • Government initiatives are distrusted • Government initiatives are distrusted	
Apprehension	
• Too many courses on offer • Too many agencies • They may be sold something they don't need • It's an admission of defeat	

seen as the benefits of a network or part of social capital, and they may be the traditional base upon which many small firms' support agencies have been built. But while they may be important characteristics of an active network they are not the only ones:[9]

- *Information*: Entrepreneurs use their social networks to signal their intentions, and to gather information about potential opportunities.

- *Sponsorship and support*: Family and friends will not only provide introductions into appropriate networks, but will also offer emotional and tangible support.

- *Credibility*: Membership of the network gives added weight to the evaluation of skills. Family and friends can provide credibility in areas unfamiliar to the entrepreneur.

- *Control*: Membership of the network, and assistance from it, require certain standards of behaviour. Owner-managers who do not conduct their business in a way that is acceptable to the community will quickly find themselves and their businesses isolated.

- *Business*: There are market networks of customers, suppliers and partners as well as production networks of subcontractors, consultants and service suppliers. In addition, there are networks of firms that may work together on projects on a basis of collaboration. This structure can provide all the components necessary for a project without the need for 'vertical integration'.

- *Resources*: Friends and family can also be sources of resources for a new small business, and many businesses are assisted by the informal venture capital market that their owners access through their networks.

These networks are complex but relatively user friendly and informal systems for the exchange of information. They have been described as 'creative communication in the business milieu'. They are not rigidly bounded and exclusive, and individuals often belong to more than one network. In general they facilitate the economic co-operation that is a feature present to at least some extent in all markets.

Networks involving small firms have a number of particular features. They are usually based on personal contacts, not official links, they are informal and are not openly advertised. They are flexible, being built up and maintained specifically to suit the purposes of their members. It is often these networks that give their member entrepreneurs the potential to react quickly to new developments. Having 'know-who' competency, networking skills and social capital can therefore be essential for success in dynamic environments.

And the result

Possessing or acquiring some or all of the possible components of the pre-start stage does not guarantee that a business will be started. The decision still has to be made actually to do it, although this is often triggered by an external event. It has been suggested that the decision is essentially a choice about the balance of risk. While the chances of success increase as relevant attributes and resources are built up, the costs of failure can also increase as personal financial commitments accumulate. It has therefore been suggested that there is a window of opportunity when the balance between benefits and costs is at the optimum, typically when people are in their thirties or early forties.

Getting started

The typical small business start-up is a new business venture; in temporary, small or unusual premises; nearly always financed from within, plus bank borrowings and with little or no long-term borrowing; usually small in terms of employment, often with only family members involved.[10] Table 7.6 presents an analysis of such a business. The reasons for starting a business may vary, but the main values driving the firm will be those of the founder(s). The basic skills of the founder will also determine the functional emphasis of the business. Normally management will be by direct supervision. The main efforts will hinge around developing a commercially acceptable product or service and establishing a niche for it in the marketplace.

The result will normally be one working unit, operating in a single market with limited channels of distribution. Sources of funds will be haphazard, and will place heavy demands on the founder, his/her partner(s) and friends and relatives. With the high level of uncertainty the level of forward planning is low.[11]

Needs

At the stage of starting up a business, the entrepreneur doing it and/or the business can have many needs. This is one list:

- capital
- family support
- customers
- suppliers
- employees
- premises
- company formation: a business name, stationery, management procedures
- infrastructure
- management skills: provided externally (consultants), or internally (training)
- information and advice
- confidence.[12]

Barriers

As well as facing the start-up needs of businesses, which are in the main an inevitable aspect of the process in which they are engaged, entrepreneurs can at this stage also face a number of distinct barriers:

- *The resource/credibility merry-go-round*: This refers to the problem of how to acquire credibility in order to get the resources necessary to prove what you can do (see Figure 7.6).

- *High entry or survival barriers*: The barriers to entry into business will depend on the amount of investment, technology and labour skills required, or on the availability of niches or of growing markets. Then, once started, the business may find that there may also be barriers to survival. High survival barriers occur when there is intense competition, saturated markets, excess capacity and changing technology or product quality requirements.

Table 7.6 Analysis of a start-up business

Aspect of the business	Description
Key issues	Obtaining customers
Economic production	
Top-management role	Direct supervision
Organisational structure	Unstructured
Product and market research	None
Systems and controls	Simple book-keeping
Eyeball contact	
Major sources of finance	Owner's savings
	Owner's friends and relatives
	Suppliers and leasing
Cash generation	Negative
Major investments	Premises, plant and equipment
Product/market	Single line, limited channels and market

Source: Reprinted from M. Scott and R. Bruce, 'Five Stages of Growth in Small Business', *Long Range Planning* (1987), 20(3), p.48. © 1987, with kind permission from Elsevier Science Ltd, The Boulevard, Langford Lane, Kidlington, OX5 1GB, UK.

- *The burden of government bureaucracy*: Ignorance is no defence when dealing with the legal requirements of officialdom. There are penalties if forms are not returned or are returned incorrectly, but full and proper compliance can be costly, even if only in the time it requires, and this is proportionally more costly for small businesses than for large ones.

- *The business plan*: Business plans are often not appropriate. When asked for a plan, the new entrepreneur feels irritated because producing it takes him or her away from the real work, frightened because he or she is not sure what it means, and confused about how to plan at all when things change daily.[13]

Business regulation

As indicated above, it is often stated by many would-be entrepreneurs and those in business that 'red tape' is a prime cause of angst amongst business owners. The World Bank Entrepreneurship Survey 2007 provides a new set of indicators relating to the relationship between business creation, the investment climate and economic development.[14] In the World Bank study a total of 84 countries were included in the analysis, and whilst the researchers did reiterate the views of other researchers[15] on the positive correlation between economic expansion, renewed optimism and incidences of entrepreneurship, the researchers discovered that the barriers to starting a business were significantly and negatively correlated with business density and the entry rate. In essence the fewer the procedures required to start a business, the greater the number of registered firms – and the higher the entry rate.

In the UK this concern about the impact of business regulation is reflected in the title of the new government department concerned with the promotion of business and enterprise, which is the Department for Business, Enterprise and Regulatory Reform (BERR).

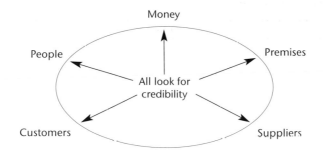

Figure 7.6 The resource/credibility merry-go-round

Source: S. Birley, personal communication (1987).

The business plan

> Before launching any new venture, the first step is to draw up a business plan.
> > Introduction to a fact sheet on business plans.

Business plans are another area in which the appropriate approach for larger businesses is not necessarily also appropriate for small ones. The view that a business plan is essential for anyone starting a small business is, to some people, so obvious that it does not need to be proved. Others however believe that, at least for some businesses, a formal written business plan in the recommended format would not only be a waste of time but could even be a misleading distraction. To understand each point of view it is necessary to look more closely into the limitations of plans and what benefits business planning and plans can offer.

> I only did it for the bank, and a year later it was obvious that the bank had not looked at it.
> > A successful businessman describing his first business plan.

> I had to present a business plan for my grant application and now, actually, I find it very useful. At the end of each week, if the sales are above the projected levels, I get a lot of comfort because it means that the business is actually succeeding. If I didn't have that reassurance I would have a lot of sleepless nights worrying whether the business was a good idea.
> > Owner of a newly opened small shop.

Owing, at least in part, to the way it has been presented, many people starting a business often see the business plan primarily as an obstacle – one that they have to address somehow, because it seems to be a compulsory part of the process. Professional advisers have told them that they should do it and may have indicated that its completion is a precondition for further help. The people thinking of starting a business may have been provided with some guidance on how to do it and given examples of suggested layouts. They may not, however, have been persuaded that it is anything but an unnecessary chore and they do not see it as a helpful tool for the venture they are about to undertake. This is especially so if all a potential investor appears to require in a plan, apart from a CV, are some financial projections (cashflow, profit and loss, and balance sheet) and the entrepreneurs cannot see how they can possibly make meaningful forecasts of what they can achieve before they have the experience of actually being in business to guide them. Of course often what the investor really needs is the assumptions underlying the projected figures, but that is rarely apparent or disclosed to the entrepreneur.

Therefore, for the person starting a small business, the basic question to be answered in relation to the business plan is not how to do it, but why. Of what real use is a business plan to a small business? Only when this is understood may the question of 'how' be relevant.

If the question 'why' is honestly addressed, it will appear that there are some new business starts for which a formal written business plan may not actually be essential. To some advisers that is heresy, which may be why the concept of business plans can get a bad reputation. If the assumption is made that they are essential then there is a temptation to assume that others share this view, and so the reason for it does not have to be explained. Advisers then address the question of how to do it, while those being advised still do not see why. If there is no good reason why, the result is unlikely to be helpful. This is compounded when it is the possession of a business plan, rather than the process of its preparation, which is seen to be the key.

It is generally accepted that there are two ways in which the preparation of a good business plan can be of very real and direct help to a new business.

Funding the business

The simplest application of the business plan to understand may be its role in 'selling' the business, in other words, putting across its merits. Potential investors in the business often need to be persuaded of its worth. A business gets financial support because the providers of that support think that they will themselves benefit from its provision. Banks seek to get paid for an overdraft or loan (interest) and grant-givers seek a contribution to the achievement of their aims (often improvements in the economy). They do not have to help a business. It is like a supplier–customer relationship: both have to benefit for it to work. In this case, however, the funds have to be provided some time before the benefits can be delivered, and the investors have to be able to trust the recipients to do that. In such circumstances, the business plan can be an essential tool for persuading investors that if they provide the funds then the business will be able to deliver the benefits and will survive long enough to do so.

The business plan is in effect the sales document for the business, and an understanding of the benefits the funders seek can be helpful in its preparation, for the following reasons:

- Government agencies want a lasting contribution to the economy, by means such as increased business and exports and more jobs. They may use terms such as 'viability', 'additionality' and 'admissibility', so that is what the plan or sales document has to convey.

- Banks want interest on their capital, and eventually their capital back, so they will want to see how the business will be able to afford this.
- Business angels and venture capitalists want to see that their investment in the business will increase in value and can ultimately be realised.

Whilst most business start-ups are small in terms of the finance required to get them off the ground, a small but growing number of businesses may be funded in part from either business angel money or money from venture capitalists. These larger-scale investors will put money into a business in exchange for an equity stake, and they expect to see a business plan to indicate what returns might be expected. It is important, therefore, for the entrepreneur to understand just what an investor wants to see from a business plan and in essence there are four main features:

- why the proposition is unique
- how it will make money (cash and profits)
- how it will be delivered effectively
- why it is a suitable investment vehicle.

The plan needs to be realistic and believable, understated rather than overstated, and grounded in hard facts. There are two crucial requirements. The plan must show how the management will deliver and what milestones are involved. The relationship between management and investors is crucial and should be one of mutual interest and trust.

Managing the venture

> The plan is nothing: planning is everything.
> Napoleon

Advice about business plans may vary, but it is generally agreed that one of the most important uses of a business plan – or rather of the process of preparing it – is that it can help the business owner to see that all relevant aspects of the potential business are addressed and allowed for. Further, the subsequent monitoring of events against the projections can show where action is needed, if any, to keep the business on course. Can someone, in a new business, in a venture and in a field that is to some extent new or novel, allow for everything without thinking it through, and probably putting it on paper? Is he or she prepared to invest savings in the business without analysing the risk? Can he or she do that without going through the analysis needed for a plan? The answer to these questions may be 'yes', but it may require some thought. The process of producing the plan can assist in focusing strategic thinking; and the plan, when completed, can provide a benchmark against which to measure subsequent performance.

When a business plan does not help
From the above it will appear that if someone starting a business does not need to raise funds, and understands what he or she is about to do and the process of doing it, then

a written business plan may not be needed. That at least is the view of some small business commentators, although it may be a controversial one. They believe that strategy is often in the head of the small business owner, and he or she may see no need to write it down. All that is required is that the person starting a business has some idea of the goal and the route to be taken to it. In these circumstances, asking an aspiring entrepreneur for a formal business plan can actually be detrimental to the business. In deference to the apparent expertise, and therefore presumed superior knowledge, of the person making the request for the plan, the emerging entrepreneur may try to produce one in line with a prescribed format. If he or she does not understand what a business plan means, or the logic behind the format, then the plan may be a bad one and the time wasted on it may be considerable.

Demystifying the business plan

> Whereas anyone can make a plan it takes something quite out of the ordinary to carry it out.
>
> General Sir Frederick Morgan

It may help to understand what a plan is and what it is not:

- *What a plan is*: Planning is an essential part of the process of getting positive results. It is the working out of how those results can best be obtained. It is a means of communicating your thoughts on this to others. The emphasis is on the plan being a vehicle to communicate your idea to others.

- *What it is not*: A plan is not holy or magical. It is a forecast. It should not be a pious hope or fixed and absolute.

Professional help: a word of caution

Why don't businesses get someone else to prepare plans for them? Others can help, but they should not do it all – unless the sole reason is to get a grant. Getting someone else to prepare it will not give the entrepreneur an insight into the issues to watch for or an understanding of what will make the business work best. Apart from possibly securing a grant or a loan, a plan prepared by someone else, without the owner-manager's involvement, probably at best gives the business nothing and could actually do harm (see Illustration 7.3). Generally, the process of preparing the plan is much more valuable than the plan itself. What, however, if all the business wants is a grant or a loan? The business should invest the minimum of resources required to produce a plan with acceptable content.

Summary

Everyone plans in some way or other, but not always on paper. Properly used, a business plan is a help, not an obstacle. A lot of nonsense has been talked about it and it has in some cases been promoted as the answer to almost every business ill. A formal

---

ILLUSTRATION 7.3
The failed plan

Sue and Mary were two partners who started a clothing design business with financial backing from their parents, who put up their houses as security. Because they were too busy setting up the business, an adviser prepared most of their business plan for them, including the financial projections. The business looked attractive and the bank supported them. Probably because of their personal appeal and enthusiasm, they even won a small business start-up award. Unfortunately, however, they had never understood cashflow forecasts and the adviser's business plan only served to disguise this. Almost inevitably they lost control of their cashflow, and the business collapsed. The parents of one of them lost their house as a result.

---

written plan is not the essential starting point for every successful business but there have nevertheless been many businesses that suffered because they were not planned properly, and plans are often essential for securing the support of others.

For those who do want to prepare a business plan, or at least to know what that might involve, a brief guide to compiling one is provided at the end of this chapter.

Financing the start-up

To some extent small business financing issues vary from country to country. In many former communist countries in Central and Eastern Europe, the banking system has been very undeveloped and unreliable and, especially when this is combined with the need to charge very high interest rates in times of high inflation, the result had been that businesses there rarely used bank financing. Even in Western Europe the use of bank financing varies from country to country. This is shown by a survey that produced the results shown in Table 7.7. The majority of small businesses however rely on internally generated funds to finance new activities. According to one survey[16] between 70 and 80 per cent use retained profit and cashflow to fund activities and it has been reported that in the UK a third of small businesses do not borrow at all from banks, another third regularly move into and out of an overdraft, and a third are consistent borrowers.[17]

In many countries there are claims that small businesses are particularly disadvantaged because it is harder for them to find appropriate sources of funding than it is elsewhere. In almost every country there are claims of disadvantage because finding funding is harder for small businesses than it is for bigger ones. There is no doubt that the difficulty of financing small businesses is one of the most frequently heard complaints. The reasons why there is this difficulty include those shown in Table 7.7.

- Small businesses are not a good risk. Suppliers of business finance, when they exist, want something in return for their money. Usually this is a financial return, either interest or dividends, plus some way eventually of getting back the initial investment or a multiple of it. If the finance sought is a development grant then returning it may not be an issue, but there will nevertheless still be an expectation that some

Table 7.7 Debt structure by country (percentage of total borrowings)

Type of facility	Britain	France	Germany	Italy	Spain	Overall
Overdraft	42	23	17	32	14	29
Short-term loans (under two years)	9	18	20	20	45	20
Medium-term loans (two to five years)	13	32	20	15	19	18
Long-term loans (over five years)	19	11	36	19	20	21
Leasing and hire purchase	17	14	7	13	3	12
Total	100	100	100	100	100	100

Source: P. Burns and O. Whitehouse, *Financing Enterprise in Europe 2*, (Milton Keynes: 3i Enterprise Centre, 1995).

benefits will be delivered, such as job creation or other economic benefits. In all cases, if the money is to be provided in advance of the returns, which is inevitably the case, then there needs to be some indication that the return will come and that the business will survive to deliver it. Although the often quoted very high failure rates for young businesses are not always what they seem to be (see later in this chapter), a significant proportion of small businesses do fail soon after start-up. Small businesses are therefore more vulnerable than larger ones, and will need to provide potential investors with some evidence that in their particular cases they will not fail.

- New small businesses do not have a track record. It is said that business financiers generally assess a business on three aspects: the management, the management and the management. For a new business with no trading history, and often with untried management, it is very difficult to provide satisfactory evidence that it will not only survive but will also do well enough to provide investors with the returns they seek.

- It is not cost effective to provide small amounts of money. Any commercial source of funds will want to check the business, its backers and its proposals before investing, and will want to monitor its investment on a regular basis. This is sometimes known as 'due diligence'. The cost of these checks will have to be recouped from any eventual income from the investments made. It is therefore not cost effective to check requests for small amounts of money, because the cost of checking will not be significantly lower than for larger amounts yet there will be less interest out of which to recoup it. (However some steps can be taken to reduce the costs of small amounts of assistance. One example in the United States is the Wells Fargo Bank, which has stopped monitoring many of the small businesses to which it has advanced loans because the cost of monitoring was more than the bad debts it incurred.)

- Small businesses lack security for loans. Small businesses often lack the collateral needed to secure loans, having few or no significant realisable assets in the business.

- Small businesses can be equity-averse. There is evidence that many owners of small businesses can be averse to sharing the equity, and therefore the ownership, of the businesses with anyone else. Investors, however, often like to take some equity because it gives them some control over their investments and an opportunity to make greater returns.

- Grants produce dependency. Because of their potential contribution to economic development, grants are sometimes considered to assist small business development and in particular to fill the so-called funding gaps that are perceived. Without care in their use, however, grants can easily freeze out whatever other sources of funding there are and can build a culture of dependency on 'free' money.

The sources of finance that are generally used by small businesses, especially when they are very small and are in the early stages of development, are the owners' own savings or the resources of family and friends. The result is that a typical pattern of small business funding can be as depicted in Figure 7.7, which is based on American experience. In recent years significant amount of early-stage funding has also been found from credit card funding, often using multiple credit cards.[18]

In the UK many start-up businesses require finance of between £5000 and £25,000, and that is typically found from the famous 4Fs – founder, family, friends and foolish strangers. This money is often supplemented by a term-based bank loan and overdraft facility, and perhaps a small loan or grant from a public body.

The next level of funding can be anything between £25,000 and £250,000. This could come from a large bank loan secured on an asset and perhaps making use of the Small Firms Loan Guarantee Scheme (SFLGS) to underwrite up to 75 per cent of the loan. Again an overdraft facility will most likely be provided. This could be supplemented by anything from £25,000 to £75,000 in the form of an equity stake from a business angel. It is however still the case that up to 80 per cent or more of funding at start-up does not involve an equity stake from an outside partner. The funding package still mainly remains personal funding and bank funding secured on an asset.

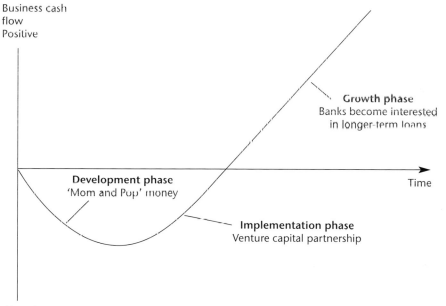

Figure 7.7 Early stage small business finance

Source: Based on author's personal contacts relaying US experience.

The third stage is the £250,000 to *c*.£1 million stage, where the funding is more likely to be of the package type, from a number of sources, perhaps combining personal, bank, public sector loans and grants and equity investment.

Beyond this stage is the use of large equity investment vehicles, often through a consortium of investors from different venture capital funds. In these cases the high risks of business failure are taken into account through the process of due diligence by investors seeking to manage risk.

The features of 'small' business entrepreneurs

In Chapter 6 and in this chapter the point is made that in exploring the subject of enterprise the fundamental unit to consider should be the entrepreneur, not the firm. So far in this chapter, however, the process of business start-up has been perhaps related to the perspective of looking at the process and the generally held view of how that sequence should be considered. First, the idea, then the opportunity, followed by the business plan and the acquisition of the necessary resources manifests itself in small businesses. The process as outlined does need the entrepreneur and he or she can differ in his or her attitudes and actions from the owners and managers of larger businesses especially in the transition into entrepreneurship. Also the many different profiles of entrepreneurship need to be understood in terms of the distinctive elements in women-owned enterprises, ethnic businesses and social enterprise.

The transition out of employment

The pre-start-up stage of small business development has already been described, and it has its own particular issues to be understood. Despite the emphasis that has been put on the benefits of small business, the predictions of increasing numbers of people who will not have the option of lifetime employment, and the varieties of help available to ease the business start-up process, moving from employment to self-employment can be traumatic. Business planning can help to indicate the physical and financial provisions necessary to establish a business, but not the mental changes necessary.

Especially if the change is an enforced one, such as when it is occasioned by redundancy, the range of mental adjustments that have to be made can be considerable. One study identified six phases in the process of leaving employment in this way:[19]

Immobilisation	The change in status shocks and overwhelms to the extent that understanding, reasoning and planning are not possible.
Minimising change	The first reaction to change is to try to minimise it and to try to carry on as if it hadn't happened.
Depression	When the reality of change can no longer be avoided depression sets in; change has happened, but is neither desired nor understood.

Acceptance	Eventually however the reality of change is accepted, the turning point has been reached.
Testing	Previous attitudes and assumptions are relinquished; new concepts, methods and ways of coping are tested.
Meaning	As this progresses, stereotypes are abandoned, new possibilities emerge and success can be possible in the search for a new meaning.

If the process of leaving employment is continued into starting one's own business, then other changes have to be made. Lessem suggests that they include:[20]

Employee to employer	You become the giver, not just a receiver. You set the standards, not just adhere to them. You accept responsibility for other people's jobs. Money becomes important.
Salary to profit	You need to spend before you receive. Income becomes uncertain. Your family cannot be kept at arm's length.
Evaluator to decision-maker	You need to consider the options, evaluate them, and then make tough choices.
Specialist to generalist	You need to call on technical, marketing, financial, administrative, people and management skills, and possibly all of them from yourself.

Part-time businesses

Another category of small business with its own particular issues is the portfolio or part-time business. This is not the same as portfolio entrepreneurship (see Chapter 6), in which one entrepreneur simultaneously has a portfolio of businesses, each of which may employ other people. Instead it is when one person engages in more than one activity, which may be a combination, or 'portfolio', of self-employment activities, or a combination of part-time work and part-time self-employment.

Like other aspects of small business, portfolio or part-time businesses can seem different when viewed from different perspectives. From the perspective of the business they can seem to be incomplete, and a less than whole-hearted dabbling in business, which may be why business support agencies often refuse to support them. Alternatively, from the point of view of the person concerned, they can be parts of a complete life, and can both be complementary and together provide a balance and diversity which might otherwise be lacking. Thus there are many artists who teach part time and produce art part time, some of whom find that the combination of working with people and producing their own work is more rewarding than doing either alone. Also, in rural areas, many people combine part-time farming with another form of income generation, often a part-time business. Without the part-time off-farm income they might have to give up farming completely, which they do not want to do. Both these examples illustrate cases where small businesses are part of the life of the owner, not the ends in themselves, and therefore need to be understood from that perspective.

Identification with the business

Once the business has started, the founding entrepreneur is likely to identify with it closely. No matter how dedicated he or she may be, a professional manager brought in to run a business is unlikely to identify with that business to the extent many business founders do. 'The business is the ego', as Gibb points out, 'and therefore even objective criticism of the business is taken personally.'[21] The implications of this include the facts that:

- A business 'consulting' approach, which attempts to analyse and list what is wrong with a business before suggesting corrective actions, will be rejected because it is perceived as a personal criticism. Instead, a 'counselling' approach, which seeks to help the owner to identify some of the issues, stands a better chance of being accepted and producing change.

- Perceived social status or acceptability may be linked to business success. Indications of business problems will therefore be played down, hidden or even denied, not just in public but also in private, in case they might have an impact on social status.

The values embodied in the business will often be those of the owner-founder and can be revealed in the products or services supplied, growth orientation, quality standards and employee relations. Where these values of the owner differ from those of business advisers, the input of the latter is likely to be rejected and, indeed, small business owners often lack the confidence to discuss problems with professionals. For these reasons, an owner's support network is likely to be based on personal friendships and contacts, rather than on the formal support network.

The influences on the small business owner

In seeking to understand the behaviour of a small business, what matters is often not so much the influences on the business as the influences on its owner. It is not always obvious however what these influences will be or what will be the interplay between the different influences. The relative strengths of the influences of different groups of people are indicated in a diagram produced by Gibb to indicate the layers of small business support networks (see Figure 7.8). One implication of this is that the closer, and more personal, layers may always have a much stronger influence than the outer, and more official, layers.

The totality of influences on a small business is often not appreciated. For instance, if assistance is made available to encourage small business development, it may be designed to add a positive influence, but it is unlikely to work if it does not outweigh other existing negative influences. If friends when consulted are negative in their advice then this will probably be far more influential than any positive input from government agencies. It can be helpful to portray the possible influences on a business as being of three types: those that may influence the business to be more competitive; those that may influence it to be less competitive; and those that may influence it to stay where it is. The latter can be the most powerful. Trying to make a business more competitive can be likened to trying to move a heavy weight uphill. Gravity may tend to drag it back, friction and inertia tend to keep it where it is, and only the push

The Purposive Support Network

Commercial Contacts – Customers, Suppliers etc

Professional Advisers With Whom He/She Must Deal

Close and Trusted Business Acquaintances

Close Friends, Relatives, Family

The Small
Business

Figure 7.8 The layers of the small business support network

Source: A. A. Gibb, 'Towards the Building of Entrepreneurial Models of Support for Small Business', Paper presented at the 11th (UK) National Small Firms Policy and Research Conference, Cardiff, 1988, p.17.

applied uphill will tend to move it in the desired direction. This analogy is pursued further in Chapter 8.

It may also be relevant to compare the prime influences on, and sources of advice for, small businesses with those relating to big businesses. The most powerful influence in a small business often comes from the ownership. This is often one person or a small group who take an active role in the business. They are much more influential on the business than the shareholder owners of a bigger business who, because they are external and disparate, have less immediate impact. In contrast, however, suppliers and customers, although they are external, can have a much bigger influence on a small business than a big one. Some reasons for this are that a small business generally has less market influence in pricing or advertising than a big organisation, and is likely to have fewer customers and to work more closely with them. Other external influences on big businesses can include trades unions, public bodies and pressure groups. Small businesses, in contrast, are less likely to be unionised, are more likely to try to ignore regulations, and are a less rewarding target for campaigns.

Inside a small firm the owner-manager is often all-powerful. While in a big business the chief executive can be very powerful, he or she still has to answer to a chairman and board, and to work with professional senior managers who often have expert knowledge relevant to their particular functions. In big businesses a unionised workforce can have the influence of its combined strength exercised through the union structure. Also, in big businesses professional sources of advice are generally used. The small business owner-manager, in contrast, has fewer such sources of influence and will instead be more likely to listen to his or her own inclinations, to rely on his or her own experience and to seek advice, if necessary, from a network of personal contacts. The small business owner-manager, in comparison with the manager of a larger business, often has less general professionalism but more flexibility and knowledge of his or her particular niche.[22]

Women-owned businesses

A number of issues particular to women-owned small businesses have already been considered in Chapter 6, and are not therefore repeated here. It has however been suggested that, in general, because women's life experiences are very different from men's, they do business differently from men.[23] Men are said to aim for profit and growth whilst women focus on relationships and integrate business relationships into their lives. Others however do not feel that such conclusions can be drawn from the evidence.

The issue of whether or not female owned firms have different management styles from male-owned firms has moved the research focus on from broad descriptions of personal and business characteristics.[24] Additionally, as outlined by Carter and Shaw, recent research review papers have stressed very similar findings on the characteristics of female-owned enterprises. [25] These are:

- Women's experiences of business ownership are remarkably similar irrespective of international context.

- Women's businesses appear to take longer at the gestation stage.

- Female-owned businesses tend to be started by individuals rather than teams.

- They do not demonstrate the same level of business performance as businesses owned by men or co-owned by men and women.

- They exit at a faster rate.

- The presence of dependent children constrains entrepreneurial actions.

- Female-owned businesses use about one-third of the starting capital used by men.

The survival of female-owned businesses

There is, however, *prima facie* evidence that female-owned businesses do not survive as long as male-owned businesses, which might be because of the under-capitalisation of female firms at start-up. A recent British study investigated this issue but argued that research on the performance of women-owned firms is complicated by the different theoretical stances adopted by various authors; by the fact that only sole business owners are investigated; by assumptions that male and female entrepreneurs are homogeneous, and by conflicting ideas on whether biological differences between men and women cause them to adopt different socio-economic roles.[26] It was also pointed out that there were lots of contradictions in quantitative studies of the performance of male and female-owned firms and that some studies do not allow for the fact that women tend to set up businesses in sectors which traditionally have higher failure rates.

Ethnic businesses

Just as there are well-known and crucial questions relating to women-owned businesses, so too there can be particular issues in ethnic and minority community enterprise. The main theories concerning the basis of the disadvantage faced by the ethnic minority population fall under three main headings of human capital, social capital and economic capital. The human capital approach stresses the role of education, experience, job-related skills and training and language fluency.[27] The social capital approach emphasises the importance of networks and ties within the community, whereas economic capital explanations are based on the fact that many people in the ethnic minority community came from economically underdeveloped, war-torn, or former colonial countries. They did not arrive with much in the way of economic capital and have not really accumulated much after their arrival. However it has been argued that as time has gone by since the first arrival wave of ethnic minority immigrants into the UK, these groups have had the opportunity to some extent to accumulate both the human and economic capital to seek mainstream employment and possibly entrepreneurship (self-employment) as an effective form of upward social mobility.[28]

Academic spin-outs

The importance of knowledge transfer has been increasingly recognised by UK universities, particularly since the 1990s. The present interest in knowledge transfer has been linked to the enactment of the Bayh–Doyle Patent and Trademarks Amendment Act in the United States in 1980 which provided incentives for US universities to patent scientific breakthroughs with the help of Federal funding.[29] The desire to maximise the return on invention coming from universities is not a new one as the following comment from 1919 illustrates:

> the small band of British scientific men have made revolutionary discoveries in science yet the chief fruits of their work have been reaped by businesses in other countries, where industry and science have been in close touch with one another.[30]

The modern concern that the economic benefits of discoveries being made in the UK are only being felt in California has led various UK governments towards attempts to stimulate the commercialisation of university knowledge and technology. In 2001 the Government established the Higher Education Innovation Fund (HEIF) and this has continued into 2007, with the latest round of HEIF worth £238m over two years.[31]

The university knowledge transfer sector is commonly referred to as the 'third stream', following on from teaching and research. The 'third stream' agenda seeks to encourage four types of university activity:

- formation of university spin-out companies
- licensing of university technology to industry
- academic collaborations with industry and contract research
- knowledge-transfer activities including entrepreneurial teaching, student industry placements, encouragement of student start-up companies and university interaction with local SMEs.

The Sainsbury Report in 2007 found that there had been an impressive increase in the amount of knowledge transfer from British universities.[32] In 2005–6 over 1500 patent applications were filed and almost 2700 royalty licences executed, and 187 spin-out companies were formed by UK universities. There are currently over 9000 active patents held by UK higher education institutes, over half of which protect IP outside the UK.[33] Also in the three years from 2004 to 2007 a total of 25 UK university spin-outs were floated on the stock exchange and a further six university spin-outs, mostly from the biotechnology sector, had been acquired for £1.8 billion.[34] The Library House Report on university start-up companies found that UK start-ups are of similar quality to US university start-ups in terms of the venture investment they attract and their downstream durability.[35]

Spin-outs and the entrepreneur

In any potentially successful spin-out situation there are a number of key features that need to be in place or put in place if the venture is to succeed. These are:

- intellectual property and its evaluation
- management resources
- suitable capital structures.[36]

The majority of academic spin-outs are considered to be somewhat different from the typical small business start-up. In a spin-out, instead of just one entrepreneur, the management resources most frequently will comprise the founding scientist(s), a manager recruited to help at the initial stages and a representative from the university. Often the scientist will have little commercial acumen and will not be motivated primarily by any thoughts of financial return. The typical traits of the start-up entrepreneur (e.g. need for achievement, motivation, locus of control, risk taking) are not likely to be much in evidence. Instead the founder scientist will be product-driven, not business-driven. If it is to succeed however, a spin-out will need the focus of the research to be on commercial priorities rather than academic priorities: 'Most spin-outs, by definition, have unproven or immature business models, combined with inexperienced founders and incomplete management teams with little or no know-how from a commercial perspective.'[37]

If the spin-out is to work what usually has to happen is that an experienced CEO or chairperson needs to be brought in, usually by the investor(s). Here it is crucial that the scientist and the entrepreneur can understand each other's role in the development of the business and work together. This is the start of the build-up of the management team. Often the new CEO or chairperson will be by necessity someone with an extensive track record in several spin-outs. If the spin-out is to build to a major business then other common features will be introduced. They will take the form of the creation of a company board to act as a vehicle for stakeholders to provide guidance and expertise. Often this will mean one or two independent non-executive directors (NEDs) will be recruited alongside, if needed, an experienced marketing director and finance director.

Although easy to describe in terms of the process, this development of an executive team working alongside the scientist(s) and a board representing the interests of investors is not an easy situation and conflict of some kind is inevitable between the various stakeholders.

Business failure

According to Storey, the fundamental characteristic, other than size per se, which distinguishes small businesses from larger ones is their higher probability of ceasing to trade.[38] Ceasing to trade does not necessarily mean failure, but in at least some cases business are closed because they have failed to deliver the benefits their owners required. Why small businesses fail however is less easy to state with certainty, both because failure itself is not clearly defined and because the precise causes of it are hard to diagnose.

In theory post-mortems could be carried out on individual business failures but this is rarely done. What is more common is to ask small businesses which have not yet failed (and therefore still exist to be asked) to indicate what their problems are. This produces lists such as that in Table 7.8. But the problems are inevitably linked and it is hard to say which problems are causes and which are symptoms. For example, low turnover can mean it was a poor business opportunity, or poor selling skills.

Another approach is to look at the businesses which have failed and to try to establish correlations with other factors. Storey presents the following useful summary of factors which appear to influence the probability of failure of a business:[39]

- *Age*: As firms get older their chances of survival increase, and this is sometimes attributed to the liability of newness. There is a great deal to learn about running a business and expertise grows with time. Other researchers talk about the 'liability of adolescence'.[40] However most firms when they start have a stock of resources and energy, which sees them through their early months or years. When this stock is used up many firms will fail. Thereafter the usual liability of newness arguments apply.

Table 7.8 Small business problems

Problems cited by a sample of 726 businesses	Proportion of all citings
Low turnover	31.8%
Regulation and paperwork	14.4%
Lack of skilled employees	10.9%
Cash flow/debtors	9.0%
Total tax burden	6.7%
Competition from big business	6.2%
Premises/rent/rates	2.9%
Internal management difficulties	1.9%
Access to finance	1.8%
High rates of pay	0.8%
Interest rates	0.4%
Shortage of supplies	0.4%
Inflation	0.1%
Other	11.0%
No response	1.8%
Total	100.0%

Source: Based on the Nat West/SBRT *Quarterly Survey of Small Business in Britain*, Vol. 17 (March 2001), p.20. Reproduced with permission from the Small Business Research Trust.

- *Size*: Failure rates are inversely related to the size of the firm at start-up. It has been suggested that larger firms are less likely to fail because if a firm is relatively large at start-up then it will quickly benefit from economies of scale. Furthermore, it will probably have sufficient financial resources to see it through its teething problems and it may also be in a good position to raise additional capital.

- *Sector*: Firms in different sectors of the economy exhibit different failure rates. In Britain, for example, the failure rates in manufacturing are greater than in various service sectors, although Storey notes that variations across sectors are not as great as economists would expect. Indeed, differences in failure rates within sectors are greater than across sectors.

- *Past performance*: Those firms which are able to grow are less likely to fail than those which maintain the status quo. Growth signifies development and learning, which are crucial ingredients for survival. Interestingly, survival rates are not linked to the rate of growth. Achieving some growth is the determining factor.

These are the more important factors connected with survival but there are others such as:

- *Ownership*: There is some evidence that the form of ownership can reverse the finding that, other things being equal, smaller firms have higher failure rates than larger firms. It has been argued that larger firms with less personal ownership will more readily leave an industry if demand is falling whilst smaller firms will struggle on. This might arise because larger firms have several plants and they may well close their non-economic ones promptly. In addition, larger firms may have multiple interests and they will divert their resources from an area of declining demand to more profitable sectors.

- *People/management*: It is likely that the kind of managers and non-managerial personnel who work in a firm will influence performance. At the very least there would seem to be a link between competence and success. Storey reviewed a number of studies which attempted to assess how work history with particular reference to previous business ownership and management experience, education, family background and personal characteristics such as gender, age and ethnic background influenced business performance. He concluded that whilst there is much speculation on the impact of these variables, 'it is difficult to draw clear patterns from the results so far.'[41]

- *Location*: Research reveals that there are pro rata many more business failures in urban as opposed to rural areas in the United Kingdom. However, urban areas also have the greatest number of business formations, and since young firms are vulnerable it is not surprising that high start-up and failure rates are connected. Another finding in this area is that those locations which provide support for SMEs in the form of loans or business advice are likely to have lower failure rates than other areas. Support could be vital for success if crucial resources were being provided, but it might also be that the existence of support agencies is indicative of a supportive climate for business formation. Sometimes support is in essence a subsidy for the SME, and it is interesting to note that there is little association between subsidy and success. A subsidy is no substitute for a lack of ability or motivation.

- *Firm type*: The final issue investigated by Storey is the connection between the type of business and propensity to fail. Franchise businesses have been found to be less risky ventures than VAT-registered businesses in general, and limited companies are less risky than sole proprietorships or partnerships. Co-operatives however have similar failure rates to VAT-registered businesses in general.

- *Macro-economic conditions*: It would seem logical to expect that macro-economic conditions would have an influence on failure rates, and some studies have attempted to explore this. For instance the influence of interest rates, which might be thought to be a condition with a very direct influence, has been examined. In this case, however, the evidence seems to be inconclusive and it has been suggested that this may be because SMEs do not experience credit squeezes in the way that larger firms do. So too with other conditions and so, while there is some evidence that macro-economic conditions affect failure rates, overall it may not be as strong as might be expected.

An understanding of the connection between these factors and failures is very useful for economic planners, but few of the factors are amenable to manipulation by owner-managers. To identify things that owner-managers can do to minimise the chances of failure it is necessary to appreciate the everyday problems that they experience. An analysis carried out in Australia indicated that among those problems were:[42]

- Sales and marketing difficulties were the most common problems encountered. Owners had little appreciation of the marketing concept, had few marketing skills and considered that marketing was synonymous with public relations and advertising. More specifically they had considerable difficulty with market research and promotion. In view of the importance of developing markets for continued business success, interventions to increase marketing awareness and skill seem appropriate.

- The survey also found that the businesses were deficient in general management skills. They found it difficult to produce business plans and manage growth, but one particular area of concern at the time of the study was the need to have appropriate quality assurance systems. With respect to human resources the biggest problems by far concerned training and development, but recruitment and selection also created dilemmas. Some attempt was made to discover if this varied with the size of the firms but for all categories paying wages and benefits, obtaining good people and training were critical issues.

- Several firms were attempting to grow, and product development difficulties arose. A range of difficulties including pricing and promotion were raised but the biggest concern was over intellectual property protection. There is legislation in Australia for the protection of these rights but the high cost of the service means that many new product ideas are not exploited commercially. The firms also had difficulty in raising start-up finance and in managing cashflows.

Results from this study are largely in keeping with the findings from previous research in the UK and elsewhere, and provide a useful guideline for those whose aim is to support the owners and managers of small firms. It is possible to develop marketing, management, people and financial skills as well as the technical skills which are specific to a particular business enterprise, and improving competencies in these areas should improve business performance.

An understanding of the problems that small firms face and the environmental forces that put pressure on them is useful but problems can be overcome. Smallbone et al. argue that a key factor in survival is the adjustments that firms make to overcome their difficulties.[43] Adjustment requires diagnosis, decision making and action, and depends on effective change management. However, it can be argued that the very characteristics which are needed by entrepreneurs can prevent proper managerial adjustment. For example, high achievers can undertake high profile but unprofitable projects to feed their egos, independent entrepreneurs can reject the advice proffered by outsiders, and self-confidence can border on the delusional. These ingredients are present within many firms but failure does not always occur. However, small firms often do not have the financial resources to absorb environmental shocks, their owners and management teams are often deficient in managerial knowledge and skill, company structures are often weak, and the dominant position of the owner-manager means that any of his or her character flaws cannot easily be offset even by a strong management team. Consequently, any or all of these factors can prevent adjustment and trigger a decline and subsequent failure.

There is therefore no simple solution to the problem of failure. Enterprise does have an inherent element of risk, and failure might be reduced but will never be eliminated. The recipe for failure will vary from situation to situation but the ingredients for it are at least known. They are summarised by Burns in Figure 7.9.

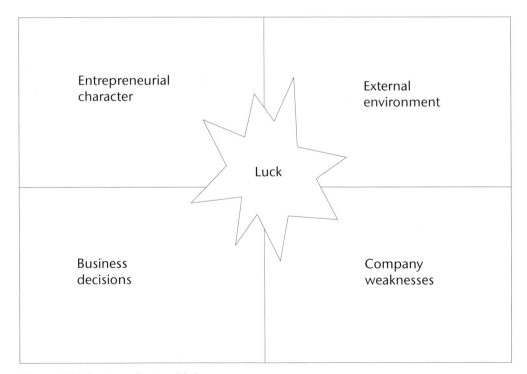

Figure 7.9 The ingredients of failure

Source: Slightly modified version of P. Burns, *Entrepreneurship and Small Business*, Second Edition, (Palgrave Macmillan, 2007), p.329. Reproduced with the permission of Palgrave Macmillan.

Models of success and failure

Another factor which is only perceived when a business is considered from the point of view of its owner is that there can be different models of what constitutes business success or failure. When looking from a business perspective it might be thought that success or failure should be obvious, but a failure to appreciate the owner's perspective can lead to a misunderstanding of what is actually happening.

What constitutes business success is an aspect of thinking about small business that has not been much commented upon, but which nevertheless probably affects many people's thinking on the subject. The model of success that people have in mind when they talk about small businesses and consider how well they are doing is likely to fall into one of two categories, depending on whether they are looking primarily at the business or at the person behind it:

- *The business professionals' model*: Many business professionals (which term could include the professional managers of larger businesses, as well as business commentators, advisers, institutional shareholders and academics) look primarily at the business and have as their model of the successful, or 'perfect', business one that is achieving its highest potential in terms of growth, market share, productivity, profitability, return on capital invested or other measures of the performance of the business itself. Professionals may not be conscious that they are adopting this model, because they may fail to see that there is an alternative but, whether it is consciously adopted or not, the result is that a business is often judged by how close it comes to what a 'perfect' business might do in particular circumstances. Small businesses often score badly in such comparisons.

- *The small business proprietors' model*: Many owner managers of small businesses do not have the same model as the one just described. Their main concern is whether the business is supplying the benefits they want from it. These benefits are often associated with a lifestyle and an income level to maintain it. If, as already noted, that is achieved satisfactorily then there is no need to grow the business further. Business success for them is being able to reach a level of comfort ('satisficing') rather than achieving the business's maximum potential.

This difference of appreciation may be linked to the different ways in which persons making the appreciation are linked to the business concerned. Even if the 'professional' is employed as the chief executive of a business, he or she probably still sees the business simply as a business, and can compare it therefore with an ideal. It, and its success or failure, may be very important to such persons, but they can and do see those aspects of their life that are not involved with the business as being completely separate. For the small business owner, however, the business is such a crucial and integral part of his or her life that the business and non-business parts of life are not considered separately. Thus the business is seen in terms of life as a whole, including family life, and is subject to more than purely business considerations. The model of a 'perfect' business that the owner has is therefore one that best fits with desired personal goals and values. The stress of further business improvement may be too high a price to pay for a better business if it detracts from other aspects of life, and continuity of employment for well-known employees may be more important than increased efficiency.

The implications of having these two different models is that the professionals may see a business as under-performing in terms of its potential as a business, while the owner may see it as successful in terms of what he or she expects from it. In such cases the owners will not automatically share a professional's agenda of pursuing continued business improvement if that involves more effort but has no commensurate increase in benefits.[44]

That does not mean that there will not be scope for further improvement, but it will have to be improvement that also increases the returns desired by the owner from the business. Professionals advising small businesses will be puzzled and ineffective unless they understand this. There is room for their assistance, but they must look at the negative impact of business improvement on the owner's requirements as well as the positive impact, and ensure that the positive outweighs the negative. The professionals' business model assumes that growth in a business is almost always automatically positive in its effect; the owners' model may not share that assumption. This means that in the extreme case, which is not uncommon, it may be in the owner's perceived best interests to close the business completely, and that obviously does not lead to the business performing better. Such a closure is not a failure, but would be counted as such on the professionals' model.

One area where this lack of appreciation of two models is very significant is in business accounting. Traditional accounting focuses on money and therefore has a key place in businesses, because a lack of money is the final symptom of business failure. Thus it needs to be watched closely, and traditional accounting provides the methods of doing this. However, traditional accounting is often linked to business audits and then to reporting on business success or failure. Here the traditional approach is based on the professionals' model or at least on a similar way of thinking. It appraises a business in terms of its financial or other tangible returns and not on any other requirements a business owner may have. Provided that is realised and accepted by the appraisers no problems should emerge. Nevertheless, its very universality of usage means that the traditional method is usually taken as the whole picture, which leaves many business owners feeling that they may be perceived as having failed but not understanding why.

If this two-model concept is correct then it suggests that relatively low productivity in small businesses may sometimes be due, not to a failure of management, but to a different vision of management and of what management should be trying to achieve. The 'may' is because there is undoubtedly a considerable amount of management failure in small business, and by no means all of it is due just to differing agendas being pursued by the various stakeholders. It may be hard however initially to distinguish between 'satisficing' and a mere lack of competence.

Business survival rates

One of the main ways of estimating the success rates of new small business in the UK is the one-year and three-year survival rates based on Value Added Tax (VAT) registrations. The one-year survival rate in 2004 was 92 per cent, down slightly on the 2003 figure. The three-year survival rate was 71 per cent, also for 2004.[45] On this measure there has been a gradual increase in the one-year survival rates over the time period 1995–2004 and in the three-year rate since 1998.

Survival rates differ across the regions, with London having the lowest three-year survival rate at 67 per cent and Northern Ireland having the highest three-year survival rate at 79 per cent. The low survival rates in London and the high rates in Northern Ireland can be partly explained by differing start-up rates in both places. In London business start-up rates as a percentage of the population are high, leading to greater competition and making it more difficult for businesses to survive. In Northern Ireland business start-up rates are relatively low, leading to less competition and hence higher survival rates. Barclays Bank also produces small business survival rate surveys of its business customers, available online from the bank. The most recent survey for the second half of 2004 indicates increased levels of small business survival. The bank believes the improvement to be based on better use of business planning and better use of advice from business support organisations.

In the United States a study on survival and longevity in business covered some 212,182 new establishments tracked over the period March 1998 to March 2002.[46] The data collected across all sectors indicated the following survival rates:

81 per cent after one year

66 per cent after two years

56 per cent after three years

44 per cent after four years.

Interpreting closure

Statistics on registrations and de-registrations are considered to be the best official guide to the pattern of business start-ups and closures. They are an indicator of the level of entrepreneurship in the economy as manifested by actual business start-ups and of the health of the business population. As such they are used widely in regional and local economic planning. However they are based on VAT registrations and de-registrations. These do not necessarily represent business start-ups and terminations, and neither when a business terminates, is that necessarily a failure.

Just as caution is needed in evaluating the success of a small business, care must also be taken when considering so-called small business failures. Again the problem is one of interpretation and of a propensity to assume that a business closure and a business failure are the same thing.

Just as there are different models of what constitutes the success of a business, so too there are different models of what constitutes its failure. It may seem that the closure or termination of a business and its ceasing to exist as a trading entity is *prima facie* evidence that the business has failed, but that assumption presupposes that the purpose of the business could only be achieved if it continued to exist. That would be the case if the purpose of the business was to maximise the returns from its activities but would not necessarily be so if its owner had other aims in mind for it. If for instance a business is started to provide an income for someone until a pre-planned retirement, and if it does so and is then closed when that retirement time arrives, then the business will both have succeeded in its purpose and been closed. Alternatively, if a business is started as an investment and is then sold for a profit, but the new owner transfers the process to an existing business and closes down the bought business, then again the business has achieved its purpose despite being closed.

It is, however, relevant to point out here that instances of business closure are often wrongly described as business failure. Statistics on business failure should therefore be treated warily. The corollary of this is that there are some businesses that do fail, as least in terms of failing to meet their owner-founder's objectives for them, but which don't close. Such a business may still be kept in existence, for instance, either for possible revival in the future, or because it continues to fulfil at least some needs, or to deliver at least some benefit to its owner. The benefit may only be a sop to the owner's pride, but it may be enough to prevent the termination of the business's existence. In such cases, business failure may not lead automatically to business closure.

Conclusions

The process of starting a business is not a simple one-stage process. If the starting point is a culture which encourages, or at least tolerates entrepreneurship, then the successive stages variously involve an inclination to start a business, an opportunity and an idea, some assessment of feasibility, and a search for resources and/or the funding to pay for them. Only then can the business start, and success is not guaranteed. Starting a business is risky and businesses do fail, especially at an early stage. Much depends on the entrepreneur, but if the issues that he or she faces are understood, the risks can be minimised.

THE KEY POINTS OF CHAPTER 7

- Between its conception and its eventual termination a business can go through many stages, although there are no clear boundaries between the different stages.

- Among the first requirements for the development of a business are the sort of culture that encourages, or at least tolerates, business formation and then a source of business ideas.

- Another requirement is the entrepreneur who can both see an opportunity in an idea and is willing to try to turn it into reality.

- The start-up stage is where the business itself is formed. Often a business plan will be helpful either to help to plan to deal with likely funders or to persuade backers that the business is worthy of support, but sometimes a plan may not be needed. Finding sufficient funding is likely to be crucial.

- Just as it is wrong to assume that small businesses will behave and respond like big businesses, so too is it wrong to assume that all small businesses are alike. Small businesses in different sectors have their own particular characteristics, as do businesses of different ages and different sizes.

- The entrepreneurs behind small businesses can also differ in both their profile and their reasons for going into business. Also the influences on a small business are often much clearer if viewed with a focus on the owner rather than on the business.

- It is not always obvious, however, who or what will influence a small business or what the interplay will be between different influences. Often at an early stage close families and friends can have more influence than professional business advisers. As well as positive and negative influences on a business, there will also be influences that encourage a business not to change. A positive influence may therefore have no effect if there is a stronger contrary influence.

- In considering small business success there are two main models. Many business professionals have as their model of business success one that involves the business achieving its highest potential. On the other hand, many small business owners have as their main concern whether the business is supplying the benefits they want from it. Care must also be taken when considering business failures and closures because some failed businesses do not close and some businesses close which have not failed.

A BUSINESS PLAN

Why are you preparing a business plan? Normally there are two purposes which a business plan might serve:

- *To assess feasibility and/or aid control*: Are you checking to see whether your idea might work or how it might be made to work? A business plan can serve as your implementation plan, to help you prepare for and implement the process of creating a viable business. If you are considering feasibility and methods then there are two conflicting pieces of advice:

  - The military maxim that time spent on reconnaissance is seldom wasted.
  - The rock climbers' approach that studying a hard climb for too long before you climb may put you off. There comes a time when you must either start or go away.

- *To communicate*: Are you trying to communicate your idea to others? A plan can serve as a sales document, for instance to help to persuade a bank or other funder to support your venture. If so then you should try to ensure that it addresses any queries they might have and indicates how they should benefit from supporting your venture. Don't tell them that the plan has been written as a sales brochure just to persuade them, but make it persuasive nevertheless.

For either use a business plan is, in effect, the answers to a series of questions. Here are some of the usual ones:

The executive summary: What does the plan say?
This is the bit that people will read first to get an introduction to your venture. Some people may then read the rest of the plan and some may look at parts of the plan to get more detail on specific issues. Many however will not get past the executive summary, so make sure that it provides a good clear summary of the key points.

Write the summary last, so that it does reflect what is in the plan. Make sure that it highlights your aim and objectives and the key issues in realising them.

> Tip: If the plan is to communicate your vision, think about the gliding analogy (see the Hierarchy of Needs Model in Chapter 11). Why should someone think that you will be able to launch and then to fly your glider? Demonstrate that you should be able both to get your venture started and then to keep it going once it is launched. If you can't keep it going then it won't survive to deliver the benefits offered.

Introduction to the business: What is the business about?

- *Who is involved?* Give relevant information and stress anything which demonstrates your competence to run the business: in other words, establish your credentials. If other key persons are involved, give their details also.

- *What were the origins of the idea?* Describe how your business idea came about, for example from a hobby, previous work experience, replicated from elsewhere.

- *What is the basic proposal?* Describe clearly but briefly what the business is: that is, the product or service; manufacture, wholesale or retail; customer groups.

- *How was it developed?* What have you done to develop the idea to the stage where it might be a viable business proposal?

- *What form will the business take?* Indicate whether you will be a sole trader, partnership or limited company. Also indicate if there are any special features such as joint venture, franchise or licence arrangements. Give details.

- *What is the present position?* How far have you got in developing your idea?

- *What is your aim now?* What do you now want to do?

> Tip: A business is not an end in itself – but a means to an end. So why are you proposing to start or grow this business?

The product(s) or service(s): What do you propose to offer?

Expand upon the initial product/service description you provided in the introduction:

- What is the product or service which you propose to offer and what will be its key features? (If it is a technically complex product, confine details to an appendix and concentrate only on the main features.)

- How have you developed it and what have you done to test that it works? What is the present stage of development, e.g. R&D, prototype, production model?

- How will you produce or supply it? What you will manufacture, assemble or buy in?

- What future developments do you plan to ensure the longer-term viability of the business, such as new products or improvements?

The market: How will your offering be received?

The details given here form the basis of your expected sales and crucially affect the credibility of your business proposition. Do not assume, therefore, that your reader knows as much about the market as you do. Include the following:

- *What is the size and growth rate of the market?* If possible, indicate the value, volume, and number of customers for the product/service you offer and how the market is changing.

- *Where is the market?* Indicate the geographical areas where you intend to sell at first and in the future.

- *What is the customer profile?* Describe the typical person who will buy from you (age, sex, income group) or, if you are selling to an organisation (such as a manufacturer or wholesaler), is it to be large/small, high quality/low quality, specialist/general?

- *What is the competition?* Who will be competing against you?

- *What will be your competitive edge?* Explain why your product/service will be bought instead of your competitors' (for instance for its quality, design, packaging, after-sales service, price or your contacts). Have you got patent, copyright or trademark protection?

- *What is the evidence that there will be a demand for your offering?* Provide as much evidence as possible to indicate you will be able to sell your product/service (such as the findings of any market research or any invoices, orders or letters of intent). If you have carried out market research, put the finer details of method, questionnaires etc. into an appendix.

> Tip: While it is true that some new products create their own market (there was no significant demand for mobile phones until they were available), funders will like to see evidence that you should be able to sell what you propose to supply, and sell it at an acceptable price. Also remember that your competition may not be other suppliers of the same product or service but suppliers of other products or services which are after the same customer spend.

Costing, pricing and sales forecasts

Will you be able to sell enough?

- *Costing:* What will it cost you to provide your product/service?
  - Show how you have arrived at the estimates of material, labour and overhead costs for each of your products/services.
  - Indicate the level of sales (in value/volume) needed to break even.
- *Pricing:* What price are you going to put on your product or service?
  - Explain how you have arrived at the price for your product/service and relate the price to the cost of providing the product/service.
  - Indicate the expected mark-ups at each stage in the subsequent distribution chain so that the price to the final customer is known.

- *Sales forecast*: How much do you think you will sell?

Based on market and price analysis above, you may now be able to draw up forecasts of sales for each product/service you are supplying. These should usually be given monthly by value and volume where appropriate. (If you have difficulty in arriving at sales figures, it is sometimes useful to ask yourself: 'What sales do I need to achieve a break-even situation?' – and judge how much better or worse than that level you expect lo perform/achieve.)

> Tip: Don't confuse cost and price. If you are buying something then the cost to you is the price you have to pay. If however you are selling something then the price is what you ask for it and the cost is what you have had to expend to provide it. If the price is more than the cost you make a profit, if it is less you make a loss and, if that continues, you go out of business.

Marketing plan
How will you get customers to buy your product or service?

- How you will you get your product to the final customer (for instance through wholesaler to retailer, direct to retailer, or mail order)?
- Who will do the selling and what promotional activity will be needed to support sales (for instance media advertising, introductory offers, mail shots and follow-up)?
- What will your promotion and distribution cost you?

Manufacturing plan
How will you produce your product/service?

The process: What is the process involved? Describe the production process in outline (if it is not obvious to a layman) and specify proposed quantities on a (monthly) forecast basis. Make clear whether:

- you will make to order only or for stock (if for stock, at what levels?)
- work will be subcontracted or bought in.

Capital equipment: What equipment will you need? List all the items of plant and machinery, fixtures and fittings, office equipment etc. that you need and include:

- description
- purpose
- cost (and whether purchased or leased), and

Premises: What space will you need? Include the following:

- location, size and layout
- build, purchase or rent
- lease arrangements
- circumstances as to planning permission/building control
- costs: start-up and continuing.

Organisation and staffing

What people do you need and how will the business be managed?

Organisation: How will the venture be run? How will it be:

- established
- owned
- directed
- advised
- organised
- managed?

Staffing: How will the venture be staffed?

- Show how many people you intend to employ, when, and how much you will pay them.
- Highlight any particular skills that are needed and how you intend to recruit them, whether management or operative.
- A salary and wages budget should also be prepared for the financial forecasts.

> Tip: You need to show that you have, or will be able to access or hire, the skills you need to launch the business and to keep it going once it is launched.

Financial forecasts: Will it fly?

You should now be in a position to put together the financial aspects of all this and to see if can both be launched and then keep going.

Launching the business

What resources will you need to launch the venture and how much will they cost? You might need:

- Premises, and fitting out
- equipment
- materials
- prototypes and testing
- promotion and advertising
- staff recruitment and training
- early operations until you break even.

And where will you get the money for this?

- your own investment?
- other investments?
- loans?
- overdraft?

Keeping the business going

Once it is launched will the venture generate enough income to cover its costs? What will your costs be?

Direct costs:	Overhead costs:
Materials?	Management?
Direct labour?	Administration?
	Office costs?
	Computers, phones, stationery etc?
	Advertising and selling?
	Cleaning and maintenance?
	Insurance?
	Rent and rates?
	Interest – the cost of borrowing money?
	Depreciation?

What will the business earn? You should assess this from your sales forecast.

Putting it all together

Support this analysis with financial projections to show the overall result:

- *Cash flow*: to see if you will run out of money.

- *Profit and loss*: to establish how much profit you should make.

- *Balance sheet*: to see what shape the business will be in.

> Tip: Financial projections may seem tiresome and boring – until you can't persuade someone to fund you or you find that the business has run out of money. Then you discover why they matter.

Other points

Although not always included in business plan formats, the following can also help to persuade people to support you.

Risk assessment: What are the risks? There will be risks associated with your business: so state what they are and what you will do to minimise them.

> Tip: Being honest about the risks will be much more convincing than trying to pretend there are no dangers ahead.

Projected benefits: What are the rewards that the business should deliver?

> Tip: Projected benefits don't often feature on official business plan formats, but this is where you try to persuade people to help you by indicating what is going to be in it for them.

QUESTIONS, ESSAY AND DISCUSSION TOPICS

- Why can the stage model not be used to predict what will happen next to a small business?
- What are the key features to examine when evaluating a business opportunity?
- Producing a business plan is the key to a small business's success. Discuss.
- Small businesses start-ups are so varied that it is not practical to have a small business policy. Discuss.
- What are the main sources of funding available to the business start-up? How can they be classified?
- What are the main categorisations of small business types? Are these categorisations useful?
- Are businesses owned by women or by individuals from ethnic minorities at a disadvantage compared with those owned by indigenous males, and what if any could be done to help them?
- Conduct research into business failure rate and survival rate statistics. What are the key variables that affect a small business's chances of surviving three years or more?

Suggestions for further reading

P. Burns, *Entrepreneurship and Small Business*, 2nd edn (Basingstoke: Palgrave, 2007).
S. Carter and D. Jones-Evans (eds), *Enterprise and Small Business*, 2nd edn (FT/Prentice Hall, 2006).
D. A. Kirby, *Entrepreneurship* (McGraw-Hill, 2003).
D. Rae, *Entrepreneurship from Opportunity to Action* (Basingstoke: Palgrave, 2007).
D. Storey, *Understanding the Small Business Sector* (London: Routledge, 1994).

References

1. S. Shane, *A General Theory of Entrepreneurship* (Cheltenham: Edward Elgar, 2003), pp. 10–11.
2. W. K. Bolton and J. L. Thompson, *Entrepreneurs: Talent, Temperament, Technique*, (Oxford: Butterworth Heinemann, 2000).
3. L. Klapper, R. Amit, M. Guillen, and J. Quesada 'Entrepreneurship and Firm Formation Across Countries', *World Bank Entrepreneurship Survey*, 2007. p. 16.
4. P. Wickham, *Strategic Entrepreneurship*, 4th edn (FT/Prentice Hall, 2006).
5. Bolton and Thompson, op. cit. (2000).
6. P. Drucker, *Innovation and Entrepreneurship* (London: Heinemann, 1985), p. 132.
7. HM Treasury News Release, 23 June 2000.
8. S. Birley, 'The Start-Up', in *Small Business and Entrepreneurship*, edited by P. Burns and J. Dewhurst (Basingstoke: Macmillan (now Palgrave Macmillan), 1989), p. 16.
9. S. Birley and S. Cromie, 'Social Networks and Entrepreneurship in Northern Ireland', Paper presented at the Enterprise in Action Conference, Belfast, September 1988.
10. Forum of Private Business, 'The Internal and External Problems That Face Small Businesses', Paper presented at the Sixteenth ISBC Annual Conference, October 1989, p. 6.

11. M. Scott and R. Bruce, 'Five Stages of Growth In Small Business', *Long Range Planning*, 20(3) (1987), pp. 45–52, at p. 49.
12. Forum of Private Business, op. cit., p. 6.
13. S. Birley, 'The Way Ahead for Local Enterprise Centres', Presentation at Enniskillen, Northern Ireland, January 1988.
14. L. Klapper, R. Amit, M. Guillen and J. M. Quesada, 'Entrepreneurship and Firm Formation Across Counties', World Bank Group Entrepreneurship Survey, 2007.
15. J. Brander, J. K. Hendricks, R. Amit and D. Whistler, 'The Engine of Growth Hypothesis: On the relationship between firm size and and employment growth.' Working Paper; University of British Columbia, 1998.
16. Bank of England, *Finance for Small Firms, Third Report*, January 1998.
17. P. Burns, *Entrepreneurship and Small Business* (Basingstoke: Palgrave, 2007).
18. T. Ashbrook, *The Leap: A Memoir of Love and Madness in the Internet Gold Rush* (Boston: Houghton and Mifflin, 2001).
19. J. Hayes and P. Nutman, *Understanding the Unemployed* (London: Tavistock, 1981).
20. R. Lessem, 'Getting into Self Employment', *Management Education and Development*, Spring (1984), pp. 44.
21. Gibb (1988), op. cit., p. 14.
22. For a discussion on the various sources of influence on organisations, see H. Mintzberg, *Power In and Around Organisations* (Englewood Cliffs, NJ: Prentice-Hall, 1983), pp. 32–46.
23. C. G. Brush, S. Marlow and A. Strange, 'Female Entrepreneurs: Success by Whose Standards?' in *Women in Management: A Developing Presence*, edited by M Taunton (London: Routledge, 1994).
24. S. Carter, S. Anderson, and E. Shaw, 'Women's Business Ownership: A Review of the Academic, Popular and Internet Literature', London: Small Business Service Research Report, RR002/01, 2001.
25. S. Carter and E. Shaw, 'Women's Business Ownership: Recent Research and Policy Developments' Report to the Small Business Service, November 2006. p. 5–8.
26. E. Chell and S. Baines, 'Does Gender Affect Business Performance? A Study of Microbusinesses In Business Services In the UK', *Entrepreneurship and Regional Development*, 10 (1998), pp. 117–35.
27 G. Borjas, 'Ethnicity, Neighbourhoods and Human Capital Externalities', *American Economic Review*, 85 (1995), pp. 365–90.
28. Y. Li., 'Assessing Data Needs and Gaps for Studying Ethnic Entrepreneurship in Britain', URN 07/152, ESRC/CRE/DTI/EMDA, 2007.
29. E. M. Rogers, Y. Yin, and J. Hoffman, 'Assessing the Effectiveness of Technology Transfer Offices at U.S. Research Universities', *The Journal of the Association of University Technology Managers*, 12 (2000), p. 47–80.
30. A. Marshall (Economist) *Industry and Trade* (1919).
31. The Library House, *Spinning Out Quality: University Spin-out Companies in the UK* (London, 2007).
32. Lord Sainsbury of Turville, *The Race to the Top: A Review of the Government's Science and Innovation Policies* (HM Treasury, 2007).
33. Higher Education Funding Council for England (HEFCE), *Higher Education and Community Interaction Survey, 2007.*
34. Lord Sainsbury, op. cit.
35. The Library House, op.cit., p. 5.
36. Quester, 'A Quester Commentary' p. 6, October 2006 (www.quester.co.uk).
37. Ibid., p. 9.
38. D. Storey, *Understanding the Small Business Sector* (London: Routledge, 1994), p. 78.
39. Ibid., pp. 91–104.
40. T. Mahmood, 'Survival of Newly Founded Business: A Log-Logistic Model Approach, *Small Business Economics*, 14 (2000), pp. 223–37, at 313.
41. Storey, op. cit., p. 100.
42. X. Huang and A. Brown, 'An Analysis and Classification of Problems In Small Business', *International Small Business Journal*, 18 (1999), pp. 73–85.
43. D. Smallbone, D. North and R. Leigh, *Managing Change for Growth and Survival: A Study of Mature Manufacturing Firms in London During the 1980s*, Working paper No. 3 (London: Middlesex Polytechnic, Planning Research Centre, 1992).
44. For a discussion on the overlap between personal goals and business goals in SMEs, see R. Goffee and R. Scase, *Corporate Realities* (London: Routledge, 1995), pp. 1–21.
45. DTI 'Survival Rates of VAT-Registered Enterprises, 1995–2004: Key Results', URN 07/963.
46. A. E. Knaup, 'Survival and longevity in Business Employment Dynamics data', *Monthly Labour Review*, May (2005).

CHAPTER 8

Business growth

Contents

KEY CONCEPTS

This chapter covers:

- The stages of business development after start-up.
- The reason why government policies have focused on growth businesses.
- How business growth can be interpreted.
- The internal and external influences on business growth.
- The arguments for and against targeting growth businesses.
- The issues arising in static, declining and terminating businesses, and how and why they might also be helped.

LEARNING OBJECTIVES
_____

By the end of this chapter the reader should:

- Understand the possible stages of business development.
- Understand the rationale for a focus on growth.
- Appreciate what growth can mean.
- Understand the range of possible influences on growth.
- Appreciate why so few businesses grow to be large.
- Be aware of the case for and against a policy of 'picking winners'.
- Appreciate the main issues which can arise in the static, decline and termination stages also.

Introduction

Chapter 7 looked at aspects of the early stages in the life cycle of a business. It looked at idea development and start-up and considered a number of aspects of small business entrepreneurship. This chapter continues that sequence: looking first at business growth and then at maturity, decline and eventually termination.

Why focus on growth?

Of these stages, the one that gets most attention, encouragement and support is business growth. In the 1990s there was a substantial shift in focus and emphasis in the field of small business study towards the growing business. This shift in the UK and elsewhere was evident in policy-making, in the application of small business support, and in related research and commentaries. Fast-growing small firms have been described as 'gazelles', 'fliers', 'growers' and 'winners', and the targeting of effort towards them has been described as 'picking', 'stimulating' or 'backing' winners.

While more recently there has been a further shift back towards support for the start-up process, it is reasonable to ask why the interest in growth developed. It is likely that, just as the earlier emphasis on small businesses in general arose from a recognition of their contribution to the economy, this focus came from a similar desire to maximise that contribution. Birch's study, and other subsequent reviews, had claimed to show that the major proportion of net new jobs is created by small businesses. Governments and others saw that there could be economic benefit in supporting small businesses. More detailed analysis showed that many small businesses did not grow and therefore, once established, did not create more jobs. It was suggested that it was a relatively small proportion of small business starts that did subsequently show significant growth and were responsible for much of the main employment benefits over time. The argument, therefore, was that if small business support resources were limited, which was invariably the case, then the way to maximise results was to apply those resources where they would be most effective. The small business sector is huge and varied, and if support has to be rationed, and if growth businesses produce a disproportionately large share of the desired jobs, then the logical thing to do is to concentrate that support on growth businesses in order to secure the best return.

Associated with this line of argument have been other reasons to look favourably on growth businesses:

- There is a belief that to base support primarily on employment creation can be distorting. Instead, support should try to promote competitiveness in the economy, which should then in turn lead to jobs. Competitiveness embraces notions of innovation, dynamism, efficiency and the winning of greater market share, in particular in export markets. All these are associated with growth firms, which presumably grow because they are competitive. Promoting growth businesses therefore promotes competitiveness and ultimately wealth creation. According to the OECD, SMEs are directly producing about 26 per cent of OECD exports and about 35 per cent of Asia's exports.[1]

- There is a recognition that simply increasing numbers of small businesses may not increase total employment because of displacement effects. Those businesses that do survive may only do so at the expense of others. This is especially the case for businesses selling mainly to local markets and is one reason for the interest in hi-tech start-ups which are likely to have a much wider sales profile.

- Indigenous businesses are seen as crucial for regional development because they have the local roots that inward investments do not have. Moreover inward investment (which is also often referred to as foreign direct investment or FDI) often cannot provide the quick injection of jobs sometimes sought by regional development agencies. If a suitable indigenous business base does not exist then it has to be created from growing small firms, and there are considerable differences in the ability of certain regions to generate sufficient numbers of successful small firms.

- The UK economy is thought to suffer from the absence of a population of efficient and resilient medium-sized businesses that could provide a backbone in the manner of the German *Mittelstand* – globally competitive, usually family-owned, medium-sized businesses, often quoted as key to the success of the German economy. If such a 'backbone' is to emerge then it must come from small growth businesses. (Views on this vary, however. Levy notes that the 'distribution of manufacturing employees between small, medium and large firms' is not greatly different between the UK and Germany.[2] An alternative analysis contends that within the UK population of businesses there are more 'make-weights' and 'punchbags'. A 1995 study of 600 manufacturing companies in the UK, Germany, the Netherlands and Finland concluded that the UK had as many world-class firms as the other countries, but a significantly higher proportion of companies that lagged badly in many key aspects of performance.[3] It has also been claimed that 15,000 medium-sized businesses in the United States, while being only 1 per cent of all businesses, account for 25 per cent of all sales and 20 per cent of all private sector employment.[4])

- Growth businesses are inherently attractive to suppliers of funding and other business services, because the prospects for financial returns are greatest and because of the feeling of success through association.

- There is an increasing recognition that the proportions of established businesses which grow, and the rates at which they grow, vary much more across countries than do the rates of business start-up. That in turn suggests that there might be more potential to influence growth rates, and therefore that promoting business growth by established businesses might be a more cost-effective policy intervention than promoting business start-ups.

> We have also begun to recognise the importance of the 'gazelle' (rapidly growing businesses) phenomenon within the small business, as well as the middle size and large company universe. In fact, mobility across firm size is almost more interesting than firm size per se. I would say the number [of gazelles] is somewhere between 5 and 10 per cent. In my last look, 4 per cent of the firms were doing 70 per cent of the growth. So it's 4, 5, 6, 7 per cent. You can take it as far as you want. Rank all firms by the growth index we have developed and start peeling them off the top. Four per cent at 70; 5 per cent at 77; 10 per cent at 87.
>
> David Birch[5]

The trend towards concentrating support on growth businesses, pursued by the UK government among others, does not command universal support. Inevitably it results in relatively less support for small business creation. Many would see new businesses as potentially a vital element in a vibrant economy, even if they do not grow, since they produce a variety of products and services on which the economy and the growth businesses in it depend. It is also argued that new businesses are the seedbed for future growth businesses, and even if only a small proportion of the businesses in the seedbed do grow, the bigger the seedbed, the more seedlings that may grow. Indeed, as noted in Chapter 4, a high level of volatility or business churn (the percentage of new firms born added to the percentage of older firms that die) is considered to be the rate at which an economy rejuvenates itself on a regular basis. Within the UK, for instance, there are examples of a high level of business churn in the more economically prosperous southeast of England and low levels of business churn in areas such as Northern Ireland. Moreover there is evidence that the size category of businesses in which net job creation is greatest, over a given period of time, is the up-to-20-employee category, because it contains the greatest number of businesses, including almost all new starts.

This debate, and its implications, is an important one for those who seek to enhance the small business contribution to economic development. It is therefore a key feature of this chapter.

Looking at growth

Overall, small businesses can be divided into three broad groupings. First, there is a high proportion of small businesses that have a short life. Then there is a second large group of businesses that, although surviving, remain small. The third group is by far the smallest: it consists of those businesses that achieve rapid growth. These groups have been referred to by Storey respectively as 'failures', 'trundlers' and 'fliers', and by Birch as 'failures', 'mice' and 'gazelles'. The following empirical data help to put the last, the fliers or gazelles, into context.

On the basis of a study of manufacturing firms in the UK, Storey claims that 'over a decade, 4 per cent of those businesses which start would be expected to create 50 per cent of employment generated' (but see the comment in Chapter 6).[6] The Northern Ireland Economic Research Centre (NIERC) studied the performance of manufacturing firms from 1973 to 1986 and also found that almost 10 per cent of surviving firms created 43 per cent of employment.[7] (Applying Storey's assumption that 40 per cent of firms survive ten years, one can again conclude that 4 per cent of the original firms generated 43 per cent of employment.)

Other findings help to confirm the view that in the UK a small number of businesses have a disproportionate impact on job creation. The US experience is broadly similar. For example, a study of new firm growth in Minnesota found that 9 per cent of new firms formed in the 1980s provided over 50 per cent of employment after two to seven years.[8] While there are particular criticisms that can be made of these findings, the general picture is probably reasonably accurate: it is that a relatively small proportion of all small businesses account for the major part of the small business contribution to new jobs. In a follow-up study of all US establishments that started in the late 1990s, one of the principal findings was that employment growth was very sector-based, with growth occurring in the information, professional and business services, education and health services, and manufacturing.[9] The key employment determinant identified was sector survival rates in terms of the numbers employed per establishment that survived. Survival was therefore a crucial variable.

However it is important to note that demonstrating that, in any cohort of businesses, a few will create most jobs is not the same as demonstrating that, in any one year or combination of years, the greatest overall net job creation comes from the fastest-growing businesses. Indeed the up-to-20-employee size range appears to be the category that generates absolutely and relatively the greatest number of net new jobs. (See also Table 6.1 in Chapter 6 for statistics on employment in different size categories of business enterprises within the UK.)

The dimensions of growth

Before examining growth issues further it is logical to consider the possible dimensions, or meanings, of growth in the context of small businesses, and what observers or business owners interpret as the desirable aspects of growth. Storey, in presenting the statistics given above, makes it clear that, in common with others, he is using increases in employment as a measure of growth. Growth in a business can also be defined as greater turnover or increased profitability but, while these measures may all be seen as desirable, they may not even be positively correlated. As noted by Smallbone and Wyer, 'a number of studies have demonstrated the close correlation that exists between employment growth and sales growth in small firms over a long period of time ... although increased employment is less clearly related to a growth in profitability'.[10] Some analysts may in addition interpret growth in the context of a broader product range, or an increased number of patents or of customers, none of which necessarily imply greater turnover, profitability or employment.

People with a financial interest in small businesses often want to increase the value of their investments by growth in shareholder value, which implies a growth in business earnings and net assets, which themselves may be achieved by growth in turnover and/or profitability (or the potential for it). Employment, therefore, is not necessarily a growth goal for them, but may be a by-product of it. For government support agencies straightforward growth in employment may however be the requirement, or at least an overall improvement in the economy, which is most likely to come from a growth in exports, or a replacement of imports, and which may lead to a growth in employment.

It is important therefore to realise that, while many people may want to see growth, it will mean different things to different people. For many people, growth in employment will generally be the primary goal. For those managing economies and balances of payments, growth in export turnover, or in import substitution, is critical. For shareholders, profitability as a means to enhance dividends and share value is likely to be predominant. The individual small business owner, however, as noted previously, may have one or more of a number of aspirations. These might include being a major local employer, creating wealth, building a large income, being seen as innovative or providing jobs for the family. Many of these will be derived from, or be facilitated by, growth in aspects of the business.

While researchers frequently measure growth in terms of employment, its potential to signify different things to different people means that care must be taken in describing it. Unless its meaning in a particular situation is clear, misunderstandings may arise. It may also be necessary sometimes to remember the distinction made between forms of growth. Some of the yardsticks used for measuring growth are indicated in Table 8.1.

The components of growth

Growing a business is not easy. The natural tendency of a business, like any other system subject to natural decay, is to regress. It takes energy and effort to prevent that and instead to grow. The easiest way to understand the effort needed is to look at the needs of a growing business and the things that must be done to address them.

Under almost every definition of growth, growing a small business needs resources, for which it needs money; it needs management delegation, co-ordination, systems and control; and it needs more sales, which may in turn come from new products or markets.

Table 8.1 Yardsticks for business growth

Share value	Return on investment	Market share
Net worth	Size of premises	Exports/imports substitution
Profit	Standard of service	New products/services
Employment	Profile/image	Innovations, patents, etc.
Turnover	Number of customers	Added value

Understanding growth however requires a regard not just for these internal needs of a business, but also for the totality of the influences on it. Such influences can be external as well as internal and can hinder or help growth. They are illustrated in Figures 8.1 and 8.2 and see also Table 8.2.

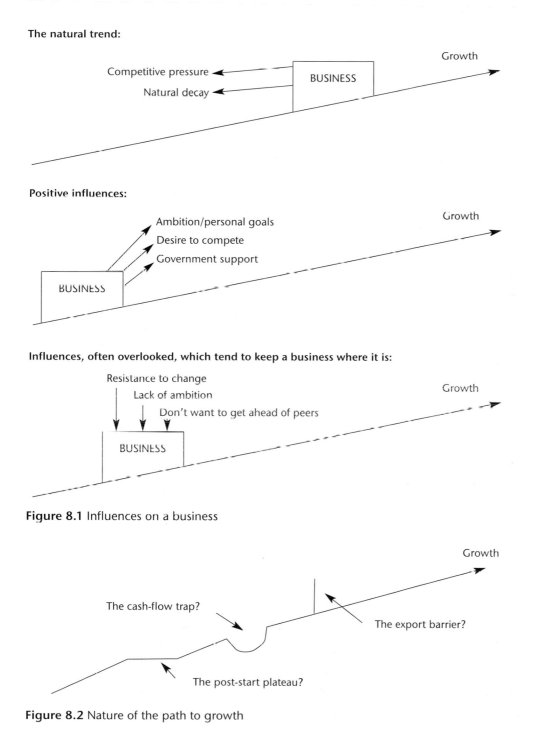

The natural trend:

Positive influences:

Influences, often overlooked, which tend to keep a business where it is:

Figure 8.1 Influences on a business

Figure 8.2 Nature of the path to growth

ILLUSTRATION 8.1
Previous academic approaches to understanding small business growth

There has been a considerable body of literature embracing very different approaches to understanding the growth process. This can be broadly divided into four categories as follows:

- Approaches exploring the impact of the entrepreneurial personality and capability on growth, including the owner-manager's personal goals and/or strategic vision.

- Approaches seeking to characterise the way the small organisation develops and influences, and is influenced by, the owner-manager. These approaches address issues of management style and stages of growth models.

- Approaches broadly embraced under the term 'business' which focus upon the importance of business skills and the role of functional management, planning, control and formal strategic orientations.

- Approaches which are more macro in scope and which usually have their academic base in industrial economics. These include sectoral approaches pertaining to regional development, a focus upon specific industry sectors or sub-sectors, for example, high-technology firms.[13]

There are obvious overlaps among these approaches. It is interesting to note however that recent economics literature on small firm growth has tended to focus on a combination of a life-cycle effect (young firms grow faster than older firms) and economic variables, especially financial variables, for an explanation of growth. Indeed in modern micro-economic theory there has been allegiance to a model of small firm growth which has led to the 'removal' of the 'human elements'.[14] Thus within economics there is a failing in empirical enquiry to address 'the key questions of entrepreneurial characteristics and motivations and how they may be translated into business strategy'.[15] Interesting studies by, for example, Barkham et al.[16] and Storey[17] have adopted a more comprehensive approach, seeking to bring together research in economics, geography, organisational studies and business strategy to examine the link between entrepreneurial characteristics, business strategy and small firm growth across a wide variety of types of small firm. Traditionally, however, the unit of study has often been the business, not the entrepreneur. The needs, aspirations and other characteristics of habitual entrepreneurs have been largely ignored by researchers, policy-makers and support agencies. 'The process of ownership diversification may shed new light on the way we can conceptualise start-up and growth dynamics.'[18]

One benefit of establishing the totality of influences on a business is that it helps to put any single influence in perspective. Without this there is a tendency to overestimate the effect of any particular influence. If, for instance, it is considered that R&D can help to build competitiveness and that a grant scheme would encourage R&D, then it might be thought that such a grant scheme would be a positive influence on a business. However, it is important to recognise the strength of the influences keeping the business where it is; they are likely to be much stronger than the more dubious incentive of a grant. This has

Table 8.2 Some of the influences on a business

Type of influence	Internal	External
Positive	Owner's desire to increase profitability and/or to prove him or herself Impetus of earlier growth	Stimulus of competition Encouragement of others Favourable tax incentives Encouragement and support from small business agencies
Negative	Bounce back from earlier uncontrolled growth Lack of ability of the owner and/or management team	Adverse tax, interest and exchange rates Improvements in the competition Product obsolescence
Those which can encourage a business not to change	Owner's lifestyle and the consequent need for the present level of return but not for more	Peer group pressure
	Inertia and the difficulty of mobilising the resources needed to do more	
	Limits on internal capacity to plan, coordinate and supervise	

been likened to pushing a heavy object: friction tends to keep it where it is, unless the pushing force is sufficiently large, and attempts to reduce the frictional resistance might be more effective than attempts to increase the amount of external push.

Growth, or its absence, can however be attributable to a wide variety of factors. There is no comprehensive theory to explain which firms will grow or how they grow, but various explanatory approaches have been used. Of course, whatever approach or combination of approaches one favours, seeking to distinguish between what is necessary and what is sufficient for growth has been and is likely to remain an unattainable goal. Indeed most of the research work in this area 'fails to provide convincing evidence of the determinants of small firm growth as a basis for informing policy-makers';[11] and again, 'Given the significance of employment created in rapidly growing small firms, it is surprising that theoretical and empirical understanding of the characteristics of these firms remains somewhat sketchy.'[12]

Influences on business growth

In the context of small businesses, what are the main influences on growth? Three types of influence in particular are examined below: first the influences of the entrepreneur, linked to his or her personality, behaviour, attitude and capability; then the influences due to the business itself, related to its structure and goals and to the performance of its management; and finally the influences of the external environment such as the business's sector, region and other strategic issues.

The entrepreneur: motivation and aspiration

The first approach focuses on the entrepreneur as a person. Personality and behaviour are believed to be causal factors for or against growth-orientated achievement.

This is understandable. It is a characteristic of small business that powers of decision are centralised at the level of the owner-manager, so his or her personality, skills, responsibilities, attitude and behaviour will have a decisive influence on business strategy.

Typical of the analysts using this approach is Kirchhoff, who develops a 'dynamic capitalism typology' to explain the relationship between innovation and firm growth.[19] The typology divides firms into four categories: economic core, ambitious, glamorous and constrained growth. Each category has its own broad growth profile.

'Economic core' businesses are low on innovation and on growth. They are the largest single category, but fast-growing firms can leap out from the core; an example is Wal-Mart, the world's largest retailer, where the most significant growth came after over 30 years of operations. 'Ambitious' firms achieve high rates of growth with one, or a few, initial innovations. Growth comes from a gradual build up of market share. However, growth cannot be sustained without additional innovations (usually in the product or service or in its marketing). With additional innovations, firms become 'glamorous'. Microsoft is a good example. Glamorous businesses, according to Kirchhoff, can have experienced periods of 'constrained growth' for two broad reasons.[20] First, growth may be self-constrained owing to the owner's reluctance to relinquish ownership and control to generate the necessary resources for growth; and second, it may be constrained where businesses are genuinely limited by a lack of resources. They can often be highly innovative, but still unable to secure early stage capital.

Kirchhoff concludes that 'what is interesting about these four classes of firms is that they do not depend upon industrial sector, business size, age nor location.'[21] This typology, he continues, 'identifies the firms' behaviours that indicate the true ambitions and goals of the owners and defines their contribution to economic growth. Aspiring entrepreneurs need to realistically assess their personal ambitions and where they wish to be in this typology.'[22]

This is a clear attribution of business growth to entrepreneurial motivation and competency, as exhibited in a willingness to innovate. It is probably reasonable to assume that the motivation to grow is likely to be the *sine qua non* of growth. Yet for many business owners the growth of their businesses is not an objective. Growth is associated with many unattractive circumstances. These may include having to find work for others, loss of management control, reliance on others, sharing responsibilities and decision making, perhaps relinquishing some ownership stake, and unnecessary risk, although there is evidence from the UK and United States that survival and growth are positively correlated. (For US data see Knaup, 2005: note 9.)

A desire to spend more time with one's family or to engage in other forms of social and leisure activity are also valid reasons. Professional and social issues combine very often, as is noted in the significant amount of literature on the family business which recognises the influence of family in respect of growth and issues of ownership. Often growth is rejected where it might lead to a conflict of interests.

There are businesses that have a no-growth aspiration. They were described in Chapter 6 as 'lifestyle' businesses, and in almost every case they are established solely to provide a satisfactory level of income. They are very often home-based, sole-trader operations employing no more than one additional person. Statistics reveal that well over half of all UK business owners in the late 1980s had no plans to grow. In addition there is a clear association between firm size and the desire to grow.[23]

Even among those entrepreneurs who seek growth, significant numbers would appear to seek only moderate or limited growth. They may reach a stage or plateau, described as a 'comfort zone', at which the owner is satisfied with his or her condition and the costs of pursuing continued growth exceed the expected benefits. These perceived costs will dominate over any material or psychological gains that might be expected from growth. As more than one owner has remarked, 'The problems grow geometrically while the firm grows arithmetically.'

> If growth of any kind is to be achieved it is important for the entrepreneur to be clear about their ambition for the business. Do they want to run a nice lifestyle business that could give them a good living for 20 years? Do they want to build the business up rapidly to sell it within five to ten years? Or do they want to build it piece by piece over time to pass it on? There is nothing wrong with any of these ambitions. They each can give the entrepreneur guidance on what risks they should be prepared to take and what they need to do to be successful in terms of the ambition they have for the business.
>
> Chris Gorman (Portfolio Entrepreneur)
>
> Source: Lecture to University of Stirling students, 2006.

With reference to the owner typologies mentioned in Chapter 3, the 'lifestyle' owners would be classified as artisans/shopkeepers but some may grow sufficiently to assume the status of Hornaday's 'professional managers'. Carree et al. claim that their 'managerial' business owners are to be found in the majority of small firms.[24] They include many franchisees, shopkeepers and people in professional occupations belonging to Kirchhoff's economic core. Indeed they further note that Audretsch and Thurik, in their analysis of how and why entrepreneurship has contributed to economic and social development, assume that their two types have different economic roles in relation to unemployment.[25] They contend that the number of what they call 'shopkeepers' is likely to go up if the level of unemployment rises, but that that level is expected to go down if the number of Schumpeterians ('real' entrepreneurs) increases. In reality, of course, it can be difficult to distinguish one type of owner from another since most owners 'share attitudes associated with these extremes in a varying degree'.[26]

The motivation of the owner is undoubtedly a very important ingredient in the (no-)growth process and, of course, the motivation can change over time as the business develops and events external and internal to the business occur. It is a dynamic situation. Firms can appear to be in a steady state for many years and then begin to grow rapidly. Growth is not necessarily a continuous process for many firms, which is an important consideration for those who rely on recent past performance as a predictor of future performance. One possible reason is a need to establish the business – to build strong roots – before moving on and upwards. The majority of firms show no growth for their first six years, while more than 50 per cent of surviving firms show growth after six years. Indeed, rapid growth, when it happens, appears to begin after six to eight years of trading.[27]

It is also worth noting that a significant number of entrepreneurs, instead of managing their established businesses whether in a growth phase or not, may be much more stimulated by, or capable of, generating new business ideas and converting them into new ventures. The excitement and fulfilment for such people may be in creating something new, not in managing an existing operation. In fact while their businesses may essentially be in the early stages of business development, the entrepreneurs themselves can become obstacles to the further development of the business as neither their interest nor competency may be at the appropriate levels. Such people may favour multiple business ownership as habitual entrepreneurs (see Chapter 6).

The role of chance

The size distribution of a population of firms can be derived from a mechanical chance model. Thus, in aggregate, firm size follows a 'random walk'. This might suggest that there is some 'iron law' of firm growth which determines the size distribution. Indeed, studies suggest that there are many factors influencing firms' growth rates, and while two or three may exert a significant influence relative to the others, they still explain a relatively small proportion of any variance produced within a given sample of firms.

It is possible to conclude, therefore, that chance or luck plays a part in determining which firms grow. To suggest that all successful entrepreneurs were merely lucky is to overstate the situation, but as Reid and Jacobsen suggest, 'it is necessary to caution those who would ignore the role of chance in determining the fortunes of the small entrepreneurial firm.'[28] In addition, as Nelson and Winter note, 'luck is the principle factor that finally distinguishes winners from near winners – although vast differences of skills and competence may separate contenders from non-contenders.'[29]

The situation can be likened to one in which racing boats in a river may or may not catch the current. To be a winner may depend on luck as well as judgement – but if, due to a lack of skills or resources, one has been unable to get one's boat as far as the river, one will certainly not win.

There is certainly no lack of anecdotal evidence from successful entrepreneurs about the role of luck, and it is surely undeniable that 'in the presence of uncertainty and bounded rationality, fortune will play a significant if variable role.'[30]

Other entrepreneurial characteristics

It will also be apparent that the will or motivation to grow by no means guarantees growth. So a growth model that focuses on the individual entrepreneur as the key to the growth process must also take into account aspects of the individual other than motivation, such as traits, behaviour and resources. These factors will influence the entrepreneur's ability to achieve growth, as well as his or her will to do so.

Storey has reviewed a number of empirical studies that examine which characteristics of the entrepreneur, including motivation, are related to growth.[31] The conclusions drawn however do not permit the development of a profile or model of the growth-achieving entrepreneur in terms of the subsequent performance of the firm. There is some suggestion that the more significant variables, in addition to motivation, are education, age and management experience, all of which are positively correlated. (Motivation, however, in this instance refers only to why the business was established – not motivation to grow.) Barkham et al. found that the entrepreneurs associated with faster-growing manufacturing firms were relatively young and members of professional organisations, that they had worked as part of a larger entrepreneurial team, and that they had a network of other business interests which were mainly legally independent and separate small firms.[32] In some cases the existence of other businesses was advantageous; in others this was not so. Interestingly, there appears to be some evidence that businesses founded by groups are also likely to grow faster than those founded by single individuals, although no definite conclusions can yet be drawn. Indeed the focus on teams of enterprising persons rather than on individuals is commanding greater interest and research in recent times. It is becoming increasingly recognised that the 'lone wolf' entrepreneur, no matter how charismatic or how enterprising, limits the growth potential of the enterprise simply because of his or her personality and the physical limitations of individuality in practising entrepreneurial management.

Another characteristic of the entrepreneur that has also been studied is his or her willingness to accept external equity. As finance from an external source is usually needed to permit rapid business expansion, accepting equity involvement and sharing ownership removes a growth constraint (and of course equity is more likely to be available to growth businesses as they will be more attractive to investors). Alternative funding sources can be used, but usually not without increasing the business's gearing. It is reasonable to infer, therefore, that a willingness by the entrepreneur to share ownership, and therefore decision making and control, is key to the growth of some businesses. When the concept of the entrepreneur is extended to embrace his or her management style and strategic management practices, including the development and use of networks, conclusions are no simpler to reach. For example, there is an increasing tendency to link the business's growth with the quality and quantity of the personal and organisational networks that the entrepreneur develops.

Some studies support the contention that a greater use of external sources of information, advice and other resources results in faster growth, particularly for a high technology business. It is logical to assume that, as the entrepreneur's resources are often limited and he or she has to gain some control over his or her socio-economic environment, networks play a more crucial role for the small business that seeks growth. Moreover the nature of networks appears to change as the business develops, which is also to be expected.

However, work on management style and networks is subject to criticisms which are frequently mentioned. To be useful, such studies need to distinguish cause and effect, and also to distinguish whether the factors being studied actually cause growth or merely facilitate (or hinder) processes determined by other influences.

Conclusion

The findings revealed by one Third World study are instructive.[33] It tested three groups of personal entrepreneurial competencies: first, those perceived to pertain to basic personality, such as assertiveness, determination and initiative; second, those relating to business management styles, such as efficiency orientation; third, those classified as business skill indicators, such as systematic planning. It was concluded from this however that personality variables are not useful predictors of business performance.

The personality-orientated competency measures represented in the data did not relate consistently, it was claimed, to the various measures of business performance for the respondents.

It is reasonable to conclude, therefore, that what the entrepreneur 'is' (traits) is less important than what he or she 'does' (behaviour), because the latter effects change. The link between what one 'is' and what one 'does' is clearly largely undetermined. Moreover Gibb and Davies contend that 'Different types of entrepreneurial behaviour are required in different marketplaces to achieve growth and different traits, skills and competencies will be needed depending upon levels of uncertainty and complexity in the market.'[34]

In conclusion, it is reasonable to deduce that the entrepreneur's (or business leader's) ambition and desire to grow are critical. In addition, the skills of the entrepreneur are particularly important in the early stages of growth. The ability to broaden and adapt to changing circumstances is likely to be of major importance in removing obstacles to growth. Different types of behaviour may be required in different market situations and different personal competencies are likely to be needed to deal with the different levels of complexity and uncertainty in the business environment. It is important that entrepreneurs are willing to delegate and, by implication, that employees must be capable and willing to accept responsibility. It is also a truism to say that an inability to manage growth, despite a motivation to do so, will prevent growth. It is undoubtedly the case that many firms fail to grow because of a variety of barriers, including those of a technical, marketing and financial nature, but not least those which are managerial (which may in fact be at the root of most of the other barriers). How some management factors can help or hinder growth at different stages is captured in Figure 8.3.

Storey's research stresses the critical importance of the attitude and quality of the initial manager(s) whom the entrepreneur recruits. Such a finding would reinforce the importance of the management team to growth achievement and of the owner's ability to build such a team. These issues of management are explored further in the next section.

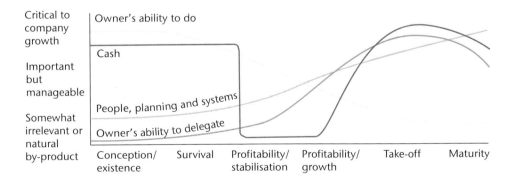

Figure 8.3 Management factors and stages

Source: N. C. Churchill, 'The Six Key Phases of Company Growth', 'Mastering Enterprise', *Financial Times* (1997), February, p.3.

The business

A second approach to explaining growth is to look at the characteristics of the business itself. These characteristics can be divided into two categories, chosen because they are firm specific:

- the firm's structure – ownership, legal form, age and size
- the firm's management skills and performance, including its access to resources.

Structure

Storey reviewed research from 11 studies on one or more of the elements in this category.[35] His conclusion was that little is known about the impact of ownership. It is not known, for example, whether a second or subsequent owner is more likely grow a business, nor is it known if an individual with more than one business is more likely to succeed in growing one or more of them, nor whether a business begun by a team is more likely to grow. Growth and the habitual entrepreneur is discussed in more detail in Chapter 6.

On the legal form of the business, it would appear that a limited company is more likely to grow as compared with a sole trader or partnership. This should not be surprising because most businesses convert to limited company status at some stage in their development and are frequently under various pressures to convert as they grow.

Most studies also conclude that younger and smaller firms grow more quickly than older and larger ones. It is important to note, however, that one reason for a correlation between size and growth is that it is easier to achieve a doubling in any growth parameter if the business is smaller to start with. Few large businesses would try a 100 per cent increase in employment at one stroke, but that is just what a previously one-person business does when it recruits its first employee. Additionally, many businesses will grow rapidly initially to reach the 'critical mass' needed to service their market efficiently, but subsequently 'plateau'.

In general findings about the firm's characteristics and growth are of very limited value for policy purposes. As with information about the entrepreneur, either the causal relationship is unclear or no meaningful basis for policy intervention has been identified. Indeed none of the structural factors identified indicates, with adequate clarity, anything about the ambitions or goals exhibited by a business's owners and managers.

Management

The second category of firm-specific characteristics relates to management performance. Many would argue that the motivation and ability of a firm to grow rests with the owner and his or her management team. Such an approach recognises that growth is related to a business's performance in the marketplace, and in particular to its ability to make rational (profitable) decisions about its products and/or services in the context of market development.

In short, a condition of growth is the ability of management to plan and implement the firm's growth in both strategic and operational terms. It is instructive to note that a European Observatory for SMEs annual report identifies four weaknesses of smaller businesses:[36]

- high mortality rates
- weak market orientation due to lack of strategic marketing approaches and to operating in small segmented markets
- low productivity of labour leading to high unit wage costs
- low equity–debt ratio and difficult and costly access to financial markets.

All of these weaknesses can be related to management inadequacy (as indeed can almost all aspects of small business performance). Even difficulty in raising finance can be attributed to a 'failure' of management adequately to search for sources, build networks, prepare suitable business plans or share ownership and control.

Evidence concerning the impact of a selection of firm-specific factors attributable to the performance of the management team is summarised by Storey.[37] These factors are: management recruitment and training, workforce training, technological sophistication, market positioning, market adjustments, planning, new product introduction, customer concentration, exporting (information and advice) and external equity. The list of factors reflects research that has been done, and is not necessarily an exhaustive list of management-related issues.

Unfortunately, as before, the findings are not conclusive. It seems to be counterintuitive that proper practice in many of these factors, which conventionally constitute good management, are as yet not found to be correlated with growth in businesses. It is, however, suggested that three aspects of management do appear to be the most closely linked with growth, as opposed to size (an important distinction): these are market positioning, new products and management recruitment.

Market positioning

A key decision for any business is the definition of its market and where it perceives itself to be in relation to its competitors. While it is difficult to define precisely, market positioning has to do with notions of who the customers are, competitive advantage, product and service range and the role of quality, service and price. Illustration 8.2 discusses this in the context of ethnic business. These are important issues for management to clarify – otherwise, the business's ability to take corrective action if things go wrong will be limited. It would appear that the ability to know of and take advantage of market positioning (in other words, to determine one's niche) is related to growth success. Barkham et al. found that undertaking formal market research had strong associations with growth, while the use of agents (as opposed to in-house sales staff) to sell products had the reverse effect.[38]

New products

Related to market positioning is the development and introduction of new products. There is some evidence, but it is by no means conclusive, that new product introductions are associated with faster growth. Introducing new products is usually seen as part of the process of innovation, which is itself in much of the literature seen as the engine driving continued growth. Innovation is often limited however to development by absorption of new techniques. Indeed, definite conclusions in this area are difficult to draw from empirical studies, although the OECD expresses a commonplace view in suggesting that 'A businessman's attitude to using

> ## ILLUSTRATION 8.2
> ## Breakout by ethnic entrepreneurs
>
> It is contended that effective market definition and positioning and the appropriate introduction of new products can allow firms to grow, but this may not be so easy for ethnic businesses. These firms can benefit from a deep understanding of the needs of their co-ethnic clients and an ability to meet them, but Ram points out that many ethnic markets are static and fiercely competitive. Growth depends on breaking into non-ethnic markets but this is predicated on the development of an effective marketing strategy. Ram notes that not many ethnic firms are sophisticated marketers and that problems with underfunding, inadequate premises and equipment, labour-intensive production methods and inadequate insurance make breakout difficult. However, some firms with innovative products, differentiated market contacts and willpower do manage to enter new markets and achieve sustainable growth.
>
> Source: M. Ram, 'Ethnic Minority Enterprise: An Overview and Research Agenda', *Journal of Entrepreneurial Behaviour and Research* (1997), 3, pp.145–56.

new technologies to ensure or increase competitiveness ... appears extremely significant. His attitude will be determined by his experience and training but also by those of his management team.'[39]

Management recruitment

Common sense dictates that as a firm grows it becomes more dependent on its management team. A CBI report revealed that there is a 'greater awareness of management weaknesses among growth firms', and that 'recruitment of outside managers also tends to increase with growth.' Table 8.3, taken from this report, highlights the perceived importance of management.[40] There is much other research evidence to show that not acquiring the right management expertise and not building the appropriate structure are amongst the main reasons why growth-orientated firms fail to achieve their objective of growth.

Other factors

Overall, one cannot deduce that other firm specific factors are not important for growth: there is merely an absence of strong evidence to demonstrate the causal relationship. Indeed, even for the factors highlighted in this section, the evidence presented remains open to challenge. Controversially, neither workforce nor management training is shown to be a causal factor influencing the growth of the business. Their association is with larger but not necessarily growing firms, and they are as likely to be a consequence as a cause.

What research there is confirms the importance of management development in a growing business, and demonstrates individual examples of its impact on performance.

Table 8.3 Management weakness as a constraint on growth: internal barriers to growth (percentage of respondents citing factor as important)

Management team too small/too stretched	65
Reluctance to dilute ownership	57
Reluctance to take on new debt	55
Lack of successful innovation	40
Preference for maintaining the manageability of small size	40

Note: Respondents were 667 private companies with turnover between £2.5 and £25 m.
Source: Binder Hamlyn and London Business School (1994), 'The Quest for Growth', reprinted from *Managing to Grow* (London: CBI, 1995), p.11.

It does not, however, isolate the impact of different approaches to management development (such as training, mentoring, counselling and the presence of non-executive directors) across a group of small businesses.

This emphasis on rational business management approaches to growth has led to an increasing flow of literature that attempts to link not only the personal characteristics of the entrepreneur but also those of the management team to planning and performance.

As with many factors studied, definitional problems make comparability of findings difficult, not least in the area of planning. Despite this, few studies demonstrate a convincing link between formalised planning and improved performance of the small firm. Planning seems to be related to size, not growth.

Many familiar with micro and small-firm behaviour will recognise that the 'informal and intuitive' dominates over formal planning procedures and is at least equally effective. Nor should the existence of a business plan be confused with planning! The OECD reports in its study on globalising SMEs that 'Successful small firms often do not rely on formal strategic planning although they are very conscious of what they want to achieve.'[41] Overall, however, it might be foolish to deny the significance of product and/or market-related decisions, cost/price decisions and constraint decisions (including time and finance) taken by a strategically aware management team as critical to business growth, despite the absence of conclusive evidence. Barkham et al. found that four business aims stated by owner-managers were significantly associated with growth: those of expansion of profits, improving margins, having a marketing strategy and improving the production process.[42] It is interesting to note that a study of 179 super-growth companies in the United States resulted in the identification of five factors leading to a 'winning performance'.[43] These were:

- competing on quality not prices
- domination of a market niche
- competing in an area of strength
- having tight financial and operating controls
- frequent product or service innovation (particularly important in manufacturing).

Barkham et al. reinforce this view in that their results reveal that it is the characteristics of the entrepreneur and the strategies he or she adopts which largely determine the growth of the small enterprise.[44] Company characteristics, including size, location and sector, appear to be influential but in a relatively minor way. To a large extent growth in small firms derives from the skills, values and motivations of the entrepreneur and the strategies adopted with regard to innovation, marketing and market research.

This approach to explaining small business growth reflects what Gibb and Davies described as a business or 'organisational' approach, emphasising the development sequence of a firm as it passes through a series of stages in its life cycle.[45] (Some of these 'stages of growth' models are described in Chapter 7.) The different stages require different roles for the direction of the business, as suggested in Table 8.4, which also draws a parallel between the needs of a developing business and Maslow's hierarchy of needs.

The external environment

Yet another approach to understanding and explaining growth lies in examining the impact of factors or constraints external to the entrepreneur or the business. These include macro-economic variables such as aggregate demand, taxation, regulations, labour market skills and labour relations, but also embrace sector and region specific matters such as product/service and/or market, competition, government assistance, location and the availability (and use) of information.

Macro-economic variables

Looking first at macro-economic variables, it is clear that policies on demand, taxation, interest rates and public spending will affect the fortunes of small firms. Indeed government policies in these areas are intended to induce behavioural change by individuals and organisations. It is indisputable that these policies have a major impact on the trading performance of small firms.

Despite the continuing calls by small firm representative bodies for reduced regulations ('less red tape') it is not clear to what extent administrative and legislative burdens hinder business growth. It is reasonable to assume, however, that anything that absorbs time and resources that would otherwise be devoted to business development is likely to have a deleterious effect.

Studies in many OECD member countries, including the UK, highlight the constraining effect of small business being unable to obtain good quality or skilled labour even in a relatively slack overall labour market. At any given time, how much the problem is on the supply side (recruitment processes, remuneration, employment rights and conditions), as opposed to the demand side, is not clear.

Table 8.4 The different role needed for business development at different stages

Business stage	Related role	Maslow's hierarchy
Maturity	Leader	Self-actualisation
Expansion	↑	Recognition
Growth	Manager	Belonging
Survival	↑	Security
Start-up	Entrepreneur	Survival

In general, governments' macro-economic policies are geared to all enterprises and not just smaller businesses. Moreover, while the impact of governments' macro policies can fall unevenly on different sectors and/or markets (and labour markets are partially differentiated), the specific effect on the growth of an individual business is likely to be much less than the effect on business in general and not least on international competitive comparisons. It is unlikely, therefore, that macro-economic and national policies will explain differential growth rates within different sectors, whatever the effects across sectors.

Sector

A number of studies in recent years indicate that the average growth rate of firms is higher in some sectors than in others.[46] Particular attention has been paid in numerous studies to businesses in the high-tech sector where, for example, Westhead and Storey conclude that high-technology small firms in the UK not only have higher growth rates but also have lower failure rates than small businesses in other sectors.[47] Kirchhoff, examining US data, only partially agrees:

> The chances of achieving high growth are almost twice as great for high-tech firms as for low-tech firms. Still, among high-tech firms terminations take a greater toll as low-growth firms are unable to hang on for as long as low-tech firms.[48]

Kirchhoff attributes their superior growth performance to the high cost of innovation, which requires growth if the firm is to survive. However high-tech sectors can suffer reverses, as was shown in the 'winter of technology' in 2000 and subsequently when many ICT businesses collapsed.

Sectoral studies serve the purpose of highlighting the particular constraints and opportunities of sectors (such as financing problems for the high-tech sector). They do not typically offer a basis for predicting the extent to which growth businesses will emerge or in what conditions, however. They also encourage analysis of the structure of an industry, and especially the role of large firms and their interaction with smaller ones. Linkages between large and small firms may play an important role in influencing small firm growth. Growth can occur on the basis of servicing the needs of large firms; large firms can spin out numbers of small ones; strategic partnerships across a variety of functions can develop; large firms can provide management and technological support and advice. On the other hand, large firms through their power in the marketplace can hinder or eliminate small business growth through acquisition, control over intellectual property, slow payment and quasi-monopolistic practices.

It is misleading however to place too much reliance on sectoral performance from a policy perspective. As research has indicated, performance within sectors varies to a much greater extent than across them.[49]

Competition

It may appear prima facie that for a given market size, the smaller the number of competitors the greater the likelihood of any given business capturing a large share of the market. However, many influences may be operating, such as (dis)economies of scale, product or market differentiation, the relative importance of large and small firms in the market and transportation costs, which make it very difficult to define the 'competitiveness' of a market or sector. It is not surprising, therefore, that no correlation appears to exist between growth and competition. Porter argues however that greater competitiveness in an industry's home market can lead to stronger export performance and growth. (See 'The cluster effect' later in this section.)

Location

The concept of location is more complex than it first seems. Locational attributes such as those of being urban, rural, peripheral or central can mean differences in many of the other factors such as competition, labour market and government support. It then becomes difficult to determine which of the influences is at work.

However, it is safe to say, once again, that there is not yet enough evidence to suggest that growth is location-determined. Possible exceptions to this conclusion are businesses (usually service or service-related firms) serving local markets, because these are likely to be small, although the benefits of larger markets may well be offset by greater numbers of competitors. A review of lists of UK fast-growth firms (such as the Sunday Times/Virgin Fast-Track 100) suggests that they are disproportionately concentrated in the south of England. The changing composition of the Fast-Track 100 list of high growth firms for sales and profits also clearly illustrates the volatility of the performance of such firms.

Findings by Vaessen and Keeble in a recent analysis of small business by regional location, on the other hand, suggest a different link between growth and location.[50] Peripheral regions are found to contain proportionately more growing small businesses than what they call the 'core' region (southeast England). A partial explanation is that greater R&D and training inputs are generated in the peripheral locations. These findings can only be tentative however: their counterintuitive nature may suggest that differences in external environments are not sufficient to explain growth differentials. Indeed, to assume otherwise would be to suggest that the entrepreneur's and the business's behaviour are largely constrained by their location, an assumption that does not allow significant scope for variable responses. Either way, the policy implications are unclear.

Information and advice

The provision of information and advice by government agencies is itself a growth sector in many countries seeking to support their small businesses. This form of support can also come from private sector sources (such as bankers, accountants, non-executive directors and consultants); and the use made of accountants and bankers, at least in developed economies, would appear to be much higher than that made of public information and advice services. Indeed the uptake of public sector provision seems generally to be very low (less than 10 per cent of potential users). However, satisfaction with information and advice, from both public and private sources, appears generally to be high. Importantly, despite the significant investment being made in these services in the United States, the UK and the European Union generally, there appears to be no convincing evidence that their uptake improves business performance and growth, although growing businesses would appear to make greater use of information and advisory networks.

Government support

Government support can take a wide variety of forms, but usually consists of grant aid, subsidised loans and/or the provision of subsidised services such as consultancy, training and the provision of information and advice.

The impact of direct financial support from government or its agencies is the issue most often studied. Such support normally comes from local or regional agencies. The small business community generally expresses dissatisfaction with the grants regime, or at least with its administration. It is reported that it feels that grants go to large or foreign firms, that application procedures are too complicated and lengthy, and that not enough information is available on how to access grants.[51] Notwithstanding these views, significant sums across many regions have been provided to small business. Once again, research findings have been inconclusive in determining whether financial support generates further growth, improved profitability or less efficient performance. (But see also Chapter 13.)

The cluster effect

There is however one theory that links issues such as location, competition and government support to the competitiveness, and hence to the potential growth, of businesses. This theory is propounded by Porter (see also Chapter 5) who, following a four-year study of ten important trading nations, ultimately concluded that nations succeed in particular industries because their home environment is the most forward-looking, dynamic and challenging.[52] These conclusions, he suggests, contradict the conventional wisdom that labour costs, interest rates, exchange rates and economies of scale are the most potent determinants of competitiveness. It is too easy, he says, for governments to adopt policies, such as joint projects for R&D, that operate on the belief that independent research by domestic rivals is wasteful and duplicative, that collaborative efforts achieve economies of scale, and that individual companies are likely to under-invest in R&D because they cannot reap all the benefits. That view, he claims, is flawed and fundamentally misperceives the true sources of competitive advantage.

Porter argues that, while successful businesses will each employ their own strategy, they achieve competitive advantage through acts of innovation. Further, he believes that it is demanding buyers in the domestic market who pressure companies to innovate faster. Why is it, he asks, that certain companies based in certain countries are capable of consistent innovation? The answer lies in four broad attributes of a region. These are: factor conditions (labour force quality, infrastructure), demand conditions (the nature of home market demand), related and supporting industries (the presence of supplier industries and other related industries which are internationally competitive), and firm strategy, structure and rivalry (the conditions in the nation affecting how businesses are created, organised and managed and the nature of domestic competition). These four determinants form the points on Porter's 'diamond', and the diamond is itself a system. Together they affect the key elements that beget international competitiveness and, by implication, firm and industry growth.

How these determinants combine to produce a successful industry is complex, but Porter notes that internationally competitive businesses are usually found in geographically concentrated clusters of related businesses. 'Among all the points on the diamond, domestic rivalry is arguably the most important because of the powerfully stimulating effect it has on all the others,' asserts Porter, adding that 'Geographic concentration magnifies the power of domestic rivalry.'[53] One of the most commonly quoted examples is that of 'The Third Italy': a proliferation of concentrations of various industrial sectors benefiting from a variety of effects that include pools of skilled workers and technicians; related input from maintenance, service and design businesses; supporting companies that offer materials, supplies and other services, including subcontracting; and specialist businesses offering consultancy and advice on logistics, advertising, finance and general support. Support agency services develop that are geared to meet a cluster's needs in the form of education and training, research and development, and fiscal and legal advice. In Italy these interrelationships are reinforced by family connections and traditional links that significantly strengthen the power of the network. Such inbuilt cultural ties however complicate the situation for those who might otherwise think that they could merely 'import' the cluster effect. Despite this, efforts continue to create clusters of mainly high-technology companies. For example in the UK in 1999 a research team under Lord Sainsbury highlighted the importance of public sector encouragement of clustering, while a joint Department of Trade and Industry and Department for Education and Employment (both since renamed) White Paper *Opportunity for All in a World of Change* (February 2001) encouraged regional development agencies to continue developing existing and embryonic clusters.[54] On the wider front the OECD notes that smaller firms are increasingly going global, 'building on local networks and inter-firm clusters to derive scale economies in international markets'.[55]

General

This brief review covers only some of the factors that have been considered as possible influences on the growth performance of small businesses. This chapter has classified the range of factors into three broad categories: the entrepreneur, the firm and the external environment. Other classifications exist. The OECD, for instance, categorises the key factors in the competitiveness of SMEs as:[56]

- The owner's/manager's basic role (drive).
- Intangible investment ('intelligence management'), including:
  - the ability to obtain information through environmental scanning and search
  - at least an intermittent R&D capability
  - the quality of the firm's organisation
  - the quality of its training.
- Tangible investment (based on new management and production technologies).
- The business's strategic capabilities (innovation and flexibility).

However, as already noted, the research on these and other classifications and their components has produced no conclusive results and no firm evidence to support interventions, either to increase the pace of growth or to increase the number of growing businesses.

Nevertheless, it would be foolish to set aside a pragmatic approach to this problem, such as to note what businesses themselves have been saying. Table 8.5 shows the barriers to growth reported in a small firm survey of 2500 businesses in the UK in 1997[57] carried out by Cambridge University's Centre for Business Research, the results of whose 1990 study[58] are also shown for comparison. The top issues in both studies revolve around market demand and competition, the availability and cost of finance, and the firm's ability to deal with them, with the scores being sufficiently close together to highlight these issues as the key to growth. These are all primarily external factors. In addition, medium-sized firms reported inadequate management skills, and to a lesser extent marketing and sales skills, as greater constraints than did smaller firms. Younger and faster-growing firms stressed financial constraints, while faster-growing ones also placed management skills shortages higher. Manufacturing firms revealed generally more constraints than service firms, and innovating firms reported more than non-innovating ones.

It may be reasonable to accept these rather typical results (albeit no mention is made of administrative and regulatory burdens!) at face value, subject to two caveats: first, businesses may tend to blame external, and therefore uncontrollable, factors before internal, controllable, factors; and second, there is a tendency to confuse causes and effects. In the latter case, financial constraints may become apparent because of a lack of demand or, in the case of a growing business, because of a reluctance to dilute ownership or control or because of poor financial management skills.

A second common-sense approach is to recognise that growth is likely to be dependent upon the interaction of a number of influences, and that these influences may be important in different combinations for different businesses. This makes generalisations very imprecise and of limited use as guides to action. Growth is likely

Table 8.5 Constraints on small business growth

Constraint	Nature	Ranking	
		1997	*1990*
Increased competition	External	1	4
Availability and cost of finance for expansion	External	2	1
Marketing and sales skills	Internal	3	5
Availability and cost of overdraft finance	External	4	2
Growth of market demand	External	5	3
Management skills	Internal	6	6
Skilled labour	Internal	7	7
Acquisition of new technology	?	8	8
Difficulty of implementing new technology	Internal	9	9
Availability of appropriate premises	External	10	10
Access to overseas markets	?	11	11

Sources: 1997: adapted from A. Cosh and A. Hughes (eds), *Enterprising Britain; Growth, Innovation and Public Policy in the Small and Medium Sized Enterprise Sector 1994–1997* (Cambridge: ESRC Centre for Business Research, 1998) (revised in P. Burns, *Entrepreneurship and Small Business, Second Edition*: Palgrave Macmillan, 2007,p. 252; Table 9.1): *ESRC Small Business Research Centre, The State of British Enterprise: Growth, Innovation and Competitive Advantage in Small and Medium-Sized Firms* (Cambridge: ESRC Small Business Research Centre, 1992).

to occur when a number of the key factors in each category combine, although it is most unlikely that there is only one or a few successful combinations, and the combinations for success could change as the business develops and market circumstances alter. The dynamic process implied in this interpretation of how growth is generated through the interaction of the entrepreneur, the firm and its environment, local and regional as well as national and international, is at the heart of understanding the growth process itself. However, given the heterogeneity of entrepreneurs and of small businesses, and the complexity and diversity of the markets in which they operate, any attempt to produce a comprehensive theory or any meaningful analysis of growth may be unrealistic, at least in the short term. One may also add that there is no single correct management of a business for growth and that growth itself, as has been noted, is not a simple linear process: rather, businesses grow, contract and grow again several times and at different rates.

Targeting growth

As has been explained earlier in this chapter, much of the interest in growth businesses arises because they represent employment potential and there is therefore a wish to target them for support to enhance that employment potential. Such a policy of targeting growth has its proponents as well as its opponents. The arguments often used by each are set out below.

Arguments for targeting growth businesses

At least five arguments have been advanced for targeting growth businesses (and see also the list of reasons to look favourably on growth businesses at the beginning of this chapter):

1. Targeting increases the effectiveness of support measures. As explained earlier, statistical evidence has been presented that, over time, a proportionately small number of firms out of any cohort of businesses will create a large proportion of new jobs. It is consequently argued that targeted support for these 'growth' businesses should be more effective in promoting jobs than more generalised support, because it has a clear focus and concentrates resources where they are most needed and where they can produce the best results.

2. It minimises support requirements. By applying support only to growth businesses, the total support requirement, and its cost, is reduced. Indeed with many hundreds of thousands of businesses starting each year, it is not feasible to deal with them all and make a sufficient impact with limited resources.

3. It encourages a clearer strategic focus on the needs of such businesses. Targeting growth businesses forces small business support organisations to identify more clearly how to support such businesses and to develop appropriate strategies for such support. It also helps agencies to develop a better understanding of the processes of growth in the target market and how best to assist such processes. High levels of expertise are thus more likely to be developed.

4. More business starts are not needed. There are situations, such as that pertaining in the UK in the 1970s and 1980s, where it has been argued that the rate of business starts was higher than that in some competitor economies. They had been developed on the back of growth in the financial services sector but many were unsustainable. More business starts were not therefore needed and attention should instead have been focused on promoting business growth, which was needed.

5. Supporting start-ups distorts the market often as a result of the displacement effect. The market mechanism serves as the most efficient means of allocating scarce resources and supporting start-up businesses will distort this. This argument however only has validity if the assumptions underlying the neo-classical approach to economic theory always hold.

Arguments against targeting growth businesses

There are also at least four arguments against targeting growth businesses:

1. It is difficult. The process of picking winners has been likened to selecting a potentially good wine. It is viewed as more of an art than a science and is the preserve of a tiny group of cognoscenti with exceptional 'noses' and 'palates'; it is a skill that takes years of training and experience to acquire, and not everyone can do it even then. (Even the wine cognoscenti generally only make predictions for wines with a good pedigree, with the result that most of them missed the potential of the 'New World' wines.) It is not therefore something that can be systemised in business agencies.

2. It is not the same as providing venture capital. The venture capital industry would pride itself on picking winners, and needs to pick them to survive. However it only needs to select a few winners that would be enough for its own purposes, and it would acknowledge that it still selects a majority of 'dogs' that have to be compensated for by the occasional correctly chosen 'star'. Public support policy, in contrast, would seek to back all the winners and avoid any losers so as to avoid the charge of wasting or losing public money.

3. It is misguided. Those who regard targeting, or 'picking winners', as a misguided policy do so for the following reasons:

   • *The structure of business*: It is argued that the quality, volume and viability of new business starts can influence the strength and competitiveness of the small business sector. This in turn is at the root of the creation of an economy which not only generates jobs but also contributes to the achievement of wider economic and social goals, including productivity, living standards, price stability, diversity, choice and personal opportunity. It is suggested that three key questions need to be asked when considering the part that start-ups play in an economy:

     – Are there enough of them?

     – Is the quality of the stock of new and small businesses adequate?

     – Are start-up rates, and net additions to the business stock, rising or falling?

     Answers to these questions will help prioritise the importance of start-up support.

- *The policy rationale for support of start-ups*: The key policy arguments for support are:
  - Start-ups are the seedbed for growth. This argument is summarised in the view that, without a healthy and quality stock of new businesses, the future supply of 'winners' or growth businesses will be curtailed. Not to support them, therefore, would be to reduce the pool of potential 'winners'.
  - Market failures constrain start-up rates. This argument seeks to highlight barriers to start-up which are attributable to organisational or institutional deficiencies. These 'market failures' are seen as impacting disproportionately on new and small businesses, disadvantaging them. These barriers include cultural/social values, difficulties in financing, legislative and administrative burdens, including reporting requirements, and access to information.
  - More employment creation. A 'picking winners' policy ignores the fact that most of the jobs in the small business sector still come from businesses with fewer than 20 employees; so not only are non-growth businesses and start-ups the source of future growth businesses, they provide employment now (between one-third and two-thirds of all new jobs in the UK). The assertion is not contrary to the findings that out of any group of existing firms measured over a discrete time period a small number will create a disproportionate number of jobs (see also Chapter 6).
  - Lower costs per job. Job creation costs are lower for start-ups than for many existing businesses. This argument is based on a perception that the costs associated with new jobs in start-ups are lower than for existing businesses including inward investment.
  - The impact of start-up rates. High start-up rates have a positive impact on regional prosperity. There appears to be a positive relationship between start-up levels and regional prosperity-including a positive correlation between levels of new venture creation and employment generation (see also Chapter 13).

4. What is needed is an enterprising culture. This set of arguments revolves around the view, explored in Chapter 4, that cultural values supportive of entrepreneurial activity and entrepreneurs can be considered a major influence on the level and success of start-up activity. In consequence it is argued that an investment needs to be made in building support and stakeholder networks positively disposed towards start-ups and growth rather than in direct intervention in growing businesses.

I haven't figured out a way [to anticipate which firms will be the gazelles and which will end up the mice]. In fact, one of the fascinating things about the gazelles is that they sometimes appear to be mice for long periods of time.

David Birch[59]

Other phases: non-growth, decline and termination

Birch's mice are businesses which stay small, but businesses of any size can remain static for periods either while they cope with issues such as survival or consolidation or because of reasons such as comfort or maturity. Such phases of business development are the reality for many businesses and therefore they are examined next along with other realities of business life such as decline and, if decline cannot be arrested, termination.

Survival, consolidation, comfort and maturity

A static stage in small business development may not sound very exciting, but it characterises the state of most small businesses. Once they have started their own business, many electricians, plumbers, chimney sweeps and consultants, for instance, rarely grow, and many other one-person businesses are the same: being static is the normal state for them.

Because, by definition, the static stage is not one that produces results in terms of more start-ups, jobs or other benefits, it is often ignored. Growth is a much more attractive stage in those terms, but in many cases it is in the static stage that the growth businesses of the future are to be found. Growth does not often follow immediately after start-up. But even if a static business is not a growth business of the future it can still perform a useful function. Together, static businesses provide significant employment. They also can be an essential part of the economic and social fabric, they can provide choice and diversity, they can provide the necessary infrastructure support for other growth businesses and they can be useful role models. They should not be ignored.

As with the separation of growth and expansion, it is possible to distinguish more than one type of stage during which a business does not grow. Survival has been the name given to that period following start-up during which a business may not grow but is nevertheless working hard to maintain its position and struggling to establish itself as a viable enterprise. Once established, a business may then have a period of building resources, of consolidation, before the next move. Just because a business shows few signs of growth for a relatively long period, this does not mean that it will never grow. In many cases the growth of a business has been likened to that of bamboo, which can lie dormant for many years before suddenly shooting up in a single season.

There is a large group of businesses whose growth is limited by their owners' ambitions or by their market niche. This stage has been labelled comfort or maturity. There may be many reasons why a business does not expand, such as the desired lifestyle of the owner-manager, the limits of his or her management capability, or even peer pressure not to get too far ahead. In general, however, this phase of development is characterised by a business which has taken up its share of the markets, has reached the limits of its capacity, or for any other managerial, political or social reason remains at the same size either in physical or economic terms.

A categorisation of static businesses can now be summarised:

- *Survival*: This is the stage which comes after start-up. Typically, a 'surviving' business has the potential to be a viable entity, but needs to work at it. It is probably a one-product or one-service business, but is concentrating on short-term issues of survival rather than the longer-term ones of future growth potential.

- *Consolidation*: After winning the struggle to survive or to grow, most businesses need a period of rest to build up the reserves they need to move forward. This may not be a conscious decision or a deliberate strategy. What was happening may only be obvious in retrospect, when subsequent growth can be seen to have been built on the contacts, the credibility and the expertise accumulated at this stage. A period of consolidation following a period of survival may be one during which even businesses that do eventually grow show few indications of their potential.

- *Comfort*: For a business that does not move on to growth, 'consolidation' can easily merge into 'comfort': the stage at which a business is doing enough to survive at least into the medium term and is providing enough profits to maintain the owner's desired standard of living. There may be little incentive to do anything different.

- *Maturity*: Maturity is generally seen as coming after some growth, and indeed there may still be slow continued growth. The businesses concerned, however, are no longer in the first stages of their existence. They may be passing the peak of their products' life cycles, or they may be on the verge of moving out of the definition of a small business because their management structure is facing a transition phase in which personal contact and word of mouth have to be replaced by more formal systems to cope with a larger organisation and more decentralisation. The onset of maturity may therefore be a transition, either onwards to bigger and better things, or sideways towards an eventual decline.

The issues

In general, the needs at this stage are for encouragement and incentive, either to prevent decline or to encourage expansion. The motivation of the owner is critical. A firm can be adapting and changing while staying still in terms of turnover or employment, but in the long term staying static is not a good strategy. It must always be presumed that competition will change or increase and in that case not to try to grow is to invite decline.

The needs of these businesses include:

- Needs of survival businesses
  - control of the business
  - generating revenues sufficient to cover all expenses
  - supervision of the work
  - both entrepreneurial and administrative management
  - simple structures, systems and controls
  - product and/or market research.
- Needs of mature businesses
  - expense control
  - increased productivity

- niche marketing, especially if the industry is declining
- watchdog top management, taking a leadership role
- product innovation, to replace products towards the end of their life cycle
- formal systems for objectives and budgets
- further long-term debt or bridging finance
- succession planning.

The succession planning issue possibly summarises one of the key dilemmas at this stage of the business. The entrepreneur behind the business has probably built it up from its inception, and has a keen sense of achievement and ownership. Now it is being suggested that he or she consider who should succeed to the management of the business. This might be advisable because the business needs it but for the owner concerned it means contemplating giving up the thing that may be the most important part of his or her life.

The longer term

As already explained, the static or survival stage can be seen as the norm for most small businesses. It is not therefore usually a stage on the way to something else, but an end in its own right. It can be preceded by start-up, growth or decline, and be succeeded eventually by growth, decline or termination. It is important to realise that, while this stage is described as static, it may only be so in the short term, and that often in the longer term not to move forward is to risk moving into decline when, because of a business's passivity, others take its market. Survival is not actually compulsory or automatic and there is a natural tendency towards regression. There is no superior power that will intervene to force all businesses to survive and so, ultimately, they must progress or die.

Decline

Decline is another of those stages of business development sometimes ignored by government agencies or support organisations when planning assistance. However, decline need not always lead to termination if the problems of the business can be addressed. Helping in the decline stage may therefore result in more surviving businesses or jobs than would otherwise be the case.

Definition

The business is losing its market share, profitability, management skills and the ability to sustain itself at a previous high level. You can often tell when a business is in trouble by looking at its staff turnover rate.

Where from and what next

Decline can come after any stage from start-up onwards. If nothing is done then it will in all probability be followed by termination. If it is arrested then it can be followed by a 'static' stage. If it is cured then a 'static' or even a 'growth' stage is possible.

The issues

The needs of the business are:

- confidence
- finance
- tolerance
- customers
- suppliers
- employees
- new management and leadership
- a strategic review and plan for a new direction, because the decline may be as a direct result of a market or other relevant business environmental change.

Termination

Businesses do terminate, as the figures in Table 8.6 indicate. In any healthy, living ecosystem there are both births and deaths. Individual business deaths may be deemed regrettable, but some are to be expected in the best of economies. It would be unhealthy to have none, and the policy should therefore to be to avoid the unnecessary ones but not to prevent terminations completely.

The terminology of termination requires care. The word 'failure' is often ascribed to the termination of a business. A business may cease to exist or otherwise change its identification for a number of reasons. A business can terminate if it is sold and its operations are absorbed into another: the operations of the business continue but its separate legal existence disappears. It can terminate when it chooses to cease to trade because those concerned see a better opportunity elsewhere, or it can terminate if it is closed when the owner retires. These are all terminations but they are not all failures. If VAT statistics are taken as guide, a business decline and subsequent VAT deregistration may be treated as a termination, and even as a failure, even if the business is actually still trading. Some of the varieties of termination are shown in Figure 8.4.

Table 8.6 Business survival rates: percentage of enterprises surviving after one, two and five years, by country

Country	Surviving after		
	One year	Two years	Five years
France	84	62	48
Germany	86	70	63
Ireland	91	70	57
Italy	87	66	54
Portugal	76	56	47
United Kingdom	87	62	47

Sources: France: INSEE and ANCE; Germany: IfM; Ireland: Department of Enterprise and Employment; Italy: INPS Data Bank; Portugal: MESS-Portuguese Enterprise's Demography; United Kingdom: Department of Trade and Industry. Reproduced from the *Third Annual Report of the European Observatory for SMEs* (Zoetermeer, The Netherlands: EIM Small Business Research and Consultancy, 1995), p.87.

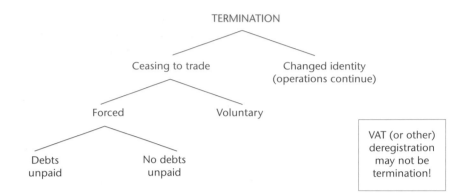

Figure 8.4 Types of business termination

Definition

Termination can be any closure of a business, but the term 'closure' can be ambiguous. It might therefore be more accurate to define it as the ending of the separate legal identity of a business and its ceasing to trade as a separate entity. Perhaps a clearer definition of failure is when a business ceases to trade involuntarily.

The issues

The need is for excellent legal advice to indicate the best way to handle employees, customers, suppliers and finances.

Intervention

It is not necessarily a waste of resources to help a business to terminate. Compared with a bad termination, too late and with many debts, a properly conducted and orderly termination can save resources. It is important not to pour good money after bad, however difficult the entrepreneur finds it to call a halt to the operation of the business. Voluntary liquidation can also avoid unpaid creditors with the consequent risk to other businesses. This activity can be described as 'ethical entrepreneurship', where the entrepreneur accepts the responsibility of closure without damaging other businesses. This means closing the business while it can still pay its creditors and before it is closed by others. This can save ideas for adoption elsewhere. It can help people to learn and re-apply the valuable lessons they have learnt, instead of being put off ever running their own business again. Assistance, in the form of advice on how to do it well, can also be provided for this stage.

Conclusions

The two stages of business development of most interest to policy-makers have been start-up and growth, and of these it is growth that is thought to have the potential to deliver most benefit. To quote Storey again, 'It is the failure of UK small enterprises to grow into large enterprises that may be at the heart of the country's long-term poor economic performance.'[60] This chapter has therefore looked at business growth and at the arguments that have been advanced for and against targeting assistance to promote it more. A policy may have been decided on at present but the targeting debate is not over and the search for the Holy Grail, the formula for creating and/or picking winners, will no doubt continue. Growth businesses may still be desirable, even if they cannot be spotted in advance.

Growth is not however either an inevitable, or the final, stage of business development. Many businesses are static for much of their lives, and those lives end with periods of decline, followed by termination. Those stages should not be ignored by those interested in businesses. Businesses still have needs during them and, if something can be done to meet those needs, decline might be halted or an end prepared in an orderly fashion with the minimum of consequential damage to others.

THE KEY POINTS OF CHAPTER 8

- After start-up, survival, consolidation, growth, maturity, decline and eventually termination are all possible stages of business.

- The growth stage has however been of particular interest. Birch and others suggested that most net new jobs were created by small businesses but further analysis appears to have shown that it is a relatively small proportion of small businesses which grow and create most of those jobs. 'Over a decade, 4 per cent of those businesses which start would be expected to create 50 per cent of employment generated.'[61] However businesses with fewer than 20 employees still generate most employment.

- Because of their job creation potential, governments and others saw that there could be economic benefit in supporting small businesses. However, if small business support resources are limited, which is invariably the case, then it has been suggested that the way to maximise results is to apply those resources only to growth businesses. Therefore there has been considerable interest in learning what makes businesses grow and how such businesses can be spotted.

- It is important to realise that growth in a business context can have many meanings. For the investor it may be growth in shareholder value. For the business it may be growth in sales and in profits, and for government it may be growth in employment. These forms of growth may not all coincide.

- In the context of small businesses, there are a number of significant influences on growth including the entrepreneur's (or leader's) ambition and desire to grow, the skills of the entrepreneur, and the impact of factors or constraints external to the firm. None of these are useful as predictors, especially as chance also appears to be a key factor.

- In the context of the external environment, 'cluster' theory is of interest. It is based on research that shows that internationally successful businesses are often found in geographic clusters where the environment is most advantageous to them; that it is innovation that makes businesses competitive, and thus provides the potential for growth; and that it is demanding buyers in the domestic market that can pressure companies to innovate faster.

- Ultimately growth is likely to be dependent upon the interaction of a number of influences, each of which may be important in different combinations for different businesses.

- As for the issue of whether to target growth businesses or not, the debate is not over. The search for the Holy Grail, the formula for creating and/or picking winners, will no doubt continue. Growth businesses may still be desirable even if they can't be spotted in advance.

- There are other possible stages of business development after start-up that should not however be ignored. All businesses will have static periods and all are likely eventually to decline and to terminate. Understanding and assisting with these stages also could have economic benefits.

QUESTIONS, ESSAY AND DISCUSSION TOPICS

- How could more small business growth be encouraged?

- How might growth as an indicator of business success be measured?

- Is the natural tendency for a business to grow or decline? Explain your reasoning.

- Describe some broad academic approaches taken to analysing the influences on the growth of firms.

- Which of the following influences on the growth of a firm are likely to be the strongest in their impact: the entrepreneur(s), the firm's strategic positioning and operational procedures, or the external environment?

- The real barriers to growth are attributable only to managerial weaknesses; everything else is just an excuse. Discuss.

- What is the role of chance in the growth of small businesses?

- Trying to 'pick winners' is either like the search for the Holy Grail or is akin to looking for a needle in a haystack. It is, therefore, no basis for policy. Discuss.

- What are the arguments for and against implementing a business birth rate strategy in your region?

- What arguments would you advance for a government-funded scheme to help declining and/or terminating businesses? What assistance should such a scheme offer?

Suggestions for further reading

A. Atherton, A. Gibb and L. Sear, *Reviewing the Case for Supporting Business Start-Ups: A Policy Overview of Current Thinking on Business Start-Ups* (Durham: Durham University Business School, 1997).

R. Barkham, E. Hanvey and M. Hart, *The Role of the Entrepreneur in Small Firm Growth* (Belfast: NIERC, 1995).

P. Burns, *Entrepreneurship and Small Business*, 2nd edn (Palgrave Macmillan, 2007), Chapters 9,10 and 11.

D. F. Kuratko, J. S. Hornsby and D. W. Nattziger, 'An Examination of Owners' Goals in Sustaining Entrepreneurship', *Journal of Small Business Management*, 35(1) (1997), pp. 24–33.

M. E. Porter, 'From Competitive Advantage to Competitive Strategy', *Harvard Business Review*, 65(3) (1987), pp. 43–59.

D. Smallbone, R. Leigh and D. North, 'The Characteristics and Strategies of High Growth SMEs', *International Journal of Entrepreneurial Behaviour and Research*,1(3) (1995), pp. 44–62.

D. J. Storey, 'Symposium on Harrison: Lean and Mean: A Job Generation Perspective', *Small Business Economics*, 7(5) (1995), pp. 337–40.

D. J. Storey, *Understanding the Small Business Sector* (London: Routledge, 1994), Chapter 5.

G. Timmons, *New Venture Creation: Entrepreneurship for the 21st Century*, 5th edn (Singapore: Irwin/McGraw-Hill, 1999), Chapter 16.

References

1. OECD, *Globalisation and Small and Medium Enterprises (SMEs)*, Vol. 1, Synthesis Report (Paris: OECD, 1997), p. 7.

2. J. Levy, *Small and Medium Sized Enterprises: A Recipe for Success* (London: Institution of Electrical Engineers) as cited in D. J. Storey, *Understanding the Small Business Sector* (London: Routledge, 1994), p. 24.

3. DTI, *Competitiveness: Helping the Smaller Firm* (London: DTI, May 1995), p. 2.

4. OECD (1997), op. cit., p. 17.

5. Extract from an interview in: 'The Job Generation Process Revisited', *ICSB Bulletin*, Spring (1995).

6. D. J. Storey, *Understanding the Small Business Sector* (London: Routledge, 1994), p. 115.

7. NIERC, *Job Generation and Manufacturing Industry 1973–86* (Belfast: Northern Ireland Economic Research Centre, 1989).

8. E. Garnsey, 'A New Theory of the Growth of the Firm', in Proceedings of the 41st ICSB World Conference, Stockholm 1996, p. 126.

9. A. E. Knaup, 'Survival and Longevity in Business Employment Dynamics data', *US Monthly Labor Review*, May (2005), p. 50–6.

10. D. Smallbone and P. Wyer, 'Growth and Development in the Small Firm', in *Enterprise and Small Business: Principles, Practice and Policy*, edited by S. Carter and D. Jones-Evans (London: Financial Times/Prentice-Hall, 2000), p. 410.

11. A. Gibb and L. Davies, 'In Pursuit of Frameworks for the Development of Growth Models of the Small Business', *International Small Business Journal*, 9(1) (1990), p. 26.

12. Storey, op. cit., p. 121.

13. Gibb and Davies, op. cit., pp. 16–17.

14. H. Barreto, *Entrepreneurship in Micro-economic Theory* (London: Routledge, 1989).

15. R. Barkham, E. Hanvey and M. Hart, *The Role of the Entrepreneur in Small Firm Growth* (Belfast: NIERC, 1995), p. 2.

16. Barkham et al., op. cit., p. 2.

17. Storey, op. cit., pp. 137–43.

18. M. Scott and P. Rosa, 'Has Firm Level Analysis Reached its Limits? Time For a Rethink', *International Small Business Journal*, 14 (1996), pp. 81–9.

19. B Kirchhoff, personal communication.

20. Ibid.

21. Ibid.

22. Ibid.

23. C. Hakim, 'Identifying Fast Growth Small Firms', *Employment Gazette*, January (1989).

24. Quoted in M. Carree, A. van Stel, R. Thurik and S. Wennekers, *Business Ownership and Economic Growth: An Empirical Investigation*, Research Report 9809/E (Zoetermeer, the Netherlands: EIM Small Business Research and Consultancy, 1999), p. 11.

25. D. B. Audretsch and A. R. Thurik, *The Knowledge Society, Entrepreneuship and Unemployment*, Research Report 9801/E (Zoetermeer, the Netherlands: EIM Small Business Research and Consultancy, 1998), p. 11.
26. Carree et al., op. cit., p. 1.
27. B. Kirchhoff, 'Twenty Years of Job Creation Research: What have We Learned?', Proceedings of the 40th ICSB World Conference, Stockholm, 1995, pp. 195–219, at p. 210.
28. G. Reid and L. Jacobsen, *The Small Entrepreneurial Firm* (Aberdeen: Aberdeen University Press, 1988), p. 8.
29. Quoted in D. Deakins and M. Freel, *Entrepreneurship and the Small Firm* (London: McGraw-Hill, 2006), p. 162.
30. Ibid p. 162.
31. Storey, op. cit., pp. 126–37.
32. Barkham et al., op. cit., p. 15.
33. Gibb and Davies, op. cit., p. 18.
34. Ibid., p. 20.
35. Storey, op. cit., pp. 137–43.
36. European Network for SME Research, *The European Observatory for SMEs: First Annual Report* (Zoetermeer, the Netherlands: EIM Small Business Research and Consultancy, 1993), p. 24.
37. Storey, op. cit., pp. 144–54.
38. Barkham et al., op. cit., p. 16.
39. OECD, *Small and Medium Sized Enterprises: Technology and Competitiveness* (Paris: OECD, 1993), p. 21.
40. CBI, *Managing to Grow* (London: CBI, December 1995), p. 11.
41. OECD (1993), op. cit., p. 9.
42. Barkham et al., op. cit., pp. 16, 39.
43. Quoted in P. Burns, *Entrepreneurship and Small Business* (Basingstoke: Palgrave (now Palgrave Macmillan), 2001), p. 272.
44. Barkham et al., op. cit., pp. 15–18.
45. Gibb and Davies, op. cit., pp. 15–31.
46. Storey, op. cit., pp. 138–40.
47. P. Westhead and D. Storey, *An Assessment of Firms Located On and Off Science Parks in the UK* (London: HMSO, 1994).
48. B. Kirchhoff, personal communication.
49. D. Smallbone, R. Leigh and D. North, 'Characteristics and Strategies of High Growth SMEs', *International Journal of Entrepreneurial Behaviour and Research*, 1(3) (1995), pp. 44–62.
50. P. Vaessen and D. Keeble, *Growth Oriented SMEs in Unfavourable Regional Environments*, Working paper (Cambridge: ESRC Centre for Business Research, 1995).
51. Institute of Directors, *Your Business Matters: Report from the Regional Conference* (London: Institute of Directors, 1996), pp. 6–7.
52. M. E. Porter, 'The Competitive Advantage of Nations', *Harvard Business Review*, March-April (1990), pp. 73–93.
53. Ibid.: 82.
54. Quoted in Bank of England, *Finance for Small Firms: An Eighth Report* (London: Bank of England, March 2001), p. 60.
55. OECD, Directorate for Science, Technology and Industry, Industry Committee, *The Role of SMEs: Findings and Issues*, DSTI/IND(2000)15/REV1 (Paris: OECD, December 2000), p. 3.
56. OECD (1993), op.cit., p. 21.
57. A. Cosh and A. Hughes (eds), *Enterprising Britain: Growth, Innovation and Public Policy in the Small and Medium Sized Enterprise Sector 1994–1997* (Cambridge: ESRC Centre for Business Research, 1998).
58. Cambridge Small Business Research Centre, *The State of British Enterprise* (Cambridge: Department of Applied Economics, University of Cambridge, 1992).
59. Extract from an interview in 'The Job Generation Process Revisited', *ICSB Bulletin*, Spring (1995).
60. Storey, op. cit., p. 159.
61. Ibid., p. 115.

CHAPTER 9

Small is beautiful: entrepreneurship in the bigger business

Contents

KEY CONCEPTS

This chapter covers:

- Why corporate entrepreneurship and innovation are desirable in big businesses.

- Different approaches to the practice of corporate entrepreneurship.

- Why corporate entrepreneurship may need to be encouraged, the barriers to it and what can be done to promote its manifestation in strategic entrepreneurship, innovation and an entrepreneurial culture.

- Areas where there appear to be disadvantages of size and where being small can be an advantage.

- Some of the implications of ICT and e-business.

Introduction

The last chapter considered the growth of small businesses because much small business policy and support have been focused on them in particular. However growth, or at least the maturity and size which come from growth, can be a disadvantage because it can be harder for the business to remain entrepreneurial. Even for big businesses, some aspects of 'small' can still seem to be 'beautiful'.

This chapter therefore looks at two aspects of 'small is beautiful' from the perspective of the bigger business. It looks at attempts by established businesses to continue to be entrepreneurial, a process which is often referred to as 'corporate entrepreneurship' or 'intrapreneurship', and it looks at situations where it really does seem to be an advantage to be small.

Entrepreneurship in bigger businesses

Growth in the early stages of a small business can be seen as a natural extension of its original formation, and at least to some extent it requires the same sense of adventure, of initiative and of opportunity. However, as has been pointed out in previous chapters, many organisations have developmental stages and different priorities and practices prevail at different stages of development. For example, Greiner suggests that after the start-up or entrepreneurial phase, many organisations focus on the efficient division of labour and the elaboration of structure, which increases the need to formalize procedures and control behaviour.[1] Management effort focuses on efficiency and the maintenance of the status quo, and change becomes something to be resisted or avoided. Yet in a dynamic business environment, where competition is severe and where market developments present new opportunities, to stand still is to court regression.[2]

Standing still and maintaining order are appropriate reactions in a stable environment but the modern business environment is extremely dynamic, and standing still is not an advisable managerial option. A turbulent business environment is commonplace nowadays but it is worth emphasising why such a state of affairs exists.

Genus[3] and Jones-Evans[4] argue that many organisational contexts are now characterised by:

- a decline in stable mass consumer markets and an increase in fragmented markets in which product life cycles are much shorter than formerly

- a significant increase in the size of the service sector

- a marked reduction in labour market rigidities with major consequences for the employment patterns of individuals and the utilisation of labour by firms

- major technological and information revolutions which have transformed industries and organisations

- the deregulation of industrial sectors and the privatisation of nationalised industries

- intense international competition and the development of global production capabilities and markets

- the glorification of entrepreneurship and the enterprise culture.

Basically 'old certainties have been superseded by new and continuing uncertainties' and consequently organisations must innovate and differentiate products and services while improving quality.[5] They must do this by modifying their internal arrangements and their association with external parties.

Innovative responses to the modern organisational world are necessary for large and small firms but the approach is somewhat different in the more mature business. Business formation and early growth, which frequently depend on the ideas, drive and personality of the founder, are seen as the essence of entrepreneurship. Growth in a mature business also requires enterprise, ideas, drive and culture, but these must come at least in part from those working in the business as well as from an owner-manager.

> Today's businesses, especially the large ones, simply will not survive in this period of rapid change and innovation unless they acquire entrepreneurial competence.
>
> Peter Drucker[6]

> It is not the strongest of the species that survive, nor the most intelligent, but the ones most responsive to change.
>
> Charles Darwin

It was an American, Gifford Pinchot, who invented the word 'intrapreneurship' to describe the practice of entrepreneurship within mature businesses, a necessary practice if those organisations are to continue to develop indefinitely.[7] Organisational development implies change and improvement; it means doing new and more productive things that can sustain or enhance profit. This development requires the application of enterprise in the mature organisation: the process which has been described as intrapreneurship or, more recently, as corporate entrepreneurship.[8] Corporate entrepreneurship has been defined in a number of ways and some of the approaches used to develop it are considered in more detail later in this chapter. But before presenting them, the connection between entrepreneurship, innovation and enterprise is summarised in order to provide a context for corporate entrepreneurship.

Entrepreneurship

Entrepreneurship has been described in terms of:

> the ability to create something from practically nothing. It is initiating ... and building an enterprise rather than ... watching one. It is the knack for sensing opportunities where others see chaos, contradiction and confusion. It is the ability to build a 'founding team' to complement your own skills and talents. It is the know-how to find, marshal and control resources. Finally it is a willingness to take calculated risks.[9]

This definition is consistent with those used in Part I but it emphasises the range of activities that are needed to initiate and to launch the development of a new business venture. It does not dwell however on the nature of the business that is then created. A great deal of entrepreneurship or enterprise must still be exercised, even in a mundane small business, if that business is to survive. The interactions 'between smallness, exposure to the environment, ownership and personal control, condition the culture of the business'.[10] The task environment is complex and changeable, and the continuing exercise of enterprise is essential for success. Problems have to be solved for which there is little or no precedent.

Learning and problem solving are common activities in many working environments nowadays, but some people consider that true entrepreneurship occurs when individuals 'ignore the established ways of thinking and action' and seek novel ideas and solutions that can meet customer needs. Entrepreneurship is therefore:

> the innovatory process involved in the creation of an economic enterprise based on a new product or service which differs significantly from products or services offered by other suppliers in content or in the way its production is organised or in its marketing.[11]

In this approach entrepreneurship is therefore concerned with newness: new ideas, products, services or combinations of resources aimed at meeting the needs of consumers more efficiently.

Innovation

Innovation has also been considered in Chapter 3, but it is appropriate to mention it again. It has been described as the successful development of competitive advantage and, as such, it is the key to corporate entrepreneurship. For example, Pinchot, in his seminal work *Intrapreneuring*, argues that entrepreneurs in businesses are:

the dreamers who do: those who take hands-on responsibility for creating innovation of any kind within an organisation. The intrapreneur may be a creator or inventor but is always a dreamer who figures out how to turn an idea into a profitable reality.[12]

More recently Kuratko and Hodgetts have argued that 'the major thrust of corporate entrepreneurship is to develop the entrepreneurial spirit within organisational boundaries, thus allowing an atmosphere of innovation to prosper';[13] the corporate entrepreneur therefore is an individual who initiates innovative change in mature firms.

It is also argued that it is the presence of innovation that distinguishes the entrepreneurial organisation from others. Covin and Miles go so far as to say that 'the label "entrepreneurial" should not be applied to firms that are not innovative.'[14] For them, innovation is necessary for corporate entrepreneurship and that means being innovative in relation to the competition. They suggest, for example, that firms which replace their basic technologies with new methods which are being disseminated throughout an industry can be regarded as innovative from an internal perspective but will hardly be considered innovative by outsiders. For Covin and Miles, innovation must 'increase competitiveness through efforts aimed at the rejuvenation, renewal, and redefinition of organisations, their markets or industries' if businesses are to be deemed entrepreneurial.[15]

Inventors are usually individuals, but corporate entrepreneurship is frequently carried out by groups or teams. Caird points out that there are leading innovators who are frequently the driving force behind innovations. They are 'the project champions', and the project 'has no chance of being realised without their belief and commitment'.[16] However, while the lead innovator may have inventing or managerial skill or both, many of Caird's innovators lacked marketing and general management skills, which were provided by members of the project team.

Innovation itself can take several forms, all relevant to corporate entrepreneurship:[17]

- Innovation in processes, including changes and improvements to methods. These contribute to increases in productivity, which lowers costs and helps to increase demand.

- Innovation in products, or services. While progressive innovation is predominant, radical innovation opens up new markets. These lead to increases in effective demand which encourage increases in investment and employment.

- Innovation in management and work organisation, and the exploitation of human resources, together with the capacity to anticipate techniques.

It is important in this context to recognise that innovation is not confined to the manufacturing sector.

Enterprise

If corporate entrepreneurship is the continuing generation of innovation by applying entrepreneurship within established businesses then it is, in turn, an example of the broad meaning of 'enterprise'. As a result the terms 'entrepreneurship', 'enterprise',

ILLUSTRATION 9.1
The Ten Commandments of innovation

1. Take risks – adopt a 'can do' philosophy.
2. Stimulate creativity and seek out new ideas.
3. Reward success and tolerate failure.
4. Set realistic targets and review.
5. Adopt an open management style.
6. Focus on the customer – cultivate partnerships.
7. Actively manage investors.
8. Know what your competition is up to.
9. Work with other companies and academics.
10. Patent/protect.

DTI presentation

'innovation', 'change', 'intrapreneurship' and 'corporate entrepreneurship' are frequently used interchangeably and, while this is sometimes due to a looseness in writing style, it is clear that there are many similarities amongst the terms.

Innovation and enterprise are known to be important in the private sector in most economies but Borins points out that they can also be commonplace in the public sector.[18] This occurs despite deterrents such as the close political management of the executive, aimed at securing a consistent implementation of policy, tight controls and checks aimed at preventing corruption, and the keenness of the media to expose any errors and mistakes that may be made. It is also part of the conventional wisdom that, because public services are generally not exposed to market forces, they are liable to operate inefficiently and that this will continue until they are forced by a public crisis to innovate. However Borins reveals that public servants often initiate external innovation to solve problems before they become crises, and that other innovations emerge in response to perceived opportunities, sometimes as a result of initiatives by politicians.

Corporate entrepreneurship

The importance of corporate entrepreneurship

Before discussing corporate entrepreneurship it may be helpful to establish the importance of this activity for business development. Management writers such as Peter Drucker have for a long time argued that entrepreneurial competency is essential for continued success. However Wiklund reviewed the literature on the connection between an entrepreneurial strategic orientation and business performance in established smaller companies and concluded that there is no simple link between them. He also raised a point about the timescale of any correlation and wondered if corporate entrepreneurship was a quick fix for firms in trouble or whether it did indeed produce long-term results.

It is recognised that size as well as maturity has an impact on corporate entrepreneurial activity, so Wiklund carried out research on Swedish businesses with between 10 and 50 employees. This is one of the few studies which utilises large longitudinal data sets in investigating the link between entrepreneurial orientation and business performance and therefore, although these were not large businesses, this research is relevant to the issues covered in this chapter.

Wiklund argues that, in the short run, proactive firms pay attention to environmental trends and can respond quickly to opportunities by introducing innovations. Their alertness allows them to target markets and charge premium prices. It also allows them to stay ahead of the competition and gain a competitive advantage. Wiklund believes that this alertness provides established smaller firms with a strategic advantage which compensates for their lack of resources. He also believes that firm-level entrepreneurship confers advantage in the longer term. Their early movement into markets allows entrepreneurial firms to dominate distribution channels and establish industry standards which consolidate their advantage.

There is some research support for the long-term benefit of entrepreneurship but, in view of the inconclusive evidence in support of the entrepreneurship–performance link, Wiklund carried out his longitudinal study to discover if performance was enhanced as a result of entrepreneurial strategy in both the short and long run. Results indicate that there is a positive association between entrepreneurship and performance in both the short and longer term, thus offering support for those who argue in favour of entrepreneurship.[19] However, it should be pointed out that the link is not a simple one. Wiklund found that availability of finance, which can be considered to be a 'pull' factor, had a stronger impact on performance than entrepreneurship, which is a 'push' factor. Having the money to complete requisite activities is very important. In another article Chandler et al. indicate that an innovation-supportive organisational culture does have a positive impact on revenue in many firms, but only under conditions of rapid environmental change.[20]

Defining corporate entrepreneurship

Corporate entrepreneurship may lead to superior performance but, as we have found with several of the issues raised in this book, there are various definitions of key concepts in this field. For example Miller, in the early 1980s, began to distinguish between conservatism and entrepreneurialism in established firms, and for him entrepreneurial businesses are proactive initiators who try to outdo the competition. They also have a proclivity for bold, risky acts and are highly innovative. In short they are innovative, proactive risk takers.[21] Recently Lumpkin and Dess have added autonomy and competitive aggressiveness to Miller's list of entrepreneurial attributes but it has been pointed out that Miller's instrument measures entrepreneurial disposition rather than entrepreneurial action.[22] Vesper has added to the debate on corporate entrepreneurship by suggesting that it is characterised by three activities:[23]

- the creation of a new business unit by an established firm
- the development and implementation of entrepreneurial strategic thrusts
- the emergence of new ideas from various levels within an organisation.

Vesper's last point is supported by Covin and Miles, who believe that in some businesses an entrepreneurial philosophy impregnates the entire organisation.[24] Zahra et al. suggest that there are many facets of firm-level entrepreneurship which reflect different combinations of:[25]

- the content of the entrepreneurship, which can be activities such as corporate venturing, innovation and proactivity
- the source of the entrepreneurship, which can be internal to the firm or external
- the focus of the entrepreneurship, which can be formal or informal.

These views cover a wide range of entrepreneurship, but from them three main ways can be identified in which larger and more mature businesses can seek to promote entrepreneurship within the business. These are the promotion of entrepreneurship through formal strategic decision making, which will sometimes require the creation of a separate corporate venture; the formal and informal development of innovative ideas by middle managers and professional staff, which often entails the creation of a new project; and the creation of an entrepreneurial philosophy throughout the organisation. Various terms have been used in the literature to describe these activities but in this chapter they are referred to as 'strategic entrepreneurship', 'developing innovation within organisations' and 'entrepreneurial culture' respectively.

Strategic entrepreneurship

In a start-up the entrepreneur is regarded as the key actor in developing a business idea, marshalling resources and creating an organisation to bring a new product or service to the market. In a competitive business environment it is clear that mature and larger organisations should continue to seek out new opportunities and make the necessary arrangements to convert them into new goods and services. At a strategic level this requires an effective plan and the proper positioning of the organisation to respond effectively to its environment.[26] Porter argues that strategic decision makers must appreciate the competitive dynamics of their chosen industry.[27] The current and predicted industrial structures strongly influence the rules of the competitive game and offer certain strategic choices for organisations. He suggests that strategic planners should analyse the current and expected state of competitive rivalry by paying attention to such matters as the threat from new entrants, the availability of substitutes and the power of suppliers and customers. Industries can be classified as attractive or unattractive, and Porter argues that the profit potential of an industry is a function of industry attractiveness coupled with an appropriate competitive strategy. He recognises that competitive forces within an industry can drive down profits but contends that organisations must position themselves properly in the industry. Strategic choice in pursuit of specific goals is more important than environment or structure in promoting innovation.

There are many criticisms of Porter's approach to strategic change but it is representative of a body of managerial thought which associates organisational development with rational, logical, strategic decision making by managerial elites in both the private and public sectors. In general this approach to corporate entrepreneurship is akin to what

Heller calls strategic forcing.[28] The innovation is 'forcibly fitted into the resisting organisation [whilst] the "champion" project leader uses a mix of political power, organisational savvy, and technical powers to get the innovation past organisational roadblocks to implementation'.

That, however, might be considered to be a top-down approach to corporate entrepreneurship. Another view presents a model of corporate entrepreneurship which suggests that external variables such as market hostility, strategic variables such as competitive orientation, and internal variables such as internal competencies and resource availability all have a strong effect on the entrepreneurial orientation of an organisation.[29] Other environmental factors have also been suggested as drivers of corporate entrepreneurship, including growth markets and the demand for new products and services.[30] Either way corporate entrepreneurship is seen as having a strong influence on firm performance.

Influencing corporate entrepreneurship

Hornsby reviewed the literature on corporate entrepreneurship and identified five inter-related internal organisational conditions that influence corporate entrepreneurship.[31] These included:

- management support of entrepreneurial efforts
- work discretion and autonomy
- rewards and reinforcement
- time availability
- organisational boundaries.

The more that such conditions are in place, and seen to be in place, then the higher the probability of an employee deciding to behave in an entrepreneurial manner. Top managers may be strategically aware and see the need for change but they often forget that there are powerful individual, managerial, organisational and cultural reasons why innovative changes are resisted. Faced with resistance, managerial elites will attempt to overcome it at individual and organisational levels, so it seems sensible for powerful elites to understand how individuals react to change.

Resistance to change by individuals

Individuals in many organisations will resist change if they feel that their skills, status, power and relationships have to be altered significantly to meet the needs of the new order.[32] They will also want to understand why change is necessary. In this context it should be realised that people from different parts of an organisation interpret events in different ways and the need for change clearly perceived by senior managers may not be shared by other individuals and interest groups.[33] Sometimes they do not 'see' a problem, and therefore see no reason to change. Senior managers must also understand that individuals proceed through recognised phases, often typified by denial, resistance, exploration and commitment, as they experience a change in their situation, and that people therefore need time to digest changes.[34] Forcing change through is a dangerous approach; it must be managed effectively if people are to commit themselves to the new order.[35]

Independent versus corporate venturing

This view of strategic entrepreneurship in established firms indicates that new strategic directions may often require the creation of a separate corporate venture to deliver results. It might be argued that a separate corporate venture developed by an established business would bear a strong resemblance to other non-corporate new business ventures. However, Jones-Evans points out that major differences exist between corporate and non-corporate ventures, not least in that with a new venture the ground rules for running it emerge as it develops, whereas the leaders of corporate ventures must conform to general corporate procedures from the start.[36] Such constraints may reduce flexibility in the corporate venture and inhibit development. Jones-Evans also argues that an existing firm will have an established product-market portfolio and the new corporate venture can expect to experience serious resistance if it attempts to compete in the same markets.

Another difference will be in financing. An independent new venture will have several potential sources of funding, and lenders will normally have considerable experience of assessing the potential of a new business. In contrast, new corporate ventures are likely to have only one source of funding, namely the corporate body; its financial custodians will seldom review more than a handful of corporate venture proposals per year and may not have the experience of evaluating emerging business proposals. In any event, evaluations will tend to be based on standard financial decision-making procedures and these may be inappropriate for evolving ventures. In addition, the initiators of rejected corporate venture proposals do not have alternative sources of funding to which they can go. In general non-corporate venture leaders are in control of financial and other decisions whilst corporate venture leaders must work within the constraints imposed by the established organisation.

Jones-Evans also points out that funding for a corporate venture will most likely be allocated at an early stage of a project's development. A return on investment will then be expected fairly quickly and if this fails to materialise all supplies of funds may dry up. In contrast the early funding of new independent ventures may be rather limited, and this may be quite appropriate. Even though new businesses tend to be under-capitalised they often obtain additional funding on a step-by-step basis. As new products or developments come on-line additional funding is sought, and this means that there may be no acquisition of major funding until it is warranted by developments.

As well as different sources of funding for new corporate and non-corporate ventures, there are also likely to be different sources of human resources. In a new venture, staff will be recruited in the labour market according to their skills and commitment to the entrepreneur's vision. In contrast corporate ventures may be staffed by existing corporate employees with more interest in developing their careers. They may see their transfer to a corporate venture as a promotion and a reward for their overall contribution to the firm. Further rewards for corporate venture staff will probably be in line with corporate remuneration procedures whereas staff in a non-corporate venture can more easily be rewarded in line with the profitability of the venture.

Jones-Evans considers that new ventures sometimes benefit substantially from having expert advice from a board of directors. Directors often have diverse backgrounds and can advise on financial, market and technical matters. Corporate ventures may not have this resource; indeed project leaders usually report to the board of the controlling firm and must compete with other shareholders to have their interests addressed.

In general there are significant differences in the strategic resource management and organisational processes in corporate as opposed to new ventures, and these differences will have an impact on the potential profitability of these dichotomous units. The differences will also impact on the likelihood of continued innovation.

Developing innovation within organisations

Aggressively and proactively seeking innovative opportunities outside the organisation is the essence of strategic entrepreneurship, but entrepreneurship is not the sole preserve of CEOs and managerial elites. Mintzberg contends that all managers, and many support staff and others, take on an entrepreneurial role as part of their work.[37] These individuals are in unique positions to understand what is happening within organisations and some of them are able to develop an interdepartmental perspective. Many will also be in touch with peers, customers, suppliers and others outside the organisation and can spot external opportunities. Many business founders are keen to retain strategic decision making themselves but as organisations grow they are rarely able to develop the skills and know-how, nor have access to all the resources needed, to continuously expand the business. Continued growth occurs when owners involve others, and not just those at the strategic apex of the business, in the entrepreneurial process. Indeed some people argue that strategy can emerge from various levels in the organisation; however the creation and development of innovatory strategic thrusts by people other than those in the top management group can only occur if appropriate managerial and organisational systems, structures, styles and cultures are in place. Not all management styles and organisational arrangements facilitate innovatory development and therefore organisational barriers to, and assistance for, innovation need to be considered.

Managerial barriers to entrepreneurship

Managers can and do act entrepreneurially as they proliferate in growing organisations and as they acquire more decision-making authority with the dispersal of company ownership amongst shareholders. It is incumbent on managers to look to the future but management is a multi-faceted job and attentions can focus on stewardship and control rather than on entrepreneurship. Stevenson and Gumpert argue that managers frequently regard themselves as trustees, and this engenders caution.[38] They are responsible for expensive human and material resources, and they feel duty-bound to use these resources wisely. They are concerned to earn an acceptable rate of return on their resources in the shorter term and to protect the lives and livelihoods of their employees.

Managers have numerous constituents who must be at least partially satisfied. Consequently, decision making and change entail a cautious process of negotiating with major players, and pursuing a less risky, middle-of-the-road strategy is preferred. Caution is also necessary, because larger organisations typically commit large amounts of resource to important projects at one time. A lot of analysis is usually done before a project is supported, but once the decision is made the organisation is committed. Entrepreneurs, on the other hand, evaluate many projects simultaneously and quickly drop those that do not look promising. Stevenson and Gumpert also point out that there is a connection between managerial power and the resources that managers control. This being so, they are reluctant to take risks and often therefore reinforce the status quo. Managers also tend to have a narrower focus than entrepreneurs and to be concerned with building the power and reputation of their departments. However the process of new product development should be holistic, and a narrow departmental focus can inhibit innovatory thinking.

Support staff are often technical experts who are keen to prove their worth to organisations by introducing as many innovative ideas as possible. By so doing they can increase the reliance of others on their expertise and consequently increase their power and status. While they are generally keen on newness and change, there are often conflicts between individual staff as they endeavour to extol to the organisation the virtues of their particular speciality. They are also likely to come into conflict with line managers who are keen to maintain the status quo as they seek efficiency gains.[39]

Barriers to innovation are commonplace in many organisations, but Borins shows that in public sector organisations there are additional obstacles.[40] His research reveals that many of the barriers emanate not only from the bureaucratic nature of public sector organisations but also from the inherent caution of various internal actors. The barriers to innovation come from 'attitudes within the bureaucracy itself, turf wars, difficulties in co-ordinating organisations, logistical problems, the difficulty of maintaining the enthusiasm of programme staff, difficulties in implementing a new technology, opposition by unions, opposition by middle management, and opposition to entrepreneurial action within the public sector'. In addition, many initiatives are opposed by politicians because they require additional resources, because of legislative constraints and because of direct political opposition. Furthermore, various external interest groups, including private sector organisations that would have to compete with the public sector, resist many innovations.

Organisational barriers

Managerial roles and responsibilities can induce caution but managers and professionals work in an organisational context and the realities of this environment can also encourage conservatism. This occurs because organisations as they grow and mature tend to install standard operating procedures and rules that constrain initiative. The first time a new job is tackled there is a time-consuming learning process, but after it has been repeated several times a satisfactory method will be identified, remembered and used again. If the task is done continuously then recommended methods will be written down and employees told to follow them as the correct procedures.[41] As the volume of output increases there is more division of labour and specialisation, which leads to the creation of functional departments. Behaviour of individuals must be predictable, and this is achieved by introducing standard work practices. To make sure that individual and group tasks coalesce, schedules, process plans and control mechanisms are introduced.

However, as the complexity of the task increases, people lose sight of the ends they are serving. 'Management must find the means to make behaviour lower down more predictable and so it turns to rules, procedures, job descriptions, and the like, all devices that formalise behaviour.'[42] Organisations, as they develop, introduce standard practices, but also develop less tangible but equally powerful cultures. They develop characteristic ways of doing things that are guided by a set of shared norms and values. Organisations are infused with values, and this culture transmits to people in the organisation what they should be doing, what they ought to believe in or what the organisation is really about. Standard procedures and culture are powerful controlling mechanisms, and can easily defeat innovatory initiatives.[43]

As mentioned above, strategic planning can assist entrepreneurship. Some writers suggest that, with sufficient will and skill, organisations can become almost anything they want to be. However, in practice this rarely happens. Organisations specialise, which can mean that a huge investment in plant, machinery and manpower may have to be written off if the specialisation changes.[44]

Drucker recognises that many of these factors affect organisations but considers that size, per se, is not 'an impediment to entrepreneurship and innovation; [the main impediment] is the existing operation itself and especially the existing successful operation'. Total commitment to the existing operation is needed to ensure continued success and to manage 'the daily crises' that normally occur. The current activity requires priority attention 'and deserves it'. Drucker goes on to argue that most successful firms of today will in ten years' time derive a significant proportion of their income from a similar product range to their present one, but for long-term survival they must also look for a new range. This is not easy. 'The temptation in the existing business is always to feed yesterday and starve tomorrow. The current business is not in trouble, and there does not seem to be any pressure to innovate.'[45] It is evident that even leading organisations such as IBM and Xerox, which have been very innovative businesses, can lose their competitive edge and be forced to withdraw from certain markets. Conditions change and the very procedures which proved very effective in one era are the source of disadvantage in another.[46]

Facilitating innovation

Porter has pointed out that continuous innovation is essential for organisational survival in competitive markets but, in view of the barriers, achieving it requires hard work, appropriate attitudes and proper structures. However, just as there is no single agreed route to developing enterprise, there are a number of suggestions as to what constitute the innovatory aspects of corporate entrepreneurship.

In considering policies, procedures, structures and cultures which help sustain corporate entrepreneurship it is possible to differentiate between, on the one hand, those activities which encourage the development of new thinking and new projects by decentralising innovation to middle managers and professional staff, and on the other those activities which extend the enterprising culture to every person in the organisation. In some cases it may prove difficult to locate a procedure in one or the other of these categories, but it seems that there are differences in the mindsets required for extending the formal and informal development of new projects to middle levels of an organisation and for creating a wider enterprise philosophy. Also, while the policies and procedures which support strategic entrepreneurship by top managers have already been discussed, some of the discussion which follows, especially that in connection with Lessem's work, is relevant to the encouragement of strategic entrepreneurship.

Roles

Lessem in particular has highlighted the importance of managerial roles and behaviour in supporting corporate entrepreneurship, although he uses the older term 'intrapreneur', which will therefore also be used here in discussing his work. He identifies the key to intrapreneurship as the intrapreneurs themselves and the roles they perform.[47] For him, the intrapreneur combines many of the qualities of the entrepreneur and the manager. The impatience of the entrepreneur with the constraints imposed by the organisation produces too much conflict with the desire of managers to control events. For Lessem, the concept of intrapreneur is important for two reasons. 'Firstly, it cuts across the division between management and enterprise. But secondly, it forms a bridge between enterprise and development.'[48]

For Lessem, there are several roles or archetypes that can elicit effective development in differing business contexts. Some support strategic entrepreneurship while others support innovation from below. In some situations rugged entrepreneurs are needed. They have an instinctive approach to opportunities and impatience when faced with obstacles. They seldom let a real or perceived lack of resources inhibit their search for new profitable opportunities. However, in a mature venture their impatience and aggression can create conflict.

It is recognised that large and mature companies may not be attractive to entrepreneurial types unless they can find opportunities in areas such as sales and new product development. The organisation should offer them the chance to take on risky projects, however. Their success should be rewarded, but failure must not lead to censure. Mature organisational entrepreneurs can develop the capacity to focus on business renewal as a goal.

In some instances entrepreneurial activity is not enough for development; what is needed is an adventurer. The latter is a major risk taker who enters uncharted waters in search of opportunity. There are difficulties in making huge changes in strategy, but in some instances this is required and the courage and forcefulness of the adventurer is indispensable. In an increasingly global economy, organisations need the drive and audaciousness of the adventurer to enter new and difficult markets.

Innovators are needed also. They are the first or early users of new ideas and are the essential link between research and accomplishment. They must create structures and a climate conducive to the generation of, experimentation with and realisation of new ideas. They encourage creativity, but they also have a strong commitment to the commercial exploitation of ideas. Innovators get their rewards from seeing the successful transformation of an idea into a successful good or service, but there can be a tendency to marginalise adventurers and innovators in successful businesses. Firms must find mechanisms to allow innovation to coexist with current product efficiency.

Exploring random innovative ideas may be exciting but firms also need a sense of direction and discipline. There must be some pattern in a firm's strategy and leaders need to ensure that new projects are aligned with their vision for the business. Leaders stand back from the intensive competition in firms and act as somewhat impartial arbitrators, co-ordinators and conflict handlers. The leader takes an overview, reconciles differing perspectives, and creates a climate of co-operation, but also exercises authority when necessary to keep the business on the rails. Like the leader of an orchestra, the business leader has concern for the final product and for the people, and uses a range of methods of influence to make sure that all play in tune.

In addition, the role of effective change agents can be crucial. They bring new products to market, implement new management systems and reorganise working arrangements. Change agents like freedom from controls and are not bound by convention, but they also possess the managerial and political skill to manage change programmes. They appreciate the importance of creating a general awareness that the status quo will not do in a turbulent era and in creating an image of the future and letting key players know what it will look like. Further, using change management theory, they can design and implement the practical first steps to bringing about change. They also recognise and can deal with resistance to change. Change agents are keen to do new things, and get their motivation from the mental excitement that accompanies change.

Change agents are important, but they cannot function on their own. Another key intrapreneurial type therefore is the enabler. Many authors point out the importance of creating a climate or culture for enterprise and innovation, and the lack of appropriate cultures in many organisations. Therefore a facilitator or enabler aims to:

develop self-renewing, self-correcting systems of people who learn to organise themselves in a variety of ways according to the nature of their tasks, and who continue to expand the choice available to the organisation as it copes with the changing demands of a changing environment.[49]

Enablers use 'soft' behavioural skills to encourage people to question ideas, challenge conventions and seek, through collaboration with insiders and outsiders, to come up with forward-looking ideas.

Lessem also describes one more intrapreneurial type: the animateur. Organisations are technical and economic tools, but they are also living social systems, which need to be humanised and enlivened. An esprit de corps or sense of community is vital for a developing organisation, and this is where the animateur assists. The emphasis is on teams and on development through co-operation, problem solving and concern for the organisational community. Enablers and animators develop the supportive atmosphere and trust that is essential for individual and group risk taking in pursuit of better options.

Lessem's approach is useful in that it recognises the importance of numerous roles, from the aggressive and competitive adventurer and entrepreneur to the people-oriented enabler and animateur, in the continued development of mature organisations. Several of these intrapreneurial types can deliver innovation in appropriate situations, but others provide the change leadership skills to guide a project to fulfilment and create the flexible structures to sustain change.

Systems and structures that support innovation

Peter Drucker, in writing about innovation and entrepreneurship, like Lessem highlights the importance of managerial decision making but considers also that

ILLUSTRATION 9.2
Who is the intrapreneur?

Primary motives: the intrapreneur wants freedom and access to corporate resources and is self-motivated, but responds to corporate rewards.

Time orientation: the intrapreneur has end goals of three to 15 years, depending on the nature of the project, and strives to meet self-imposed and corporate timetables.

Action: the intrapreneur does whatever is needed to accomplish tasks and is not interested in status.

Skills: the intrapreneur knows the business intimately, but recognises the importance of managerial and political skill.

Confidence: the intrapreneur is self-confident and courageous and, if necessary, will outwit the organisational system.

Focus: the intrapreneur focuses both inside and outside the business. The intrapreneur pays attention to customers and gets insiders to do the same.

Risk: the intrapreneur likes moderate risk and undertakes market research in order to understand the risks.

Failure and mistakes: the intrapreneur regards mistakes as a learning experience, but is sensitive to the needs of the organisation for stability and hence may hide risky projects from view.

Decisions: the intrapreneur is adept at communicating his or her own private vision to others and is willing to compromise to make progress with this vision.

Attitude towards the system: the intrapreneur dislikes the system, but learns to manipulate it.

Background: the intrapreneur is often from an entrepreneurial, small business, professional or farm background and is often middle class and highly educated, particularly in technical fields.

Source: 'Who Is the Intrapreneur?', adapted from G. Pinchot III, *Intrapreneuring* (New York: Harper & Row, 1985), pp.54–6. Copyright © by Gifford Pinchot III. Reprinted by permission of the author.

appropriate policies and procedures are needed. He considers that the essence of innovation and corporate entrepreneurship is the development of new or different processes, products or services that utilise resources more productively than before. He contends that innovators must systematically review the changes taking place in society to identify and exploit business opportunities. Entrepreneurial managers must also scan the environment to become aware of changes in those management principles and practices, production processes, and market structures and requirements that can conceivably have an impact on their organisations. They must also be aware of changes in knowledge, but are warned against an over-emphasis on knowledge-based innovations. Some are spectacular and transform markets, but although the vast majority of innovations are more mundane they have a much greater cumulative impact on profits and employment.

It is important to emphasise the weight that Drucker attaches to solid, systematic investigation in the process of modernisation. This is seldom the result of genius or high-technology discoveries; more often it is the application of systematic search and logic to a host of organisational procedures and practices. Instalment credit or hire purchase, for instance, had a much greater impact on the business sector than more novel and spectacular changes. There are barriers to successful organisational innovation but, if the right managerial policies and practices are put in place, then innovation can become normal.

Many managers protect what they have currently, but if they are to change they must become aware that it is company policy systematically to give up those products and practices that are unproductive. They must therefore place all activities periodically 'on trial for their lives'. Managers should answer critical questions on the contribution products make to productivity and should be encouraged not to shore up the obsolete. Obsolete or declining products absorb scarce resources at the expense of the new. The best people tend to be charged with overcoming the problems associated with old products, whereas they should be encouraged to develop the new. Entrepreneurial business 'management must take the lead in making obsolete its own products and services rather than waiting for a competitor to do so'.[50]

Another approach is to use successful innovators as role models. They are asked to make presentations to their peers to explain their actions, to outline those factors that lead to success and those that cause difficulties. The fact that senior managers encourage this activity sends a clear message that innovative behaviour is appreciated. Then, if innovation is to become an important business function, mechanisms must be initiated to assess innovative performance. It is important to know what the expected outcomes of the innovation are likely to be, what resources are necessary and when results are to be achieved. Innovation concerns the new and largely unknown, but serious attempts must be made to gain feedback on progress to assess performance.

Policies, practices and appraisals assist innovation, but innovative ideas and their commercialisation are generated by people. Since behaviour is influenced by context, the organisational context must support innovative behaviour. Successful innovation emerges when organisations have appropriate personnel in post, when management systems support change and when a suitable climate obtains. The complexity of large organisations can stifle classic entrepreneurs, even if they are the company founders. Without appropriate policies the organisation is likely to become performance oriented rather than innovation oriented. 'Companies that have built entrepreneurial management into their structure ... continue to be innovators ... irrespective of changes in chief executives or economic conditions.'[51]

Just what is meant by entrepreneurial management and the creation of an appropriate climate? Jones-Evans argues that managers cannot tell people to engage in innovation: they self-select and will only continue to develop their ideas if appropriate organisational arrangements are in place.[52] An important requirement is to have clearly defined roles for those involved in the change process. In change management projects Jaffe argues that it is important to identify:[53]

- the top executive team of the whole organisation in which the innovation will develop
- the project sponsor – the person who makes the decision to make the change
- the project leader, who is often the person who has developed the new ideas
- the change navigator – the person with knowledge of and skill in implementing change programmes.

Innovatory change will not succeed unless the top management group supports it, and it will be problematic if there is not a skilled change agent in the entrepreneurial group. The leader has the detailed knowledge and enthusiasm to energise people but the sponsor must also be active in:

- overcoming the financial concerns of other managers regarding risky ventures, in both initial review and follow-up evaluations
- curing the need for resources by defending proposals in evaluation meetings, allocating initial exploration funding to new ideas and permitting flexibility in budgets in terms of money, people and equipment
- ensuring that corporate venturing develops quickly within an organisation by putting the rewards and initiatives in place for intrapreneurs
- fighting internal departmental issues, such as the hoarding of resources in one division, and empire-building.[54]

Jones-Evans also argues that it is important to retain those who initiate innovations in the corporate entrepreneurial team even if they lack managerial or organisational skill. If they are removed their strong motivational drive will be lost. Quite often the initial innovator does lack certain skills but this can be accommodated by creating a project team, which includes those with technical, economic, managerial and change management skills. It is also important for the project team to be kept intact even after the initial completion of the project. The team may have to respond to outsiders who develop new variants of the idea.

Corporate entrepreneurship is not easily confined within an organisational department. Bringing an idea to market will involve a great deal of knowledge which is located within functional departments. It is important therefore that corporate entrepreneurs and their associates have the power to make decisions and the political skill to obtain the level of co-operation they require. To avoid the damaging conflicts that can arise between departments, it may also be sensible to define innovation as a crucial business process and reorganise the business along business process lines (where a process is 'a specific ordering of work activities across time and place with a beginning, an end, and clearly identified inputs and outputs: a structure for action'[55]).

Corporate entrepreneurs have a strong proclivity for advancing risky projects, but as we have already seen, organisational policies and procedures often discourage managers and others from taking risks. Indeed failure is often seen as a barrier to career advancement. A mature business which wants to encourage corporate entrepreneurship must find ways of encouraging risky initiatives without damaging the careers of those individuals who lead these projects.

Resources must also be provided for corporate entrepreneurs. In the early stages of project development, time is a vital resource and those with an interest in developing new ideas must get away from regular duties. If a new idea looks promising then adequate funds must be made available. In general, there must be a degree of surplus or slack in organisations, which can be allocated to the generation and development of new business ideas.

If mature organisations are to continue to encourage entrepreneurship then corporate entrepreneurs must be appropriately rewarded. Organisations have been devising reward systems to motivate staff for a long time, but in view of the recent emergence of corporate entrepreneurship this presents a new challenge. Balkin and Logan have examined this issue and concluded that corporate entrepreneurs should be paid at or below market rate but that a significant bonus should be linked to the success of an innovative project.[56] In the short run, new venture personnel could be offered a profit-sharing option where profits from the new venture are paid to individuals in line with their current salaries. In the longer term, personnel could be offered shares in the new venture in proportion to their basic salaries.

CASE 9.1
New products at 3M

The Minnesota Mining Company (3M) has a reputation as one of the most innovative companies in the world. In the late 1980s it had developed more than 60,000 products, and almost a third of sales in 1988 came from products developed in the previous five years. Sales exceeded $10 billion in 1988 yet it was exceedingly entrepreneurial.

A major mistake by the founders around 1900 forced the company to innovate or go under and it has remained innovative for most of its subsequent existence. One early innovation was in the company's approach to selling. Rather than selling to purchasing officers, salesmen tried to meet their ultimate customers in the operating core of firms. They talked to production people and tailored their products to their needs.

These days 3M encourages innovative behaviour amongst all of its staff. It realises that many ideas will not reach fruition or become commercially successful but it works on the principle that the more attempts at innovation the more 'hits' there will be. Things that get in the way of innovation, like company politics or over-zealous planning, are stamped out. Co-operation, sharing information and informal communication are encouraged. Divisions are kept small — there were 42 in 1988 — and functional structures are discouraged. A product or process approach to departmental structures is favoured, individuals are multi-skilled and they are expected to accept responsibility. There is also a strong focus on teamwork. When an individual has a new idea he or she forms an action team drawn from manufacturing, technical and commercial staff. The team design and develop the idea and they are rewarded as the project passes important hurdles. Furthermore, the initiator of a successful development is given the chance to manage it as a founding entrepreneur. He or she runs a micro-company within 3M.

At 3M innovative thinking is encouraged and systems and structures are put in place to support it. However, resources are also made available. For example, there is a 15-per-cent rule which allows anyone to spend up to 15 per cent of their time on what they want to do so long as it is related to production. 'Genesis grants' of $50,000 are also available to allow people to progress projects beyond the ideas stage.

3M empowers its staff but there are guidelines and behavioural controls. The 25-per-cent rule is important and bonuses are based on achieving it. The rule states that 25 per cent of annual sales must emanate from products introduced during the previous five years. 3M is also keen on cost control. When Jake Jacobson became CEO in 1985 he said that manufacturing costs had to be reduced by 35 per cent by 1990 and the company initiated an innovative programme to achieve this goal. People are free to debate and discuss issues but they are subject to rigorous questioning by their peers. In effect individuals are controlled by means of peer review and feedback.

3M has a focus on innovation, and the company philosophy and culture are instrumental in sustaining this. Innovation as a means of getting close to customers and their needs is the philosophical bedrock on which the company is built. Another basic belief is that managers must support and facilitate innovation and be constructive in their dealings with others. 3M's values seem to build loyalty. Staff turnover is low and the company seldom hires from outside.

Source: Based on R. Mitchell, 'Masters of Innovation: How 3M Keeps Its New Products Coming', *Business Week* (1989), 10 April, pp.58–63.

Points raised

This is an example of the sort of deliberate steps taken by a company to ensure that innovation continues at a high level.

ILLUSTRATION 9.3
The reality?

Not all organisations are like 3M. For many the reality of attempts to be entrepreneurial in larger organisations are more likely to be one of unfriendly, protective secretaries and of unsympathetic bosses who are difficult to approach, and who are even more suspicious of ideas coming from the 'ranks'. Permission, support and resources are more likely to be refused and withheld rather than freely given. Modern bosses may have been taught to be more sensitive to employee ideas and be less prone to reject them openly, so instead they may listen politely and then quietly and slowly sabotage the project through inertia or a failure to deliver a vital resource.

How then can an intrapreneur go about succeeding in indifferent and even potentially hostile corporate environments? Part of the answer lies in becoming a 'guerrilla' working underground and unnoticed until success begins to speak for itself. Another aspect is resourcefulness, a dogged and creative ability to mobilise support. Finally there is courage and the determination to carry on despite all the odds.

Adhocracies

A theme of this chapter is that enterprise is both necessary and possible in organisations which, once established, need to continue to develop by introducing new products, processes or services while maintaining the efficiency of their existing portfolios.

There are organisations where innovation is the norm and which will continue to innovate boldly unless and until evidence emerges that there are dangers from excessive innovation. Miller and Friesen[57] point out that in these organisations the impetus for innovation comes primarily from the goals espoused by senior managers and associated strategies, but Covin and Slevin suggest that appropriate structural arrangements are also necessary.[58] Organisations in the computer, biomedical and film industries are constant innovators and require appropriate structures if they are to remain successful.

Mintzberg indicates that ad hoc flexibility is the key to this type of organisation.[59] This flexibility extends to the domain of strategy. Since these are innovative, problem-solving ventures, and individuals and teams are constantly working on new projects, no one can be sure how things will work out. So long as they fit in with the broad vision of the firm, successful projects which emerge from below will strongly influence strategy. Their structures are also highly flexible. There is no extensive division of labour or departmental specialisation, and little reliance on procedures, rules and plans. The reason is clear: as innovators they do not follow standard operating procedures and must devise new ways of tackling new jobs.

Because they are refined and complex innovators, these firms rely heavily on the knowledge of their expert staff, and quite often senior managers do not fully understand the intricate details of the work done by these staff. The power of knowledge becomes important and managers must delegate and have confidence in the ability of their experts. In addition, the experts will come together in ad hoc project teams to work on client problems. Teamwork is not easy, but the managers of project teams must be skilled in group dynamics, facilitation and motivation. The intrapreneurial roles of enabling and animation are vitally important and, because the work can only be done well in small groups, managerial spans of control are limited.

These structural arrangements are the antithesis of bureaucratic principles. Bureaucracies are control-oriented organisations, adhocracies are freedom seekers, and if both are housed in the same location then the culture of one will adversely impact on the effectiveness of the other. Drucker therefore argues for a physical separation of the innovative from the performance parts of businesses.

Coupling innovative projects and host organisations

Calls for the separation of innovative projects from mature organisations are common from popular management writers like Drucker, but Heller argues that two contrasting models of the link between host organisations and projects are common. In some cases an innovative project is developed by a 'product champion' who then, using his or her political skills, foists it upon and embeds it into a reluctant host organisation. Alternatively projects are 'imbued with the values and strategies of the firm and thereby channel their creations to be consistent with established consistencies'.[60] In this mode of development managerial elites monitor and encourage the alignment of new projects and corporate strategy. Heller believes, however, that it is more sensible to look at the link between host organisation and innovative project as a 'relationship of mutual influence between innovation and host organisational systems'. Loosening the link can allow the innovative unit to be creative in an atmosphere of psychological safety. It can also allow the innovators to deviate from the legitimate behaviour of the host organisation and can prevent problems in the innovative unit from percolating into the host organisation. Conversely, tight coupling can allow the innovative unit to benefit from the technical, human and financial expertise of the host organisation. Heller's research reveals that there are eight devices for coupling routine with innovating systems, as shown in Table 9.1.

It seems likely that in practice there will be less separation, forcing and assimilation of projects and hosts and more management of a dynamic interface between the two through everyday decisions. There are some additional points of interest emerging from this research. Heller points out that coupling occurs at different levels and may lead to pseudo-looseness. This occurs when a project is given considerable flexibility at a total

Table 9.1 Categories of loosening and coupling mechanisms

There are three mechanisms which rely heavily on assumptions about what the organisation does with respect to:	
• strategy	Projects which conform to the established understandings are closely coupled with the host while those which do not are unshackled.
• existent technology	
• and established markets	
and an additional five devices which connect projects by means of:	
• funding	Decisions on these variables determine the extent of the coupling between host and project. Coupling brings advantages such as legitimacy and funding and drawbacks such as interference and rejection.
• senior management attention	
• structural location of the new product development activities	
• standard operating procedures	
• and human resources deployments[61]	

Source: Modified version of Table 1, p.28 of T. Heller, 'Loosely Coupled Systems for Corporate Entrepreneurship: Imagining and Managing the Innovative Project/Host Organisation Interface', *Entrepreneurship: Theory and Practice* (1999), 24, p.25–31. Reprinted by permission of Baylor University, publisher of *Entrepreneurship: Theory and Practice*.

level but is expected to conform to senior management's decision-making parameters. She also argues that the oft-claimed motivational benefits of decentralisation may be more to do with changes in delegation than with an outcome of a particular structure. Tightly coupled projects which are set loose engender exhilaration. Nevertheless, while it might be attractive to separate innovative projects and host organisational systems completely, management of the interface is a more common occurrence.

Entrepreneurial competencies

It has been suggested that some business strategies, such as downsizing, have actually caused organisations to reduce their capacity to innovate and to identify and build on new opportunities. To offset such tendencies, and in recognition of their need to continue to develop opportunities, businesses are adopting specific strategies to build entrepreneurial competencies.

There are several strands to this approach in the strategic change literature but their primary focus is on the effective management of internal resources and the emergence of special competencies as a result of the intelligent utilisation of resources.[62] The creation of unique competencies allows organisations to rid themselves of outmoded procedures and develop new routines which allow the organisation to meet the changing needs of customers. Competencies also assist in altering the nature of competition in industries. Organisations redefine the nature of competition in a way which allows them to use their special combinations of production, service and infor- mation provision skills. Competent organisations provide customers with both tangible and intangible benefits. Some writers in this area concentrate on combining product and process technologies to afford competitive advantage, while others focus on the structural and cultural changes needed to create advantage.

A variant on this theme is provided by the 'capabilities school' promoted by authors such as Nonaka.[63] They take a more holistic approach to the effective leverage of resources and emphasise the importance of values in promoting special capacities. They recommend the use of language, metaphor and analogy in enhancing the creation of knowledge which can lead to improved customer-related capabilities.

Entrepreneurial culture

Mention of values leads into the final area for consideration in the corporate entrepre- neurship debate. The ideology and values of senior managers are important determinants of entrepreneurialism in mature ventures but this must be supported by entrepreneurial management, organisational systems and structures.

Managers and professional staff at all levels will be expected to look to the future on occasions but there are those who argue that everyone in organisations must be entre- preneurial, including first-line supervisors, staff in the operating core, clerical workers and security personnel. Senior managers and others can create an environment which is conducive to entrepreneurship, but they cannot order it. If the dominant organisa- tional form for most of the twentieth century was a bureaucracy which relied on standardisation, specialisation, rules and procedures, and obedient service by opera- tors,[64] then the inculcation of an all-pervasive entrepreneurial orientation in bureaucratic businesses represents a huge shift in the organisational paradigm. It implies a shift in the culture and many of the elements of the cultural web that sustain the paradigm.

Table 9.2 illustrates some of the changes that emerged when the Baxi Heating company changed from a 'solid, slow manufacturing organisation to a more dynamic, market-focused organisation'. It can be seen that the structures, behaviours and assumptions needed to support the new paradigm are very different from those underpinning the old.

There are many contributors to the organisational culture debate but Peters and Waterman were early and influential protagonists. They believe that managers should not aim to control individual behaviour by issuing directives but should try to influence the way people think.[65] The goals are to win their hearts, to engender absolute commitment to the organisation, and to encourage them to challenge the status quo and try out new solutions to problems. This is a very different mindset from that which pertains in a bureaucratic organisation, and is brought about by various mechanisms, as shown in Table 9.3.

Genus argues that, while the proponents of the 'excellence school' are wary of concentrating too much on structural form, they believe that certain structures are crucial in promoting innovation and entrepreneurship.[66] To support an entrepreneurial culture it is essential that the structure be simple, non-hierarchical, decentralised, flat, team-oriented and flexible.

Managers, especially senior managers, play a key role in articulating and creating the culture of entrepreneurship, but they will only be successful to the extent that individuals identify with this ideology. Some individuals will identify naturally with managerial values, some will be selected to important teams because they so identify, many others will be successfully socialised and indoctrinated by management endeavour; but some will merely identify because they calculate that it is in their best interest to do so. Peters and Waterman give the impression that the modification of culture and its assimilation by all participants is a practical possibility for many organisations, but many other authors are less sure about the possibility of changing culture to order.[67] Even those authors who consider that cultural change is important and feasible believe that it is a long-term endeavour which requires leadership backed up by the other elements of the cultural web.

Table 9.2 The old and new paradigms at Baxi Heating

Old	New
Solid	Dynamic and responsive
Stable/safe	Market-focused
Excellence	Continuous learning
Proud	Proud and profitable
Lifetime employment	Open communication and trust
Slow	Continuous improvement

Source: Based on J. Balogun and V. Hope-Hailey, *Exploring Strategic Change* (London: Prentice-Hall, 1999), pp.50–1. Copyright © Prentice-Hall, 1999. Reprinted by permission of Pearson Education Ltd.

Table 9.3 A motivational framework

Feature	Remarks
Value-driven	It is vital that basic beliefs and values concerning what the organisation stands for should be communicated to all employees by managers who speak with one voice. Managers take the process of inculcating values seriously and preach it using analogy and metaphor rather than more direct methods.
Simultaneous loose-tight properties	Individuals are encouraged to challenge, debate and engage in innovation and entrepreneurship but these activities are the means. The ends are highly prescribed through adherence to basic beliefs, which are strongly reinforced by the cultural web. Workers are empowered but within tight confines.
People-orientated	People, who have the capacity to be extremely creative and flexible, are regarded as the greatest asset of excellent companies and a family atmosphere is frequently engendered. People are treated with respect and are well trained but are expected to perform.
Entrepreneurship	A critical feature of excellent companies is their ability to create an entrepreneurial orientation. This state of affairs is promoted by granting autonomy to the individual and 'product champions' are encouraged to run their own 'independent businesses' under the corporate umbrella. Entrepreneurship is also fostered by intense, open and informal communication facilitated by the provision of flip charts, whiteboards and tables in many locations throughout the organisation.
Customer and action-focused	Excellent organisations believe that the customer is king and that customers can be a fine source of new ideas. Excellent firms have a bias for action rather than analysis. Complex jobs are broken down into manageable bits and small is beautiful: it assists the management of units and creates a sense of ownership.
'Stick to the knitting'	Excellent firms stick to what they know well. They do not move readily into uncharted industrial sectors and, if they do, they first test the water adequately.

Source: Based on T. Peters and R. H. Waterman, *In Search of Excellence* (London: Harper and Row, 1982).

A new mindset

It is important for managers to set the tone and adopt a new mindset if they want all employees to act entrepreneurially, but as with culture, it is unlikely that they can produce innovation to order. In a real sense they must empower their innovative personnel rather than exercise power over them. Hales notes that much endeavour by managers is geared towards overcoming resistance to their authority and, in spite of a host of techniques such as participative management, quality circles and incentive schemes, many managers still exercise an autocratic form of power over others. However, he notes that many organisations are recognising that power in the sense of 'transformative capacity' or 'power to ...' now resides in the interdependence which is characteristic of work organisations.[68] For innovation and enterprise, 'power to ...' is more important than 'power over'.

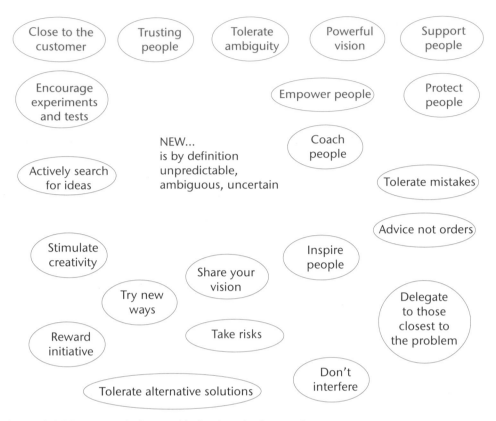

Figure 9.1 Manager mindset and behaviour for innovation

Source: Slightly modified from © The ForeSight Group Diagram, S Hamngatan 37, 41106 Göteborg, Sweden.

Many of the attitudes, behaviours and organisational arrangements which support innovation are presented by Sven Atterhed and his colleagues, from the ForeSight Group, as in Figure 9.1.

Flexibility, experimentation, empowerment and risk taking are crucial in engendering an innovative spirit and capacity in mature organisations. Imported techniques can assist, but Atterhed argues that such mechanisms will achieve little if managers still try to reduce uncertainty and protect existing practices. He suggests that it is important to have a 'managerial mindset and behaviour that encourages enterprise and innovation and equips people to be open to the new'.[69] The new mindset 'requests and requires' that innovation be the responsibility of all. For Atterhed this will not happen unless management develops a new mindset.

A modern study of entrepreneurial culture

Hornsby et al. note the increasing interest in entrepreneurial culture in recent years but argue that very few studies have empirically tested the existence of factors thought to be important in creating such a culture.[70] They reviewed the literature on those factors in the corporate environment which are conducive to corporate entrepreneurship and conclude that five are important:

- management support
- work discretion
- rewards/reinforcement
- time availability
- permeable organisational boundaries.

In view of some claims in the literature that the managerial culture is different in Canadian and US firms, the authors looked at the initiatives coming from 353 mid-level managerial workers from 12 Canadian firms and from 174 managers from six US firms. They asked respondents to complete a Corporate Entrepreneurship Assessment Instrument to discover if the five supporting mechanisms were present in the two countries. They also asked six open-ended questions to assess the extent of entrepreneurial behaviour. The questions referred to:

- the number of ideas suggested in the last six months
- the number of ideas which were implemented
- the number of ideas implemented without official organisational approval
- the amount of time spent thinking about new work-related ideas
- the number of times managers talked outside their own departments about new ideas
- the number of times managers bypassed normal channels to pursue an innovative idea.

The results revealed that there were no differences between the perceived entrepreneurial cultures in US and Canadian firms. Furthermore, there were no significant differences between the reported entrepreneurial behaviours of the US and Canadian managers, although the former had greater absolute scores on all six indicators of behaviour. There was a positive connection between work discretion, managerial support, rewards and low organisational boundaries. Results also indicated that, while there was no difference in the overall level of innovative behaviour in US and Canadian firms, US managers were more likely to respond to an encouraging corporate culture than Canadians. The authors speculated that the more security-conscious Canadian managers did not respond very positively to expressions of support for innovation from senior managers. This study is useful for its timely review of the literature but even more so for its operationalisation of key variables and the introduction of a cross-cultural perspective on this subject.

A similar pattern to the Canadian results was also found among Japanese managers within a major multinational. In a study of a small sample of Japanese managers within NEC, the prime concerns of the managers were with the traditional Japanese lack of acceptance of failure and low tolerance of risk.[71] As Helms indicates:

> The traditional Japanese 'sarariman' or salary man takes great pride in his title and position within the [organisation] which provides him with status in society, security and a social life. To many, venturing outside the corporation with the knowledge of how difficult or impossible it would be to get back in, would be akin to the highest of gambles, with personal, family, social, and financial status at stake.[72]

Networks

So far, corporate entrepreneurship has been described as largely an intraorganisational process, as that is the original essence of the concept. However, there are situations where inter-firm contact and co-operation can help the process, especially in terms of innovation. Firms can search for opportunities and try to realise them by developing products to meet market needs. If, however, having seen an opportunity, a business does not have the wherewithal to address it, it may help if it collaborates with one that can supply the missing component(s). This can also bring benefits of shared knowledge, reduced development and process costs, reduced risks of failure and knowledge of key benchmarks. In some markets it is also common for customers to initiate innovations.[73] Users are often the first to recognise a need and may then pass such information on to manufacturers, or use it in co-operation with them to develop an appropriate new product.

A level of collaboration has long characterised innovation, but it has been argued that inter-organisational co-operation is much more common in today's world. One reason argued for by Alter and Hage is that, with the pace of change in technology and markets, the risks in carrying out innovation have increased considerably.[74] Innovators need time to recoup development costs but, in current conditions, product life cycles may be too short to guarantee recovery. They also argue that the state plays an increasing role in much industrial innovation. Often it encourages lots of players to get involved and promotes collaborative practices to let many of the players share in the benefits. Porter argues against encouraging joint ventures between domestic competitors, because this reduces the incentive to maintain a competitive advantage. However collaboration and the development of long-term relationships with customers and suppliers can help to reduce costs and enhance competitiveness.

Such inter-organisational relationships, however, are unlikely to develop instantaneously. Parties must be sensitive to one another and feel that the others have something of use to them. They must also communicate to explain their needs and examine possibilities for exchange. A degree of consensus is also important. They must have reasonably compatible values and be able to work problems through by means of 'adjustment and compromise: a process that entails negotiating and bargaining'.[75]

Market uncertainties, experience in developing long-term relationships, and the complexity of the innovation process have led many firms to form links with a number of outside organisations when generating ideas, developing prototypes and testing markets. As James notes, 'The significant change in the business environment … has changed the focus of alliance strategies (for innovation) to the point where they are now becoming the rule rather than the exception.'[76]

When smaller is an advantage

Introducing corporate entrepreneurship into bigger businesses, and making them more entrepreneurial and innovative and thus more like small businesses in their market responses, is not always the best way to take advantage of new business opportunities, however. As Charles Handy argues, economic prosperity needs both elephants and fleas.[77] Sometimes it is better to be a flea. Other examples of this can be found with high technology businesses and in the 'new economy' outlined in Illustration 9.4.

ILLUSTRATION 9.4
The rules of the new economy

The rules as applied to our economies by traditional economists have changed. In the old economies, convergence within and across countries was possible as, in the longer term, capital migrated to lower wage areas. But there is no such convergence in a knowledge economy. Knowledge doesn't spread so easily. It tends to stay 'regional', as evidenced by what some have alluded to as the knowledge 'black holes' of Silicon Valley, Route 128, Atlanta and Austin in the United States and of Cambridge in the UK. Knowledge develops within and through close personal networks which are facilitated by geographical proximity. Indeed it is also now well known that 'business angels', who are important to high-growth start-ups, concentrate their investments within easily accessible distances. It is an apparent paradox that in an era in which data and information can be transmitted globally in fractions of a second, knowledge is relatively immobile and still requires geographic proximity for its spread.

Factor	New economy	Old economy
Unit of analysis	The entrepreneur	The plant/business
Policy instrument	Knowledge infrastructure	Interest rates
Entry criteria	Knowledge (available to all)	Financial capital (available to a few)
Growth drivers	Entrepreneurs	Managers
Source of competitiveness	Knowledge and value added	Economies of scale and cost reduction
Infrastructure required	Knowledge infrastructure	Transport infrastructure Labour supply
Convergence	Knowledge stays regional	Capital moves to lower wage areas

It is interesting to note that in this context countries can be placed within one of three categories:

- Creators of knowledge: about 30 countries are, according to the number of patents filed, significant creators of knowledge.

- Users of knowledge: many countries, such as the former Soviet Bloc countries, use knowledge but do not appear to create it.

- Others: those countries which are neither creators nor users of knowledge, such as parts of Africa and Latin America.

To convert from a 'user' to a 'creator' it is necessary to have an infrastructure that both generates and applies knowledge. As well as universities and research institutes, that also requires, for example, market researchers and marketing organisations as well as knowledge-based businesses.

ICT and e-business

The 'new economy' has also been described as the knowledge economy. The term 'new economy' is used to encompass issues of the globalisation of business, the expansion of information and communication technology (ICT) and the increasing importance and pervasiveness of knowledge.[78] Indeed many now see the availability of appropriate knowledge as a key driver of competitiveness, superseding the availability of raw materials, energy or labour, which had been predominant. Information technologies, which facilitate the application of knowledge, promote new business methods and specialisations. The new economic conditions promote new opportunities for enterprise.

Knowledge, in comparison with other products of business, is also strange stuff. It can be sold, and yet still be retained by the seller after it has been sold. It can be shared indefinitely but not diluted. It can be valuable and, as intellectual property, its ownership can be protected, yet it is of most use when it is fresh, and it is hard to keep because if it is retained for too long it tends to leak out. It can belong to a company but it resides in the employees and, if they leave, it can go too.

The emergence of these new forms of economic activity creates new opportunities which are often taken up by small businesses, rather than through innovation in bigger businesses. As already noted, small businesses, especially at the time of their start-up, are often more flexible than big businesses and their speed of response is generally quicker. They can therefore occupy, and capitalise on, a niche opportunity more quickly than their bigger rivals. Their owner-managers do not have other operations to distract them and typically are fully committed to the new venture depending, as they often do, on it alone for their future. However it is not just small businesses which have made use of the Internet. Home shopping and airline booking are examples used by many people of bigger businesses using the technology to gain or maintain their market positions.

The introduction of ICT has been likened to the earlier introduction of the telephone or of the railways in the opportunities it offers and in its potential to change business. For other businesses the opportunities, Burns suggests, lie in the following areas:[79]

- The opportunity to establish the network through which other traders can gain access to the new marketplace. Businesses doing this can be likened to the railway companies which built and operated the early railways and may, like them, find that it is not in reality a source of long-term profit.

- The opportunity to use the technology to do business by becoming a trader in the e-marketplace, like the businesses which used the facilities provided by the railway companies to do their work better. These opportunities can in turn be of two sorts:

  - the opportunity to establish innovative trading businesses which exploit the unique characteristics of the Internet. These are businesses which could not exist without the Internet.

  - the opportunity to use the Internet to reach a global market and to compete there on price, on the differentiated qualities of the product or service, or by focusing even more effectively on particular market segments. This is done by businesses which could probably operate without the Internet but which use it to reach a wider market.

It is the last of these areas of opportunity which will in particular have implications for businesses which are not themselves e-businesses. While they may not be using the Internet, many of their customers are, and by doing so they are finding other suppliers. Almost all businesses therefore need to see what ICT is doing to their market and to take appropriate steps to respond. Those steps may involve the businesses concerned using the Internet themselves, by becoming 'connected'. However in some cases it might be appropriate to change, or even end, the business. The growth of low-cost airlines with online direct booking of flights has taken business away from travel agents and they will not get it back just by using the Internet themselves.

The new economy is nevertheless an area in which it can help to be small and where there do appear to be disadvantages of scale, and there are other areas where this applies also. As a result some entrepreneurs prefer to grow the totality of their portfolio not by growing their existing business or businesses, but by forming new businesses. Richard Branson is an example of someone who has grown Virgin by new ventures, not by organisational control, but by his interest and the Virgin label. However not all of this 'growth' would be seen from a business-centred perspective because it arises not only from growth in the businesses themselves but from new business formations.

Conclusions

> Innovation is at the heart of the spirit of enterprise. Practically all firms are born from a development which is innovative, at least in comparison with their existing competitors in the marketplace. If they are subsequently to survive and develop, however, firms must constantly innovate – even if only gradually. In this respect, technical advances are not themselves sufficient to ensure success. Innovation also means anticipating the needs of the market, offering additional quality or services, organising efficiently, mastering details and keeping costs under control.
>
> EU Green Paper on innovation[80]

Small businesses are a reservoir, a source, both for the creation of jobs and for the development of diversity within economies. Capitalising on this reservoir means growing those small businesses and maintaining the attitudes of enterprise in the business upon which that growth will depend. That internal enterprise, in larger businesses, requires some different approaches from the enterprise which typically starts a small business. It has been called corporate entrepreneurship.

THE KEY POINTS OF CHAPTER 9

- Growth in the early stages of a small business can be seen as a natural extension of its original formation, but when a business reaches a steady state different attitudes can prevail and further change can be resisted. Maintaining growth in a more mature business can therefore require a different approach, a process of internal enterprise, which has been called 'intrapreneurship' or more recently 'corporate entrepreneurship'.

- Corporate entrepreneurship is therefore connected to the concepts of entrepreneurship, enterprise and innovation. Entrepreneurship has typically described the drive that starts a business, and a similar drive is needed to maintain its advance. Innovation is the successful development of competitive advantage and, as such, can be said to be the key to corporate entrepreneurship. That innovation can take several forms: innovation in processes and methods, innovation in products or services, and innovation in work organisation. Entrepreneurship and innovation, applied to the continued development of a business, are still enterprise even if the business is a larger one.

- There are however inherent difficulties in corporate entrepreneurship. These are such that some writers on corporate entrepreneurship, or formerly on intrapreneurship, have contended that many large corporations will in practice survive only by restructuring their businesses as confederations of small businesses. There are barriers of human resistance to change, barriers of management roles and motivation, and barriers of organisational structures and systems. Size, per se, is not an impediment to entrepreneurship and innovation, but the attitude and methods that size can bring are.

- The process of corporate entrepreneurship itself has been analysed in terms of the roles a corporate entrepreneur must play, including those of entrepreneur, adventurer, innovator, leader, change agent, animateur and enabler, many of which do not fit in easily with a large company ethos. The structures that best support the processes of corporate entrepreneurship have also been considered, with recommendations for solid systematic investigations into the relevance of current products and procedures and into the process of modernisation.

- Some organisations, in industries such as computers, biomedical products, and management consulting, are constant problem solvers and innovators. Flexibility is the key to their success. They are also frequently knowledge based and have structural arrangements that are the antithesis of bureaucracy. Empowerment is important, as well as having the right mindset.

- Corporate entrepreneurship can be seen as a response by bigger businesses to some of the perceived advantages of small businesses. However, despite this, there are areas of business, such as those in the 'new economy', where small businesses sometimes really do seem to have an advantage. In that situation some entrepreneurs, instead of trying to grow their existing businesses by making them behave like small ones, increase their portfolios by starting new separate small businesses.

QUESTIONS, ESSAY AND DISCUSSION TOPICS

- What can enterprise add to big business?
- What are the differences between the practices and processes of creating a new independent venture and the launching of a subsidiary venture by an established firm?
- How would you define the terms 'corporate entrepreneurship' and 'intrapreneurship'?
- Identify and describe three broad approaches which encourage the development of innovative projects within large organisations.
- Describe the types of managerial role which are conducive to innovation in an organisation.
- What might be done to create an entrepreneurial ethos throughout an established organisation?
- What are the principal determinants of business culture?
- Contrast this with your national business environment.
- Can you identify in business terms another example of the successful 'flea'?
- What is the future for e-businesses?

Suggestions for further reading and information

C. Handy, *The Elephant and the Flea* (London: Hutchinson, 2001).

P. Burns, *Corporate Entrepreneurship: Building the Entrepreneurial Organisation*, 2nd edn (Basingstoke: Palgrave, 2008).

P. Drucker, *Innovation and Entrepreneurship* (London: Heinemann, 1985).

I. Eltring (ed.), *Corporate Entrepreneurship and Venturing: International Studies in Entrepreneurship*, Vol. 10, 2005 (Springer).

D. F. Kuratko and R. M. Hodgetts, *Entrepreneurship: A Contemporary Approach* (Orlando, FLA: Harcourt College Publishers, 2001), Chapter 6.

References

1. L. E. Greiner, 'Evolution and Revolution as Organisations Grow', *Harvard Business Review*, July–August (1972), pp. 40–7.
2. P. Drucker, 'Our Entrepreneurial Economy', *Harvard Business Review*, January–February (1984), pp. 59–64.
3. A. Genus, *The Management of Change* (London: Thomson Business Press, 1998).
4. D. Jones-Evans, 'Intrapreneurship', in *Enterprise and Small Business*, edited by S. Carter and D. Jones-Evans (Harlow: Financial Times/Prentice-Hall, 2000).
5. Genus, op cit., p. 5.
6. P. Drucker, *Innovation and Entrepreneurship* (London: Heinemann, 1985), p. 132.
7. G. Pinchot III, *Intrapreneuring: Why You Don't Have to Leave the Organisation to Become an Entrepreneur* (New York: Harper & Row, 1985).

8. See for example S. A. Zahra and J. G. Covin, 'Contextual Influences On the Corporate Entrepreneurship-Performance Relationship', *Journal of Business Venturing*, 10 (1995), pp. 43–58.

9. J. A. Timmons, *The Entrepreneurial Mind* (Andover: Brick House, 1989), p. 1.

10. A. A. Gibb, 'The Enterprise Culture and Education', *International Small Business Journal*, 11 (1993), pp. 11–34, at 16.

11. J. Curran and R. Burroughs, 'The Sociology of Petit Capitalism: A Trend Report', *Sociology*, 20 (1986), pp. 265–79, at p. 269.

12. Pinchot, op. cit., p. 46.

13. D. F. Kuratko and R. M. Hodgetts, *Entrepreneurship* (Fort Worth: Dryden Press, 1995), p. 95.

14. J. G. Covin and M. P. Miles, 'Corporate Entrepreneurship and the Pursuit of Competitive Advantage', *Entrepreneurship: Theory and Practice*, 23 (1999), pp. 47–66, at p. 51.

15. Covin and Miles, op cit.: 52.

16. S. Caird, 'How Important Is the Innovator for the Commercial Success of Innovative Products in SMEs?', *Technovation*, 14 (1994), pp. 71–83, at p. 81.

17. 'Green Paper on Innovation', *Bulletin of the European Union*, Supplement 5/95 (Brussels: ECSC-EC-EAEC, 1996).

18. S. Borins, 'Loose Cannons and Rule Breakers, or Enterprising Leaders? Some Evidence About Innovative Public Managers', *Public Administration Review*, 60 (2000), pp. 498–507.

19. J Wiklund, 'The Sustainability of the Entrepreneurial Orientation–Performance Relationship', *Entrepreneurship: Theory and Practice*, 24 (1999), pp. 37–48, at p. 41.

20. G. N. Chandler, C. Keller and D. W. Lyon, 'Unravelling the Determinants and Consequences of an Innovation-Supportive Organisational Culture', *Entrepreneurship: Theory and Practice*, 24 (2000), pp. 59–76.

21. D. Miller and P. H. Friesen, 'Innovation In Conservative and Entrepreneurial Firms: Two Models of Strategic Momentum', *Strategic Management Journal*, 3 (1982), pp. 1–25.

22. G. T. Lumpkin and G. G. Dess, 'Clarifying the Entrepreneurial Orientation Construct and Linking It To Performance', *Academy of Management Review*, 21 (1996), pp. 135–72.

23. K. H. Vesper, 'The Three Faces of Corporate Entrepreneurship: A Pilot Study', in *Frontiers of Entrepreneurial Research*, edited by J. A. Hornaday et al. (Wellesley, Mass.: Babson Colleges, 1984), pp. 294–320.

24. Covin and Miles, op. cit., p. 52.

25. S. A. Zahra, D. F. Jennings and D. F. Kuratko, 'The Antecedents and Consequences of Firm Level Entrepreneurship: The State of the Field', *Entrepreneurship: Theory and Practice*, 24 (1999), pp. 45–63.

26. For a short critical review of the strategic planning approach to change see Genus, op cit., pp. 15–25.

27. M. Porter, *Competitive Strategy* (New York: Free Press, 1980).

28. T. Heller, 'Loosely Coupled Systems for Corporate Entrepreneurship: Imagining and Managing the Innovation Project/Host Organisation Interface', *Entrepreneurship: Theory and Practice*, 24 (1999), pp. 25–31, at pp. 25–6.

29. J. G. Covin and D. P. Slevin 'A Conceptual Model of Entrepreneurship as Firm Behaviour', *Entrepreneurship: Theory and Practice*, 16 (1991), pp. 7–25.

30. B. Antoncic and R. D. Hisrich 'Corporate Entrepreneurship Contingencies and Organisational Wealth Creation', *Journal of Management Development*, 23 (2004), pp. 518–550.

31. J. S. Hornsby, D. F. Kuratko, and S. A. Zahra 'Middle Managers' Perception of the Internal Environment for Corporate Entrepreneurship: Assessing a Measurement Scale', *Journal of Business Venturing*, 17 (2002), pp. 253–273.

32. L. Clarke, *The Essence of Change* (Hemel Hempstead: Prentice-Hall, 1994).

33. G. Zaltman and R. Duncan, *Strategies for Planned Change* (New York: Wiley, 1977).

34. D. Jaffe, *Leading Change* (Washington, DC: NTL Workshop, 1999).

35. C. Handy, *The Age of Unreason* (London: Arrow, 1990).

36. Jones-Evans, op. cit., pp. 244–6.

37. H. Mintzberg, *The Structuring of Organisations* (Englewood Cliffs, NJ: Prentice-Hall, 1979).

38. H. H. Stevenson and D. E. Gumpert, 'The Heart of Entrepreneurship', in *The Entrepreneurial Venture*, edited by W. A. Sahlman and H. H. Stevenson (Boston, Mass.: Harvard Business School Press, 1993), pp. 9–25.

39. H. Mintzberg, *Power in and Around Organisations* (Englewood Cliffs, NJ: Prentice-Hall, 1983).

40. Borins, op. cit: 504.

41. Mintzberg (1979), op. cit., p. 233.

42. Ibid., p. 233.

43. P. Selznick, *Leadership in Administration* (New York: Harper & Row, 1957).

44. W. Starbuck, *Organisational Growth and Development* (Harmondsworth: Penguin, 1971).

45. Drucker (1985), op. cit., p. 137.

46. D. Miller, *The Icarus Paradox* (New York: Harper Business, 1992).

47. R. Lessem, *Intrapreneurship* (Aldershot: Gower, 1987).

48. Ibid., p. 7.

49. J. Sherwood, 'An Introduction to Organisational Development', in *Sensitivity Training and the Laboratory Approach*, edited by R. T. Golembiewski and A. Blumberg (New York: Peacock, 1973), at p. 431.

50. Drucker (1985), op. cit., p. 142.

51. Ibid., p. 156.

52. Jones-Evans, op. cit., pp. 247–51.

53. Jaffe, op. cit.

54. Jones-Evans, op. cit., p. 247.

55. T. Davenport, *Process Innovations: Reengineering Work Through Information Technology* (Boston, Mass.: Harvard Business School Press, 1993), p. 5.

56. D. B. Balkin and J. W. Logan, 'Reward Policies That Support Entrepreneurship', *Compensation and Benefit Review*, 20 (1988), pp. 18–25.

57. Miller and Friesen, op. cit.

58. J. D. Covin and D. P. Slevin, 'The Influence of Organisational Structure In the Utility of an Entrepreneurial Top Management Style', *Journal of Management Studies*, 25 (1988), pp. 217–34, at p. 222.

59. Mintzberg (1979), op. cit., p. 433.

60. Heller, op. cit:. 26.

61. Ibid.: 28.

62. See Genus, op. cit., pp. 28–33, for a critique of the organisational capabilities school.

63. I. Nonaka, 'The Knowledge-Creating Company', Harvard Business Review, November–December) (1991), pp. 96–104.

64. See J. Balogun and V. Hope-Hailey, *Exploring Strategic Change* (London: Prentice-Hall, 1999), pp. 48–52 for a discussion of the paradigm.

65. T. Peters and R. H. Waterman, *In Search of Excellence* (London: Harper and Row, 1982).

66. Genus, op. cit., p. 35.

67. See Genus, op. cit., pp. 36–8; C. Mabey, G. Salaman and J. Storey, *Strategic Human Resource Management* (Oxford: Blackwell, 1998), Chapters 15 and 16 for a discussion of culture.

68. C. Hales, *Managing Through Organisation* (London: Routledge, 1993), p. 44.

69. G. Haskins, 'Entrepreneurship Inside Corporations', *efmd Forum*, 2 (1994), pp. 12–15. The ForeSight Group, 1990, diagram and quotation at p. 15

70. J. S. Hornsby, D. F. Kuratko and R. V. Montagno, 'Perceptions of Internal Factors for Corporate Entrepreneurship: A Comparison of Canadian and US Managers', *Entrepreneurship: Theory and Practice*, 24 (1999), pp. 9–29.

71. M. Helms, 'Japanese managers: Their candid views on Entrepreneurship', *Competitiveness Review*, 13(1) (2003), pp. 24–34.

72. Helms, op. cit.

73. See W. G. Biemans, *Managing Innovation Within Networks* (London: Routledge, 1993) for a discussion of networks and innovation.

74. C. Alter and J. Hage, *Organisations Working Together* (Newbury Park, Calif.: Sage, 1993).

75. A. H. Van de Ven and D. Ferry, *Measuring and Assessing Organisations* (New York: Wiley, 1980), p. 312.

76. B. G. James, 'Alliance: The New Strategic Focus', *Long Range Planning*, 18 (1985), pp. 76–81, at p. 76.

77. C. Handy, *The Elephant and the Flea* (London: Hutchinson, 2001).

78. E. Garnsey, 'Knowledge-Based Enterprise In A New Economy', in *New Economy: New Entrepreneurs* (Zoetermeer, the Netherlands: EIM Business and Policy Research, January 2001), pp. 51–69, at pp. 51, 75.

79. Based on P. Burns, *Entrepreneurship and Small Business* (Basingstoke: Palgrave (now Palgrave Macmillan), 2001), pp. 177, 178.

80. 'Green Paper on Innovation', *Bulletin of the European Union*, op. cit., p. 19.

Introduction

Part I of this book looked at the concept of enterprise and showed that the word 'enterprise' has a range of meanings. It includes what has been described as the narrow meaning, referring specifically to the development of small business, which was the prime focus of Part II. Small businesses are important for reasons of innovation, diversity and social stability, and for supporting the competitiveness of other businesses. Particular attention has been focused on them because of the indicated links between small businesses and job creation. Governments, especially in times of high unemployment, want more jobs. For these reasons they are prepared to intervene in the economic process to secure the development of more enterprise.

Part III therefore looks at this intervention: intervention which cannot of itself create enterprise but, at least in theory, can promote it. It is people who can act in an enterprising way and it is people who can start and develop small businesses, and intervention can seek to encourage them to do it more and to make it easier or more rewarding for them. That is what is meant by promoting enterprise.

Chapter 10, therefore, after first reviewing the concept of intervention, examines the motivation for intervention and the justification for it, which may not be the same thing. It considers the pressure that sometimes exists for intervention, even if only to appear to be doing something. It looks at the benefits sought and the arguments that there are barriers to enterprise and its benefits which might be addressed by intervention.

The forms of intervention to be used will, at least in part, depend on theories and assumptions about the nature of the enterprise process and about the barriers it faces. It is necessary to have some understanding of the process, from culture through to growth business, in order to see how intervention might work and what intervention might be successful. These issues are examined in Chapter 11.

As well as ideally having a sound theoretical and practical basis, intervention, if it is to succeed, should also be based on clear objectives, be delivered through appropriate structures and use relevant approaches. Chapter 12 therefore builds on Chapter 11 and looks at these issues, at the possible areas for intervention, and the forms it might take.

The variety of interventions that are practised raises the question of how successful they are. Evaluating enterprise intervention is not easy. The requirements for it can be complex and there are many difficulties in doing it. These issues are covered in Chapter 13, which also looks at the findings of some of the evaluation research to date and at the current state of knowledge about the effectiveness of intervention.

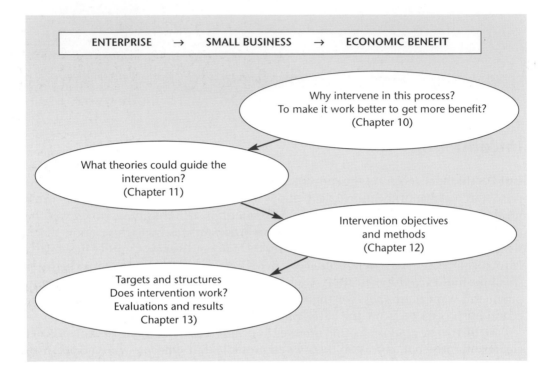

Contents

KEY CONCEPTS

This chapter covers:

- What is meant by intervention.

- The motivations for intervention and the benefits it is expected to deliver, including the creation of employment and other economic and social benefits.

- The justification advanced for intervention, including the arguments that there are failures in markets, governance and economic systems which adversely affect entrepreneurship and small business development and which it would be beneficial to correct.

- Barriers to enterprise development at the cultural and educational levels.

- Some of the arguments against intervention.

- Why governmental intervention is nevertheless still likely.

LEARNING OBJECTIVES
_____

By the end of this chapter the reader should:

- Have an understanding of what is meant by intervention.
- Be aware of the benefits enterprise, entrepreneurship and/or small businesses are supposed to deliver and why governments therefore consider intervening to promote them.
- Understand the conceptual case for intervention based on market, governmental or systemic failure.
- Have an understanding of the arguments against intervention.
- Appreciate the pressures that can exist for intervention.

Introduction: what is intervention?

Throughout the world governments and governmental organisations, national, regional and local, intervene in the economies of their countries, regions or localities. In the context of this chapter intervention is taken to be the attempt by a governmental or other body to affect the behaviour of an economy, or to improve an input to an economy, in a way which is intended to produce an increase in economic benefit which would not have happened had it been left solely to market forces.

However much market forces may be praised, and laissez-faire economics promoted, no government, it seems, can resist the pressure to intervene in some way to promote or protect the economy for which it is perceived to be responsible. That intervention may not always be effective, or may have effects contrary to what was intended, but there is still always a pressure to do something, and often to be seen to do something.

Some of this economic intervention is intended to have the effect of promoting more enterprise, usually in the form of business and not least of small business. Before looking at the methods that might be employed in such interventions, however, it may be relevant to consider why intervention to promote enterprise and/or small business development may be desired, and how it might be justified.

Why intervene? The motivations

Small firms were the source of the majority of net new jobs created between 1969 and 1976 in the USA.

David Birch[1]

The UK results are broadly similar to those of the United States... indicating that smaller firms provide a disproportionate share of new job creation.

Colin Gallagher[2]

Small firms play an important role in the economy, in creating jobs, in innovation and in regenerating regions.

Andrea Westall and Marc Cowling[3]

There was a net gain of 800 thousand jobs, in the period (1995–1999), and small businesses accounted for around 70 per cent of this.

DTI's Small Business Service[4]

Faced with a serious unemployment problem, such as that in the UK in the 1980s and 1990s, and persuasive evidence that small businesses are effective as job creators and are particularly resilient in an economic recession, there would seem to be a strong prima facie case for government intervention in support of small businesses.

Jobs are the usual, and apparently obvious, argument for intervention to promote enterprise. Therefore, if intervention can mean that there will be more, and faster-growing, small businesses, intervention can achieve the desired benefit of more jobs.

There are however other factors at work which may affect this reasoning and which are not always considered. For instance:

- Some jobs in small businesses may be the result of transfers of work from bigger businesses, which in turn may have resulted in efficiency gains but may not lead to net job creation. Productivity gains in bigger businesses can result in greater output but fewer jobs. Therefore the existence of figures showing net job creation in smaller businesses does not necessarily mean that they are better wealth creators.

- The creation and growth of new small businesses can result in considerable displacement of jobs from existing businesses, although there can still be benefits in wealth creation if more efficient businesses replace the less efficient.

- A strong emphasis on jobs in economic interventions may result in a bias against improvements in productivity, because such improvements, which can benefit an economy, may actually result in net job losses.

These are not criticisms of small businesses, and do not mean that they are not important. It is just a caution that small business development need not inevitably result in net economic growth, and that increases in employment in some small businesses do not necessarily mean more jobs overall. However the indications from the Global Entrepreneurship Monitor (GEM) (summarised in Chapter 4), and other research (see Chapter 7), appear to suggest that there is a strong correlation between the level of entrepreneurial activity and growth in GDP, at least in the GEM countries, and possibly between the level of entrepreneurship and increases in employment.

However, the 'more small businesses equals more jobs' approach would seem to be so obvious that it would appear that it is often followed without further exploration or consideration. Storey pointed out in 1994 that in Europe there was a wide range of policy initiatives to assist small businesses, but that the governments concerned have yet to formulate a coherent policy towards the sector, and that is still largely true today:

In no country, as far as we are aware, is there the equivalent of a 'White Paper' which articulates the range of public policies towards smaller firms which currently exist, which provides a justification for the existing configuration of policies, and which provides criteria for judging whether or not policies are successful.[5]

If policies are to be successful, it will be helpful if the argument for the policies is correct. For the employment argument to hold, small businesses must provide net jobs, more and/or faster-growing small businesses must provide more net jobs, and intervention must promote more and/or faster-growing small businesses. The evidence that small businesses create jobs has been considered earlier, in Chapter 7. Whether intervention is actually effective however is a different issue. It depends on whether intervention can have a positive effect on small businesses and whether the cost of that effect, in terms of both the cost of the intervention and the cost of any side-effects, is less than the benefit gained and less than the cost of alternative interventions to produce the same benefit. Intervention must not just make the recipient businesses better off, it must overall make a positive net contribution to the economy, and a better contribution than might be achieved from any alternative interventions. As well as employment, that economic contribution might also include wealth creation, choice, variety and not least innovation which can accelerate many of the other gains (see Chapter 13 for further elaboration of this issue).

There are arguments that intervention is only justified if it will achieve a net economic benefit and that, if there is to be such a net benefit, then there must be a market or other 'failure' to be addressed (see later in this chapter), and addressing it must increase the economic welfare of society as a whole. There are reasons however to think that intervention in some form is inevitable because it is politically desirable. This obviously introduces into the argument a political element based on the perceived attractiveness of the benefits to be gained. Consideration of the justification for intervention therefore requires a look at the range of benefits that might be derived from intervention (including political benefits), at the barriers or obstacles preventing or hindering those benefits which intervention may help to overcome, and at the overall balance between costs and benefits.

The benefits sought

Intervention has a cost and should be considered only if it is likely to result in a net benefit. Therefore, if there is to be intervention to promote more enterprise, then it should be because of the benefits more enterprise can provide.

The economic benefits of enterprise

> Entrepreneurship and innovation are central to the creative process in the economy and to promoting growth, increasing productivity and creating jobs.
>
> UK Department of Trade and Industry 1998[6]

Small and medium-sized enterprises are the backbone of the European economy and the most important creators of new jobs and economic growth.

European Commission DG Enterprise and Industry[7]

Some of the economic benefits of enterprise have been considered in earlier chapters. However, because they are also relevant here, a summary is provided:

- Enterprise, in its narrow definition of small business, can create wealth (but so also can larger businesses).

- Small businesses can provide jobs (see Chapter 7).

- It has also been argued that small businesses have a greater proclivity to innovate than their larger counterparts and are therefore crucial in helping a country respond to the myriad changes in the economic, technological and social environment.[8] For instance, the OECD points out that small firms are innovative in different ways and are especially active in developing new approaches to management and marketing.[9]

- Small businesses can make an important contribution to the infrastructure needed to support larger competitive businesses (see Chapter 5 for cluster theory). Particularly today, when 'downsizing' has been more common than vertical integration, it is almost impossible to find a business that does not in some way depend to a considerable extent on small business subcontractors as an integral part of its supply chain.

- Small businesses can help to counter regional economic decline. This assertion is sometimes made but finding evidence to support it is difficult. It seems to be based on the view that, in relatively deprived areas, it would be easier to start smaller businesses than bigger ones or that small businesses could survive in limited markets when bigger businesses could not. (That might be so but it does not mean that starting a small business in such an area will be easy or, from the perspective of the entrepreneur, sensible. On the contrary, it would seem preferable to start a small business in a more prosperous area where there might be more niche opportunities, where it would be closer to a larger market, and/or where disposable income and price expectations might be higher.)

- Other potential benefits provided by small businesses are increased competition, choice and diversity; regeneration and revitalisation of sectors; and political stability and social cohesion.

- Enterprise in its 'broad' definition includes forms of individual behaviour which lead to accelerated development of organisations of all types – private, public and third sector – with possible benefits for an economy and individual well-being (see below).

Whether actual interventions are based on all these benefits is a different issue. In many cases the objectives of the interventions are not clearly stated, and have to be deduced from other information. Storey has inferred objectives from observing public policy towards small businesses in the UK. His list is presented in Table 10.1.

Table 10.1 Objectives of small firm policy

Intermediate	Final
1 Increase employment	Increase employment
	Reduce unemployment
2 Increase number of start-ups	Increase number of start-ups
	Increase stock of firms
3 Promote use of consultants	Promote use of consultants
	Faster growth of firms
4 Increase competition	Increase competition
	Increase wealth
5 Promote 'efficient' markets	Promote 'efficient' markets
	Increase wealth
6 Promote technology diffusion	Promote technology diffusion
	Increase wealth
7 Increase wealth	Votes

Source: D. J. Storey, *Understanding the Small Business Sector* (London: Routledge, 1994), p.260.

In 2003, the UK Government developed an action plan for small business 'based around seven themes identified as key drivers for economic growth, improved productivity and enterprise for all:

- building an enterprise culture
- encouraging a more dynamic start-up market
- building the capability for small business growth
- improving access to finance for small businesses
- encouraging more enterprise in disadvantaged communities of under-represented groups
- improving small businesses' experience of government services
- developing better regulations and policy.'[10]

The social and wider benefits of enterprise

As noted above, enterprise and small businesses can provide a range of social benefits. They can provide jobs in areas where few big businesses can operate, such as very rural areas, and in this way they can distribute jobs more widely. Small businesses can supply a range of personal and community services, such as those of restaurants, window cleaning, household repairs and local corner shops. Most artists are, in effect, small businesses, as also are legal and medical practices. Small businesses are therefore essential to the way of life many people enjoy.

Enterprise in its broad sense also provides many benefits. People who have been successfully encouraged to be more enterprising will be more confident and self-reliant. They are a good illustration of the change principle which states that successful people who are experiencing problems are the most likely to enthusiastically embrace change.[11] Such people may suffer less from social exclusion and from deprivation. This is not to say that enterprise will solve all their problems, but that it can help them to start to overcome some of them. Many immigrant communities often seem to thrive because they are enterprising, even if that enterprise has been born of necessity; although it may be that it is mainly the more enterprising who leave their original countries and become immigrants. Enterprise sustains change and encourages new approaches that allow individuals, organisations and societies to adjust effectively to changing environments. Whether it is in business, in politics, in the arts or in community work, enterprise in its broad sense is beneficial in responding to change, which, in all except the short term, is inevitable.

Why intervene? The justification

Intervention to promote more enterprise, more entrepreneurship and/or more growth in small businesses is proposed because these are thought to be beneficial. However, intervention should only be considered if it will enhance the level of enterprise, entrepreneurship and/or growth of small businesses and deliver the benefits sought. The argument that it will do so is generally that there are obstacles and barriers preventing their development, that these obstacles and barriers occur because there has been failure of some sort, and that intervention can correct this failure. Whether that failure is in the market, in governance or in economic systems will determine what sort of intervention should be considered but, the argument goes, if there is no failure there is no justification for intervention. The various forms of failure are examined below.

Market failure

It is argued that SMEs face particular challenges compared to larger businesses. They face discriminatory barriers that prevent a 'level playing field', and these are generally classified as 'market failures'.[12] According to neo-classical economic theory there is a tendency towards perfect markets. Attempting to intervene in a perfect market would not result in any improvement in that market. The value of any apparent benefits in one area would be outweighed by the cost of displacement effects elsewhere, and there would be no net economic benefit. However, after a disruption in the market, there may be some factors that delay the return of the market to perfection. Intervening to address these inherently temporary factors could therefore produce benefits. Such factors are market failures in that they represent a failure of the market to perform perfectly.

The term 'market failure' therefore can mean different things to different people. To the neo-classical economist, if it exists it is only a temporary phenomenon that will eventually go. If it is not temporary, it is not a market failure, and trying to address it will not result in a net benefit. To others, however, a market failure is potentially a permanent feature, which will continue to disrupt unless addressed. They point out that the neo-classical perfect market is a myth and that many of the assumptions about markets made by neo-classical economists do not hold true. There are always imperfections in markets. Many organisations have the power to dominate markets, and use it. Large corporations dominate markets, product differentiations by means of marketing manipulations are manifold, and predatory practices are commonplace. The result is many 'market failures' which place small businesses at a disadvantage and are likely to be permanent unless steps are taken to address them.[13] (See also Table 10.2.)

The UK's Small Business Service defined market failure as a situation in which markets left to themselves do not deliver outcomes which are 'optimal from society's perspective or to achieve equity objectives that ensure prosperity for all'.[14] It claims that 'the evidence from the research' indicates that there are four broad types of market failure which 'act to constrain new business formation and growth'. They are described by the SBS as follows:

- Imperfect and asymmetric information
  - Imperfect information can lead to uncertainty and a reduced ability to assess the risks of starting a business or project (including training and R&D).
  - Asymmetric information (the distribution of information between small businesses and those with whom they contract) could affect the supply of resources to small business, e.g. premises, consultancy, advisory services. It may affect the willingness of third parties to purchase from or otherwise contract with them especially in the case of finance. The provider of finance cannot observe all the relevant information and costs of monitoring are high with collateral more likely to be sought in the case of small businesses.

Table 10.2 A view of market imperfections, their causes and the actions needed

Market gap	Cause of market gap	Action needed
Supply of entrepreneurs	Social and economic bias in favour of employment rather than self-employment	Social security system Education Tax system
Supply of innovations	Inadequate R&D	Education and research policy R&D expenditure Tax system
Lack of capital	Distortions in capital markets	Tax system Subsidised lending Monopoly policy Credit guarantees
Labour shortage	Imperfections in the labour market	Social security system Social environment Housing policy Training and education Monopoly policy Labour relations policy
Lack of premises	Imperfections in property market	Urban redevelopment Planning regulations Infrastructure investment Tax system
Bureaucracy and compliance costs	Growth of government	Simplification, exemption, changes in local taxation Reorganisation of central and local government
Purchasing Marketing	Imperfections in supplier markets Imperfections in seller markets	Monopoly policy, tax system, government 'crowding out'

Sources: Developed from D. Keeble and S. Walker, 'New Firms, Small Firms and Dead Firms: Spatial Patterns and Determinants in the United Kingdom', *Regional Studies* (1994), 28(4), pp.411–27; and P. Westhead and A. Moyes, 'Reflections on Thatcher's Britain: Evidence from New Production Firm Registrations 1980-88', *Entrepreneurship and Regional Development* (1992), 4(1), pp.21–36.

ILLUSTRATION 10.1
Policy rationale 1: an OECD view

'It is often argued that governments should promote SMEs because they face special challenges, as well as special opportunities, compared to larger firms. SMEs have been shown to be important for the economy, particularly for job creation. But is this sufficient justification for special treatment or schemes for smaller firms? Policies and measures targeted on SMEs should be adopted only to the extent that there is a clear rationale for doing so, particularly in terms of market and other failures [governmental or systemic – see Illustration 10.3]. In addition, there is a broader, wide-ranging set of government policies (competition, fiscal, and so on) which affect SME performance, and these must also be reviewed in terms of their implications for smaller firms.

'Traditional market failure arguments, when cited in the case of SMEs, usually concern problems related to economies of scale, asymmetric information and imperfect appropriation of returns. Smaller firms generally have fewer financial, human and technical resources which [constrains] their ability to take advantage of given opportunities, particularly those associated with economies of scale. Small firms also suffer more from information gaps and have difficulty evaluating the benefits of, for instance, adopting new technologies or entering distant markets. SMEs may be at a disadvantage in adopting new technology due for example to greater dependence on external sources of scientific and technological information and the need for tailored technical responses. With regard to financing, small firms have more problems obtaining bank loans and other capital due to a lack of collateral, unproven track record and risk-adverse investors; at the same time, they may lack information on alternative financing sources. In general, the social returns of SME activities are higher than the expected private returns, but more difficult to appropriate, resulting in under-investment by the market.'

Source: OECD, *Working Paper On the Role of SMEs: Findings and Issues* (Paris: OECD/DSTI/IND, 2000), p. 7. Personal communication from members of The Working Party on SMEs.

- Externalities and incomplete property rights

Externalities, or spillover effects, occur when the actions of one party confer benefits or costs on other parties. Combined with incomplete property rights, externalities may prevent small businesses from acquiring the full benefit of their investments, particularly, it is argued, in relation to R&D and training. In these cases, their rights to the benefits of their investment are weak and costly to defend. Left to the market, small businesses may under-invest, therefore. The externality argument may be extended to the issue of the distribution of resources and so to equity (in that an unequal distribution can lead to adverse consequences for some groups of people). It can be on equity grounds that support for such groups within society is promoted, – promotion of entrepreneurial activity among disaffected youth, women, ethnic minorities, for example – but it can also be on market failure where lack of resources reduces economic welfare by preventing viable businesses from developing.

- Imperfect market structure

Anti-competitive behaviour may prevent new business with new products or more efficient processes from driving innovation and raising productivity in the economy. Lack of competition in labour, financial and consultancy services can lead to higher prices for smaller businesses or services not geared to their needs.

- Poor regulation

Compliance burdens are often regressive in that they bear more heavily on smaller than larger businesses as well as reducing the efficiency of markets when they are excessive, unnecessary or poorly implemented.

Government and systemic failures

Much attention has been given to market failure as a justification for intervention but, it would seem, there has been less recognition of the problems of relevant 'failure' in areas such as government and economic systems. Initiatives have been introduced to try to correct market failures but, the Organisation for Economic Cooperation and Development (OECD) argues, this has often been a piecemeal development of policy measures and 'Insufficient co-ordination between different government bodies and policies has reduced the efficiency of SME policies and thus limited their potential to fuel economic growth.'[15]

On the same theme, the Chief Executive of the UK's Small Business Service claimed:

> to pursue needs of small business and to bring some intelligence and rationalisa-
> tion to Government's efforts, all of which stand up in their departmental silos --
> but when taken in the round and viewed from the customer's point of view -- do
> not necessarily add up. ... I[I]t is a similarly complex problem to what we are
> trying to do with the simplification of business support. Successive governments
> have created and presided over such complexity.[16]

Thus with the predominance of the market failure model of justification there has been less recognition of the problems of relevant 'failure' in areas such as government and economic systems. Johnson offers a number of other theories that are also used to explain the existence and nature of policy interventions. These are the public choice model, the economic theory of bureaucracy and the more radical approaches focusing on the power relations between different interest groups and those which emphasise the ideological dimension of SME policies.[17] A summary of each model follows.

Public choice and the role of politicians
Underlying this model is the argument that politicians will maximise their own welfare and so will 'instigate and promote policies that will maximise their chance

of remaining in office through re-election'.[18] What can be called their 'rent-seeking' behaviour may improve economic welfare but need not, for two reasons. Their time horizons are limited to the election cycle and so they will favour short-term gains but will also consider the gains to only that part of the electorate to which they hope to have appeal. Following such a logic will not necessarily correct market failures or increase economic welfare.

The economic theory of bureaucracy

Another tradition focuses upon government officials and their motivations. It is recognised that state bureaucrats also have vested interests which can mean that they wish to be associated with prominent and apparently successful initiatives. While they are not subject to re-election, power, job prospects, remuneration and other benefits can flow from association with what is perceived to be successful. The results of pursuing their own welfare can be 'more resource intensive programmes ... over-bureaucratic management and control structures, reluctance to undertake robust evaluations and a reluctance to curtail ineffective programmes for fear of loss of power or status'.[19]

There is regular criticism by commentators of the existence of too many 'supply-led' programmes not based on the needs of business

Power relations, pressure groups and ideology

This approach emphasises the power relations within society and suggests that it is 'the outcome of conflict between powerful groups in society that ultimately determine (sic) the direction of public policy'.[20]

Some would base their views on the Marxist concept of a class struggle with the state supporting specific ideologies which support the status quo – with SMEs representing the free market capitalist economy, for example. Others perceive a thriving SME sector as essential to a healthy democracy. Indeed in the United States the role of the Small Business Administration was seen as supporting small business as, inter alia, essential to the 'security of this Nation'.[21]

In this type of model, one looks to relative strength of groups in their abilities to influence government policies. Johnson notes that 'it is puzzling to observe that SME policy has been particularly prominent in the UK since the early 1980s, whereas SME organisations have only appeared to be in positions of influence in relation to government since ... 2000.'[22] He suggests on such evidence that power relations between business groups can only be a small part of the continuing popularity of SME policies across Europe and the world.

Conclusion

Johnson concludes that: 'Market failure alone does not justify or explain the existence of SME policy in most countries of the world, nor does it explain why these policies differ over space and time.' It is impossible to ignore that issues of equity, the self-interest of politicians and government officials, political lobbying, societal power structures and ideological considerations all play a role in making and shaping SME policies.[23]

ILLUSTRATION 10.2
Policy rationale 2: an OECD view

Government failures occur when government intervenes where markets would have worked better if they had been left alone. SMEs tend to shoulder a relatively heavy burden in terms of regulation since overly bureaucratic administrative practices can impose high fixed costs on individual firms. For example, when implemented inadequately, standardisation can prevent flexibility, which is an important source of competitiveness for SMEs, especially in the case of new, technology-based firms. Another example relates to networks which are proving to be instrumental in increasing SME performance: their development is often confronted with various information and regulatory barriers, which may prevent them from taking shape spontaneously or, at least, significantly slow their development. Also, lags and deficiencies in information, complexity of regulatory measures, delays in their implementation and poor quality delivery limit the scope for successful government involvement in rapidly evolving fields. These problems led to OECD recommendations on easing the regulatory burden on smaller enterprises, such as:

- The regulatory reform process should be based on an explicit understanding of the overall economic importance of the SME sector.
- Regulatory policy should be forward-looking, part of a broader strategy to foster a large and healthy community of SMEs, and needs to be considered in the context of structural reforms which include other factors such as taxation.
- Regulatory reform for SMEs should not take a 'good or bad' regulation approach but a 'better' regulation approach in all policy areas.
- Regulations should ensure an economic structure within which SMEs, and in particular micro-enterprises, are given a fair opportunity to compete.
- Mechanisms should be established to ensure that SME concerns are considered and debated in the regulatory process.
- Attention should be given to the cumulative effects of regulations on SMEs, particularly micro-enterprises, for both regulatory and economic reasons.
- Special attention should be given to regulations that affect flexibility for entrepreneurial activities, which is a major SME advantage.
- All types of SMEs, including those which are not technology-based, innovative or high-growth, should be considered when vetting regulations and reviewing regulatory effects.

Systemic failures, which are related to institutional interactions in the economy, occur partly because SME policies remain the concern of specific ministries and/or government agencies directly in charge of SME development, even though responsibilities in areas affecting SMEs are scattered among different ministries and agencies. In the past, SME policies were viewed as having a distinctive role, targeting a specific and disadvantaged group of firms, and as different from other economic policies in that they were serving not only economic but also social objectives. In many countries, there has been a lack of understanding among government officials not directly in charge of SMEs of the importance and special economic issues relating to SME performance. There has been insufficient attention to SMEs in the broader economic context, reflecting an outdated perception that SMEs are of limited importance to technology development or growth despite their potential for job creation. This has resulted in a piecemeal development of policy measures, aiming to deal with specific problems at a given time and often protecting small firms from normal business pressures. Insufficient co-ordination between different government bodies and policies has reduced the efficiency of SME policies and thus limited their potential to fuel economic growth.

Systemic failures also exist on an international scale as national policies regarding SMEs sometimes contradict and cancel each other. National policy measures may lead to unintended impacts on smaller firms in other countries, in particular smaller countries. Various factors may interact to cause discrimination against newcomers (such as registration procedures, norms and standards, labour and product market regulations and so forth) which are particularly disadvantageous for smaller firms trying to bridge national borders. National competition policies also vary widely across countries in their treatment of SMEs, for which the abuse of market power is a formidable problem. Such cross-boundary effects raise the question of how countries can take advantage of the opportunities created by the trend towards globalisation and how together they can alleviate unnecessary obstacles to the international activities of smaller firms.

Source: *OECD, The Role of SMEs: Findings and Issues* (Paris: OECD/DSTI/ IND, 2000); personal communication from members of the Working Party on SMEs.

Examples of market failure?

Of the varieties of market failure in which it is argued that small businesses are at a disadvantage, two of the most common relate to the advantages of big business and the need for external support. They are examined here to highlight the nature of the arguments.

The advantages of big business

There are multinational firms with turnovers that exceed the gross national product of most nations. The sheer size and economic power of such firms allow them to dominate consumer and factor markets. They can use huge advertising and marketing expenditure to make it very difficult for new entrants to gain a foothold in their markets. They can benefit from economies of scale. In the procurement field, large firms can secure discounts and organise just-in-time contracts that shift the burden of stockholding to their suppliers. In the labour market they can attract the best staff with their competitive remunerative packages and career prospects for employees.

Some of the reasons for their advantages are as follows:

- Their ability to spread fixed costs over a larger output confers significant advantages on large businesses. Larger businesses may have higher fixed costs than small ones, but such costs tend to increase in discontinuous steps that are proportionately higher for small producers than for larger ones.[24]

- Large businesses use their size and power to advantage in other areas. When they need finance they can use the capital market with greater facility than small businesses, and they can benefit from considerable economies of scale. Indeed, it has long been argued that an equity gap exists for small businesses which cannot find market sources for the type and amount of capital they need.[25] (This is explored in more detail in Chapter 12.) This gap exists in part because of the inefficiency of the capital market with respect to small businesses. In an efficient market, buyers and sellers of finance act through intermediaries and legal remedies are available in cases of dispute. However, many small businesses are unquoted companies and the divestment and exchange of information between the parties is less than perfect. Firms are reluctant to divulge sensitive data and investors are reluctant to lend in the absence of detailed information. In this situation an effective working relationship must be built up between the principals before business can be done, but this is time-consuming and costly for both the small businesses and the venture capitalists involved.[26]

- It is also argued that small firms are at a relative disadvantage when complying with a range of statutory and administrative regulations imposed by government.[27] Governments introduce all manner of regulations, and compliance with them can impose relatively heavier fixed costs on individual SMEs. Regulatory systems are often characterised by delays and poor implementation, and compliance with them can reduce flexibility and diminish some of the competitive advantages of SMEs. Compliance with regulations on the collection and disclosure of information can also prevent the development of efficient information networks.[28]

- Entrepreneurialism is concerned with spotting and realising opportunities but small firms rarely have sufficient resources to exploit them, particularly those openings which offer economies of scale. Small firms also suffer from a lack of information on environmental trends and they often have insufficient data to evaluate new developments and insufficient finance for R&D.

- Large firms can afford to employ their own in-house expertise. Smaller businesses arguably are less competent at recruiting 'the right person' and additionally are more dependent on external support.

A counter to this is the argument that in many cases large firms have earned these cost advantages. Developing a business can require considerable skill and capital, and cost advantages are the reward for this endeavour. In this sense these are not market failures. It can also be pointed out that large firms are currently breaking themselves up into smaller strategic business units and are reducing the size of these units by outsourcing services. If this trend continues then some of the benefits of size may no longer be available to large firms.

Despite these arguments, supporters of small firms feel that large ventures do have real advantages and that the perpetuation of those advantages will damage the prospects for the small business sector to realise its maximum economic benefit. Thus intervention to reduce the relative advantages is justified.

The need for external support

Businesses, if they are to develop, need access to a range of skills and abilities in areas such as organisation, management, production, marketing, selling, strategy, finance and law. Bigger businesses can have all of these competencies in-house, but smaller businesses must inevitably depend on external agencies to provide at least some of them. They need such support but are often reluctant to seek it.

It has been argued that if the felt need for services is great enough then small businesses will seek out the services on offer and pay the market price for them. This economic argument for the free functioning of markets is persuasive but it has been pointed out that small businesses frequently do not seek out the providers of services, even when the need is great, and that they give a variety of explanations for this:

- The need for support is not appreciated. It can be difficult to analyse fully the complexities of a business organisation and identify needs precisely.

- Owners fear that exposing their efforts to others may lead to their ideas being stolen.

- There is a reluctance to approach experts because owners fear that the experts may despise their efforts and because they believe that they do not have the interpersonal and technical skills to deal with sophisticated advisors.

- Perceptions of how consultancies approach assignments is off-putting to many small businesses.

- They do not have sufficient information about the availability and cost of services to make a rational choice.

- They feel that the available support is not appropriate to their needs.

- They might also be discouraged by the price of advice.

A counter-argument might be that making a special case for small business support is a paternalistic approach. Business founders have to learn to stand on their own feet, and in doing so will develop an invaluable set of skills and contacts. Gibb argues that the development of transactions with the suppliers of needed services is a crucial aspect of entrepreneurial learning.[29] Owners must understand their environments and learn how to acquire resources on favourable terms. Services from accountants, market researchers and consultants are commercial offerings and there are adequately developed markets in these areas. It could also be pointed out that there is no overwhelming demand for the services of small business support agency services, and that this might well be because there is little need for the services.

Another argument against the provision of support is that large firms have gone through a learning phase and have survived, so why should emerging small businesses now be pampered? However a view put forward by Bannock is that large firms are disproportionately represented in the British economy to the detriment of economic development. He argues that the percentage of small businesses should be increased, and contends that 'We cannot leave it to the market.'[30] If small businesses face temporary market or managerial problems then financial and other

ILLUSTRATION 10.3
A low take-up of small business support

Specific government-funded programmes have been provided to try to provide services in a way which avoids or minimises some of these issues, but they too can suffer from low levels of take-up. Curran suggests that there are three reasons in particular for this:[31]

- Owner-managers frequently claim that the support provider 'does not understand' the business. So common is this response that it suggests it does not simply refer to an external adviser's lack of close knowledge of the business, nor to a lack of understanding of problems in particular sectors. Instead Lightfoot suggests that this extreme reluctance to accept external advice has its roots in small business owners' psychology, which shows a strong commitment to independence resulting in a stubborn 'I did it my way' individualism.[32]

- The content of the support appears to be 'top down' in character. Providers see what they offer as the know-how for business success and distil that know-how from standard texts and large firm practice. But small businesses are not large businesses scaled down (see Chapter 7), and good practice in a large business may be poorly suited to the needs of a small business.

- Government departments favour standardised approaches which are easy to cost, administer and monitor, but which ignore the heterogeneity of small firms or the special characteristics of localities.

means of support could provide a vital breathing space until circumstances improve. If we want small firms to make the maximum contribution to the economy then it makes sense to assist businesses that are basically viable until their expertise and experience improve and allow them to reap the benefits which size and age confer on organisations. Of course such a policy will not add overall to the economy if the supported small businesses, by virtue of that support, force out of the market existing businesses that are fundamentally no less competitive. The displacement effect must always be considered.

In addition to the usual arguments for support there are additional reasons for supporting embryonic small businesses. Economists extol the virtues of small businesses in facilitating structural changes in industries. As old and inefficient firms expire, new, more productive small businesses fill the gap. But numerous studies have pointed to the vulnerability of small businesses, especially in their formative years. If individuals are to be encouraged to set up in business, then they might warrant assistance in the dangerous early years. Many small business people are in need of help as they struggle with the multiple and complex tasks of business formation, launch and early development; and it seems sensible to offer them assistance, especially if the assistance is based on a deep understanding of the 'world' of the entrepreneur.

CASE 10.1
'Small business growth stunted by reluctance to seek advice'

Survey finds biggest barrier to advice is a psychological one

The vast majority of the UK's small businesses do not ask for business advice because they don't think they need it. According to leading psychologist, Dr Peter Collett, entrepreneurs are less likely to ask for advice due to their psychological make-up.

A survey of small businesses conducted by NOP and commissioned by Business Link, the information and advice service for small businesses, found that 82 per cent of businesses said the reason they do not seek business advice was because they don't need it. Surprisingly this ranked way above other barriers to advice like cost, which was stated by 5 per cent of respondents, and lack of time which was cited by only 1 per cent of the sample.

Dr Peter Collett, a psychologist specialising in culture and management style, believes that attitudes have to be changed to encourage people to ask for advice. He explains:

'People who run their own business are usually extremely confident and self-assured: they need to be in order to survive. But they sometimes feel hesitant about asking for help, particularly if they feel they ought to know the answer. What makes them so effective up to now often prevents them from being even more successful in the future.'

David Irwin, Chief Executive of the Small Business Service, the agency within Government tasked with managing Business Link, said:

'There is a common misconception that you only need to ask for advice when your business is in trouble. It is our job to challenge this view and ensure that UK businesses benefit from the wealth of expertise that Business Link has to offer.'

During his analysis of the results Dr Peter Collett identified the following types of business that appear to be most in need of advice:

1. Small businesses that have just started up and which need to learn the ropes.

2. Those that have been in existence for a long time and which have become set in their ways.

3. Small businesses with a small turnover, which are particularly vulnerable.

4. Those that don't have many employees, and which therefore have less internal expertise and diversity of opinion.

5. Those that don't get a lot of advice from institutions like banks.

On this basis one would expect to find that these five types of business ask for advice more often. The survey results indicate that the opposite is true – those that are most in need of advice are least likely to ask for it.

Source: Business Link Press Release, 8 October 2001.

Points raised

This report is a reminder that meeting an apparent need is not always a straightforward process.

Other barriers

Government and economic system failures do exist, but they apply across wide areas and do not explain, for example, the variations in business start-up between different regions in the same jurisdiction (see Table 10.3). Market failure may explain part of this variation but that applies to the narrow aspect of enterprise as small business. There are other barriers that are more apparent when the development of enterprise in its broad sense of an enterprise culture is considered, and these will be relevant when an 'entrepreneurship' as opposed to a 'small business' policy is being considered. Barriers of culture or of education exist that prevent people from starting businesses, or even thinking of starting them, as well as from being enterprising in the broad sense, and intervention might be considered to address these also.

Cultural barriers

One way of identifying the presence of other barriers is to look at the variations between levels of enterprise in different regions and countries. Within the UK there are variations in the level of enterprise, as has been pointed out in Chapter 4 and as is indicated in the variations in VAT registration rates, and proportions of fast-growing firms, which may be seen as an observable proxy for the levels of enterprise. It has been argued that some societies have economic and social structures that encourage and facilitate enterprise while others do not. For example, within the UK, Northern Ireland's recent economic history is characterised by a reliance on a self-sufficient agricultural sector, large employing organisations in declining industries and a dominant public sector. Its social and political problems have been severe, and some suggest that it has a dependency culture. It lacks therefore a strong non-agricultural small business tradition and the culture that might support one. That is an obstacle to enterprise.

In this situation social conditions are such that the option of entrepreneurship as a form of employment is not commonly recognised. There are very successful entrepreneurial ventures in Northern Ireland, but most individuals lack the knowledge, skills and mindset to pursue this career option successfully. They see two economic possibilities: if they are lucky they can have a job working for someone else, or if they are unlucky they will be unemployed and reliant on social security benefit payments. In this, and in other situations of economic and social deprivation with second and third-generation unemployment, the facilitation of the entrepreneurial process could be viewed as one means of overcoming social disadvantage. However it is not easy: the problems are long-term ones that are likely to require long-term solutions, and many government activities in this sphere are viewed with suspicion because they can have strong political overtones.

The typical Northern Ireland view of a market economy may not be very close to the American or liberal model of capitalism, but markets do exist there. In some of the former Soviet Bloc countries, however, markets were slow to develop. Under the so-called communist system the state determined what was to be produced and how, and many employees aimed to extract the greatest benefit from the state at minimum effort to themselves. This was a situation where the entrepreneurship option, far from not being recognised, often simply did not exist or was not developed. Under these conditions the removal of state controls tended in some cases to lead not straight to a market economy but instead to chaos and opportunities for the criminal fraternity.

Table 10.3 Variations in business start-up rates across the UK (as indicated by VAT registrations per 10,000 resident adult population in 2006)

UK overall	**37**	Northern Ireland	33
City of London	1951	Glasgow	31
Borough of Islington, London	187	Cardiff	30
Shetland Islands	44	Cambridge	28
Bristol	39	Dover	28
Cornwall	37	Oxford	26
Edinburgh	37	Liverpool	25
Aberdeen	35	Merthyr Tydfil	25
Highland Scotland	35	Fife	21
Leeds	33	South Tyneside	17

Source: http://stats.berr.gov.uk. Accessed 16 Feb 2007. Crown copyright material is reproduced with the permission of the Controller of HMSO.

These countries want a market economy, and enterprise is no longer actively discouraged. Possibly the neo-classical economists might be proved correct and perfect markets might evolve, given enough time. However, the countries concerned want improvements quickly and are willing to consider intervention to get them.

Thus certain countries appear to be more enterprising and entrepreneurial than others. Many factors create an enterprise culture and the values, beliefs and assumptions that are widely shared by members of a community will not be the same in Britain, in Scandinavia and in Eastern Europe. The discussion in Chapter 3 of cognitive approaches to entrepreneurship by individuals indicated that more people are likely to become entrepreneurs when attitudes and general opinion support the notion of entrepreneurship. If the government, media and popular opinion are supportive of entrepreneurship, it is likely that individuals will develop positive attitudes towards this form of work and it will be regarded as important.

Nevertheless, attitudes alone are unlikely to produce entrepreneurs. What has been identified as important however is whether individuals have perceived behavioural control and 'whether people feel that entrepreneurship is a feasible option for themselves'.[33] People with strong attitudes seek out people who share their point of view, and in an entrepreneurially rich locality there will be opportunities to meet or observe people who could well act as positive role models.

Within countries, certain regions also appear to be more enterprising and entrepreneurial. Economic theory suggests that a market-driven reduction in wage rates and other costs, plus the exit of firms from certain industries, would provide opportunities for profit in some areas and therefore encourage an influx of entrepreneurial firms. However, economic forces alone are unlikely to redress the balance between regions.[34] That implies that if an imbalance is to be redressed then intervention of some sort will be necessary.

Barriers for ethnic and women-owned ventures
It is argued by some that ethnic business firms and those owned by women face discriminatory barriers and that special support should be offered to help them over-

come these. Although many people from immigrant communities do start businesses this may be, at least in part, because they have little choice as they perceive that language problems, a lack of recognised qualifications, glass ceilings or just racism reduce their chances of finding suitable employment, and not because they find it a particularly easy thing to do. It was a cultural norm in many Western societies until recently that women and ethnic groups played subordinate roles, and over recent years support agencies in Britain have been keen to assist where possible in the formation and development of ethnic business enterprises. Interestingly, Phizacklea and Ram report that when the director of a business start-up agency in Venisseux, France, visited England, he was impressed by the 'proliferation of business agencies which specifically target ethnic minority populations, not just at the inception but by providing business support services as well'.[35] Help is offered but there is a low take-up of support; recent studies of ethnic firms in Britain give the following reasons for the reluctance to use formal support services:[36]

- Language difficulties.
- 'I started on my own therefore I don't need help.'
- 'Agencies are only interested in larger firms.'
- 'I can't afford the time to attend meetings and courses.''
- 'West Indians are stereotyped as incapable of running a firm.'
- 'We are discriminated against for being Nigerian.'

Ram approached the topic of under-use from the perspective of providers and concluded that problems arose because:[37]

- There were no precise data about ethnic entrepreneurs.
- Providers were unsure of the rationale for intervention.
- There was competition between the agencies.
- It was more important to meet 'targets' than specific needs.
- Providers perceived themselves as marginal.

Curran has mentioned that the take-up of support services by small firms is patchy, and in the case of ethnic businesses this might be because there is a network of local support for embryonic firms. It is mentioned in Chapter 3 that Ismaili-Pakistani immigrants in the south western United Sates have their own self-help community support programme and that this has many advantages compared with officially sponsored aid programmes.

Just as some people feel that it is important to assist ethnic entrepreneurs, so some feel that women entrepreneurs face particular obstacles and should be assisted. Additional business obstacles may exist for women entrepreneurs if they cannot acquire resources as easily as men, if their work and life experiences have not allowed them to develop entrepreneurial competence, or if they face gender discrimination. We should note, however, that some recent studies on discrimination against women in acquiring start-up capital, for example, point to the complexity of the topic.[38] Evidence in this area suggests that discrimination against women arises for economic reasons. Women tend to operate riskier firms than men and are less well prepared for management. Consequently lenders are reluctant to divert funds to these ventures.

Walker and Joyner argue that women's difficulties in getting business finance

WHY INTERVENE?

can arise because of pure gender discrimination, institutionalised gender discrimination, statistical gender discrimination or economic gender discrimination.[39] Gender discrimination occurs when women are offered different financial terms simply because they are women. Institutional discrimination occurs when it is presumed that a woman is less likely to operate a firm successfully. Statistical discrimination occurs when women as a group are less well qualified as borrowers, and economic discrimination occurs when a woman does not meet the criteria for financing and this arises from the fact that she is a woman. These authors point out that various forms of government assistance have different impacts on these four kinds of discrimination. For example government procurement programmes in the United Sates, which ration contracts on the basis of gender, can remove pure and institutional discrimination but not statistical and economic discrimination. On the other hand business counselling and training can reduce all four kinds of discrimination. Walker and Joyner argue that care should be exercised when developing special support programmes. Specific policies impact on specific kinds of discrimination, and policies in support of women or other groups can create resentment and actually increase discrimination. Furthermore, support can discourage those who are supported from seeking 'new and creative ways of overcoming obstacles'. Entrepreneurs must use their own skills to overcome obstacles. Support in the form of grants or loan guarantees can also cause women to enter more risky ventures than they ought to and this may lead to the subsequent failure of the business. Subsidies can cloud economic judgement It seems attractive to offer support to disadvantaged groups but Walker and Joyner show that caution should be exercised when advocating such policies.

Why not? The arguments against intervention

It is almost universally accepted among politicians that more small enterprise is unquestionably beneficial to the economy. Yet this can be questioned. ... Several frequently offered justifications for policies appear dubious. For example, the alleged existence of shortages of start-up finance or the negative impact of employment legislation on small business expansion and job creation have been overwhelmingly rejected by research. Yet Conservative and Labour administrations [in the UK] have continued to cling to these assumptions and policy continues to be influenced by them strongly.

James Curran[40]

Economic arguments justify intervention in a market economy when there is market failure. Some economists, however, maintain that market failure, although a necessary condition, is not alone a sufficient condition for intervention. There must in addition be evidence that the overall welfare improvements resulting from the intervention will be sufficient to justify the cost of that intervention, and that there is no better way of achieving the same improvements.

It might be expected that attempts to promote enterprise and entrepreneurship would find favour in most quarters, but this is not necessarily the case. It is said that enterprise thrives in a free enterprise economy, and many advocates of this economic system caution against interference with market forces. These people argue that the laws of supply and demand, operating through the price system, send signals to interested parties who respond to market opportunities and threats. Those persons who are able to interpret market forces accurately will reap economic rewards, and this pursuit of self-interest leads to the most efficient utilisation of economic resources. Enterprising individuals are inclined to be energetic, forward-looking people who take bold steps to realise opportunities, and it can be seen that free enterprise economic systems are an attractive milieu for enterprising individuals to display their skills. It is argued therefore that there is no point in promoting entrepreneurship and enterprise: the enterprising will avail themselves of opportunities, and the aggregate outcome of their decisions will produce greater welfare than decisions made by central authorities.

This argument assumes perfectly competitive markets, yet many maintain that markets are far from competitive. Nevertheless, it is still contended that there is no generalised market failure in the small business sector. Bennett, like Gibb, points to the size and growth of the sector as evidence of advance. He argues that, when asked about those factors that inhibit the development of small businesses, owners comment on general economic and regulatory factors such as the condition of the economy and the inhibiting impact of statutory regulations. Where specific needs are highlighted they arise in areas such as venture capital, marketing advice, training and cash flow problems: 'areas where well developed markets already exist'.[41]

Two comments in particular may be made in response to these views. First, many small businesses may be unaware of the immense power of large corporations and their subtle ability to inhibit competition. Those small businesses may occupy niche markets where, unless they threaten industrial giants directly, they may be tolerated or, with the advent of strategic outsourcing, they may be positively welcomed by some large businesses. Second, the methods used by those who seek to identify the problems experienced by small firms rarely delve, in a detailed way, into the problems small firms experience. Researchers commonly present entrepreneurs with lengthy lists of problems and ask them to say which of the problems apply to them. Just as Bennett argues that it is only by means of in-depth discussion with small business owners that the effectiveness of policy initiatives can be judged, so it can be argued that quantitative studies of the problems faced by small businesses will merely elicit pre-programmed responses. It is important to understand how entrepreneurs perceive and construct problems, and there may also be a tendency for small business owners to project their problems away from themselves towards more distant perceived impediments such as the government or the European Commission.

On the issue of the provision of needed services, such as information, advice and training, Bennett argues that if the felt need of businesses is great enough then they will pay the market price for the consultancy services on offer. As mentioned above, however, economic reasoning ignores many of the personal and interpersonal aspects of seeking external advice, whether it is from consultants, counsellors or mentors. Many owners have a real need for such assistance but lack the information and confidence needed to identify, approach, and if necessary negotiate terms for, suitable help.

ILLUSTRATION 10.4
An analogy?

In some respects classical economic theory is like the theory of natural selection in nature. According to that theory, in the long term the fittest for survival will survive and nature itself is an effective way of ensuring that this happens. However, in a system in which natural selection rules, what then is the role of selective breeding and intensive farming, both of which are much practised in agriculture? The answer may be that the question is to some extent itself misleading. Left to itself nature has produced a very wide variety of life forms, all of which thrive in their own niches. However, for our own purposes we want to encourage the growth of some of these life forms and to make them better suited to our requirements. That is what agriculture does: it intervenes to create circumstances in which those that survive and grow are those that we want to harvest.

May it not be that markets, left to themselves, will also produce a variety of businesses? However, if we specifically seek to influence the course of development in the population of SMEs, may we not also have to intervene to create the conditions that specifically encourage their development?

Intervention exists

The Government announced in the 2006 Budget that it intended to cut the number of small business support programmes from 3000 to fewer than 100.

Source: House of Commons Committee of Public Accounts 'Supporting Small Business'. Eleventh Report of Session 2006–07 HC 262 6, February 2007, p. 5.

Given the large number of small businesses ... the many sectors in which they operate and the variety of economic social and governmental influences to which they are subject, any moves to improve small business performance are inherently complex.

Source: Ibid., p. 5.

Research sponsored by SBS reported that in 2003–4, 15 central government departments provided 265 programmes to support small business in England. A survey of three of the nine English regions identified over 800 further services being provided at a local level.

Source: Ibid., p. 9.

A pragmatic view of intervention is to recognise that it exists and will, in some form or another, continue to exist. One form of existing intervention is laws and regulations to control business: laws that require businesses to be registered, laws that seek to control monopolies and laws that stipulate permitted labour practices are all interventions.

In addition to this precedent there is an almost irresistible temptation for governments to intervene. If it is understood that small businesses create jobs, and if significant numbers of people are unemployed and want jobs, then government will find that intervention to promote small business will be a popular option. Politically motivated behaviour is also prevalent in conditions of uncertainty. The SME area is complex and there is limited knowledge about the connection between policy and its outcomes. In this context few governments will wish to irritate electorates with subtle arguments on the pros and cons of intervention.

There are many advocates of a laissez-faire economic policy, but no government, even among those that purport to champion liberal capitalist economics, appears to have adhered strictly to such a policy. Governments intervene in numerous ways to manage their economies and redistribute wealth. As the editors of *Business Week* note, the most successful economies, in spite of huge differences among them, all have 'broad support throughout their societies for basic national economic goals and for measures of industrial policy to achieve them'.[42] In many respects the debate about intervention is not therefore about the principle of intervention but about the means that are to be used.

There is debate about the wisdom and efficacy of state intervention in support of enterprise and entrepreneurship, but the sheer size of the small business sector makes it very difficult for governments to ignore the real or perceived needs of the sector. In addition the variety of the goals pursued by small business policy-makers, and the lack of measurement of their success, create ideal conditions for the political manipulation of policy. There are many people in the 'small business support industry', and any apparent willingness to promote small businesses, especially when combined with any uncertainty surrounding policy objectives, provides them with ample opportunity to use their creativity in providing and developing small business support services. The great difficulty of conducting scientific evaluations of policy measures only adds to this problem.

The call for intervention will continue to be made given the number of groups who have a vested interest in it – researchers, policy-makers, support agencies and SME groups.

> Providers of business information, support and training rely heavily on programmes – the jobs of policy-makers and officials ultimately resolve around designing, developing and managing support programmes. A large part of the role of SME membership bodies is concerned with lobbying government to introduce new forms of support . Researchers spend substantial amounts of time (and often money) on evaluation of SME support programmes and writing about them. [43]

It is not surprising therefore to discover that so much of the literature in this field is focused on the 'how' as opposed to the 'why' of SME policy.

Part of the debate should be about the effectiveness of those means, yet, as a number of writers have pointed out, there has been a paucity of sophisticated, systematic evaluations of specific interventions to enhance the achievements of small businesses. The result is that many uncertainties arise in connection with the usefulness of various policies. These uncertainties permit, or even encourage, a political dimension of policy to develop. If actions appear to look good and there is no clear evidence for what they achieve, or fail to achieve, then the actions may be pursued, not for the results they bring, but for the credit that applying them will earn for those responsible.[44]

This is politically motivated behaviour, and it is particularly prevalent when an objective is desired but its achievement cannot easily be measured. These conditions apply in small business support. There is a considerable willingness to support small businesses, combined with a lack of information on what really works. In these circumstances, intervention, if at least superficially justified, may actually be engaged in for political reasons, connected with the desire for recognition or advancement by the people involved, rather than because of any real desire to promote enterprise.

Requirements

If interventions are to happen then they should be evaluated to see if they produce useful benefits in terms of their intended purpose. Evaluating interventions is not however always straightforward (a subject developed further in Chapter 13), and there are also problems in establishing what intervention is required in the first place. This arises because it is difficult to find out what help businesses need. Established firms may not request specific assistance from government in overcoming their difficulties because they are more concerned with aggregate demand and general labour market issues. Nevertheless, this does not mean that they do not have problems which could be overcome with help.

THE KEY POINTS OF CHAPTER 10

- Intervention is the attempt by a governmental or other body to affect the behaviour of an economy or to improve an input to an economy in a way which produces an increase in economic benefit which would not have happened had it been left to market forces.

- The purpose of small business intervention is not often made clear, but it would appear to be to promote economic and/or social welfare benefits, of which the most obvious is employment. Small businesses can create jobs, but they can also provide more innovation, which is needed for future competitiveness, and they can provide essential support for other businesses. Enterprise in its broad manifestation can also provide social and political benefits.

- The rationale for intervention is that there are barriers to the development of enterprise, entrepreneurship and/or small businesses due to failures in markets, governance or economic systems, and that intervention can correct them.

- To be justified, intervention must be based on a valid way of achieving the outcomes sought. Usually that way is by addressing obstacles and barriers to enterprise, of which there are many. Some of these are classified as market failures, and there are economic welfare arguments about the value of intervening to address these. Classical theory may suggest that the market will make its own adjustments, but others maintain that there are real and lasting imperfections which will only be corrected by external intervention. These problems include the power of big businesses, the imperfections of the capital market, the impossibility of small businesses employing directly all the skills and expertise they need, the excessive regulatory regimes that governments impose on SMEs, information deficits and a reluctance by small businesses to seek the help they need.

- There can also be barriers of culture and education to the development of enterprise. In the former communist countries of Eastern Europe and the Soviet Union, for instance, there had for many years been no tradition of enterprise or role models for it.

- While there seems to be very wide acceptance of the rationale for intervention, there are arguments that several of the justifications offered, especially those for providing small business assistance, do not stand up well to close scrutiny.

- To be justified, intervention must make a positive change, the value of which exceeds the cost of the intervention. Classical theory suggests that, while the direct results of intervention may be positive, the indirect results, such as displacement, can negate the direct benefits. Others argue that imperfections exist, and that if more enterprise is required, and if there are barriers to its development, then intervening to reduce the barriers will be beneficial.

- However, whatever the arguments, intervention is practised. Governments are subject to political pressures as well as economic ones, and the political pressures for supporting enterprise seem irresistible. Governments do intervene therefore to promote enterprise, even if the objectives of their interventions, and their results, are often unclear.

CASE 10.2
The rationale for an industrial policy

From an address by Mary Harney, Tánaiste and Minister For Enterprise, Trade and Employment, to Dail Eireann on the second stage of the Industrial Development (Enterprise Ireland) Bill on 18 June 1998:

'The Bill before you today provides for the creation of a new support structure for enterprise development. First and foremost, that structure entails the creation of a new agency, "Enterprise Ireland", through the amalgamation and restructuring of Forbairt, An Bord Tráchtála and relevant elements of the Services to Business function of FÁS. But this Bill is about much more than a technical change in agency configuration – it is also about a fundamental reappraisal of industrial policy.

'I believe that industrial policy needs to be founded on clear principles. The following are critical:

- Firstly: it is the people, not Governments, that create successful businesses. The primary role of Government is to help create the environment in which people want to start new businesses, to grow those businesses and to explore new directions when entrepreneurial ideas fail, as some inevitably must.

- Secondly: Government must respond to the dynamic inherent in business. For too long, Irish industrial policy has been dominated by a protectionist tendency, propping up and protecting businesses which have no inherent competitive advantage or long-term prospects of survival. The plain truth is that Ireland's economy is constantly changing and our industrial base must undergo a similar process of transformation and upgrading.

- Finally: we need to recognise that not all companies want, or have the potential, to grow. Many firms are lifestyle businesses which will not grow beyond a certain point. Such businesses are a normal healthy part of any market economy. However, their existence serves to underscore the point that State assistance, if it is provided at all, must necessarily be limited. The risks of deadweight and displacement are ever present, threatening to dissipate Government's development efforts and waste taxpayers money.

'On coming into Office, I directed my Department to undertake a root and branch review of industrial policy. That review of policy started from a zero base: nothing was ruled in or out. Indeed, the first option considered was the abolition of all direct State supports to industry and the consequent dissolution of the agencies providing those supports. This option was considered on the basis of the following potential benefits:

- One – the Exchequer resources freed up by this approach could be used to improve the enterprise environment through, for example, investment in infrastructure or tax reductions;

- Two – the elimination of direct supports would effectively end the "grant mentality" and leave companies free to focus on their competitive strategy instead of trying to exploit complex and unwieldy agency structures; and

- Thirdly, market forces would promote the survival of companies fit to compete in the global free market.

'I decided not to pursue this option because of the clear evidence that Irish industry has still not reached the stage where it is fully self-sufficient. Various market failures and other barriers to development still exist. Some examples are in the areas of:

- Finance, where the key market failure is in the provision of affordable equity and working capital to developing firms, especially those competing in international services and technologically intensive sectors.

- Lack of scale is also a major issue. Eighty-four per cent of Irish-owned manufacturing firms are SMEs employing less than 250 people, and 53 per cent employ between 11 and 100 employees.

- Related to the lack of scale are issues of accumulated experience and depth of infrastructure. Virtually all advanced economies display strong groupings of firms in specific sectors or in related and supporting industries. Such groupings create a positive mix of competition and co-operation which strengthens the industry as a whole.
- Because of Ireland's late industrialisation we have yet to develop such mutually reinforcing groupings of firms and the associated depth of infrastructure (in areas such as technology and logistics, for example) to support them.
- These deficiencies in scale and experience give rise to information deficits at firm level. Many small or developing firms are not in a position to undertake strategic analysis and to identify their strengths and weaknesses or to take the necessary steps to address them.
- Key information deficits at firm level involve research, development and design; knowledge of and access to markets; and training and human resource development, generally.

'I am convinced, therefore, that a role exists for the continued provision of some direct State supports to industry. However, I am far from satisfied that the existing structures, programmes and approaches are delivering optimum results.

'The traditional approach can be characterised as supply driven. Under this approach, the development agencies channel their cash into a wide range of schemes which they have established, and the onus is largely on the firm to match its needs to those schemes.

'The effect of this supply driven approach is that there are too many schemes and too little focus on the real needs of the client firm. At best, this gives rise to a scattergun approach in the hope that if enough clients get support across enough categories at least some of it will hit the mark.

'This approach is wasteful, inefficient and less than optimally effective. Moving away from it requires a much greater focus on identifying the real needs of client firms and addressing those needs in a streamlined, flexible way. Such a move will result in better value for money, better targeting of supports and better perform-ance from the assisted companies.

'Simple support structures meeting real business needs and efficient client-friendly delivery – these are the goals. Self evidently, three separate agencies operating in excess of 45 different schemes is not the way to achieve this. If we want to continue with a policy which is unfocused and which fails to target the State's resources at the real developmental needs of firms then, clearly, we should leave the existing agency structures as they are.

'If, on the other hand, we intend to take an integrated, holistic approach to the development of enterprise and to make a real impact on industrial performance, we need to have an integrated agency; hence the creation of Enterprise Ireland.'

Source: Extracts from a press release from the Department of Enterprise and Employment, Dublin. Reproduced with the kind permission of the Department of Enterprise and Employment.

Points raised

This statement by a government minister presents the rationale behind a real example of the creation of a revamped enterprise support structure. It presents a summary of the issues in the economy, a criticism of past intervention efforts, an appreciation of the option of ending intervention and a way forward.

QUESTIONS, ESSAY AND DISCUSSION TOPICS

- Comment on the social and economic benefits which SMEs deliver to communities.
- Examine the barriers which prevent small firms from making a full contribution to the development of modern economies.
- 'Intervening to assist SME owners is a misguided activity.' Discuss.
- 'You can take a horse to water but you cannot make it drink.' Do psychological barriers (see Case 10.1) mean that intervention to support small businesses will be unproductive?
- Why do almost all governments ignore the arguments of neo-liberal market economists and intervene to support small firms?
- How might a government strategy for promoting wealth differ from one designed to promote employment?
- Is it possible to separate the economic and social benefits provided by small businesses?
- Is market failure a good reason for intervening to support small businesses, or is it only advanced as a justification? Is intervention only justified when there are market failures? Identify the failures, whether market, governmental or systemic, quoted by the Tánaiste in Case 10.2.
- What arguments for not intervening do you think should have been considered in the analysis behind Case 10.2?
- Identify and compare the arguments for and against intervention to promote small business formation and development.

Suggestions for further reading and information

J. Curran, 'What is Small Business Policy In the UK For? Evaluation and Assessing Small Business Policies', *International Small Business Journal*, 18(3) (2000), pp. 43–5.

D. J. Storey, *Understanding the Small Business Sector* (London: Routledge, 1994), Chapter 8, 'Public Policy'.

OECD-UNIDO, 'Effective Policies for Small Business' (www.unido.org/doc) (33172–accessed 15 January 2008) (Paris: OECD/DSTI/IND, 2000).

DTI's Small Business Service, *A Government Action Plan for Small Business: The Evidence Base* (2004).
Forfás, 'Towards Developing an Entrepreneurship Policy for Ireland' (Dublin, www.forfas.ie) (The National Policy and Advisory Board for Enterprise, Trade, Science, Technology and Innovation, September 2007).

References

1. D. Birch, cited in D. J. Storey, *Understanding the Small Business Sector* (London: Routledge, 1994), p. 161.
2. C. Gallagher, cited in Storey, op. cit., p. 165.
3. From the back cover of A. Westall and M. Cowling, *Agenda for Growth* (London: Institute for Public Policy Research, 1999).
4. Small Business Service, *A Government Action Plan for Small Business: The Evidence Base* (Departmnet of Trade and Industry, 2004), p. 15.
5. Storey, op. cit., p. 253.
6. DTI, *Our Competitive Future: Building the Knowledge Driven Economy* (London: HMSO, CM4176, 1998), pp. 14–15.
7. European Commission DG Enterprise and Industry, *Putting SMEs First* (2007), in the introduction.
8. Z. J. Acs and S. Gifford, 'Innovation of Entrepreneurial Firms', *Small Business Economics*, 8 (1996), pp. 203–18.
9. OECD, *The Role of SMEs: Findings and Issues* (Paris: OECD/DSTI/IND, 2000), pp. 1–20, at p. 11.
10. Small Business Service, op. cit., p. 4.
11. D. Pugh, 'Understanding and Managing Organisational Change', in *Managing Change*, edited by C. Mabey and B. Mayon-White (London: Paul Chapman, 1994), pp. 108–12.
12. OECD, op. cit., p. 7.
13. See H. Mintzberg, *Power In and Around Organisations* (Englewood Cliffs, NJ: Prentice-Hall, 1983), p. 636, for a discussion of the fallacy of economic markets.
14. Small Business Service, op. cit., pp. 5, 6.
15. OECD (2000), op. cit., p. 2.
16. Committee of Public Accounts, Oral Evidence on 19 June 2006 on Report by the Controller and Auditor General, 'Supporting Small Business', HC962.
17. S. Johnson, *Public Policy and the Small Firm*, book proposal reviewed by authors (2006) Chapter 2.
18. Johnson, op. cit., p. 17.
19. S. Johnson, *Public Policy and the Small Firm*, book proposal reviewed by authors (2006) p 18.
20. S. Johnson, *Public Policy and the Small Firm*, book proposal reviewed by authors (2006) p 18.
21. G. Bannock, *The Economics and Management of Small Business: An International Perspective* (London: Routledge, 2005), p. 111.
22. Johnson, op. cit., p. 17.
23. Johnson, op. cit., p 19.
24. See W. R. Scott, *Organisations* (Englewood Cliffs, NJ: Prentice-Hall, 1992), Chapter 10, for a discussion of the impact of size on organisations.
25. C. Mason, R. Harrison and J. Chaloner, *Informal Risk Capital In the UK* (Southampton: Venture Finance Research Project, 1991).
26. M. B. Slovin and J. E. Young, 'The Entrepreneurial Search for Capital: An Investment in Finance', *Entrepreneurship, Innovation and Change*, 1 (1992), pp. 177–94.
27. G. Bannock and A. Peacock, *Governments and Small Business* (London: Paul Chapman, 1989).
28. OECD, *Regulatory Reform for Smaller Firms* (Paris: OECD, 1999).
29. A. A. Gibb, 'SME Policy, Academic Research and the Growth of Ignorance: Mythical Concepts, Myths, Assumptions, Rituals and Confusions', *International Small Business Journal*, 18(3) (2000), pp. 13–35.
30. Bannock and Peacock, op. cit.
31. J. Curran, 'What is Small Business Policy In the UK For? Evaluation and Assessing Small Business Policies', *International Small Business Journal*, 18(3) (2000), pp. 43–5.
32. G. Lightfoot, *Financial Management and Small Firm Owner-Managers*, unpublished PhD thesis, quoted by Curran, op. cit.

33. F. Delmar, 'The Psychology of the Entrepreneur', in *Enterprise and Small Business*, edited by S. Carter and D. Jones-Evans (London: Pearson Education, 2000), pp. 132–54, at p. 148.
34. Mintzberg, op. cit., p. 636.
35. A. Phizacklea and M. Ram, 'Ethnic Entrepreneurship In Comparative Perspective', *International Journal of Entrepreneurial Behaviour and Research*, 1 (1995), pp. 48–58.
36. A. Fadahunsi, D. Smallbone and S. Supri, 'Networking and Ethnic Minority Enterprise Development: Insights from a North London Study', *Journal of Small Business and Enterprise Development*, 7 (2000), pp. 228–40.
37. M. Ram, 'Unravelling Social Networks In Ethnic Minority Firms', *International Small Business Journal*, 12 (1994), pp. 42–53.
38. S. Carter and P. Rosa, 'The Financing of Male- and Female-Owned Businesses,' *Entrepreneurship and Regional Development*, 10 (1998), pp. 225–41.
39. D. Walker and B. E. Joyner, 'Female Entrepreneurship and the Market Process: Gender-Based Policy Considerations', *Journal of Developmental Entrepreneurship*, 4 (1999), pp. 95–116.
40. Curran, op. cit., pp. 38, 42.
41. R. J. Bennett, 'SMEs and Public Policy: Present Day Dilemmas, Future Priorities and the Case of Business Links', Paper presented at the 19th ISBA National Small Firms Policy and Research Conference, Birmingham, 1996, p. 6.
42. Business Week Editors, *The Reindustrialisation of America* (New York: McGraw-Hill, 1982), cited in K. Vesper, *Entrepreneurship and National Policy* (Chicago: Heller Institute for Small Business Policy Papers, 1983), p. 74.
43. Johnson, op. cit., Chapter 2.
44. See Mintzberg, op. cit., pp. 171–83, for a discussion of the conditions that favour political behaviour in organisations.

Contents

KEY CONCEPTS

This chapter covers:

- Theories, models and assumptions about enterprise, entrepreneurship and small business development that might help to guide interventions to promote more or better enterprise.

- A possible hierarchy-of-enterprise-needs model.

- The difference between hard and soft intervention.

- The need for insight in understanding enterprise and entrepreneurship research and the apparent lack of evidence on which to base policy.

LEARNING OBJECTIVES

By the end of this chapter the reader should:

- Have an understanding of some of the main theories and models of enterprise and entrepreneurship and how they might be used to suggest intervention methods.

- Appreciate the different theories and models that might apply to entrepreneurship and to small business development.

- Appreciate the possibility of a hierarchy of enterprise needs which could explain why different needs may be apparent at different times or to different people.

- Understand the difference between hard and soft intervention.

- Understand the possible limitations of research results and of the indicated evidence base.

Introduction

Chapter 10 considered some of the arguments for and against intervening to try to promote more enterprise and entrepreneurship. If, for whatever reason, the decision has been made to intervene, however, then on what basis might it be done? What theories and models are there to guide that intervention?

This chapter looks at some of the assumptions that have been made about enterprise and entrepreneurship, and the theories and models of them which have been advanced, that might indicate where intervention could be effective and what form it might take. Examples of specific areas and types of intervention are given in Chapter 12, but before they are discussed it may be helpful to have some ideas about how enterprise can be influenced. This will not only indicate the theory which underlies some of the intervention methods currently practised but also provide the basis for new approaches.

Some of these ideas have been described in previous chapters but are referred to again here in order to show a comparative selection of these ideas without the need to refer back frequently. There is however no guarantee that all the theories are correct. Like any theory in science, they are useful, not for explaining the past, but to model behaviour in a way which predicts what will happen in the future as a result of any action taken. The theories do not have to conform to some absolute level of truth to be helpful, nor do they all have to be consistent one with another. Newton's proposals for laws of gravity may have been proved to be less accurate than Einstein's ideas on the behaviour of space, but they are still good enough for many predictions about the movement of objects in space. The wave theory of light may help to explain light interference, although it is apparently inconsistent with particle theory, which can better explain other observable phenomena.

Approach

There are a variety of theories and models about how entrepreneurs and businesses behave and, because they have to be described in some sort of order, they are presented here in the sequence in which they might apply to the emergence and development of an enterprise, from the culture in which the initial idea may be sown through to the establishment and growth of a subsequent business, or other venture. This therefore follows broadly the stages of development of a business which were outlined in Chapter 7.

The earlier stages in this sequence cover the readiness of people to display enterprise and the development of their ideas to the stage where they put them into action. The subsequent stages concern the development of the businesses that may be started as a result of that enterprise. This division is consistent with the distinction which is drawn between an entrepreneurship policy, which is aimed primarily at increasing the business start-up rate, and a small business policy, which is aimed primarily at assisting those small businesses which have been established.

The early, or 'entrepreneurship', stages therefore focus primarily on the behaviour and development of people and the later or 'small business' stages on the behaviour and development of any businesses which those people may start. This distinction can also be seen to follow to some extent the different perspectives on enterprise, mentioned in Chapter 6, which are obtained when the unit of analysis is taken to be the person or the business.

Together, these stages and their relevant policies can be given the label 'enterprise'. This book has looked at both the broad and narrow definitions of enterprise and this label conforms to the broad definition, while the stages and policies to which the label 'small business' is applied conform to the narrow definition.

Early stages: entrepreneurship development

The development of a readiness to display enterprise, or of an enterprise culture, may be a particularly appropriate starting point because of the belief, which conforms to many observations, that enterprising people are 'made not born'. The exercise of enterprising behaviour is not, it is suggested, something that depends solely or largely on inherited characteristics, but instead is to a very considerable extent something that is cultural and/or can be developed by learning. If that is so then intervention to promote more of it may be both possible and practical. Promoting awareness of it may be the start.

Awareness

The pursuit of entrepreneurship can be likened to choosing an occupation. To be successful it requires an initial awareness of entrepreneurship, an interest in it, a desire to try it and the decision and action to do it, followed by a sufficient degree of attainment in it. That process must start with an awareness of the possibility of doing it.

It would be wrong to assume that everyone is aware of the possibility that he or she might be entrepreneurial, or that entrepreneurship might have potential for him or her. Research by Curran and Blackburn indicated that sixth-form pupils in Britain, unless they have a parent or a close relative in their own business, were unlikely to be interested in entrepreneurship as a career.[1] People may not want to try entrepreneurship, either because it is not desirable, or because they don't think that they would be able to do it, or because the possibility has never occurred to them. A first intervention step therefore may be an act of social persuasion to raise awareness of entrepreneurship and its potential benefits: a process of encouraging people to want to be entrepreneurs.

A time when awareness might most appropriately be raised by or with young people is during the time they are in school. Interventions at this stage are generally based on communicating enterprise awareness through the consideration of the process of starting or running a business. There are programmes that try to introduce young people to the notion of small business and the possibility of setting up a new business. However, Gibb suggested that many of these programmes have not themselves been delivered in an enterprising manner.[2] They focus on the technical aspects of managing a small firm, and fail to provide participants with insights into the dynamic and ultimately enterprising nature of small business management. Instead it is important to incorporate the 'essence of small enterprise' into the learning method. If this is done then participants will acquire useful technical knowledge but will also learn how to cope with the complex, variable and ambiguous world of the small business.

The small scale of operation in an SME renders the owner vulnerable to environmental uncertainties and a reliance on outside stakeholders. In addition, owners and their staff must complete numerous tasks and develop a holistic view of their work. The ensuing task environment is complex and changeable, and the fact that owners are in charge means that they cannot walk away from problems – they must see tasks through to completion. As a result, owners experience a strange mixture of freedom and flexibility coupled with customer-led demands to meet various wants. Myriad demands create a need to develop problem-solving skills and a capacity to obtain requisite information and resources through networks of personal contacts. To survive in this environment, owner-managers in small businesses must be adaptable and able to learn from experience. They learn by doing, by taking risks, by problem solving, by interacting with others and by tolerating ambiguity. They also initiate more than they react to situations. If the essence of entrepreneurship is to be inculcated into potential entrepreneurs then the essential elements of a small business environment must be created in the learning situation. It is important to create an uncertain task environment and to encourage learning by 'self-discovery'. Teachers must be facilitators rather than fonts of knowledge, and must create an effective learning environment that uses a project of suitable complexity as a learning vehicle. Table 2.4 in Chapter 2 summarises some key differences between an educational and an entrepreneurial focus.

As well as school-based programmes, other means can be employed to raise enterprise awareness. Again, Gibb has indicated some of them in his illustration of the components of an enterprise culture shown in Figure 2.1 in Chapter 2.

However, there may be dangers in being too positive in promoting enterprise. Creating a rosy picture of the entrepreneurial world and ignoring the difficulties that can arise may not help; and neither may talking about 'the enterprise culture' for apparently political reasons without any attempt to explain what it means and to acknowledge what might be the emotional, psychological, social and financial costs of unsuccessful participation (see Chapter 5 for some of the disadvantages of enterprise).

Developing a preference for enterprise

Raising the level of awareness may stimulate interest in enterprise and entrepreneurship, but if entrepreneurial behaviour is to be increased then more individuals must develop a preference for it.

Krueger believes 'perceptions of the entrepreneurial climate are critical. ... To encourage new business founders, communities must cultivate an environment that they will perceive as being favourable.'[3] To do this it is helpful to understand the process underlying the intention to become an entrepreneur. Krueger, like many others, notes that intentions have antecedents that are derived from a person's experiences and the meaning an individual ascribes to them. His intentions model and cognitive psychological theories (summarised in Chapter 3) suggest that the act of creating a venture must be considered to be desirable and feasible by would-be entrepreneurs. Interventions should aim therefore to reinforce these perceptions.

Perceived desirability

Potential entrepreneurs should perceive that a new venture can deliver what they want. They must believe that the experience will be rewarding and enjoyable. Research on the motivation of entrepreneurs reveals that they have multiple motives and that economic ones rarely predominate. Highlighting the potential autonomy and sense of achievement that can be gained may therefore be more important than the potential financial rewards. Research has also revealed that many people consider entrepreneurship when they are experiencing dissatisfaction with other jobs or careers. This finding may indicate when it might be most appropriate to reinforce an entrepreneurial message and those at whom it might most effectively be targeted.

The personal desirability of entrepreneurship is important, but if the entrepreneurial act is also perceived as socially desirable then this is likely to encourage prospective entrepreneurs. A positive community attitude to enterprise is important, because often the capacity for enterprise is embedded in a community. Markets, resources, information and support, both practical and psychological, all originate there, and if that community is perceived as hostile many potential entrepreneurs may be deterred. The absence of entrepreneurial role models or of a positive encouragement to enter one of the 'professions', while not actually being hostile towards enterprise, nevertheless act counter to it.

Perceived feasibility

In developing a preference for an occupation, as well as evaluating the attractiveness of the potential outcomes, individuals generally assess their chances of attaining those outcomes. To do this they consider whether they can obtain:

- the necessary knowledge and skill
- the resources required
- the means to overcome any shortfall.

If individuals have the opportunity to develop and manage enterprising projects in their existing employment, or to practise entrepreneurship on a part-time or temporary basis, they will have an appreciation of what is involved and can assess their attributes against the perceived requirements. As it has been put by Delmar:

> What stands out ... is whether people feel that entrepreneurship is a feasible option for themselves. In other words a person will try to start a business if he or she can do it in terms of possessing the ability and knowledge required to carry it out.[4]

Entrepreneurial counselling can also help people to assess their competence in this area. Krueger believes that if the process of review is carried out sensitively, and if the emphasis is on positive steps to develop skills and overcome environmental obstacles, then this can be effective in building confidence and enhancing a person's perceived self-efficacy.[5]

Preparation

> Success = Idea + Know-how + Know-who
> Rein Peterson and Robert Rondstadt[6]

Building an appropriate culture does not itself create more enterprise. It does however provide an important precondition, like preparing a seedbed before sowing seeds: seeds sown on rocky ground will not find any sustenance and the energy in them will be wasted. But, given a seedbed of sorts, the formula for success given above can also be interpreted to indicate that entrepreneurial success starts with the idea: both the idea of starting a business in the first place and the idea of what business to start. Technical know-how appropriate to that business idea will be needed, as well as business know-how to guide the establishment and running of the venture as a business. Know-who is also highlighted to indicate the importance of developing and using a network of contacts to obtain resources, advice, guidance and other forms of assistance.

The early stages of development can be seen as preparation for the possibility of a business at some time, before any decision may have been made about start-up. The later stages can be preparation for a venture that has already been decided upon. Chapter 3 included a view of enterprise based on self-efficacy or the attributes and resources which an individual may possess (see Table 3.1). If these attributes and resources are appropriate for an entrepreneurial venture then it makes it more likely that the individual will engage in such a venture, given the right opportunity or 'trigger'. Therefore if the individual thinks that entrepreneurship is something that he or she might like to try at some time, then he or she might endeavour to acquire the appropriate attributes and resources.

Acquiring and developing such attributes and resources in preparation for the possibility of enterprise can be seen as necessary foundation work. Preparing to start an enterprise, once the decision has been made to do it, is to prepare to build a structure on those foundations. Actually the distinction is not hard and fast. If the necessary foundations are not in place when the decision is made to build, it will be necessary to address them at that time. Nevertheless, the analogy does help to separate the general preparation from the specific.

Later stages: business development

At this stage in the development of a business the focus for intervention starts to shift from the person to the business. It becomes less about helping a person to develop than about helping an enterprise to overcome specific barriers.

The barrier analogy may be a helpful one. Realising an idea or starting a business inevitably means encountering a number of difficulties and obstacles. To get to the desired destination it will be necessary to reduce them, cross them, avoid them or find ways through and around them as appropriate. Intervention can help by signposting pitfalls, by removing obstacles, by lowering barriers, and also by improving jumping capability, by raising the take-off point for jumping fences and by raising confidence: showing that in general it is possible to complete the course.

Start-up

There are numerous barriers which can impede the launch of new businesses or other enterprising projects. Interventions in support of them can try to remove or reduce the tangible restrictions or to enhance the capacity of the actors to overcome the constraints. These can be addressed in both the short and the long term. (See Table 11.1.)

In the short term, intervention to remove barriers is usually one-off help to overcome problems, and intervention to improve competence is mainly basic training in issues such as business plans, cashflow management and selling. Sometimes the training may be tied to a grant to ensure that it is taken up by making its completion a condition of the grant. This is the equivalent of providing fish to feed the hungry, and possibly combining pills with it to provide some medication.

In the longer term, barriers can be addressed by effective management of the economy to increase aggregate demand, increase financial stability, meet changing labour market and educational needs, and improve the context within which business development takes place. In the longer term, competence can be enhanced by increasing the

Table 11.1 Schema of small business intervention strategies

Time frame	Type of problem	
	Barriers to overcome	Capability to be acquired
Shorter	The direct provision of help to entrepreneurs to overcome obstacles, for example by offering grants, loans, advice, consultancy, and so on	Provide basic knowledge and skills training and lay the foundations for future development
Longer	Reduce or remove obstacles by addressing market failures, by improving the infrastructure, by changing regulations, and so on	Develop owner-manager and in-company capacity for learning, for analysis and for accessing appropriate assistance

organisation's own capacity to learn through skills in accessing information, in analysis, in planning, and in using appropriate outside sources of advice without the need for 'hand-holding'. In essence, owners and businesses are assisted to develop the attributes, knowledge and skills that are needed for sustainable development.

The latter is the equivalent of teaching the hungry to fish, but can have its problems when free fish are readily available without the need to learn how to catch them. Grant regimes can result in an attitude of dependency, including examples of a refusal to contemplate action without a grant, even when the action concerned would most likely be profitable without one.

Growth

Up to start-up the focus for intervention has been on the individual, the development of his or her entrepreneurship, and the minimisation of barriers. As the business comes closer to reality, different issues such as the securing of markets and the marshalling of resources become critical and, at start-up, a new range of problems can emerge. Once trading commences, however, intervention typically switches from entrepreneurship to business development, with the focus being on the firm, not the individual. The aim of intervention becomes the growth of the business, for which business and management knowledge and skill become crucial, so it is important to consider how small business managers are to acquire them. Individual owner-managers are responsible for their own self-development. However, as their ventures move from owner-managed to owner-directed status they will have to develop a management structure and delegate key roles. The changing roles for self and others will bring a requirement to master new skills. Some of these skills can be learned on the job, but a lack of previous relevant experience is likely to be a handicap. Help in this area would therefore seem to be particularly beneficial. One way of addressing this is, for instance, through the mentoring of owner-managers by other, more experienced, owner-managers, and there are now formal schemes in the UK to organise this.

Like start-up businesses, growing businesses also face external barriers, especially those associated with finance and employment. For instance, an important source of finance for growth is the venture capital sector. However, only a small proportion of formal venture capital tends to find its way to small businesses. In contrast to the formal venture capital industry, 'business angels' do seem to make a significant contribution to the development of small businesses. Nevertheless, there are still considered to be some funding gaps in the private financial market that intervention might try to address.[7]

Another popular target for intervention is the promotion of innovative and high-technology businesses. Innovation is widely regarded as a key factor in business survival, development, growth and competitiveness, and high-technology businesses are thought to offer the potential for greater growth, higher returns or longer life than 'low'-technology businesses, which are easier for others to copy. The apparent link between innovation and economic prowess in the United States is often cited as an example in making this point.

For small businesses to become innovative, or to remain so, they will need to have access to new ideas developed by others and/or to develop and protect their own ideas. In addition they will need financial resources to tide them over the non-revenue-generating phases of research and development. Other suggestions for intervention in this field include addressing the system for registering and protecting intellectual property, either by making it easier for small businesses to take out patents and other protection or, alternatively, by making it more difficult for large firms to defend their patent rights. This would encourage small businesses to adapt and develop technological ideas developed by others.

Decline and termination

One stage of business development not often considered for intervention is that of decline and ultimately termination. Nevertheless, there could be economic benefits to intervention here also. The benefits of reversing a decline may seem more obvious, but there may be benefits to be gained even in termination. Not only is the turnover of less effective businesses and their replacement by new ventures necessary for the health of an economy but also, if a business is going to terminate, then it is better for its owners, its staff, its customers and its creditors if it does so in an orderly and controlled way, rather than trading beyond the point of insolvency and subsequently collapsing in debt. An orderly termination would minimise knock-on effects on creditor businesses, and the business proprietors may even be prepared to learn from their experience and try again, instead of being discouraged, perhaps permanently, from developing further business ventures. The medical profession acknowledges that, while a terminally ill patient is by definition past the stage when medicine can effect a cure, there are still three things that can be offered to help at such times: support, information and choices. Similarly, there may be forms of intervention that provide benefits even in the termination stage of a business.

A hierarchy-of-needs model

It has been observed that, if people who are starting new enterprises are asked what they need to help the process, the answer is very often 'money'; whereas if people seeking to help that process are asked, they will often mention other areas of assistance such as premises, training, advice and mentoring, and some people go as far as to say that money is not the issue. However, frequently there appears to be a connection between the assistance that those seeking to help are best able to supply and what they claim is the main need: trainers for instance often seem to see skills as the key issue.

So is the main need money or not? What explains this apparent difference of opinion? How is it that different people, each of whom ought to be in a position to know, can provide different answers? Is it like the case of three blind people each seeking to identify an elephant by what they could feel, and who therefore variously described it as a rubbery hose, a tree, or an unravelled rope, depending on whether they felt the trunk, a leg or the tail?

One model (shown in Figure 11.1) developed to explain the variety of answers obtained to this question borrows a concept from Maslow in his analysis of human needs. He postulated that those needs could be placed in a hierarchy in which

Figure 11.1 A hierarchy of enterprise needs

lower-order needs are dominant until they are satisfied, whereupon the higher-order needs start to be felt. The higher-order needs are there, but may not reveal themselves until the lower-order needs are satisfied. It has been suggested that a similar hierarchy could apply to enterprise needs, which would explain why they appear differently to different observers. Thus, without an idea, no need is felt for the resources to develop it and, until those resources are provided, no need is often apparent for any extra enterprise skills. Ultimately, if the enterprise is to be a success, it needs an environment which, given a sound approach by the enterprise, is capable of sustaining it.

An enterprise, in this context, can be any form of human endeavour in which enterprising attributes might assist. This definition would include artistic and social endeavour as well as business entrepreneurship. A successful enterprise is considered to be one which has gone from the idea stage to implementation on a basis which is sustainable because the income attracted by that enterprise – whether earned income from sales, income from investments, sponsorship attracted from patrons or charitable donations – is consistently high enough to pay for the outgoings of the enterprise.

The model appears, for instance, to work for artistic as well as for business enterprise. For example there is a need for pump-priming support for the artist until he or she can become established, and becoming established can mean earning enough to support the art from direct sales or through some sort of benefaction. Given artistic skill there is still a need for skill in marketing and money control if the venture is to succeed.

In this presentation, money is often a complicating factor. It has not been included in the hierarchy because it is not a direct need but is sought because it can be used to buy what is needed. It is a means not an end. Money is needed at an early stage to buy the resources required for start-up and then it is needed at a later stage to sustain the venture once it is launched. At the later stage however, the money required should be found from the earnings of the venture itself. These two types of funding can be likened to the flight of a glider. At its launch a glider needs external help to get into the air, but then, if it is successfully launched and piloted, it should itself be able to find enough lift to sustain its flight. But if the glider pilot does not have sufficient skills to do this, the glider will descend and will once again need external help if it is to rise again. It is however only when the glider has been launched that such a lack of skills will be apparent. Similarly in enterprise, if some of the higher-order needs are not then satisfied, the enterprise will not be operated viably and will need more 'pump-priming' money as a result. Therefore, given an initial idea and then some form of start-up finance, failure to meet higher-level needs can appear as a further need for finance, just as if it were still a lower-level start-up finance need. This can be further complicated when higher-level needs are combined with some, but inadequate, start-up finance.

Given an idea, which is often the starting-point without which the needs issue will not arise, the lowest, and therefore the most obvious, need is likely to be resources, to which money appears to be the obvious answer. Therefore this hierarchy-of-needs hypothesis explains why the needs of enterprise are, at an early stage, often expressed as a need for money, and why the other needs are hidden until that need is apparently satisfied. Hence it explains why there can be confusion and disagreement about what is the most appropriate assistance to offer. It also explains why, when asked, most people will say that money is the key issue, yet there are other people who will talk not about money, but about training and mentoring needs for example. It also explains why providing more money often does not solve the problem.

The model can also be expanded and explained further. A level below the idea might be added, which is the need for a culture in which ideas for enterprise can arise and which encourages people to be enterprising. Further explanation could also be added of the sorts of needs at the various levels.

The model also highlights the reason for a not-infrequent temptation to use money as the tool with which to help enterprise. Often bodies which are created to help enterprises are given a budget with which to operate. Then, when they ask people engaged in enterprise what would most help them, they are told it is money. In such circumstances it is very easy for them to believe that money is the tool to use, instead of seeing that it has to be converted into something else if it is actually to achieve the desired effect. The model also indicates that anyone seeking to assist the enterprise process should not believe that it is possible to intervene at one stage only and succeed in addressing in one way all the main needs of enterprise development.

Advocacy

One further explanation might also help. In the hierarchy model 'advocacy' has been included as a possible source of advice or help on presentation, which is a separate requirement from that of mentoring. The concept of 'advocacy' has been borrowed from the legal world. In that area lawyers are hired to argue cases, not because they know the case better than the litigants, but because they know the system and how to present the case so that the system can best understand it and recognise its good points. Similarly, when making applications for support for ideas, it can help to know those who might either speak for the venture or advise on how best to present a case.

The issue of advocacy is recognised in legal circles, even though all are equal before the law. It is often not recognised amongst funders, however, where those who administer the funding like to believe that they can judge a case on its merits without some third party explaining it to them. Some of those who have worked in the funding system may recognise that the way a case is presented can influence the funding decision and that, because those making the decision work in a different culture from those making the applications, good communication between them may only be possible with the help of interpreters who can understand the concerns of both sides.

Advocacy, in the sense in which it is used in the model, is not the same as mentoring. In this context advocacy is taken to mean help with the presentation of a proposal or venture to those who are being asked to make a decision on it, whereas mentoring is taken to mean one-to-one personal help with different aspects of the business or idea development process (although not all uses of the words 'mentoring' and 'advocacy' conform to these definitions).

Hard and soft

One category of initiatives to promote small businesses is one which, instead of offering direct help to the individual entrepreneur or business, attempts to create conditions in which businesses can better germinate and grow. A clear example of this sort of initiative is the creation of science parks and business incubators. These have been called 'hard' assistance, in comparison with 'soft' assistance such as training provision and mentoring, presumably because they involve the creation of 'hard' physical structures (buildings) rather like the physical hardware of computers.

There are a number of places including, in the United States, Silicon Valley in California and Route 128 in Massachusetts, and around Cambridge in England (sometimes referred to as Silicon Fen), where there has been an extraordinary growth of productive clusters of high-technology firms. In these clusters, the conditions which produce innovative business communities, with significant outputs of patents and innovations and new businesses, are thought to include a university or other technological research facility; the close proximity of other innovative firms, which encourages the spread of ideas and helps small businesses to access the expertise of other businesses around them; and informal networks incorporating business angels, venture capitalists, professional firms including accountants and lawyers, and a business school. Providing help with these conditions is soft assistance.

Science parks seek to replicate at least some of these conditions. As well as science parks there are also research parks, technology parks and innovation parks but, whatever the name used, they all generally share a number of common components, which include:

- a property base which provides suitable business premises
- close links with a source of technology expertise and possible spin-off ideas. Often these are formal and operational links with a university or other higher education body or major centre of research
- assisted access to finance and advice
- a management function which is actively engaged in the transfer of technology and business skills to the organisations on-site and in encouraging the formation and growth of knowledge-based businesses.

This list highlights the university or other research links and the transfer of technology as key components in a science park and it is this link that distinguishes science parks from many business incubators. Science parks may be business incubators but business incubators are not necessarily science parks. Incubators may concentrate more on providing nursery space, often at subsidised rents, and access to support services such as word-processing, copying, telephone answering and telecommunications. The theory behind the creation of this environment is that it provides services which might otherwise be beyond the means of the small start-up business, but it also provides what it is possible and, once premises are available, easy to provide.

However, there appears to be little convincing evidence yet that a science park, or other form of business park, necessarily has a significant impact on the innovative performance of its tenant firms. In England it was Segal Quince Wicksteed that did most to highlight the spin-off from technical developments at Cambridge University facilitated by the Cambridge Science Park, now known as the 'Cambridge Phenomenon'.[8] Some other studies of individual parks and incubators have also indicated that they can be successful but Deakins, in reviewing this area, finds that the overall picture is less certain.[9] He reports on a study for the DTI which found that there was little difference in performance between firms on and off science parks and indicates that other studies based on incubator facilities also contain similarly equivocal findings.[10]

ILLUSTRATION 11.1
Does location matter in Israel and Ireland?

Innovation activities of Israeli firms are found to be much more locationally sensitive than those of Irish companies. In other words, in Israel a metropolitan location gives firms an advantage in terms of the probability of innovating. Locations in Belfast and Dublin, however, are no more propitious for innovation than other areas of Northern Ireland or the Republic of Ireland. One plausible explanation is that the more R&D-intensive activities of Israeli high-tech firms mean that these firms benefit more from a metropolitan location than their Irish counterparts.

In terms of policy, the implication is that dispersing high-tech industry in Israel is likely to be more 'costly' in terms of its negative impact on innovation than in Ireland. For policy-makers in Ireland this is a heartening conclusion, suggesting that the policy of dispersing high-tech activity over the last three decades is likely to have had little detrimental effect on the overall level of innovative activity. For Israel, however, more tension is evident between industrial and regional policy. The pattern of industrial incentives, and particularly high levels of public support for R&D, have stimulated investment in highly R&D-intensive sectors which are unlikely to fare well in more peripheral areas. For these areas, offering high levels of R&D support may actually be an inappropriate policy, at least in the absence of measures designed to improve other aspects of the operating environment for R&D-intensive businesses (such as developing local higher education institutions).

Source: Northern Ireland Economic Research Centre, *Does Location Matter for Innovation? A Comparison of High-Tech Firms In Israel and Ireland*, Research briefing (Belfast: NIERC, 2001).

Research evidence

> It ain't what you don't know that gets you into trouble, it's what you know for sure that ain't so.
>
> Mark Twain

It might be expected that guidance for intervention to promote more enterprise might come from research and, in the last two decades of the twentieth century, there was an 'explosion of research into entrepreneurship and the small and medium enterprise'.[11] However Gibb points out that, despite the resultant increase in academic knowledge, or even perhaps because of it, there has also been a growth in ignorance about entrepreneurship and small and medium enterprises.[12]

Earlier Gibb had looked at the problem of trying to ensure that small firm research was relevant to policy-makers.[13] He highlighted issues such as the relationship between academic knowledge and insight, showing, for instance, that insight into small businesses was needed if research findings were to be interpreted in a meaningful way. The assumption that objectivity was a prerequisite for good research could, he suggested, mean that the need for insight was often overlooked on the grounds that those who knew enough about small businesses to have insight might be too close to their subject to be fully objective.

Gibb has identified a number of 'mythical concepts' which he describes as important policy development areas around which there is an expanding mass of literature but also a considerable degree of confusion and ignorance. These include entrepreneurship and the enterprise culture, network development, the 'growth' company, local 'bottom-up' development, and competency and learning. He has also highlighted 'a number of more straightforward myths which have influenced key policy objectives in the 1990s and continue to do so'. These are:[14]

- that three out of every five new businesses started fail within the first three years
- that growth companies are the major job creators
- that in the United States failure is regarded positively by banks and other stakeholders compared with the UK
- that there is a major gap in bank finance for SMEs in the UK.

CASE 11.1
The start-up failure myth

'Among the more straightforward myths which have influenced key policy objectives in the 1990s and continue to do so is the myth that three out of every five new businesses started fail within the first three years.

'Much has been written about the failure of new business starts. All these studies indicate that of all business exits (as measured by VAT de-registrations, exits from self-employment or from the companies register), only a small fraction are due (in the case of individuals) to bankruptcy and (in the case of companies) to compulsory involuntary liquidation. ... It is evident, however, that a useful distinction can be made between the legal entity, the business activity and the entrepreneur. Casual observations would indicate that even in apparently stable business conditions there can be a great deal of 'churning' in respect of registration with little else changing.

'Table 11.2 demonstrates the movement into and out of various forms of business registration in 'Brigadoon', a 'mythical' village (known well to the author). It indicates that there were, in the space of six years, 14 'starts', 12 'failures' and eight 'new entrepreneurs'; [but overall there was only] one business activity loss and one business activity gain. The explanation mainly lies in changes in legal status arrangements. For example the architect resident in the village went into two partnerships, each of which lasted only a short time, before resuming independent status.

Table 11.2 The Brigadoon economy: change over six years

Business	De-registration	New registration	Persons change	Activity change
Architect	4	4	0	0
Pub	2	2	2	0
Post Office	3	3	3	1
Bus	1	1	1	0
Electrical contractor	1	1	1	0
Plumber (informal)	0	1	0	0
Garage/caravan site	0	1	1	0
House cleaner (informal)	0	1	0	0
Weaving	1	0	0	-1

'Other changes related to marital arrangements, to deaths and, perhaps not uncommon in the rural community, to (in the case of the Post Office) families running this community service who added a small store for a short period of time as a duty before transferring it to someone else. Other explanations related to the movement from the informal to the more formal economy, and to a wife's ambition to run part of an existing business and subsequently to register it. The economic life of the village looks extremely turbulent if a business registration approach is taken to describe it. In practice, little has changed in terms of activity.

'The start-up failure myth needs to be more clearly exposed as it is frequently quoted by politicians and easily leads into other policy assumptions, for example that investment in training in start-ups is undesirable because such training is written off with failure; that the majority of those who start businesses are poor managers; and that start-ups are not a source of employment growth, which is untrue. It also lends credence to the belief that microenterprises are not entrepreneurial or in dynamic sectors of the economy.

'An alternative view, coloured by the notion that individuals may move into and out of self-employment, is that starting a business can be seen as an intrinsic part of the flexible labour market, and that start-up might be one of the best ways of experiencing, learning and practising enterprise. When combined with the notion that the learning curve during the start-up process, particularly for the novice start-up, is probably greater than any other time during the life of the small business then the potential for reconsideration of the rate of return to the training investment is considerable.'

Sources: A. A. Gibb, 'SME Policy, Academic Research and the Growth of Ignorance, Mythical Concepts, Myths, Assumptions, Rituals and Confusions', *International Small Business Journal* (2000), 18(3), pp. 22–3; A. A. Gibb, 'SME Policy, Mythical Concepts, Myths, Assumptions, Rituals and Confusions', 21st ISBA National Small Firms Conference, Durham, 1998, p. 12.

Points raised

This example is extracted from a longer paper by Allan Gibb. It illustrates how the statistics of business registration and de-registration can give a very misleading impression of what is actually happening to those engaged in business and can appear to suggest a much higher failure rate than is actually the case.

Each myth, Gibb indicates, is shared in different ways by different groups and each has influenced policy, being treated as a 'fact' rather than as an assumption with little or questionable supporting evidence. If there is this 'growth of ignorance' then, Gibb argues, there are three contributory factors:[15]

- The first factor is that of the nature of the relationship and involvement between SMEs, policy-makers, other stakeholders and academics. Between and within these groups there are substantial differences concerning beliefs, values and assumptions about the ways that things work, and these differences influence the processes by which the groups learn from each other.

- The second factor relates to understanding of the way that governance works and the kinds of assumptions made in establishing priorities for policy action, as well as assumptions concerning the process by which these priorities are met. If academics do not understand the process of governance, and believe, for instance, that it pursues a rational discovery and problem-solving model, then their contribution is likely to be marginalised.

- The third factor arises in respect of the way in which academics approach their policy-related work. There is a need for researchers to attach greater value to insight into the way that others see and feel things and to distinguish data, descriptions of empirical results, constructs and hypotheses from useful theory.

The evidence base

One attempt in the UK to collect and present the evidence relevant to the field of enterprise and small business was made by the Small Business Service (SBS). In 2004 it published *The Evidence Base* for a government action plan for small business.[16] In the foreword the document indicates that the SBS's aim 'is to ensure that all decisions which affect small business are only taken after reviewing the evidence on what is needed and what actually works – and where the lessons learned in the delivery of products and services are fed back into the further development of policy'. The Introduction then states that:

> This paper sets out a more detailed analysis of the evidence base underpinning the Action Plan. It aims to provide a resource which policy makers and analysts across government and external researchers in the small business field can draw upon, and to make transparent the evidence on which policy is made.

The document is structured around the following seven themes 'identified (in the government's action plan for small business) as key drivers for economic growth, improved productivity and enterprise for all':[17]

- 'Building and enterprise culture.
- Encouraging a more dynamic start-up market.
- Building the capability for small business growth.
- Improving access to finance for small businesses.
- Encouraging more enterprise in disadvantaged communities and under-represented groups.
- Improving small businesses' experience of government services.
- Developing better regulation and policy.'[18]

The first section of the document presents a statistical overview of the nature and characteristics of small businesses and their importance to the economy. This section is not prescriptive and does not suggest any evidence that the seven themes are indeed the key drivers for economic growth, improved productivity and enterprise. It is followed by sections providing a summary of the evidence underpinning each of the seven key themes. These sections generally present the evidence that is available about each theme. With the exception of the section addressing 'Improving small businesses' experience of government services', each section indicates that it has a twofold purpose: first, to provide an overview of the evidence to explain why the government is putting in place a range of activities and actions to address that issue, and second, to outline how the government will monitor success in achieving its objectives in that area. The sections do not suggest any evidence to indicate that the government is pursuing an appropriate policy in each area, although they do indicate that specific research and evaluation will be carried out to fill gaps in knowledge about what policy actions work and why.

It could therefore be argued that *The Evidence Base* is more a distillation of the evidence available than an attempt to identify and present the evidence needed. It does not, for instance, provide the following:

- Evidence of why enterprise/entrepreneurship and/or small business should be promoted. Which will depend on:
  - evidence of what people want or need
  - if that is jobs, evidence for what sort of jobs (and for what 'quality' jobs)
  - evidence that enterprise/entrepreneurship and/or small business will provide what is sought.
- Evidence that enterprise/entrepreneurship and/or small business can usefully be promoted.
- Evidence of how enterprise/entrepreneurship and/or small business can be promoted.
- Evidence that enterprise/entrepreneurship and/or small business are being successfully promoted.

ILLUSTRATION 11.2
Evidence and the development of knowledge

In science the development of knowledge about a particular issue often involves trying to establish a proven theory (a 'law'), which can be used to predict how the issue will behave, and on which actions to influence the issue can be based. The usual approach to establishing a theory is to identify what is known about the phenomenon in question, to build a hypotheses which is consistent with those facts, to test that hypothesis with new experiments and then, if they do not disprove it, to use it until it is disproved.

What, in that context, is the evidence base? Is it the facts known about the issue, which are the evidence on which a hypothesis might be based, or is it the results of tests made on the hypothesis, which might provide evidence that the hypothesis appears to work? Of those alternatives the only one on which policy/actions might be based is the latter: the evidence that there is a working hypothesis.

How does that approach compare with the SBS 'evidence base'? The SBS document does not appear to provide evidence in support of a hypothesis or model of enterprise development and/or small business growth, upon which enterprise or small business policy might be based. Instead it appears to be a collection of information about aspects of enterprise and small business which provides a description of some of their characteristics without indicating how they might be influenced. Indeed the document does not itself claim to offer evidence in support of a model, but tries instead to provide evidence for why (but not how) the government should seek to support enterprise and businesses and how it will monitor success in achieving its objectives.

The link between evidence and policy

In the UK, in the area of enterprise and small business development, government objectives appear to be multiple. For instance the relevant objectives that provide a context for much enterprise policy appear to include stimulating economic growth, promoting employment opportunities and helping disadvantaged areas. However *The Evidence Base* does not offer evidence that enterprise and small business can contribute to all those objectives, or that they are being promoted in the best way to achieve those objectives. If, in the field of enterprise and small business promotion, myths prevail, and if little or no evidence is offered that the government is pursuing appropriate policies for achieving its objectives, this suggests that current policy is not actually 'evidence based'. Where evidence is offered it appears to be evidence associated with existing policy, rather than evidence on which to base new policy.

The other view: the perspective of the individual

In considering intervention in enterprise it is important not to see it only from the point of view of the intervener, but also to consider the view of the individuals engaging in it. In making their occupational choice, individuals will, at least to some extent, conduct appraisals although, as in other 'consumption' decisions, issues of 'fantasy, feeling and fun' also play a part.[19] Macro-economic issues such as the general health of the economy will be considered, along with the personal attributes deemed necessary for occupational success. If the potential outcomes of an endeavour are valued, and if individuals consider that their efforts in that endeavour will lead to the requisite performance and associated rewards, then they are likely to expend energy in its pursuit.[20] That applies both to enterprise in a business context and to enterprise applied in other situations.

At an early stage, perceptions are all-important, and there are possibilities of misconceptions because appraisals are conducted on the basis of suppositions. While entrepreneurial choice has quite a lot in common with occupational choice in general, it has some unique features that should be borne in mind when considering intervention. As individuals move through life, their career choices are moulded by 'the opportunity structures to which individuals are exposed, first in education, and subsequently in employment. Individuals' ambitions in turn, can be treated as reflecting the influence of the structures through which they pass.'[21] However, education and work opportunities have not often exposed people to the realities of entrepreneurship. Until some recent examples, few educational courses have delved into the nature of enterprise/entrepreneurship, and most individuals experience employment as employees. If they learn anything about work, they learn the skills of job-readiness and successful employment. They will be 'job takers' not 'job makers'. People generally choose occupations that they know something about, and in the absence of a conception of entrepreneurship it may not be a realistic option for many.

Furthermore, enterprise is a somewhat heterogeneous occupation. Entrepreneurs run manufacturing firms and service organisations. Similarly enterprising individuals may display their talents in healthcare, education or the church. These individuals are responsible for the technological aspects of their ventures, and the socio-economic tasks of administration, co-ordination and leadership. A range of technical and managerial abilities is needed, and previous education and work will rarely prepare individuals fully for these tasks.

In addition, entrepreneurs must develop a viable business idea and marshal appropriate resources to create a business venture. The multiple technical and management skills, coupled with the need for ideas and resources, contribute to the complexity of entrepreneurship as an occupation and the need to consider many leverage points for intervention. Entrepreneurship also differs from normal employment in that potential entrepreneurs are not screened in the way that potential employees are. In many countries there are no formal entry qualifications, there is no formal selection and interview process, and there is no appointment and review procedure.[22] Business counsellors, bankers and other advisers may proffer advice, but no one can, or should try to, prevent a person starting a business if he or she decides to do so whatever his or her abilities. Further, when it is done, there is no compulsory process for identifying and rectifying any deficiencies in relevant skills and knowledge.

The absence of selectors and the complexities of entrepreneurial choice should indicate the need for wariness about prescribing simple solutions to the problem of attracting and developing entrepreneurs. This complexity is confirmed by the fact that many business founders tend to choose entrepreneurship only after trying other jobs or career paths. By their mid-thirties, potential entrepreneurs will tend to have been exposed to a selection of jobs or roles, and while they may not have had direct experience of entrepreneurship, they may have had an opportunity to assess interests, values, abilities and opportunities. This being so, intervention in this area may need to address a number of issues experienced by people at different stages of entrepreneurial development. Since each individual is unique, a very wide range of interventions would be needed to reach all of them in an appropriate way.

It is also relevant to remember that intervention can be direct or indirect. It can seek to target the individual or business directly, or it may seek to change the context or conditions in which they operate, which will in turn influence the individuals or businesses concerned. Gibb's diagram, presented in Chapter 7 (Figure 7.10), helps to make this point by showing that the purposive support network, through which much of the intervention might come, may in reality have much less direct influence on entrepreneurs and small businesses than many of their other layers of contacts. It may be more effective for organisations in that network to try to work through some of the other layers than to try to go directly to the business owners concerned.

THE KEY POINTS OF CHAPTER 11

- As entrepreneurs and businesses go through different stages of their development their influences and needs change, and so therefore do the opportunities for intervention.

- Intervention in the early stages of development may be referred to as entrepreneurship policy, and intervention in the later stages, after a business has started trading, as small business policy.

- The first stage is the development of an enterprise culture which can provide both an awareness of the possibility of enterprise and the development of a preference for it. The society in which individuals live, the education they receive, and the environment in which they work can all be very influential in this and are therefore possible targets for intervention.

- Preparation for enterprise involves the identification of an idea or opportunity to pursue; the building of experience, skills and other attributes relevant to its pursuit; and the acquisition of the finances, networks and other resources necessary for it. Intervention might help in all these areas.

- Start-up is a common focus for intervention, in particular to help those wishing to start businesses to overcome the barriers they face. Such intervention may attempt to reduce the barriers or to raise ability to overcome them. It can use measures with short-term or immediate effects, such as grants to overcome financial difficulties, or it may seek longer-lasting effects by seeking to address market failures or by developing a capacity to learn. However entrepreneurship is a heterogeneous occupation and the requisite resources, knowledge and skills will be diverse.

- Intervention to assist declining, or even terminating, businesses may also produce benefits, and should not therefore be discounted automatically.

- Simplistic, direct solutions to intervention should be suspect however. There are no formal selectors for entrepreneurship that can prevent occupational entry by those who are unsuited to it. The variety of people trying it is therefore considerable, and so are the influences on them. Direct intervention may be considered, but it may also be effective to seek to influence people through others.

- Entrepreneurs starting businesses also have a variety of needs, not all of which will be equally apparent at any one time. It will therefore rarely be possible to help them significantly by meeting just one need.

- One vehicle for help has been the provision of physical facilities, such as premises, which are designed to stimulate the conditions in which at least some businesses seem to thrive. This is 'hard' assistance, in contrast to the 'soft' assistance such as training and mentoring provided directly to improve individual businesses.

- Research into entrepreneurship and small businesses has not necessarily led to increased understanding. In this area ignorance, not least in the form of false concepts and myths about small businesses and their behaviour, still persists and clear evidence on which to base policy is lacking.

- The perspective of the individual engaged in enterprise is also of relevance when considering intervention.

QUESTIONS, ESSAY AND DISCUSSION TOPICS

- Is it true that intervention is often based more on what can be provided than on what is needed?
- What interventions might be desirable but impractical?
- Is it always a good thing to get more people to start their own businesses?
- 'Backing winners' was a popular small business development strategy in the 1990s. What was the theory behind it, and was it valid?
- 'Don't worry too much about why. It's more important to start something. Then we will be able to see if it really works.' Is that a good basis for introducing new enterprise initiatives?
- 'It will always be possible to find a theory to support any strategy you want to adopt.' Is this true of enterprise support?

Suggestions for further reading and information

J. Curran and R. A. Blackburn, *Researching the Small Enterprise* (London: Sage, 2001).
A. A. Gibb, 'SME Policy, Academic Research and the Growth of Ignorance: Mythical Concepts, Myths, Assumptions, Rituals and Confusions', *International Small Business Journal*, 18(3) (2000), pp. 13–35.

References

1. J. Curran and R. Blackburn, *Young People and Enterprise: A National Survey*, Occasional paper No. 11 (Kingston: Kingston Business School, 1989).
2. A. A. Gibb, 'Enterprise Culture and Education: Understanding Enterprise Education and Its Links With Small Business, Entrepreneurship and Wider Educational Goals', *International Small Business Journal*, 11 (1993), pp. 11–34.
3. N. F. Krueger Jr., *Prescriptions for Opportunity: How Communities Can Create Potential for Entrepreneurs*, Working paper 90–03 (Washington, DC: The Small Business Foundation of America, 1995).
4. F. Delmar, 'The Psychology of the Entrepreneur', in *Enterprise and Small Business*, edited by S. Carter and D. Jones-Evans (London: Pearson Education, 2000), pp. 132–54, at p. 148.
5. Krueger, op. cit.
6. R. Peterson and R. Rondstadt, 'A Silent Strength: Entrepreneurial Know-Who', *The 16th ESBS/efmd /IMD Report* (86/4), pp. 11–15. at p. 11.
7. See R. T. Harrison and C. M. Mason, 'Finance for the Growing Business: The Role of Informal Investment', *National Westminster Bank Review*, May (1993), pp. 17–29 for a discussion of business angels.
8. Segal, Quince, Wicksteed, *The Cambridge Phenomenon* (London: Segal, Quince, Wicksteed, 1985).
9. D. Deakins, *Entrepreneurship and Small Firms* (London: McGraw-Hill, 1999), pp. 150, 156–8.
10. P. Westhead and D. J. Storey, *An Assessment of Firms Located on and off Science Parks: Main Report* (London: DTI / HMSO, 1994).
11. A. A. Gibb, 'SME Policy, Academic Research and the Growth of Ignorance, Mythical Concepts, Myths, Assumptions, Rituals and Confusions', *International Small Business Journal*, 18(3) (2000), pp. 13–35, at 13.
12. Ibid., p. 13.
13. A. A. Gibb, 'Can Academe Achieve Quality In Small Firms Policy Research?' *Entrepreneurship and Regional Development*, 4 (1992), pp. 127–44.

14. Gibb (2000), op. cit., p. 22.

15. Gibb (2000), ibid., pp. 24–31.

16. Small Business Service, *A Government Action Plan for Small Business: The Evidence Base* (Department for Trade and Industry, 2004) (http://www.sbs.gov.uk).

17. Ibid.

18. Ibid., p. 4.

19. M. B. Holbrook and E. C. Hirschman, 'The Experiential Aspects of Consumption: Consumer Fantasies, Feeling and Fun', *Journal of Consumer Research*, 9 (1982), pp. 132–40.

20. P. M. Blau, J. W. Gustad, R. Jessor, H. S. Parnes and R. C. Wilcox, 'Occupational Choice: A Conceptual Framework', *Industrial and Labour Review*, 19 (1956), pp. 531–43.

21. K. Roberts, 'The Social Conditions, Consequences and Limitations of Careers Guidance', *British Journal of Guidance and Counselling*, 5 (1977), pp. 3.

22. V. H. Vroom, *Work and Motivation* (New York: Wiley, 1964).

CHAPTER 12

Intervention methods (objectives, structures and approaches)

Contents

KEY CONCEPTS

This chapter covers:

- The reasons why governments feel the need to intervene to promote aspects of enterprise, but often do so without an overall strategy.
- The frequent lack of clarity of intervention objectives.

- The very wide variety of possible structures for, and methods of, intervention.
- Developments in enterprise policy and delivery systems in the UK and the evolution of EU policy towards enterprise development.
- Typical instruments for intervention in the UK and other EU countries.

LEARNING OBJECTIVES

By the end of this chapter the reader should:

- Understand the reasons why governments intervene to support entrepreneurship and small business.
- Appreciate that governments do intervene but often do not have clear objectives or overall strategies.
- Appreciate the range of possible areas and methods for intervention in the UK and other EU countries.
- Understand the main developments in policy towards entrepreneurship and small business and how the policy is being delivered in the UK.
- Be aware of the major developments in EU policy for entrepreneurship and small business.
- Understand the range of forms of assistance and their application in specific fields.

Introduction

Because of the growth in the perceived importance of smaller firms for economic development, virtually every country in the developed and developing world is now intervening in some way to promote enterprise skills, to encourage more entrepreneurs and to grow more indigenous businesses. These same countries are looking at 'best practice' in places such as the United States, the UK and Ireland. But are they importing the cure or the disease?

Some of the motivations and justifications for these interventions have been described in Chapter 10, and some of the theories, models and assumptions behind them in Chapter 11. This chapter describes the array of objectives, structures and approaches used for intervention. These are the means, not the strategies, used for the promotion of entrepreneurship and small business, and indeed often the strategies appear to be missing. Indeed, despite apparently hundreds of initiatives in the UK since the end of the 1970s, an overall strategy, in the sense of a coherent set of objectives and associated means of achieving them, was lacking at least until 2002. Up to then, the last real attempt in the UK to articulate a coherent SME policy in a single document, some claim, was the *Bolton Report On Small Firms* in 1971. A brief overview of the UK approach to policy in this field follows.

Enterprise policy in the UK

The demand for entrepreneurs has probably never been greater than at the present time. Since the 1970s, however, there have been successive attempts to increase the supply of entrepreneurs across all developed economies. Indeed it is possible to identify four main types of enterprise policy over the period.[1]

Prior to the 1980s support was based around corporate capitalism and large enterprises, and often aimed to make them larger through mergers. There was no meaningful small business policy, although some support began to emerge following the *Bolton Report* in 1971. During the 1980s a major emphasis was placed on increasing the quantity of enterprises, not least in the face of persistent unemployment and the desire to create an enterprise culture. The number of enterprises grew from 2.4 million to 3.6 million in the decade but many would dispute that this was mainly due to policy support (see Chapter 13).

The 1990s it is argued was a period when the emphasis shifted to improving the quality of new and small enterprises. Of particular interest were businesses with significant value added, in the new technologies, knowledge driven and export or internationally orientated. This emphasis was driven by the desire to push up productivity (not least relative to the United States and Germany), concerns about the high failure rate of new enterprises and recognition of the role of deadweight and displacement effects. Nor was it clear that start-ups would provide sufficient jobs to replace those being lost from large organisations. Indeed, 'perhaps for the first time, there was an explicit DTI target. The target was to concentrate on businesses between 10 and 200 employees which had the potential to grow.'[2]

This explicit emphasis upon growth 'did not survive for long for several reasons'.[3] These had to do with the problems inherent in offering advice effectively as well as to a change in government in 1997. In addition, as the 1990s passed, greater awareness of how economic growth occurs and the role of innovation through people put the spotlight on the way in which skilled people could commercialise their innovations.

Initiatives to improve the education and skills of the population and increase linkages between industry and universities became popular. Thus there has been an attempt to rebalance support between new start-ups and growth business, often with a sectoral emphasis. Cluster policies emerged, based on the premise that knowledge is transferred within social networks of professionals. The general idea is that 'social networks of professionals ... with access to highly valuable specialist tacit knowledge, interact with each other to produce new forms of knowledge. ... These knowledge spillovers subsequently create competitive advantages.'[4]

The other discernible policy aim of this period has been to seek for equality of opportunity to participate in enterprise, especially amongst disadvantaged groups (particularly women and ethnic minorities). The emphasis on social enterprise is also a noticeable development as an attempt at, *inter alia*, regeneration and greater social inclusion.

Greene et al. conclude that 'little has changed over the last ten years, bar an unprecedented growth in the "enterprise industry" and that enterprise policy has long been concerned with cutting off the corners of regional disadvantage.'[5]

At least part of the reason for the absence of a coherent strategy is the fact that the small business sector is characterised by very considerable diversity, with competing interests making the prioritisation of needs very difficult for politicians and policy-makers. This has led Bennett among others to suggest that 'Fragmentation of government programmes for SMEs appears to reflect the fragmentation and variety of the problems that SMEs confront.'[6] On the other hand the Audit Commission saw the situation just as 'a patchwork quilt of complexity and idiosyncrasy'.[7]

A more recent attempt at a coherent strategy was formulated in December 2002 by the Small Business Service (SBS) (created in the year 2000 as part of the then Department of Trade and Industry and reformed in 2006). It published *Small Business and Government: The Way Forward*, which sought to lay out a strategic framework for a government-wide approach to helping small business.[8] This policy paper under-pinned *A Government Action Plan for Small Business*, produced in February 2004 and formalising the government's commitment to delivering the strategic framework.[9] It identified seven strategic themes as follows:

- building an enterprise culture
- encouraging a more dynamic start-up market
- building the capability for small business growth
- improving access to finance for small business
- encouraging more enterprise in disadvantaged communities and under-represented groups
- improving small business experience of government services
- developing better regulation and policy.

According to the SBS, the Action Plan contained 69 'actions' and 21 'measures of success'.[10]

The report of the Public Accounts Committee (PAC) notes that the SBS created a performance management framework (see Figure 12.1 – and also the section on 'the evidence base' in Chapter 11) to assist it to pursue its vision for small business.[11] The framework comprised three aims, three targets and the above-mentioned strategic themes. The PAC report referred to the 'complexity of the performance management framework' and reflected that 'as there is no direct correlation between the strategic themes and government aims and targets, satisfying each of the strategic themes may still not be sufficient to meet all the government aims and targets'.

In this the UK is not alone. An OECD paper reviews the experience of its member countries in encouraging entrepreneurship and their contribution to job creation.[12] Amongst its observations are:

- Member governments lack a comprehensive strategy towards entrepreneurship and job creation.
- The explicit promotion of entrepreneurship as a source of job creation is rare in policy formulation.
- Better policy co-ordination is needed to exploit more fully the potential of entrepreneurship and new business in order to help start-ups and existing firms in the creation of new jobs.

Lundström and Stevenson reflect that:

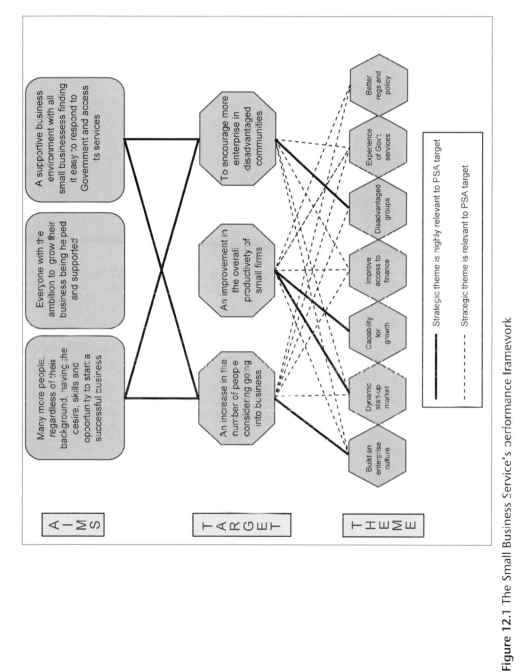

Figure 12.1 The Small Business Service's performance framework

Source: House of Commons, Committee of Public Accounts, 'Supporting Small Business', HC262 (London: The Stationery Office, 2007).

[because] entrepreneurship itself is still not a well defined concept and the differences between SME and entrepreneurship policies are unclear, efforts to become a more 'entrepreneurial economy' are somewhat impeded. Instead of assuming an integrated approach to stimulating a higher level of entrepreneurial activity, governments currently tend to add on projects and activities in a piecemeal incremental fashion.[13]

Enterprise, entrepreneurship and small business policies

One consequence of the lack of clear definitions of words such as 'enterprise' and 'entrepreneurship' is that there is a related confusion about what is meant by enterprise, entrepreneurship and small business policies. They can be perceived as interchangeable, overlapping or quite separate and, as a result, important policy differences can often be obscured or ignored.

There can be at least three distinct policy areas which some people now distinguish with the labels 'small business', 'entrepreneurship' and 'enterprise', although those labels have also been used with less discrimination. These policy areas are:

- *Small business policies*: These are policies for stimulating growth of already established small business, variations of which have also been called a 'growth' or 'business growth' policy and a 'backing winners' policy. This sort of policy tends to focus on the businesses and what will help them to grow, not the entrepreneurs behind them.

- *Entrepreneurship policies*: These are policies for encouraging and facilitating more people to take up self-employment. These policies are centred on people and on what will persuade or help them to start businesses; they can also be referred to as 'business start' or 'business birth rate' policies.

- *Enterprise policies*: These are policies for encouraging enterprise in its broad sense, much – but not all – of which may be manifest as new business starts. These policies are clearly focused on people, both as individuals and in groups, and seek to develop skills and attitudes likely to assist people to be more successful in any chosen career or endeavour. However the description 'enterprise' may also be applied to policies which try to incorporate the promotion of both entrepreneurship and small business growth, or the term 'enterprise policy' may be used to describe a combination of both entrepreneurship and small business policies. It can also be used to refer to a policy for business and industry generally.

This terminology, because it can at least separate entrepreneurship from small business policy, facilitates a distinction which is important because these policies require very different approaches. A small business policy should be about business development while policies for entrepreneurship and enterprise should be about wider personal, social and economic development. In a recent government report in the Republic of Ireland *Towards Developing an Enterprise Policy*, the authors note that the overriding objective of SME policy 'is to strengthen existing business', while the main focus of entrepreneurship policy is to stimulate 'a greater supply of entrepreneurs'.[14] Building on Lundström and Stevenson, they assert that an entrepreneurship policy should have the following characteristics (see Figure 12.2):

- be focused primarily on individuals, not firms
- support the needs of people as they move through the earliest stages of the entrepreneurial process from awareness to intent to pre-start-up to early post-start-up
- make extensive use of soft policy supports
- in its implementation, incorporate a broad set of institutional partners in the make up of the support environment (e.g. educators, the media and a diverse set of government ministries) which necessitates intergovernmental, horizontal approaches and strategies involving a range of departments, regulating bodies and other agencies.

They add 'the focus of entrepreneurship policy is on the individual entrepreneur and the economic, technological, institutional, cultural, personal and local communitycontext.'

Indeed, there is evidence that it is an oversimplification to perceive that all business start-ups are influenced by the same determinants. Burke and Shabbir, utilising US data, suggest that while the factors emphasised in labour economics (unemployment push effects, negatively affected by wage increases and stimulated by the amount of venture capital under management) 'give a good account of microfirm start-ups, these factors do not stimulate large firm start-ups'.[15] Larger ventures are associated with factors emphasised in industrial and finance economics (fiscal initiatives, namely corporation and income tax, and new investments undertaken by venture capitalists).

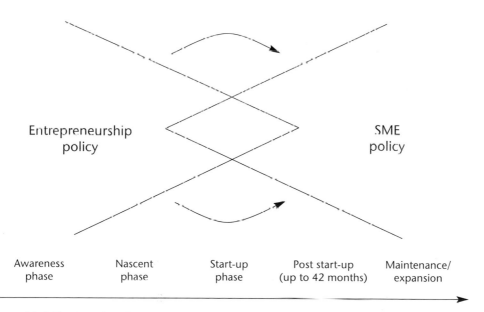

Awareness phase   Nascent phase   Start-up phase   Post start-up (up to 42 months)   Maintenance/ expansion

Figure 12.2 The interface between entrepreneurship policy and SME policy

Source: L. Stevenson and A. Lundström, *Beyond the Rhetoric: Defining Entrepreneurship Policy and its Best Practice Components* (Stockholm: Swedish Foundation for Small Business Research, 2002), p. 27.

Lundström and Stevenson developed Figure 12.2 to illustrate the interrelated, but at the same time distinctive, policy domains of entrepreneurship and small and medium-sized enterprise (SME) policy.

Unfortunately this distinction is often not appreciated, with the result that even those who formulate the policies sometimes mix them up, and therefore mix different objectives or fail to select appropriate means for achieving them. Different words can mean the same or different things depending upon who is using them and in what context. In this chapter the labels used are generally those applied by the policy originators or 'owners', but an explanation is offered where this is thought to be necessary.

> The scope of entrepreneurship policy is very broad and is differentiated from SME policy by its breathe (sic) and horizontal nature.
>
> Entrepreneurship policy is primarily focused on individuals and the economic, technological, institutional, cultural and personal context in which he/she chooses entrepreneurship over employment.
>
> It seeks to ensure that the needs of people are met, and unnecessary barriers removed, as they move through the earliest stages of the entrepreneurial process from awareness to intent, to the active planning and gathering of the necessary resources, to the early days of the new venture as it gets off the ground.
>
> In its implementation, entrepreneurship policy must incorporate a broad set of institutional partners, which necessitate the involvement of Government and a wide range of public and private interests.
>
> The degree to which entrepreneurship is given due political recognition, relevant to its central importance in creating competitive advantage in a knowledge economy, will be highly influential on the eventual success of the policy.
>
> Source: Forfás, *Towards Developing an Entrepreneurship Policy*, Dublin, September 2007, p. 78.

Linking entrepreneurship to economic growth

As noted in the previous section, it is important, one might even say necessary, when viewing the role of policy and how it might influence the achievement of objectives, to have some kind of picture of how key components and elements in the system relate to one another. GEM (see Chapter 4) is one example of a project which has established and is exploring a correlation between entrepreneurship and economic growth, but it has not yet determined just what the link between them is. Nevertheless, if economic growth is an objective, an apparent relationship between entrepreneurship and economic growth might suggest that an entrepreneurship policy should at least be tried. Having a theory tried and tested in terms of a working model of this relationship would be ideal. It is evident, however, that there is still some way to go before there is such an understanding of how economic systems operate. Specifically the nature and functioning of the link between individuals, entrepreneurship and economic growth is not yet adequately

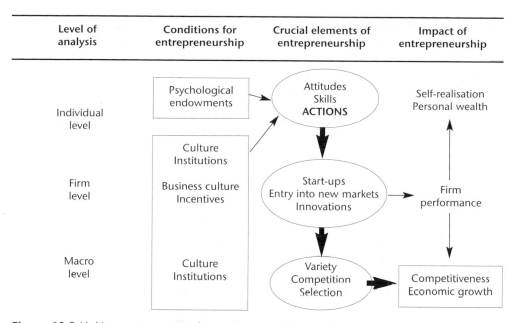

Level of analysis	Conditions for entrepreneurship	Crucial elements of entrepreneurship	Impact of entrepreneurship

Figure 12.3 Linking entrepreneurship and economic growth

Source: from S. Wennekers and R. Thurik, 'Institutions, entrepreneurship and economic performance', in A. Lundström and L. Stevenson, *Entrepreneurship Policy For the Future*, Special edition (Stockholm: Swedish Foundation for Small Business Research, 2001), p.70.

understood. It is not surprising, therefore, that there is also a general lack of clarity about whether and how to develop integrated entrepreneurship and small business development policies. Lundström and Stevenson have proposed, however, an illustrative model of the linkages between entrepreneurship and economic growth (shown in Figure 12.3) which highlights some areas where more research is required to establish, *inter alia*, the nature of any linkages, their causal relationships, their magnitudes and the lead times.

Objectives

To be able to understand and evaluate strategies, the objectives must be explicit. Having a strategy implies having objectives and targets, and therein lies a problem for policy-makers. The objectives of entrepreneurship or small business strategies are often not explicit.

Storey claims that the objectives of public policies to assist small firms are rarely specified directly.[16] Instead, it is necessary for analysts to infer objectives by observing the policies in operation, rather than by finding them clearly stated as a coherent response to an agreed role that government plays. According to de Koning et al. this is true of most European countries.[17] Inferring objectives is made harder by the frequent failure of policy-makers to distinguish between means and ends. However, the following objectives appear to be generally agreed:

- increased wealth through economic growth
- job creation
- increased competition
- promotion of and spread of innovation and technology
- greater diversification and choice
- revitalisation of traditional sectors/international competitiveness
- expanding and strengthening the production chain
- more efficient markets
- greater social cohesion (including removal of discrimination).

ILLUSTRATION 12.1
The common objectives of 'small firm policy'*

The objectives of government SME policies – intermediate and final, stated and unstated – are likely to be one or more of the following:

1. Increase employment.

2. Increase number of start-ups.

3. Promote use of advisors.

4. Increase competition.

5. Promote 'efficient' markets.

6. Promote technology diffusion.

7. Increase wealth.

8. Get re-elected.

David Storey[18]

*   Here the term 'small firm policy' covers the full range of policies, including both those for entrepreneurship and those for small business.

Organisation, confusion and churn

Another problem which, at least in the UK, can make it hard to identify objectives is articulated by Perren et al. as:[19]

> a plethora of organisations and initiatives that have been identified as having some part to play in this area. ... The continuing churn and name changes adds to the challenge.
>
> The majority of the organisations identified and many of the initiatives are funded through the public purse, either fully or through part subsidy. Therefore the government is largely responsible for the volume and fragmentation of organisations and initiatives in the area. Indeed the inflexibility of funding

regimes often appears to encourage the development of new initiatives even if there are similar schemes already in operation. The aim may have been to respond to perceived needs, but ... it appears to have resulted in a tangled and confusing assortment of dislocated organisations and initiatives. ... Many organisations in the area appear to be driven by government agendas and funding rather than any direct demand from SMEs themselves.

Informants, and by implication their organisations, appear to have a relatively narrow sphere of knowledge and relationships. ... They can be seen as occupying micro-worlds that are embedded within a wider system of which they have partial knowledge. No single organisation emerges as providing a central bridge between the various ... worlds. The inevitable consequence is that any new initiatives run the risk of being developed in isolation from what presently exists.

While it might seem surprising to some people that apparently little regard should be paid in this way to the consumers' needs, this is yet another example of market forces. If the government is funding the initiatives, then the government is the customer. It is not surprising therefore that the organisations delivering initiatives pursue the money and follow the customer's agenda, not that of the consumers.

The result, however, is a small firms policy (and it is still largely about small businesses) that has been described as 'a patchwork quilt'[20] and 'an excess of loosely connected and apparently uncoordinated policy initiatives shooting off in all directions, generating noise and interest, but not commensurate light'.[21]

Targets

> Too often the target is anything you happen to hit.
>
> David Storey[22]

While there may be a range of objectives which are generally agreed, it is unusual for governments to set targets for their (enterprise) policies in the sense of measured outputs to be achieved within a given time frame. Some would argue the need for such targets if government's attention is to be adequately focused on what it is trying to achieve and how it expects to do so. On the other hand it is problematical to argue for targets for interventions when it is not known whether they will work, how they work, within what time scales they will achieve what outputs, or how those outputs will in turn lead to the desired outcomes. To be able to predict outcomes in a system requires knowledge not just of its inputs but also of the process which links them to outputs and in turn to the outcomes. This process, as previously noted, is often not sufficiently understood in the field of enterprise development for it to be possible to predict outcomes accurately.

Nevertheless governments have been attracted occasionally to setting targets for programmes as, without them, it is argued that 'If you don't know where you are trying to go, any road will take you there.' Intermediate targets, or 'milestones' can also provide a form of progress measurement. A recent example of the problems inherent in setting targets was in Scotland where, early in the 1990s, Scottish Enterprise embarked on a 'business birthrate strategy'.

This strategy reflected what was felt to be an entrepreneurial deficit in Scotland compared with the most prosperous areas of the UK, and sought an increase in the country's historic rate of new firm formation. The target set was that this rate should be increased by a factor of 3.5. This was not, in the event, achieved, leading many people to regard the strategy itself as a failure. However, an alternative view was that it appeared to have been more successful in changing attitudes to enterprise and entrepreneurship in a positive direction than in increasing the business birth rate within the relatively short timescale originally set (see also Case 12.1).

CASE 12.1
Scotland's Birthrate Strategy

In Scotland, at the beginning of the 1990s, Scottish Enterprise introduced its 'Birthrate Strategy'. This initiative derived from the knowledge that Scotland's business start-up rate was considerably below that of the most prosperous regions of the UK. The target set was to increase the start-up rate by a factor of 3.5. It was recognised subsequently that setting such an ambitious target (higher than the prosperous south-east of England) was counterproductive, in that failure to achieve it induced some to view the strategy overall as a failure. A review of the strategy in 2001 concluded that its impact on new firm formation was an increase of around 3 per cent. In reality, whatever the pressures to achieve an explicit definition of success, it needs to be recognised that creating a more entrepreneurial economy, the real aim of the strategy, requires a focus on the longer term. Moreover an entrepreneurial economy exhibits itself in more than the rate of business start-ups which is only one expression of enterprise.

The former Welsh Development Agency had set itself a target of a 65 per cent increase in the rate of new firm formation, and Northern Ireland sought to bring its start-up rate up to the UK average. These regions seek to overcome what they regard as an 'entrepreneurial deficit' in similar ways to Scotland.

Points raised

Scotland's experience showed a downside of setting targets when the socio-economic dynamics are not fully appreciated and of setting a too ambitious timescale for achieving them. Nevertheless the public sector environment is such that similar targets are still being set by others.

It should be recognised that seeking a more entrepreneurial economy requires the changing of attitudes to entrepreneurship and other fundamental changes which themselves are long term and will not be apparent solely in the number of new firms (or jobs) created, and that even these may take many years to be realised. Inevitably measurement of deeper changes will take time and involve other indicators. When setting performance targets, governments and agencies appear to rely often on short-term indicators to measure what is inevitably long-term change. There continues to be the tendency towards policy and programme implementation being 'target driven' to achieve an easily measurable definition of success in the shorter term. (The possible counterproductive/dysfunctional side effects of such an approach were evident in the early 2000s in the UK in the health sector, where the length of hospital waiting lists was seen as a key indicator of the success of its National Health Service. The result however was that patients where taken off the lists by a variety of means, many of which did not actually involve treating them. This had the effect of reducing the numbers on the lists but had nothing to do with providing a better service.) Thus:

> adoption of a set of intermediate targets employing traditional measures does not accurately reflect an agency's contribution towards improving the entrepreneurial culture. Such targets do not show the nature of change within an economy and offer little scope for subtlety of focus.[23]

ILLUSTRATION 12.2
Government policies are not adequately promoting entrepreneurship

Overall, Danish experts did not, in 2000, believe that government policies were aimed at, or gave priority to, entrepreneurship. Entrepreneurship, according to the experts, was subject to political whim (according to ideology) and was used as a regulating means to other ends rather than being an issue of self-standing interest. The experts were also highly critical of those government policies which are aimed at promoting entrepreneurship, claiming that they were short-sighted and produced equally short-term initiatives which lacked continuity and therefore had less effect. Accordingly, there was a need for a long-term strategy that provided a sense of stability in this area. Further criticism was levelled at the government's lack of concern about the administrative burden faced by small firms, the taxation system, a lack of co-ordination between ministries and a general lack of understanding of entrepreneurship on the part of politicians.[24] (But see Illustration 12.4.)

Structures for intervention

The following description of organisational arrangements focuses primarily on aspects of small business support in the UK. It serves to highlight the relevant problems and principles which have a wider relevance for the formulation and implementation of entrepreneurship and small business policy in many other countries.

Responsibility for small business policy lies primarily within the newly created Department of Business, Enterprise and Regulatory Reform (BERR) but is influenced and affected by the actions of the Department for Innovation, Universities and Skills, the Department of the Environment, Food and Rural Affairs and the Department of Culture, Media and Sport, not to mention the Treasury (finance and taxation). Guaranteeing consistent and coherent treatment of the sector is made difficult by this dispersal of policies across ministries. As a result, support schemes have tended to grow piecemeal.

The Public Accounts Committee (in reviewing the performance of the Small Business Service (see below) in 2007) commented that: 'The SBS was only ever responsible for a small part of the total government budget that provided support to small business and it had no formal authority over the actions of other government bodies'[25] and 'the performance of the SBS depends to a large degree on the performance of the rest of government.'[26]

An important distinction also has to be made between the formulation of small business policy and its implementation. In the UK, as in many EU countries, the formulation of such policy is very largely determined at the level of central government, while the implementation of measures is achieved through a network of regional agencies. Within the overall framework of policy, these agencies can, and indeed are often expected to, alter the emphasis and priorities of implementation according to local needs and circumstances. Indeed this change towards decentralisation of the delivery of support services has been a significant trend in many countries over recent years. In the UK, for the most part, the public sector business support structure has been undergoing yet further restructuring and refocusing as described below. This constant process of change, which is intended to produce greater effectiveness and efficiency in support, is viewed by some as self-defeating in that structures are not allowed to settle. Until April 2001 the situation which prevailed was one which included such agencies as the Training and Enterprise Councils (TECs) in England and Wales and the Local Enterprise Companies (LECs) in Scotland. In addition regional and local authorities contribute a network of support services, while Scottish Enterprise (SE) in Scotland and the Welsh Assembly government in Wales have countrywide jurisdictions like their Northern Ireland counterpart: Invest Northern Ireland.

The TECs and LECs were complemented in Great Britain by the establishment of the DTI-initiated Business Links in England, by Business Connect in Wales and by Business Shops in Scotland. Business Links were funded by the DTI, but this funding came through the TEC network, which was the responsibility of the then Department for Education and Employment. TECs and Business Links therefore found themselves under the direction of two different government departments.

The UK government established a new Small Business Service in April 2000 to provide a single organisation within government dedicated to promoting the interests of small firms. Its chief executive reported to the Secretary of State for Trade and Industry. In addition, the chief executive was supported by a Small Business Council and a Small Business Investment Task Force (see Illustration 12.3).

ILLUSTRATION 12.3
The UK Small Business Service (SBS)

The objectives of the SBS were:

- to provide a strong voice for small firms at the heart of government
- to simplify and improve the quality and coherence of public support for small businesses
- to help small firms deal with regulation and compliance, and to ensure that small firms' interests are properly considered in future regulation.

In addition, the SBS aimed to 'promote enterprise across society and particularly in under-represented and disadvantaged groups'.[27] It sought to develop a single gateway for business advice, enabling businesses to access an extensive range of information via the Internet or the telephone.

In March 2001 a new Business Links network was launched, reducing the number of Business Links from 81 to 45 as part of the SBS's drive to streamline and improve the network of organisations running business support services (and further rationalised with the creation of Regional Development Agencies).

In January 2001 the SBS launched its strategy paper *Think Small First*, outlining a framework for government support for UK SMEs. It highlighted three priority areas:

- the prevailing culture and environment, including macro-economic stability and the policy environment
- the regulatory framework for business
- support for business at each stage of the business life cycle, including people, skills, advice, workspace, IT, finance and international trade.

Its overall aim was that by 2005, 'the UK should be the best place in the world to start and grow a business.' The SBS also runs national initiatives to help small firms, such as the Small Firms Loan Guarantee Scheme (SFLGS) and grants for technology transfer.

Business support in Scotland, Wales and Northern Ireland

The SBS's services were largely offered only in England, unless it was responsible for delivering specific schemes which it is agreed should continue on a UK-wide basis.

Scotland has its own business support structure in place through Scottish Enterprise and Highlands and Islands Enterprise. The Scottish Parliament and executive are trying to create a simpler and more cohesive structure and to improve support for small businesses. For example, the Enterprise Networks are being reviewed, Local Enterprise forums are being established, services are being brought together under the Small Business Gateway brand, and a Business Growth Unit and Business Growth Fund have been established.

In Wales, the Business Connect network is a single gateway to business support for small firms. The management has recently been strengthened by the establishment of a business-led Management Board, Business Connect Wales

Ltd. This development is one part of the agenda to improve the existing support network.

In Northern Ireland, since April 2002 LEDU has merged with both the Industrial Development Board of Northern Ireland, which provided support for bigger businesses and inward investment, and the Industrial Research and Technology Unit to provide one comprehensive business support network. The new body is known as Invest Northern Ireland and is a company limited by guarantee, which is intended to give it greater flexibility than if it were part of the Civil Service.

Source: Based on *Finance for Small Firms: An Eighth Report* (London: Bank of England, 2001), pp. 21–2.

The SBS, at an early stage of its life, was the subject of further restructuring due to a review of the Department of Trade and Industry to which it reports. The main aim was the desire to separate its policy and regulatory functions from its business support functions. In October 2006, a ministerial announcement indicated that the SBS would be reformed to operate as a policy unit within the DTI's Enterprise and Business Group. It would focus on influencing the business environment and supporting entrepreneurs, but lose its 'next step' executive agency status and its service delivery role. In July 2007, a further ministerial announcement renamed the SBS as the 'Enterprise Directorate' within the newly created Department for Business, Enterprise and Regulatory Reform (BERR), itself a re-creation of the DTI. With substantial staff reductions over the years, the Enterprise Directorate 'continues to be the expert policy unit on small business issues throughout Government'.[28] Since its creation in 2000 it has undergone a gradual transition from being a deliverer of services to influencing government to take appropriate actions to support small business.

The business support landscape was further altered in England in 2001 by the creation of business-led Regional Development Agencies (RDAs) and the Learning and Skills Council for England (LSC), while greater powers were also devolved to the Scottish Parliament and Welsh Assembly. The RDAs are an attempt to give greater influence at a regional level to economic policy. The LSC is the leading body in post-16-years learning and skills development and operates through 47 local arms known as local LSCs. They have a key role in human resource development for small businesses and replaced the Training and Enterprise Councils (TECs).

Business Link and most business development initiatives were devolved to RDAs from 2005, with the result that different 'business support' strategies now operate within each region of England as well as Scotland, Wales and Northern Ireland.

The role of Business Links and their counterparts is to create partnerships of providers of small business services in their region. Such providers include LSCs, chambers of commerce, local authorities and enterprises agencies. The aim is to ensure that the small business consumer is presented with a seamless collection of services accessed through 'one-stop shops', or through 'first-stop shops'. The expected benefits are:

- bringing the main suppliers of enterprise support together in partnership arrange-ments so as to bring about their meaningful integration and coherence, and for the client, a single point of contact
- upgrading the quality of services and support
- having a strong and visible network across Britain with a high degree of physical concentration of supply partners in each location.

Although greater efficiency, professionalism and quality of impact are believed to be possible where services are concentrated, it is difficult and very unusual to bring together individuals and organisations offering support services into close physical proximity. Mostly, what is achieved or sought is in fact a 'first-stop shop' where users can receive advice and information from a range of services immediately available and can be signposted to those others believed to be most useful to them.

Two different approaches actively evolved for such networking: Business Links in England aimed to be 'one-stop shops', while Business Shops in Scotland are based on a 'first-stop shop' approach. The distinction between the concept of a 'one-stop shop' and a 'first-stop shop' is however often missed. While both derive from a desire to reduce proliferation and dispersal of support services and to make accessing them easier and less confusing for the potential user, the 'one-stop shop' approach aims to concentrate them, or at least their representatives, into one location. On the other hand the 'first-stop shop' concept assumes that it will often not be feasible to concen-trate all the relevant sources of support in this way. Instead it is suggested that there should be initial contact points, the 'first-stop shops', which will either offer assis-tance directly if they can, or will be able to signpost the inquirer to the right place for specific assistance. The aim is that the knowledge throughout the network about the other organisations in it should be such that an inquirer to one, if he or she does not get the right place initially, will be so directed that his or her second stop will be correct. (The right place might therefore be the second place to be contacted, which is why this approach is also sometimes referred to as the 'second-stop shop' concept.) This is a different approach from a 'one-stop shop' and indeed it has been further observed that one does not get a 'second-stop shop' by aiming at a 'one-stop shop' and missing.

Part of the problem for the 'one-stop shop' is that, while government-organised or government-controlled organisations can be instructed by government to behave in a particular way, others cannot. Because of the potential social and other benefits of enterprise and small business, many other organisations have sought to offer support or assistance. Small businesses are more likely to want to maintain their independence and sense of identity and are therefore more likely to resist conform-ing to the mould of a 'one-stop shop'. Indeed there would seem to be an element of incongruity in requiring organisations, whose aim is essentially to support enter-prise and its associated varieties, themselves to conform to an externally deter-mined strategy or mode of operation. The first-stop shop approach can have problems in that the staff can be of variable quality, creating in the minds of users the impression that people within the system are unlikely to be able to offer the quality and range of support needed across the range of business issues. The issue of one-stop shops has gained additional prominence in the EU as the Commission seeks to ensure its member countries make the challenge of developing a business no more difficult for migrants than for their own citizens. Ensuring an adequate information and guidance service, easily available to all regardless of language, is feared by some to impose undue costs on business service organisations (see Case 12.3 and Chapter 13).

> The notion of a one-stop shop is, for serious entrepreneurial regions, simply untenable.
>
> Ron Botham [29]

The result of all these efforts is, as already noted, a rather fragmented structure assessed variously as a 'labyrinth of initiatives' and 'a muddle'. The Better Regulation Task Force 'struggled with the justification for so many bodies on the ground'.[30]

Approaches

There are essentially two broad approaches to achieving entrepreneurship or small business policy objectives, however ambiguously those objectives are stated:

- The first approach is the one that concentrates on the creation of a favourable environment for business creation and growth. This policy approach results in measures to liberalise trade, to deregulate, to privatise, and to reform legal and taxation regimes as well as to create a positive climate to reinforce a culture of enterprise. Not all these measures are designed with only, or even mainly, small businesses in mind, but a number are aimed at addressing distortions or areas of market failure that are believed to harm smaller businesses specifically.

- The second approach is that of supporting the actual start-up and growth of individual businesses by providing direct assistance to the individuals or businesses concerned.

These two approaches are not mutually exclusive, and in nearly all countries they are adopted simultaneously. This was for instance specifically acknowledged in the UK by the former Department of Employment, which stated:

> There are three strands in the Government's approach to small firms. First, and of most importance, the role of the Government is to ensure that small firms can flourish in conditions of fair competition and to create space and incentives for enterprise by minimising taxation, regulations and red tape. Second, the Government strongly supports and reinforces the change to more positive social attitudes towards the small business sector. Third, the Government helps to fill gaps in the supply side by providing commercial services for small firms, largely to improve their access to finance, information, professional advice and training. Wherever possible the Government's approach is provided in partnership with the private sector.[31]

A multi-strand approach is not however universally accepted. It has for instance been argued by many, on the basis of numerous surveys, that the main factors which restrict the growth of businesses relate to the macro-economy. Accordingly the Confederation of British Industry's (CBI's) SME Council has claimed:

> It is through the creation of a healthy economy and conditions for growth that employment will be generated. ... The CBI therefore believes that Governments should focus on creating the right conditions for SMEs to start and grow rather than introducing individual policy objectives aimed at market distortions.[32]

Policies and instruments

To achieve the objective of intervention, policies and instruments are adopted which tend to operate to achieve three main effects:[33]

- *Risk reduction*: the use of macro-economic policies (e.g. taxation, interest rates) to stabilise the economy and reduce uncertainty.
- *Cost reduction*: the use of grants, subsidies or low-cost loans to reduce the cost of inputs to the business. These can be targeted (e.g. a grant to a specific business) or general (e.g. to reduce energy/fuel costs or labour costs).
- *Increase the flow of information/advice*: to make information more readily available on trends in international markets, national/local issues and government programmes for small business. This can be through targeted supports (and information services) or general publicity.

The main UK government small business policies have been categorised as shown in Table 12.1.

The annual reports of the European Observatory for SMEs have distinguished between policy fields and instruments. To quote one of them:

> Although the instrumental design of schemes aiming at the same target can differ by Member State, the fields SME policy measures focus on tend to converge towards a set of nine fields of activity. These are:

Start-ups and growth	R&D	Capital and finance
Investment	Exports	Co-operation
Subcontracting	Education	Job creation[34]

The instruments of intervention identified, each of which can be applied to one or more fields, are:

- direct subsidies or grants
- subsidised loans
- loan guarantee/participation
- tax relief
- service

- export guarantees
- subsidised start-up for unemployed
- subsidised personnel
- subsidised buildings, power, communication networks, sites.

All the instruments of intervention listed above are geared towards the second of the two approaches described earlier: intervention at the level of specific businesses or individuals. The Observatory report also indicates that, of these instruments, financial inducements are the most popular form of intervention in support of many policy fields. Inducements commonly take the form of direct subsidies, grants or loan guarantees, and subsidies are used to reduce the cost of loans, employees, premises and various services.

Van Wijngaarden and Van der Horst offer a similar framework. They identify the most important 'fields' and 'instruments' (measures taken in the different policy fields to achieve the objectives) as shown in Table 12.2.[35] Again, the fields are a mix of more general and specific areas, and combine market segments and functions with processes. Indeed, information and counselling appear both as a policy field and as an instrument!

The frameworks shown in the table make no real attempt to relate intervention

Table 12.1 UK government SME policies

Macro policies
- Interest rates
- Taxation
- Public spending
- Inflation

Deregulation and simplification
- Cutting 'red tape'
- Legislative exemptions
- Legal form

Sectoral and problem-specific policies
- High-tech firms
- Rural enterprises
- Social enterprises / social economy
- Ethnic businesses
- Women-owned businesses

Finance assistance
- Enterprise Investment Scheme
- Small Firms Loan Guarantee Scheme
- Venture Capital Funds
- Grants

Indirect assistance
- Information and advice
- Training
- Consultancy counselling / mentoring
- Network development (for example for owners and business angels)

Source: Adapted from D. J. Storey, *Understanding the Small Business Sector* (London: Routledge, 1994), p.269.

Table 12.2 Policy fields and instruments

Field	Instrument(s)
General tax facilities	
Regional development	Financial means (guarantees on loans, venture capital, insurance)
Technology and R & D	
Export	
Employment	Fiscal regulations (tariffs, exemptions)
Start-ups	
Information and counselling	Information and counselling
Finance	
Education	Training
Business licensing	
Administrative simplification	Others (programmes and legislation)
Environment / energy	

Source: Adapted from K. de Lind Van Wijngaarden and R. Van der Horst, 'A Comparison of SME Policy In the EU Member States', *Business Growth and Profitability* (1996), 2(1), p.40.

measures to the stages in the growth of a business, as described in Chapter 7, or to the pre-start-up stage, which influences the number of new businesses created. Therefore the framework shown in Table 12.3 is offered in an attempt to categorise fields and instruments according to a stages-of-development model of business formation and growth. It suffers from the limitations associated with such modelling, summarised in Chapter 6, but it is intended to assist by providing greater coherence across target markets, ends and means.

While instruments (support measures) are general in description, the table outlines a representative range of the very many variations that apply. It is apparent that certain measures, such as information and counselling, finance and training, are available throughout most or all of the development stages of a business. However, both the nature and extent of delivery mechanisms can change at each stage.

Targeting

Policies that target some small businesses as opposed to others have been increasingly popular as they are perceived to offer more efficient and effective use of scarce resources. Targeting can be towards new start-ups, established businesses, export-oriented businesses, 'growth' sectors or women/ethnic businesses (and see Chapter 8).

The usual methods of targeting policy is to target those businesses which either:

- will benefit to the greatest extent from assistance (a 'need' measure)
- will yield the greatest policy benefit ('leverage' or 'value for money' measures) or
- avoid as far as possible displacement and non-additionality effects (additionality measures).[36]

The benefits of targeting a policy, as stated by Bauer, are that it can reduce the range of expenditure, it may focus resources where they are needed and it is easier to market.[37]

Table 12.3 A taxonomy of enterprise initiatives

Stage of business	Policy field or need	Instrument
Culture	A positive, encouraging and	Media advertising
Community programmes	supportive environment	Community programmes
		Capacity-building
		Role models
		Enterprise in education
Pre-start	Ideas	Spin-off ideas
		Technology transfer
		Ideas generation workshops and publications
	Small business know-how (accounts, finance, selling, marketing and so on)	Small business skills training
		Training trainers
	'Know-who' networks	Networking advice
		Network access points, for both business and technical assistance
	Advice	Pre-start counselling/mentoring
Start-up: external	Customers	Purchasing initiatives
	Suppliers	Local sourcing initiatives
		Trade directories
	Advice / consultancy: business	Business expertise available
		Coordination of third party provision (Business Links)
		Training, counselling and mentoring
		Websites
	Advice / consultancy: technical	Technical advice, research and so on
	Networks	Business clubs
		Export clubs
	Information	Databases
		Internet portals
	Producing the business plan	Business plan services
	Premises	Incubation centres
		Managed workspaces
		Business/science parks
Start-up: internal	Finance	Grants, loans, loan guarantee schemes
		Business angel networks
	Market expertise	
	Administration expertise	Training services
	Financial management	Advice/counselling
	Employment expertise	Mentors
	Company formation	

Table 12.3 (continued)

Stage of business	Policy field or need	Instrument
Established	Ideas	Ideas generation workshops
		Spin-off ideas
		Technology transfer programmes
	Encouragement	Guidance services, including 'one-stop shops'
	Specialist guidance	Banks, accountants
	Investment	Solicitors
Growth	Market opportunities, including exports	Trade missions
		Market visits
		Export development advisers
		Export credit insurance
		Market information: trends, contacts and so on
	Product development	Technical advice / support for product development
	Strategic approach	Development courses
	Management skills	Salary support
		Subsidised staff attachment programmes
		Benchmarking
	Finance	Grants and loans
		Business angel networks
Decline	Confidence	Mentors
	Customers	
	Money	
	Strategic review and planning	Advice and guidance
Termination	Legal and other advice	Provision of advice and counselling
Other dimensions	Business sector	Sector initiatives, including Sector-based training
	Business support environment	Information and education
All	Information on small business needs and behaviour	Research coordination
		Research databases
		Research centres
	General information and advice	Internet portals and other online assistance
	Legislative and other administrative developments	

He further states that a focus on growth businesses (10–200 employees) 'yields a target of 200,000 businesses', a focus on exporting businesses 'yields a target of about 100,000 businesses', and a focus on innovation or high-technology businesses 'yields a target of perhaps 100,000 businesses'.[38] The SMEs within each group would reduce the figures further. Warning of the dangers of targeting, he explains that:[39]

- Targeting can only be 'of the crudest kind – identifying a target for possible take-up rather than identifying a specific group where all will need to respond', on the basis that many businesses may choose not to take-up the support offered.

- Target groups are rarely stable. Businesses that exhibit growth, innovation or export behaviour in one period may not do so in another (albeit the tendency is in that direction)

- There is a certain in-built contradiction in a policy that seeks to give support to those which are already successful.

- It can be self-defeating to distinguish between growth and lifestyle businesses when the latter can be the growth business of tomorrow. 'The managerial gateway to access policy benefits must, therefore, be a flexible one, both for entry and exit.' And, he concludes, 'the safest policy of all is not to target, and leave open the choice of policy supports used to those best able to access them – the small business itself.'

Areas of intervention

The analysis framework in Figure 12.4 is an attempt to highlight the main fields of public policy in enterprise (including entrepreneurship and small business) support, and it includes the broad elements indicated below, which are considered in more detail on the following pages.

- The business environment is included. It affects the performance of all firms, not just small businesses, but it is nevertheless crucial to a healthy small business sector, regardless of firm size, motivation or stage of development. Improvement of the business environment, the first of the two broad approaches to small business support, as described above, is defined as comprising six broad categories: the economy, skills, infrastructure, regulations, fiscal policy and societal attitudes.

- Individuals and their businesses are also included. This field embraces:
  - The development of enterprising people (in the broad sense) and the supply of entrepreneurs who start businesses. (see Illustration 12.5).
  - Assisting the start-up business in its birth stages and subsequent aftercare. Such assistance is often viewed as critical not only to survival rates but also to the quality and quantity of the subsequent growers.
  - Removing the barriers and giving incentives to established businesses wishing to grow. The growth of businesses is often perceived as central to policy, and support for it is now quite common. Less common is support for the other, non-growing, businesses although they are still considered by some as potential growth businesses and therefore worthy of some attention. Intervention

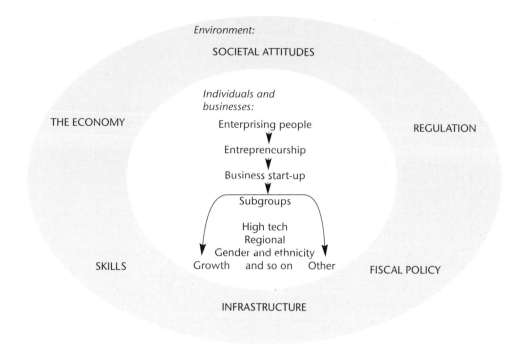

Figure 12.4 Enterprise policy analysis framework

often takes the form of support of specific sub-groups such as high-tech or exporting businesses, and there can also be a focus on selected sectors, geographic regions or sections of the population which are under-represented and/or which may have unrealised potential such as women, ethnic minorities and older people.

ILLUSTRATION 12.4
Identifying entrepreneurship framework conditions in Denmark

Denmark is a member of the International Consortium on Entrepreneurship (ICE), which is a consortium of leading entrepreneurship countries working to improve the analytical foundation for entrepreneurship policies. Working closely with the OECD, Denmark has recently endeavoured to identify the key factors conducive to entrepreneurship. The National Agency for Enterprise and Construction (FORA) has identified five factors, each of which comprises a number of policy areas believed to have an impact on those factors and thus on entrepreneurship (see Figure 12.5 and 12.6). NB: In the context of this policy, entrepreneurship is considered to be the entry and exit of firms and the creation of high growth firms.

Source: Based on Entrepreneurship Index 2006, available on http://ice.foranet.dk (accessed 2 July 2008) pp.24–5.

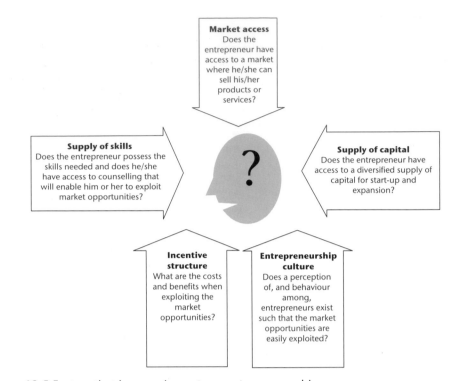

Figure 12.5 Factors that have an impact on entrepreneurship

Factors:

Market access	Supply of capital	Supply of skills	Incentives (motivation)	Culture
		Policy areas:		
Access barriers	Loan capital	Traditional business education	Income tax	Cultural and social norms
Access to international markets	Wealth and bequest tax	Entrepreneurship education	Corporate tax	Targeted initiatives
New knowledge transfer	Venture capital	Restart possibilities	Administrative burdens – start-up	Introducing entrepreneurship in primary education
Private demand	Stock markets	Entrepreneurship infrastructure (public)	Administrative burdens – operation	Communication on 'heroes'/'awards'
Public demand	Capital tax	Entrepreneurship. infrastructure (private)	Labour market regulation	
Testing facilities	Business angels		Bankruptcy legislation	
			Financial incentives	
			Social and health insurance	

Figure 12.6 Policy areas with an impact on the five factors

The business/enterprise environment

Addressing the business environment will affect all businesses, not just specific sectors such as small businesses. However Bannock argues that, rather than focusing on specific policies and programmes for small businesses, it is more productive to concentrate on improving what he calls the framework conditions for all enterprises, as these will often have a disproportionately beneficial effect upon small enterprises.[40]

The economy

Most governments strive for stable growth, low inflation, low interest rates and a steady exchange rate as the economic backcloth against which it is thought that businesses can plan effectively in the context of reasonable certainty about future trading circumstances. It is thus supposed that the impacts of taxation and public spending are critically important policy intervention measures. The effects of the trade cycle upon the birth, death and growth-rates of all businesses may generally override the impact of all interventions, and the effects can be particularly severe on the more vulnerable small firms sector.

Fiscal policy

There are various fiscal measures aimed at helping the growth and survival of small businesses. These range from a reduced rate of corporation tax to inheritance tax concessions and extended value added tax (VAT) exemption thresholds, as well as tax incentives for business angels and investors.

Although, when asked, small business owners will say that they want lower taxes to allow them to keep more of the rewards for enterprise, the relationship between lower taxes (more disposable income) and economic activity does not appear to be straightforward. For example, Rees and Shah investigated the hours worked by self-employed persons and found that personal and family factors like age and number of children were key determinants.[41] However, when these variables were controlled, they found that the number of hours worked fell when personal taxation rates fell.

Skills

The business need for labour market skills is apparent at all levels from management to operative. The ability to access appropriate skills at affordable prices is an essential ingredient in any supportive economic environment. Small businesses, especially growing ones, would appear to have more acute difficulties in accessing skills. Indeed, small firms would appear to experience genuine problems in dealing with the formalities and legalities of recruitment in an increasingly sophisticated environment. In particular, there is evidence that the small business sector is reluctant to recruit graduate labour and has difficulty in doing so. Changes in the tax treatment of share options in the UK, however, has allowed many more firms, and particularly small high-growth companies, to use them as a carrot to attract key staff.

Infrastructure

An efficient and effective infrastructure is needed, including appropriate transportation systems and networks, communication networks and an adequate supply of

ILLUSTRATION 12.5
Issues relevant to an entrepreneurship policy, according to the Global Entrepreneurship Monitor

1. Promoting entrepreneurship and enhancing the entrepreneurial dynamic of a country should be an integral element of any government's commitment to improving economic well-being.

2. Government policies and programmes targeted specifically on the entrepreneurial sector will have a more significant, direct impact than programmes simply aimed at improving the national business context.

3. To be effective, government programmes designed to encourage and support entrepreneurial activity must be carefully co-ordinated and harmonised so as to avoid confusion and to enhance their utilisation by those for whom such programmes are designed.

4. Increasing entrepreneurial activity in any country will entail raising the participation level of those outside the most active age group of 25–45 years old.

5. For most GEM countries, the greatest and most rapid gain in firm start-ups will be achieved by increasing the participation of women in the entrepreneurial process.

6. Long-term, sustained enhancement of entrepreneurial activity requires a substantial commitment to and investment in education at the third level.

7. Developing the skills and capabilities required to start a business should be integrated into specific educational and vocational training programmes at all educational levels.

8. Regardless of education level, emphasis should be placed on developing an individual's capacity to recognise and pursue new opportunities.

9. The capacity of a society to accommodate the higher levels of income disparity associated with entrepreneurial activity is a defining feature of a strong entrepreneurial culture.

10. Government and public policy officials and opinion leaders from all spheres have a key role to play in creating a culture that validates and promotes entrepreneurship throughout society.

Source: Authors' interpretation, developed from various reports from the Global Entrepreneurship Monitor (Kansas City, Mo.: Kauffman Centre for Entrepreneurial Leadership at the Ewing Marion Kauffman Foundation, various years).

business premises, appropriately located. Indeed with the knowledge economy becoming all-pervasive, speedy and reliable transfer of more and more information has put increasing pressure on regions and nations to ensure that they are abreast of the latest developments in information and communication technology (ICT) and have the infrastructure to support it.

(De)regulation and administrative simplification

It is noticeable that regulation, and the volume, complexity, rate of change and interpretation of it, or more colloquially 'red tape and bureaucracy', tend to come at or near the top of any list when surveys are made either of the problems of small businesses or of the constraints on their growth. Clearly, a certain level of regulation is needed to create a healthy business environment; adequate standards are needed in the areas of health and safety, employment rights, environmental protection and reducing anti-competitive practices, and, as is often claimed, one man's right is another man's burden. Nevertheless, it has been argued that statutory regulations in the above areas and in taxation, statistical reporting and company registration are disproportionately burdensome for small businesses. It is asserted that employment legislation prevents small businesses from employing more labour, and that requirements such as the statutory audit for incorporated businesses discourages them from availing themselves of this legal form of business. VAT compliance, data protection legislation and other statutory requirements have also been listed as barriers. However, it has been suggested that, while these and other burdens have been identified by lobby groups as barriers to small business development, they are not necessarily perceived as such by all small businesses. (See also Table 12.4.)

Governments across the world pay at least lip service to reducing the burdens on small business. In the UK there has been increasing emphasis on deregulation since the publication of the White Paper *Lifting the Burden* in 1985. The OECD and the EU have also had task forces or equivalents examining the issue. The UK established the Deregulation Unit within the DTI in 1985, and in 1994 the Deregulation Task Force was set up. In 1997 it was renamed the 'Better Regulation Task Force' and subsequently it became a Better Regulation Executive. These and other initiatives including the creation of a Regulatory Impact Unit implied that increasing attention may be paid to:

Table 12.4 The Dirty Dozen

The 12 regulatory provisions which hit UK small firms hardest are reported to be:

- the EU Working Time Directive;
- provisions for parental leave;
- provisions for trade union recognition;
- other aspects of the Employment Relations Act;
- unfair dismissal rules;
- the Disability Discrimination Act;
- the National Minimum Wage;
- time off for study or training for 16 to 18 year olds;
- the Working Families Tax Credit;
- the Asylum and Immigration Act;
- the EU Part-Time Workers Directive;
- tax and payroll burdens.

Source: 'The Dirty Dozen' from by 'Help for Small Firms to Beat Bureaucrats', Clare Oldfield, *The Sunday Times*, 14 November 1999. © Times Newspapers Limited.

- measuring the impact of new regulations on small businesses
- critically examining existing legislative measures affecting business with a view to eliminating many of them
- increasing emphasis on making regulations 'goal-based' and not over-prescriptive (that is, emphasising outcomes, not processes, in enforcement procedures).

A significant constraint on better regulation/initiatives is that these bodies work outside the government departments which make the regulations in the first place. (They have been administered in the Cabinet Office.) Overall the result is a history of slow and doubtful progress in these areas which is reflected in reports over time such as:

- One proposal is a crackdown on enforcing strict rules on consultation over proposed legislation. This would introduce a new transparency to policy-making that is likely to be uncomfortable for ministers and civil servants. Regulatory impact assessments have been ignored by several departments, a failure which is being investigated by the National Audit Office.[42]
- The Small Business Council, established in 2000 to act as the voice of small business across government and since disbanded, stated that 'it is time that the cost of being governed should start to reduce year on year. The regulatory burden needs measuring, particularly as it has a disproportionate effect on small firms.'[43]
- The Public Accounts Committee commented that 'the Government has currently no official statistics on the national cost to business of regulation or on the overall burden of compliance. The absence of such figures makes it impossible to set targets for managing and ultimately reducing the burden.'[44]

Shortly before its absorption into the Enterprise Directorate of DTI, the Small Business Service said it had helped to persuade the government to embark on an exercise to measure the burden of regulations, the results of which are awaited.

Recent efforts within the UK include changes in solvency laws, while in the European Union efforts continue to be made to cut start-up costs for new businesses. Contrasts are being drawn between the United States where it 'takes about a week and costs $500 to set up a business' and Europe where 'on average it takes 12 weeks and costs $2000.'[45] Illustration 12.6 elaborates further on this issue.

It is not the purpose of this chapter to argue for or against regulation; however, it is worth noting the opinion that 'there needs to be a more coherent and systematic investigation of the precise nature of the disadvantages facing small firms in this domain as the basis for a policy thrust', the aim of which is to remove or at least reduce the disadvantages affecting small businesses as against large ones.[46]

Societal attitudes

A government's position is usually that it supports and encourages more positive attitudes in society to enterprise, entrepreneurship and the small business sector. The phrase most commonly used to describe the approach is 'creating an enterprise culture'. Certainly, the language of enterprise has never been more popular in politics, economics and business. Critics, however, say it has simply become a synonym for success or a political slogan or is a search for a Heffalump – a creature of supposed vast importance that no one has ever actually seen.

ILLUSTRATION 12.6
Setting up a private limited liability company

In the Netherlands, setting up a private limited liability company takes three to four times as long as it does in the United Kingdom or the United States. These disparities can to some extent be explained by differences between Anglo-Saxon and Dutch Law systems. But apart from this, a study of international laws and regulations reveals a number of differences which in the Netherlands present bigger obstacles to entrepreneurs wanting to start a new company. For example, the Netherlands requires a mandatory minimum capital of NLG 40,000 (before conversion to euros). Countries such as Australia, Ireland and the United Kingdom apply only a symbolic amount. In the United States, there is no minimum capital requirement at all. It is striking that some branch organisations in the Netherlands impose added requirements with regard to operational activities. In the transport sector, for example, this NLG 40,000 is imposed per existing truck rather than per new private limited liability company.[47]

The time authorities need for processing other applications highlights additional aspects of the administrative burden in the European Union. Lundström and Stevenson note that this particularly holds for the permits that companies often need for types of machinery and other capital items.[48] The longer authorities take to issue these permits, the longer the investments are delayed. They point out that the French government took a bold step on this issue and decided that any application not answered within three months shall be considered granted. On the other hand, the United Kingdom abolished some regulations related to permits, while the Belgian and Danish governments have passed acts according to which any proposed legislation must be checked regarding its administrative impact on business before passing through parliament (with an attachment which indicates the impact).

The different interpretations of the word 'enterprise' and aspects of its development have already been described in earlier chapters. It is true to say, nevertheless, that governmental efforts in this area have concentrated generally on the 'narrow' approach of business entrepreneurialism. The broad 'educational' interpretations have not been ignored, but little of significance has been done. A notable exception in the UK was the 'Enterprise in Higher Education' initiative of 1990–5 in the universities, followed by more recent initiatives such as the Science Enterprise Challenge and National Council for Graduate Entrepreneurship. The latter initiatives have the narrower approach at their core however. In addition following the Davies Review, enterprise education is now becoming a curriculum requirement in schools, albeit not on a significant scale in terms of curriculum hours (see Illustration 12.7).

The lack of an enterprise culture has been variously identified through, for example, low business start-up and growth rates, significant external ownership of businesses, an over-large public sector and high unemployment rates. Specifically, policy in this area would seek to create a climate that enhances perceptions of the feasibility and desirability of entrepreneurship. Overall, it is accepted that the image of enterprise in a community will impact on the perception of enterprise on the part of potentially enterprising people within it. The instruments used in fostering such a policy include publicity campaigns, highlighting successful role models, business start-up and awareness programmes, and seminars, information and advice.

ILLUSTRATION 12.7
Enterprise education

The view is often articulated that the supply of entrepreneurs will ultimately be increased more if awareness of the feasibility and desirability of starting a business is established at a young age. Thus the education system is assisted in fostering, supporting and encouraging those interested in knowing what it is like to run a business. Young Enterprise, a mostly privately funded charity, is the leading UK organisation engaged in this process. Its aim is to develop 'enterprise skills' and currently its major programme involves setting up and running mini-businesses.

Similarly, government and others have assisted entrepreneurship programmes for final-year undergraduates. In 1999 the UK's Office for Science and Technology (part of the then DTI) funded selected universities through a competitive tendering process to expand entrepreneurship education across their courses, especially among students of science and technology. The UK government, following a review into how to nurture an enterprise culture through schools and colleges, is introducing enterprise education into the curriculum, albeit in a limited way.

The perceived potential role for education to develop enterprise is being increasingly stressed. The Enterprise Directorate General of the EU claims that general knowledge about business and entrepreneurship needs to be taught right through primary, secondary and tertiary education, 'Yet many [school leavers] know little of enterprise and almost nothing of the opportunities offered by entrepreneurship.'[49] A Danish report sums up the views of many as follows:[50]

> The experts in each one of the 21 GEM (Global Entrepreneurship Monitor) nations consistently placed the provision of individuals with high quality entrepreneurship education as a high priority. Danish experts do not believe that the current education system provides adequately for the promotion of entrepreneurship. They believe that the education system does not focus sharply enough on entrepreneurship and that there is a paucity of formal courses in the subject. Furthermore, they were of the opinion that the quality of both teachers and the material taught in entrepreneurship is low. According to the experts, there are more opportunities for entrepreneurship in Denmark than there are people equipped and skilled to take advantage of them. Other programmes have targeted youth, the unemployed, corporate employees, women and the disabled.

There have also been examples of programmes that have attempted to improve a community's or society's self-image and self-confidence, and to change it from a 'can't do' to a 'can do' attitude. This has been done on the grounds that such an improvement will in turn make it easier for other enterprise ideas to take root. To use a horticultural analogy (see also Figure 12.7), such schemes aim to prepare the soil so that seeds are more likely to germinate in it and so that it is better able to support and sustain any seedlings that may then appear. Needless to say, there is not mutual agreement on the efficacy of such interventions (see Chapter 3).

Individuals and businesses: the enterprise process

The second broad approach to policy described earlier in this chapter is that of promoting the enterprise process by interventions targeted at the level of the individual business or at the person preparing to start a business. This is in contrast to the interventions just considered, which are at the meso or macro-economic level – albeit there is no clear division between where one approach ends and the other begins.

These interventions, aimed either at individual people or at individual businesses, generally target segments or sub-groups of this population categorised by age, by stage of development, by business sector, by geographic region, by market area or by type of ownership: categories where unique sets of problems and/or opportunities are perceived to exist. Some of these categories are described further below.

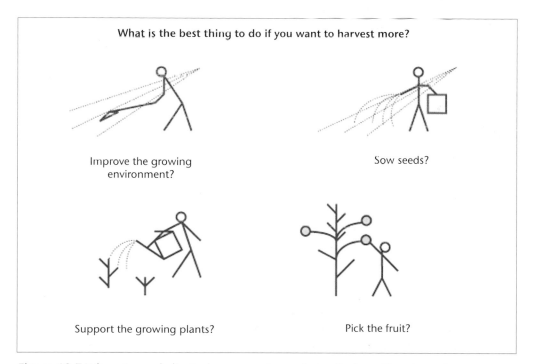

Figure 12.7 Where to apply limited resources to maximise the benefits returned

Pre-start-up

The pre-start-up stage could be perceived as including all those who have not even considered self-employment or business creation as a career option. However enterprise policies addressing this issue are considered under the earlier heading of 'Societal attitudes'. Instead attention is focused here on those working to attempt to become entrepreneurs. There are interventions to help people who are thinking about, or preparing for, business start-up. The most common form of intervention in this area is probably business skills training in its various forms, but there are also interventions to assist and guide market research, and schemes to help with early product/service development. Included in the latter are initiatives that try to help inventors to meet business people capable of understanding the potential of new ideas. In the field of ideas, however, a phenomenon encountered by many who offer assistance is the 'mad inventor', someone who believes that his or her invention is wonderful and the basis for certain commercial success. The inventor believes that the 'hard' bit has been done, so all that is needed is help with the 'easy' bit of turning the invention into a thriving business. In this situation the appropriate intervention can be to disillusion the inventor and to reduce his or her unrealistic expectations.

There are also variations of intervention that help with the sourcing, identification and development of business ideas, and with the formation of enterprise teams to combine the different strengths of individuals in order to promote one successful venture. The former Welsh Development Agency in its national business start-up programme sought to use:

> a realistic approach based on 'the escalator principle', i.e. working with individuals in the process of developing an idea, starting the business and providing the necessary support needed for that business to achieve its full potential. It is intended to move away [from] a purely programmatic approach and instead to focus on continuity of service for new starts through a National Business Centre Network which is to be created under the aegis of Business Connect which will deliver the 'Gateway' service.[51]

Start-ups

It has been noted that, while a healthy level of start-ups is essential for new ideas, innovation, competitiveness and the overall vibrancy of the economy, policy emphasis through much of the 1990s was increasingly placed on the perceived quality of start-ups, such as their potential for growth or for exporting. It has been argued that non-discriminating support to start-ups is counterproductive because many will fail, and that this implies that a more selective approach to business support should be adopted. (The arguments for and against this were described in Chapter 8.) Thus in Britain the role of the Business Links and the TECs and LECs was to offer, as the 1990s progressed, most support to firms with the motivation to grow (and to target companies with between 10 and 200 employees). As previously noted, since the new millennium and creation of the Small Business Service, however, a more balanced approach was evidenced as the attention of political leaders becomes more focused on the volume of start-ups as well as their 'quality'. Government policy reverted to its previous position, offering practical support (in the form of advice and training) to all start-ups, but with particular sectoral biases.

Interventions in the field of start-ups have included financial assistance, training, networking, information, advice and counselling. They have also included the provision of workspace geared specifically to meet the needs of small businesses. This has taken the form of managed workspace ('MWS'- premises with easy leasing terms and, typically, with the availability of central services such as secretarial support and business advice), often on attractive leasing terms. In addition, there have been variations on the business incubator concept. Special attention was also paid to enabling the small business sector to take advantage of the information and communication technology revolution.

High-tech businesses

> Probably the greatest and most salient shift in SME policy over the last 15 years has been a shift from trying to preserve SMEs that are confronted with a cost disadvantage due to size inherent scale disadvantages, towards promoting the start-up and viability of small entrepreneurial firms involved in the commercialisation of knowledge, or knowledge-based SMEs.
>
> Zoltan Acs and David Audretsch [52]

Businesses in the high-tech category are believed to have particular problems needing tailored solutions. Specific support for them is now a strong feature in many countries because of their contribution to innovation and their potential for growth, and because they are likely to be the seeds for the new industry sectors of the future. Their particular needs are seen to arise from the relatively high cost of research and development and its associated risks, which makes them unattractive to conservative or risk-averse lending institutions. High-tech businesses can also have the potential for fast growth, which means that the need for finance will be even greater. Such problems are frequently compounded by other aspects of these businesses, for example:

- a value which is often linked primarily to longer-term growth, based on scientific knowledge and intellectual property
- a lack of tangible assets in their initial development to use as collateral when significant up-front investment may be needed (and little evidence that the businesses can trade profitably)
- products with little or no track record, untested in the marketplace and possibly subject to a high rate of obsolescence
- the funders' lack of understanding of the potential of the products or processes, which is due very often to their specialist nature
- their owners' frequent failure to pay enough attention to communicating meaningfully in a non-technical way.

The overall result is that funders have difficulties in assessing the viability of the proposals, particularly in terms of judging the technology, estimating prospective demand and quantifying the risks.

Since the 1980s, therefore, a range of schemes have been introduced to help high-tech businesses financially and in other ways. Examples of such help are shown in Illustration 12.8.

ILLUSTRATION 12.8
Public sector initiatives for high-tech businesses

Various public sector initiatives and fiscal incentives have been provided in the UK in recent years to encourage greater investment in high-tech small firms. These include initiatives aimed specifically at improving the provision of small amounts of risk capital at the seed and start-up stages, and at tackling both demand and supply-side constraints. Examples are given below:

- *Clustering*: US high-tech companies are believed to have benefited greatly from the clustering of firms and finance providers together, for example in Silicon Valley. The former DTI developed plans to use a regional innovation fund to facilitate the formation of local clusters of high-technology companies. Regional Development Agencies (RDAs) are also being encouraged by government to continue developing existing and embryonic clusters.

- *Business incubators*: These are viewed as an effective means of encouraging innovation and the wider dissemination of technology. UK Business Incubation (UKBI) was established in 1998, jointly funded by the public and private sectors.

- *Innovation and technology counsellors*: The Business Links offer an innovation and technology counselling service and most employ experienced independent counsellors.

- *Enterprise Centres*: In November 1998 the creation of the Science Enterprise Challenge was announced, targeted on developing entrepreneurial skills among university scientists and engineers. Eight enterprise centres were established in universities around the country, with the help of a £25 million contribution from the government. A further public sector allocation has added to the number of centres and a special allocation was made towards the cost of a joint institute to be established by the Massachusetts Institute of Technology and Cambridge University. This is designed to stimulate, *inter alia*, spin-outs from the university's academic base.

- *The Small Firms Merit Award for Research and Technology (SMART)*: This provided grants of amounts varying from around £2500 to £150,000 to help SMEs to access technology and research, and develop innovative products and processes. (Now discontinued.)

- *The Enterprise Fund*: With public funds worth £180 million over three years, this has been developed to stimulate the provision of both debt and equity finance to UK SMEs with growth potential. The Fund expects to lever in significant amounts of private sector funding. The Fund has four main elements: the UK

High-Tech Venture Capital Fund, Regional Venture Capital Funds, the Small Firms Loan Guarantee Scheme (see text) and the National Business Angel Network (NBAN).

- *The UK High-Tech Venture Capital Fund*: This is a public/private partnership designed to encourage institutional investors currently not active in this market to invest in the early stage high-technology sector. It started with £126 billion.

- *Regional Venture Capital Funds*: These are another joint public/private partnership initiative. The government sought at least one venture capital fund, with a minimum fund size of £10 million (both public and private investors), in each English region (and totalled £24 million in 2004). The Fund is not restricted to high-technology investments. The aim is to increase the supply of equity in amounts of less than £500,000 available to SMEs with growth potential, whilst stimulating the creation of venture capital funds that will address the 'equity gap'.

- *The Early Growth Fund*: A venture capital co-investment fund set up with UK government capital to assist early stage businesses with growth potential. It matches risk capital provided by other private investors and is administered by the RDAs.

- *University Challenge Fund*: Intended to encourage the transfer of science, engineering and technology from the universities into the commercial world and to demonstrate that very early stage investments can be profitable. In conjunction with major charities, the government has provided £65 million for seedcorn venture capital funds, enabling the universities to develop their business proposals and start up companies.

- *The Enterprise Management Incentive (EMI) Scheme*: Intended to promote and improve the supply of labour to SMEs in general and technology-based small firms in particular, as well as facilitating the flow of finance to such companies. The EMI Scheme permits tax-advantaged share options to be given in small higher risk companies.

- *Taxation of corporate venturing*: The Budget in 2000 introduced up-front corporation tax relief at 20 per cent on investments by corporate venturers in small higher-risk trading companies. The Corporate Venturing Tax Relief Scheme provides tax incentives for corporate equity investment in the same types of companies as are eligible under the Enterprise Investment Scheme (EIS) and Venture Capital Trusts (VCT). (The rate of relief is due to change at time of writing.)

- *Tax credit for R&D*: An R&D tax credit for SMEs based on the total cost of their R&D expenditure was introduced in 2000.

- *EU initiatives*: There are a range of European-funded initiatives which will work to increase the supply of funds to high-tech small firms. These include: the European Investment Bank's (EIB's) European Technology Facility, which will support business through business incubators and seed funds; I-TEC, which covers 50 per cent of the costs of administering funds making early stage investments in technologically innovative SMEs; and the EIB's Innovation 2000 Initiative (i2i), which is reorientating lending resources towards the dissemination of innovation, SME development and information and communication technologies. Furthermore, by the end of 2000, the EIB/EIF had invested £20 million in the UK High-Technology Venture Capital Fund (see also Case 12.3).

Source: Based on *Finance for Small Firms: An Eighth Report* (London: Bank of England, 2001), pp. 71–2. With kind permission of the Bank of England.

Geographical areas of disadvantage

Policies have been adopted to assist in the regeneration, through enterprise and small business development, of areas of special disadvantage. Deprivation is a complex issue and the nature and extent of its impact vary, not least between urban and rural areas:

> Deprived areas have particular features which include high mortality rates, poor physical environment, low levels of educational attainment and participation, high crime rates, and poor housing. The promotion of enterprise can play an important role in addressing social exclusion. ... It should not, however, be viewed as a panacea for social and financial exclusion. High levels of displacement of existing businesses, the risks involved in setting up in business and the propensity to create marginal businesses are potential limitations to the contribution of small firms in deprived areas.[53]

On the other hand, run-down inner cities and depressed rural areas have benefited from initiatives designed to promote social enterprises, such as 'community enterprises' and co-operatives. In addition, managed workspace has been publicly funded in whole or in part in an attempt to provide localised support that is relevant and real (and visible).

This provision often takes the form of local enterprise agencies, which can become the centrepiece of policies to create a focus for urban or rural regeneration involving local people in their management and activities. Such local roots can greatly strengthen the ability of local agencies to be true centres and role models for stimulating a local enterprise culture. As well as premises, they can offer various other forms of business support – particularly training, advice and information – and can be vehicles for moulding regional programmes to meet local needs. Some UK initiatives are described in the next section.

Population sub-groups

Efforts to encourage the population in general, and certain sub-groups in particular, to become more aware of and receptive to the possibilities of enterprise have already been referred to in earlier chapters.

ILLUSTRATION 12.9
Population sub-groups

A variety of (usually business start-up) programmes have targeted graduates, youth, the unemployed, corporate employees, ethnic minorities, women and the disabled. Across Europe, it is perceived that an effective enterprise policy will seek to improve the start-up rate among some or all of such sub-groups. It will for instance aim at 'improving the start-up rate among women, young people and unemployed'.[54] Indeed, the Global Entrepreneurship Monitor (see Chapter 4) identified three main demographic characteristics as impacting on entrepreneurship, of which one was 'the level of female participation in entrepreneurial activity', women being the largest 'sub-group' in the population.[55]

Many such interventions begin with young people when they are in school. Schools have cross-curricular themes to pursue such as 'economic awareness' and more recently an enterprise component, which create an opportunity to develop a positive culture, attitude and motivation towards enterprise and business. In most instances they are used to give an introduction to what is loosely referred to as the 'world of work'. In the UK, the Young Enterprise's Company Programme (an initiative, described in Chapter 2, enabling (*inter alia*) teams of students in secondary and tertiary education to run their own businesses) applies from the age of 16. Other Young Enterprise programmes are aimed at younger age groups. The Shell Livewire Scheme and the Prince's Trust both seek to help young people who wish to start a business.

Special programmes, usually awareness-raising or start-up seminars and training, have, as already noted, been targeted on groups that are believed to be under-represented in entrepreneurship or that may share common problems or disadvantages. Barriers to the potential for women, for example, to run their own businesses has led to special funding from the European Union and a range of national and transnational programmes to enable that potential to be realised. In Northern Ireland a portfolio of training programmes has also been developed ('target programmes') for sub-groups of the population deemed to have particular disadvantages or potential. They have covered women, youth, the unemployed, the employed, the disabled and graduates. In Great Britain the danger of some members of ethnic minorities being economically and socially marginalised by a vicious cycle of dependency is well recognised. It derives from the lack of a business tradition, the shortage of entrepreneurs, the dearth of enterprise, the absence of role models, and institutional barriers, all of which reinforce lack of confidence. As a result, special funds and initiatives to break that cycle have been created.

Exporters

There is a danger that support for specific small businesses will result in displacement of other local small business activity and so will not result in net local benefits. If the businesses assisted are exporting, this danger will be largely avoided. Because of this and because of their growth potential there has been a variety of incentives to encourage greater export performance by the small firm sector, mainly through financial subsidies and information-based assistance (such as travel and trade show subsidies, export credit guarantees, subsidised market research, free access to databases, and information on trends, market requirements and potential contacts). Growth has become associated, in the minds of many, with the need to export, and such businesses are finding an increasing amount of support from the private sector (particularly the banks), as well as from the public sector.

Forms of assistance

Where assistance is directed at filling perceived gaps on the supply side, it usually takes the form of providing various services to small businesses. Such services are not necessarily available to all small firms, but, as indicated above, may often be targeted on specific groupings that apparently share a number of common needs. Some examples of such assistance are described below.

Financial assistance

Since 1931, when the Macmillan Committee reported and identified what has since been known as the 'Macmillan Gap', shortage of finance has been one of the central issues in discussions of the support needs of small firms. The 'gap' refers to a situation where a firm has profitable opportunities but there are no, or insufficient, funds (from internal or external sources) to exploit the opportunity. This need was reiterated in the *Bolton Report* (1971) and in numerous other reports and papers since.[56] Burns presents the problem thus:

> The question remains as to whether there is a funding gap (defined as an unwillingness on the part of suppliers of finance to supply it on terms and conditions that owner-managers need). Owner-managers who are unsuccessful in obtaining finance will always say that there is. Survey after survey of owner-managers will reveal this to be a major 'barrier to growth'. However, just because the owner-manager might want finance, on specific terms, does not necessarily mean that it should be provided, either for the good of the owner-manager, the financier or the economy as a whole.
>
> Economists would criticise the use of the word 'gap' and prefer to use the term 'market failure' or 'credit rationing' because there may be a 'gap' even in a perfect market simply because, for example, an owner-manager is unwilling to pay higher rates of interest or investors judge a project to be too risky. ... 'Gaps' can easily arise, largely as a result of information asymmetry, the fixed costs of providing small amounts of capital, and the requirement of bankers for collateral. Also there is the inherent reluctance of the owner-manager to share equity in their business. The question is, however, whether there is evidence that the gap actually exists.

On the one hand there is the evidence of numerous surveys which ask owner-managers what they perceive to be barriers to the growth of their firm. Almost inevitably lack of appropriately priced finance will be cited as a major constraint, particularly for fast-growing and newer firms. However this proves nothing: perception is one thing and reality another. Even if accurate, the lack of appropriately priced finance for certain projects may actually indicate that the market is working perfectly well.[57]

Burns goes on to claim that numerous surveys 'have been unable to objectively establish that a 'gap' exists in any systematic way'.[58]

Despite Burns's conclusions and the availability of other sources of finance, the issue continues to be central to many intervention strategies. There is, at least in some economies, a strongly held view that the major problem now for the funding of small businesses lies not in an overall shortage of finance, but in the appropriate means of focusing that finance and, for instance, avoiding an over-reliance on overdrafts and security-based lending. As a result, in the UK, the relationship between banks and small businesses has been under strain and scrutiny for some time, and the subject has probably been the single most prominent issue in the small business literature over many years. It led in part, in 1998, to the commissioning of a review in the UK which resulted in the publication of *Competition in UK Banking* in March 2000. Key elements of this report (called the Cruickshank Review after the review body's chairman) are shown in Illustration 12.10.

Cruickshank's findings triggered a Competition Commission inquiry which found 'a complex monopoly' which distorted price competition in banking services to small businesses from within the 'Big Four' (clearing banks) which control 90 per cent of the market.[59] The Competition Commission's report, which went to the Secretary of State for Trade and Industry in October 2001, estimated that 'excessive charges' of £725 million had been imposed on the sector and recommended that 'price controls are temporarily imposed', believing that excessive prices and profits 'arise from failure of the banks to pay interest on business current accounts'.[60] In March 2002, in anticipation of government action, the British Bankers' Association issued a voluntary code of conduct for the treatment of small business customers, which was widely seen as an attempt to head off moves by the government.[61] Jarvis notes that since 1997 'deposits have exceeded total lending' to the SME sector, based on Bank of England figures, and suggests that 'small firms in general, are not finding it difficult to access debt finance.'[62] He extends this conclusion, based on recent surveys, to all sources of finance while acknowledging 'there is evidence that a number of groups and sectors face distinct challenges when accessing finance.'[63] Firms wishing to grow are included in this category, as are women and graduates also.

To help in the area of small business finance a number of initiatives have been developed over the years in the UK, most of which are quite common in many other countries. Governments are tending to focus on both the demand and supply sides of the issue, promoting both the knowledge of and ability to access finance, and the availability of finance. Descriptions of some of the different types of such initiatives are given in the following paragraphs.

ILLUSTRATION 12.10
The Cruickshank Review

The Cruickshank Review posed two main questions relating to SMEs:

- whether they have access to appropriate external finance
- whether there is effective competition in the provision of banking services to SMEs.

As part of this, three banking services for SMEs were examined in detail: money transmission, debt and savings.

On banking services, Cruickshank concluded that:

- There was no evidence to suggest that SMEs currently have difficulty accessing debt finance from banks.
- There were a limited number of suppliers.
- The banks were making excess profits in the SME market.
- There was almost no new entry into the SME banking services market.

As far as equity finance was concerned, the Review:

- highlighted some key barriers to entry in the SME equity markets, including asymmetric information
- confirmed the existence of an equity gap for firms who seek to raise between £100,000 and £500,000
- criticised the Small Firms Loan Guarantee Scheme for not addressing these market imperfections.

Source: Bank of England, *Finance for Small Firms: An Eighth Report* (London: Bank of England, 2001), pp. 63–4, with kind permission of the Bank of England.

Reducing late payment of debts

Late payment by customers can be a severe handicap to small businesses, and the consequent adverse effect on cash flow and viability has been a constant complaint by small firms and their representative organisations. Various initiatives have been identified to address this. In the UK the legal procedures for recovery of debts through the courts have been simplified and a statutory right to claim interest on late-paid commercial debts now exists. Under the Late Payments of Commercial Debts (Interest) Act (1998) originally small businesses (up to 50 employees), and now all businesses, may charge interest to all businesses and public sector debtors. The European Commission adopted a Directive on Combating Late Payment in Commercial Transactions in February 2001, for implementation by all EU member states by August 2004. In addition, the CBI promoted a Prompt Payment Code, encouraging organisations to adhere to agreed payment terms and to publish details of their payment performance.

Small Firms Loan Guarantee Scheme (SFLGS)

A Small Firms Loan Guarantee Scheme was introduced in the UK as a pilot. It was based on the commonly held belief that the ability of small firms to borrow for expansion was limited by the lack of security or lack of a track record they could offer lenders, in particular the banks. Under the scheme, the government, through its Small Business Service, provides a guarantee to the banks (or other approved institutions) of a percentage (variously between 70 per cent and 85 per cent) of specified loans. The lending however must still be justified on normal commercial criteria, and the borrowers must pay an interest rate premium on the loans provided. Loans extend from two to ten years on amounts from £5000 to £250,000 (with a ceiling of £100,000 for those trading less than two years) and by 2005 had guaranteed £4 billion of loans.

Enterprise Investment Scheme (EIS) and Venture Capital Trusts (VCT)

The Enterprise Investment Scheme and its precursors, the Business Start-Up Scheme (BSUS) and Business Expansion Scheme (BES), were introduced in the UK to increase the supply of relatively small amounts of equity capital to mainly manufacturing and tradeable service businesses. EIS, introduced in 1993, provides tax relief to individuals (business angels) investing in qualifying unquoted companies. Unlike its predecessors, EIS allows the investor to be a manager or director of the businesses concerned. The venture capital trusts (VCTs) introduced in 1995 are a pooled investment mechanism to enable private investors to spread the risk of investing in private companies. They aim to increase the supply of risk capital for businesses with growth potential. As with EIS, tax relief (on income and capital gains tax) is a prime incentive, but the investors are also expected to benefit from the greater marketability of their shares as VCTs are quoted companies.

Alternative Investment Market (AIM)

Replacing the Unlisted Securities Market (USM) in the UK, the Alternative Investment Market was introduced by the Stock Exchange, in 1995, as a second-tier market to target small or young companies whose shares are not publicly traded. It provides easier entry requirements and less rigorous continuing obligations than the main market, thereby encouraging smaller companies to access public equity. However, 'costs are considered by some companies to be not much lower than those required for a full listing.'[64]

Business angel networks

'Business angels' is the term often used for informal investors in small businesses who tend to operate on the basis of personal knowledge and contacts rather than through formal equity markets. These high-net-worth individuals invest risk capital (up to £100,000 typically) in small unquoted companies. They provide not only capital but often experience and advice to assist the company also. In the UK pools of potential business angels are being developed by the restructured Business Links, banks and others through a variety of local and regional networks. However, many business angels wish to remain anonymous making it difficult to measure their overall impact.

It has been estimated that there are between 20,000 and 40,000 business angels in the UK investing £500 million to £1 billion annually, mostly for start-up and early stage finance (many will use the Enterprise Investment Scheme as a tax-efficient vehicle for their investments).[65] The government seeks to strengthen the UK informal investment market by, for example, support for the National Business Angel Network

(NBAN) as a national conduit for matching investors and investees. Such initiatives aim to promote more investment, cut the costs of finding suitable partners and make the process speedier and more efficient.

Grants and loans

As well as schemes of the kinds considered above, there is a wide variety offering direct grant aid to encourage business development. Often such support is targeted on increases in competitiveness through improvements in key areas of the business such as management, marketing, design, production, research and development, quality systems and training. Grants may also be available to assist with the cost of capital acquisitions such as premises, machines and equipment.

Instead of grants, assistance may sometimes be provided in the form of subsidised low-interest loans ('seedcorn' loans). The costs of administering such funds may be subsidised, but usually interest and repayments are expected to provide a continuing source of revolving support without the need for additional capital injections.

Grants have been suspected of developing further dependence on them. There is an impression that in many cases grants were introduced because government wanted to assist small businesses, and a financial budget was the facility it could most easily make available to the relevant agencies. However, not perceiving a hierarchy of needs (see Figure 11.1 in Chapter 11), the agencies often in effect took that money as the tool they were to use, especially because money was what small businesses frequently said they wanted. Agencies therefore gave out money in the form of grants, instead of asking what tool would be most effective for achieving their purpose and then considering how to convert the money into it. (See Illustration 12.7 which includes a summary of some UK and EU financial initiatives to help small firms and especially those with a strong emphasis on technological innovation.)

Exporters

Small exporting businesses have had difficulty in acquiring attractive credit insurance from the private sector. The causes of this were noted in a Bank of England report and, while new products have been introduced, take-up is low.[66] In 2000 the DTI's Export Credit Guarantee Department announced a new export credit package for SMEs, indicating that it would work with other government agencies to give export advice to SMEs. Subsidised trade fairs and outward missions as well as funds to develop specific overseas markets have been given a particularly strong emphasis in an attempt to increase the exporting performance of SMEs. The European Observatory reported only 8 per cent of SMEs as having export turnover.[67]

Support for particular sub-groups

Support for ethnic minority businesses (EMBs)

There is a recognition that ethnic minority businesses have special financing needs, given that they can face 'difficulties in raising external finance [which] can be more acute' than for small businesses as a whole.[68] Any real problems of discriminatory practice become mixed up with issues such as the disproportionately high representation of

EMBs in inner city areas, and in rented accommodation, and a tendency towards concentration in sectors with above-average failure rates (such as catering and retail). Recent evidence suggests that 'as a group EMBs are not disadvantaged in terms of start-up capital from banks and other formal sources' and that there is more variation 'within EMBs (as a group) than with white-owned firms'.[69]

Many EMBs have benefited from their own community finance schemes used instead of, or in addition to, bank finance. For example, 'partnering schemes' which involve members paying an agreed amount of savings into a mutual savings fund are important for African-Caribbean businesses. The success of many UK-based Asian business start-ups can be put down, at least in part, to the 'flexible' repayment conditions set by the often extended family group, removing the normal bank lending repayment pressures on a new business.

There is also concern that the take-up of official business support by EMBs is lower than for other businesses with both demand and supply-side factors being used as explanations. An Ethnic Minority Business Forum was set up in 2000 to highlight issues of concern to EMBs and to consider how government policies might meet them.

Support for women-owned businesses

Women-owned businesses are another sub-group which may need special forms of support (see also Chapters 3 and 7). Despite the significant recent growth in women owned businesses in the UK, the absolute rise in female self-employment appears to have been largely caused by an increase in the number of women in the labour market as a whole. The rate of female self-employment has increased less than in the United States, but is still a substantial growth, from approximately 3 per cent of total females economically active in 1979 to 7 per cent in 2007. During the same period the rate of male self-employment increased from 9 per cent of total males economically active to 15 per cent in 2007.[70]

Similar trends have been seen in many other Northern European countries. In the United States however there has been strong growth in the number of women starting in business. There women account in 2007 for nearly 40 per cent of self-employed business owners, growing from 26.80 per cent in 1976 (equating to the current UK figure). Across the EU in comparison with men, there are fewer self-employed women in all age groups and across all business sectors.

Within the EU generally and the UK in particular there is a range of initiatives seeking actively to promote women entrepreneurs. The importance attached in the Global Entrepreneurship Monitor to the role of women as entrepreneurs has already been noted and is believed to be enhanced as information technology and the Internet cause changes in how business is structured and operated. The UK government has a Women's Unit at the Cabinet Office while the Small Business Services (SBS) strategy document *Think Small First* stated that the government 'will seek to increase the number of women entrepreneurs to levels in comparable economies such as the United States by researching and understanding their needs. As with EMBs, issues of discrimination in relation to bank finance become intermingled with 'factors such as lower expected, and actual, turnover and a greater desire to work part-time which might reduce the ability of women-owned businesses to raise finance'.[71]

Deprived areas

Following the establishment of the UK Government's Social Exclusion Unit in 1997, a report was published entitled *Enterprise and Social Exclusion*, focusing on access to finance and support services by small firms in deprived areas. It called upon the Bank of England to report on a regular basis on finance for business in these areas. The Bank accepted this remit, citing several factors that may limit lending by external agents such as a 'lack of business experience, lack of collateral and personal equity; concentration in business sectors subject to higher failure rates; remoteness; small and localised markets and high crime rates'.[72] The Bank followed up with a special report in 2003, *The Financing of Social Enterprises*.[73] The report found that 'Social enterprises are more likely to have been rejected for finance, although the majority of those rejected by one lender appear subsequently to be successful with another.' It adds that while there is no obvious simple reason for such higher rejection rates, possible contributing factors are:

> lack of available security and personal financial stake; use of organisational structures and grant funding schemes with which lenders may be unfamiliar, and which may result in lengthy arrangement times; some elements of credit and behavioural scoring; reputational risk to lender; and low levels of investment readiness among some social enterprises.

It further suggests that there is 'evidence of demand for some form of "patient" finance, particularly at the start-up and expansion stages'.

Recognising the potential of a strong community development sector to promote enterprise in deprived areas, a Social Investment Task Force was established in 2000 to explore suitable ways in which social investment and financing might be developed. (Its recommendations are summarised in Illustration 12.11.) In addition the Phoenix Fund operated from 1999 until 2006 to further assist businesses in deprived communities (see Illustration 12.12).

Additional developments include the Government's Inner City 100 initiative, a scheme to profile the fastest-growing unquoted companies in the most disadvantaged areas of ten major cities to serve as role models, and the Adventure Capital Fund, which supports social enterprises to overcome barriers to growth (in England).

Community and group self-help schemes

An alternative to externally supplied grants or loans for small businesses may be found, in various parts of Europe, in community or group self-help financing schemes such as credit unions and mutual credit guarantee schemes. The logic behind such schemes is that each individual in a community may be able to save a small amount, and if these amounts are pooled they are together much more effective than they would be separately. Alternatively, shared resources can be used to guarantee a bigger loan than any one person could manage alone. Mutual credit guarantee schemes apply the same principle to small businesses, which combine into self-help groups to pool their financial resources in order to fund, or secure credit for, significant projects for the member businesses as appropriate. Thus, one or two at a time, the members can afford to undertake projects they could not have afforded on their own. Such schemes

---

ILLUSTRATION 12.11
The Social Investment Task Force

Set up in February 2000, the Social Investment Task Force is independently managed by the UK Social Investment Forum in partnership with the New Economics Foundation and the Development Trusts Association (the Treasury has an observer role).

The Task Force aims to find out how entrepreneurial practices can be applied to obtain higher social and financial returns from social investment and financing in regeneration and community economic development. It seeks also to unleash new sources of private and institutional investment in low income areas.

The Task Force has made five recommendations that it suggests would create the environment in which a 'vibrant, entrepreneurial community development sector' could emerge. The proposals were for:

- A community investment tax credit – *since introduced as a Community Investment Tax Relief providing an incentive for private investment in community development.*

- Community Development Venture Funds – the initially committed £10 million of matched funding to the first Community Development Venture Fund (*an equity and non-equity fund*).

- Disclosure of individual bank lending activities in under-invested communities. Banks *are now reporting on their activities and performance.*

- Greater latitude and encouragement for charitable trusts and foundations to invest in community development initiatives, *for which initiatives have been taken, including the Charity Bank.*

- Support for Community Development Financial Institutions (CDFIs). *Lending by 2005 amounted to £27 million to social enterprises.**

* HM Treasury/Cabinet Office, *The Future Role of the Third Sector in Economic and Social Regeneration: Final Report*, CM7189 HM Treasury (July 2007), p. 79.

Source: Based on *Finance for Small Firms: An Eighth Report* (London: Bank of England, 2001), p. 66. Reproduced with kind permission of the Bank of England.

---

apply ideas similar to those on which the early building societies were based. Intervention may help to get them started by providing encouragement and by making available information on how to set up and run them.

Summary

Governments are thus tending to focus on both the demand and supply sides of the financing issue. On the demand side, the major approaches seek to improve the information flow between SMEs and investors and to provide counselling services to SMEs to improve their willingness and ability to find and secure debt and equity financing.

ILLUSTRATION 12.12
Government initiatives for deprived areas

Government support for businesses in deprived communities included the Small Business Service's increased focus on providing advice to such businesses, and the establishment of the Phoenix Fund (now discontinued) to encourage entrepreneurship in disadvantaged areas and within disadvantaged groups. The fund was, however, part of a much wider regeneration programme, outlined below.

- *The Phoenix Fund*: This fund, designed specifically to encourage entrepreneurship in disadvantaged areas and within disadvantaged groups, was launched in 1999. The Fund, initially worth £30 million and trebled in the 2000 Budget, had four key elements, which together aimed to assist businesses in deprived communities indirectly by providing assistance to intermediaries, most notably business support providers and Community Finance Initiatives (CFIs).

- *The Challenge Fund*: This helped resource CFIs in England and to provide capital for on-lending.

- *Loan guarantees*: These encourage commercial and charitable lending to CFIs in the UK. A CFI borrows money for on-lending within the community, servicing the bank loan with the funds obtained from their clients' repayments. (A proportion of the lending by the CFI could be covered by guarantees from the Phoenix Fund in the event of default, in order to assist the CFI with the repayment of its bank borrowings.)

- *The Development Fund*: This is designed to support innovative ideas of how to promote enterprise in deprived areas and under-represented groups in England.

- *Business Volunteer Mentors Association*: £3 million was allocated in 2000 from the Phoenix Fund to support such an association. As with the pilot initiative, it is being run by the National Federation of Enterprise Agencies for delivery through local enterprise agencies and other local partnerships. It is based on a core of volunteers drawn from all sections of the business community, who provide mentoring advice aimed at pre- and early start-up businesses and micro-businesses, including those in disadvantaged communities.

Source: Based on *Finance for Small Firms: A Special Report* (London: Bank of England, 2001), pp. 67–8. Reproduced with kind permission of the Bank of England.

On the supply side the major approaches have been to encourage banks to do more small business lending and make them accountable (through loan guarantees, statistical reporting and setting minimum targets for SME loans), to provide tax incentives for equity investments, and to provide government financial assistance programmes (such as micro-loans, subsidised interest rate loans, and R&D funds).

This is how Lundström and Stevenson sum up international trends in financing:

> With the growing understanding of 'gaps' in small business financing and the differences in financing needs, governments are ensuring that multiple sources and types of financing are available (such as micro-loans, seed capital, venture capital and informal investment capital) to different types of entrepreneurs (such as women, ethnic minorities) and firms (such as high-growth firms, technology firms) at different stages of development (such as R&D stage, start-up stage, growth stage).[74]

Other assistance

Although financial assistance may be the most obvious kind, there are many other types of assistance measures. Subsidised provision of a variety of forms of information, advice, training and counselling is a very large and fast-growing part of attempts to improve the internal efficiency of small businesses. Some such forms of assistance are described below.

They are often referred to as 'soft' support as opposed to the 'hard' support of finance, premises and plant, for example.

Information and advice

Small businesses are believed to be at a disadvantage relative to larger ones because of their limited ability to scan the environment and filter for information relevant to their progress. Indeed it can be argued that a lack of relevant and timely information, delivered in a manner which can be quickly and easily absorbed and used, is a critical problem for most small businesses and that this example of market failure in access to information needs to be addressed if small businesses are to realise their growth potential. Consequently, the major part of the remit of the network of business support agencies is to remedy this information gap.

With the huge expansion of the Internet as a means of communicating vast amounts of data, this medium has assumed a significant role in providing information for SMEs. International, national, regional and local agencies as well as private sector organisations are developing websites and knowledge portals dedicated to supplying information believed to be useful for SMEs. The European Commission reported in 2007 that 'access' to ICT was no longer a barrier to e-business uptake, with connectivity at 84 per cent for small businesses.[75] Such a high level of connectivity reveals the potential for reaching SMEs.

Another method, employed by Business Links and their equivalents, is the use of personal business advisers (PBAs) offering person-to-person and face-to-face communication, which is an approach preferred by many business owners. Subsidised consultancy can also enable businesses to engage professional specialists to help them to analyse their situations and prescribe improvement actions. Another type of special initiative relies on experienced business people acting as 'mentors' to selected local businesses. Working typically only for expenses, the mentors assist owner-managers with information, advice and counselling, usually over a 6 to 12-month period. The UK has initiated a Business Volunteers Mentors Association, and in the Republic of Ireland the government's business support agency, Enterprise Ireland, has delivered the Mentor Programme nationally to SMEs for almost 15 years. A similar national scheme also exists in Scotland linked to the Business Gateway and to the Scottish Chambers of Commerce, and in Northern Ireland through its local enterprise agency network (Enterprise N. Ireland). Examples can be found in many other countries, often using retired business people.

Management and workforce development and training

Support for management development in small businesses has developed significantly over recent years, as both the private and the public sectors have identified a gap in the market. It is well known that the right mix of management skills is important for any business and is critical if a business is to grow successfully. Yet a consistent finding of research on training provision in developed countries is that workers (managers and employees) in small firms are less likely to be in receipt of formal training than those in larger enterprises.[76] For instance the Council for Excellence in Management and Leadership reported (see also Chapter 6):[77]

> Joyce et al.[78] found that only 43 per cent of businesses with under five employees provided training compared with 92 per cent of businesses with over 200 employees, while Hankinson's[79] interviews with key personnel from engineering firms with under 100 employees found that 'Hardly any firms had specific policies of staff training by in-house seminars, conferences, short courses, etc.' Matlay found that only 2 per cent of micro-businesses (under ten employees) provided 'formal or mixed learning' opportunities compared with 60 per cent of medium-sized businesses (50 to 250 employees).[80]
>
> In addition Sargent found that, on average, 'Small businesses spent £103 per annum per employee on staff development, compared to £182 from a previous study of medium- and large-sized businesses.'[81] Extracts from Hankinson's interviews with owner-managers provide further evidence: ' ... small firms would find it costly to provide training over and above a minimum level'; '... training beyond a "hands-on" approach would be too expensive for us'.[82]
>
> While there is a proliferation of providers of training and development opportunities, there is strong evidence that amongst the reasons for low uptake is dissatisfaction with much of the current offering. Sargent suggests from his survey of 77 'small businesses' in Devon that 'Many small business owners feel that management courses lack practicality and are too academic in terms of their style of delivery.' This evidence is supported by Gibb's suggestion that education and training will need to move away from 'detached provision' based around abstract/functional knowledge, towards 'embedded provision' based around 'context and processes'.[83] Perren et al.'s exploratory case studies provide support for Gibb suggesting that owner-managers' learning is often problem-focused and motivated by dealing with

current concerns.[84] There is also evidence that 'on-the-job' learning is preferred to 'off-the-job' courses, perhaps as a means of overcoming *inter alia* problems of cost and relevance.

Bannock notes that while 'Survey results vary according to sample composition and how questions are phased and, in particular to how training is defined', nevertheless 'there is no doubt that SMEs carry out less training (as conventionally defined) for all their staff.'[85] Kitching and Blackburn record in their analysis of training that established staff are most commonly trained in working methods, IT and product knowledge; for the owner manager the content was working methods, IT and health and safety.[86] Training in general management processes and techniques and finance were much lower.

Government intervention over many years has been designed to enhance management and workforce training in small businesses (perceiving a market failure to exist in that small businesses do not see the benefits of training). Others, like Bannock, will argue that there is much more on-the-job informal training going on in SMEs than is appreciated. 'It is not possible to capture fully the training and learning that actively goes on.'[87] In the UK, Small Firms Training Loans were introduced in 1994 to help pay for training by subsidising the interest payments on bank loans which small firms took out to invest in training. The scheme is administered by LSCs in England, which consider applications before they are sent to the lending bank, and offer help and advice where necessary. In the 1980s Business Growth Training offered a consultant paid from public funds to train and develop management in small firms. More recently there has been strong encouragement for smaller firms to engage in Investors in People (IIP) while, in 2000, the then

---

ILLUSTRATION 12.13
Graduates and small businesses

Small business and graduates each perceive the other as a high risk, though they have much to offer each other. Small businesses can benefit from the abilities of graduates, yet many small businesses have a resistance to the perceived cost of employing them, requiring immediate added value from the extra cost of a graduate's salary. Graduates, in particular those who might want a business of their own eventually, have much to gain from working for small businesses, but do not want to find that they are working for employers who will not value their skills. Moreover, graduates tend to perceive that larger employers offer more formalised development programmes, greater opportunities for advancement and greater security of employment.

Specific schemes have therefore been devised aimed at encouraging the recruitment of graduates by small businesses. They include measures such as match-making between individual graduates and businesses, training for graduates in small business issues, and subsidies for graduate salaries for an initial settling-in period or longer.

DfEE/DTI in a joint initiative established a Council for Excellence in Management and Leadership. It aimed 'to develop a strategy to ensure that the UK has the managers and leaders of the future to match the best in the world'. It further sought, in the context of SMEs, 'to establish a coherent approach to the confusing plethora of management and leadership development initiatives' and to introduce schemes which offer entrepreneurs 'a range of solutions which work with the grain' and mimic their informal procedures.

Market, product and process development

Small businesses may have difficulty finding and researching new markets, especially export markets. Equally, in the longer term the survival and growth of businesses will require the constant development of new or improved products or services. Various programmes of support to help businesses in these areas have been devised. They include R&D assistance, export marketing grants, trade missions and shows, market intelligence reports and export credit guarantee schemes, as well as assistance with the development and production of sales literature and advertising materials. Productivity increases through, for example, process development are encouraged by assisting benchmarking studies, quality initiatives and best-practice visits. The linking of markets and products – or services, suppliers and customers – has also been facilitated by the Internet and e-commerce, and therefore there have been various initiatives to promote and assist increased small business connectivity.

Technology

The importance of technology in stimulating innovation, competitiveness and growth of businesses is well understood. It is believed, however, that the potential of many smaller businesses to identify and exploit new and existing technologies is limited by lack of information on their availability and potential, or by cost factors (another example of 'market failure'?). A wide range of schemes exist to ensure that the process of technology transfer is enhanced. Additionally, all Business Links offer an Innovation and Technology Counselling Service using independent counsellors, and the Technology Strategy Board offers the Knowledge Transfer Partnership (formerly the Teaching Company Scheme): a scheme which brings SMEs and universities/FE colleges into co-operative alliances through (up to) three-year placements for highly qualified graduates.

Networking

If 'Success = Idea + Know-how + Know-who' (see Chapter 11) then intervention to help networking to provide the 'know-who' is clearly appropriate. Generally however it appears not to be addressed nearly as often as 'idea' and 'know-how'. As noted by Bennett and Smith,[88] 'Cluster theory developed from the work of Porter[89] suggests that local interactions ... improve the competitive position of the SME.' Also, 'Local networks allow SMEs to gain advantage from being embedded in local institutions that can offer knowledge pools of advice and support.' While there is 'substantial evidence' to indicate that entrepreneurial networks are important to the growth of the firm, opening up new opportunities and resources, it is also suggested that social networks may play both positive and negative roles.[90]

UK and European small business support: a summary

UK

Overall the characteristics of the UK approach to small business support may be summarised as:

- creating a healthy business environment, with increasing emphasis on deregulation and reduced and simplified administrative burdens
- selective intervention where market failure can be demonstrated
- developing forms of support geared to improving the competitiveness and export performance of small firms, emphasising marketing, quality, productivity, benchmarking, product development, management and workforce skills
- encouraging greater private sector involvement in the delivery of services through 'partnership' arrangements
- decentralised delivery combined with variations in the priorities and scope of support services to cater for differences in local and/or regional needs.

The reality however is that UK governments have not usually looked to small business for a significant contribution to economic renewal and development. Attracting inward investment has been seen as a much more fruitful focus for support. However inward investment is now much reduced as a reality, in part due to the major shift of large-scale businesses from high-labour cost areas to countries whose labour costs are significantly lower. With this in mind, small indigenous businesses may become much more important as innovators and job creators and mechanisms for economic regeneration.

European Union

Within the EU as a whole, policy towards small businesses may be summarised as focusing on two approaches (as in the UK): first, addressing the economic environment with the emphasis on fiscal measures and increasing labour market flexibility, and second, developing additional enterprise support schemes, with the emphasis on R&D, internationalisation and the supply of finance. (See Case 12.3.)

In fact, the majority of measures in the EU countries are concentrated on three instruments:

- grants and tax reliefs
- counselling and information services
- subsidised loans.

There is little evidence of tension between support for new enterprises as opposed to established and growing ones. In the EU the two approaches are considered to be complementary. A noticeable trend in a number of EU countries and in the European Commission itself is an increasing emphasis on 'the entrepreneurial economy' and internationalisation. Indeed, it is interesting to note that over 40 countries are now participating in the Global Entrepreneurship Monitor project to benchmark themselves according to their total entrepreneurial activity (see Chapter 4).

Small business policy in most countries of the EU is closely linked to regional policy. The UK has tended to be an exception with most policies being national in coverage.

However with the establishment of a Parliament in Scotland, Assemblies in Wales and Northern Ireland and Regional Development Agencies in England, there is a strong trend towards greater regionalisation within the constraints of the UK-wide regulatory and fiscal regime.

Recent research indicates that, while policy fields and instruments may be similar from country to country, their implementation and delivery mechanisms can vary considerably, resulting in significant differences in the perception of their effectiveness. It is further contended that European Commission programmes, while providing a useful range of funds for SMEs and their support organisations, 'can prove very difficult to access, and in some cases the costs of advice, and time, required to put forward a satisfactory application can outweigh the benefits'.[91] Overall, there has undoubtedly been a fundamental shift in many countries over recent years, with the locus of enabling policies being increasingly at the local or regional level, as opposed to the federal or national level.

In January 2008, the European Commission launched a pubic consultation on the content of its proposed European 'Small Business Act' targeted for June 2008. This proposal has followed from a number of Commission publications on entrepreneurship in the EU. In 2000, the Lisbon Declaration committed the EU to becoming, within a decade, the most competitive and dynamic knowledge-based economy in the world. In 2003, there followed a Green Paper on Entrepreneurship to help it achieve its goals. The Paper addressed two key issues:

- Why do so few people start a business relative to those who express their interest in entrepreneurship?
- Why do so few enterprises grow and at such a modest rate?

Following the debate on the Green Paper, the Commission launched an Entrepreneurship Action Plan based on the feedback it received. The Plan outlined key actions related to five strategic areas:[92]

- fuelling entrepreneurial mindsets
- encouraging more people to become entrepreneurs
- gearing entrepreneurs for growth and competitiveness
- improving the flow of finance
- creating a more SME-friendly regulatory and administrative framework.

Other related issues identified for action within the strategy were: reducing the stigma of failure, providing support for women and ethnic minorities, facilitating business transfers, facilitating SME business co-operation in the EU, fostering innovative clusters and reducing the complexity of complying with tax laws. The 'Small Business Act' is the next significant step in putting SMEs at the forefront of decision-making in the EU. The Act intended to include measures to:[93]

- unlock SMEs' growth potential
- reduce the regulatory burden
- facilitate access to Single Market/public procurement
- help provide necessary financial/human resources for SME development
- help SMEs face the challenge of globalisation and climate change.

The document underpinning the consultation identified six areas to be examined:

- better regulation for the benefit of SMEs
- putting SMEs at the forefront of society
- SMEs' access to markets
- SMEs' access to finance, skills and innovation
- turning the environment challenge into opportunities for SMEs
- enhancing the implementation of EU SME policy principles.

Making a choice

This chapter has indicated that there is a wide range of possibilities for intervention, and therefore some choice will inevitably have to be made between them. That choice will depend on many factors, including local policies and priorities, but a key influence will be the perceived effectiveness of the different options. Evaluation of the results of intervention is therefore the subject of the next chapter.

Comparing methods is not easy, however. Not only, as the next chapter indicates, is the evidence of effectiveness not clear, but different methods can apply at different stages of the process. Thus it is not usually a choice among alternatives where the decision is for one or the other, but among approaches which can work together, which means that the choice is among a whole range of possible combinations. Figure 12.3 illustrates this dilemma using a horticultural analogy.

THE KEY POINTS OF CHAPTER 12

- Because of the perceived importance of smaller firms for economic development, virtually every country in the developed and developing world is now intervening in some way to promote more enterprise. However, such interventions often lack an overall strategy in the sense of a coherent set of objectives and the co-ordinated means of achieving them. Aspects of enterprise, entrepreneurship or small business policy and intervention are often dispersed across different government departments and, as a result, support schemes have tended to grow piecemeal. Their objectives appear to include increased wealth and economic growth, job creation and other benefits, including greater social cohesion.

- Agencies are often established to deliver much of the direct intervention, but the dispersal of policy and the involvement of different organisations can result in a confusing variety of apparent sources of help. Attempts to co-ordinate this and give it some form of structure can follow the 'one-stop shop' approach of trying to concentrate services into one location, or the 'first-stop shop' approach of ensuring that different sources of support are well signposted from single access points.

- The means of achieving enterprise, entrepreneurship or small business policy objectives include two broad approaches which are not mutually exclusive. They are:
  - Creating a favourable environment for enterprise. This can involve actions in the areas of the economy, fiscal policy, skills, infrastructure, regulations and societal attitudes.
  - Intervening to support the enterprise process, by direct and indirect support to individuals and businesses. This is often tailored to specific stages of development and to sub-groups such as pre-start and start-up, high-tech businesses, geographic areas of disadvantage, population sub-groups and exporters. The forms of assistance used include financial assistance (such as grants, loan guarantees, business angel and venture finance), information and advice, management development and training, marketing, R&D, networking and technology transfer.
- While differences in delivery systems and policy emphasis exist, there is, across Europe, much more that is common than is different.

CASE 12.2
A Letter from David Irwin, Chief Executive of the Small Business Service, to the Institute of Business Advisers and others

The Small Business Service
1 Victoria Street, London SW1H OET

9 May 2001

ONE YEAR ON

The Small Business Service came into being on 3 April 2000. It started in a blaze of publicity and with ambitious plans. What has it achieved in its first year? And what are its future plans?

Encouraging government to think small first

A major role for the Small Business Service, particularly in relation to regulation, is to ensure that government departments really are thinking about the effects of their actions on small businesses. To promote this objective, the government published *Think Small First* on 15 January. This document, developed by the SBS, sets out for the first time a national framework for business support for all government departments. *Think Small First* is intended to encourage departments to consider all alternatives to regulation, before deciding to regulate, and then, if they really need to regulate, adopting the principles of better regulation promulgated by the Better Regulation Taskforce. Not only do I sit on the ministerial panel for regulatory accountability, but also the SBS's Regulatory Action Team has been developing good bilateral relationships with all other government departments. SBS has recently represented small businesses on childcare standards, passive smoking in the workplace, environmental legislation, care standards, the private security industry, company merger fees and the interception of employees' electronic communications. We pushed hard for the changes to the rules governing Employment Tribunals to make it harder to bring frivolous and vexatious cases. SBS is organising focus groups of small businesses in order to secure qualitative feedback. Recent focus groups have concentrated on the timescale for the introduction of requirements for the employment of people with disabilities, the Green Paper on parental leave and the proposed regulation for waste electrical and electronic equipment.

Think Small First also encourages departments, when they want to initiate schemes to help small businesses, to do so in partnership with the Small Business Service and the Business Link network. A good example of this during the year was MAFF [Ministry of Agriculture, Fisheries and Food] and SBS working together to launch the Farm Business Advisory Service, giving all Business Link operators additional resource to enable them to provide specialist support to farms.

The government has also agreed to introduce a minimum period of 12 weeks for consultation regarding possible new regulations and a 12-week period of grace after regulations are finally agreed, before they are enforced, in order to give small businesses an opportunity to consider the implications and make changes if required, to personnel policies or to procedures.

We have been successful in persuading DETR [Department of Environment, Transport and the Regions] that they should replace their proposal for a supplementary rate with the concept of Business Improvement Districts, which has the support of all parties including businesses.

Developing a world class business support service

At end of March, we launched the new Business Link network. We have reduced the number of Business Link contracts from 81 to 45. Following an intensive competitive contracting process, we are confident that all Business Link partners will have the needs of small businesses uppermost in their minds. This is being reinforced by a commitment to improve the quality of all those working in the Business Link network. We are adopting revised standards for business advisers and other staff. All staff will be assessed against those standards. We have ambitious plans to launch the SBS'U' to provide appropriate professional development to every one of the staff working within the Small Business Service and the Business Link network. We have been engaged in a major exercise to offer every member of staff at the Business Link contractors and their key partners the opportunity to participate in Imagine – a vision-and-values event designed to ensure that everyone understands and shares our purpose. We estimate that the Business Link operators helped over 300,000 businesses and individuals last year and distributed over 8 million leaflets and publications.

The SBS has brought the benefits of benchmarking to 1600 businesses, up by over 600 over 1999's total. 9800 business visitors have learnt about good management practices through our company visit programme, Inside UK Enterprise, up 3000 on 1999. 10,000 participants have viewed one of our CONNECT programmes on good management practice, with about 80 per cent going on to further work in their business.

The UK online business adviser network will be fully integrated as part of the new Business Link network in England. We will be spending an additional £15 million over the period 2000/03 to provide additional UK online for business front-line advisers and services to help small companies to take advantage of information and communications technologies.

We helped 1200 undergraduate students gain a work placement in a small business through the STEP programme jointly supported by Shell.

We increased the number of companies working with universities on technology and knowledge transfer via the TCS programme from 703 to around 800.

We are working with DfEE's [now DES's] new National & Local Learning & Skills Councils on workforce and management development, and also with managing the transition of IiP [Investors in People] delivery to small businesses from the TECs to the local Business Link operators.

The website, www.businesslink.org will be launched at the end of this month, though we will continue to add new functionality and services over the next few months.

Improving access to finance

The SBS inherited the responsibility for the Small Firms Loan Guarantee Scheme and the SMART Awards. Last year we guaranteed over 4300 loans worth £240 million. Our long-term net loss rate is 18 per cent. For SMART, we made 590 commitments worth nearly £29 million. In July, we launched a high-tech Venture Capital Fund providing £20 million which levered £106 million from the private sector to invest in a number of venture funds which are themselves investing in technology-based businesses. We intend to launch Regional Venture Capital Funds in every region of England as soon as we receive clearance from the EU, which we now anticipate within the next couple of months. We have plans to create catalyst funds that will invest small amounts of equity finance to support businesses in their early stage of development. The SBS has teamed up with the clearing banks and other organisations to support the National Business Angel Network in an effort to increase the level of angel finance provided to small businesses. The SBS is also exploring ways to encourage corporate venturing.

Reaching the parts other schemes fail to reach

SBS is investing in deprived areas and among groups who are under-represented in business. Earlier this year, we agreed to award £15 million to 50 community and business support organisations to launch innovative projects to encourage and support entrepreneurship in disadvantaged areas. In March we launched a second round, inviting more proposals. In addition, the Phoenix Fund has agreed to provide financial support to 15 community finance initiatives, in an effort to increase the availability of non-bank finance to small businesses primarily in disadvantaged areas. The first year of the Business Volunteer Mentors Association appears to have been a success and we will be continuing to support that initiative.

Changing the culture

If the UK is genuinely to become an enterprising society, there is no doubt that more needs to be done to encourage everyone in society to believe that they can really make it in business. It is also important that failure is seen as a learning experience and that people are encouraged to try again. The SBS wants to see a culture that respects and values entrepreneurs and enterprise in the same way that it values pop stars and footballers. That is why we are supporting Enterprise Insight, launched by the Prime Minister at Number 10 [Downing Street], and which will initially concentrate on promoting enterprise in schools and amongst young people.

Future priorities

The White Paper on enterprise, skills and innovation (Opportunity for All In a World of Change) published in February announced a new £75 million fund to support the development of many more incubator and managed workspaces. This will be managed in partnership with the RDAs [Regional Development Agencies].

We are working with the Treasury to develop the concept of City Growth Strategies which will build on the work of Professor Michael Porter's US-based Initiative for a Competitive Inner City.

We are looking forward to the results of the consultation on tax credits for Community Development Venture Funds.

We are intending to strengthen our work in Brussels by setting up a UK SME liaison point to help build up the voice of small business in Europe. This will be operational from June.

We expect to publish our three-year strategy and one-year business plan within the next month or so and will ensure that you are sent a copy.

I believe that we are making a difference – but perhaps more importantly we have laid some excellent foundations for our work over the next few years. With best wishes

David Irwin

Source: Extracts from a letter from David Irwin, chief executive of the Small Business Service, to the Institute of Business Advisers, dated 9 May 2001. Reproduced with the permission of the Small Business Service.

Note

On 23 November 2001 the *Financial Times* reported that, following a DTI reorganisation, changes were to be made to the Small Business Service. The SBS was to continue to deliver its core services, but the role of advising on the impact of new regulations was to be separated. During 2007, the SBS was downsized and renamed the Enterprise Directorate with a remit to influence SME policy. The DTI subsequently changed its name to the Department of Business Enterprise and Regulatory Reform.

Points raised

This real example shows how the Small Business Service interpreted its remit and approached the early stages of its existence.

CASE 12.3
EU and OECD perspectives

The perspective of the European Union on enterprise and small business is presented briefly below.

When the Rome Treaty was signed in 1957, unsurprisingly nothing was said about either issue, the focus being on the establishment and growth of large-scale enterprises (with particular attention being paid to the industries of shipbuilding, coal and steel and textiles, where the workforces were under threat or in decline).

As evidence of the probably important role of SMEs, a first Community programme in their support was adopted in 1983 by the European Parliament and the Economic and Social Committee.[94] The same year was designated the European Year of SMEs and Craft Industries. In the following couple of years moves were made to emphasise the importance of improving the environment for SMEs.

A Commission working party reported in 1985 leading to the establishment of an independent SME Task Force the following year. Also in 1986 the Community launched an Action Programme for SMEs, the first occasion on which a coherent framework for a Community business support policy was defined.[95]

The Action Programme focused on what were regarded as areas of identified need:[96]

- a simple and open administrative and regulatory environment
- availability of capital
- increased and efficient information flows and networks
- tailored training.

Following on from the Action Programme, the Council of Ministers adopted a decision in 1989 'on the improvement of the business environment and the promotion of the development of enterprises, and in particular small and medium-sized enterprises, in the Community'.[97]

The essence of the Community Enterprise Policy was similar to the content of the Action Programme (the ensuing programme was to be implemented from 1991 to 1993).

Also in 1989 the SME Task Force in the Commission was transferred to the Directorate-General XXIII (DGXXIII) responsible for Enterprise Policy, Distributive Trades, Tourism and Co-operatives (which in turn was integrated into DG Enterprise and Industry (the 'Enterprise DG') in 1999, starting its work in January 2000 – with a 'mission' to address the entire business environment to enable enterprises to strengthen their competitiveness, growth and development in a way which is compatible with the overall EU goal of sustainable development).

A second and subsequent programmes were developed as follows:

- the Multi-Annual Programme on Community Measures, covering the period 1993–6, to identify priority areas and to ensure the continuation and consolidation of policy for enterprises, in particular SMEs, in the Community[98]

- the Third Multi-Annual Programme for Small and Medium Sized Enterprises in the European Union 1997–2000[99]

- the Multi-Annual Programme for Enterprise and Entrepreneurship and in particular for small and medium-sized enterprises (SMEs) (2001–5).[100]

The latter programme was influenced by external evaluation of the Third Multi-Annual Programme. The evaluation concluded, *inter alia*, that 'There is a need for an active voice in favour of SMEs within the Commission and the policy work is important and appreciated.'

In 2002 an SME post was designated in the Enterprise DG to act as a liaison between the Commission and the SME community. (since referred to as the 'SME Envoy').

Not only was the Multi-Annual Programme influenced by the above evaluation outcomes and the experience of previous programmes but it also took account of the European Charter for Small Enterprises and the Bologna Charter on SME Policies (see below).[101]

The Programme was seen as instrumental in fulfilling the objectives of the European Charter. The five main goals of the Programme were:

- enhancing the growth and competitiveness of business in a knowledge-based internationalised economy of entrepreneurship

- promotion of entrepreneurship

- simplification and improvement of the administrative and regulatory framework enabling research, innovation and business creation to flourish

- improvement of the financial environment

- easier access for business to Community support services, programmes and networks and improvement in the co-ordination of such facilities.

In 2004 an Action Plan for Enterprise was published,[102] while in 2005 the European Commission adopted its 'Modern SME Policy for Growth and Employment' to 'ensure that all aspects of EU policy to help SMEs are co-ordinated'[103] and based on the needs of SMEs.

The Commission announced in 2008 its intention to produce a Small Business Act with objectives largely similar to those of previous initiatives. At the same time it also announced the establishment of an Enterprise Europe Network – a support network of one-stop shops developed to offer business advice and support to SMEs throughout the enlarged EU (and beyond). This initiative was taken under the 'Entrepreneurship and Innovation Programme', an operational programme of the 'Competitiveness and Innovation Framework Programme' to support mainly SMEs and launched in 2007.

OECD and the Bologna Charter

SMEs and entrepreneurship are receiving increasing attention as OECD member countries are concerned about ways to strengthen long-term growth performance. The Bologna Conference for Industry Ministers and Ministers Responsible for SMEs (June 2000) has contributed to putting 'SMEs at the forefront of the international policy agenda'.[104] The Bologna Charter on SME Policies has developed from the conference. It articulates certain principles and calls for greater dialogue and co-operation amongst countries and international institutions.

The Bologna Charter articulates certain principles shared by OECD member and participating non-member countries regarding SME policies. It considers implicitly that business challenges have to be addressed on the basis of the firm itself, the entrepreneur (including women and young entrepreneurs) and the business life cycle. Therefore, in addition to fostering market liberalisation and securing appropriate framework conditions that affect firm creation and expansion, governments should:

- promote entrepreneurship
- facilitate firm start-up and expansion (and not hinder exit)
- improve access to venture capital and other types of financing
- improve access of new firms and SMEs to information, innovation networks and business services
- reduce the regulatory burden on smaller firms
- promote enterprise partnerships, networks and clusters which can enhance SME performance and competitiveness.

The Bologna Charter also calls for intensified dialogue and co-operation between OECD member and non-member countries in this area, as well as between international institutions. It implies a willingness on the part of governments to redesign SME policies and insert them into a coherent and integrated approach to economic growth and social development both in OECD countries and in the rest of the world. The Bologna Charter provides a framework of reference for countries concerned that more could be done to improve the efficacy of policies and programmes directed at fostering entrepreneurship and assisting the development of smaller firms. To promote the potential of SMEs and their contribution to growth, there is a need for policy-makers to identify and take into account the opportunities as well as the problems facing SMEs in this new context.[105]

Points raised

These examples indicate how the EU and OECD have approached the needs they perceived for promotion of, and support for, SMEs.

QUESTIONS, EXERCISES, ESSAY AND DISCUSSION TOPICS

- How do the things that small businesses want from intervention compare with the objectives of that intervention?
- Compare the advantages and disadvantages of intervention to create a favourable environment for business creation and growth with intervention directly to support actual start-up and growth.
- It has been said that 'SME intervention methods are as fragmented as SME needs.' Should they be?
- Why is there an absence of coherent national strategies for entrepreneurship and small business?
- Describe the structure for small business support in your region.
- Might it be possible to set meaningful targets and avoid the problems identified in Case 12.1?
- Identify the main policy fields and instruments being used to support entrepreneurship and small business in your region.
- What are the relative roles of the public and private sectors in support of entrepreneurship and small business in the UK or in your region?
- What approach should be taken to expand entrepreneurship education in the schools or outside the formal schooling system?
- Is there too much or too little public support being offered to small businesses nationally or in your region?
- Compare the EU and OECD approaches (see Case 12.3) to the perceived needs for promotion of, and support for, SMEs.
- Have the remit and policies of the former Small Business Service been consistent with the distinction that can be drawn between entrepreneurship and small business policy. Which direction has it taken (see Illustrations 12.3 and 12.6 and Case 12.2)?

Suggestions for further reading and information

R. Aernoudt, 'European Policy Towards Venture Capital: Myth or Reality?', *Venture Capital*, 1(7) (1999).

Department of Trade and Industry, *Opportunity for All in a World of Change*, White Paper on Enterprise, Skills and Innovation (London: DTI, 2001).

European Observatory for SMEs Sixth Report, L-2985 (Luxembourg: Office for Official Publications of the European Communities, 2001).

A. Lundström and L. A. Stevenson, *Entrepreneurship Policy: Theory and Practice.* (New York: Springer Publishing, 2005).

HM Treasury/Cabinet Office, 'The Future Role of the Third Sector in Social and Economic Regeneration', CM7189 (July 2007).

Websites

Note: Website information presented here was correct at the time of finalising the material for this book, but is of course subject to change.

A site for online advice	www.businesseurope.com
Business Link	www.businesslink.org
	www.businessadviceonline.org
Chambers of Commerce	www.britishchambers.org.uk
Companies House	www.companies-house.gov.uk
Confederation of British Industry	www.cbi.org.uk
Quarterly SME Trends Report	
Confidential free advice through the National Federation of Enterprise Agencies	www.smallbusinessadvice.org.uk
Connecting entrepreneurs to venture capital and service providers	www.e-start.com
Details of The Mentor Programme Ltd	www.enterprise-ireland.com
BERR services and reports	www.berr.gov.uk
Global Entrepreneurship Monitor reports	www.entreworld.org
Small Business Research Trust	www.sbrt.co.uk
Mentoring	www.mentorsforum.co.uk
	www.smallbusiness.info.au
Networking	www.enterpriseforum.co.uk
	www.firsttuesday.com
	www.newbusiness.org.uk
N Ireland Department of Enterprise Trade and Investment	www.detini.gov.uk
Scottish Enterprise's services	www.scottish-enterprise.com
Small Business Research Portal (an overall resource on small firms with useful links for advisers)	www.smallbusinessportal.co.uk
Enterprise Directorate reports	www.berr.gov.uk/bbf/enterprise-smes/index.html
	www.sbs.gov.uk
	www.sbs.gov/research
The Institute of Business Consulting	www.ibconsulting.org.uk
UK Business Barometer	www.ukbb.ac
Monthly Survey	
UK Government response to the Cruickshank Review	www.hm-treasury.gov.uk
USA's Small Business Administration site	www.sba.gov
Welsh Assembly Government services	www.wales.gov.uk

References

1. See Chapter 3 of F. J. Greene, K. F. Mole, and D. J. Storey, *Three Decades of Enterprise Culture* (Basingstoke: Palgrave, 2008).
2. F. J. Greene, K. F. Mole, and D. J. Storey, *Three Decades of Enterprise Culture* (Basingstoke: Palgrave, 2008), pp. 69.
3. Ibid., p. 70.
4. Ibid., p. 75.
5. Ibid., p. 71.
6. R. J. Bennett, 'SMEs and Public Policy: Present Dilemmas, Future Priorities and the Case of Business Links', Paper presented to 19th ISBA National Small Firms Policy and Research Conference, November 1996, p. 3.
7. Quoted in J. Curran, 'What Is Small Business Policy in the UK For? Evaluating and Assessing Small Business Policies', *International Small Business Journal*, 18(3) (2000), pp. 36–50, at p. 43.
8. DTI, *Small Business and Government: The Way Forward* (London: The Stationery Office, 2002).
9. www.sbs.gov.uk/action (accessed 16 January 2008).
10. House of Commons, Committee of Public Accounts, 'Supporting Small Business', Eleventh Report of Session 2006-07, HC262 (London: The Stationery Office, 2007).
11. Ibid., p. 8.
12. L. Stevenson, *Lessons Learned From the Implementation of Entrepreneurship Development Strategy in Canada: The Case of the Atlantic Region* (Moncton, NB: Atlantic Canada Entrepreneurship Agency, April 1996, unpublished), pp. 2, 4.
13. A. Lundström and L. Stevenson, *Entrepreneurship Policy for the Future: Final Report*, eu2001.se (Brussels: European Commission, Directorate General Enterprise, 2001), pp. 34–5.
14. Forfás, *Towards Developing an Entrepreneurship Policy* (Dublin, 2007), p. 23–4.
15. A. Burke and A. Shabbir, 'Are the Causes of Business Start-up Different or Affect Small Firm Size?' Paper presented to the 30th Institute for Small Business and Entrepreneurship conference, Glasgow 2007, p. 36.
16. D. Storey, *Understanding the Small Business Sector* (London: Routledge, 1994), p. 258.
17. A. C. P. de Koning, J. A. H. Snijders and J. G. Vianen, 'Policies On Small and Medium Enterprises in Countries of the European Community', *International Small Business Journal*, 10(3) (1992), pp. 25–39.
18. D. Storey, 'Six Steps to Heaven: Evaluating the Impact of SME Policies', Paper presented to 23rd ISBA Small Firms Conference, Leeds, 1999; also published in *Handbook of Entrepreneurship*, edited by D. L. Sexton and H. Landstrom (Oxford: Blackwell, 2000), pp. 176–94.
19. L. Perren, M. Davis and R. Kroessin, *Mapping the UK SME Management and Leadership Development Provision* (London: Council for Excellence in Management Leadership, 2001), p. 14.
20. Storey (1994), op. cit., p. 304.
21. J. Curran and D. Storey, *Small Business Policy: Past Experiences and Future Directions* (The Small Business Service and Kingston University Small Business Research Centre SME Seminar Series 'Linking Research and Policy', DTI Conference Centre, December 2000), p. 2.
22. Storey (1999/2000), op. cit.
23. Scottish Enterprise and Paisley Business School, 'Discussion Paper for "A Celtic Comparison"', distributed at the UK Evaluation Society Symposium, Belfast, 6–8 Dec 2001.
24. M. Hancock, K. Klyver and T. Bager, *Global Entrepreneurship Monitor: Danish National Executive Report* (Prepared at the University of Southern Denmark, for the Danish Agency for Trade and Industry, Danish Ministry for Trade and Industry, 2000), p. 22.
25. House of Commons, Public Accounts Committee, op. cit. p. 14.
26. Ibid., p. 8.
27. Small Business Service promotional leaflet: *Small Business Service: The Vision* (London: Small Business Service, 2000).
28. http:/www.dti.gov.uk/bbf/small-business/ (accessed 13 January 2008).
29. R. Botham of the Training and Employment Unit, University of Glasgow, speaking at a Scott Policy Seminar in Belfast, 12 November 2001.
30. R. J. Bennett, 'Government and Small Business' in *Enterprise and Small Business: Principles, Practice and Policy* edited by S. Carter and D. A. Jones-Evans (London : Financial Times/Prentice Hall, 2nd Edn, 2000), Chapter 4, at p. 69.
31. J. Stanworth and C. Gray, *Bolton 20 Years On: The Small Firm in the 1990s* (London: PCP, 1991), p. 20.

32. CBI SME Council, Internal working paper (unpublished).
33. Based on Bennett in Carter and Jones-Evans, op. cit. p. 60.
34. European Network for SME Research, *The European Observatory for SMEs Second Annual Report* (Zoetermeer, the Netherlands: EIM Small Business Research and Consultancy, 1994).
35. K. de Lind van Wijngaarden and R. van der Horst, 'A Comparison of SME Policy in the EU Member States', *Business, Growth and Profitability*, 2(1) (1996), pp. 36–48, at p. 40.
36. Carter and Jones-Evans, op. cit., p. 58.
37. Ibid., p. 58.
38. Ibid., p. 59.
39. Ibid., p. 59.
40. G. Bannock, *The Economics and Management of Small Business*: *An International Perspective* (London: Routledge, 2005) p.134.
41. H. Rees and A. Shah, 'The Characteristics of the Self-Employed: The Supply of Labour', in *Employment, The Small Firm and the Labour Market*, edited by J. Atkinson and D. J. Storey (Routledge: London, 1993), pp. 317–27.
42. H. Arnold, extract from 'Police Castigation from the Voice of Small Business Owners', from the *Financial Times* ©, 13 July 2001.
43. Carter and Jones-Evans, op. cit., p. 62.
44. House of Commons, Public Accounts Committee, op. cit., p. 11.
45. Extract from DTI news release, 'Byers Calls For a European Charter for Small Firms', 8 February 2000.
46. Stanworth and Gray, op. cit., p. 20.
47. *Entrepreneurship in the Netherlands: New Economy: New Entrepreneurs* (Zoetermeer, the Netherlands: EIM Business and Policy Research, 2000), p. 37.
48. A. Lundström and L. Stevenson, *Entrepreneurship Policy for the Future* (Stockholm: Swedish Foundation for Small Business Research, 2001), pp. 124–6.
49. Commission of the European Communities, *Towards Enterprise Europe: Work Programme for Enterprise Policy 2000–2005* (Commission Staff working paper, Brussels 08.05.2000, SEC(2000)771), p. 7.
50. Hancock et al., op.cit., p. 22.
51. Scottish Enterprise and Paisley Business School, op.cit., p. 3.
52. Z. J. Acs and D. B. Audretsch, *The Emergence of the Entrepreneurial Society*, Presentation for the acceptance of the 2001 International Award for Entrepreneurship and Small Business Research (Stockholm: Swedish Foundation for Small Business Research, April 2001), p. 23.
53. Bank of England, *Finance for Small Firms: An Eighth Report* (London: Bank of England, March 2001), pp. 63–4.
54. Commission of the European Communities (2000), op.cit., p. 7.
55. Hancock et al., op.cit., p. 59.
56. See Wilson Committee 'The Financing of Small Firms: Interim Report of the Committee to Review the function of the Financial Institutions', (London: HMSO, 1979).
57. P. Burns, *Entrepreneurship and Small Business* (Basingstoke: Palgrave Macmillan, 2007), pp. 368.
58. Ibid., p. 368.
59. Patrick Tooher, *Financial Mail On Sunday*, 27 January 2002.
60. J. Moore, 'Banks Face Price Controls Aimed At Curbing Charges', *Times* ©, 15 March 2002.
61. D. Smith, 'Brown to End Banks' Abuse of Small Firms', *Sunday Times* ©, 10 March 2002.
62 R. Jarvis, 'Finance and the Small Firm', in Carter and Jones-Evans, op. cit., p. 342.
63. Ibid., p. 342.
64. Bank of England, op. cit., p. 54.
65. C. Mason, 'Venture Capital and the Small Business', in Carter and Jones-Evans, op. cit., p. 364.
66. Bank of England, *Small Exporters: A Special Report* (London: Bank of England, January 1998).
67. http://ec.europa.eu/enterprise/enterprise_policy/analysis/observatory_eu.htm (accessed 3 February 2008).
68. D. Smallbone, R. Baldock, M. Ram and D. Deakins, 'Access to Finance by Ethnic Minority Businesses: Some Results from a National Study', Proceedings of the 24th ISBA National Small Firms Policy and Research Conference, November 2001, pp. 1115–36, at p. 1134.
69. Bank of England (March 2001), op. cit., p. 76.
70. S. Carter, 'Improving the Numbers and Performance of Women-Owned Businesses: Some Implications for Training and Advisory Services', *Education and Training*, 42(4) (2000), pp. 326–34.
71. Bank of England, *Finance for Small Firms: An Eighth Report*, (London: Bank of England, March 2001), p. 2.
72. Ibid. p.64.

73. Bank of England, *The Financing of Social Enterprises, A Special Report by the Bank of England* (London: Bank of England, Domestic Finance Division, May 2003).
74. Lundström and Stevenson (2001), op. cit., p. 185.
75. European Commission http://www.ebusiness-watch.org/(accessed 5 January 2008) *Economics*, 1(1) (2004), pp. 51–64.
76. S. Fraser, D. Storey, J. Frankish and R. Roberts 'The Relationship Between Training and Small Business Performance: An Analysis of the Barclays Bank Small Firms Training Loans Scheme', 20 July 2001, version of paper presented to the 23rd ISBA National Small Firms Policy and Research Conference, Aberdeen, November 2000, made available to the present authors by personal communication.
77. Council for Excellence in Management and Leadership, *Excellent Managers and Leaders: Meeting the Need: A Consultation Paper* (London: CEML, 2001), p. 24.
78. P. Joyce, T. McNulty and A. Woods, 'Workforce Training: Are Small Firms Different?' *Journal of European Industrial Training*, 19(5) (1995), pp. 19–25.
79. A. Hankinson, 'Small Firms' Training: The Reluctance Prevails', *Industrial and Commercial Training*, 26(9) (1994), pp. 28–30.
80. H. Matlay, 'The Learning Small Business: Myth or Reality?' Paper presented to the 21st ISBA National Small Firms Policy and Research Conference, Durham, November 1998.
81. A. Sargent and R. Matheson, 'Management Training: Are Business Schools Out of Touch With Their Market?', The Thornlea Papers, University of Exeter, 1995, cited in A. Sargent, 'Training For Growth: How Can Education Assist in the Development of Small Businesses?', *Industrial and Commercial Training*, 28(2) (1996), pp. 3–9.
82. Hankinson, op. cit.
83. A. A. Gibb, 'Small Firms' Training and Competitiveness: Building Upon the Small Business as a Learning Organisation', *International Small Business Journal*, 15(3) (1997), pp. 13–29.
84. L. J. Perren, A. Berry and M. Partridge, 'The Evolution of Management Information, Control and Decision-Making Processes in Small Growth Oriented Service Sector Businesses: Exploratory Lessons From Four Cases of Success', *Journal of Small Business Enterprise and Development*, 5(4) (1998), pp. 351–62.
85. G. Bannock, op. cit., p. 147.
86. Ibid., p. 148.
87. Ibid., p. 154.
88. R. J. Bennett and C. Smith, 'The Influences of Location and Distance on the Supply of Business Advice', Proceedings of the 24th ISBA National Small Firms Policy and Research Conference, Hinckley, November 2001, pp. 487–507, at p. 489.
89. M. E. Porter, 'On Competition', *Harvard Business Review*, November-December (1998), pp. 72ff.
90. S. Conway and O. Jones, 'Networking and the Small Business' in Carter and Jones-Evans op. cit., p. 321.
91. Bank of England (March 2001), op. cit., p. 62.
92. http://ec.europa.eu/enterprise/entrepreneurship/promoting_ entrepreneurship/doc/com_70_en.pdf (accessed 3 February 2008).
93. http://europa.eu/rapid/pressreleasesAction.do?reference=IP/08/1658format=HTML 02/02/2008 (accessed 3 February 2008).
94. Commission of the European Communities, *Action Programme for a Community Policy on SMEs* (Strasbourg: The Commission, 9 December 1983).
95. COM (86) 445,1986.
96. EEC Commission, *Problems of SMEs: National and Community Policies* (Brussels: The Commission, March 1986).
97. 89/490/EEC, 28 July 1989; OJL 239, p. 33.
98. Council Decision 93/397/EEC; OJL 161, 2 July 1993, p. 68 (based on COM (92) 470).
99. Council Decision 97/15.EC; OJL 006, 10 January 1997, p. 25.
100. Council Decision 2000/819/EC; OJL 333, 29 December 2000, p. 84.
101. OECD, *Bologna Charter On SME Policies: Follow up to the Bologna Conference for Ministers Responsible for SMEs and Industry Ministers On Enhancing the Competitiveness of SMEs In the Global Economy: Strategies and Policies* (Paris: OECD, 2000), p. 135.
102. Action Plan: The European Agenda for Entrepreneurship COM (2004) 70, 11/02/2008.
103. http://eu.europa/enterprise/entrepreneurship/sme_policy.html (accessed 10 Feb 2008).
104. OECD, *The Role of SMEs: Findings and Issues* (Paris: OECD Directorate for Science, Technology and Industry, Industry Committee DSTVIND (2000) 1S/REV1, December 2000), p. 5.
105. Ibid., pp. 5–6.

CHAPTER 13
Intervention evaluation and results

Contents

KEY CONCEPTS

This chapter covers:

- The need for evaluation of interventions.
- The need for rigorous and comprehensive evaluation criteria and methods.
- The distinction between monitoring and evaluation.
- The principles of evaluation studies.
- Theoretical and practical problems inherent in evaluation studies, including issues of deadweight, displacement, multiplier effects, effectiveness, efficiency and economy.

- The strategic implications of inadequate evaluation.
- Current trends, practices and measures adopted in monitoring and evaluation studies of enterprise development policies.
- Current understanding of the impact of various policy interventions and instruments on small businesses.

LEARNING OBJECTIVES

By the end of this chapter the reader should:

- Understand the various objectives of evaluations and the different stakeholder requirements.
- Have an appreciation of the differences between monitoring and evaluation.
- Understand the general principles underlying evaluation studies.
- Understand the problems of carrying out evaluations.
- Be able to identify some of the key policy issues, the application and impact of which require evaluation.
- Appreciate some of the results of evaluation studies of enterprise programmes.
- Recognise where more effort is needed to improve understanding of the efficacy of enterprise policy interventions.

Introduction

It would be expected that intervention would be justified, or not justified, as the case may be, by the results it achieves. While there may be some circumstances where being seen to intervene is itself thought to be important, most people would expect that, if intervention is to continue, then there should be clear evidence that it achieves its purpose. If that is so then the fact that many governments across the world, including that of the UK, devote substantial resources to assist enterprise and small business development suggests that the results are indeed positive.

However the evidence for positive results is not as clear as might be expected. Relevant results are frequently hard to measure or to ascribe to any particular intervention. Unambiguous evidence of direct positive outcomes appears to be sparse. It is also recognised that there is ambiguity, inconsistency and even confusion in the thoughts and words of those who influence policy makers, as well as in the actions of those policy makers themselves. This has produced a spreading belief that there may be too many policies and/or programmes of uncertain effectiveness.

As a result, it is not surprising that increasing attention is being paid to evaluating the efficacy of policies in the whole area of enterprise. Measuring the results of the substantial resource investments in promoting and pursuing enterprise development is climbing up the agenda, not just for the public sector, but also for private sector investors in this process. Issues of efficiency, economy and effectiveness are becoming an integral part of the formulas that determine priorities, and monitoring and evaluation are being called for and are becoming a required component to be built into new initiatives at the planning stage.

Consequently, the requirements for the measurement and assessment of results, the development of rigorous and comprehensive evaluation criteria, the methods available, and the problems that these entail, all need to be considered. The results already obtained need to be examined, along with any conclusions that can be drawn from them. These issues form the subject of this chapter.

ILLUSTRATION 13.1
The difference between appraisal and evaluation

Appraisal is the process of defining objectives, examining options and weighing up the costs and benefits and risks and uncertainties before a decision is made.

Evaluation is the retrospective analysis of a project, programme, or policy to assess how successful or otherwise it has been, and what lessons can be learnt for the future. The terms 'policy evaluation' and 'post-project evaluation' are often used to describe evaluation in those two areas.

Source: H. M. Treasury, *Appraisal and Evaluation In Central Government: 'The Green Book'* (London: The Stationery Office, 1997), pp. 96–7.

Requirements

Many people would like to know the results of intervention programmes, not least those responsible for their design and implementation. Providing meaningful information about results is not however just a simple matter of measurement. Before that can be done a number of issues have to be considered.

Who are interested in the results, and what do they want, or need, to know? The stakeholders in intervention include the consumers or recipients of the intervention, who are often considered to be the customers of intervention but who rarely pay more than a small portion of its costs. If the customer is the one who pays, then government is frequently the customer as it often pays the major share of the cost and therefore has a legitimate interest in knowing what it is getting for its money. Then there are other stakeholders, including the deliverers of the intervention and in the case of public-sector-funded interventions, the voters and taxpayers in whose name it is done.

What do these stakeholders want to know? For government, at least in the UK, there is a desire for evaluations to provide answers to major policy questions, some of which are listed in Table 13.1. For other stakeholders the position is less clear, although they will generally share the same concerns.

Answering the questions in Table 13.1 requires rigorous and comprehensive evaluation criteria and methods: the 'what' and the 'how' of measurement. The question of what to measure itself raises a number of other questions, however:

Table 13.1 Major UK small business policy questions

- What is the appropriate balance to be accorded to assisting start-ups, existing businesses and growing businesses? Is there a case for a selective targeting and, if so, then on what basis should it be undertaken?
- How can the business birthrate be increased, especially that of fast growing, knowledge-based businesses with international market potential?
- To what extent can more firms be encouraged to grow beyond the 20 employee threshold?
- Will the restructured (RDA) Business Link delivery system prove effective in generating meaningful demand for and supply of services to small business?
- What form and structure should business support take?
- Is the current analysis of the financial needs of new and growing firms correct?
- How critical is the role of management training and development in the small firm sector?
- How can the sector be facilitated to expand its exports and keep abreast of technological developments?
- Should policy-making and its delivery be more, or less, centralised?
- Which interventions 'work' (however defined) and which don't?
- Who should pay, the client or the provider/government?
- What is the role of publicly funded business support?

- What are the links between enterprise, jobs and other benefits?
- With what should the results be compared? What results might be expected (benchmarks) and how does this compare with the results required?
- Over what timescale is it reasonable to expect and measure results?
- What value could or should be attached to results which cannot easily be measured (due to their intangibility or difficulties in isolating cause-and-effect relationships)?
- To whom do the benefits or the drawbacks accrue (the 'stakeholders') and who bears the costs?

Of the two main aims of evaluation indicated in Illustration 13.2, it is that of proving, or examining the difference made by an intervention, that is often the trickier. Seeking to examine the impact of a policy requires knowing what would have happened in the absence of the initiative in question and then determining what has changed as a result of the initiative. The changes considered should not be restricted to the direct recipients of assistance only (for instance a small business being assisted), but should also embrace the effects on the wider economy, community and society (for instance on the other businesses that did not receive assistance). This implies clearly identifying the stakeholders interested in changes or, more importantly, affected by them.

Different individuals, groups or organisations in society may well seek different outputs or combinations of outputs from policy interventions. These outputs can range broadly across economic, social and political aspirations, with the different stakeholder interests not infrequently being incompatible or in conflict.

In short, society is made up of many and varied customer groupings with different requirements. Thus a conclusion, such as 'the policy worked', often raises the

---

ILLUSTRATION 13.2
Monitoring and evaluation

In his work in this area, R. Scott emphasised the distinction between monitoring and evaluation, because these concepts are often confused with each other.[1]

Monitoring has narrower objectives than evaluation. It is limited to observing and recording partial indicators of inputs and outputs. Typical inputs would be that conditions of assistance have been met, a description of the programme of assistance and the scope, level and types of activity undertaken. These findings would usually be rounded off with some partial indicators of outputs such as jobs created or qualifications gained.

Evaluation is broader and usually has two primary aims:

- an improving and learning aim, to provide information that will help those involved to learn and so improve the design, operation and outcomes of policy initiatives

- a proving aim, to examine what difference the policy initiative has made to the individuals or firms or to the wider economic and social parameters it seeks to influence.

Evaluation studies will have additional benefits if they also indicate how and why initiatives have their effects. Such learning enables initiatives to be enhanced in an informed way. This can be particularly valuable when more than one initiative is aimed at a particular objective. In this case, it may be important to analyse not only individual impacts but also whether the combined effects are greater than the sum of those individual impacts.

---

question: 'in whose terms?' The need to take a wide view of the effects is reinforced by current emphasis on the concepts of social accounting and the social audit. Traditionally, recorded effects have tended to be limited to the direct and easily measurable effects, especially those that could be expressed in money terms. Now, with increasing concern for the environmental and social impact of policies and the functioning of organisations generally, wider measures, new measures and new measuring techniques are becoming imperative. Traditional accounting systems are too narrow in scope to deal with many of the complexities and interest groups in the modern world. Even if financial assessments of some effects were possible, such an assessment might be too costly, too uncertain or could take too long. Projects which target social need, for example, will have a number of objectives, the achievement of which will be evidenced not only in some economic measurements but also in other qualities or values that cannot be added together and then scientifically compared. If a project produces apples and pears they cannot all be considered to be apples. Assuming that they could, or alternatively ignoring the pears, does not help!

ILLUSTRATION 13.3
The Macnamara fallacy

The first step is to measure whatever can be easily measured. That is OK as far as it goes. The second step is to disregard that which can't easily be measured or give it an arbitrary quantitative value. This is artificial and misleading. The third step is to presume that what can't be measured really isn't important. This is blindness. The fourth step is to say that what can't be easily measured really doesn't exist. This is suicide.

Source: Daniel Yankelovich (1972).[2]

Methods

CASE 13.1
Two guides to evaluation

From the UK Government Green Book[3]

Evaluation examines the outturn of a project or policy. When carried out it adds value by providing lessons from experience to help future project management or development of a specific policy. It may also contribute to the quality of wider policy debate. ... The evaluation itself should normally follow this sequence:

1. Establish exactly what is to be evaluated and how the past outturns can be measured.

2. Choose alternative states of the world and/or alternative management decisions as counterfactuals. (The decision on exactly what should be compared with what needs clear thinking. ... The outturn of any complex activity will never be exactly as projected in advance. However the reasons for the outturn being in some respects better or worse than expected may be attributable to the 'state of the world'. Or it may be attributable to actions under the control of the responsible body.)

3. Compare the outturn with the target outturn, and with the effects of the chosen alternative states of the world and/or management decisions.

4. Present the results and recommendations.

5. Disseminate and use the results and recommendations.

From David Storey's Six Steps to Heaven[4]

The six steps of increasing level of sophistication of evaluation (of small-business support programmes) are:

Step 1   The take-up (numbers)?

Step 2   Do they like it (happy sheets)?

Step 3   What difference did it make?

Step 4   Compare assisted firms with 'typical' firms (but assisted firms are not typical).

Step 5   Compare assisted firms with 'match' firms (but there is still selection bias).

Step 6   Compare assisted firms with 'match' firms taking account of selection bias.

Note

In most OECD countries evaluation rarely passes Step 3 and in many instances does not pass Step 1.

Points raised

The results of evaluations are often quoted but the process of evaluation is rarely written about, and its limitations are not highlighted. These extracts summarise two approaches.

Some general principles of evaluation studies can be enunciated:

1. Clearly understand the objectives of the initiative, so that evaluation can be related as closely as possible to them. (But, as noted in Chapter 12, determining the objectives of policy initiatives is often very difficult, because they may not be made explicit.)

2. Look for and record not just intended effects but other effects as well, both direct and indirect. This may mean broadening the scope of the evaluation study. Policy initiatives can have effects beyond those intended, both positive and negative. For instance, will an increase in business start-ups reduce the growth prospects of some existing businesses? Moreover, as already noted, the scope of an evaluation may need to embrace social and environmental as well as economic effects.

3. Record the effects as they impact on the various stakeholders.

4. Have common measures of the effect, so that comparisons can be made across different initiatives.

5. Decide upon the basis on which the effect of any initiative is to be judged. Is it to be compared with the situation in the absence of that initiative, or against the effect of a previous initiative, or of a (future) alternative initiative, or of the effects of the best parallel initiative elsewhere (a benchmark)? In short, it is necessary to determine whether there are better ways to achieve similar results.

6. Determine what the effects of more, or less, expenditure on the initiative might be, not just the effect of all or nothing.

7. Determine whether the policy initiative would be more effective if it were implemented within a different institutional framework and delivery mechanism.

The core of an evaluation should be the extent of the net benefit, or additionality, attributable to the intervention in question. Implicit in the foregoing however are two concepts that are often ignored in evaluation studies of small business policies: the deadweight and displacement effects. They have the effect of reducing the net benefit of interventions. Multiplier effects have the opposite effect. They enhance the benefits and should also be considered. Effectiveness, efficiency and economy are measures of different aspects of the process.

- *Additionality*: This is the measure of the net benefit: the benefit which accrued as a result of the measure, whether intended or not, which would not otherwise have accrued.

- *Deadweight*: This is a measure of 'what would have happened anyway' without the measure. Because of deadweight, even the direct effects alone of intervention are often not easy to ascertain. It may be possible to show that a business has received assistance and has subsequently improved; but to what extent is that improvement due to other factors and would therefore have happened anyway, even had there been no intervention?

- *Displacement*: This is a measure of 'how much of the gain in one area is offset by losses elsewhere'. It may be that a business directly benefits from intervention and increases its employment as a result. However if the employment in a rival business is reduced because the first business takes its market, the total employment between the two may not increase and therefore overall there may be no benefit. The increase in activity in one business merely displaces activity in another, albeit the quality of the jobs may change. While, superficially, improved small business creation and growth may appear to be beneficial, this is so only if there is net growth and wealth creation as opposed to redistributing existing wealth, and there are no adverse effects on non-economic benefits. (In addition the benefits of a measure should exceed the cost of the measure.)

- *Multiplier effects*: There can be additional benefits from the indirect or side effects of intervention. If an increase in activity in a directly affected business results in an increase in activity in another business, for instance because it is a subcontractor, that is a beneficial multiplier effect which increases the extent of the additionality.

- *Effectiveness, efficiency and economy*: This is a trio of measures concerned with value for money. Effectiveness is the extent to which an intervention achieved its aims; efficiency measures the amount of direct output that the inputs achieved; and economy is concerned with the cost of those inputs.

Observance of the principles described above, coupled with a practical and useful evaluation method, would provide a sound basis for determining the value for money of an economy's (or region's) support programmes. It strongly suggests that the implications of enterprise development polices have to be examined in a wider framework than has traditionally been the case.

ILLUSTRATION 13.4
Economic appraisals

Although a prior appraisal of a project is not an evaluation of its eventual results, there is a connection in that the issues raised in the appraisal are likely to influence the agenda for a subsequent evaluation.

In the UK at least, the established government system for the prior appraisal of projects is essentially an economic one. The *Green Book*[5] produced by H. M. Treasury to guide government departments in project appraisal describes a method of economic appraisal based on a comparison of net present values.* Those values can only include items to which a monetary value can be assigned. The book does acknowledge that, in making a choice among options, there will frequently be a need to consider factors that cannot usefully be valued in money terms. However, by concentrating primarily, and in some detail, on the more easily appraised economic aspects, it can have the result of encouraging appraisers to ignore the other factors, or at least to treat them as if they were less important. This is particularly serious when the other factors are the main point of the project, or where they could be the deciding factor in prioritising projects.

It is only to be expected that the issues raised by the appraisal are then likely to feature in the requirements set for monitoring during the project, which will in turn influence the subsequent evaluation. A limited, and biased, agenda will have been set, even if only subconsciously.

---

*   The net present value of a project is defined as the difference between the present value of its stream of benefits and of its stream of costs. The present value of a stream of benefits (or costs) is the projected values at the time when the benefits (or costs) will occur, discounted at an appropriate rate.

Problems

It is unusual to find evaluation studies that observe the principles of evaluation fully. There are a number of possible reasons for this:

- A rigorous study may be viewed as too expensive. To establish fully all the results might cost more than the original initiative.

- Studies may be deliberately circumscribed so as to 'prove' a desired outcome. This is, for instance, particularly possible when the researchers are reliant on the policy makers or deliverers for some or all of their funding.

- In some situations it is argued that there are so many variables at work that it is not possible in practice to isolate the effects of one or two.

- Even if a correlation can be demonstrated between inputs and outputs, it does not necessarily imply causation, or clarify its direction. Research is often supposed to be better if done impartially, but someone who is impartial is often not involved, and without involvement it is hard to get the insight needed to understand cause and effect.

- It is argued that many of the effects of an initiative can be intangible and therefore difficult or impossible to measure.
- It is not easy to determine over what period results should be measured.

Some of these notions have been brought into focus by, *inter alia*, R. Bennett, who argues that '"Scientific" evaluation methods as normally applied will be unlikely to offer much useful assessment of SME policy effectiveness.'[6] He suggests that evaluation of intervention measures can only effectively be made by the business owners and managers affected.

ILLUSTRATION 13.5
Two types of evaluation

According to Curran, the evaluation of small business policies in the UK has been of two main kinds:

- Evaluations sponsored by government funding departments and/or agencies delivering the policy, conducted by private sector for-profit bodies. Most small business support evaluation in the UK is probably of this type and often the results never enter the public domain.
- Evaluations by independent (usually academic) researchers on a not-for-profit basis, sponsored by others than those funding or delivering the initiative. ... The results are normally made public with the aim of promoting constructive discussion.

The distinction between the two is important. ...The first kind is much more likely to be favourable to the policy or programme than the second kind. Where those conducting the evaluation are dependent on the initiator or deliverer for their fees and future similar work, there will be pressures to be less critical. This is less likely if evaluation is by researchers not reliant on policy makers or deliverers for their funding and the results are open to peer scrutiny. One result of such a poor record is that overall small business initiatives receive more favourable recognition for promoting small businesses, employment and economic performance than they merit.

Source: J. Curran, 'What is Small Business Policy in the UK For? Evaluation and Assessing Small Business Policies', *International Small Business Journal* (2000), 18(3), pp. 38–9.

Notwithstanding the genuine nature of some of the above problems and issues, they do not explain the poor record of evaluation work, not only in the UK but internationally also.

National trends

It is to be expected that the move to a relatively new policy area like that of enterprise development will require new thinking about how progress will be measured. Lundström and Stevenson review what they call 'interesting transitions' in measuring performance in entrepreneurship development in their review of ten economies.[7] In the more established area of 'SME policy', they identify four levels of measurement:

- At the sector level, for instance:
  - the net increase in number/share of SMEs
  - the SME share of employment and value added output
  - survival and growth rates.
- At the firm level:
  - how are individual firms performing in terms of sales, exports, productivity and employment (especially if in receipt of government assistance)?
- At the customer service level:
  - the number of clients served and degree of satisfaction.
- At the programme level:
  - the cost-effectiveness of public programmes.

They note that 'evaluation approaches in this area have been subject to considerable criticism', with evaluation measures tending to focus 'either on numbers of clients reached and satisfaction ratings or the impact on assisted firms compared to a control group of non-assisted firms'.[8]

They note certain emerging trends in measuring performance and provide a comprehensive list of specific indicators being used across a number of countries. They claim that 'Driving forces making these developments possible are current research linking entrepreneurial activity to economic growth, attempts to define the intervening variables and development of methodologies and instruments to collect data over time.' (Their summary of these trends can be found in Case 13.3 at the end of this chapter.)

Strategic implications

It has already been pointed out that, in the UK as elsewhere, there is often an absence of explicit statements of objectives and targets to guide the development of policies to encourage and support small business. This situation has led, *inter alia*, to a piecemeal development of policies. Moreover, the review and evaluation of existing support measures has often been narrow in scope, lacking in rigour and superficial. The explanations for this state of affairs are often complex and include reactions which range from 'it is very difficult', 'the data aren't there' and 'lack of resources' to 'the political will is lacking'. Certainly much more can be done and, until it is, our knowledge of policy effects will be limited and policy itself will be 'hit and miss'.

Thus the combination of these two strands, lack of objectives and inadequate review, has led to a situation where policy is formulated, and support maintained, too often on the basis of 'pressure from small business lobby groups, short-term fluctuations in macro-economic conditions and political expediency'.[9]

This same problem is further highlighted by Stevenson in explaining the difficulties of formulating and implementing an Entrepreneurship Development Strategy in the Atlantic Region of Canada.[10] She listed the following obstacles:

- *Lack of existing comprehensive models*: It is argued, in essence, that few if any models of entrepreneurship development exist that are based on a comprehensive, integrated and well-researched strategy. Because of this, 'there was a great deal of risk in the initiative.'

- *Lack of clarity about what entrepreneurship development is*: It is claimed that 'there is confusion in the minds of policy makers and practitioners alike' about the meaning of entrepreneurship development, about its relationship with small business, about how to stimulate new ventures and growth of existing ones, and about how to determine priorities.

- *Prevailing myths*: Attention is drawn to the 'born not made' ('nature versus nurture') argument about entrepreneurs. 'There are still a number of government officials, policy makers and business leaders who do not accept that the supply of entrepreneurs can be increased.'

- *Adapting to the paradigm shift in regional development policy*: It is argued that entrepreneurship development requires a different approach to economic development: that the emphasis needs to be on 'community animation' rather than on the traditional 'industrial development' approaches of developing economic infrastructure, undertaking macro-economic planning or evaluating investment projects.

The above themes are reinforced by an OECD study, which concluded that member governments lacked a comprehensive strategy towards entrepreneurship and job creation. that there was scope for more to be done in promoting the entrepreneurial culture and business start-up, and that organisational arrangements and delivery systems could be improved.[11] It also noted that few of the programmes which presently exist in member countries have been rigorously evaluated. This observation applies to EU-wide programmes as well as to national (or sub-national) programmes.

'A COHERENT FRAMEWORK?'

Given the large number of small businesses in England, the many sectors in which they operate and the variety of economic, social and government influences to which they are subject, any moves to improve small business performance are coherently complex. In an effort to reduce that complexity and help deliver quality support to all small businesses, the SBS created a performance framework bringing together multiple objectives, targets and strategic themes. Unfortunately, the resulting performance framework is complex. In particular, it has been difficult to see how success with the strategic themes would lead to the achievement of the targets, and how achieving targets would, in turn, satisfy the Government's aims and objectives.

Source: House of Commons Committee of Public Accounts 'Supporting Small Business', 11th Report of Session 2006–07. HC262 6 February 2007, p. 3.

Key policy questions

In summary, the key questions for governments seeking to support an enterprise development policy may be posed as follows:

1. Why do enterprise and small business development warrant policies of support?

2. If support is justified, what outcomes are sought and how will they be measured? This requires setting objectives and targets.

3. What are the policies and programmes for achieving the objectives set? Subsidiary questions might include:

   - What can be done to stimulate a stronger enterprise culture and entrepreneurial vitality?

   - What can be done to influence and support the process by which people decide to start their own business so as to know how to vary the number and quality of such businesses?

   - What is needed to improve the survival and growth rates of new and existing businesses and their international competitiveness?

4. What are the most effective delivery mechanisms for chosen forms of support? Subsidiary questions might include:

   - What is the appropriate balance between private and public sector delivery?

   - What is the appropriate balance between national as opposed to local initiatives?

   - To what extent is targeting relevant or necessary?

   - How can delivery be made more effective?

5. What forms of evaluation frameworks/methods are needed to evaluate the impacts of policies and programmes?

6. What works and what doesn't? Why does it work and how?

7. Is it capable of transference to another place, and if so, with what adjustments?

Results: the current state of knowledge

Despite the difficulties described there has been research into the effectiveness of the various methods of enterprise intervention. Some indications are available of the results they have achieved.

In the UK a significant research programme took place largely over the period 1989–92. It was commissioned by the Economic and Social Research Council (ESRC) and co-ordinated by Storey. Some of the published results of the programme have already been widely referred to in this book.[12] There have also been many other assessments which have sometimes produced contrary evidence. The following summary of some of these has therefore to be selective, but it seeks to give a flavour of the results reported in a variety of areas.

Attitudinal change

A number of countries/regions have attempted to increase the business birth rate through various initiatives. The Scottish seven-year Business Birth Rate Strategy appears to have been of questionable value in generating more start-ups.[13] In Northern Ireland, the Accelerating Entrepreneurship Strategy has not produced a sustained or significant change in entrepreneurial intentions as measured through Northern Ireland's GEM Total Entrepreneurial Activity (TEA) scores (see Chapter 4) which were its chosen benchmark. Greene et al. looked at three decades of intervention in Teesside and the central policy question: 'Given the objective of policy in the 1980s and 1990s was to make Teesside more entrepreneurial – did it work?'[14] They concluded that 'Teesside, along with almost every UK county and region remains in the same relative position as it did 10, 20 and probably even 30 years ago'[15] and that, 'if there has been some form of enterprise/entrepreneurship policy over these decades it has clearly not resulted in any shift whatever in the relative position of the regions.'[16] It would appear that the impact of such intervention was more firms in competitive sectors (such as hairdressing and motor vehicle repair) with consequent displacement and deadweight effects. Greene et al. therefore questioned 'whether, in low enterprise areas, it is possible to raise new business formation rates – other than perhaps inducing a recession or by offering incentives for existing informal businesses to "convert" to the formal sector by potentially reducing registration costs and times for new businesses'.[17]

High-tech firms, clusters and science parks

High-tech small firms have been viewed as the potential panacea for the effects of the decline in traditional industries, and thus there have been a plethora of initiatives aimed at them. It does appear that businesses have benefited from government grants in their ability to survive and grow. Not only did the grant amount matter, but the credibility associated with its receipt eased the problem of levering in additional external monies. Science parks also appear to meet at least some of the needs of those wishing to start high-tech businesses. The Bank of England, in concluding that there was no evidence of a major market failure as far as finance was concerned, acknowledged an improvement in the financing environment for these firms. Nevertheless it did perceive a financing gap in the provision of early stage finance. It made two suggestions in this regard:

> greater focus on the role of business angels; and further measures on the part of both the public and private sectors to assist (these firms) to become investment-ready and therefore better understand the expectations and requirements of investors.[18]

The perceived value of science parks, networks and clusters for high-tech knowledge-based firms has been high on the agenda for around two decades. This is largely attributable to the benefits gained by being plugged into national and regional innovation systems and the availability of external economies in agglomerations of small firms (as well as the success of, for example, the Silicon Valley and Route 128 clusters). Nevertheless, Bannock reports that 'despite initiatives in many countries, there are few cases where dynamic clusters have been initiated by public action', recording Sophia-Antipolis, near Nice, France, and the North Carolina–Texas clusters as exceptions, owing their existence to mainly public initiatives.[19] 'Many, if not most publicly sponsored science parks have remained small' and 'many science parks do not predominantly contain firms that can be described as innovative or high-tech, while some academic studies have been sceptical of the value of science parks.' Keeble[20] concludes, on the other hand, as does Storey[21] that science parks can contribute to high tech new firms' growth.

Rural/urban businesses

Some evidence exists that small manufacturing businesses in rural environments (but not 'remote' ones) outperform similar firms in urban locations. However, there is no suggestion that such a differential is attributable to government intervention, but rather to issues of owner motivation.

Enterprise policies in inner urban areas of main cities do reveal some interesting results in the context of managed workspace and community enterprises. Managed workspace was found, in terms of job creation, to be a more efficient use of public funds than community enterprises. Jobs in the community enterprises however were more likely to be taken by persons from the locality and thus more likely to give the long-term unemployed a 'taste of enterprise'. Such results raise questions about the objectives of public policy.

Financial assistance

Enterprise Allowance Scheme/Business Start-up Scheme

The Enterprise Allowance Scheme (EAS) was introduced as a pilot initiative in 1982 and later became the Business Start-up Scheme (BSUS). It offered financial inducement for unemployed people to become self-employed and was arguably one of the better-researched public policy initiatives. Almost 700,000 people started the scheme in the ten-year period 1982/83 to 1992/93.

The scheme could be evaluated against three criteria: job creation for the recipients (that is, the recipients leaving the unemployment register); creation of employment (for others); and net reduction in the numbers of unemployed (for example, after allowing for persons being employed who were not registered unemployed, or reduced outward migration).

The results indicated that the scheme was cost-effective. It is estimated that the scheme cost £2000 for each individual removed from the unemployment register. However, the scheme has been subject to some criticisms. For instance, a study in Cleveland in the north-east of England found that the net effect in terms of job creation was negligible, with, it is argued, many of the new businesses (in areas such as hairdressing) merely displacing existing ones. Others have argued that instead of creating a 'culture of enterprise' it has merely created a culture of 'survival', with too many self-employed, low-income businesses operating at the margin. However a further argument is that, even if the businesses eventually ceased trading, there would still be lasting personal development benefits, such as gains in knowledge, skills and confidence.

Grants

Grants are, at least in the eyes of many recipients, a popular way of intervening to promote small business development and the resultant job creation. The job creation aspect is frequently seen, by those awarding the grants, to be crucial to the extent that the amount of grant awarded in total was often reported in terms of grant-cost per job. Frequently this is specified as the cost per job promoted, because what is known at the time the grant is awarded is the number of jobs planned, or at least indicated in the business plan on which the grant award is based. If the plan works, which it does not always, the jobs will be created later. The number of jobs promoted can therefore be recorded at the time the grant award is made. The number of jobs actually created will not be known until some time later.

As well as the cost per job, therefore, evaluations have also considered the difference between the jobs planned (promoted) and the number of jobs eventually created, as well as issues concerned with the 'quality' of the jobs. Summarising the results is not very helpful, because the range of answers is so large. Costs per job can range from zero (a job which was created with no grants) to many tens of thousands of pounds. Job creation rates, for programmes in Northern Ireland, appear to have varied from only 40 per cent of jobs promised being realised to a success rate of between 70 per cent and 80 per cent. Job quality is particularly problematic. One measure of it is taken to be job duration, but this cannot actually be measured until the job ends, which may take many years.

ILLUSTRATION 13.6
A negative effect of grants

One way in which grants can lead directly to a reduction in productivity concerns capital grants. If a business can get a 50 per cent capital grant for the purchase of a new machine then it may be tempted to buy a better (faster, higher quality, greater capacity) machine than was originally envisaged. If however the business did not need the extra speed, quality or throughput, then it would not make full use of the machine and output would not in consequence increase above that which a cheaper machine might have produced. The more expensive machine would, however, probably be more complex and have higher depreciation and maintenance costs (which would not be grant-assisted). Thus the business would, as a direct result of the grant, have higher production costs and no increase in output, which means higher unit costs.

The evidence for the success of grants is mixed. Owen, who examined state aid to small businesses in three areas of Europe (South Yorkshire in England, Nord-Pas-de-Calais in France and the Hainault region of Belgium), found that in all three areas the provision of grants led to additional economic activity.[22] However, a report by Hitchens et al. on Northern Ireland's industrial productivity compared with West Germany's found that Northern Ireland firms, despite lower productivity, were at least as profitable as their German counterparts.[23] This was attributed in a large part to lower wages and to the level of government financial assistance. It was suggested that the level and nature of such assistance (which in the 1980s amounted to about 20 per cent of manufacturing GDP) impeded the efficient operation of some local businesses by reducing their incentive to carry out essential research and development, training, and product innovation and design. In effect, the grant tended to become almost a straight addition to the firm's profit (although, it is argued, it has sometimes led to lower, and therefore subsidised, pricing).

This work was instrumental in triggering a change in the emphasis of Northern Ireland's grant strategy away from capital grants towards assistance with planning, product development, marketing, strengthening management and applying quality standards, as well as training and development of staff.

A subsequent study in Northern Ireland appeared to be much more positive about the effectiveness of grants. Scott's work used control groups in Leicestershire in England and in the Republic of Ireland to demonstrate the effect of the work of the government-funded Northern Ireland small business agency LEDU (which was subsequently absorbed into Invest Northern Ireland).[24] He found that LEDU-assisted businesses had higher employment growth rates than comparable but non-assisted businesses and that the cost per job year was estimated at between 3 per cent and 5 per cent below the estimate for the Regional Investment Grant in Great Britain.

It is worth noting, however, that the additional employment creation by grant-assisted small firms was due more to a higher survival rate 'than to variations in subsequent employment growth'. It may also be relevant that LEDU engaged in a variety of interventions in addition to grants, including work to promote a more positive enterprise culture. The employment growth benefits may not therefore be due solely to grants. They may be more likely to be an indication of the overall effectiveness of LEDU than simply the result of a single intervention.

Trade credit and late payment

The Late Payment of Commercial Debts (Interest) Act (described in Chapter 12) took effect in the UK in 1998 and introduced, on a three-phase basis, the statutory right to interest on late payments of debt. Research claims to show, nevertheless, that:

> over 90 per cent of small businesses have not noticed any improvement in late payment since the introduction of the Act. ... Many small businesses are reluctant to pursue their customers in the courts. The CRMC (Credit Management Research Centre) at Leeds University found that over 90 per cent were aware of the first phase of the Act and 80 per cent were aware of the second phase. Although only 4 per cent of respondents indicated that they had seen an improvement in payment times, 22 per cent stated that they thought the legislation would have an advantage in the long term.[25]

In October 2006, the CRMC released data to suggest that late payment by UK companies is still higher than seven years ago, and this despite further European Late Payment legislation introduced in 2002.[26] In examining the SME position, it is noted that 'large firms are currently receiving more credit than they are extending and SMEs are being forced to extend more credit than they are receiving', adding that 'the clear imbalance could be evidence that large firms use their dominant position at the expense of the small firm.' While a fairer comparison would be SME indebtedness to large firms now as against their indebtedness in 1998, nevertheless there appears to be little of significant gain for the sector overall.

Small Firms Loan Guarantee Scheme

A rigorous assessment of the impact of the Small Firms Loan Guarantee Scheme (SFLGS) was carried out by National Economic Research Associates in 1990. Overall, it concluded that the impact of the scheme on the small business sector was negligible, although it may have had some initial effect 'in providing a demonstration to the clearing banks that there were opportunities for profitable lending in the small business sector'.[27]

Other independent evaluations of the scheme (for example that by KPMG in December 1998) have suggested that it continues to play an important role in businesses that lack a track record or collateral. Another study found evidence that the scheme did help to meet genuine market gaps in the provision of finance to SMEs.[28] Nevertheless the Cruickshank Review recommended that the government 'should progressively switch financial support away from the Scheme and instead focus on market imperfections in the provision of small-scale risk capital to certain segments of the SME population'.[29]

The results of the Graham Review[30] of the scheme were published in September 2004, as a result of which the Scheme has been focused on start-ups and young businesses, two groups viewed as suffering most from the lack of collateral and a business track record. One of the main criticisms of the scheme was that it was over-regulated; consequently lenders were required to refer loans to the (then) Small Business Service for approval.

More recently, the Public Accounts Committee referred to the Graham Review and its estimate 'that the Scheme has a default rate of 35 per cent compared with a commercial default rate for small business of 4 per cent', adding that the default rate 'is partly attributable to intervening when the market will not but, with a default rate so much higher than the commercial rate, it is questionable whether the scheme is best calculated to promote the generation of viable businesses'.[31]

Parker finds that loan guarantee schemes generally 'to be, at least ineffective: while they do not do much obvious harm they do not appear to do very much good either'.[32].

Enterprise Investment Scheme

A 1986 review by Peat Marwick judged that the Business Expansion Scheme (BES), the forerunner of the Enterprise Investment Scheme (EIS), was 'effective in terms of generating additional jobs, at a cost to the Exchequer of between £8000 and £10,000'.[33]

However, as investments moved into non-productive areas and as the amounts invested became larger, the scheme failed to add value by assisting businesses that needed small amounts of equity, which was the original purpose of BES. Again, while the scheme probably had some clear demonstration or 'symbolic' benefits, those benefits were that it 'encouraged financial institutions to take an interest in ... small firms, encouraged private investment in small firms ... and educated some small business owners in the benefits of external equity'.[34] For both investors and small business owners, its measurable impact appeared to be minimal. It was replaced in 1993 by the Enterprise Investment Scheme, which allows investors to play a role in their investee companies. It also offers individuals up-front income tax relief, capital gains tax exemption and tax relief on losses.

As noted in Chapter 12, changes to this scheme and to venture capital trusts have been made to improve their effectiveness and to benefit small, higher-risk companies. It has not yet been possible to make a judgement on the scale of the impact of these changes or on these schemes generally. The amounts of investment through them is small relative to the other forms of external finance in SMEs. In Europe generally, the various incentives have been criticised as having been 'insufficiently targeted, or at least ineffective in getting funds into new-technology based enterprises or into depressed regions'[35] with venture funding having a bias towards expansion and buy-in–buy-out finance. Bannock further argues that the most fundamental criticism of the schemes is that they 'provide no help for SME owners, who are invariably forced to invest personal funds in their own business out of taxed income',[36] while tax relief is offered on investment in their pension funds (which rarely invest in SMEs). Finally, there is a view that VCTs 'have had a favourable impact'[37] on the success of the Alternative Investment Market (AIM).

Counselling and advisory services

Counselling has been one of the fastest growing areas of small business support. Evaluation of these services tends to typify the superficial nature of studies in this area. Such studies concentrate on headcounts (how many use the service) and satisfaction indicators (how many clients say they find it useful). The critical question, however, is how the service affects the performance of the business in terms of turnover, profitability or other measures.

On the issue of satisfaction indicators it would appear that reaction is largely positive from clients of these services. However, some studies reveal that small businesses found greater satisfaction with their banks and accountants than with public support services.[38]

The evaluation of improved business performance appears to be inconclusive. Relatively little research has been done in this area, and most of what has been done does not stand up to rigorous critical analysis. The conclusion of Storey is that 'We are not aware of any studies which demonstrate that the provision of information and advice is a significant factor influencing the survival of the business.'[39] It must be remembered, however, that the absence of proof does not mean that the influence of this form of support is not positive in terms of business performance; it may merely remain to be demonstrated.

A recent study by Bennett shows government advice services to be strongest where the SME clients are most focused in what they seek and where the quality expectations are not too demanding.[40] He concludes, therefore, that Business Link should 'focus on the primary aim of specialist advice links to subsidised services, primarily with a skill or other technical focus'. Bennett further adds that, while in terms of the impact and use of Business Links, some important advances have been made, nevertheless 'average customer satisfaction levels – with about 79 per cent of clients reporting they are fully or partly satisfied with the service they receive – still fell short of the 90 per cent target sought by the DTI.'[41] Moreover:

> while the DTI has a strategic objective that 50 per cent of businesses should improve productivity or competitiveness after receiving advice, small businesses themselves use it for 'softer' outcomes such as reassurance, confirmation of prior expectations, and adding value to management's skills/knowledge base, rather than providing an immediate impact on the bottom line.[42]

Bennett states that 'many of the impact targets sought by government ... are inappropriate: and that Business Link needs to be far more sensitive to client needs, and to be client-driven', rather than policy or political-driven. Robson and Bennett concluded in a previous review that 'There is little evidence of statistically significant relationships between government-backed providers of business advice, such as Business Links, and firm performance.'[43]

Another study of this area was undertaken by Hart and Roper, who looked at the impact of Business Link assistance on the performance of small firms, using methods which allowed for both 'assistance' and 'selection' effects. They found 'little evidence that BL assistance over the 1996–8 period was having any significant effect on firms' sales, employment or productivity growth performance over the 1996–2000 period'.[44]

To the extent that advisory services provide some genuine benefits, a study by Bennett and Smith highlights a potential public policy issue. It analyses the influence of location and distance on the supply of external business advice. It focuses on the demand side and the supply side of such services, confirming that it is the supply structure which is often most influential on the choice of adviser. Amongst its conclusions is the finding that some locations offer SMEs a better market in which to find the best advisers than others do:

> In weaker markets, which are generally those which are smaller and more peripheral, an SME may suffer disadvantage in the ability to choose advisers. These locations may therefore be the main ones in which a public policy support may be most useful.[45]

Indeed the issue of the relatively low take-up of external advice by SMEs (evidence suggests less than 10 per cent of businesses, while between 8 and 15 per cent use Business Links) has been a cause for concern.[46] The European Observatory in its *Fifth Annual Report* identified three main factors which affect the use of external advice while classifying such advice into three groups according to the life cycle of the enterprise:[47]

- external advice related to the start-up phase
- advice connected to growth and change
- external advice linked to crisis.

In various phases of the business life cycle, the type of advice and the reasons for usage differ accordingly. The report identifies what hampers the use of external advice as follows:

- barriers related to resources
- barriers related to content
- barriers related to the availability of information
- barriers related to implementation.

Management training and development

The conclusion reached in relation to advice and information applies equally to another area of considerable investment by the public sector: management training development. Improving the quality of management is self-evidently the *sine qua non* of improved business performance. The question posed is 'To what extent does management development lead to improved management and therefore to improved business performance?'

While a great deal of research has been carried out in the field of management development (and to a lesser extent of consultancy), its value is limited. What research there is confirms the importance of developing management, especially in the growing firm, but it does not isolate the benefits either of management development in general or of different types of management development appropriate to the particular circumstances of groups of businesses.

Storey and Westhead concluded that there was 'little evidence that management training programmes clearly led directly to better performance amongst participating SMEs', and also criticised most studies as methodologically flawed.[48] However, an analysis by Fraser et al. of the impact of the Small Firms Training Loans Scheme did find that it enhanced business performance.[49] This latter finding was not supported in the major study undertaken by Cambridge University et al. of training for the British Bankers' Association (the Golden Key Package).[50] While reaction to the scheme by the parties involved was positive, there was no statistically significant impact on business performance.

Overall this is clearly a cause for concern, which applies also to the role of consultancy in the small business. The DTI's 'Consultancy Initiative' was designed to encourage small businesses to use commercial management consultants. However, little is known of what benefit was achieved and under what circumstances. Official evaluations concentrated mainly on take-up and subsequent use of consultants and were inconclusive as regards the impact on the businesses.

The reasons for the lack of useful research evidence in the areas of advice, information, training and consultancy, and indeed other areas, are essentially twofold:

- There is a lack of rigour in much of the research, and the methodology adopted is inappropriate to the objectives of the research (in so far as the objectives are genuinely to assess impact). There are various reasons for this, including a failure to distinguish between the training of managers and that of other employees, the time scales not being adequate, the sample sizes being too small, the impact of multiple variables not being allowed for, and the absence of control groups for comparisons.

- The area of training and advice is a very complex one. It can be difficult even for rigorous research to demonstrate clearly the benefits of management development. Distinguishing between correlation and causality, and knowing the direction of causality, is particularly problematical. Moreover, the effectiveness of management development activity in any business is subject to many influences, not least the size and structure of the management team itself, the nature of its products or services, its stage of development and, of course, the quality of the management development input provided.

CASE 13.2
Why workers in smaller businesses are less likely to receive training

A consistent finding in research on training provision in developed countries is that workers in small firms are less likely to be in receipt of formal training than those in larger enterprises.[51]

Two explanations can be provided for this. The first is that small firm owners are unaware of the benefits to their enterprise of the provision of training. Storey and West-head refer to this as the Ignorance Explanation: that is, small firm owners are, for some reason, less aware than those managing large firms of the benefits which training provides for their enterprise.[52] There is evidence that government certainly appears to believe small firm owners underestimate (are ignorant of) the benefits of training. Thus the official Investors in People (IIP) literature highlights the benefits which firms themselves will gain from enhanced workforce procedures. It seeks to show that firms which have participated in the past have obtained 'bottom line' benefits. A similar pattern is observed in the promotional literature on Small Firms Training Loans (SFTL).

Government support for these initiatives, which focused on smaller firms, appears to be based on persuading firms that there are tangible benefits from the firm's training provision and, by implication, that the small firm owner is imperfectly aware of these benefits.

In contrast, the second explanation does not imply imperfect knowledge on the part of the small firm owner. Instead it assumes the small firm owner-manager makes a (fully) informed judgement but is more likely than a large firm counterpart to conclude that the benefits of training are insufficient to offset the costs.

To some extent these explanations are open to empirical assessment. It is possible to assess whether small firms which provide training, in some sense, perform better than otherwise compatible firms which do not. If there is no evidence of enhanced performance on the part of the firm providing training then this would favour the second explanation over the first.

This issue is of central policy importance, at least in the UK. Here there has been a major effort, for many years, to enhance management and workforce training in smaller enterprises. For example, in the late 1980s government introduced Business Growth Training (BGT) Option 3, under which a consultant was paid from public funds to train and develop management in small firms. More recently there has been a drive to encourage smaller firms to participate in Investors in People. There have also been pilot schemes, initially developed at the City College Norwich, in which the

Nat West Bank provided financial inducements to start-up and pre-start firms to seek training with the college.

A final example is the Small Firms Training Loans Scheme (SFTLS), through which government subsidised the interest payments on bank loans which small firms took out to invest in training.

Source: Based on: S. Fraser, D. Storey, J. Frankish and R. Roberts, 'The Relationship Between Training and Small Business Performance: An Analysis of the Barclays Bank Small Firms Training Loans Scheme', Paper presented at the 23rd ISBA National Small Firms Policy and Research Conference, Aberdeen, 2000, pp. 1–2.

Points raised

The fact that there is a diagnosed need for training does not mean that training will be consumed if it is supplied, even when it is subsidised. This extract explores some of the issues behind the observed lack of training up-take.

The impact of interventions

The main impression given by the sources summarised above is that the case for many forms of assistance in the UK is 'not proven'. Clearly the government, LSCs and Business Links will need to make greater efforts to determine the value added from these schemes. Also, the research community will need to adopt a more rigorous approach to the 'proving' element of evaluation studies (as opposed to the 'learning' and 'improving' elements).

If interventions are to be successful both in rates of take-up and ultimately in impact, more attention will need to paid to why so many business owners decline help despite '20 years of substantial government funding, the setting up of hundreds of dedicated local support agencies and ... at least 200 initiatives'.[53]

Common reasons, as noted previously, may lie in the owner's desire for personal autonomy and 'doing it my way'; the large company mindset of some advisers; the delay factor in delivery and other bureaucratic implications of government administered schemes; compounded by general confusion as to what is available, to whom, on what conditions and how it can be accessed readily.

Curran, in questioning the need for and cost-effectiveness of, at least national (if not regional), small business policies comments:

Despite the strong consensus among policy makers that policies are needed to promote the small firm and its role in the economy ... it is difficult to see how the large and growing support for the small enterprise could be having any great impact. Too few small businesses appear willing to accept the support and, among those that do, the evidence of any significant impact on the performance on the business appears to be scant.[54]

Bannock questions why governments persist ('and not just in the UK – Germany spends far more than the UK does') with support services of the present kind. The answer he suggests is that:

> There is a paternalistic view that, whether SMEs want these services or not, they need them. The underlying assumptions are that SME owners, or many of them, are not very competent and need educating. There may be some truth in this though ... on the whole, small business owners are rational and are forced to be rational and realistic by their circumstances. ... There is no doubt a further reason for the continuing emphasis on the first strand of SME policy (support services): the second strand (that of offsetting discrimination against SMEs or improving the enabling environment) is difficult, and potentially politically painful, though there are encouraging signs that nettles are being grasped.[55]

Ultimately, the recipients of these support services should engage in a more systematic approach to gauging the benefits for their investment of time and money and/or clearly articulate their own specific requirements. The recipient businesses could and should have an important role in shaping provision. It is regularly argued and generally agreed that small businesses lack management skills and information and advice, as noted above. However, the recognition of need does not define intervention to meet it. This dilemma derives from the unique nature of each business; while they have many generic and common features, each has its own internal characteristics and relationship to various stakeholders (customers, suppliers and funders, for example).

This theme is also taken up by Westall and Cowling of the Institute for Public Policy Research, who comment that recent studies show that the 'take-up of services is significantly biased towards manufacturing', that 'support is too heavily focused on manufacturing and influenced by its models of growth and business practice', and that 'small business owners might be more receptive to advice being offered by people who know their industry'. They further contend that:

> policy initiatives ... seem to be aimed at a manufacturing model of business and fail to recognise the heterogeneity of small business. Policy solutions have tended to adopt a 'one-size-fits-all' approach and have not taken into account the impact of differences in small firms – for example, sector, size, age or business models.[56]

This approach, it is argued, adversely affects the implementation of policies.

Bennett concludes that:

> whilst there is some scope [for] government to help small businesses, much of this effort has to be focused on general rather than specific schemes. This is because the government is not going to have the technical capacity to be able to segment its strategies in an effective way. This means that government action can be most effective where it improves the generic environment – (through education policy, skills training, infrastructure) rather than specific and targeted initiatives.[57]

In short, identifying an appropriate management training, counselling or information supply response means determining, for each business, what its deficiency in the area is, what form of assistance is required, who needs it and how best to meet the need. Even when such questions are answered for a business, the opportunity cost of meeting the need has to be assessed. As the circumstances of each business are often so unique, generalised solutions, such as offering more management training or information and counselling, will ignore the specifics of each business's market, trading situation and internal characteristics. Hence, it is often argued that there is a need to put more onus on the individual business to identify and seek out provision appropriate to its own circumstances.

This need was recognised by the then DfEE/DTI-initiated Council for Excellence in Management and Leadership which states that:

> Support agencies have tried it all but have failed to engage with the world of the entrepreneur. They have tried to encourage the entrepreneur to come out of his or her world and engage in initiatives created by providers supported by public funds.[58]

The Council argued for a new approach to be 'based on joining entrepreneurs in their world and tapping seamlessly into the activities undertaken as a normal part of running the business'.[59] It anticipated that the most sought-for solutions will be those which 'mimic the informal development opportunities which many entrepreneurs experience'.[60] Examples offered of such solutions include self-managed mentorship, entrepreneurial shadowing, skill sharing and action-centred networking opportunities.

Bannock concludes:

> The history of SME support service is not a very satisfactory one anywhere. Once started, they have never been withdrawn, but many problems have been encountered. These problems include: low awareness and take-up, complaints about quality and consistency, lack of evidence of effectiveness in improving business performance, vacillation between targets for support (start-ups and growth firms) and confusion about the extent to which services should be changed for.[61]

Conclusions

Evaluating enterprise policy interventions is not easy. In commenting on this Bennett notes:

> Thus for small businesses we have the general conclusion that age, size, sector and location are crucial distinctions of small business characteristics (e.g. Storey 1994) but beyond that we know that a multiplicity of other variables is also important in different combinations for each business.[62]

Thus, he argues, in researching small businesses to assess policy interventions, there are two possible courses of action. The first, typified by 'matched pairs' research, involves so subdividing the population by careful sampling that any conclusions relate only to very constrained circumstances from which generalisations are difficult or impossible. The second involves taking large samples that include businesses from a wide range of different ages, sectors, locations and other distinguishing factors. The problem with such approaches is that 'It is usually impossible to obtain the sample size necessary to say anything useful about specific business problems: generalisation to the population is emphasised at the expense of detailed or specific assessments.' The range of different business circumstances is however such that even surveys with samples of up to 2000 can focus only 'on a restricted range of issues that does not allow each business to be put in a proper context'.[63] This view is also articulated by Curran, who claims that:

> a serious problem with quantitatively based aggregate evaluations of small business policies (by far the most common) is that they offer little on how individual firms respond to policies. Given the heterogeneity of small firms the asymmetrical impact of policy is likely to be great. How owner-managers integrate any support with their business goals, how it impacts on operational procedures and relates with those outside the firm, is hidden where evaluation offers aggregate findings only. Yet without knowing how a policy goes through 'the black box' which is the firm and its activities, no evaluation can properly estimate impact on business performance.[64]

Bennett contends that it is in 'the area of evaluation of SME programmes that there is also one of the greatest methodological challenges'.[65]

The extent of the challenge facing governments can be summed up in the following extracts from recent publications, the first applying to the UK and the second to OECD countries in general:

- In recognising growing pressures on limited government revenues, Curran asks:

    > Is public support for small enterprise value for money? To what extent has it helped to promote the increase in small business since 1979? Even if it can be shown to have been effective, is it still justified in the late 1990s?[66]

    He argues that the reason why evaluation of policies and initiatives has lagged behind their growth and proliferation is the consensus that supporting small enterprise undoubtedly promotes entrepreneurship, employment and national economic performance.

- In the 1990s, however, concerns emerged. In 2000 the OECD commented:

    > In most OECD countries, there is a need to deal with a maze of SME-specific programmes, which have tended to proliferate over the years with inadequate rationale or evaluation. Just the cost of administering these programmes is becoming a burden to governments which need to streamline their activities in cost-cutting efforts. ... Governments need to engage in more systematic evaluation of these programmes to ensure they are justified and efficient. They need to avoid incoherence and contradictions in existing or future policies while ensuring transparency and 'value-for-money'. As yet, most OECD countries have not acquired an 'evaluation culture'.[67]

And the verdict?

Policy makers would like to know how effective the possible forms of intervention are in order to select the ones that will be most cost-effective in achieving their purposes.

However, due to reasons such as the complexity of the subject area and the time it would take any results to become clear, as well as to avoidable shortcoming in evaluations, the evidence available to them is often imperfect, ambiguous and even contradictory. Nevertheless there appears to be no strong body of evidence to say that intervention has worked and a number of studies, some of which are reviewed above, which suggest that so far much intervention had failed. It seems reasonable to conclude that, overall, the evidence is that the methods so far applied have not worked in that they have not had the effect intended in improving rates of entrepreneurship or levels of business performance. Despite the similarity of policies and interventions across the world, there are few proven examples of successful 'best practice'. The adoption of interventionist policies appears to be due more to a 'me too' approach than any rigorous examination of their impact. If governments still want to intervene, and they will, and if they want to achieve more than just being seen to do something, they will need to change their intervention methods. For this they will need new models of what actually influences entrepreneurs and enterprises. Doing more of the same seems unlikely to yield significantly different results.

ILLUSTRATION 13.7
The evidence of businesses

Most surveys of business opinion in the UK point to a number of simple conclusions, similar to those already articulated by a number of other commentators. Based on what businesses say their needs are, these surveys have suggested that:

- A key role for government should be to create a stable and positive economic environment, and encourage an enterprise culture.

- The needs of small businesses for government support do not differ significantly from those of bigger firms (except in the special cases of the impact of regulations and diseconomies of scale).

- There is no strong case for a large array of firm or sector-specific policies.

- Where services are required and supplied, the most common need is not for more but for better. Moreover, the case for public, as opposed to private, provision is often highly questionable.

THE KEY POINTS OF CHAPTER 13

- There are a number of stakeholders in the process of intervention to promote more enterprise. They include the initiator(s) of the intervention, which is often government, those who deliver it and those who receive it. They all have an interest in knowing how effective it is or what its impact is on its recipients.

- To answer their questions, rigorous and comprehensive evaluation criteria and methods are needed. Evaluation can have a number of aims, including both an 'improving' and 'learning' aim to provide information which will help to improve policy initiatives, and a 'proving' aim to examine what difference the policy initiative has made to the individuals or firms or to the wider economic and social parameters it seeks to influence. Evaluations also have to contend with issues such as 'In whose terms is success to be measured?' and 'How can both economic and social benefits be assessed?'

- The methods employed should be carefully considered and should address issues such as additionality, deadweight, displacement and multiplier effects as well as effectiveness, efficiency and economy.

- The problems of doing this are considerable. For instance, they include a lack of clear objectives, a lack of existing comprehensive models, a lack of clarity about what entrepreneurship development is, prevailing myths and adapting to paradigm shifts in regional development policy.

- There are some indications that interventions can work, but overall the evidence for positive results is not as clear as might be expected. There appears to be ambiguity, inconsistency and even confusion in the thoughts and words of policy makers, as well as in their actions. Relevant results are frequently hard to measure or to ascribe to any particular intervention, and clear evidence of direct positive outcomes appears to be sparse.

- Overall there appears to be no strong body of evidence to say that intervention works, and a number of studies that suggest that it has failed.

- There is increasing recognition of the need to determine the efficacy of enterprise policies and initiatives.

CASE 13.3
Measuring performance: the trends, indicators and outcomes observed by Anders Lundström and Lois Stevenson

The move to any new policy area, like that of entrepreneurship, demands new thinking about how progress will be measured. What performance indicators are needed? What types of evaluation should be undertaken? What are the appropriate benchmarks against which to monitor developments over time or in relationship to other regions or nations? This section focuses on some of the emerging developments in this area of entrepreneurship policy, based on the insights gained from a study of ten economies.

First of all, we see some interesting transitions. In the more established area of SME policy, there appear to be at least four levels of measurement:

1. *At the level of the sector*: How well is the SME sector doing in terms of net increases in the number/share of SMEs, growth in SME share of employment, increased SME value-added output, aggregate SME survival and growth rates?

2. *At the level of the firm*: How well are individual firms performing in terms of growth in productivity, employment and sales, particularly if they have accessed government assistance programmes?

3. *At the customer service level*: How many clients have been served, and how satisfied have they been?

4. *At the programme level*: How effective are government programmes on a cost–benefit basis?

Evaluation approaches in this area have been subject to considerable criticism. Because a lot of measures are targeted towards individual firms or sectors and the majority of support is in the form of direct assistance programmes (of a financial or non-financial nature), evaluation measures have tended to focus either on reach (numbers of clients) and client satisfaction or the impact of assistance on the firms of assisted clients versus a control group of non-assisted firms.

In the area of measuring performance, a number of emerging trends are worth highlighting. First of all, with the increasing emphasis on the 'entrepreneurial economy', we notice less interest in measures motivated from a neo-classical point of view, for instance less about external effects or imperfections in the market, and less interest in individual firms such as measuring the impacts of 'picking the winner' strategies. Instead a whole new category of performance indicators is emerging. These are referred to as measurements of 'general entrepreneurship trends' and of the entrepreneurship climate/culture.

From our case studies, it is evident that Finland and the Netherlands are particularly focused on articulating these measures. Indicators of increases in the entrepreneurial climate/culture include things like increases in the entrepreneurial potential of the population, increases in the preconditions for becoming an entrepreneur and decreases in obstacles, and changes in social attitudes towards entrepreneurship. Finland proposes to track, at the community level, changes in entrepreneurial attitude, role identity, motivation level and intent to start a business, changes in the self-employment level, and changes in the level of entrepreneurial activity among women, youths, immigrants and academics. These could be classified as measures of the environment for entrepreneurship.

In the Netherlands, the government has established a set of performance indicators which include the level of business start-ups, exits and growth firms (measures of 'dynamism'), increases in the number of sole traders (measure of social value attached to entrepreneurship), reduced cost and time needed to start a business/reduced barriers to hiring the 'first' employee (measure of reduced administrative burden), the number of professors who teach entrepreneurship and the attitudes of students towards entrepreneurship (measures of impact of entrepreneurship education inputs), and business entry, exit and turbulence rates in each of 25 cities.

In the UK, changes in social attitudes towards entrepreneurship and the number of nascent entrepreneurs are being used to measure increases in the entrepreneurship climate/culture, and reduced burden to comply with government regulation to measure reductions in obstacles to business entry. In Atlantic Canada, the government is tracking increases in the intent to start a business by asking the question 'How likely is it that you will start a business within the next two years?' on regular omnibus household surveys.

We also observe a trend to develop performance indicators for specific entrepreneurship policy/programme areas like entrepreneurship education, entrepreneurship promotion, entrepreneurship network activity, start-up financing, and administrative obstacles to business entry. The measures themselves, the outputs being measured and the longer-term orientation of many of these measures are also apparent. In addition we see the development of new categories of entrepreneurs (even people who are not yet entrepreneurs, as in the nascent entrepreneur category) and the use of new indices like 'business formations per capita' (a measure of the business start-up propensity in the population), 'enterprises per capita' (a measure of density of entrepreneurs in the population), the Total Entrepreneurial Index (used by the Global Entrepreneurship Monitor to measure the prevalence rate of entrepreneurial activity in a region/country) and business 'turbulence' (measurement of the business dynamics of entries and exits).

These new indices are being used as indicators of the level of entrepreneurial vitality in a country or region. Static and dynamic measures like this allow international comparisons on a country-by-country basis, which in turn is leading to international benchmarking of entrepreneurship levels. This capability mirrors the existing capability and practice of countries to benchmark their SME sector against that of others (a pattern we also see in many of the cases in this study). Governments are benchmarking themselves against the performance of other countries in a number of SME/entrepreneurship-related areas; this is particularly evident in Taiwan, the Netherlands, Ireland and the UK. They are tracking their performance against that of other countries on such indicators as SME share of businesses, SME share of employment, SME share of value added and exports, new business entry and exit rates, net increases in SME population, SME survival rates over time, percentage of high-growth SMEs, self-employment rates, attitudes of the population towards entrepreneurship, and more recently, the rate of nascent entrepreneurship.

At this point, the development and adoption of these sorts of performance indicators and measures are in very early stages and certainly not widespread. Only a few of the economies in this study have made progress in this area, and then only recently. What may be most important here is that what gets measured gets attended to and what is attended to tends to get measured. Either way, the importance of entrepreneurship in a government's policy mix is being raised as a result of the ability to identify and quantify inputs, outputs and outcomes in the area.

Points raised

This case reviews the measurement of the performance of entrepreneurship policy and summarises the different approaches taken in different countries.

Source: A. Lundström and L. Stevenson, *Entrepreneurship Policy for the Future* (Stockholm: Swedish Foundation for Small Business Research, 2001), pp. 144–6. Reproduced with the permission of the Swedish Foundation for Small Business Research.

QUESTIONS, ESSAY AND DISCUSSION TOPICS

- What would the various stakeholders of an entrepreneurship or small business support initiative hope to learn from an evaluation of it?

- Outline the key steps involved in a rigorous evaluation of policy.

- Are the two guides to evaluation presented in Case 13.1 contradictory or complementary?

- Identify the main problems associated with assessment of policy and support for small businesses.

- If an evaluation of small business support measures finds evidence of a low take-up, what might be the explanation(s) and how should that be tested in order to learn from the problem?

- How could the impact of management training on business performance be evaluated?

- If the overall verdict on the effectiveness of small business intervention is still undecided, should small business intervention still continue?

- Are SME policies and programmes satisfactory? Are they critically evaluated? Are bad policies phased out or refocused? Illustrate your answer with examples.

- Which are the most important policy instruments for improving SME performance, and what should change in government policies if more favourable conditions are to be obtained?

- If workers in small businesses are less likely to be in receipt of formal training than those in larger enterprises (see Case 13.2), what might be the implications and how might they be addressed?

- Case 13.3 summarises the different approaches being taken in different countries to measure the performance of entrepreneurship policy. What do you conclude should be included in a perfect approach, and why?

Suggestions for further reading and information

G. Bannock, *The Economics of Management and Small Business: An International Perspective* (Routledge, 2005).

J. Curran, 'What Is Small Business Policy In the UK For? Evaluating and Assessing Small Business Policies', *International Small Business Journal*, 18(3) (2000), pp. 43–5.

J. Curran and R. A. Blackburn, *Researching the Small Enterprise* (London: Sage, 2001).

A. A. Gibb, 'SME Policy, Academic Research and the Growth of Ignorance, Mythical Concepts, Myths, Assumptions, Rituals and Confusions', *International Small Business Journal*, 18(3) (2000), pp. 13–35.

F. J. Greene, K. F. Mole and D. J. Storey, *Three Decades of Enterprise Culture* (Basingstoke: Palgrave, 2008).

H. M. Treasury, *Appraisal and Evaluation in Central Government: 'The Green Book'* (London: The Stationery Office, 1997), for its small section on evaluation.

References

1. R. Scott, personal correspondence based on work for Northern Ireland's Department of Economic Development.
2. D. Yankelovich, *Corporate Priorities: A Continuing Study of the New Demands on Business* (Stanford, Conn.: Daurer Yankelovich Inc., 1972).
3. H. M. Treasury, *Appraisal and Evaluation in Central Government: 'The Green Book'* (London: The Stationery Office, 1997), p. 12.
4. D. J. Storey, 'Six Steps to Heaven', Presented to the 22nd ISBA National Small Firms Policy and Research Conference, Leeds, 1999; also published in *Handbook of Entrepreneurship*, edited by D. L. Sexton and H. Landström (Oxford: Blackwell, 2000). pp. 176–94.
5. H. M. Treasury, op. cit.
6. R. J. Bennett, 'SMEs and Public Policy: Present Dilemmas, Future Priorities and the Case of Business Links', Keynote address to the 19th ISBA National Small Firms Policy and Research Conference, Birmingham, November 1996, at p. 20 of paper handed out.
7. A. Lundström and L. Stevenson, *Entrepreneurship Policy for the Future*, Volume 1 of the 'Entrepreneurship Policy for the Future' series (Stockholm: Swedish Foundation for Small Business Research, 2001).
8. Ibid., p. 144.
9. D. Storey, quoted in D. Smallbone, 'Policies to Support SME Development: The UK Experience', Paper presented at a conference in Novara, Italy, June 1995, p. 3.
10. L. Stevenson, *Lessons Learned From the Implementation of an Entrepreneurship Development Strategy In Canada: The Case of the Atlantic Region*, April 1996 (unpublished), p. 2.
11. OECD, *Jobs Study Follow up: Thematic Review of Entrepreneurship and Job Creation Policies* (Paris: OECD, 1996).
12. D. Storey, *Understanding the Small Business Sector* (London: Routledge, 1994).
13. Quoted in D. Deakins, and M. Freel, *Entrepreneurship and the Small Firm* (London: McGraw-Hill, 2006), pp. 162, 243.
14. F. J. Greene, K. F. Mole, and D. J. Storey, *Three Decades of Enterprise Culture* (Basingstoke: Palgrave, 2008), p. 233.
15. Ibid., p. 245.
16. Ibid., p. 234.
17. Ibid., p. 243.
18. Bank of England, *Finance for Small Firms: An Eighth Report* (London: Bank of England, March 2001), p. 73.
19. G. Bannock, *The Economics and Management of Small Business: An international perspective* (London: Routledge, 2005), pp. 131–2.
20. Ibid p., 140 (Note 42).
21. Ibid p., 140 (Note 42).
22. G. Owen, *Aid Regimes and Small Business In the UK France and Belgium*, efmd report to ESRC (Brussels: efmd, 1992).
23. D. M. W. N. Hitchens, K. Wagner and J. E. Birnie, *Northern Ireland Manufacturing Productivity Compared With West Germany* (Belfast: Northern Ireland Economic Research Centre, 1989).
24. R. Scott, 'Does a Regime of Intensive Grant Assistance to Small Firms Create Jobs?', Paper presented to the 23rd efmd European Small Business Seminar, N. Ireland, September 1993.
25. Bank of England, op. cit., pp. 30–1.
26. http://www.cmrc.co.uk/october_2006.pdf (accessed 10 February 2008).
27. Storey (1994), op. cit., p. 227.
28. M. Cowling and P. Mitchell, *Is the Small Firms Loan Guarantee Scheme Hazardous for Banks or Helpful to Small Businesses?* (Birmingham: Birmingham Business School Research Centre for Industrial Strategy, March 2000).
29. Bank of England, op. cit., p. 29.
30. Graham 'Graham Review of the Small Firms Loan Guarantee' H M Treasury (2004).
31. House of Commons Committee of Public Accounts 'Supporting Small Business' 11th Report of Session 2006–7 HC262 (February 2007), p. 5.
32. Parker quoted in F. J. Greene, K. F. Mole, and D. J. Storey, *Three Decades of Enterprise Culture* (Basingstoke: Palgrave, 2008), p. 153.
33. Storey (1994), op. cit., p. 229.

34. Ibid., p. 229.
35. Bannock (2005), op. cit.
36. Ibid.
37. Ibid.
38. Bennett, op. cit., pp. 3–4.
39. Storey (1994), op. cit., p. 291.
40. R. J. Bennett 'Expectations-based evaluation of SME advice and counselling: an example of business link services' *Journal of Small Business and Enterprise Development*, 14(3) (2007), p. 435–57 (23).
41. See also R. J. Bennett, 'SME Expectations from Business Link Services: How Are They Met?' Paper presented at the 28th Institute for Small Business and Entrepreneurship conference, Blackpool, 2005.
42. www.cbr.cam.ac.uk/research/SMEsurvey.
43. P. J. A. Robson and R. J. Bennett 'SME Growth: The Relationship with Business Advice and Extended Collaboration', *Small Business Economics*, November (2000), quoted in G. Bannock, *The Economics and Management of Small Business: an international perspective* (Routledge, 2005), p. 158.
44. M. Hart and S. Roper, 'Small Firm Growth and Public Policy in the UK: What Exactly Are the Conclusions?' Paper presented at the EISB Conference, Turku, Finland, 2004, p. 21.
45. R. J. Bennett and C. Smith, 'The Influence of Location and Distance on the Supply of Business Advice', Paper presented at the 24th ISBA National Small Firms Policy and Research Conference, Hinkley, November 2001.
46. Bannock (2005), op. cit.
47. *The European Observatory for SMEs, Fifth Annual Report*, Report submitted to DGXXIII by European Network for SME Research, October 1997.
48. D. J. Storey and P. Westhead, *Management Training and Small Firm Performance: A Critical Review*, Working paper No. 18 (Coventry: Warwick University Centre for Small and Medium-Sized Enterprises, 1997), p. 1.
49. S. Fraser, D. Storey, J. Frankish and R. Roberts, 'The Relationship Between Training and Small Business Performance: An Analysis of the Barclays Bank Small Firms Training Loans Scheme', Paper presented to the 24th ISBA National Small Firms Policy and Research Conference, Hinkley, November 2001.
50. Cambridge University et al. for The British Bankers' Association, *The Evaluation of the Golden Key Package Component of the Small Business Initiative* (London: The Association, April 2001).
51. For the US: L. M. Lynch and S. E. Black, 'Beyond the Incidence of Employer Provided Training', *Industrial and Labour Relations Review*, 52(1) (1998), pp. 64–81. For the UK: A. L. Booth, 'Job Related Formal Training: Who Receives It and What Is It Worth?', *Oxford Bulletin of Economics and Statistics*, 53(3) (1991), pp. 281–94.
52. D. J. Storey and P. Westhead, 'Management Training In Small Firms: A Case of Market Failure?' *Human Resource Management Journal*, 7(2) (1997), pp. 61–71.
53. J. Curran, 'What is Small Business Policy in the UK For? Evaluation and Assessing Small Business Policies', *International Small Business Journal*, 18(3) (2000), pp. 36–50, at p. 43.
54. Curran, ibid.: 45.
55. G. Bannock, 'Letter: A Comment on Gibb and Curran', *International Small Business Journal*, 18(4) (2000), pp. 85–6.
56. M. Westall and M, Cowling, *Agenda for Growth* (London: Institute for Public Policy Research, 1999), pp. 5–6 and back cover.
57. R.J. Bennett 'Governments and Small Business', in *Enterprise and Small Business: Principles, Productivity and Policy*, 2nd edn, edited by S. Carter and D. Jones-Evans, (FT/Prentice Hall, 2005), p. 74.
58. Council for Excellence in Management and Leadership, *Excellent Managers and Leaders: Meeting the Need: A Consultation Paper* (London: CEML, 2001), p. 10.
59. Ibid., p. 10.
60. Ibid., p. 10.
61. Bannock (2005), op. cit.
62. Bennett, op. cit., p. 3.
63. Ibid., p. 4.
64. Curran, op. cit., p. 41.
65. Bennett, op. cit., p. 20.
66. Curran, op. cit.: 38.
67. OECD, *The Role of SMEs: Findings and Issues* (Paris: OECD, Directorate for Science, Technology and Industry/Industry Committee, December 2000), p. 16.

Afterword

CHAPTER 14
Science, art or magic?

It is time for change. Time to realise that Governments on their own cannot provide us with permanent secure jobs and a growing standard of living. ... Time to accept that the solutions to our problems lie in our own hands. We need to foster a spirit of self-reliance and determination to take charge of our future. The next decade will provide greater opportunities for enterprise and initiative than we have ever seen before. The extent to which our community will accept this challenge will determine our future levels of employment and national wealth.

The Culliton Report, Ireland, 1992.[1]

Who should provide opportunities in our lives, and particularly in our economic lives? Is a job something which is a right and which should therefore be provided for us? If there is a problem is it someone else's task to sort it out, and is that someone usually the government? Many people alive today were brought up in a culture where lifetime employment was seen as being both available and the norm, and therefore as the desired and natural state for individual economic activity, even though in reality it had not been the norm for very long, if at all. Many of the large businesses, which for a lot of the last century seemed to provide the core employment in most economies, are dying, or are at least in decline. Like human beings, businesses are born, live and then die, and generally they die at an earlier age than humans. Lifetime employment is not to be expected in those circumstances. Should we instead view employment rather as Buddhists view life? Should we expect that after our present life ends we will be reborn into a different existence; that when one form of employment ends there can be another? If there is continuity it will be seen in the life of the individual person and in its progression, not in his or her employment which must be expected to change. Who though will provide the other forms of employment?

We have, in recent years, seen a growing recognition of the importance of small businesses and the significance of entrepreneurship. That is not to say that small businesses ever went away. There have always been there in the form of farms, shops and many personal services such as those provided by hairdressers, restaurateurs, plumbers and window-cleaners. What is now recognised is the contribution of small businesses and their distinctiveness. Small businesses are understood to have particular features which distinguish them from larger businesses and to have a distinct role to play in a modern economy; whereas it used to be the case that, while it was recognised that many businesses were small, their size was not thought to be a crucial distinction and the business population was thought in effect to be relatively homogeneous.

It is also recognised that entrepreneurship is a key factor in economic development. It is entrepreneurs who spot ideas and opportunities, who innovate and explore, and who start the small businesses which provide many of the new jobs and the source of bigger businesses in the future. Even for those being employed in them, the new small businesses do not offer the same employment prospects as used to be offered by the declining big businesses. For both employers and employees, economic security will increasingly depend on entrepreneurship: on having the skills, ideas, and the ability to learn and to adapt to meet changing requirements. That means having people who are enterprising and entrepreneurial, and there is therefore an interest in building an enterprise culture in which people feel that they can and should use their own initiative to secure their economic future.

This represents a challenge that is social as well as economic. It has been observed that in the United States, 'the nature of work has changed, but the nature of education has not. ... Global competition and new technology are overthrowing the assumptions behind mass production and, simultaneously, the lessons taught in American classrooms.'[2] People need a different approach: an enterprising approach.

Enterprising behaviour, however, is not something just limited to, or reserved for, a business context. Being enterprising and seeking to contribute in that way can impact on, or be affected by, many of aspects of our lives. Enterprise is a mode of behaviour that can be subject to both social and economic influences and can have a wide range of applications which can, in turn, have both social and economic impacts:

> A close-knit social fabric can be good for democracy and the economy. A study of Italian regions ... suggested that membership of choral societies is one of the three best predictors of a robust and effective local democracy and economy.[3]

If private sector small business enterprise is growing, so too is social enterprise. Examples of social economic actions now include community businesses, development trusts, housing associations, credit unions, country markets, managed workspace, community recycling schemes, city farms and local exchange trading schemes (LETS).

It is one thing, however, to see the potential for such initiatives and another thing to achieve them. There are many obstacles between potential and achievement, including habits, attitudes, beliefs and expectations. If people are used to seeing the economic cake as essentially fixed in size, where every gain by one person means a corresponding loss by another, they are likely to be concerned primarily with the distribution of that cake. If, however, they can see that a bigger cake is possible then they might look for creative ways of enlarging it.

If European politics in the nineteenth century was about dividing up the cake, Marxism was supposed to make the reallocation permanent. To the astonished Virginian in his buckskins, the idea must have seemed absurd. Everything you could possibly want or need was there, waiting for you, only provided you were prepared to cut it down, dig it out or plough it. That was the deal God had offered: you could have it, but only if you did the work.

Simon Hoggart[4]

Getting more enterprise involves addressing obstacles: obstacles to enterprising behaviour and entrepreneurship such as belief, individual and society values and attitudes, and obstacles to its application to (small) business such as a shortage of ideas, finance and advice.

If we want more enterprise then it helps to have some idea of what it is, and how to stimulate and support it. Is enterprise a science? Are there theories about enterprise that can be used to predict accurately when it will happen and how it will behave in specific circumstances? Is enterprise an art? Is it something that is hard to define, but that can be recognised when it is seen, that can be followed by many or demonstrated only by a few, and that, while it has rules, often appears to succeed by breaking the rules? Or is enterprise a magic, because it is a mystery to us, because it is unpredictable and because we have no control over it?

In this book some of the issues relevant to such a debate have been presented. There is no one, single accepted view on enterprise, what it means, what gives rise to it, what its implications are, or how it can be promoted. However, 'One of the commonplace yet probably essential characteristics in the development of any new body of knowledge is the competing values of those who generate and use that knowledge.'[5] The authors hope that this book helps to present the emerging body of knowledge on enterprise.

References

1. Industrial Policy Review Group, *A Time For Change: Industrial Policy for the 1990s* (Dublin: Stationery Office, 1992), p. 7.
2. M. Penrose, 'Is America In Decline?' *Harvard Business Review*, July–August (1992), pp. 34–45, at p. 44.
3. S. Zadek and E. Mayo, 'Ten Reasons Why Society Does Count', *New Economics Magazine*, 41 (Spring 1997), pp. 5
4. S. Hoggart, *America: A User's Guide* (London: Fontana, 1991), p. 6.
5. A. Pettigrew, in the Foreword to C. B. Handy, *Understanding Organisations* (Harmondsworth: Penguin, 1976), p. 7.

Index

In this index case studies are indicated by c., figures by f., illustrations by i., and tables by t. (e.g. Asia 116(c.4.1) indicates that Asia is mentioned on page 116 in Case 4.1). Published documents are presented in italics.